SHARE the MUSIC

MACMILLAN/McGRAW-HILL

COORDINATING AUTHORS
Judy Bond, Marilyn Copeland Davidson, Mary Goetze, Vincent P. Lawrence, Susan Snyder

AUTHORS
René Boyer-Alexander, Margaret Campbelle-Holman, Robert de Frece, Doug Goodkin, Betsy M. Henderson, Michael Jothen, Carol King, Nancy L.T. Miller, Ivy Rawlins

Macmillan McGraw-Hill

New York   Farmington

HAL•LEONARD®

Published by Macmillan/McGraw-Hill, of McGraw-Hill Education, a division of The McGraw-Hill Companies, Inc., Two Penn Plaza, New York, New York 10121.

1 2 3 4 5 6 7 8 9 027 07 06 05 04 03 02

CONTENTS

TIME FOR SINGING!

Experience the joy of singing together with this collection of favorite songs to start off the year.

UNIT PLANNER

Charts showing assessment objectives, lesson content, materials, concepts, and skills. Quick reference to multicultural materials, integrated curriculum, and technology opportunities.

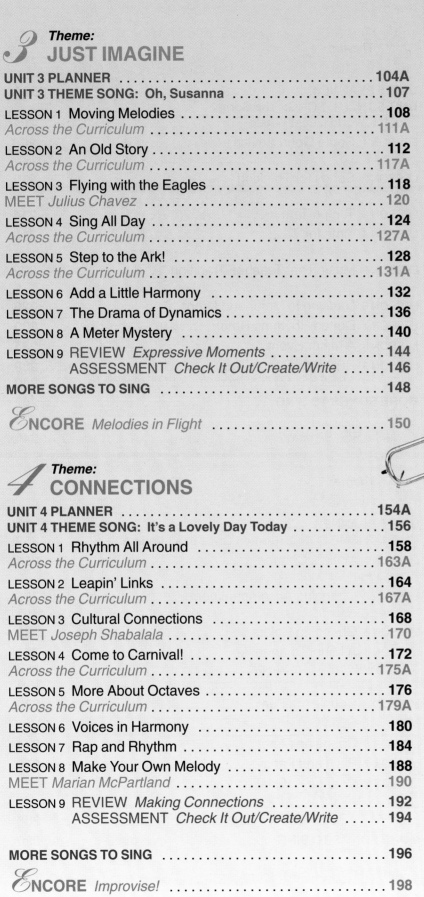

*U*NIT THEMES

Unit themes connect music to real-life experiences. An opening theme song and theme projects set the stage for thematic ideas woven throughout each unit.

*A*CROSS THE CURRICULUM

Two pages follow each CORE lesson for connections to other curriculum areas, including related arts.

TECHNOLOGY

- **Music With *MIDI*,** correlated to Grades 1–8, allows students to create and revise music with a MIDI sequencing program.

- ***SHARE THE MUSIC* Videos,** for K–8, make music come alive through movement, signing, technology, and performance.

- **MUSIC ACE™** software, Grades 1–6, reinforces pitch concepts in a lively, interactive environment.

- **MUSIC ACE 2™** software, Grades 3–6, reviews pitch concepts and teaches rhythm concepts with a fresh, creative approach.

- **MUSIC TIME™** notational software develops music literacy through creative activities and projects correlated to CORE lessons in Grades 3–8.

- ***SHARE THE MUSIC* MIDISAURUS,** Grades 1–3, CD-ROM, reinforces music concepts and provides elementary keyboard experiences.

- ***SHARE THE MUSIC* INTERACTIVE RECORDER,** Grade 3, CD-ROM, offers beginning recorder students video demonstrations and instant feedback on their playing.

- **ORCHESTRAL INSTRUMENTS** and **WORLD INSTRUMENTS,** Grades K–8, CD-ROMs, reinforce instrument identification with videos of performers.

All are sold separately.

CELEBRATIONS

MUSIC LIBRARY

CELEBRATIONS

Cross-referenced section of patriotic, seasonal, and holiday materials that allows flexibility in planning your instruction.

MUSIC LIBRARY

Cross-referenced "More Songs to Read," "Choral Anthology," (Grades 4–6) and "Listening Anthology" plus a new musical for each grade level.

PHILOSOPHY

SHARE THE MUSIC is a child-centered K–8 music program designed and written by teachers. Sequenced and thematic activities build musical concepts and skills the way students learn.

SHARE THE MUSIC enables you and your students to be successful.

HERE'S HOW!

- Familiar, age-appropriate songs that students love to sing.

- Sequenced lessons that provide continuity and ensure musical learning.

- Unit themes that connect music to real-life experiences.

- Appealing music that celebrates traditional American heritage and reflects cultural diversity.

- A fully integrated curriculum across all content areas, including phonics reinforcement and related literature.

- Related arts and movement throughout every book.

- Flexible and authentic assessment strategies for every lesson and unit.

- Integrated music technology that motivates and inspires.

- Lessons that reinforce the National Music Standards.

A FLEXIBLE PROGRAM

FOR DIFFERENT TEACHING NEEDS

- LESSONS THAT CAN BE ARRANGED FOR EITHER A 9- OR 12-MONTH SCHOOL YEAR
- LESSONS RELATED TO UNIT THEMES AND OBJECTIVES
- ENGAGING, EASY-TO-USE PLANS FOR EITHER MUSIC SPECIALISTS OR CLASSROOM TEACHERS

SPECIAL SECTIONS K–6

- **Encore**
- **Celebrations**
- **Music Library** *NEW*
  More Songs to Read
  Choral Anthology (Grades 4–6)
  Listening Anthology *NEW*
  Musical
- **Hal Leonard Showstoppers** *NEW*

GRADES K–5 ORGANIZATION

6 SEQUENCED THEMATIC UNITS

- **Unit Opener:** An appealing theme song and poem emphasizing the theme and introducing the unit projects.

- **Core Lessons (1, 2, 4, 5):** Introduction and teaching of tested objectives and skills

- **Across the Curriculum:** Classroom connections after every Core lesson

- **Non-Core Lessons (3, 6, 7, 8):** Creative lessons reinforcing concepts and skills

- **Unit Review and Assessment (Lesson 9):** Performance assessments and written evaluations

SPECIAL UNITS IN GRADE 6

UNIT 1

- A basic unit which can be used for a 9- or 12-week course.

UNIT 6

- From Rag to Rap: Lessons featuring popular music of the 20th century with songs, playalongs, and dramatic recorded lessons that set the historical and cultural context of each decade.

Basic Program activities in each lesson are indicated by ▶ and can be taught by classroom teachers with a minimal background in music and by substitute teachers.

THE LESSON PLAN *DESIGNED FOR*

SHARE THE MUSIC builds on our tradition of sequential teaching from lesson to lesson and unit to unit.

CORE LESSONS 1, 2, 4, and 5 introduce and use new concepts and skills.

NON-CORE LESSONS 3, 6, 7, and 8 reinforce and extend concepts and skills taught in CORE lessons.

LESSON PLANNER
A quick outline of the lesson.

CD NUMBER AND TRACK
Quick reference at the point of use.

BASIC PROGRAM
Activities for **classroom teachers** can be taught with a minimum background in music and are indicated by a ▶.

MEETING INDIVIDUAL NEEDS
Optional resources for alternate strategies, extension, higher-level activities, special learner strategies, critical thinking, background information, and pronunciation guides.

Approximate lesson length:
Grades K–1, 25 minutes
Grades 2–5, 30 minutes
Grade 6, 35 or 50 minutes

CORE
UNIT TWO
LESSON 2

RELATED ARTS MOVEMENT THEATER VISUAL ARTS

LESSON PLANNER

FOCUS Duration, three and four sounds to a beat

OBJECTIVES
OBJECTIVE 1 Signal when a rhythm pattern with sixteenth notes is heard (tested)
OBJECTIVE 2 Match word patterns with sixteenth-note durations to rhythm pattern pictures (tested)

MATERIALS
Recordings
The Old Carrion Crow — CD2:17
Recorded Lesson: Catch Those Phrases — CD2:18
Listening: Karşi Bar — CD2:19
En la feria de San Juan — CD2:20
Recorded Lesson: Instruments for Sale — CD2:21

Resources
Resource Master 2 • 1 (practice)
Recorder Master R • 3 (pitches A B)

▶ = **BASIC PROGRAM**

A Story

Before radio and television were popular, songs like "The Old Carrion Crow" were passed from person to person. As you sing, see how the clear story, repeated melodies, and funny nonsense syllables could make this song easy to remember.

D Dorian

The Old Carrion Crow

Nova Scotian Folk Song

Verse *mf* Dm ... C ... Dm ... Am

1. Oh, the old car-rion crow was sit-ting on an oak,
2. Hur-ry now bring me my cross- and my bow,
3. Oh, the tai- lor shot and missed his mark,
4. The old sow died and the bells did toll,
5. Oh, now the old sow's dead and gone,

Dm ... C ... Dm

Fol the rid- dle, all the rid- dle hey ding
(1.) doh,
(2.) doh,
(3.) doh, And he
(4.) doh, And he
(5.) doh, And the

62

MEETING **INDIVIDUAL** NEEDS

MULTICULTURAL PERSPECTIVES: *Folk Songs*
Like folktales, songs were often part of the cultural riches brought by the peoples who settled the Americas. "The Old Carrion Crow" probably descends from an English folk song that immigrants brought to North America. Another version can be heard in Appalachia, where many people have English ancestors. The song's clear musical form made it easy to remember, while the nonsense syllables made it fun to sing. Lyrics such as *fol the riddle* link the song to traditional English folk songs, but others such as *kimo* seem to have been added after the song reached this continent.

MOVEMENT: *Sensing Sixteenth Notes*
Divide the class in half with several students left over. Half of the class walks in a circle and steps quarter notes. The other half circles in reverse direction inside the walking students and jogs eighth notes. The several students left clap sixteenth notes, sitting inside the two circles. Lead one group at a time to move by playing its note value on a drum or other instrument then changing to another note value.

62 Lesson 2 A STORY IN A SONG

CREATIVE INSTRUCTION AND MANAGEABILITY

in a Song

Dm   C   Dm   Am

(1.) Watch - ing   a   tai - lor   cut - ting   out   a   coat.
(2.) That   I   may   shoot   yon   car - ri - on____   crow.
(3.)shot the   mil - ler's   sow   right   through____   the____   heart.
(4.) lit -tle   pigs____   cried   and   prayed____   for   her   soul.
(5.) lit -tle   pigs____   play   and   wad - dle____   on,

mp   slightly held back
Dm   *in tempo*

Sing   he,   sing   ho,   the   old   car - rion crow,   Fol the rid -dle,   all the rid -dle

Refrain   *slightly held back*
C   Dm   Am   G   F   C

hey   ding   doh.   Ki - me-lea-ro   kill my kea-ro,   ki - me-lea-ro   ki - mo,

in tempo
Dm   C   Dm   Am Dm   C Dm

To me   bump, bump, bump, jump Pol-ly wol-ly lee,   Lin - ko kil-ly cum   ki - mo.

Unit 2 *Traveling On* **63**

1 GET SET

"Does your family have stories they like to
tell? Sometimes stories are handed down in
songs." Have students:

▶ • Listen to "The Old Carrion Crow" CD2:17
and identify the parts that tell the story and the
sounds that are just fun to sing.

"Today you'll be listening for special rhythms
in this song and in others."

2 DEVELOP

**1. Identify similar phrases and three and
four sounds to a beat in "The Old Carrion
Crow."** Have students:

Recorded Lesson CD2:18
▶ • Listen to "Catch Those Phrases;" echo-sing
and pat *Fol the riddle, all the riddle, hey ding
doh* and *linko killy cum kimo*, then discover
that the phrases are similar.

• Find the similar phrases in the notation.

▶ • Sing the song.

• In two groups, determine how many sounds
occur on each beat by having one group clap
with the beat and the other pat *fol the riddle*
four times.

• Describe *fol the riddle* as having four sounds
to a beat.

• Repeat with *killy cum* and describe it as having three sounds per beat.

(Change every eight beats.) Groups rotate. To cue two
groups to respond at the same time, have a student play
quarter notes while you play either eighth or sixteenth
notes.

CRITICAL THINKING: *Oral Tradition*
Have students compare "The Old Carrion Crow" with
songs they learned through oral tradition, such as "Pat-a-
cake," and discuss why they think these songs survived.

CAREERS: *Music Journalism*

Tracing the roots of folk songs is one of many possible
challenges for the music journalist. Some journalists research and write about music; others review it. Have
students imagine interviewing their favorite singer.

MUSIC BUILDS READING SKILLS

Phonological Awareness and **Listening**
In identifying the number of sounds to a beat,
students will be identifying the number of
syllables in words.

Unit 2 TRAVELING ON **63**

Related Arts strategies in "Meeting Individual
Needs" are highlighted by logos:

MOVEMENT   THEATER   VISUAL ARTS

MUSIC BUILDS SKILLS
Highlights specific ways that music helps to
reinforce math and reading skills.

Piano Accompaniments conveniently bound
in a separate booklet for each grade.

THE LESSON PLAN (continued)

3 APPLY
Lesson steps that present new materials for application and synthesis of concepts.

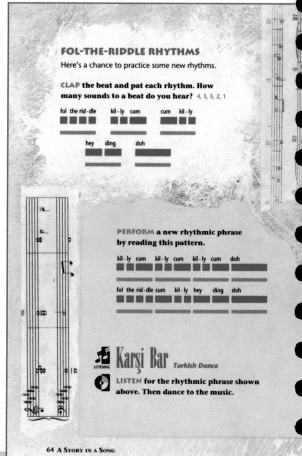

CORE
UNIT TWO LESSON 2

continued from previous page
2. Introduce "Karşi Bar" CD2:19. **Identify a phrase by the rhythm.** Have students:
• Perform the rhythm patterns on page 64.
▶ • Listen to "Karşi Bar" (kar **shi** bar) and walk to the beat, walking straight, curved, or zigzag pathways.

OBJECTIVE 1 Informal Assessment
• Listen to "Karşi Bar" with eyes closed and raise a hand as soon as they hear the rhythm phrase. (beginning of B section)
▶ • Dance and create movement for "Karşi Bar." (See *Movement* on the bottom of page 65. This recording contains spoken dance instructions over the music. You may adjust the stereo balance control to hear the music alone.)

3 APPLY

Introduce "En la feria de San Juan" CD2:20. **Match word patterns with rhythm patterns.** Have students:

Recorded Lesson CD2:21
• Listen to "Instruments for Sale" and clap each instrument's word pattern.
▶ • Listen for these patterns in "En la feria de San Juan" (en la **fe** rya ðe san **xwan**).
▶ • Work in four groups, one for each instrument, and determine which rhythm pattern picture on page 65 matches their assigned word patterns. (Optional: Use **Resource Master 2 · 1**, in which students match word phrases to rhythm pattern pictures.)

FOL-THE-RIDDLE RHYTHMS
Here's a chance to practice some new rhythms.

CLAP the beat and pat each rhythm. How many sounds to a beat do you hear? 4, 3, 3, 2, 1

fol the rid-dle   kil-ly cum   cum kil-ly

hey ding doh

PERFORM a new rhythmic phrase by reading this pattern.

kil-ly cum kil-ly cum kil-ly cum doh

fol the rid-dle cum kil-ly hey ding doh

♫ **Karşi Bar** *Turkish Dance*
🎵 **LISTEN for the rhythmic phrase shown above. Then dance to the music.**

64 A STORY IN A SONG

MEETING **INDIVIDUAL** NEEDS

ALTERNATE TEACHING STRATEGIES

OBJECTIVE 1 Have students walk to the beat as they pat the rhythm phrase in the middle of page 64. Then have them signal each time they hear the phrase as you perform the following. Clapping or drumming, play eight beats of quarter notes, the phrase, eight beats of ♩ ♩, the phrase, eight beats of ♫♫ ♩, and finally the phrase.

OBJECTIVE 2 Have students pat one sound to a beat, then two, then four. Draw both rhythm patterns from "En la feria de San Juan" on the board, and have students practice switching as you point to the patterns in turn.

MULTICULTURAL PERSPECTIVES: *"Karşi Bar"*
"Karşi Bar" is a traditional folk dance from eastern Anatolia in Turkey. *Karşi* means "welcoming," and a *bar* is a line dance that usually features several distinct sections, one after another. The dance leader triggers section changes by signaling the musicians to change rhythms, then the dancers change their movements.

64 Lesson 2 A STORY IN A SONG

TEACH TOWARD CAREERS

Help students discover career opportunities in:

• PUPIL EDITION sections such as *Encore*, *Meet* (recorded interviews), *Spotlight On*, and instrument-playing activities.

• TEACHER EDITION sections such as *Meeting Individual Needs* (biographies and careers).

• MUSIC WITH MIDI, *Music Ace™*, and *MusicTime™* through hands-on experiences in music making.

NEW for *SHARE THE MUSIC 2003*

1. "Time for Singing!"—A sing-along opens each book.
2. Expanded thematic content of units: opening theme song and lesson, unit theme projects, and "More Songs to Sing."
3. Enhanced curriculum correlations and related arts content.
4. "Music Builds Math Skills," "Music Builds Reading Skills."
5. National Standards correlated to each lesson, Units 1–6.
6. Music literacy reinforced in "More Songs to Read," Grades 1–6.
7. New "Choral Anthology" for Grades 4–6.

SING and pat the rhythm for each instrument.

piti, piti, piti, el pítío

ton, ton, ton, el tambor

tara, tara, tara, la guitarra

Which word patterns in the song match these rhythms?

pitío or guitarra

tambor or violín

lin, lin, lin, el violín

THINK IT THROUGH
What are some ways you could use the rhythm patterns or parts of the patterns to create other rhythm patterns?
Students may combine beats to create new 4-beat patterns, or they may add patterns together to create longer ones.

Unit 2 *Traveling On* **65**

OBJECTIVE 2 Informal Assessment
▶• After you name an instrument and speak its word pattern, signal with one or two fingers to show which rhythm pattern matches the phrase they heard.
▶• Discuss the *Think It Through.*

4 CLOSE

"How many sounds to a beat did you listen for today?" (three and four) Have students:
• Clap the rhythm patterns from "En la feria de San Juan," and say the words that fit each pattern.

LESSON SUMMARY

Informal Assessment In this lesson, students:

OBJECTIVE 1 Signaled when they heard a rhythmic pattern with sixteenth notes in "Karşi Bar."

OBJECTIVE 2 Matched word patterns with sixteenth-note durations from "En la feria de San Juan" to rhythm pattern pictures.

National Standards for Music Education
1b Sing with appropriate dynamics, phrasing, and interpretation.
6e Respond to musical characteristics through movement.
9d Identify and describe the various roles of musicians.

MORE MUSIC: Reinforcement
More Songs to Read, page 351 (four sounds to a beat)
"When I Was a Lad," page 96 (sixteenth-note rhythms)

---

4 CLOSE
A creative summary that provides teachers with a check for student understanding.

LESSON SUMMARY
Indicates how each *Objective* was accomplished.

NATIONAL STANDARDS FOR MUSIC EDUCATION
Standards covered in the lesson are summarized.
Chart with National Standards for the entire grade level appears on pages HL18–HL19.

MORE MUSIC: Reinforcement
References to lessons in "More Songs to Read" as well as alternate songs in *Encores, Celebrations,* and the balance of the *Music Library.*

LESSON ASSESSMENT steps:
● **Informal Assessment** activities (Lessons 1–8) correlate to *Objectives* and *Alternate Strategies.*
● **Lesson Summary** indicates how each objective was accomplished.

UNIT ASSESSMENT steps:
● **Review and Assessment** (Lesson 9) provides a recap of unit song materials and measures objectives taught in CORE lessons.
● **Recorded Assessments** provide two options for quick informal assessment in the pupil edition or for formal written responses using the Resource Masters.

OTHER OPTIONS
● **Portfolio Options** for music and related arts are given in each *Unit Planner.*
● **Music Journal** opportunities are listed in each *Unit Planner.*

MOVEMENT: *Preparation for "Karşi Bar"*
Review side-closes. (Left foot steps left, right foot closes and steps next to it.) In Lesson 4, page 73, *Movement,* students learn the traditional dance and compare it to movements they create for this B section.

Form: A B A B A B

A section (sixteen beats): eight side-closes, four beginning with the left foot and moving left, then four to the right. Perform every fourth side-close as a side-touch. Arms move in windshield-wiper fashion from side to side with bent elbows.

B section: Invite groups of six to eight students to create four-beat locomotor sequences that can be performed in one direction, then repeated in the opposite direction, then again in the original direction, then one last time in the opposite direction. The entire sequence will take sixteen beats. For example, walk forward four steps, backward four steps, forward four, backward four.

Final Form: Perform the A section; have each group perform its own movement for the B section simultaneously; return to the A section.

Unit 2 TRAVELING ON **65**

---

8. New musical for every grade.
9. "Hal Leonard Showstoppers," 56 popular songs, grades K–6.
10. Orff books: new in Grades 1–2, expanded in Grades 3–6.
11. *Playing the Recorder* book, Grade 3.
12. *Share Caribbean Music* book/CD, new songs with activities.
13. CD-ROMs: *Share the Music* MiDisaurus, *Share the Music* Interactive Recorder, Orchestral Instruments and World Instruments.

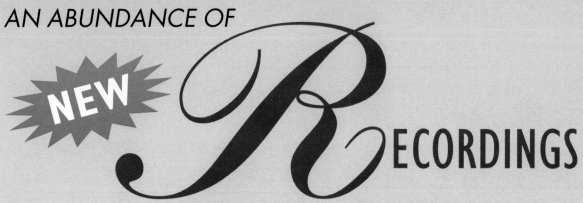

AN ABUNDANCE OF NEW Recordings

OUTSTANDING SOUNDS AND INNOVATIVE CHOICES

SONG RECORDINGS

- Voices that provide motivating vocal models—including children, young teens, and adults.

- Rich, artistic instrumental accompaniments in a variety of folk, popular, and contemporary styles.

- **DIVIDED TRACKS** allowing students to hear either the vocal or the instrumental tracks separately.

- **PERFORMANCE MIXES** providing a stereo instrumental accompaniment without vocals for "Time for Singing!," Unit Theme Songs, selected Celebration songs, musicals, and many other selected songs.

- **A VARIETY OF VOCAL PERFORMING GROUPS,** chosen from regions throughout the country, including California, Florida, Georgia, Maryland, New Jersey, Texas, Indiana, Tennessee, Virginia, Washington, Wisconsin, and Utah.

RECORDED LESSONS Dramatized, interactive recorded lessons reinforce instruction in a lively, interactive format.

GUIDED LISTENING Pronunciation for all non-English songs and movement instruction provide valuable teaching tools.

RECORDED INTERVIEWS motivate students toward lifelong musical involvement. Famous choreographers, actors, and musicians such as Linda Ronstadt, Jean Ritchie, Wynton Marsalis, Bobby McFerrin, and others share experiences with students.

RECORDED UNIT ASSESSMENTS use both familiar and new material to validate learning.

RECORDED PERFORMANCES by leading performing artists such as Yo-Yo Ma, Billy Joel, Alicia de la Roccha, Gloria Estefan, Paul Winter, and Andre Watts.

MUSIC ACROSS CULTURES

- Authentic song recordings from many cultures that open a new world of understanding to your students.

- Recorded pronunciation lessons by native speakers for every non-English song.

- Variety of ethnic instruments seen in illustrations and heard on recordings.

- Native singers, speakers, and instrumentalists provide authentic regional music and cultural background.

INTEGRATED ARTS

VISUAL ARTS • DANCE • THEATER • MUSIC

Motivating materials invite students to explore connections among the visual arts, dance, theater, and music.

Related arts strategies in *Share the Music* are found:

- Integrated within lessons throughout Student Book and Teacher Editions.

- In "Meeting Individual Needs." These are highlighted by logos:

 THEATER   VISUAL ARTS   MOVEMENT

- On "Across the Curriculum" pages in Teacher Editions.

- Throughout *Share the Music* videos.

Preparation for the Chinese New Year begins at least a month in advance. In addition to cleaning the house, families paint their front doors red—the color red means happiness. When the new year actually arrives, the celebration lasts for fifteen days.

BAILE EN TEHUANTEPEC
When Mexican artist Diego Rivera traveled to the Tehuantepec region of Mexico, he sketched hundreds of scenes, some of which he turned into paintings years later. In this painting, the people are dancing to lively Mexican folk music.

Los Angeles County Museum of Art

Unit 3 *Just Imagine* 141

the Golden Goose

An original musical by Linda Worsley
based on a story by the Brothers Grimm

HAPPINESS

Words and Music by Linda Worsley

Music by Linda Worsley

390 THE GOLDEN GOOSE

CUSTOMIZE YOUR CURRICULUM

WITH

- **ENCORES**
  Special related arts and multicultural sections after every unit

- **CELEBRATIONS**
  Holiday and seasonal materials for classroom and performance

- **MUSIC LIBRARY**
  More Songs to Read: Sequentially arranged supplementary reading practice for Core lessons
  Choral Anthology: Program music for Grades 4–6, including Vocal Development suggestions
  Listening Anthology: Additional listening lessons, with engaging listening maps
  You're Invited: Special listening lessons emphasizing audience etiquette
  Musical: Including staging suggestions

- **HAL LEONARD SHOWSTOPPERS**
  Eight highly motivating popular songs

- **TEACHER'S RESOURCE MASTERS**
  Scripts, games, special projects, cultural enrichment, and reading worksheets

- **SPECIAL SUPPLEMENTAL BOOKLETS**
  Playing the Recorder (Grades 3–6)
  Orchestrations for Orff Instruments (Grades 1–6)
  Playing the Guitar (Grade 6)
  Songs to Sing and Read: Additional folk songs for supplemental reading experience
  Música para todos: Favorite songs in Spanish and English with song maps for easy teaching and compact discs
  Share World Music: Folk melodies from Asia and the Pacific, with song maps and compact discs

- **TECHNOLOGY COMPONENTS**
  Music Ace™ and Music Ace 2™: Note-reading tutorials, with guides for *Share the Music* users
  MusicTime™: Notation program with special creative projects for every unit, Grades 3–6
  Music With MIDI: Enjoyable, integrated lessons using a music sequencing program
  Videos: A variety of original videotapes made especially for *Share the Music*
  Share the Music **MiDisaurus:** Games and keyboard experiences
  Share the Music **Interactive Recorder:** Beginning recorder lessons with instant feedback
  Orchestral Instruments and **World Instruments:** Demonstrations of a wide range of musical instruments

For more details on planning, see Options for Scheduling in the back of the Teacher's Edition.

UTHORS

JUDY BOND
COORDINATING AUTHOR
Judy is Coordinator of Music Education at the University of Wisconsin Stevens Point. Her public school experience includes teaching elementary and middle school general music and high school choral music. She is a past president of the American Orff-Schulwerk Association and has presented workshops and teacher training courses nationally and internationally.

DR. RENÉ BOYER-ALEXANDER
René is Professor of Music Education at the University of Cincinnati's College Conservatory of Music and is widely known for her work in multicultural music and international presentations. A well-known national clinician, René is also president of the National Black Music Caucus of MENC and the Coordinator and Director of the Orff-Schulwerk Certification Program at the University of Cincinnati.

MARGARET CAMPBELLE-HOLMAN
Margaret has been a music specialist in the Nashville, Tennessee, public schools for 15 years. She is widely known for her national and state presentations in the United States and Canada, and for her university-level Orff-Schulwerk training courses. Margaret was a contributing composer to the *Music and You* series, and she has published numerous original songs.

MARILYN COPELAND DAVIDSON
COORDINATING AUTHOR
Marilyn is a celebrated author, arranger, and composer. Her teaching experience spans over thirty years and ranges from kindergarten through graduate courses. Marilyn has presented teacher-training sessions and workshops on the national and international level. She is a past national president of the American Orff-Schulwerk Association and is a principal author of the *Music and You* series (Grades K–6).

DR. ROBERT DE FRECE
Robert is a Professor of Music and Music Education at the University of Alberta in Edmonton, Alberta, Canada. He is director of the University of Alberta Mixed Chorus, the Faculty of Education Handbell Ringers, and Edmonton's Greenwood Singers, a chamber choir that he founded in 1980. Despite his busy schedule, he finds time to teach several kindergarten music classes each week.

DR. MARY GOETZE
COORDINATING AUTHOR
Mary is an internationally known clinician, composer, arranger, and guest conductor. She has published many choral pieces and written numerous articles about children's singing and children's choirs. Mary is currently an Associate Professor of Music at the Indiana University School of Music, where she teaches music education and directs a children's choir program.

DOUG GOODKIN
Doug is a music specialist at The San Francisco School in California, where he has taught preschool through middle school since 1975. He has presented workshops and teacher-training courses in Orff-Schulwerk throughout the United States, Canada, Europe, and Australia. Doug has published numerous articles on music education in contemporary culture and is a founding member of the Orff performing group *Xephyr*.

BETSY M. HENDERSON
Betsy is the Elementary Fine Arts Coordinator and an assistant principal for the Garland Independent School District in Texas. She is a church organist, children's choir director, workshop/festival clinician, and a director of children's musicals. Betsy has served as Elementary Chairperson for both the Texas Choral Directors Association and the Texas Music Educators Association.

DR. MICHAEL JOTHEN
Michael is an Associate Professor of Music and Coordinator of the Graduate Program in Music Education at Towson State University in Maryland. He is a nationally-known music educator, choral clinician, and conductor. Michael has received many commissions for choral compositions and has been recognized by ASCAP for his contributions as a composer. He is an author of *Music and You*.

CAROL KING
Carol is currently an elementary school Orff specialist in the Memphis City Schools, where she also served as acting supervisor for three years. Over the years she presented numerous sessions at state and national music conferences in the United States and Canada. Carol has also published books for recorder and for Orff instruments and has co-authored many curriculum guides.

DR. VINCENT P. LAWRENCE
COORDINATING AUTHOR
Vincent is a sought-after clinician and consultant in music education. He was formerly Professor of Music at Towson State University in Maryland, where he directed the University Chorale. At the same time, he was actively involved in teaching general music in the middle school. Vincent is an author of *Music and You* and of the high school text *Music! Its Role and Importance in Our Lives*.

NANCY L.T. MILLER
Nancy is a performing arts specialist at The College School of Webster Groves, Missouri, and also teaches the Orff certification courses at the University of Kentucky, Webster University, and St. Thomas University. In her teaching she has developed approaches that integrate music, dance, literature, and theater and has written and produced over 25 musical plays.

IVY RAWLINS
Ivy lives in Indiana, where she is currently pursuing doctoral studies. Prior to this she taught methodology and supervised student teachers in the Kodály certification program of the Hartt College of Music, University of Hartford. She has also taught at Holy Names College; in Budapest, Hungary; and while serving with the Peace Corps, in Uganda, East Africa.

DR. SUSAN SNYDER
COORDINATING AUTHOR
Sue has taught elementary music for over twenty years and is a prominent consultant in general music, curriculum development, early childhood, integrated language arts, multicultural education, and cooperative learning. Currently, Sue teaches at Hunter College, New York City. She is an author of the *Music and You* series.

TIME FOR SINGING!

RELATED ARTS | MOVEMENT | THEATER | VISUAL ARTS

PLANNER

FOCUS Music Makes the World Go 'Round

OBJECTIVES
- Sing songs that express hopes and dreams
- Present a sing-along program

MATERIALS
Recordings
Don't Let the Music Stop	CD1:1
Oh, Won't You Sit Down?	CD1:2
Let Music Surround You	CD1:3
Somos el barco	CD1:4
Recorded Lesson: Pronunciation for "Somos el barco"	CD1:5
The Wabash Cannonball	CD1:6
This Is My Country	CD1:7
Recorded Lesson: Octave Skip	CD1:8

Performance Mixes for all songs CD10:1–6

Resources
Orff Orchestration O•1 (Oh, Won't You Sit Down?)
Signing Master S•4•1 (This Is My Country)

Time for Singing!

Once you start this song, it may not stop just because you finish singing it. Some songs are like that. You may find yourself hearing or singing them the rest of the day.

DON'T LET THE MUSIC STOP

Words and Music by Eugene Butler

Don't let the mu-sic stop,___ let's keep it firm and strong;

Don't let the mu-sic stop,___ let's sing the whole day long.

Don't let the mu-sic stop,___ don't let it ev-er cease, 'Cause the

mu-sic that I sing makes the world go round,___ It brings

love and joy___ and peace!

MEETING **INDIVIDUAL** NEEDS

ENRICHMENT: *Inner Hearing*

Have students sing the song and keep clapping quietly. Pretend they are turning the volume down as you signal to get quieter until they are simply moving their lips and hearing the song internally. Next, ask them to sing only these words aloud while hearing the rest inside: *Don't let* (3 times), *love and joy and peace!,* and *I hear.* The challenge is to be together when they sing these words.

For an extra challenge, ask them to sing the first page aloud, then concentrate on hearing the song inside during the second page. See if they are together when they start singing the first page again. This is easier if they tap the beat quietly through the second page.

LITERATURE CONNECTION: *Walt Whitman*

Walter Whitman (1819–1892) was an American poet. He was born on Long Island and grew up in Brooklyn, New York. His poems reflect his love of the United States and its democratic ideals. The words *I hear America singing* and *varied carols I hear* in "Don't Let the Music Stop" are from Whitman's poem "I Hear America Singing." This poem is in his famous 1860 collection "Leaves of Grass."

I hear___ A - mer - i - ca sing - ing, I hear her sing - ing,

Var - ied car - ols I hear.___

I hear___ A - mer - i - ca sing - ing, I hear her sing - ing,

Go back to A *and sing to end*
(Da Capo al Fine)

Var - ied car - ols I hear.___

A famous American poet, Walt Whitman, wrote the words that inspired this song over 100 years ago. You'll find other "varied carols" or songs that Americans love to sing on the pages that follow.

Time for Singing! **1**

Don't Let the Music Stop CD1:1

Learn a song with two sections. Have students:

• Listen to the first page of the song and raise their hands each time they hear the words *Don't let the music stop.* (3 times)

• Listen again, singing along each time they hear that phrase.

• Read about the song and recall if they have a favorite song that they can hear inside.

• Listen to the first page again, following the notation.

• Form two groups, one to sing the first half of each line and the other to sing the last half. Both groups join in on *'Cause the....*

• Listen to the second page of the song and tell how it is different from the first. (different text, longer sounds, less rhythmic, more sustained)

• Listen again, then sing the second page.

• Sing the entire song.

• Watch and imitate you clapping on the off-beats of each measure.

• Sing the whole song, clapping on the off-beats as they sing the first page.

VOCAL DEVELOPMENT: *Breathing*

Ask students to clap the rhythm of the first two phrases. Then, sitting with sternum high, have them take a deep breath. Using a *ts* sound, they should perform the rhythm of each phrase in one breath. Be sure they give the whole notes their full value. Try this in these ways: sharply articulated, loudly, softly, and with a crescendo.

PROGRAM IDEA: *Sing-Along*

Help students organize a school-wide Sing-Along. Have them develop a plan for organizing the project and divide into groups to carry out such tasks as gaining support for the project from school administrators and faculty, selecting a date and location, advertising, choosing songs, selecting a song leader, rehearsing any narration, determining the order of the songs, and inviting instrumentalists to accompany them. This program could serve as "practice" for a more ambitious Community Sing.

TIME FOR SINGING!

Oh, Won't You Sit Down?

CD1:2

Sing an African American spiritual in call-and-response form. Have students:

• Read about the song on page 2.

• Echo you as you sing the first phrase *Oh, won't you sit down.*

• Listen, raising their hand each time they hear that phrase. (3 times)

• Echo you as you sing *Lord, I can't sit down.*

• Sing through the refrain, standing up during *Lord, I can't sit down.*

• Listen to the call-and-response section (verse) and describe the rhyming pattern of the words.

• Form two groups, one to sing the call while the other sings the response, then exchange parts.

• Sing the entire song.

• With you, choose volunteers to sing the calls while the whole group sings the responses. Sing the entire song, with soloists as planned.

Were you ever so excited that you could not sit still? The enslaved African Americans who created "Oh, Won't You Sit Down?" sang about heaven because their lives on earth were difficult. Joyful songs like this one gave them hope.

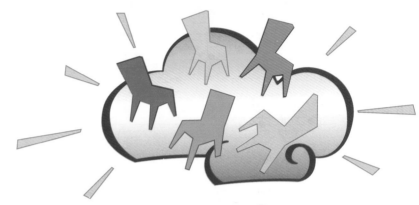

2

MEETING **INDIVIDUAL** NEEDS

LANGUAGE ARTS: *Rhyming*

Invite pairs of students to write additional verses to be sung during the call-and-response section. Encourage pairs to think of calls to which someone could improvise a response that rhymes. Alternately, one member of the pair could sing the call and the other the response, with the whole class repeating their couplet after them before returning to the refrain.

ORFF: *"Oh, Won't You Sit Down?"*

See **O•1** in *Orchestrations for Orff Instruments.*

PLAYING INSTRUMENTS: *"Let Music Surround You"*

Ask volunteers to play these patterns on resonator bells or Orff instruments to accompany the round.

After you have learned the song below, you can sing it as a round. When your class sings all of the phrases at one time, music really will surround you!

Time for Singing! **3**

Sing a round. Have students:

• Read page 3 and review how one sings in a round to create harmony.

• Listen and signal when they hear the song sung as a round on the recording.

• Read the words in rhythm.

• Whisper the words as they trace the contour of the four phrases on the page.

• Sing the whole song.

ENRICHMENT: *Relative Pitches in "Let Music Surround You"*

Draw four Xs denoting relative pitches on the board.

X (highest)   Phrase 3
X   Phrase 2
X   Phrase 1
X (lowest)   Phrase 4

Explain that each of the song's phrases starts on a different pitch. Have students listen to find which phrases start on the highest and lowest pitches (Phrases 3, 4). Show the answers next to the Xs, then determine the positions for Phrases 1 and 2. Have volunteers play resonator bells D G B D' as appropriate at the beginning of each phrase.

MOVEMENT: *Creating Signs*

Have students suggest signs to convey the meaning of these words and phrases: *music, surround, fill, heart, sing, harmony, grow apart.* They may use traditional sign language or create their own signs. After they have agreed on a sign for each phrase, have them sing the song internally (see *Enrichment* on page xvi) while signing. Then repeat in four parts.

TIME FOR SINGING!

Somos el barco CD1:4

Learn a song that has both Spanish and English words. Have students:

- Read about the song on page 4 and listen to it.

Recorded Lesson CD1:5

- Listen to "Pronunciation of 'Somos el barco'" to learn the Spanish words.
- Echo you as you sing the melody for the refrain while showing the shape of each phrase with your hand. (The English words are a translation of the Spanish.)
- Listen to the verse (your singing or the recording) and join in on the refrain.
- Knowing that this song is about peace, discuss the symbolic meaning of the voyage described in the verses.
- Sing the whole song.

Songs can inspire people to pull together. "Somos el barco" has been sung around the globe by people who want a peaceful world.

Somos el barco
We Are the Boat

Words and Music by Lorre Wyatt

A Refrain

Spanish: So - mos el bar - co,___ So - mos el mar.
Pronunciation: so mos el bar ko so mos el mar

Yo na - ve - go___ en ti, Tu na - ve - gas___ en mí.
yo na βe go en ti tu na βe gas en mi

We are the boat, We are the sea.

Last time only: repeat this line

I sail in you, you sail in me.

1. B Verse

1. The stream sings___ it to the riv- er,___ The

riv - er sings it to the sea. The sea sings it

4

MEETING **INDIVIDUAL** NEEDS

BACKGROUND: *"Somos el barco"*

This song was created in 1973 by Lorre Wyatt to promote global unity. It has been sung by Pete Seeger, Arlo Guthrie and HARP, Gordon Bok, and the Clancy Brothers. The verses evolved as people in different countries adapted the song and joined in the effort for world peace. There are verses in many languages.

MULTICULTURAL PERSPECTIVES: *Creating a New Verse*

If someone in the class or community is fluent in another language, have them translate the refrain into that language and, with your help, fit it to the melody to make a new verse. Share the results with the class.

to the_ boat that car - ries you_ and me._ So-mos el
so   mos   el

C **Verse**
2. - 4.

2. The boat we are_ sail - ing in_ was
3. With our hopes we raise the sails_ to
4. The voy-age has been_ long and hard_ and

built by man - y_ hands, The sea we are_
face the wind once_ more, With our hearts_ we_
yet we're sail - ing_ still, With a song to help us_

Go back to the sign
D.S. %

sail - ing on_ Touch-es ev' - ry sand. _
chart the wa - ters Nev - er sailed be - fore. _ { So-mos el
pull to-geth - er If we on - ly_ will. _ { *so   mos   el*

Time for Singing! **5**

ART CONNECTION: *Making Boats*

VISUAL ARTS

Have students work in pairs to make boats. Suggest that they collect shoe boxes or other forms for the boats, popsicle sticks or tree twigs for the masts, and colorful fabrics for the sails. Have them cover the boxes with paper or paint them any color. Display the boats in the classroom.

PRONUNCIATION: *"Somos el barco"*

a father	e ch<u>a</u>otic	i b<u>ee</u>
o <u>o</u>bey	u m<u>oo</u>n	
β b without lips touching		ɾ flipped r

The Wabash Cannonball

CD1:6

Learn a traditional song about a train. Have students:

• Listen to Verse 1 and the refrain and guess what the Wabash Cannonball might be, then open their books to page 6 to read about the train.

• Read and discuss the text of the verses.

• Review Verse 1 and the refrain until the melody is familiar.

• Listen to all of the verses, joining in on the refrain.

• Sing the entire song, patting with the beat each time they sing the refrain.

The Wabash Cannonball was a famous train running between large cities in the midwest beginning in 1851. But originally this song was about an imaginary train that went all over North America. The more the song was sung, the more fantastic the train became.

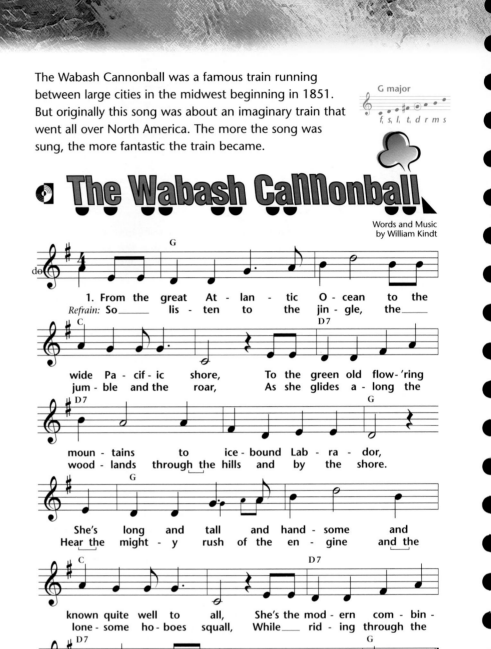

The Wabash Cannonball

Words and Music
by William Kindt

6

MEETING **INDIVIDUAL** NEEDS

SOCIAL STUDIES CONNECTION: *Mapping*

Have students use a map of the United States to find the cities and states that are mentioned in Verses 3 and 4. Invite them to create their own maps and mark the cities and states on it. Then have them search in a library or on the Web to find the train routes between these cities and draw the routes onto their own maps.

ENRICHMENT: *Creating Verses*

Have students clap the rhythm of the first two lines of the verse. Guide them to discover the rhyme scheme of the verses, then have them make up a new verse about where this imaginary train might go in the year 2010 or 2050.

2. Now she came in from Birmingham on a cold and frosty day,
   As she rolled into the station you could hear the people say,
   "There's a gal out there from Tennessee, she's long, boy, and tall,
   She's the modern combination called the Wabash Cannonball."
   Refrain

3. Now the Eastern states are dandy, so all the people say,
   From New York to Saint Louis and Chicago by the way,
   From the lakes of Minnesota where the rippling waters fall,
   No change in standard gauging on the Wabash Cannonball.
   Refrain

Words like these take on even greater meaning when they are set to such powerful music. Think of what makes you proud to be an American as you sing this song.

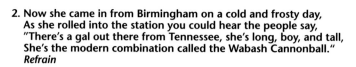

C major

d m f s l t d' r'

Music by Al Jacobs
Words by Don Raye

1.–2. This is my coun-try! Land of my { birth. / choice.

This is my coun-try! { Grand - est on earth. / Hear my proud voice.

I pledge thee my al - le - giance, A - mer - i - ca the bold, for

This is my coun-try, to have and to hold!

Time for Singing! 7

This Is My Country CD1:7

Sing a patriotic song. Have students:
• Recall the first line of the Pledge of Allegiance and listen for this phrase in the song.
• Read about the song on page 7.
• Echo you singing the phrase, *This is my country!*, and count how many times they see it on the page. (3 times)
• Listen and join in on this phrase each time it occurs, drawing the shape of the phrase in the air with their hands.
• Sing the whole song.

VOCAL DEVELOPMENT: *Singing Wide Intervals*

Have students echo you as you sing the patterns below. Be sure students sing in the lighter register with an open mouth when they begin on the higher pitches. Have them retain this openness when they drop to the lower octave, without losing the lighter quality. When starting on the lower pitch, be sure they maintain this lightness in order to produce a consistent quality on the higher pitch. The higher pitch will be difficult to sing if they carry the heavy register into that range.

loo loo loo   loo loo loo   loo loo loo

SIGNING: *"This Is My Country"*

Signing Master S•4•1 has sign language for this song.

ENRICHMENT: *Octaves*

Have students look at the notation to locate the words *is* and *my* in Line 1. If they are able, have them name the pitches as C and C' and identify the interval as an octave. Listen to "Recorded Lesson: Octave Skip" **CD1:8** to sing intervals including octaves. Then practice the first phrase of the song, assessing the accuracy of the octave.

WHERE IN THE WORLD?

MULTICULTURAL PERSPECTIVES

Through exposure to diverse materials, students develop an awareness of how people from many cultures create and participate in music. This unit includes:

African/African American and Caribbean
- **I Let Her Go, Go,** folk song from Trinidad and Tobago, 15
- **Mañana Iguana** by Bobby McFerrin, 20
- **Sir Duke,** by Stevie Wonder, 10
- **'Way Down Yonder in the Brickyard,** American game song, 17

Asian/Asian American
- *Chinese Mirror Painting,* 18
- **Mongolian Night Song,** traditional Inner Mongolian song, 19

Europe/European American and Canadian
- **Dancing the Troika,** Russian dance, TE 34
- **Fed My Horse,** Southern Appalachian song, 31
- **The Foxhunter's,** Celtic folk music by Canadian group The Barra MacNeils, 42
- **Hi! Ho! The Rattlin' Bog,** Irish folk song, 23
- **Les saluts,** French Canadian dance, TE 18
- *St. Basil's Cathedral,* model of Russian church, 32
- *Still Music,* by American painter Ben Shahn, 26
- **Troika,** by Russian composer Sergei Prokofiev, 34
- **Voices of the World,** by poet Stefi Samuelson, 8

For a complete listing of materials by culture throughout the book, see the Classified Index.

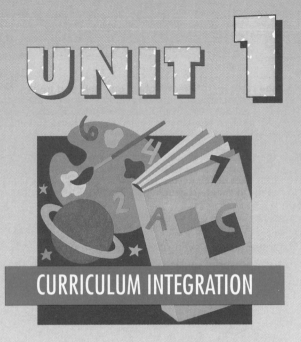

UNIT 1

CURRICULUM INTEGRATION

Activities in this unit that promote the integration of music with other curriculum areas include:

Art
- Make a picture of the poem, 15A
- Make a picture-story of the song, 19B
- Make a papier-mâché horse, 31B

Math
- Explore repeated addition, 15B
- Represent time using hands, 27B
- Estimate measurements, 27A
- Sketch a floor plan of a home, 27A
- Make a pendulum, 27B
- Measure a horse, 31B

Reading/Language Arts
- Create call-and-response phrases, 19A
- Write new verses to a song, 32
- Compare and contrast the definitions of two words, 40
- Write an essay about a favorite musician, 47

Science
- Make a model bog, 15B
- Research various animals, 31A
- Make an animal chart, 31A

Social Studies
- Research great names in jazz, 15A
- Research geography of Mongolia, 19B

New! **UNIT OPENERS WITH THEMATIC TEACHING PROJECTS**

PLANNER

ASSESSMENT OPTIONS

Informal Performance Assessments

Informal Assessments correlated to Objectives are provided in every lesson with Alternate Strategies for reteaching. Frequent informal assessment allows for ongoing progress checks throughout the course of the unit.

Formal Assessment

An assessment form is provided on pupil page 46 and Resource Master 1•9. The questions assess student understanding of the following main unit objectives:

- Identify phrases
- Read rhythms ($\quarternote$, $\eighthnote\eighthnote$, $\halfnote$, $\quarterrest$) in $\frac{4}{4}$ and $\frac{2}{4}$ meters
- Recognize patterns using *do re mi so la* from staff notation

Music Journal

Encourage students to enter thoughts about selections, progects, performances, and personal progress. Some journal opportunities include:

- *Think It Through,* 25, 39
- Response to fine art, 26
- Critical Thinking, TE 27, 38
- Write, 47

Portfolio Opportunities

Update student portfolios with outcome-based materials, including written work, audiotapes, videotapes, and/or photos that represent their best work for each unit. Some portfolio opportunities in this unit include:

- Identify and create graphic representations of beat groupings (Resource Master 1•1), TE 14
- Performance of Orff Orchestrations (audiotape), TE 19, 31
- Cooperative Learning: Vocal Exploration (audio-tape, graphic score), TE 20
- Draw bar lines for rhythms in $\frac{4}{4}$ meter (Resource Masters 1•2, 1•3), TE 26, 27
- Cooperative Learning: Melodic Contours (graphic notation), TE 29
- Reading and writing pitch syllables (Resource Masters 1•4, 1•5, 1•7), TE 30, 34, 36
- Creating and performing a melody for "I Wish," (Resource Master 1•8, audio/videotape), 38
- Creating a movement ostinato for "The Foxhunter's," (videotape), 43
- Check It Out (formal assessment), 46; Resource Master 1•9
- Portfolio Assessment (Resource Masters TA•1–5), TE 46
- Create 47; Resource Master 1•10
- Write, 47

MY MUSIC NOTEBOOK

			LESSON 1 CORE p.12	**LESSON 2 CORE** p.16	**LESSON 3** p.20
FOCUS			Duration/Meter	Phrase	Tone color
SELECTIONS			Where in the World? (listening) Take Me Home, Country Roads Hi! Ho! The Rattlin' Bog I Let Her Go, Go	Sir Duke 'Way Down Yonder in the Brickyard Mongolian Night Song Les saluts (listening)	Mañana Iguana (listening) I Wish (speech piece) I Let Her Go, Go Hi! Ho! The Rattlin' Bog

MUSICAL ELEMENTS	CONCEPTS	UNIT OBJECTIVES Bold = Tested	LESSON 1 CORE	LESSON 2 CORE	LESSON 3
EXPRESSIVE QUALITIES	Dynamics				• Discuss vocal performance, including loud and soft
	Tempo			• *Change tempo of instrumental phrase*	
	Articulation			• Hear and sing legato phrases	
TONE COLOR	Vocal/ Instrumental Tone Color	• Identify heavier and lighter vocal registers	• *Play unpitched percussion accompaniment*	• Hear Chinese flute	• Hear and discuss vocal performance • Define registers, tone color • Speak in 2 vocal registers • Sing in heavier register
DURATION	Beat/Meter	• **Read rhythms in ¾ and ⁴⁄ meters** • Identify beat and rhythm of words	• **Perform a pattern showing ⁴⁄ (E/D)** • **Identify sets of beats and locate meter signature in ⁴⁄ (I/P)** • **Move to show beats in sets of 4 (E/D)** • **Identify ⁴⁄ meter, perform song in ⁴⁄ (I/P)** • *Conduct in ⁴⁄ (E)* • Compare patting with beat and clapping the rhythm of the words • Change from performing beat to rhythm of melody	• *Move with beat while singing*	• Speak in duple meter • See graphic notation for beat and rhythm • *Change body facing with strong beat in ⁴⁄ meter*
	Rhythm	• **Read rhythms (♫, ♩, ♩, 𝄽)** • Identify beat and rhythm of words	• Compare patting with beat and clapping rhythm of the words	• **See notation and sing ♫, ♩, ♩ (E)** • Clap rhythm of recurring phrase	• See graphic notation for rhythm and beat
PITCH	Melody	• **Recognize patterns using *do re mi so la***		• **Sing *do re mi so la* (E)** • Define pitch and melody	
	Harmony				
	Tonality major/minor			• Sing in minor	
DESIGN	Texture	• Speak in canon	• *Accompany song with unpitched instruments*		• Define, perform canon
	Form/ Structure	• **Identify phrases**	• Sing refrain of song • Move during the interludes of song	• **Show with movement, define, and sing phrases (E/D/I/P)** • **Trace phrases on notation (Rd)** • **Recognize phrases (Rf)** • **Show phrases of different lengths (Rf)** • Sing call-and-response song with 3 sections • Learn folk dance with phrases	• Perform canon • Define and sing cumulative song
CULTURAL CONTEXT	Style/ Background	• Hear and sing music from diverse cultures • Develop undertanding of musical concepts using selections from diverse cultures	• Hear and discuss languages and instruments from diverse cultures • Sing and move to folk song from Trinidad and Tobago	• Sing and move to African American song from the Georgia Sea Islands • Sing song from Inner Mongolia and hear Chinese flute • Learn French Canadian folk dance	• Sing Irish folk song

Learning Sequence: E = Explore, D = Describe, I = Identify, P = Practice, Rf = Reinforce, Rd = Read, C = Create   See also *Scope and Sequence*, page 402.

OVERVIEW

LESSON 4 CORE p.24	LESSON 5 CORE p.28	LESSON 6 p.32	LESSON 7 p.36	LESSON 8 p.40
Duration—quarter note, eighth note, half note, quarter rest	Pitch, *do re mi so la*	Design—same, different, and similar phrases	Pitch	Duration
I Wish (speech piece) / Mongolian Night Song	'Way Down Yonder in the Brickyard / Fed My Horse	Fed My Horse / Troika (listening) / Dancing the Troika (listening) / Hi! Ho! The Rattlin' Bog	'Way Down Yonder in the Brickyard / I Wish (speech piece)	Voices of the World (poem) / I Let Her Go, Go / The Foxhunter's (listening)
		• Hear contrasting dynamics		
• *Point to rhythmic symbols, increasing tempo*	• Use slow tempo to practice singing with pitch syllables			
				• Hear short crisp singing style
• *Play unpitched percussion ostinato*	• Hear Appalachian string band	• Listen to orchestral selection / • *Play unpitched percussion and pitched bordun*	• Add unpitched percussion to composed melody	• Play ostinatos with unpitched instruments
• **Perform pattern from notation in ² (Rd)** / • **Pat and tap to determine ¹ meter (Rf)** / • **Indicate placement of bar lines in ¹ (Rd)** / • **Define meter signature, measure, bar line**	• **Sing song in ² (Rf)**	• *Play with beat*	• Compose melody in duple meter	• **Jump with strong beat to show ¹ meter (Rf)** / • **Create 8-beat ostinatos in ¹ (Rf/C)** / • *Move to beat and strong beat to show meter*
• **Move to show ♫, ♩, ♩ (D)** / • **Learn symbols ♫, ♩, ♩, ♩ (I)** / • **Perform rhythm patterns from notation (P/Rd)**	• *Perform rhythmic movement*	• Clap rhythms of phrases	• Compose to a given rhythm / • *Improvise to a given rhythm*	• **Perform ostinatos with ♫, ♩ (Rf)** / • **Read notation with ♫, ♩, ♩, ♩ (Rd)** / • **Create with ♩, ♩ (C)**
	• Draw melodic contour and match to graphic notation (D) / • Sing with pitch syllables from notation (I/P) / • Recognize *do re mi so la* (Rf) / • Study notation, compare pitch positions (Rd)	• Identify melodic phrases as being same, different, or similar	• **Echo phrases with pitch syllables (Rf)** / • **Create melody (C)** / • *Improvise melodically*	
	• *Sing countermelody*	• *Add I-V bordun*	• *Add I-V bordun*	• *Accompany in thirds*
	• Use pitch syllables for 2 songs in major		• Try different beginning and ending pitches	
	• *Add body-percussion pattern*	• *Accompany with bordun and unpitched percussion*	• Accompany with Orff, unpitched percussion	• Perform mouth-music accompaniment
• Define and perform coda	• **Match phrases to graphic notation (Rf)**	• **Indicate phrase form (a b, a a¹) (Rf)**	• **Put phrases in correct order and label phrase form (Rf)** / • Compose melodic phrases / • *Analyze form of class melody*	• Define and create ostinatos / • Move and perform ostinatos during interludes
	• Sing Southern Appalachian song	• Listen to music by Sergei Prokofiev / • Learn Russian folk dance		• Listen to Celtic folk music, learn about the instruments / • Sing mouth music

UNIT 1 PLANNER

UNIT

SKILLS

SKILLS		LESSON 1 CORE p.12	LESSON 2 CORE p.16	LESSON 3 p.20
CREATION AND PERFORMANCE	Singing	• *Practice good posture and deep breathing for singing*	• Sing call-and-response song • Sing legato phrases • *Practice diaphragmatic breathing and singing phrases*	• Speak and sing in heavier and lighter registers, canon • *Practice finding lighter register* • Create unique ways to say things
	Playing	• *Play unpitched instruments to show meter*	• *Play pitched introduction, change phrase lengths* • *Play Orff orchestration*	
	Moving	• Pat with beat and clap rhythm of words • Perform pat-clap pattern in meter • *Conduct in meter* • Show meter by changing body movement	• Change body facing and body percussion, perform circle dance to show phrases • *Learn "step-it-down" step and move with beat* • Draw curved pathways for phrases of unequal length • *Walk with beat to show phrase lengths*	• *Change body facing with strong beats*
	Improvising/ Creating			• *Plan performance using various vocal qualities* • Create unique ways to say things
NOTATION	Reading	• See graphic representation of meter	• Trace phrase lines on notation	• See graphic notation for beat and rhythm • Compare two pitch sets
	Writing			• *Make score with graphic notation*
PERCEPTION AND ANALYSIS	Listening/ Describing/ Analyzing	• Listen to and describe languages and instruments from diverse cultures	• Listen for and compare phrase lengths • Discuss characteristics of song's phrases	• Describe vocal qualities and changes heard • Determine which register is heard

 TECHNOLOGY

SHARE THE MUSIC VIDEOS

Use videos to reinforce, extend, and enrich learning.
· Lesson 1, p. 13: Introduction to Computers in Music
· Lesson 3, p. 20: Making a Music Video (vocal techniques)

MUSIC WITH *MIDI*

MIDI technology allows students to manipulate musical elements and make musical decisions with this song:
· Lesson 2, p. 17: 'Way Down Yonder in the Brickyard

MUSICTIME™

This notational software develops students' music reading and writing skills through activities correlated to these lessons:
· Lesson 4, Project 1 (create a percussion pattern)
· Lessons 5 & 7, Project 2 (create a melody)
· Lesson 9, Project 3 (compose and notate a melody)

OVERVIEW

Italic = Meeting Individual Needs

LESSON 4 CORE p.24	LESSON 5 CORE p.28	LESSON 6 p.32	LESSON 7 p.36	LESSON 8 p.40
	• Sing with pitch syllables • *Practice matching pitch* • *Sing countermelody*	• Sing phrases with pitch syllables	• Echo-sing phrases with pitch syllables • Sing phrases from notation • Sing melody composed in class	• Sing mouth music
• Perform rhythm pattern with ♩, ♩ • *Play unpitched percussion ostinato* • *Perform phrases in ⁴*	• *Play Orff orchestration*	• *Play bordun, unpitched percussion, and pitched phrases*	• *Play Orff instruments* • Play unpitched percussion	• Play unpitched instruments
• Create nonlocomotor movements • Tap with beat, pat with strong beats	• Draw melodic contours in air • *Use body staff to show pitch changes* • Add body-percussion pattern • *Perform rhythmic movement*	• Draw melodic contours of phrases • Perform movement to show phrases • Follow a listening map, raising hand to show phrase form • Stand upon singing assigned phrases	• *Use hand signs or body staff to identify pitch syllables*	• Create movement ostinatos in ⁴ • *Move to the beat and strong beat to show meter*
• *Create 4-measure patterns in ⁴*		• *Create new verses to familiar melody* • *Create different and similar pitched phrases*	• Create melody for poem • *Improvise melodic phrases for B section*	• Create 8-beat ostinatos in ⁴ with ♩, ♩
• Read rhythm pattern with ♩, ♫, ♩, and ♩	• Sing with pitch syllables from notation • Match graphic notation to phrases • Study notation to find *la*		• Put notated phrases in correct order • Play unpitched percussion from diagram	• Read notation with ♩, ♫, ♩, ♩
• *Write 4-measure patterns in ⁴*			• Notate composed melodies	
• Listen for beginning of each measure	• Listen for *mi so* and *do re mi* patterns, and for *la*	• Distinguish same, different, similar phrases	• Identify *mi so la* and *do re mi* phrases • *Analyze class melody for form*	• Listen for mouth music in Celtic folk music

MUSIC ACE™

Music Ace reinforces musical concepts and provides ear-training opportunities for students.
- **Lesson 5, p. 28: Lesson 1 (staff); Lesson 7 (pitch names); Lesson 10 (ledger lines)**
- **Lesson 7, p. 36: Lesson 7 (pitch names)**

NEW! MUSIC ACE 2™

Music Ace 2™ introduces basic rhythm concepts and furthers the melodic and harmonic concepts covered in Music Ace.

UNIT 1 PLANNER

FOCUS We can explore music from all over the world.

OBJECTIVE To set the stage for Unit 1

MATERIALS
Voices of the World (poem)
Sir Duke   CD1:10
Sir Duke (performance mix)   CD10:7
unpitched instruments

The Unit Opener suggestions throughout the book give teachers and students an opportunity to reflect on the theme of the unit. The theme poem and song may be introduced as a preview as the prior unit is completed, or may be presented as an introduction to Lesson 1. The Unit Theme Projects and the Unit Music Project, which may be completed on an ongoing basis throughout the unit, offer suggestions for creating music and for integrating the students' musical learning with other curriculum areas.

INTRODUCE THE UNIT THEME

1. Discuss the theme. "In music class, we will explore music from close at hand and from far away. Getting to know music is like getting to know new friends. As we become familiar with them, we find we grow to enjoy them." Have students:

• Look around the room and raise their hands if they see faces that were (are) new to them on the first day of school.

VOICES OF THE WORLD

There is music
in the hearts of people—
the music of joy
turned into song—
a roundelay of happiness—
lifting all voices
in one choir
of the world.

There is a dance-step
to the heart-beat of people—
a timing of gladness—
of nimble feet
and clapping hands—
widening around
the magic circle
of the world.

There is music
in the gypsy-tune
of violins—
a piper's flute—
the roll of an organ chord—
a tinkling chime—
the drum-beat
of a town-band on parade. . .
Music is the sound of life awakening
The voices of the world!

—*Stefi Samuelson*

U N I T 1 T H E M E P R O J E C T S

The songs in this unit will give students the opportunity to become more familiar with different cultures. As the students experience the music, they will discover ways in which cultures differ from each other. They will also realize that people of different cultures are more alike than different.

CREATE A BULLETIN BOARD OF A MUSICAL JOURNEY
Cover a bulletin board with a map of the world. Have students find the place of origin of each of the songs that they learn, and on that spot on the map have them place a picture they create that illustrates the song. *(Lessons 1, 2, 3, and 5)*

CREATE A WHERE-IN-THE-WORLD ATLAS After learning a song from a particular culture, have students research the area and write an essay or a poem about it. They may wish to draw a picture of the traditional dress, if any, of the area. Add the essays, poems, and drawings to the "Musical Journey" bulletin board. *(Lessons 1, 2, and 3)*

2. Introduce "Voices of the World."
"There is music in the hearts of everyone. The poem 'Voices of the World' expresses one person's view of hearing music everywhere." Have students:

• Read the poem aloud in groups. (Divide the class in three groups with each group reading a separate stanza.)

• Read the poem again and identify as many musical images as they can.

WRITE A POEM IN FOLK STYLE Have students keep the rhythm of "Fed My Horse" (page 31) but change the words of the verse. For example: "Brought my dog to the park today, Brought my dog to the park today, Brought my dog to the park today, all he did was run and play." Students may work individually or in small groups. Have them write out their words and add them to the bulletin board under the heading "New Words to an Old Tune." *(Lesson 5)*

THEME: WHERE IN THE WORLD?

3. Introduce "Sir Duke" CD1:10. "Jazz is a very popular form of music. 'Sir Duke' is a tribute to many famous jazz musicians. This song will be our theme song for Unit 1." Have students:

• Listen to "Sir Duke" and pat with the beat.

• Listen again (Verse 1 and refrain), following the notation.

• Find the names mentioned in the song. [Explain that they are great jazz musicians—Duke Ellington (1889–1974), jazz composer and big band leader; Count Basie (1904–1984), jazz pianist and band leader; Glenn Miller (1904–1944), trombonist and swing band leader; "Satchmo"—Louis Armstrong (1900–1971), trumpeter and singer; Ella Fitzgerald (1917–1996), jazz singer.]

4. Set the stage for Unit 1. Have students:

• Describe where they hear music in the "voices of the world," that is, all around us. (background music on radio or television, rhythmic movement of stepping, heartbeats, clocks)

• Look through the unit and find all the different countries that are mentioned in the songs. Identify one song that they would especially like to learn. (Play the recording as a preview if time permits.)

• Read "Voices of the World," tapping with the beat on unpitched instruments.

• Hum along with "Sir Duke."

UNIT 1 THEME SONG

In cultures throughout the world, people enjoy expressing their thoughts and feelings through music. A song's origin can often be identified by the way the melody and rhythms sound, the instruments used, and the words.

Duke Ellington

Eb major

Sir Duke

Words and Music by
Stevie Wonder

Verse   Eb   Cm

1. Mu - sic   is   a   world with - in   it - self____   be
2. Mu - sic knows it   is   and   al - ways   will____   be

Cb   Bb

with   a   lan - guage we all   un - der - stand,____
one   of   the things that life   just won't   quit.____

Eb   Cm

with   an   e - qual   op - por - tu - ni - ty____
But   here   are   some   of   mu - sic's   pi - o - neers,____

Cb   Bb   A7

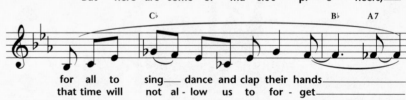

for   all   to   sing____ dance and clap their hands____
that time will   not al - low   us   to   for - get____

10

UNIT 1 MUSIC PROJECT:

Students should keep a folder to save their work as they complete various stages of this project. As they complete these activities, students will grow in understanding of reading and writing rhythms in ⅔ and ¼ and of recognizing patterns using *do re mi so la*. Completion of this project will help students achieve success in the "Create" activity in Lesson 9.

1 WRITE A THREE-NOTE MELODY Have students clap the pattern on page 26, then assign pitches from resonator bells F G A to the rhythm. Have them practice singing their pitches with *do re mi*, using hand signs. Finally, have them write the letters and pitch syllable names under the rhythm and put it in their folders.
(After Lesson 4)

but just be-cause a re-cord has a groove don't make it in the groove
for there's— Ba-sie, Mil- ler, Satch-mo,— and the king of all, Sir Duke,

but you can tell right a - way at let - ter A— when the
and with a voice like— El - la's ring - in' out,— there's no

Refrain

peo-ple start to move. They} can feel it all— o - ver.—
way the band can lose. You}

They} can feel it all— o - ver,— peo - ple.— {They can feel it all—
You} {You

o - ver.— {They can feel it all— o - ver,— peo - ple, go!
{You

Is there anyone
you look up to?
Stevie Wonder
expresses his
admiration for
some of his
heroes in
"Sir Duke."

Louis Armstrong

Ella Fitzgerald

Program Idea: A United Nations Meeting

Have students develop a program based on a scenario of a United Nations meeting. Delegates from different nations are getting to-gether to share their cultures with each other in order to promote more understanding among different peoples. The delegates (students) sing songs from various cultures and share some facts about these cultures. If possible, have students make or bring artifacts or traditional garb from various countries. Suggest the following songs and ideas:

• People feel comfortable at home, wherever that may be: "Take Me Home, Country Roads" (page 12)

• Singing and dancing are ways that people have fun. Here is a joyful melody from Trinidad and Tobago: "I Let Her Go, Go" (page 15) And an-other joyful song of African American origin: "'Way Down Yonder in the Brickyard" (page 17) And still another song just for fun from Southern Appalachia: "Fed My Horse" (page 31)

• Different places have different names for the same thing. In Ireland a swamp is called a bog: "Hi! Ho! The Rattlin' Bog" (page 23)

• Songs can tell us about the way people live in different lands. In this we learn about tending sheep in parts of China: "Mongolian Night Song" (page 19)

• Sometimes people leave their homes and travel to new places in order to better themselves: "The California Song" (page 48)

CREATE A MELODY

2 DEVELOP THE PATTERN Have students use the same pattern from page 26 as in the above activity. Ask them to practice the pattern they wrote using *do re mi* (F G A). They should then write a second line based on the same rhythm, only this time using *do re mi so la* (F G A C D). *(After Lesson 5)*

UNIT ONE
LESSON 1

RELATED ARTS MOVEMENT | THEATER | VISUAL ARTS

LESSON PLANNER

FOCUS Duration/Meter

OBJECTIVES

OBJECTIVE 1 Change from clapping the rhythm of the words to patting with the beat in response to a visual cue

OBJECTIVE 2 Perform a pattern showing ₂ meter in time with a song (tested)

OBJECTIVE 3 Identify the meter of a song in ₄ meter (tested)

MATERIALS
Recordings
Listening: Where in the World?   CD1:9
Take Me Home, Country Roads   CD1:11
Take Me Home, Country Roads
  (performance mix)   CD10:8
Hi! Ho! The Rattlin' Bog   CD1:12
I Let Her Go, Go   CD1:13

Other ball

Resources Resource Master 1 • 1
(practice)

VOCABULARY
beat, meter signature

▶ = **BASIC PROGRAM**

A MUSICAL WORLD

Take Me Home, Country Roads

Words and Music
by Bill Danoff, Taffy Nivert,
and John Denver

F major

12

MEETING **INDIVIDUAL** NEEDS

ALTERNATE TEACHING STRATEGY

OBJECTIVE 1 Ask students to choose a familiar song or rhyme, such as "Yankee Doodle" or "Humpty Dumpty." Clap the rhythm of the words, then explain what you were doing. Have them clap and sing with you. Repeat as you clap with the beat. Have them describe the difference, using their own words. Finally, have the class identify whether a student is clapping the rhythm of the words or is clapping with the beat.

SPECIAL LEARNERS: *Showing Beat and Rhythm*

MOVEMENT

Assign students of varying abilities to groups of three, with no more than one disabled student per group. Have each group select two movements—one for rhythm and one for beat—that all group members can do. As the class sings familiar songs or says rhythms, have a few groups perform one of their movements. Emphasize that this activity is practice and that group members should encourage each other to move correctly to the beat and rhythm. Working in small groups will help special learners develop skills and experience friendly relationships with nondisabled peers.

moun - tain mom - ma,___ Take___ me home,___ coun - try roads.___

I hear her voice, in the morn - in' hours she calls___ me, the ra - di - o re - minds me of my home far a - way, and driv - in' down the road I get a feel - in' that I should have been home yes - ter - day,___ yes - ter - day.___

Go back to 𝄋 and sing to the end (D.S. 𝄋 al Fine)

When you tap your foot to a song, you're tapping to the **beat**, or the steady pulse that you feel.

The long and short sounds and silences that occur when you sing the words are called the rhythm of the words.

Unit 1 *Where in the World?* 13

"Some faces in this class may be familiar to you and others may not. That will change as you get to know one another. As you listen to 'Where in the World?' you may find that some words and sounds will be familiar to you and others won't." Have students:

▶ • Listen to "Where in the World?" CD1:9 in which they hear languages and instruments from diverse cultures. Then discuss what they recognized.

"This year you will become familiar with voices and music of our world through singing and playing, reading and listening. Today you'll work with how beats are grouped as you sing some new songs."

2 DEVELOP

1. Introduce "Take Me Home, Country Roads" CD1:11. **Pat with the beat.** Have students:

▶ • Listen to the song and pat with the beat.

▶ • Listen again, following the notation.

2. Identify beat and word rhythm in "Take Me Home, Country Roads." Have students:

▶ • Read about beat and rhythm of the words on page 13.

OBJECTIVE 1 Informal Assessment

• Listen to the song, clapping the rhythm of the words of the verse, then patting with the beat for the refrain.

VOCAL DEVELOPMENT: *Posture and Breathing*

Posture: Have students sit forward on the edge of their chairs. They should sit tall, sternum high, shoulders down. If standing, students should have their feet slightly apart and shoulders back and down. This is the "singing position."

Breathing: Breathing for singing is deeper than everyday breathing. Have students put one hand on their chest and the other hand just below their waist. Over three beats inhale. Over five beats exhale with a hissing sound. Only the bottom hand moves as they inhale and exhale. Over three beats have the students inhale, then sing the alphabet to K, repeat to M, and so on.

MUSIC BUILDS READING SKILLS

Listening In listening to a song and clapping the rhythm of the words of the verse, students will be listening critically and responsively.

MOVEMENT: *Moving in Unison*

Have students listen to the recording, patting with the beat. Then have small groups choreograph simple 4- or 8-beat stepping patterns, refining movements.

UNIT ONE
LESSON 1

continued from previous page

2. Introduce "Hi! Ho! The Rattlin' Bog"
CD1:12. Perform a pattern to show ₂ meter.
Have students:

▶ • Read about "Hi! Ho! The Rattlin' Bog."

▶ • Sing the refrain, patting on the strong beats
and clapping on the weak beats as you bounce
a ball with the strong beats and catch it with
the weak beats.

OBJECTIVE 2 Informal Assessment
• Perform the pat-clap pattern while singing
the refrain of "Hi! Ho! The Rattlin' Bog."

▶ • Read about sets of beats on page 14.

• Describe the way beats are grouped in "Hi!
Ho! The Rattlin' Bog," then locate the meter
signature on the notation.

3 APPLY

**Introduce "I Let Her Go, Go" CD1:13. Iden-
tify meter.** Have students:

▶ • Explore different body designs or shapes.
(See *Movement* on the bottom of page 15.)

▶ • Listen to "I Let Her Go, Go," changing body
shape on each strong beat.

▶ • Make one shape on the strong beats and flick
fingers on all other beats.

▶ • Count the beats in each set. (four)

OBJECTIVE 3 Informal Assessment
• Point to the pattern on page 4 that shows the
meter of the song. (set of four beats)

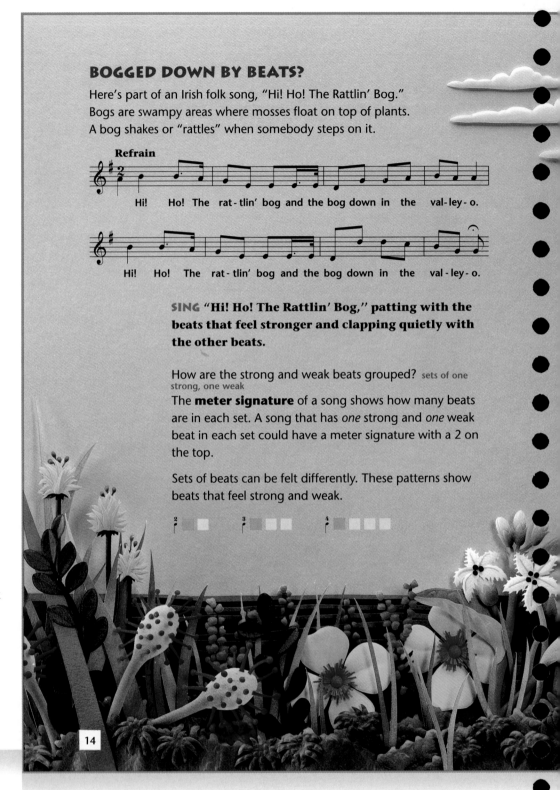

BOGGED DOWN BY BEATS?

Here's part of an Irish folk song, "Hi! Ho! The Rattlin' Bog."
Bogs are swampy areas where mosses float on top of plants.
A bog shakes or "rattles" when somebody steps on it.

Refrain

Hi! Ho! The rat-tlin' bog and the bog down in the val-ley-o.

Hi! Ho! The rat-tlin' bog and the bog down in the val-ley-o.

SING "Hi! Ho! The Rattlin' Bog," patting with the
**beats that feel stronger and clapping quietly with
the other beats.**

How are the strong and weak beats grouped? sets of one
strong, one weak
The **meter signature** of a song shows how many beats
are in each set. A song that has *one* strong and *one* weak
beat in each set could have a meter signature with a 2 on
the top.

Sets of beats can be felt differently. These patterns show
beats that feel strong and weak.

14

MEETING **INDIVIDUAL** NEEDS

ALTERNATE TEACHING STRATEGIES

OBJECTIVE 2 Have students use **Resource Master 1 • 1** to
practice identifying beats in sets of two, three, and four.
Draw the first pattern on the board and have students watch you
tap the symbols as they listen to the refrain of "Hi! The
Rattlin' Bog." (Pattern repeats.) Then have them perform the
pat-clap pattern as they sing the refrain and watch you bounce-
catch the ball.

OBJECTIVE 3 Form groups of five, each with four singers
and one beat-tapper. Sing "I Let Her Go, Go" while the

beat-tapper of each group taps the hands of each singer in
the group four times in turn, starting on the first *go*.

PLAYING INSTRUMENTS: *Unpitched*

Transfer the pat-clap pattern to sticks, tapping both sticks
on the floor with Beat 1 and clicking them together with
Beat 2 during the refrain of "Hi! Ho! The Rattlin' Bog."

ENRICHMENT: *Conducting in ₂*

Reinforce strong and weak beats in ₂ by teaching students to
conduct. Have them make a downward motion with their

"How is the rhythm of the words different from the beat?" (beat is steady; rhythm of words has long and short sounds) "What sets of beats did you work with today?" (two and four) Have students:

• Sing "I Let Her Go, Go," clapping on each *go* and patting with the rhythm of the other words.

▶ • Show the meter by making shapes on strong beats and flicking fingers on weak beats during the instrumental interludes.

Here's a folk song from the islands of Trinidad and Tobago. As you listen, see if you can feel the beat.

I Let Her Go, Go

Folk Song from
Trinidad and Tobago
Adapted by Carol King

I let her go, go, Ee ay I let her go, go,

Ee ay I let her go ___ I let her go, go, go.

FIND the pattern on page 14 that shows the set of beats used in this song. What is the meter signature? 1 strong, 3 weak; 4/4

LESSON SUMMARY

Informal Assessment In this lesson, students:

OBJECTIVE 1 Changed from clapping the rhythm of words to patting with the beat while singing "Take Me Home, Country Roads."

OBJECTIVE 2 Performed a pattern showing 2/4 meter with the refrain of "Hi! Ho! The Rattlin' Bog."

OBJECTIVE 3 Identified the meter of "I Let Her Go, Go" by pointing to the pattern that shows a set of four beats.

National Standards for Music Education

1b Sing with appropriate dynamics, phrasing, and interpretation.

2b Perform easy patterns on various classroom instruments.

6d Identify instrumental and vocal sounds from various cultures.

MORE MUSIC: Reinforcement
More Songs to Read, page 346 (4/4 meter)
"Festival," page 296 (beat, rhythm of words)

---

hands when they feel the strong beats and an upward motion on the weak beats. Compare the conducting motion with the bounce-catch motion. Then conduct, saying *1, 2.* Draw the figure on the board and allow students to trace the pattern as they say *down, up* or *1, 2.* Some students may benefit if you take their hands and guide them physically in the correct manner.

MOVEMENT: *Exploring Body Design*

MOVEMENT

Body design, or shape, is an important movement concept. The following activities will help students to develop a large vocabulary of body design. Have students stand in a scattered formation where they are not touching anyone or anything. Have them make: **(1)** Statues or shapes, using images such as tall, skinny, curvy, pointed, fat, flat, tiny, or strong. **(2)** Shapes with a designated number of body parts touching the floor. For example, if three body parts must touch, they might stand on one leg with both hands on the floor. **(3)** Letters of the alphabet with their bodies.

ACROSS the

MULTICULTURAL PERSPECTIVES

ART

EXPRESSIVE ART

"Voices of the World"

INDIVIDUAL   **30 MIN OR LONGER**

MATERIALS: art paper, scissors, glue, tissue paper, crayons, markers

Read "Voices of the World." Have students think of what music means to them. Ask them to close their eyes and think how they might paint this poem. Then give each student a sheet of paper and art materials. Ask them to make a picture of the poem. Remind them to consider shape, line, color, symbols, and patterns. Encourage creativity and freedom of expression.

(As starter ideas, you might suggest that students read the poem themselves and pick out words that suggest images: *heart-beat, clapping, dance-step*, and so on.)

COMPREHENSION STRATEGY: Visualizing

I who ran the fastest in our school track day

SOCIAL STUDIES

NAMES

"Sir Duke"

INDIVIDUAL   **30 MIN OR LONGER**

MATERIALS: optional—reference books

Have students find names in the song. Explain that they are famous musicians: *Basie*—Count Basie; *Miller*—Glenn Miller; *Satchmo*—Louis Armstrong; *Sir Duke*—Edward Kennedy ("Duke") Ellington; *Ella*—Ella Fitzgerald.

Have students tell which of these names they think were not the actual first or last name of the person. (*Satchmo* and *Sir Duke*)

Ask "If you were to give yourself a name that told something about you, what would it be?" Have each student decide on a new "personal" name and describe what it signifies. Suggest the way Native Americans were named. A Native American name may have included a person's clan, accomplishments, appearance, or an event in a person's life: *Man-Afraid-of-His-Horse*.

Students might research any of the jazz greats named in the song and write a short biographical sketch of the artist's accomplishments.

COMPREHENSION STRATEGY: Summarizing

CURRICULUM

MATHEMATICS

CALCULATOR

"I Let Her Go, Go"

PAIR   15–30 MIN
MATERIALS: calculator

How many times is the word *go* sung in the first line of music? How many times is it sung in the second line of music? How many times is it sung in the whole song? (4, 4, 8) Once students have answered these questions, have them explore repeated addition using calculators.

How many times would you sing the word *go* if you sang the song four times? Students can multiply 4 x 8 to get 32. However, ask them to find a way of answering by pressing the addition key once and then only the equal-sign key.

(The equal-sign key repeats operations: press 8, press + , press 8, and press = to show one addition of 8. Then press = two more times to show repeated additions of 8 to get a total of 32. Or press 8, press +, and press = four times.)

Have students use this method to write problems of their own and share them with a partner.

COMPREHENSION STRATEGY: Determining steps in a process

SCIENCE/ART

BOG SETTING

"Hi! Ho! The Rattlin' Bog"

WHOLE CLASS   15 MIN OR LESS
MATERIALS: large glass jar, water, sand or soil, shredded newspaper, kitchen sponges, scissors; alternatives—drawing paper, crayons, markers

A bog is an area of wet, spongy land. It develops in a lake that has little drainage. Moss grows over the surface of the water, forming a thick mat that looks like solid ground. It "rattles" when stepped on. Forest animals often fall through it into the lake.

Decaying matter from the mat, and decaying plants and animals in the lake, drift down and form a thick, slushy "false bottom" over the solid bottom, which eventually forms peat.

As moss gets thicker at the top and the false bottom gets thicker, the lake gradually fills in—but does not become solid enough to prevent an animal from falling in.

Have students make a model to show these facts. They can pack the bottom of a jar with soil or sand. Wet, shredded newspaper can be used for the "false bottom." Fill half the jar with water and float thin strips of sponge at the top (moss).

Children may wish to draw their bogs. If so, they may add pictures of animals—such as dragonflies, mosquitoes, ducks, and frogs—and plants like shrubs and trees that root in the mat as well as on the shore.

COMPREHENSION STRATEGY: Visualizing

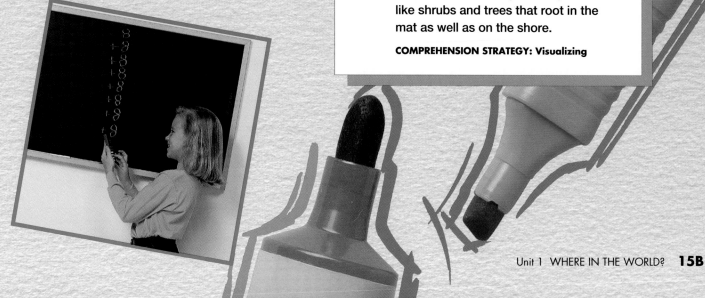

UNIT ONE
LESSON 2

RELATED ARTS | MOVEMENT | THEATER | VISUAL ARTS |

LESSON PLANNER

FOCUS Phrase

OBJECTIVES

OBJECTIVE 1 Signal to show recognition of phrases in a song (tested)

OBJECTIVE 2 Move to show recognition of phrases of different lengths (tested)

MATERIALS

Recordings

Sir Duke	CD1:10
'Way Down Yonder in the Brickyard	CD1:14
Mongolian Night Song	CD1:15
Listening: Les saluts	CD1:16

Resources

Signing Master S • 4 • 2 (Mongolian Night Song)

Orff Orchestration O • 2 (Mongolian Night Song)

Technology Music with MIDI: 'Way Down Yonder in the Brickyard

VOCABULARY

phrase, pitch, melody, call-and-response

▶ = **BASIC PROGRAM**

Musical Ideas Are Everywhere

Have you ever read a story without words? Try this one! Each picture stands for one idea. When all the ideas are put together, they tell a story.

Music is also made up of ideas. A complete musical idea is called a **phrase.** A phrase is made of high and low sounds, or **pitches.** When phrases are put together, they make up a song or a **melody.**

16

MEETING **INDIVIDUAL** NEEDS

ALTERNATE TEACHING STRATEGY

OBJECTIVE 1 As two groups listen to the A section, one group stands only on *Remember me*, the other only on any other phrases. Have two students from each group draw phrase lines on the board while their group stands. (They should draw four phrase lines of equal length.)

MULTICULTURAL PERSPECTIVES: *Gullah Songs*

"'Way Down Yonder in the Brickyard" is one of many songs performed by Frankie and Doug Quimby. They are the two remaining members of the Georgia Sea Island

Singers, a group formed to preserve the Gullah culture of these isolated islands. Since enslaved Africans had limited access to musical instruments, the Quimbys sing a cappella or with rhythm instruments.

MUSIC BUILDS READING SKILLS

Listening In listening to a song and identifying the phrase that occurs most often, students will be listening critically to evaluate.

In a **call-and-response** song, call phrases are sung by a leader and response phrases are sung by the group. Find the phrases as you listen to this song.

Pentatonic

d r m s l d'

'Way Down Yonder in the Brickyard

Traditional African American Game Song As Performed by the Georgia Sea Island Singers

A Call **Freely** Response G C

'Way down yon-der in the brick-yard, Re-mem-ber me.

Call C Response G C

'Way down yon-der in the brick-yard, Re-mem-ber me.

B Call Am Response C G C

Oh, step it, step it, step it down.—— Re-mem-ber me.

Call Am Response C G C

Oh, step it, step it, step it down.—— Re-mem-ber me.

C Call F C Response G C

Oh, swing your la-dy, turn her a-round,—— Re-mem-ber me.

Call F C Response G C

Oh, swing your la-dy, turn her a-round,—— Re-mem-ber me.

Unit 1 *Where in the World?* **17**

"As we listen to this song, do what I do." Have students:

• Listen to "Sir Duke" CD1:10 and imitate your movement after you demonstrate facing a different wall in the room when each phrase begins. (See phrase lines in notation on pages 10–11.)

"These movements showed something special about how this song is put together—something you will learn about today."

2 DEVELOP

1. Introduce phrases in "Sir Duke" (pp. 10–11). Have students:

▶ • Read about phrases on page 16.

▶ • Sing each phrase of the refrain of "Sir Duke," then sing the song and trace the phrase lines over the notation on pages 10–11.

2. Introduce "'Way Down Yonder in the Brickyard" CD1:14. Identify phrases and learn the song. Have students:

▶ • Listen to the song and identify the phrase that occurs most often (*Remember me*), then clap the rhythm of that phrase.

OBJECTIVE 1 Informal Assessment
• Close eyes and listen to the A section, showing phrase recognition by raising hands during the first phrase, dropping hands for the next, and so on. (four two-measure phrases)

• Discuss how these phrases differ from those of "Sir Duke." (these—all same length; "Sir Duke"—varying lengths)

▶ • Read about call-and-response phrases.

▶ • Learn to sing the song.

▶ • Sing with movement. (See *Movement: "'Way Down Yonder in the Brickyard"* below.)

MOVEMENT: *"'Way Down Yonder in the Brickyard"*

MOVEMENT

Practice a "step-it-down" step. (Verbal Cue—*touch, close, touch, close*) Touch right foot forward and lean slightly into it but do *not* transfer weight completely, then close (step) right foot back into place. Repeat with left foot. Do this flat-footed, as if softly stamping. **Step facing a partner.** As students touch forward, the inside of the right foot will be next to their partner's. The same will happen when they touch the left foot forward.

Formation: partners in two parallel lines, with lines two arm-lengths apart

Start each pattern with the right foot.

A section: (Verbal Cue—*step, clap, step, clap*) Step in place on Beats 1 and 3, clap on Beats 2 and 4.

B section: Meas. 1–2; 5–6—Step-it-down, alternating right and left feet; **Meas. 3–4; 7–8**—same as A section.

C section: Meas. 1–2—right-elbow swing with partner, exchanging places; **Meas. 3–4**—same as A section, except head dancer of one line step-claps down the outside to foot of set and rest of line moves up. **Meas. 5–6**—head dancer continues, others swing new partners; **Meas. 7–8**—same as A section, head dancer reaches foot.

UNIT ONE LESSON 2

continued from previous page

3 APPLY

1. Introduce "Mongolian Night Song" CD1:15. **Identify phrases.** Have students:

▶ • Read about the song on page 18.

▶ • With eyes closed, listen to the song, drawing a curved pathway in the air for each sung phrase.

▶ • Discuss characteristics of the phrases: some feel longer than others, some are sung, and some are played by instruments.

OBJECTIVE 2 Informal Assessment
• Listen again, drawing the sung phrases in the air with curved pathways (eight phrases of unequal length) and remaining still during the interlude. (Students may be in scattered formation around the room—some sitting, some kneeling, some standing. They may use ribbon-sticks or crepe-paper streamers for a visual effect.)

▶ • Learn the song.

2. Introduce "Les saluts" CD1:16. **Perform movement to show phrases.** Have students:

▶ • Learn the French Canadian dance to "Les saluts" (le sa lü) for more practice with musical phrases and to review body design and various ways to move in a circle. (clockwise, counterclockwise, in and out) (See *Movement* on the bottom of page 19; form is intro [8 beats], A B six times.)

A SONG FROM INNER MONGOLIA

Inner Mongolia is part of China. Some people live by herding animals, and the children help by watching over their families' sheep. The children may sing or play flutes to calm the flocks, just as you'd sing a lullaby to comfort a baby.

CHINESE MIRROR PAINTING
This mirror was painted when Qian-long was emperor of China (1735–1796). One woman plays a traditional flute, the other a frame drum and wooden clappers.

18 MUSICAL IDEAS ARE EVERYWHERE

MEETING **INDIVIDUAL** NEEDS

ALTERNATE TEACHING STRATEGY

OBJECTIVE 2 Eight walkers stand along one wall. The class claps to the beat of "Mongolian Night Song," changing body percussion (snap, pat) on each new phrase. The first walker walks with the beat until a new phrase begins, then freezes while the second one walks with the next sung phrase. Continue until the song ends, then look at the walkers' positions (distances from wall) to compare phrase lengths. For visual reinforcement, each walker may unroll a ribbon, attached to the wall, when walking away.

VOCAL DEVELOPMENT: *Diaphragmatic Breathing*

Have students put their hands just below their waists and laugh a deep *hah, hah, hah*. They will feel their abdominal muscles move. Now ask them to breathe "down" to where they felt the impulses, and sing the first phrase of "Mary Had a Little Lamb" on one breath. Have them sing each phrase of "Mongolian Night Song" on one breath.

SIGNING: *"Mongolian Night Song"*
Signing Master S • 4 • 2 has sign language for this song.

MOVE your arm in an arch to show each phrase you hear in "Mongolian Night Song." Then sing the song.

Mongolian Night Song

Traditional Inner Mongolian Song
Collected and Translated by Gloria Kiester

1. Lit - tle girl who tends the sheep, Brings them to the fold to sleep.
2. In the moon-light's gold - en glow, Soft the wind be - gins to blow.

Lit - tle lambs are bounc - ing by to their moth - er's bleat - ing cry,
Lit - tle lambs are fast a - sleep, ly - ing by the oth - er sheep.

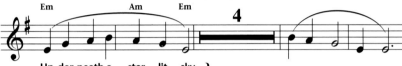

Un-der-neath a star - lit sky. }
Still a si - lent watch she keeps. }
All a - lone she waits.

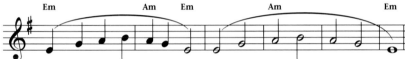

"In the dark I'm not a - fraid. I've a lamp to light the way."
"When I'm tend-ing all a - lone, All I think a - bout is home."

Four-tone

l, d r m

"Today you learned about phrases in music. How can you describe a phrase?" (a musical idea, part of a song) Have students:

▶ • Sing "Mongolian Night Song" once more, drawing in the air to show phrases of different lengths.

LESSON SUMMARY

Informal Assessment In this lesson, students:

OBJECTIVE 1 Signaled at the beginning of phrases in "'Way Down Yonder in the Brickyard."
OBJECTIVE 2 Moved to show phrases of different lengths in "Mongolian Night Song."

National Standards for Music Education
1b Sing with appropriate dynamics, phrasing, and interpretation.
2c Play repertoire from diverse genres and cultures.
6b Describe, in words or movement, music from diverse cultures.

MORE MUSIC: Reinforcement
More Songs to Read, page 347 (phrases)
"America, the Beautiful," page 300 (phrases; patriotic)
"Allundé, Alluia," page 376 (call and re-sponse)

PLAYING INSTRUMENTS: *Keyboards*

Have a student play this phrase three or more times as an introduction to "Mongolian Night Song." Change the tempo, thus the duration of the phrase, each time. Have others draw a curve for each phrase, then describe how the length of the curve changed as the tempo changed.

MOVEMENT: *"Les saluts"* MOVEMENT

Formation: single circle, facing clockwise

A section: Walk 16 beats clockwise; change body facing direction at end of phrase; walk 16 beats counterclockwise.

B section—Beats 1–4: Face in, take four steps into center.
Beats 5–8: Four steps back out. **Beats 9–12:** (and fermata of varying length) Make a shape in place, hold through fermata.
Beats 12–16: Face clockwise, ready to walk.

ORFF: *"Mongolian Night Song"*
See **O • 2** in *Orchestrations for Orff Instruments.*

ACROSS the

LANGUAGE ARTS

COMMUNICATION

"Sir Duke"

GROUP — 15–30 MIN

This song describes music as *a language we all understand.* Have students work in groups to describe other examples of how messages can be communicated universally. They can start with their own experiences in their neighborhoods:

- road signs (stop signs, crossing signs, parking signs),
- danger signs,
- no-smoking signs.

They might mention speaking in sign language, body language, sports symbols or sports talk, or using words that have become universal— such as brand names of products that are sold around the world.

Have each group use any of these examples of universal language (or use several combined) to communicate a message. Each group gets a chance to "perform" the message and other groups get a chance to interpret the message.

COMPREHENSION STRATEGIES: Expressing main ideas, visualizing

LANGUAGE ARTS

DRAMATIZATION

"'Way Down Yonder in the Brickyard"

GROUP — 15 MIN OR LESS

Review the song "'Way Down Yonder in the Brickyard" with the class. Discuss the fact that in a call-and-response song, call phrases are sung by a leader and response phrases are sung by the group. Have them find the call phrases and the response phrases in the song.

Then have students divide into groups and create their own call-and-response phrases, based on things that they are familiar with. They might fit their phrases with a melody, although they could also use a rap style.

As a starter, suggest that they think of some main idea—some recent event, a videogame they enjoy, a film they have seen, and so on. That main idea can be the basis of the call. The response should be the same for each call phrase—or there might be two alternating responses.

Have each group perform their call-and-response phrases for the class.

COMPREHENSION STRATEGY: Expressing main ideas

CURRICULUM

ART

SEQUENCE PAINTINGS

"Mongolian Night Song"

GROUP   **30 MIN OR LONGER**

MATERIALS: long sheets of paper, black paint, brushes, examples of Chinese art

If possible, begin by introducing an example of Chinese art in which black ink or paint has been applied with a brush. You might show painted scrolls and screens on which a story is told through a sequence of pictures.

Divide the class into small groups and give each group a sheet of paper long enough so that they can divide it into separate squares (one for each student) by folding it accordion style. Students listen to the song and discuss what they think it is about. Each group then paints a sequential picture-story of the song, using each folded square to tell part of the story.

COMPREHENSION STRATEGIES: Visualizing, sequencing

SOCIAL STUDIES

CLASS PRESENTATION

"Mongolian Night Song"

GROUP   **30 MIN OR LONGER**

MATERIALS: globe or map of the world, reference books

Help students locate Inner Mongolia (a region of northern China) and the neighboring country of Mongolia (north of China) on a map. Have students assume the role of explorers. Divide the class into groups. Students research the geography and history of Mongolia and Inner Mongolia—their history (from the Mongol Empire and Ghengis Kahn up to the present), land areas they share (such as the Gobi desert), the nomadic lifestyle of people of the Mongolian plains, and so on.

Have the groups organize their findings into written and oral reports, as well as drawings and map displays. Students can put on a class presentation, with members of each group presenting their findings.

COMPREHENSION STRATEGY: Organizing information

UNIT ONE
LESSON 3

LESSON PLANNER

FOCUS Tone color

OBJECTIVES
OBJECTIVE 1 Speak a speech piece in two vocal registers
OBJECTIVE 2 Sing a song using the heavier register
OBJECTIVE 3 Signal to identify lighter register

MATERIALS
Recordings
Listening: Mañana Iguana by
  B. McFerrin   CD1:17
Speech Piece: I Wish (unison)   CD1:18
Recorded Lesson: Speaking in
  Two Registers   CD1:19
Speech Piece: I Wish (canon)   CD1:20
Recorded Lesson: Singing in
  Two Registers   CD1:21
I Let Her Go, Go   CD1:13
Hi! Ho! The Rattlin' Bog   CD1:12

VOCABULARY
lighter register, heavier register, canon, tone color, cumulative

▶ = **BASIC PROGRAM**

CHOICES WITH VOICES

Have you ever disguised your voice or tried to sound like somebody you know? Then you know you can change the sound of your speaking and singing voice.

🎵 **Mañana Iguana**
LISTENING
by Bobby McFerrin

Bobby McFerrin uses his voice to make all sorts of interesting sounds. What are some things he does to change his voice?

One way to change your voice is to change the register. The **lighter register** is quieter and generally higher in pitch. The **heavier register** is usually louder, fuller, and lower in pitch.

20

MEETING **INDIVIDUAL** NEEDS

ALTERNATE TEACHING STRATEGY
THEATER

OBJECTIVE 1 Have students use their voices in a variety of ways—low, high, light, heavy, and so on. Give the class many opportunities to produce and imitate sounds so they gain control over a wide range of pitches in both registers.

COOPERATIVE LEARNING: *Vocal Exploration*
THEATER

Have small groups plan a way of performing "I Wish" using the range, registers, pitch, duration, loudness, and quality of their voices, modeled after "Mañana Iguana." Encourage them to make a score using graphic notation.

BIOGRAPHY: *Bobby McFerrin*

Bobby McFerrin (b. 1950) is an American jazz singer from a family of singers. His father sang on the soundtrack of the film *Porgy and Bess*; his mother works for the Metropolitan Opera. His unique vocal style shows his imagination—he can sound like an entire doo-wop group, tapping percussion on his body and using even the sound of his breathing as music. One of McFerrin's biggest successes was his light-hearted hit, "Don't Worry, Be Happy." He has appeared on television shows such as *Sesame Street*.

SPEAK "I Wish" in the two registers.

I Wish

Nancy M. Hayes
Adapted by Carol King

1
I   wish,   how I   wish,   that I   had a   lit - tle house,

With a   mat   for the cat   and   a   hole   for the mouse,

And a   clock   go - ing "tock"   in   the cor - ner of   the room

And a   ket - tle, and a   cup - board, and a   big   birch broom.

In a **canon**, all parts perform the same song or poem, but start at different times. Change the sound of the poem by speaking in canon. One group speaks in the heavier register, the other in the lighter register.

Unit 1 *Where in the World?* 21

"Think of some ways you can say goodbye to someone." (bye-bye, so long, see you later, ta-ta) "On this recording by Bobby McFerrin, all of the phrases you hear mean 'Good-bye, I'll see you again.' See how many you can re-member." Have students:

▶ • Listen to "Mañana Iguana" (ma **nya** na i **gwa** na) CD1:17.

▶ • List ways McFerrin said "good-bye."

▶ • Tell how McFerrin changed his voice on the different phrases. (Possible answers: high, low, light, heavy, loud, soft, descriptions of varied sounds)

"Today you will learn about using your voice in a variety of ways."

2 DEVELOP

1. Introduce "I Wish." Read the speech piece, using two vocal registers. Have students:

▶ • Listen to "I Wish" (unison CD1:18).

▶ • Read about vocal registers.

Recorded Lesson CD1:19
▶ • Listen to "Speaking in Two Registers" and learn how to speak "I Wish" in two registers.

OBJECTIVE 1 Informal Assessment
• Speak "I Wish" once in each register.

• Read about canons on page 21, then divide into two groups, one for each register.

• Listen to "I Wish" (canon CD1:20), then speak it in canon. (The second voice enters four beats after the first; one group uses the lighter register, one group uses the heavier register.)

ENRICHMENT: *Vocal Exploration* THEATER

Have students listen again for all the ways Bobby McFerrin uses his voice as he sings "Mañana Iguana." Have several students say their favorite expression from the song in both registers and make up their own unique way to say their favorite expressions.

CAREERS: *Arranger*

The *Cooperative Learning* exercise (on the bottom of page 20) gives students a chance to plan a performance of "I Wish" using a variety of ranges and pitches. This is very similar to what an arranger does. An arranger's main func-

tion is to score the various parts of a musical composition. The arranger may put together a musical composition for an orchestra, band, or individual artists. This is accomplished by determining voice, instrument, harmonic structure, rhythm, tempo, and tone balance to achieve the desired effect. By working closely with the artist and producer, the arranger can take a song and, by creative arranging, turn it into a hit tune.

continued from previous page

2. Review "I Let Her Go, Go" CD1:13 **(p. 15). Sing in heavier register.** Have students:

Recorded Lesson CD1:21
- ▶ • Listen to "Singing in Two Registers" and sing phrases in two registers.
- ▶ • Listen to "I Let Her Go, Go" to determine that the singers use the heavier register.

OBJECTIVE 2 Informal Assessment
- ▶ • Sing "I Let Her Go, Go" using the heavier register.
- ▶ • Sing the song again with movement. (See *Movement: "I Let Her Go, Go"* on the bottom of page 23.)

3 APPLY

Review "Hi! Ho! The Rattlin' Bog" CD1:12 **(p. 14). Determine appropriate vocal register.** Have students:

OBJECTIVE 3 Informal Assessment
- ▶ • Listen to Verse 1 of "Hi! Ho! The Rattlin' Bog" and place their hands on their heads when they hear the singers use the lighter register (mostly lighter register).
- ▶ • Read page 22, then compare the two sets of pitches to determine that higher pitches are more easily sung in the lighter register, and lower pitches in the heavier register.
- ▶ • Read about cumulative songs and sing all the verses, using the lighter register to accommodate the higher pitches.

SING HIGH! SING LOW!

Using different registers, you change the **tone color** of your sound. You can sing different styles and make singing some pitches easier.

Compare two melodies. Most of the notes in "I Let Her Go, Go" are on the lower part of the staff. The lower pitches are probably easier to sing in the heavier register.

I let her go, go,

Now look at the second melody. Are these notes mostly higher or lower than the ones in "I Let Her Go, Go"? Which register will you probably use to sing this part of "Hi! Ho! The Rattlin' Bog"? higher; lighter

Verse

Now in this bog there was a tree, a rare tree, a rat-tlin' tree;

"Hi! Ho! The Rattlin' Bog" song is called a **cumulative** song because each verse adds to the story. Have a rattlin' good time!

22 CHOICES WITH VOICES

MEETING **INDIVIDUAL** NEEDS

ALTERNATE TEACHING STRATEGIES

OBJECTIVE 2 Students with narrow singing ranges in the heavier register may be more successful singing lower pitches. Have them sing the first phrase, *I let her go, go,* and then only on each *go* after that.

OBJECTIVE 3 Have students listen to the recordings of "Hi! Ho! The Rattlin' Bog" and "I Let Her Go, Go." Compare the sounds by having them speak the words of the songs in the same quality in which they are sung. (lighter quality for higher parts of "Hi! Ho! The Rattlin' Bog," heavier for "I Let Her Go, Go") Switch by speaking "I Let Her Go, Go" in the way they spoke higher parts of "Hi! Ho! The Rattlin' Bog," and vice versa. (Sing "Hi! Ho! The Rattlin' Bog" in E♭ or "I Let Her Go, Go" in G to try more of each song in the heavier or lighter register, respectively.)

VOCAL DEVELOPMENT: *Lighter Register*

To help students find their lighter register, have them stand tall, take a deep breath, and call *Yoo-hoo* or sigh lightly. Have them put their hands lightly on their cheeks. It is also easier if they do not sing too loudly. Have a child who succeeds model this for those having difficulty.

G major

s, l d r m f s

Hi! Ho! The Rattlin' Bog

Irish Folk Song

Refrain

Hi! Ho! The rat-tlin' bog and the bog down in the val-ley-o.

End here, last time

Hi! Ho! The rat-tlin' bog and the bog down in the val-ley-o.

Verse

1. Now in this bog there was a tree, a rare tree, a
2. Now on this tree there was a limb, a rare limb, a
3. Now on this limb there was a branch, a rare branch, a
4. Now on this branch there was a nest, a rare nest, a
5. Now in this nest there was an egg, a rare egg, a
6. Now in this egg there was a bird, a rare bird, a

Add a repeat with each verse

rat - tlin' tree; The
rat - tlin' limb; The limb on the tree and the
rat - tlin' branch; The branch on the limb and the
rat - tlin' nest; The nest on the branch and the
rat - tlin' egg; The egg in the nest and the
rat - tlin' bird; The bird in the egg and the

(Skip this measure for verse 1)

1.-6. tree in the bog and the bog down in the val-ley-o.

4 CLOSE

"By using your voice in a variety of ways, you'll be able to sing songs in many styles." Have students:

▶ • Count backward from ten to one in their heavier register, then in their lighter register.

▶ • Sing the refrain of "Hi! Ho! The Rattlin' Bog" using their lighter register.

LESSON SUMMARY

Informal Assessment In this lesson, students:

OBJECTIVE 1 Spoke "I Wish" in two vocal registers.

OBJECTIVE 2 Sang phrases of "I Let Her Go, Go" in the heavier register.

OBJECTIVE 3 Signaled upon hearing the lighter register in "Hi! Ho! The Rattlin' Bog."

National Standards for Music Education
1d Sing ostinatos, partner songs, and rounds.
6d Identify instrumental and vocal sounds from various cultures.

MORE MUSIC: Reinforcement

"The Star-Spangled Banner," page 298 (vocal register; patriotic)

"The Twelve Days of Christmas," page 330 (cumulative song)

"You're Invited: Choral Concert," page 382 (vocal tone color)

"And Where Is Home?," page 378 (vocal tone color)

"Hallelujah Chorus" from *Messiah,* page 385A (vocal tone color)

MOVEMENT: *"I Let Her Go, Go"*

This activity prepares students for the game on page 41.

Formation: partners facing

Song: Clap own hands on each *go* or *go, go*.

Interlude: (8 measures) Jump once in place with each strong beat, changing body facing (see definition following) with each jump to complete a rotation. First jump—partners land side by side, shoulder to shoulder; second jump—land back to back; third jump—land side by side; fourth jump—land front to front again. Repeat sequence.

MOVEMENT: *Body Facing*

Body facing is a movement term used to describe the way the front of the body is facing. It differs from direction because one must be traveling to have direction (such as walking forward or running backward). It is possible to change body facing without traveling at all. Body facing can be described in terms of the clock (face twelve o'clock), of objects in the room (face the board, face the window), of other people (face your partner), or of the line of motion (forward, backward).

UNIT ONE
LESSON 4

RELATED ARTS | MOVEMENT | THEATER | VISUAL ARTS

LESSON PLANNER

FOCUS Duration—quarter note, eighth note, half note, quarter rest

OBJECTIVES
OBJECTIVE 1 Perform a rhythmic pattern in ² from notation (tested)
OBJECTIVE 2 Indicate placement of bar lines in notated phrases in ² (tested)

MATERIALS
Recordings
Speech Piece: I Wish (unison)   CD1:18
Recorded Lesson: Grandfather
  Clock   CD1:22
Mongolian Night Song   CD1:15

Instruments unpitched instruments

Resources
Resource Master 1•2 (practice)
Resource Master 1•3 (practice)

VOCABULARY
quarter note, eighth note, half note, quarter rest, coda, bar line, measure

▶ = **BASIC PROGRAM**

TIME OUT

Playing and resting are part of both sports and music.

Musical sounds have different lengths. Musicians know how long to play or sing by following written music. Look at the chart to see how musical sounds can be written when a quarter note gets the beat.

♩	**quarter note**	one sound to a beat
♫	two **eighth notes**	two sounds to a beat
♪	**half note**	sound lasting two beats
𝄽	**quarter rest**	silence the length of a beat

PAT each quarter note, snap the eighth notes, and brush your hands for each half note.

24

MEETING **INDIVIDUAL** NEEDS

ALTERNATE TEACHING STRATEGY THEATER

OBJECTIVE 1 Write ♫, ♩, ♪, and 𝄽 on the board. Have students choose three clock-sounds they can make with their voices and assign each sound to one of the three durations. (For example, say *tick* for eighth notes, cluck tongue for quarter notes, and say *bong* for half notes.) Have them perform these as you point to each rhythmic symbol on the board, making no sound on the quarter rest.

MUSIC BUILDS MATH SKILLS

Number and Operations When identifying quarter, eighth, and half notes, students use their knowledge of unit fractions.

EXTRA HELP: *Rhythmic Preparation*

Have students review in rhythm the words of "I Wish." Then have them write a large ♫, ♩, ♪, and 𝄽. Have students point to each symbol as you play four beats of each duration. Gradually increase the tempo.

FOR RHYTHMS

THINK IT THROUGH

What are some movements you can make to show 𝄽 ?
Why did you choose those movements?

A **coda** is a special ending for a song or poem.

CREATE a coda for "I Wish" by performing the pattern on page 24 two times after you speak the poem.

"What are some things you wish for?" Have students:

▶ • Listen to "I Wish" CD1:18.

▶ • Read the speech piece (on page 21), patting with the beat.

"Why do you think the poet wrote her ideas down?" (to remember and/or share it)

"Writing songs is a way to remember and share music. Today you will find out more about writing the rhythm of songs."

2 DEVELOP

1. Move to show note values. Have students:

Recorded Lesson CD1:22

▶ • Listen to "Grandfather Clock" and create nonlocomotor clock movements for each duration. (See *Movement* below.)

2. Introduce rhythmic notation. Have students:

▶ • Read about note values on page 24.

OBJECTIVE 1 Informal Assessment

• Read and perform the pattern with body percussion.

• Discuss the *Think It Through*.

• Read about coda, then perform the pattern two times as a coda to "I Wish," playing the pattern on woodblocks or other unpitched instruments.

PLAYING INSTRUMENTS: *Unpitched*

Using unpitched percussion or a percussion setting on an electronic keyboard, have three students perform the coda on page 24 as an ostinato to "I Wish."

MOVEMENT: *Clock Movements*

If students need help inventing clock movements, suggest that when moving to the eighth notes (gears) they move (bend and straighten) only their hands, fingers, and wrists. Move to the quarter notes (pendulum) by bending arms in and out, forward and back. Finally, move to the half notes (chimes) by swinging arms forward and back or from side to side.

UNIT ONE
LESSON 4

continued from previous page

3. Introduce measure and bar line. Have students:

▶ • Read about meter symbols on page 26.

▶ • Signal with the correct number of fingers to show the number of measures in the rhythm pattern on page 26. (four)

▶ • Read about meter signature on page 27.

3 APPLY

Review "Mongolian Night Song" CD1:15 **(p. 19). Determine meter.** Have students:

▶ • With eyes closed, listen for, then pat, the strong beats in "Mongolian Night Song."

▶ • Divide into two groups and listen again as one group taps lightly with the beat on their shoulders, and the other group pats only the strong beats. Tell how many beats they feel in a set. (four)

• Perform the rhythm on page 27, clapping the quarter notes and brushing hands for the half notes.

• In groups of three, listen to the two phrases shown on page 27. One student taps shoulders for all beats while the second pats with the strong beats and the third makes note of which words were sung on the pats. (*Lit-, tends, Brings, fold*)

STILL MUSIC
This painting shows a stage after a rehearsal or concert. Why do you think the artist, Ben Shahn, called it "Still Music"?

© The Philips Collection, Washington, D.C.

To see how sets of beats are felt in a song, look at the meter signature. The top number tells how many beats are in a set. The **bar lines** divide the notes into sets, or **measures**, based on the top number.

meter signature   measure bar line

26 TIME OUT FOR RHYTHMS

MEETING **INDIVIDUAL** NEEDS

ALTERNATE TEACHING STRATEGY

OBJECTIVE 2 Write the first two phrases of "Mongolian Night Song," as shown on page 27, on the board. Play the phrases while a student follows along by tapping with the beat on the notation on the board. The class pats with each strong beat. Help them realize that because they feel four beats in a set, the bar lines will be placed after every four beats. Have the student at the board mark the bar lines where the class indicates.

BIOGRAPHY: *Ben Shahn*

VISUAL ARTS

The painter Ben Shahn (shän), 1898–1969, was born in Lithuania and moved to New York City at age eight. As a teenager, he spent many hours wandering around the Brooklyn Museum of Art, teaching himself about art. He became famous for paintings and huge murals about the hardships people faced and their struggles for justice, fair working conditions, and better lives. Shahn enjoyed meeting musicians, and musical instruments and scenes appear often in his artwork.

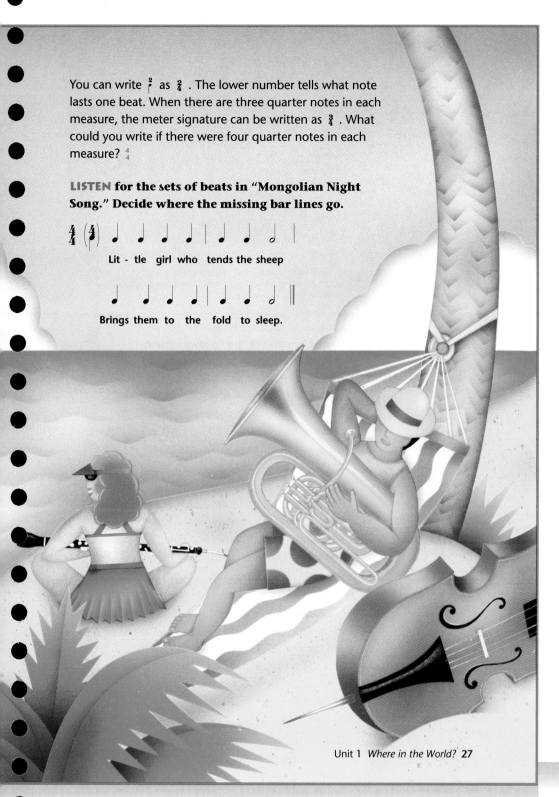

You can write $\frac{2}{?}$ as $\frac{2}{4}$. The lower number tells what note lasts one beat. When there are three quarter notes in each measure, the meter signature can be written as $\frac{3}{4}$. What could you write if there were four quarter notes in each measure? $\frac{4}{4}$

LISTEN for the sets of beats in "Mongolian Night Song." Decide where the missing bar lines go.

Lit - tle girl who tends the sheep

Brings them to the fold to sleep.

OBJECTIVE 2 Informal Assessment
• Point on page 27 to the places where the bar lines go as you read the words in rhythm. (between *who* and *tends*, *sheep* and *Brings*, *the* and *fold*, after *sleep*) (Optional: For more practice with bar lines use **Resource Master 1 · 2.**)

4 CLOSE

"What do bar lines help us see?" (how sets of beats are felt) "In $\frac{2}{?}$ meter, which kind of note stands for one sound per beat?" (quarter note) "Which note lasts for two beats?" (half note) "Which notes mean two sounds to a beat?" (two eighth notes) Have students:

• Sing "Mongolian Night Song" from page 19, patting each time a new measure begins.

LESSON SUMMARY

Informal Assessment In this lesson, students:

OBJECTIVE 1 Performed a rhythm pattern in $\frac{2}{?}$ from notation.
OBJECTIVE 2 Indicated placement of bar lines in $\frac{2}{?}$ phrases from "Mongolian Night Song."

National Standards for Music Education
5a Read standard note values in duple and triple meters.
6b Describe, in words or movement, music from diverse cultures.
6e Respond to musical characteristics through movement.

MORE MUSIC: Reinforcement
More Songs to Read, page 348 ($\quarternote$, $\eighthnote\eighthnote$, $\halfnote$)
"When I First Came to This Land," page 148 ($\dottedquarter$, $\halfnote$)
"Donna, Donna," page 291 ($\quarternote$, $\eighthnote\eighthnote$, $\halfnote$, $\quarterrest$)

CAREERS: *Session Musician*

The kind of musician who appeared in the artwork of Ben Shahn may have been a session musician. Also known as a studio musician, session player, or backup musician, the main responsibility of this musician is to back up the leader of a group in the recording studio. He or she may at times play backup in a live concert or for commercials. It is his/her responsibility to play what is assigned in the manner that the group leader or the producer wants it played. Working for other musicians may mean few chances for individual creativity, but the job offers opportunities to work steadily and to meet other musicians.

CRITICAL THINKING: $\frac{2}{?}$ *Meter*

Have students brainstorm and write ways to fill a measure in $\frac{2}{?}$ using quarters, eighths, halves, and rests on the board. Then have them arrange the measures into various four-measure phrases. They should select and perform the phrases they like best, then explain why they chose those phrases. (Optional: Use **Resource Master 1 · 3** for practice arranging rhythms to fit measures of $\frac{2}{?}$ meter.)

ACROSS the

FLOOR PLANS

"I Wish"

INDIVIDUAL   **15–30 MIN**

MATERIALS: graph paper, straightedge, pencil

A floor plan is a mathematical map of one floor of a building. It is a drawing of the outline of the floor that indicates how long each wall will be, and where to build doors and windows.

Have each student sketch a simple design for a floor of their "ideal" home. Then have them draw the plan carefully on graph paper. Set a standard measurement scale that corresponds to a square of the graph paper—for example, have each side represent the length of one meter or one foot.

Then on their finished drawings, have students indicate how long each wall is, and how far from each corner a window or door is. Also, they should find the perimeter of the floor.

COMPREHENSION STRATEGIES: Visualizing, drawing a scale model

MEASURING CAPACITY

"I Wish"

GROUP   **15–30 MIN**

MATERIALS: teakettle or teapot with a 1-quart capacity, 4-ounce paper cups, set of measuring cups, water

Give each group a measuring cup that holds one of the following: one-quarter cup, one-half cup, one cup, one pint, or one quart. Ask them to estimate how many of each measure they will need to fill the kettle or teapot.

Students estimate how many and record their guesses. Then they test the estimate by using the group's container to fill the kettle with water. They record the answer. Have groups share their results and discuss the relationship between each quantity and the number of times that the cup needed to be filled.

Then ask how many of the paper cups students think you can fill with the water in the kettle. Write the different estimates on the board. Fill the cups until the water in the kettle is gone.

You can extend this activity by introducing tablespoons and teaspoons and having students calculate how many of each are in a quarter-cup. Then multiply to find how many tablespoons and teaspoons it would take to fill the other cups.

COMPREHENSION STRATEGY: Estimating

CURRICULUM

MATHEMATICS

TELLING TIME

"Grandfather Clock"

GROUP   **15 MIN OR LESS**

Have students work in small groups to play "time pantomime." In each round of the game, one student writes down a secret time, such as 3:30 or 4:15. The times should be to the quarter of an hour.

Then that student has to use his or her arms to show the secret time. A student uses one fully extended arm to represent the minute hand of a clock. The student bends the other arm at the elbow to represent the hour hand. For example, to show 3:00, one arm is held straight up from the shoulder. The other arm has the elbow bent. The portion of the arm from elbow to fingers is held horizontally, as if pointing to the number 3 on a clock face.

The first student in the group to tell the time correctly becomes the next person to pantomime a time.

COMPREHENSION STRATEGY: Visualizing

MATHEMATICS

MEASURING TIME

"Grandfather Clock"

GROUP   **15–30 MIN**
MATERIALS: clock with second hand, thread, nails, metal nuts, yardstick or tape measure

Students can make a pendulum like one that goes "tock" in a grandfather clock. Their goal is to make a pendulum that measures exactly one second for each swing.

Give groups of students several pieces of thread, each 40 inches long. Students tie a loop at one end so that they can hang the thread from a nail and let the pendulum swing freely. Then tie the nut to the other end of the thread and let the pendulum swing back and forth 60 times (or 30 complete swings).

One person counts the swings while the partner times them by the clock. At the end of 60 seconds, students record how many swings the pendulum has made. If it has made more than 60 swings, students lengthen the thread by tying another piece of thread to the original. If it has made less than 60 swings, students shorten the thread. (Students can use short cuts—aim for swings in 10 seconds— and then test the final try a full 60 seconds.)

COMPREHENSION STRATEGY: Trial and error

UNIT ONE
LESSON 5

RELATED ARTS | MOVEMENT | THEATER | VISUAL ARTS

LESSON PLANNER

FOCUS Pitch, *do re mi so la*

OBJECTIVES
OBJECTIVE 1 Sing a song from notation with pitch syllables
OBJECTIVE 2 Identify the pitches heard in a melodic phrase (tested)

MATERIALS
Recordings
'Way Down Yonder in the
  Brickyard   CD1:14
Recorded Lesson: Melodic
  Patterns   CD1:23
Fed My Horse   CD1:24

Resources
Resource Master 1 • 4 (practice)
Orff Orchestration O • 3 (Fed My Horse)

VOCABULARY
pitch syllables, staff, ledger line

▶ = **BASIC PROGRAM**

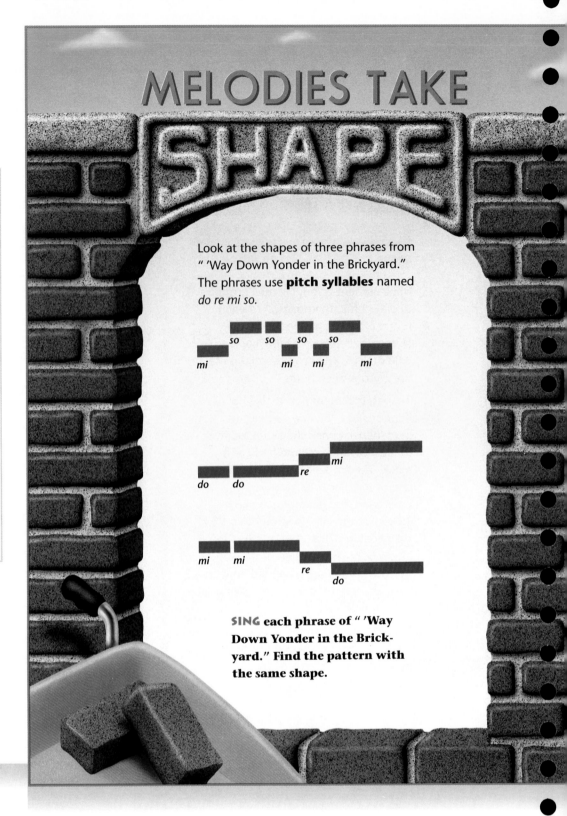

MELODIES TAKE SHAPE

Look at the shapes of three phrases from " 'Way Down Yonder in the Brickyard." The phrases use **pitch syllables** named *do re mi so.*

SING each phrase of " 'Way Down Yonder in the Brickyard." Find the pattern with the same shape.

MEETING **INDIVIDUAL** NEEDS

ALTERNATE TEACHING STRATEGY

OBJECTIVE 1 Write a staff with C D E G on the board, showing pitch syllable names *do re mi so* underneath. Give each of four students one resonator bell. Have the class sing and play the pitch syllables as you slowly point to the notes on the staff. Conduct patterns that include repeated pitches and ones that move back and forth between pitches. Give the bells to four other students, erase the pitch syllable names, and repeat. Have students do the activity in groups of five so that each student takes a turn conducting and playing each pitch.

SPECIAL LEARNERS: *Pitch Syllable Names*

Since words and melody are often integrated in memory, some students may have difficulty transferring syllable names to the pitches of " 'Way Down Yonder in the Brickyard," for which they have already learned words. Teaching a new melody that has no associated words and uses only syllable names as "words" may help. Write short, unfamiliar melodies on the board and have students sing pitch syllables to these new melodies. For familiar songs, encourage students to think of the pitch syllables as new "words" that also name the pitches.

Melodies can be written on a **staff** of five lines and four spaces. In " 'Way Down Yonder in the Brickyard," *do re mi so* look like this.

do   re   mi   so

Because *do* is below the staff, an extra line called a **ledger line** is used.

'Way down yon-der in the brick-yard,

Re - mem - ber   me.

'Way down yon-der in the brick-yard,

Re - mem - ber   me.

MATCH these phrases with the patterns on page 28. First, third phrases-first pattern; second phrase-second pattern; fourth phrase-third pattern.

1 GET SET

"You've shown the phrases and played the game for ' 'Way Down Yonder in the Brick-yard.' As we sing the song today, follow me in a different way." Have students:

▶ • Sing "'Way Down Yonder in the Brickyard" CD1:14 on page 17.

   • Imitate you as you draw the melodic contour in the air.

   • Determine that the gestures matched the high and low pitches they sang.

"Today you will learn another way to show how the melody moves."

2 DEVELOP

1. Identify melodic patterns in "'Way Down Yonder in the Brickyard" (p. 17). Have students:

▶ • Read page 28 about melodic shape and pitch syllables.

▶ • Sing each phrase of the A section and find its matching icon.

   • Sing each phrase with pitch syllables. (A slower tempo is recommended.)

▶ • Read page 29 about the staff and match the A section notation with the icons on page 28.

OBJECTIVE 1 Informal Assessment
   • Sing the A section with pitch syllables while pointing to the notation. (A slower tempo is recommended.)

▶ • Perform the song with the movement. (See *Movement*, Lesson 2, on the bottom of page 17.)

VOCAL DEVELOPMENT: *Matching Pitch*

Students who are not able to match pitch need to practice individual pitches or short melodic patterns before singing songs. This should help them sing on pitch.

MUSIC BUILDS READING SKILLS

Viewing In singing a song from notation with pitch syllables, students will be interpreting information from various formats.

COOPERATIVE LEARNING: *Melodic Contours*

Have small groups of students work to find ways of showing melodic contours, then explain their "pictures" to you and the class. Assign roles and set a time limit for the activity. Offer the melody below as a starting point by playing it or writing it on the board, then have students choose another melody.

UNIT ONE
LESSON 5

continued from previous page

2. Sing with pitch syllables. Have students:

▶ • Read page 30 about moving pitches to different staff positions. (Optional: Use **Resource Master 1·4** for practice placing *do re mi so* on a staff.)

Recorded Lesson CD1:23

▶ • Listen to "Melodic Patterns," and echo phrases that use *mi so* or *do re mi*, then listen to four patterns sung on a neutral syllable.

OBJECTIVE 2 Informal Assessment

▶ • With eyes closed, signal by raising one or two fingers to show which pitch set is used in each example.

3 APPLY

Introduce "Fed My Horse" CD1:24 **Introduce** *la*. Have students:

▶ • Read about and listen to the song.

• Study the notation to find the pitch *la*.

• Listen to the verse, while following the notation, and raise a hand each time *la* occurs. (Phrases 1 and 3, *pop-*)

• Describe *la* and its relationship to the other pitches. (higher, on line above *so*)

▶ • Sing the song with movement. (See *Movement* below.)

MOVING ON

You often hear *do* at the beginning and end of a song. *Do* can be written on any line or in any space of the staff. If *do* moves, the other pitches also move.

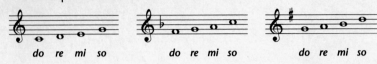

do re mi so   do re mi so   do re mi so

When *do* is on a line, where are *mi* and *so*? When *do* is in a space, where are *mi* and *so*? on the lines above it; in the spaces above it

LISTEN to some melodies. Which set of pitches do you hear?

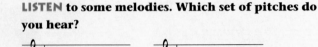

do   do re mi   do   mi   so

People traditionally gathered to share folk songs, learning them from family and friends. Playing along on instruments, which were sometimes made at home, added to the fun.

30

MEETING **INDIVIDUAL** NEEDS

ALTERNATE TEACHING STRATEGY

OBJECTIVE 2 Teach students the "body staff": touch knees for *do*, waist for *re*, shoulders for *mi*, and head for *so*. Now sing a phrase on *loo*. Have the class sing it back with pitch syllables and body staff, and then point to one or both staffs in the middle of page 30 to show the pitch set used. (Start with four-beat phrases.)

MOVEMENT: *"Fed My Horse"*

MOVEMENT

Line 3: (Verbal Cue—*stamp, clap, hambone, hambone*) Stamp, clap, hambone on legs with this pattern.

Hambone directions: alternate lightly slapping the back of the fingers on top of thighs, and the palm on outside of thighs.

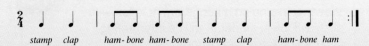

stamp clap ham-bone ham-bone stamp clap ham-bone ham

Pentatonic

d   r   m   s   l

Fed My Horse

Southern
Appalachian
Folk Song

Fed my horse in a pop - lar trough, Fed my horse in a pop - lar trough,

Fed my horse in a pop - lar trough, Then she caught the whoop - ing cough.

Coy ma - lin - do   Kill - ko, kill - ko;   Coy ma - lin - do   Kill - ko me.

Which pitch sounded just right to end on? *do*
Find the pitch in this song that is <u>not</u> *do re mi* or *so.*
The name of that pitch is *la.*

"Think about the pitch syllables you learned today. Who can tell me the name of the highest one?" (*la*—Continue asking students to name the pitch syllables in order from high to low—*so mi re do.*)

"Now let's sing 'Fed My Horse' for fun."

LESSON SUMMARY

Informal Assessment In this lesson, students:

OBJECTIVE 1 Sang pitch syllables from notation of "'Way Down Yonder in the Brickyard."
OBJECTIVE 2 Signaled to show which pitches made up the patterns in the recorded lesson "Melodic Patterns."

National Standards for Music Education
1a Sing accurately, on pitch and in rhythm.
5b Use a system to read notation in treble clef in major keys.
6b Describe, in words or movement, music from diverse cultures.

MORE MUSIC: Reinforcement

More Songs to Read, page 349 (*do re mi so la*)
"The California Song," page 48 (*do re mi so la*)

ENRICHMENT: *Countermelody for "Fed My Horse"*
Students will hear this countermelody with line 3 on the recording. When students are secure singing the melody and countermelody separately, have them sing both parts together.

Coy   ma - lin - do.   Coy   ma - lin - do.

PITCH SYLLABLES: *"Fed My Horse"*
Sing this song using pitch syllables and hand signs.

do   re   mi   so   la

ORFF: *"Fed My Horse"*
See **O·3** in *Orchestrations for Orff Instruments.*

ACROSS the

SCIENCE

CLASSIFYING ANIMALS

"Fed My Horse"

GROUP   **15 MIN OR LESS**
MATERIALS: optional—research books on animals

Brainstorm with the class to make a list of animals—ranging from familiar pets to animals of different parts of the world and different kinds of surroundings, such as ponds, forests, and deserts. Be sure to include insects, worms, and other less familiar animals. Write the names on the board.

Then organize students into groups. In each group, have students make a description of characteristics of horses, based on what they may know or have seen of horses—shape, number of legs (limbs), hair on its body, rearing of young, and so on.

Then based on their descriptions, have each group of students pick four animals from the list on the board that they think have the most similar characteristics to those of a horse. Encourage students to consider physical characteristics—not necessarily size.

Have students look up information on a horse—as well as information on the animals listed on the board—to confirm whether they did pick the animals most similar to the horse.

COMPREHENSION STRATEGIES: Compare and contrast, researching information

SCIENCE

CARE FOR ANIMALS

"Fed My Horse"

INDIVIDUAL   **15–30 MIN**
MATERIALS: reference books, chart paper

Have students discuss their pets, or animals they would like to have for pets. Students make a chart showing the following headings:

    Type of Pet
    Class of Animal
    Food
    Natural Habitat
    Where It Lives Outside Its Natural
      Habitat

Students research their chosen animals and complete the chart. They may wish to add categories, such as Most Common Ailments, Age, or Size and Weight.

COMPREHENSION STRATEGIES: Researching information, displaying information

CURRICULUM

ART

HORSE MODELS

"Fed My Horse"

INDIVIDUAL   **30 MIN OR LONGER**

MATERIALS: flour, water, shredded newspaper, pipe cleaners, mixing bowl, paper towels; optional—white glue, drops of wintergreen oil

Here are some directions for making a papier-mâché horse:

● Make a horse's body with pipe cleaners. First fold one pipe cleaner 2/3 of the way from one end. Then fold the shorter part toward the end again. The longer part is the trunk of the body. The shorter part is the neck and head. Twist a pipe cleaner around each end of the trunk to make legs.

● Cover the body with papier-mâché pulp. To make papier-mâché pulp, mix two parts water with one part flour in a bowl, and stir in shredded bits of newspaper. Squeeze the mixture together until it feels like clay. A few drops of wintergreen oil keeps the mixture from hardening too quickly to use.

● Squeeze the papier-mâché pulp over the horse's body to give it an even shape. Let the models dry for about a day or two.

Students can also experiment with other materials—centimeter cubes, modeling clay—to make their own models.

COMPREHENSION STRATEGIES: Visualizing, following directions

MATHEMATICS

MEASURING LENGTH

"Fed My Horse"

PAIR   **15–30 MIN**

MATERIALS: mural paper, markers, rulers

When people measure horses, they talk about how many "hands tall" a horse is. The horse is measured from the ground to its shoulder. Have students measure how many "hands" tall they are. Tape strips of mural paper to a wall. One student stands against the wall. The partner draws a line to show where the first student's shoulder comes to. Then they measure how many "hands" it is from the floor to the shoulder mark.

Explain to the students that the "hand" used in measuring horses is a fixed length of four inches. Ask them to see if it makes a difference whose hand they measure with. Why would this way of measuring make it hard to know the actual height?

After partners have taken turns being measured, have them find out how many inches tall they are from shoulder to foot. Then they divide the total by four to find how many horse "hands" tall they are.

COMPREHENSION STRATEGIES: Compare and contrast, estimating

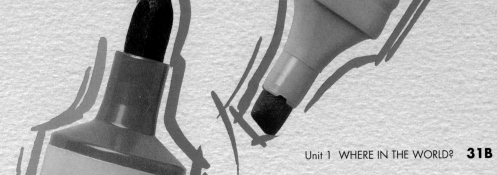

RELATED ARTS | MOVEMENT | THEATER | VISUAL ARTS |

LESSON PLANNER

FOCUS Design—same, different, and similar phrases

OBJECTIVES
OBJECTIVE 1 Signal to indicate that two phrases are different (tested)
OBJECTIVE 2 Signal to indicate that two phrases are similar (tested)

MATERIALS
Recordings
Fed My Horse	CD1:24
Recorded Lesson: "Troika" Phrases	CD1:25
Listening: Troika (excerpt) from *Lt. Kijé Suite* by S. Prokofiev	CD1:26
Listening: Dancing the Troika	CD1:27
Hi! Ho! The Rattlin' Bog	CD1:12
Listening: Troika (entire) from *Lt. Kijé Suite* by S. Prokofiev	CD1:28

Resources
Resource Master 1 • 5 (practice)
Resource Master 1 • 6 (listening map)
Listening Map Transparencies T • 1 (Troika, excerpt), T • 2 (Troika, entire)

VOCABULARY
form

▶ = **BASIC PROGRAM**

Just to Inform You

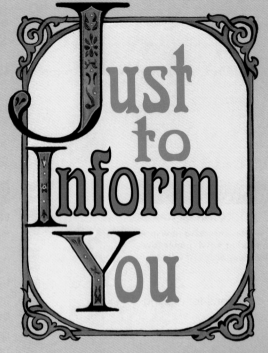

When you look at the shape or outline of something, you see its **form.** The form can be made up of one large shape or many smaller shapes.

DESCRIBE the forms in this building. Encourge students to describe the model as a whole and by its varied parts.

Music has form, too. You can hear the form of a song by listening to the order of its phrases or sections.

The order of a song's phrases is called its phrase form. To describe the form when two phrases are the same, use a a. When two phrases are different, use a b.

LISTEN to two phrases from a piece of music called "Troika."

Model of St. Basil's Cathedral, Moscow

32

MEETING **INDIVIDUAL** NEEDS

ALTERNATE TEACHING STRATEGY

OBJECTIVE 1 Have students listen to the phrases several times to become familiar with them. Have them compare the phrases by clapping the rhythms, then by drawing the melodic contours in the air.

BACKGROUND: *St. Basil's Cathedral*

St. Basil's Cathedral (1555) is near the Kremlin in Moscow, Russia. Asymmetrical in design, no two domes are exactly

alike. (The model shown is simplified.) The church was originally white. Its dazzling colors were added later.

ENRICHMENT: *New Verses for "Fed My Horse"*

Have students work in small groups or with a partner to write new verses to the song. Provide some examples to get students started, such as: *Fed my horse from a spoon of gold, then she got an awful cold;* or, *Fed my horse some oats and hay, she jumped up and ran away.*

SPOTLIGHT ON
SERGEI PROKOFIEV

Sergei Prokofiev (1891–1953) was a renowned Russian pianist, conductor, and composer. His first piano teacher was his mother. He began composing when he was five, and tried to write an opera when he was nine. Prokofiev became a very good pianist, and once won a piano in a competition.

Prokofiev loved theater, and composed operas, ballets, and film music. He also wrote symphonies and concertos. Unusual stories attracted him. For example, he wrote music for Lieutenant Kijé, a movie about an imaginary man.

Prokofiev's music was criticized at first because people were not used to his modern harmonies and rhythms. However, others found his music brilliant and appealing, and he received many invitations to compose. Now he is remembered as one of the greatest modern composers.

"Listen to this song and raise your hand when you recognize it." ("Fed My Horse" CD1:24) Have students:

▶ • Name the song and sing it, doing the hambone pattern on the third line. (See *Movement* on the bottom of page 30.)

▶ • Tell which phrases of the verse have the same words (1, 2, and 3) and which of the phrases have the same melody. (1, 3)

"Today you will listen for phrases that are the same in the songs you sing."

2 DEVELOP

1. Read phrases that are the same in "Fed My Horse." Have students:

• Sing Phrases 1 and 3 on page 31 with pitch syllables. (*mi so so mi mi la so so*)

▶ • Choose and perform movement for Phrases 1 and 3. (for example: walk forward four beats)

▶ • Sing the verse, moving only on Phrases 1 and 3, then add hambone pattern on the refrain. (See *Movement* on the bottom of page 30.)

2. Introduce phrase form. Have students:

▶ • Read about form and discuss the forms visible in the model on page 32. (cylinders, spheres, rectangular prisms or blocks, cones)

▶ • Read about phrase form of a song.

Recorded Lesson CD1:25

▶ • Listen to "'Troika' Phrases" to hear the first two phrases of the music and draw a curved pathway in the air for each phrase.

OBJECTIVE 1 Informal Assessment

▶ • With eyes closed, show the form of the two phrases. (a b: one closed fist, one open hand)

▶ • Read about Sergei Sergeyevich Prokofiev (sɛr gɛ sɛr gɛ ə vɪch prɔ kɔf i ɛf).

BIOGRAPHY: *Sergei Prokofiev*

Sergei Sergeyevich Prokofiev (1891–1953) began composing at age five and gave his first piano concert in Moscow when he was 18. During the Russian Revolution, Prokofiev thought of moving to Europe or the United States. However, after lengthy stays in other countries, he returned to live in Russia. Support for the arts was strong in the Soviet Union, and he went on to compose ballets, film scores, operas, symphonies, and piano pieces. One of his best-known works is *Peter and the Wolf*.

PLAYING INSTRUMENTS: *Keyboard/Pitched*

Play this accompaniment to "Fed My Horse" as an F/C' chord bordun on bass xylophone or piano, as a drone on dulcimer, or on an electronic keyboard. (Set tone to guitar or dulcimer).

UNIT ONE
LESSON 6

continued from previous page

3. Introduce "Troika" (excerpt) CD1:26 and **"Dancing the Troika" CD1:27. Follow a listening map.** Have students:

▶ • Read about "Troika" on page 34.

▶ • Listen to the excerpt from "Troika" while following the map, raising a hand when the first two phrases return. (Optional: Use **Listening Map Transparency T • 1**.)

▶ • Learn the dance by listening to "Dancing the Troika," in which they hear the directions for this lively Russian folk dance. (See *Movement* below. This recording contains spoken dance instructions over the music. You may adjust the stereo balance control to hear the music alone.)

3 APPLY

Review "Hi! Ho! The Rattlin' Bog" CD1:12 (p. 23). Identify phrase form. Have students:

▶ • Sing and draw the melodic shape of the first two phrases in the air.

▶ • Read about similar phrases on page 35.

▶ • Form two groups, one singing Phrase 1, the other singing Phrase 2.

OBJECTIVE 2 Informal Assessment

▶ • With eyes shut, show one finger for a a' or two for a b to indicate the correct form of the phrases. (one: a a')

▶ • Discuss their responses, then sing the song for fun. (Optional: Use **Resource Master 1 • 5** to compare same, different, and similar pitch patterns.)

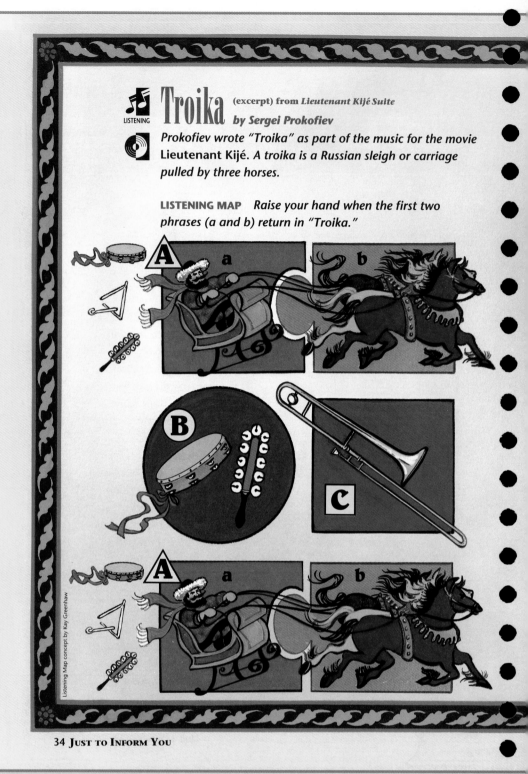

♫ LISTENING
Troika (excerpt) from *Lieutenant Kijé Suite*
by Sergei Prokofiev

Prokofiev wrote "Troika" as part of the music for the movie Lieutenant Kijé. A troika is a Russian sleigh or carriage pulled by three horses.

LISTENING MAP *Raise your hand when the first two phrases (a and b) return in "Troika."*

Listening Map concept by Kay Greenhaw

34 JUST TO INFORM YOU

MEETING **INDIVIDUAL** NEEDS

ALTERNATE TEACHING STRATEGY

OBJECTIVE 2 Have each group chant the words to their phrase, in turn, to find that they are the same, then clap the rhythms to find they are the same. Have them trace the contours and find that they begin the same but end differently. For reinforcement, perform each step simultaneously.

MOVEMENT: *"Dancing the Troika"*

Formation: lines of three, holding hands, facing counterclockwise in "spokes of a wheel" formation

Students in each line are numbered as shown.

```
            1
        1   2   1
          2   2
         3  3  3
    1 2 3      3 2 1
         3  3  3
          2   2
        1   2   1
            1
```

Part 1: All run forward using small, light steps, keeping the spoked formation. (16 beats)

Part 2: Dancers 2 and 3 lift their joined arms, forming an arch. Dancer 1 goes under the arch and returns to place. This movement turns Dancer 2 in place under his or her

SIMILAR PHRASES

These snowflakes are similar, but not the same.
How are they different from one another?

Sometimes musical phrases are almost the same, or similar.

When you describe a form that has similar phrases, add a mark (') called a prime to the letter for the similar phrase. The form can be called a a' or b b'.

Is the phrase form a a' or a b in the first two lines of "Hi! Ho! The Rattlin' Bog"? Where does the difference occur?

a a'; last 2 measures of each phrase

4 CLOSE

"Today you've learned to listen for the phrase form of songs. Now pretend that you're testing me about this lesson." (Encourage students to question you about the definition of *form*, how to tell whether two phrases are the same, different, or similar, and how to label phrase form.) Have students:

▶ • Sing "Hi! Ho! The Rattlin' Bog" in two groups. Each group stands when its members sing their assigned phrase.

LESSON SUMMARY

Informal Assessment In this lesson, students:

OBJECTIVE 1 Signaled to indicate the phrase form (a b) of first two phrases of "Troika."

OBJECTIVE 2 Signaled to indicate the phrase form (a a') of the refrain of "Hi! Ho! the Rattlin' Bog."

National Standards for Music Education
I b Sing with appropriate dynamics, phrasing, and interpretation.
2f Play parts while others perform contrasting parts.
6a Identify simple musical forms by ear.

MORE MUSIC: Reinforcement

"Garden Song," page 290 (phrase form)
"The Ghost of John," page 306 (phrases; Halloween)

---

own arm. (8 beats) Repeat: 1, 2 form arch; 3 goes under; 2 again turns under own arm. (8 beats)

Part 3: Each trio forms a circle and runs clockwise (leaning slightly backward) for 12 beats, then stamps three times in place. (4 beats) Reverse, circling counterclockwise. (12 beats) Dancers 1 and 3 drop hands and return to spoked formation; all stamp three times. (4 beats)

ENRICHMENT: *"Troika" from Lieutenant Kijé Suite*

Invite the students to enjoy "Troika" **CD1:28** in its entirety. Have them follow the listening map on **Resource Master 1 · 6** or **Listening Map Transparency T · 2**.

PLAYING INSTRUMENTS: *Orff*

"Troika" A section: Play tambourine and jingle bells with each beat. Add whip on first beat of each four.

Phrases: Have partners create eight-beat call-and-response phrases using F G A C' D'. They should play responses that are different or similar to the call phrase.

UNIT ONE
LESSON 7

LESSON PLANNER

FOCUS Pitch

OBJECTIVES
OBJECTIVE 1 Echo instrumental phrases with pitch syllables
OBJECTIVE 2 Create and perform a melody for the text of a poem (speech piece)

MATERIALS
Recordings
'Way Down Yonder in the
Brickyard   CD1:14
Recorded Lesson: Name
Those Pitches   CD1:29
Speech Piece: I Wish (unison)   CD1:18

Instruments
resonator bells or other pitched instruments (C D E G A), unpitched instruments

Resources
Resource Master 1 • 7 (practice)
Resource Master 1 • 8 (practice)
Musical Instruments Masters—gong, güiro/maracas, triangle

▶ = **BASIC PROGRAM**

IT'S A PITCH PUZZLE!

Are you ready for a puzzle? The first four phrases of " 'Way Down Yonder in the Brickyard" are all mixed up.

SING each phrase with pitch syllables.

a
dǝ 'Way down yon-der in the brick-yard,

b¹
dǝ Re-mem-ber me.

a
dǝ 'Way down yon-der in the brick-yard,

b
dǝ Re-mem-ber me.

What is the correct order for the phrases, a b b¹ a or a b a b¹? a b a b¹

36

MEETING **INDIVIDUAL** NEEDS

ALTERNATE TEACHING STRATEGY

OBJECTIVE 1 Have students echo phrases as a group, gesturing for each pitch. Use hand signs (or *la*: hand over head, *so*: touch head, *mi*: touch shoulders, *re*: touch waist, *do*: touch knees). Then have them gesture as they respond to the recorded lesson "Name Those Pitches."

SPECIAL LEARNERS: *Pitch Syllable Recognition*

Students who have trouble singing back pitch syllable names they hear may succeed by first singing the pitches on a neutral syllable. Play several three-note patterns using *do*

re mi so la on resonator bells. Instruct students to sing the melody on *loo* for some examples, then to sing pitch syllable names for other examples. Since it is easier to match a vocal model than an instrumental model, sing the pitches on *loo* as you play the bells.

CRITICAL THINKING: *Pitch Patterns on the Staff*

Have the students complete **Resource Master 1 • 7**, on which they identify *mi so la* or *do re mi* patterns, then play their own "Name Those Pitches" games. (This activity will also prepare students to add pitches to "I Wish" on page 38, *Apply*.)

NAME THOSE PITCHES!

You are listening to the radio, and you decide to join in the "Name Those Pitches" game. You try to recognize the mystery melody. It could be a melody with *mi so la* or one with *do re mi*.

do re mi

mi so la

How will you figure out the winning pitches? Listen carefully!

"Let's begin by singing "Way Down Yonder in the Brickyard." Listen for any phrases that repeat." **CD1:14** Have students:

▶ • Sing the A section, page 17.

▶ • Identify Phrases 1 and 3 as being the same and Phrases 2 and 4 as having the same words but different melodies. (form: a b a b')

"The words *Remember me* use the same pitches each time, but they're in a different order. Today you will use the pitches you've learned in new ways."

2 DEVELOP

1. Place the melodic phrases of ""Way Down Yonder in the Brickyard" in order. Have students:

• Read page 36 and sing the pitch syllables for each phrase.

• Identify the correct phrase order on page 36. (Have students sing the A section, tracing the contour of each phrase in the air and on the board, then match the contours with the notation on the bottom of page 36.)

▶ • Sing the song with movement. (See *Movement* on the bottom of page 17.)

2. Practice pitch syllables. Have students:

▶ • Read page 37.

Recorded Lesson CD1:29
▶ • Listen to "Name Those Pitches" and echo phrases with pitch syllables.

OBJECTIVE 1 Informal Assessment
• Echo phrases played on resonator bells, using either *mi so la* or *do re mi* pitch syllables.

IMPROVISATION: *A B A Form*

Have students set up resonator bells in C pentatonic (C D E G A). (If using a keyboard, tell them to use only these keys.) They then choose one pitch on which to play the rhythm of all the words in ""Way Down Yonder in the Brickyard" except *Remember me*, which they sing. Next, they play the same rhythms, using a different pitch for each syllable of the words. Continue to sing each *Remember me*. Finally, have them create in A B A form by singing the entire song once, improvising with different pitches once, and then singing the entire song once more.

PLAYING INSTRUMENTS: *Orff*

Play all the *mi re do/do re mi* patterns from ""Way Down Yonder in the Brickyard" on resonator bells or soprano xylophones. Add a I-V accompaniment on basses and altos.

continued from previous page

3 APPLY

**1. Review "I Wish" (unison) CD1:18 (p. 21).
Create a melody.** Have students:

▶ • Speak "I Wish" while clapping the rhythm on page 21.

• With a partner or small group, take one line of the speech piece and create a melody using the suggested pitch syllables. (Optional: Have students notate their melody on **Resource Master 1 • 8**.)

• Include same, similar, different phrases; try different beginning and ending notes to see which pitches they prefer. (This will help prepare them for the idea of a tonal center, taught in Unit 2.)

• Share their ideas, then choose one setting for each line.

OBJECTIVE 2 Informal Assessment

• Perform the speech piece with their new melody.

▶ • Add unpitched percussion to the designated words and sing. (See *Playing Instruments* on the bottom of page 39.)

• Discuss the *Think It Through*.

FROM POETRY TO PITCHES

Have you ever tried to set a poem to music? That's what songwriters do all the time! This activity may give you some ideas.

CREATE a melody for "I Wish."

Use the pitches shown with the lines of the poem. Match them by color.

do   mi   so   la

do   do   re   mi

Here are more ideas for your melody! Include same, similar, and different phrases. Try different beginning and ending pitches.

MEETING **INDIVIDUAL** NEEDS

ALTERNATE TEACHING STRATEGY

OBJECTIVE 2 Have resonator bells or other pitched instruments available for the students to check their pitches. Mark and arrange the bells for them: *mi so la* (E G A) and *do re mi* (C D E). Have the students sing and play along as you point to the five pitches on a staff or pitch stairs. Then have the students notate each phrase of the speech piece.

EXTRA HELP: *Singing "I Wish"*

To help students move from speaking to singing, practice singing all on one pitch, *so*, then try two pitches: *so mi*, and so on.

CRITICAL THINKING: *Analyzing the Class Melody*

Invite each group to write on a large staff its part of the melody created in the lesson. (Optional: Make a transparency of **Resource Master 1 • 8** for the whole class.) Work as a class to analyze the melodic contour and sing

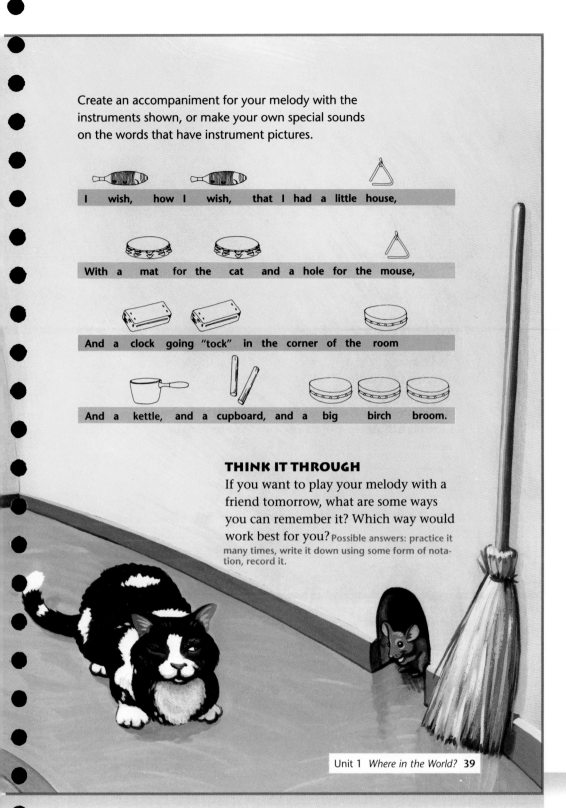

Create an accompaniment for your melody with the instruments shown, or make your own special sounds on the words that have instrument pictures.

I wish, how I wish, that I had a little house,

With a mat for the cat and a hole for the mouse,

And a clock going "tock" in the corner of the room

And a kettle, and a cupboard, and a big birch broom.

THINK IT THROUGH

If you want to play your melody with a friend tomorrow, what are some ways you can remember it? Which way would work best for you? Possible answers: practice it many times, write it down using some form of notation, record it.

4 CLOSE

"Today you all helped to write a song. What three things did you start with?" (words, rhythm, and pitches). "How did you decide how the melody should go?"

"Let's sing our own song version of 'I Wish' once more."

LESSON SUMMARY

Informal Assessment In this lesson, students:

OBJECTIVE 1 Echoed instrumental phrases with pitch syllables in the Recorded Lesson: Name Those Pitches.

OBJECTIVE 2 Created a melodic setting for "I Wish" using *do re mi so la.*

National Standards for Music Education
1e Sing in groups, responding to the conductor.
3c Improvise rhythmic variations and melodic embellishments.
6e Respond to musical characteristics through movement.

MORE MUSIC: Reinforcement

"Theme in Yellow," page 307 (accompaniment to a poem; Halloween)

---

with pitch syllables. Ask students to determine the form, then give letter names to each phrase.

PLAYING INSTRUMENTS: *Unpitched/Keyboards*

Unpitched Instruments: Play a game with "I Wish." Sit in a semicircle or circle. Hand an unpitched instrument to every third or fourth student. Make a large visual of the poem on page 39, showing which instruments to play on which words. Have the students sing the poem, playing on assigned words, then pass the instruments and repeat. To unify the song and help maintain a beat, have one or two

students play a beat pattern, alternating between C and G on a bass xylophone. (You might play a one-chord accompaniment on autoharp or a bordun on keyboard.)

Keyboards: Have students perform their melody to "I Wish" on keyboards.

RELATED ARTS [MOVEMENT] [THEATER] [VISUAL ARTS]

LESSON PLANNER

FOCUS Duration

OBJECTIVES
OBJECTIVE 1 Perform an ostinato using eighth and half notes (tested)
OBJECTIVE 2 Create and perform an eight-beat pattern in ⁴⁄₄ with quarter notes and quarter rests (tested)

MATERIALS

Recordings
I Let Her Go, Go   CD1:13
Recorded Lesson: Interview
  with the Barra MacNeils   CD1:30
Listening: The Foxhunter's
  from *Flower Basket Medley*
  arranged by S., K., S., and
  L. MacNeil   CD2:1

Resources
Musical Instruments Master—
  güiro/maracas
Recorder Master R • 1 (pitch B)

VOCABULARY
ostinato

▶ = **BASIC PROGRAM**

Rhythms that Repeat

If you have a melody in mind, why not add some rhythms? Try an **ostinato,** a pattern that repeats many times.

CREATE a rhythm ostinato by repeating this pattern. Snap the eighth notes and brush your hands for the half notes.

Two instruments can also share the ostinato.

maracas   güiro

PERFORM the ostinato with the instrumental section of "I Let Her Go, Go."

40

MEETING **INDIVIDUAL** NEEDS

ALTERNATE TEACHING STRATEGY

OBJECTIVE 1 Have students play the "Switch" Game. As you point to the symbols ♩, ♫, ♩ on the board, changing every eight beats, have students switch from performing one snap per beat to patting two times per beat, then to brushing hands for two beats. Have them repeat as you cue a change of symbol at four-beat intervals. Then, as one student snaps quarter notes, have them watch you perform eighth notes or half notes with maracas or güiro and identify, by symbol, which rhythm you played.

EXTRA HELP: *"Troika" Rhythm Warmup*

Have students listen to "Troika" on page 34. Have half the class pretend to shake the horses' reins in time with the beat, while the other half shows strong beats by pretending to crack a whip. Ask students how the beats are grouped. (sets of four)

LANGUAGE ARTS CONNECTION: *Compare/Contrast*

Have a few students look up *obstinate* in dictionaries while the rest of the class gives ideas about what the word means. After defining *obstinate*, work together to compare

OSTINATO "TO GO"

You can add a playful movement ostinato to "I Let Her Go, Go."

FOLLOW the pictures to find out what to do each time you sing *go.*

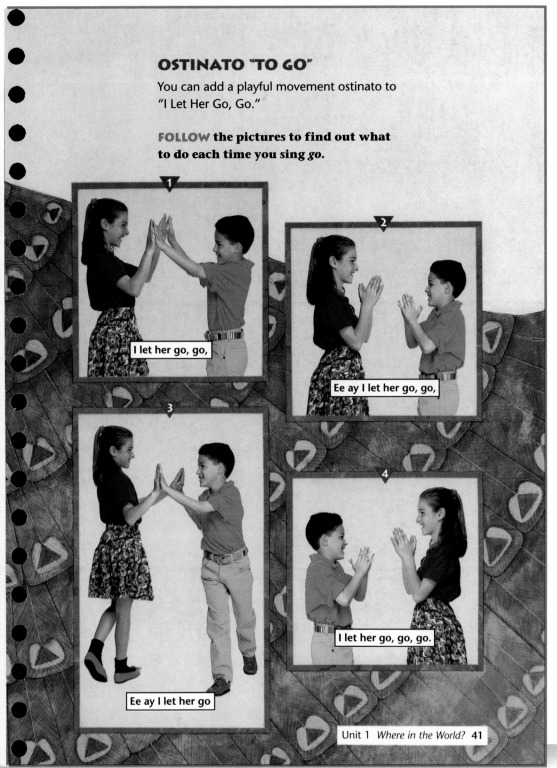

1 I let her go, go,

2 Ee ay I let her go, go,

3 Ee ay I let her go

4 I let her go, go, go.

Unit 1 *Where in the World?* 41

1 GET SET

"Let's read 'Voices of the World.'" (See page 8G.) "What does it describe?" (voices, dance, instruments) "Today you'll use your voices with instruments and movement." Have students:

• Listen to "I Let Her Go, Go" **CD1:13** (page 15) and jump in place with each strong beat when they hear only instruments. (See *Movement* on the bottom of page 23.)

"In what meter did you move?" ($\frac{4}{4}$) "Today you'll perform and create patterns in this meter."

2 DEVELOP

1. Perform an ostinato to "I Let Her Go, Go" (p. 15). Have students:

• Sing "I Let Her Go, Go," imitating you as you perform the ostinato on page 40 during the interludes.

• Review the rhythmic symbols on page 24 and match them with the movements you performed (snap ♫, brush ♩).

• Read about ostinato on page 40.

• Perform the ostinato with body percussion.

OBJECTIVE 1 Informal Assessment
• Sing the song, performing the ostinato with unpitched and/or body percussion during the instrumental interludes.

2. Learn the game to "I Let Her Go, Go." Have students:

▶ • Read about and perform the game. (See *Movement* below.)

• Perform the song and game, with a group assigned to play the ostinato during the interludes.

it with *ostinato.* Discuss how the definition of *obstinate* applies to their experience of *ostinato.*

PLAYING INSTRUMENTS: *Drums/Keyboards*

Drums: Ask volunteers to play conga or small hand drums on each *go,* to reinforce the clapping in the game.
Keyboards: Have students perform the rhythmic ostinato from page 40 during the interludes of "I Let Her Go, Go." Use a steel drum tone on electric keyboard if available.

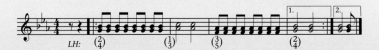

LH: (²/₄)   (¹/₃)   (³/₅)   (²/₄)   1.   2.

MOVEMENT: *Game for "I Let Her Go, Go"*
Preparation for this game is in Lesson 3, page 23, *Movement.*

Formation: partners facing, in scattered formation
1. Clap both hands of partner on the first *go, go.*
2. Clap own hands on the second *go, go.*
3. Touch partner's palms and exchange places on the long *go.*
4. Clap own hands on the last set of *go*'s. Partners are now standing in each other's places.

continued from previous page

3. Introduce "The Foxhunter's" from *Flower Basket Medley* CD2:1**. Experiment with mouth music.** Have students:

Recorded Lesson CD1:30
▶ • Listen to "Interview with the Barra MacNeils," in which the group discusses Celtic music.

▶ • Read about the Barra MacNeils on page 42.

▶ • Listen to "The Foxhunter's."

▶ • Try mouth music.

3 APPLY

Create two-measure patterns in ⁴⁄₄ in "The Foxhunter's." Have students:

• Listen to "The Foxhunter's" again, walking eight beats through shared space, then standing in place eight beats, and repeating this pattern.

• Create and clap four-beat combinations of quarters and rests.

• Read the patterns on page 43.

• Choose and perform a four-beat pattern as an ostinato, walking through shared space. (See *Movement* on the bottom of page 43.)

OBJECTIVE 2 Informal Assessment
• Perform an eight-beat pattern with a partner as a movement ostinato for "The Foxhunter's."

Meet
THE BARRA MACNEILS

The Barra MacNeils are from Nova Scotia, Canada. They perform traditional Celtic and Canadian music and write their own songs as well.

LISTEN to the Barra MacNeils discuss their music.

The Foxhunter's from *Flower Basket Medley*

LISTENING

Arranged by Sheumas, Kyle, Stewart, and Lucy MacNeil

Listen for the mouth music in "The Foxhunter's." Mouth music is created by singing very fast rhythms with nonsense syllables. It can be dance music when no instruments are handy. Try this mouth music.

die od-dle dee-dle i-dle did-dle-y i-dle dee-dle dum

Can you keep up with "The Foxhunter's"?

42 RHYTHMS THAT REPEAT

MEETING **INDIVIDUAL** NEEDS

ALTERNATE TEACHING STRATEGY

OBJECTIVE 2 Have students watch you perform the ostinato patterns on page 43 in random order, and match the movement patterns to the written ones. Next, write the patterns on the board or a transparency. Have students practice combining patterns by walking the first pattern as an ostinato, then changing each time you point to a different pattern.

MULTICULTURAL PERSPECTIVES: *Bodhran*

The bodhran (**bɔ** rɔn), or frame drum, held by Lucy MacNeil in the photo on page 42, is used in Irish folk music. The drum has a single head of animal skin stretched across a round, wooden frame. The player, or *bodhran stricker*, strikes the bodhran with the hand or with a carved wooden stick known as a *tipper*. The word *bodhran* comes from *bodhar*, meaning deaf or dull sounding. This drum was traditionally played in religious processions, and it may have originated as a tray used to hold grain during festivals.

RHYTHMS HIT THE ROAD!

CREATE a dance of movement ostinatos. First, choose a pattern to perform with your feet.

Find a partner and teach one another your steps. Together, create an ostinato using both patterns. How many beats long is it? 8

PERFORM your ostinato to "The Foxhunter's."

"Name two ways you performed ostinatos today." (body percussion, movement) "How many measures were in each ostinato?" (two measures of ⁴⁄₄) Have students:

• Break into pairs and perform their movement ostinatos. As each pair performs its ostinato, the rest of the class determines which patterns on page 43 are being performed.

LESSON SUMMARY

Informal Assessment In this lesson, students:

OBJECTIVE 1 Performed a two-measure ⁴⁄₄ ostinato using eighth and half notes to accompany "I Let Her Go, Go."

OBJECTIVE 2 Created and performed a two-measure ⁴⁄₄ movement ostinato for "The Foxhunter's" from *Flower Basket Medley,* using quarter notes and quarter rests.

National Standards for Music Education
1a Sing accurately, on pitch and in rhythm.
3c Improvise rhythmic variations and melodic embellishments.

MORE MUSIC: Reinforcement

"Campo," page 52 (maraca)
"El Marunguey," page 53 (rhythm reading in ⁴⁄₄ meter; güiro)
"Sing a Song of Peace," page 301 (⁴⁄₄ meter)
"The Boogie Woogie Ghost," page 304 (eight-beat patterns in ⁴⁄₄ meter; Halloween)
"The Ghost of John," page 306 (vocal ostinato; Halloween)
"Scary Music Montage," page 307 (Halloween)
"Dry Bones," page 308 (movement ostinato; Halloween)

MOVEMENT: *Ostinato to "The Foxhunter's"*

Have the class experiment with various ways to perform each rhythm pattern as a walking ostinato. For example, ♩ 𝄽 ♩ 𝄽 could be forward, rest, backward, rest, or step, rest, touch, rest; ♩♩♩ 𝄽 could be side, close, stamp, rest, or forward, forward, forward, rest.

After experimenting, let each student choose a favorite pattern, then find a partner. The partners teach each other their patterns, then combine the two, one after the other, to make an eight-beat pattern. Have the pairs perform the new pattern to "The Foxhunter's." (See *Apply,* page 42.)

IMPROVISATION: *Making Mouth Music*

Encourage groups of three or four students to create and perform a mouth-music accompaniment to "Fed My Horse" (page 31) or "Hi! Ho! The Rattlin' Bog" (page 23). Suggest that they start by choosing syllables to go with various durations. For example, try *dum* for ♩, *dum-dee* for ♫, and *dee-dle* for faster or uneven rhythms such as ♫ or ♫ for which they have not yet studied the notation.

RELATED ARTS MOVEMENT | THEATER | VISUAL ARTS

LESSON PLANNER

OBJECTIVES
To review songs, skills, and concepts learned in Unit 1 and to test students' ability to:

1. Identify phrases
2. Read rhythms (♩, ♫, ♩, 𝄽) in ⁴/₄ and ²/₄ meters
3. Recognize patterns using *do re mi so la* from staff notation

MATERIALS
Recordings

Fed My Horse	CD1:24
Mongolian Night Song	CD1:15
Hi! Ho! The Rattlin' Bog	CD1:12
Sir Duke	CD1:10
Unit 1 Assessment A	CD2:2–5
Unit 1 Assessment B	CD2:6–9

Other

4 or 5 tennis balls; Optional—map of the world

RESOURCES
Resource Master 1 • 9 (assessment)
Resource Master 1 • 10 (assessment)
Resource Master TA • 1 (assessment)

▶ = BASIC PROGRAM

REVIEW

MUSIC IS A WORLD WITHIN ITSELF

People all over the world enjoy music. The songs in this unit come from near and far.

Name each song pictured on the map, then name the country from which each song comes. Plan a travel route that includes all the orange countries.

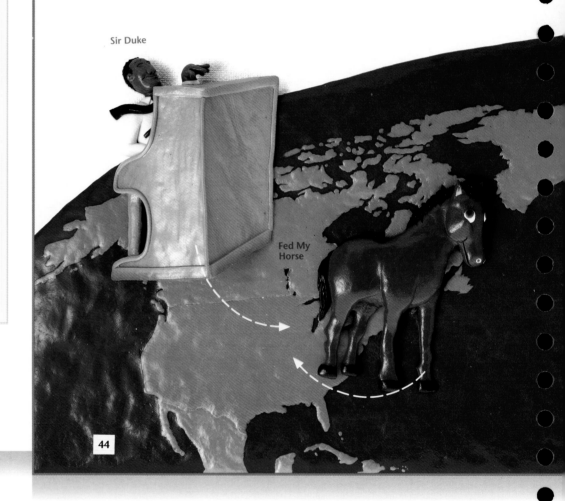

Sir Duke

Fed My Horse

44

MEETING **INDIVIDUAL** NEEDS

PROGRAM IDEA: *Music Is a World Within Itself*

This review can be enjoyed in the classroom or presented as a simple program. Additional materials from Unit 1, *Celebrations,* or the *Music Library* may be added, as well as original work from the students.

"There are many songs from different countries in our musical world. As you sing songs from different places, you can often find out about how people live in that country. First let's sing a song from our own country." Have students sing the Southern Appalachian folk song "Fed My Horse."

"Raising sheep is an important part of life in Inner Mongolia." Have students sing "Mongolian Night Song" and draw a curved pathway in the air for each phrase.

"In Ireland some interesting sights can be found in places that are unfamiliar to us." Have students sing "Hi! Ho! The Rattlin' Bog."

"Singing music that comes to us from around the world is fun. How about singing about people who took jazz around the world?" Have students sing "Sir Duke" and make up their own short poem about one of the musicians named in the song or another musician of their choice.

SING the songs that come from these countries as you visit around the musical world.

Which songs are in ⅜ meter? In ⁴⁄₄?

Which songs have phrases of different lengths? The same length?

Hi! Ho! The Rattlin' Bog

Mongolian Night Song

1. Review "Fed My Horse" CD1:24 (p. 31). Distinguish between phrase and melody. Have students:

▶ • Sing the song and find the United States on the map on pages 44–45 or on a world map.

• Find which phrases include *la* (1, 3) and which include *re* and *do* (2, 4).

▶ • Sing the song in two groups—one group standing to sing Phrases 1 and 3; the other, Phrases 2 and 4—all singing the third line with the hambone pattern. (See *Movement* on the bottom of page 30.)

2. Review "Mongolian Night Song" CD1:15 (p. 19). Review rhythms and ⁴⁄₄ meter. Have students:

▶ • Sing the song and find Inner Mongolia, in China, on the map.

• Review the rhythms and metric signs found in the first five phrases. (quarter, eighth, half notes, meter signature, bar line)

• Divide into two groups, one group singing the song, the other clapping this ostinato:

3. Review ⁴⁄₄ meter in "Hi! Ho! The Rattlin' Bog" CD1:12. Have students:

▶ • Sing the refrain of "Hi! Ho! The Rattlin' Bog" (page 14) and find Ireland on the map.

• Sing the refrain again (or the entire song, page 23), showing the meter of the refrain with a bounce-catch motion. (See *Enrichment* below.)

4. Sing "Sir Duke" CD1:10 (p. 10) for fun. Have students:

▶ • Find the related picture on the map.

▶ • Sing the song to celebrate music and the world.

ENRICHMENT: *"Hi! Ho! The Rattlin' Bog" Game*

Have the class stand in a circle formation. Give a tennis ball to every sixth or seventh student. Have those students bounce and catch the ball to the beat during the refrain (bounce = 1 beat; catch = 1 beat). If singing the entire song, students should pass the ball to the neighbor on the right during the verses.

ART CONNECTION: *Textures in Clay*

VISUAL ARTS

Have students look at the picture on pages 44–45 and determine what media was used to create it. (clay) Because clay is pliable, textures are readily created with it. Ask students to describe the textures of the sheep, the tree trunk, the leaves, and the people's hair. What tools do they think the artist used to create the various textures? Invite students to flatten pieces of clay into pancakes and to use a variety of objects (forks, nails, buttons, garlic press, paper clips) to create textures in the clay.

ASSESSMENTS A AND B CD2:2–9

Different recorded examples for Assessments A and B allow for two uses of the same set of questions. When appropriate, recorded examples for Assessment A use familiar musical examples with which students have worked for the given concept. The recorded examples for Assessment B use musical selections the students have not previously worked with for the concept, encouraging the application of knowledge to new material.

The pupil page is intended for those who wish to assess quickly with the whole class or in small groups. Each assessment may be used as a pretest or as a final review before presenting the written test (**Resource Master 1 • 9**).

ANSWERS		
	ASSESSMENT A	**ASSESSMENT B**
1.	a	b
2.	c	b
3.	c	d
4.	d	b

CHECK IT OUT

1. How many phrases do you hear?

   a. two   **b.** three   **c.** four

2. Locate the rhythm pattern that is played. Which measure has the wrong number of beats?

   a. Measure 1   **b.** Measure 2   **c.** Measure 3   **d.** Measure 4

   Pattern 1

   Pattern 2

   Pattern 3

   Pattern 4

3. Which rhythm do you hear?

   a.

   b.

   c.

   d.

4. Which melody do you hear?

   a. 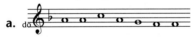   c.

   b. 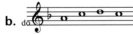   d.

46

MEETING **INDIVIDUAL** NEEDS

PORTFOLIO ASSESSMENT

To evaluate student portfolios, use the Portfolio Assessment form on **Resource Master TA • 1**. See page 8B for a summary of Portfolio Opportunities in this unit.

ENRICHMENT: *Creating Assessment Guidelines*

Discuss the following to help children create their own assessment guidelines for compositions and performances.
Facts and feelings: What musical elements did the composition or performance contain? Name three things you liked about the performance. Why? Name one thing you might change. Why?
Group processing: How did your group work successfully together to complete this task?
Use these guidelines throughout the school year whenever children create and perform for each other.

CREATE

Introduction in Eight

CREATE a melody. Use the pitches F G A C' D'. Use this eight-beat rhythm pattern.

On a piece of paper, write your melody with the letters you find on the bells you chose.

The bell with the letter F sounds like *do*. Write your melody with pitch syllables, too.

If the meter signature of this rhythm pattern is ⁴⁄₄ , where do the bar lines go?

Play your melody as an introduction to "Fed My Horse."

Write

Stevie Wonder wrote "Sir Duke" in honor of jazz musician Duke Ellington. Think of a musician you admire.

Write a poem telling who the person is and why you look up to that person.

CREATE AND WRITE

1. Create introductions. Have students:

• Work in small groups and follow the instructions on page 47 to create introductions to "Fed My Horse." (Optional: Use **Resource Master 1 • 10** to organize this activity.)

2. Write poems. Have students:

▶ • Write poems as described. (Invite volunteers to read their poems to the class.)

> **National Standards for Music Education**
> **4b** Create and arrange short songs and instrumental pieces.
> **4c** Use a variety of sound sources when composing.
> **7a** Devise criteria for evaluating performances and compositions.
> **7b** Explain musical preferences, using appropriate musical terms.

LANGUAGE ARTS CONNECTION: *Essays*

Listen again to "Sir Duke." Have students write a short essay on one of their favorite musical artists and compare him or her to one of the artists featured in "Sir Duke."

MOVEMENT: *Assessing Movement*

Using the discussion process outlined in *Enrichment*, page 46, help students create their own assessment guidelines for choreography and movement performance.

Choreography: What design elements were important? What variations of these elements did you notice? What contrasting elements were there?

Performance: Was the movement performed appropriately with the accompaniment? If there was unison movement, was it precise? Did the performance have a clear beginning, middle, and end?

The California Song

Unit 1 Reinforcement
do re mi so la, page 31

1. Sing with pitch syllables CD2:10. Have students:

• Notate the pitch set of the verse on the board and sing it. (*do re mi so la*)

• Sing each pitch as you point to it. (Follow the melodic ideas of the verse.)

• Look at the pitches of the verse and notice that *so* is the most frequently sung pitch.

• Sing the verse with pitch syllables.

• Listen to the entire song, then discuss what it is about. (westward expansion, gold rush)

• Sing the entire song.

2. Sing the song in two groups. Have students:

• Form two groups. One group sings the first two lines of the verse, the other sings the last two lines. They join together on the refrain. (Optional: Use "The California Song" Performance Mix CD10:9.)

48

MEETING **INDIVIDUAL** NEEDS

SOCIAL STUDIES CONNECTION: *Gold Rush*

Have students tell which parts of "The California Song" give clues as to what life was like at the time of the Gold Rush. Have them read about the California Gold Rush and find out when, where, and how it started, who was "rushing" and where they were going, and how long it lasted.

PLAYING INSTRUMENTS: *Unpitched*

Have students accompany "The California Song" on sticks or other unpitched instruments.

On the banks of the Sac - ra - men - to shore,
They've ta-ken out lumps as big as a brick.
But pa - tient - ly wait for a - bout two year.
Ex - cept when the wolves come howl - ing round.

Refrain

Then ho, boys, ho! to Cal - i - for - nia go,

for the moun-tains bold are cov-ered with gold on the

banks of the Sac - ra - men - to,

Heigh, ho a - way we go,

Dig - ging up gold in Fris - co.

Unit 1 *Where in the World?* 49

ENCORE

MULTICULTURAL PERSPECTIVES

RELATED ARTS | **MOVEMENT** | THEATER | **VISUAL ARTS**

LESSONLINKS

Carnival Time in Puerto Rico *(10 min)*

OBJECTIVE Learn about Puerto Rican carnival customs

Reinforcement carnival, *page 163*

Campo *(10 min)*

OBJECTIVE Listen to a Puerto Rican bomba and learn about the percussion used

Reinforcement maraca, *page 43*

MATERIALS
Recording Campo (listening)   CD2:11

El Marunguey *(15 min)*

OBJECTIVE Move to the rhythm of a Puerto Rican plena

Reinforcement
rhythm reading in ⁴⁄₄, *page 43*
güiro, *page 43*

MATERIALS
Recording El Marunguey by Angel Luís Medina and José Rivera (listening)   CD2:12

ENCORE
~ Carnival Time in Puerto Rico ~

Costumes, food, parades, and music are the most important ingredients of Carnival in Puerto Rico.

Since 1858, men and boys have dressed up as *Vejigantes*, masked pranksters. The Vejigantes travel the streets, teasing children with good-natured pranks. They wear colorful costumes with wings.

50

MEETING **INDIVIDUAL** NEEDS

BACKGROUND: *"Carnival"*

The custom of Carnival grew out of both the traditional Holy Week parades of Spain and the processions of Africa. Carnival is a late winter celebration, like Mardi Gras in New Orleans and elsewhere, before the fasting and serious contemplation of the pre-Easter period of Lent. The word "carnival" comes from the Latin word *carnaval*, which means "farewell to meat." It was customary to forego eating meat during Lent, so Carnival time became the last chance to feast until Easter.

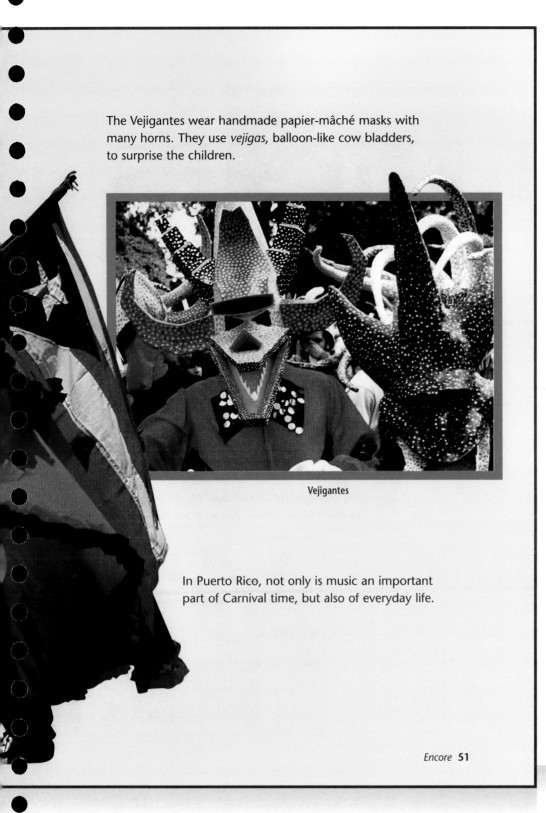

The Vejigantes wear handmade papier-mâché masks with many horns. They use *vejigas*, balloon-like cow bladders, to surprise the children.

Vejigantes

In Puerto Rico, not only is music an important part of Carnival time, but also of everyday life.

Carnival Time in Puerto Rico

Learn about Carnival. Have students:

• Share any experiences they have had in making or wearing costumes.

• Locate Puerto Rico on a map, and identify what islands are nearby.

• Look at the pictures on pages 50 and 51 and discuss Carnival.

• Read about Vejigantes and look at pictures of them.

ENRICHMENT: *Making Masks* VISUAL ARTS

Have students make colorful horned masks from papier-mâché. Invite them to examine the photographs in their book, then to draw their own ideas. Use balloons or wire mesh to make rounded forms for the faces. Suggest that students collect empty toilet paper tubes, paper towel rolls, or other forms of their own devising to make horns. Make vertical cuts at the base of the rolls to form tabs and attach them to the mask using more papier-mâché strips. When the papier-mâché is dry, have students paint the masks bright colors.

PRONUNCIATION: *Spanish Words*

Vejigantes   ve hi **gan** tes
vejigas   ve **hi** gas
bomba   **bom** ba
plena   **ple** na
pandereta   pan de **re** ta
marunguey   ma **run** gweɩ

MULTICULTURAL PERSPECTIVES

Campo CD2:11

Listen to a Puerto Rican bomba and compare the bomba drums and maraca.
Have students:

• Read about bomba and look at the picture of the instruments, paying particular attention to the bomba drum (top, center).

• Identify the drums in the picture at the bottom of page 52 as bomba drums.

• Listen to "Campo," paying attention to the percussion. (If needed, review what percussion instruments are.)

• Listen again, then compare the sound of the bomba drum and maraca. (They are both used as percussion instruments; the drum is beaten while the maraca sounds like a rattle. If possible, demonstrate a maraca or other shaker.)

• Share and discuss how music can express emotions such as suffering or joy. (Encourage them to share songs they sing, or listen to, when they are happy or sad. See *Background: Bomba* below.)

Typical Puerto Rican instruments include from left to right: rasp, pandereta (flat drum), maraca, bomba drum, güiro (snake-shaped gourd), and cuatro.

Bomba is one of the oldest forms of Puerto Rican music. It combines dance, singing, and percussion. The percussion usually features a single maraca and three differently pitched drums made from barrels. There are two kinds of calls and responses in bomba: the solo singer and chorus respond to one another, and the drummers and dancer respond to one another. They challenge each other in a lively competition. It's very exciting!

LISTENING
Campo *Puerto Rican bomba*

The singer tells of his sad, hard life. He wants to be free to dance to the bomba, hoping it will help him to be happy.

Los Pleneros de la 21 performing a bomba.

MEETING **INDIVIDUAL** NEEDS

BACKGROUND: *Bomba*

Bomba flourished wherever Africans and their descendants lived and worked on colonial plantations. It is most associated with the suffering of enslaved people. Before the abolition of slavery in 1873, bomba dances often had a subversive message: The female dancers raised their skirts in the dance, exposing their petticoats to ridicule the elaborate dresses and slips of the plantation ladies. Bomba provided social, political, and spiritual outlets for people with many burdens in life.

SCIENCE CONNECTION: *Gourds*

Have students research gourds in library books or on the internet. They can discover what gourds are and the many uses for them. Have a competition to see who can find the most uses for gourds.

El Marunguey

*by Angel Luis Medina
and José Rivera*

"El Marunguey" tells of going to the mangroves to catch crabs, fish, and eels. It is a type of music called *plena*. Plena is an exciting and joyful type of Caribbean music. It is often called *el periodico*, or "the sung newspaper," because daily events are described in improvised music. Plena combines both African and Spanish musical traditions. It usually consists of calls and responses between soloist and chorus.

Children playing a pandereta
and güiro with rasp.

Plena instruments include a güiro, made from a gourd, and three or more hand-held frame drums, each of a different size, called *panderetas*. Each pandereta plays a different rhythm.

STEP and play this rhythm to the plena "El Marunguey."

right   left   right   left   right   left   right   left   right   left

El Marunguey CD2:12

Listen to a plena and perform its rhythm pattern. Have students:

• Read about plena on page 53.

• Identify the güiro and pandereta drums in the photographs at the top of page 52 and on page 53. (Point out that the güiro is played with a rasp.)

• Listen to the plena, "El Marunguey," paying attention to the percussion.

• Read and clap the rhythm on page 53.

• Listen again, clapping the rhythm along with the selection.

• Learn the movement. (See *Movement* below.)

• Practice the movement with the music.

MOVEMENT: *"El Marunguey"*

Have students practice the step in their own space. Students should move forward on Beats 1 and 2 and step in place on Beats 3 and 4. When ready, have them form one long line, with each student facing forward and positioned directly behind the student in front of him or her. Appoint different students to lead the class around the room as they move with the music.

BACKGROUND: *Plena*

Plena music was born in the working-class neighborhoods near the city of Ponce, Puerto Rico, in about 1898. This was during the change from Spanish to American colonial rule.

Traveling On

MULTICULTURAL PERSPECTIVES

Through exposure to diverse materials, students develop an awareness of how people from many cultures create and participate in music. This unit includes:

African/African American and Caribbean

- **Four White Horses,** Caribbean song, 60

Asian/Asian American and Middle Eastern

- Chinese ensemble with instruments, 90
- **In a Mountain Path,** traditional Chinese song arranged by Han Kuo-huang, 90
- **Karşi Bar,** Turkish folk dance, 64
- *Landscape in the Style of Dong Beiyuan,* by Chinese painter Dong Qichang, 91
- Turkish instruments, 72–73

European/European American and Canadian

- **Down the Road,** American folk song, 76
- **The Old Carrion Crow,** Nova Scotian song, 62
- **Prelude,** by French composer Georges Bizet, 85
- **Promenade,** by Russian composer Modest Mussorgsky, 70
- **Roads Go Ever Ever On,** by British poet J.R.R. Tolkien, 55
- **Swapping Song,** Appalachian folk song, 82
- **Trail to Mexico,** cowboy song, 59
- Western orchestral instruments, 68–69

Hispanic/Hispanic American

- **En la feria de San Juan,** Puerto Rican song, 66

For a complete listing of materials by culture throughout the book, see the Classified Index.

UNIT 2

CURRICULUM INTEGRATION

Activities in this unit that promote the integration of music with other curriculum areas include:

Art

- Draw self-portraits in a Western scene, 61B
- Hold an art exhibition, 71

Math

- Estimate distances to Mexico, 61A
- Draw a grid map of an arrow's path, 65A
- Draw a multiplication tree, 65B
- Solve a word problem with multiplication, 75A
- Plan an elapsed-time game, 79B

Reading/Language Arts

- Play a word-substitution game with a song, 61B
- Perform a skit or short play, 65A
- Write a news story, 65B
- Write a letter about an imaginary journey, 75B
- Make a descriptive list of a route through the school building, 79A
- Write about a real or imaginary vacation, 79A

Social Studies

- Map an imaginary journey, 61A
- Research and compare cattle drive routes, 75A
- Play a map game, 75B
- Draw a map of a route between two points in the neighborhood, 79B
- Explore aspects of ethnic heritage, 82
- Research and create posters showing the history of transportation, 94

New! **UNIT OPENERS WITH THEMATIC TEACHING PROJECTS**

PLANNER

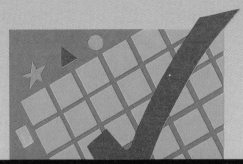

ASSESSMENT OPTIONS

Informal Performance Assessments

Informal Assessments correlated to Objectives are provided in every lesson with Alternate Strategies for reteaching. Frequent informal assessment allows for ongoing progress checks throughout the course of the unit.

Formal Assessment

An assessment form is provided on pupil page 94 and Resource Master 2•9. The questions assess student understanding of the following main unit objectives:

- Identify sixteenth notes
- Recognize patterns using pitches D E G A B from staff notation

Music Journal

Encourage students to enter thoughts about selections, projects, performances, and personal progress. Some journal opportunities include:

- Critical Thinking, TE 63, 69, 81
- *Think It Through,* 65, 79
- Write, 95

Portfolio Opportunities

Update student portfolios with outcome-based materials, including written work, audiotapes, videotapes, and/or photos that represent their best work for each unit. Some portfolio opportunities in this unit include:

- Performance of Orff Orchestrations (audiotape), TE 58, 77
- Working with rhythms (Resource Masters 2•1, 2•3, 2•4), TE 64, 74
- Sorting orchestral instruments by family (Resource Master 2•2), TE 70
- Performance of vocal ostinato with "Trail to Mexico" (audiotape), 74
- Labeling pitch letter names from staff notation (Resource Master 2•5), TE 78
- Learning to draw the treble clef (Resource Master 2•6), TE 78
- Matching notation with pitch syllables; creating a melody with given pitch patterns (Resource Master 2•7), TE 82
- Playing Instruments: performance of interludes (audiotape), TE 87
- Check It Out (formal assessment), 94; Resource Master 2•9
- Portfolio Assessment (Resource Masters TA•1–5), TE 94
- Create 95; Resource Master 2•10
- Write, 95

			LESSON 1 CORE p.58	LESSON 2 CORE p.62	LESSON 3 p.66
	FOCUS		Pitch, tonal center	Duration, three and four sounds to a beat	Tone color, instrument families
	SELECTIONS		Roads Go Ever Ever On (poem) Trail to Mexico Four White Horses Down the Road	The Old Carrion Crow Karşi Bar (listening) En la feria de San Juan	En la feria de San Juan Strings and Things (listening) Promenade from *Pictures at an Exhibition* (listening)
MUSICAL ELEMENTS	**CONCEPTS**	**UNIT OBJECTIVES** Bold = Tested			
EXPRESSIVE QUALITIES	**Dynamics**				
	Tempo			• Sing song with tempo changes	
	Articulation				
TONE COLOR	**Vocal/ Instrumental Tone Color**	• Identify families of instruments		• Hear Turkish instruments	• Name, compare and contrast orchestral instrument families
DURATION	**Beat/Meter**		• Snap on beats 2, 4 of song in 𝅘𝅥 • Move with beat in 𝅘𝅥	• Move to show beat and rhythm • Distinguish 4 equal and 3 unequal sounds to beat • Use graphic notation of beat and rhythm	• Pat, tap listening map with beat • Hear a selection and see notation with meter changes
	Rhythm	• **Identify sixteenth notes** • Create and perform 4-measure rhythmic interludes	• **See and sing sixteenth notes (E)**	• **Echo, pat, and move to show beat and rhythm (E)** • **Describe sixteenth notes (D)** • **Use graphic notation of sixteenth notes (E/D)** • **Make up rhythm patterns with sixteenth notes (E)**	• **Sing and see notation with sixteenth notes (E)**
PITCH	**Melody**	• Identify tonal center • Identify melodic contour • **Sing with pitch letter names D E G A B** • Use so₁ la₁ do re mi	• **See and sing D E G A B (E)** • Move to show melodic contour • Discover tonal center • Match melodic contour to graphic notation		• See and listen for notated melodic theme • *Play melody of refrain as accompaniment*
	Harmony				• *Play chord roots in accompaniment*
	Tonality major/minor	• Identify tonal center	• Discover and hum tonal center		
DESIGN	**Texture**				• *Play unpitched, melodic, and harmonic accompaniments*
	Form/ Structure	• Identify A B A form	• Sing song with 3 verses	• Recognize similar phrases • Listen and move to show A B A B A B • Devise and perform contrasting B section	• Sing cumulative song
CULTURAL CONTEXT	**Style/ Background**	• Hear and sing music from diverse cultures • Develop understanding of musical concepts using selections from diverse cultures	• Learn and move to Caribbean folk song	• Sing Nova Scotian folk song • Hear and perform Turkish folk dance	• Sing Puerto Rican folk song • Listen to music by Modest Mussorgsky • *Compare instruments from diverse cultures*

Learning Sequence: E = Explore, D = Describe, I = Identify, P = Practice, Rf = Reinforce, Rd = Read, C = Create   See also *Program Scope and Sequence,* page 402.

LESSON 4 CORE p.72	LESSON 5 CORE p.76	LESSON 6 p.80	LESSON 7 p.84	LESSON 8 p.88
Duration—sixteenth notes, upbeat	Pitch—low *la*, low *so*; D E G A B	Pitch—*do la₁ so₁*, G E D, tonal center	Duration, sixteenth notes	Design—A B, A B A
The Old Carrion Crow Karşi Bar (listening) Trail to Mexico	Down the Road Trail to Mexico	Four White Horses Mongolian Night Song Swapping Song	Carrion Crow Rhythm (listening) The Old Carrion Crow Prelude to *Carmen* (listening) Swapping Song	Karşi Bar (listening) Down the Road In a Mountain Path (listening) Four White Horses
		• Sing softly to correct intonation		
			• Review tempo changes • *Use slower tempo* • *Vary tempo of rhythms*	
		• Review song with legato phrases	• Hear selection with staccato articulation	• Move with marcato and legato motions
	• *Sing in jazz style* • *Sing harmony in small groups*	• Sing softly to correct intonation • *Select 3 different-sounding instruments for ostinato*	• Hear orchestral music • Choose different body-percussion sounds • *Sing solo, duo, and trio*	• Hear hammered and bowed Chinese string instruments
• Snap and move with beat • Learn upbeat • *Make up and play ostinatos with beat*	• Move with beat	• Perform body percussion with beat • Clap with beat in 4 meter • *Toss and catch with beat in ¾ meter*	• Tap graphic notation with beat • Count number of beats in phrase	• Pat, move with beat • Improvise 8-beat rhythm patterns • *Follow listening map with graphic notation of beat*
• **Define sixteenth notes (I)** • **Make up words to go with sixteenth-note patterns (P)** • **Perform an ostinato with sixteenth notes from notation (Rd/Rf)** • *Perform sixteenth notes with body percussion* • *Write rhythms with sixteenth notes*	• *Pat and clap rhythm*	• **Sing song with sixteenth note patterns (Rf)** • *Pat and put notated rhythmic phrases in order*	• **Identify motive with sixteenth notes (Rf)** • **Perform rhythm patterns with sixteenth notes (Rf)** • **Create and perform 4-measure rhythmic interludes (C)** • *Create and perform 8-beat rhythm patterns*	• Improvise 8-beat rhythm patterns
• Sing and play ostinato melody • *See graphic notation of melody*	• **Determine pitches used (D E G A B) (E/D)** • **Define D E G A B; name and sing letter names of song (I/P)** • **Sing ostinato with D E (Rf)** • Define *so₁* and *la₁* • Use *so₁ la₁ do re mi* • Sing and play song from notation	• **Sing with D E G A B (Rd/Rf)** • Sing with pitch syllables *so₁ la₁ do re mi* • Distinguish, sing *do la₁ so₁* • *Find so₁ and la₁ in notation* • *Draw melodic contour*		• **Sing with D E G A B (Rf)** • Use *so₁ la₁ do re mi* • Determine song from melody
• Sing melodic ostinato with song	• Sing melodic ostinato • *Perform Orff orchestration, countermelodies* • *Sing harmony in small groups*			
	• Recognize tonal center	• Recognize and compare tonal centers of 3 songs		
• *Make up and play unpitched ostinatos*	• *Perform instrumental countermelodies*	• *Add 4-beat unpitched ostinato*	• *Add unpitched ostinato*	
• Perform A B A B A B dance	• Sing and see sectional labels of A B song	• Sing and see notation of verse-refrain song with 14 verses	• Recall similar phrases • Recognize phrases • Define overture, motive, interlude • Make up interludes	• Learn A B and A B A form • Make up and perform contrasting B section • *Follow listening map that shows phrase, section*
• Perform Turkish folk dance • See Turkish instruments	• *Sing in jazz style*	• Play Caribbean game with song • Sing Appalachian folk song	• Hear music by Georges Bizet	• Hear traditional Chinese song • See traditional Chinese instruments

UNIT 2 PLANNER

UNIT 2

SKILLS

SKILLS		LESSON 1 CORE p.58	LESSON 2 CORE p.62	LESSON 3 p.66
CREATION AND PERFORMANCE	Singing	• *Practice singing without flatting* • Hum tonal center	• Echo-sing phrases with sixteenth notes	• Sing sixteenth notes
	Playing	• *Play Orff orchestration*		• *Play unpitched, melodic, and harmonic accompaniments*
	Moving	• Change arm levels to show melodic contour • Move with beat in ⁶⁄₈	• Walk pathways with beat • *Move to show durations* (♩, ♫, ♬) • Move to show A and B sections	• Perform cumulative body-percussion routine • *Create a dance with body facing changes* • Imitate motions of playing instrument
	Improvising/ Creating		• Create B section movement • Create rhythm patterns with sixteenth notes	• *Create a dance with body facing changes* • *Invent and describe a new family of instruments*
NOTATION	Reading	• See graphic notation for melodic contours	• Find similar phrases and see sixteenth notes in notation • Read graphic notation of beat and rhythms with sixteenth notes	• See notation with sixteenth notes • See and listen for notated melodic theme • See notated meter change • Follow listening map
	Writing			
PERCEPTION AND ANALYSIS	Listening/ Describing/ Analyzing	• Recognize tonal center	• Listen for story of song • Distinguish 4 equal and 3 unequal sounds to beat • Aurally identify rhythmic phrase	• Identify, compare and contrast orchestral instrument families • Listen for entrance of each orchestral family

 TECHNOLOGY

SHARE THE MUSIC VIDEOS

Use videos to reinforce, extend, and enrich learning.
- Lesson 1, p. 59: Making a Music Video (two-part singing)
- Lesson 3, pp. 68–69: Musical Expression (violin): Sounds of Percussion (percussion family); Introduction to Computers in Music (saxophone)
- Lesson 7, p. 85: Musical Expression *(Carmen)*

MUSIC WITH *MIDI*

MIDI technology allows students to manipulate musical elements and make musical decisions with this song:
- Lesson 1, p. 59: Trail to Mexico

MUSICTIME™

This notational software develops students' music reading and writing skills through activities correlated to these lessons:
- Lesson 4, Project 1 (create a rhythm pattern)
- Lesson 9, Project 2 (create a melody with D E G A B)
- Encore, Project (create sound effects)

LESSON 4 CORE p.78	LESSON 5 CORE p.76	LESSON 6 p.80	LESSON 7 p.84	LESSON 8 p.88
• Sing melodic ostinato with song	• Sing with pitch letter names D E G A B and pitch syllables *so₁ la₁ do re mi* • *Sing in jazz style* • *Practice singing harmony in small groups*	• *Sing softly to correct intonation* • Sing with pitch syllables *so₁ la₁ do re mi* and pitch letter names D E G A B • Sing sixteenth note patterns	• *Sing solo, duo, and trio*	• Sing and speak contrasting sections
• *Create and play ostinatos with beat*	• *Perform Orff orchestration* • *Perform instrumental countermelodies*	• *Play 3 different-sounding instruments for ostinato*	• *Add unpitched ostinato* • *Perform interludes*	
• Move with beat in A B A B A B dance	• Move with beat	• Draw melodic contour in air • Toss and catch with beat in ⅔ meter		• Move with beat to show A B form • Improvise marcato/legato mirroring movement
• *Create and play ostinatos with beat* • Make up words to go with sixteenth note patterns	• Improvise ways to walk with song • *Use hand signs for pitch syllables*		• Create interludes • *Create and perform 8-beat rhythm patterns*	• *Improvise melodies with D E G A B* • Improvise mirroring movement • Improvise 8-beat rhythm patterns
• Perform an ostinato with sixteenth notes from notation • *See graphic notation of melody* • Identify upbeat	• Read, sing, and play D E G A B from notation • Identify treble clef	• Read all pitches and rhythms of song • Identify tonal center on notation • *Find la₁ so₁ in notation* • *Put notated rhythmic phrases in order*	• Tap graphic notation with beat • Identify motive with sixteenth notes	• Sing letter names and pitch syllable from notation • *Follow listening map with graphic notation of beat, phrase, section*
• *Practice writing rhythms with sixteenth notes*	• *Practice drawing treble clef*			
• Listen for upbeat	• Listen for pitches below *do* • Compare and contrast how song sounds with and without ostinato changes a song	• Identify *do la₁ so₁* melodic pattern • Identify tonal centers of 3 songs • *Use inner hearing for certain phrases*	• Identify motive with sixteenth notes	• Identify A B and A B A form • Predict and compare A, B sections

MUSIC ACE™

Music Ace reinforces musical concepts and provides ear-training opportunities for students.
  · **Lesson 1, p. 54: Lesson 19 (C major scale)**
  · **Lesson 5, p. 76: Lessons 7 & 8 (pitch names); Lesson 10 (ledger lines)**
  · **Lesson 6, p. 80: Lesson 24 (major scales)**

NEW! MUSIC ACE 2™

Music Ace 2™ introduces basic rhythm concepts and furthers the melodic and harmonic concepts covered in Music Ace.

FOCUS We can explore ways of travel
through music.

OBJECTIVE To set the stage for Unit 2

MATERIALS
Roads Go Ever Ever On (poem)
City of New Orleans   CD2:13
City of New Orleans
  (performance mix)   CD10:10

INTRODUCE THE THEME

1. Discuss the theme. "Have you ever started to
go somewhere without being exactly sure which
roads you would take to get there? Sometimes the
journey can be as interesting as the place you are
going to." Have students:

• Share experiences they have had on trips to
different parts of town, school trips, or holiday
trips.

2. Introduce "Roads Go Ever Ever On."
"Let's look at the poem 'Roads Go Ever Ever
On.' It tells us about one person's journey."
Have students:

• Listen as a volunteer reads the first half of the
poem aloud.

• Identify and listen for the sights that are seen
along the road.

• Listen to the second half to see where the roads
lead to. (back to familiar meadow and trees)

UNIT 2

TRAVELING ON

54

UNIT 2 THEME PROJECTS

Through the songs in this unit, students will explore
different ways that people travel.

TRAVEL BY TRAIN Have the class discuss trains and train
travel. Encourage them to explore ideas such as: the importance of trains before there were cars or planes; how
railroads opened up the United States in the mid-1800s;
and what it feels like to travel by train. In small groups,
have students improvise (or write and dramatize) a scene
about a train. They may choose to depict train travel as it
was in earlier times or as it is today. They can get their

ideas from the words to "City of New Orleans" (page 56)
as well as from researching train travel through books or
personal interviews. Have each group perform its scene
for the class. *(After Unit Opener)*

BECOME A COWHAND After singing "Trail to Mexico"
(page 59), have the class discuss what it would be like to
be a cowhand. Have students research cowhand life.
Then, have small groups improvise or write and dramatize a scene about cowhands on a cattle drive. Have each
group perform its scene for the class. *(Lessons 2 and 4)*

Roads Go Ever Ever On

Roads go ever ever on,
   Over rock and under tree,
By caves where never sun has shone,
   By streams that never find the sea;
Over snow by winter sown,
   And through the merry flowers of June,
Over grass and over stone,
   And under mountains in the moon.

Roads go ever ever on
   Under cloud and under star,
Yet feet that wandering have gone
   Turn at last to home afar.
Eyes that fire and sword have seen
   And horror in the halls of stone
Look at last on meadows green
   And trees and hills they long have known.

—J. R. R. Tolkien

Meet the Poet John Ronald Reuel Tolkien (tɔl ki ɛn), 1892–1973, was a professor of language and literature at Oxford University in England. His fantasy books, The *Hobbit* and *The Lord of the Rings*, remain widely read. This poem, an excerpt from *The Hobbit* (1937), is spoken by a hobbit, Bilbo Baggins, as he returns home from his adventures. Hobbits are a good-natured, peaceable race of little people who love good food and dislike machines. Tolkien drew on ancient British legends and traditions to create the hobbits' fantasy world of Middle-earth, with its geography, calendar, and even a language.

Art Link Have students discuss how this illustration (pages 54–55) captures the vastness of the desert. The artist has used perspective to give a sense of depth and distance. Perspective can be created by overlapping objects, by making things that are in the distance smaller than those closer to us, and by showing more detail on the closer objects. Invite students to identify the techniques used in this picture, then to create their own desert scenes showing perspective.

EXPLORE THE WORLD THROUGH AN ANIMAL'S EYES

With "The Old Carrion Crow" (page 62) in mind, have students talk about the ways different animals travel and how this might influence their view of the world. For example, birds fly, fish swim, snails crawl, frogs hop, and so on. Have students write a composition or a poem from the viewpoint of an animal. If they choose a bird, for example, they can write about how it feels to glide through the air, and how the city or countryside looks from their vantage point. *(Lesson 2)*

3. Introduce "City of New Orleans" CD2:13.
"The song 'City of New Orleans' is about another way of traveling. See if you can guess what it is." Have students:

• Listen to the "City of New Orleans" to see what type of vehicle it is and where it is going. (a train traveling throughout the United States)

• Listen again, joining in each time on the refrain.

• Sing the entire song as they are able.

4. Set the stage for Unit 2. Have students:

• Think about the idea in the poem of "roads that go ever ever on," then look through the unit to find the many places that the roads in the songs can take them.

• Sing the theme song, "City of New Orleans." (This final activity should be in "performance mode" as much as possible.)

UNIT 2 THEME SONG

C major

City of New Orleans

Words and Music
by Steve Goodman

Freely

1. Rid - in' on___ the Cit - y of___ New Or - leans,

Il - li - nois___ Cen - tral Mon - day morn - in' rail.___

Fif - teen cars___ and fif - teen rest - less rid - ers,

three con - duc - tors and twen - ty - five sacks of mail.___

And the sons of old___ men por - ters and the

sons of en - gi - neers___ Ride their fa - thers'___ ma - gic car -

- pets___ made of steel.___

56

UNIT 2 MUSIC PROJECT:

This project will give students additional practice in reading and writing rhythms and will prepare them for successful completion of the "Create" activity in Lesson 9.

1 CREATE A PATTERN Have students use the nonsense syllables shown on page 64 to create their own patterns of the same length. Have them write the words down to help them recall the pattern. Then have them perform their pattern in alternation with a partner. Have partners determine their preferred order for the two patterns based on which of the two patterns sounds more like an ending. *(After Lesson 2)*

Moth - ers with their babes a - sleep are

rock - in' to the gen - tle beat and the

rhy - thm of the rails is all they feel.

Good morn - ing A - mer - i - ca, how are you?

Say don't you know me, I'm your na - tive son.

I'm the train they call the Cit - y of New Or - leans.

I'll be gone five hun - dred miles when the day is done.

2. Night time on the City of New Orleans,
Changin' cars in Memphis, Tennessee.
Halfway home, we'll be there by mornin'
through the Mississippi darkness rollin' down to the sea.
But all the towns and people seem to fade into a bad dream
and the steel rail still ain't heard the news.
The conductor sings his songs again
the passengers will please refrain
this train's got the disappearin' railroad blues.
Good night America, how are you?
Say don't you know me, I'm your native son.
I'm the train they call the City of New Orleans.
I'll be gone five hundred miles when the day is done.

Program Idea: Travel Land

Have students create a program about a theme park based on travel. A tour guide welcomes the guests (students) and brings them to the different rides in the theme park. The tour guide introduces each song with a few words about each mode of transportation. Then students sing the song:

• The old train ride—"City of New Orleans" (page 56)

• Riding horse as a cowhand—"Trail to Mexico" (page 59)

• Riding horses for fun—"Four White Horses" (page 60)

• A flying bird ride—"The Old Carrion Crow" (page 62)

• Taking a walk through a scenic valley—"Down the Road" (page 76)

• Sailing on a big ship. The tour guide can introduce the Admiral, who sings "When I Was a Lad" (page 96), with students joining in on the group response parts.

CREATE A MELODY WITH SIXTEENTH NOTES

2 PLAY ON UNPITCHED INSTRUMENTS Have partners write the rhythmic notation for the patterns they created in Lesson 2. Have them practice playing the patterns on unpitched instruments. They may share their patterns with classmates in order to practice reading other patterns. Have them save the patterns in their folder. *(After Lesson 4)*

3 DEVELOP THE MELODY Have partners assign pitches to the two patterns they combined in the previous activity. Instruct them to choose pitches from the set D E G A B. Have them make sure the second pattern ends on the tonal center. *(After Lesson 5)*

UNIT TWO
LESSON 1

RELATED ARTS | MOVEMENT | THEATER | VISUAL ARTS

LESSON PLANNER

FOCUS Pitch, tonal center

OBJECTIVES
OBJECTIVE 1 Hum the tonal center of a song
OBJECTIVE 2 Signal to identify visual representation that matches the melodic contour

MATERIALS
Recordings
Trail To Mexico (I—with
  instrumental ostinato)   CD2:14
Four White Horses   CD2:15
Down the Road (A section)   CD2:16

Resources
Orff Orchestration O • 4 (Trail to Mexico)
Recorder Master R • 2 (pitches A B)

Technology Music with MIDI:
  Trail to Mexico

VOCABULARY
tonal center

▶ = **BASIC PROGRAM**

HOME, SWEET HOME

Do you sing with your family or friends to pass the time on a trip? Cowboys sang on long cattle drives. They also sang at night to calm the herds, to keep away wild animals, and to ease loneliness.

SING "Trail to Mexico." Move your arm to show the shape of the melody.

58

MEETING **INDIVIDUAL** NEEDS

VOCAL DEVELOPMENT: *Vocal Range*

Explain that just as athletes need to warm up their muscles, singers need to warm up their voices. Remind students of the correct posture and breathing for singing. Have them listen as you demonstrate the vocalise. Ask them to breathe and feel the beginning of a yawn in the back of their throats as they sing the first *oh*. Have them raise one hand above their heads and imagine "touching" the tone as they echo the vocalise. As they echo you, have them imitate as you point your hand up and move it upward to help avoid flatting on the downward passage.

Continue up by half steps to F.

Oh,   oh_____ (breathe)   Oh,   oh_____ (breathe)

ORFF: *"Trail to Mexico"*

See **O • 4** in *Orchestrations for Orff Instruments.*

BACKGROUND: *Tonal Center*

The tonal center is the pitch which, when used as the last pitch of a song, gives a definite feeling of completion. It is

TRAIL to MEXICO

American Cowboy Song
Music Adapted by Carol King

Pentatonic

s, l, d r m s l

G   C   G   D7

1. I made up my mind _____ in the ear-ly morn
2. 'Twas in the _____ year _____ of _____ eight-y - three _____
3. 'Twas in the_____ spring - time_____ of the year _____

G

To leave the home _____ where I was born, _____
That A. J. Stin - son_____ hired _____ me. _____
I vol - un - teered _____ to_____ drive the steers. _____

G

To leave my na - tive home for a while, _____
He said, "Young man, _____ I want you to go, _____
I'll tell you, boys, _____ 'twas a long_____ hard go, _____

C   D7   C   G

And trav - el_____ west _____ for _____ man-y a mile. _____
And fol - low my herd _____ to_____ Mex - i - co." _____
As the trail rolled_____ on_____ in - to Mex - i - co. _____

When you take a trip, your last stop is probably your home. Usually, the last pitch of a melody is a note called the home tone or **tonal center.** Ending on this note makes the melody sound finished.

Unit 2 Traveling On **59**

---

1 GET SET

"Do you remember the many roads taken by the traveler in the poem 'Roads Go Ever Ever On'? Where did the roads lead at the end of the poem?" Have students:

▶ • Review the poem on page 55 and recall that the roads led the traveler home.

"Music can lead us down paths to different places. Today we will listen for ways a melody might travel."

2 DEVELOP

1. Introduce "Trail to Mexico" CD2:14. Show melodic contour. Have students:

▶ • Read about and listen to "Trail to Mexico" (with instrumental ostinato).

▶ • Learn the song.

▶ • Sing Verse 1, showing the melodic contour or changes in pitch by changing their arm levels in space. (As students sing the skip of a fifth in the second and third phrases of "Trail to Mexico," have them each raise a hand above their heads to "touch" the high D. See *Vocal Development* below. This will prevent them from straining for the high pitch from below.)

2. Introduce tonal center in "Trail to Mexico." Have students:

• Hum the last pitch.

• Read about tonal center on page 59.

---

often called the "home tone" because the melody seems to lead to that pitch. In major and minor keys, the tonal center names the key: if a melody is in F major, its tonal center is F. If a melody is in D minor, the tonal center is D. In most pentatonic music, such as "Trail to Mexico," the tonal center is also usually the last pitch of the melody and names the pentatonic. In a *do* pentatonic song, *do* is the tonal center; in a *la* pentatonic, *la* is the tonal center. Have students identify the last pitch in "Trail to Mexico" as *do*. *Do* is the tonal center.

BACKGROUND: *"Trail to Mexico"*

Different versions of "Trails to Mexico" have appeared in many collections of American folk songs, including Carl Sandburg's *American Songbag*. According to Sandburg, when cowboys sang the song, part of the fun came from everyone pretending they knew exactly who A. J. Stinson was.

MUSIC BUILDS MATH SKILLS

Geometry Changing arm levels in space to show the melodic contour reinforces understanding of relative position and spatial sense.

UNIT TWO
LESSON 1

continued from previous page

3. Introduce "Four White Horses" CD2:15. Find the tonal center. Have students:

▶ • Read about the song on page 60.

OBJECTIVE 1 Informal Assessment
• Listen to the song with eyes closed, then hum the tonal center. (E)

▶ • Learn the song.

▶ • With a partner, learn the clapping pattern. (See *Movement* on the bottom of page 61.)

3 APPLY

Introduce "Down the Road" CD2:16. Determine contour. Have students:

• Listen to "Down the Road" (A section), snapping on Beats 2 and 4 of each measure.

▶ • Listen again to learn the A section by rote. (See page 76.)

• Hum the tonal center (G) and signal that this is the tonal center by resting hands on their waists.

• Sing the A section, drawing the three phrase contours in the air, moving their hands above and below their waists as they hear the melody go above and below the tonal center.

OBJECTIVE 2 Informal Assessment
• Signal with one, two, or three fingers to show which contour on page 61 matches Phrase 3.

• Sing the song, drawing the contour as shown in Picture 2 when they sing Phrase 3.

ON YOUR WAY HOME

Children often make up their own words as they play a clapping game with this song. The words don't have to make much sense!

LISTEN to the song, then hum the tonal center.

FOUR WHITE HORSES

Caribbean Folk Song
Collected by Lois Choksy

Four white hors - es on the riv - er, Hey, hey,— hey,— up to-mor-row, Up to-mor - row is a rain - y day.

Come on up— to the shal-low bay. Shal-low bay— is a ripe ba - nan - a, Up to-mor - row is a rain - y day.

60 HOME, SWEET HOME

MEETING **INDIVIDUAL** NEEDS

ALTERNATE TEACHING STRATEGIES

OBJECTIVE 1 Remind students that the tonal center often is the last pitch of a song. Ask students to find the last word in "Four White Horses," (*day*) and then to stand and listen to the song, sitting only on *day*. They will discover that *day* occurs twice. Help them recognize that it is the same pitch both times—the tonal center. Have a student confirm this by playing the resonator bell E on each *day*. Play E throughout the song to help students keep the tonal center pitch in mind.

OBJECTIVE 2 Stack books in five piles of different heights. Place resonator bells D E G A B on the piles according to their pitch. Play the pitches so that students can relate the height of each bell to its pitch. Have students discover through trial and error the order of pitches needed to play each phrase of "Down the Road." Referring to the heights of the bells, draw the corresponding melodic contours on the board.

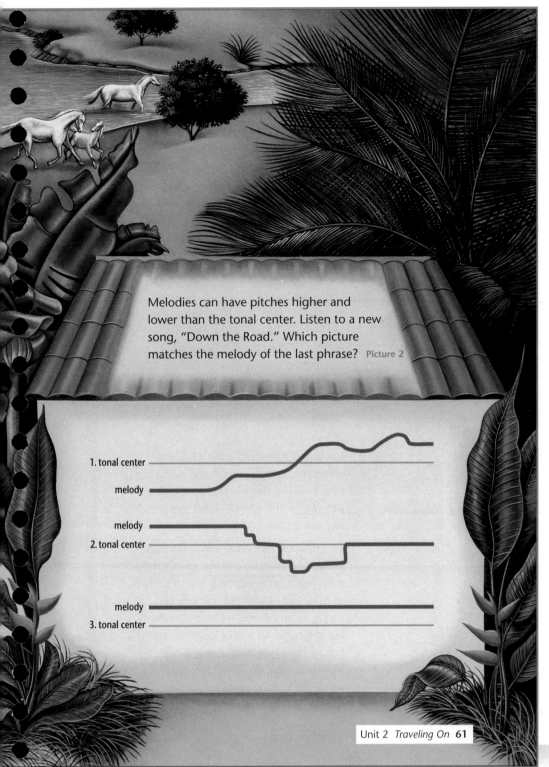

Melodies can have pitches higher and lower than the tonal center. Listen to a new song, "Down the Road." Which picture matches the melody of the last phrase? *Picture 2*

1. tonal center
melody

melody
2. tonal center

melody
3. tonal center

4 CLOSE

"Why is the tonal center sometimes called the home tone?" (Often it is the last pitch; melody sounds finished.) Have students:

▶ • Listen to a song without the last pitch. (Choose a simple unfamiliar song to play or sing for the class, leaving out the last pitch.)

• Sing together what they think the last sound should be. (Play or sing the tone for the class so they can compare it to their ideas.)

LESSON SUMMARY

Informal Assessment In this lesson, students:

OBJECTIVE 1 Hummed the tonal center of "Four White Horses."

OBJECTIVE 2 Signaled to show which visual representation matches the shape of a phrase from "Down the Road."

National Standards for Music Education
1a Sing accurately, on pitch and in rhythm.
2b Perform easy patterns on various classroom instruments.
6e Respond to musical characteristics through movement.

MORE MUSIC: Reinforcement
More Songs to Read, page 350 (*do re mi so*)

MULTICULTURAL PERSPECTIVES: *"Four White Horses"*

This folk song was collected on St. Eustatius, one of the six islands in the Netherlands Antilles, about 200 miles east of Puerto Rico. Other versions of "Four White Horses" are found elsewhere in the Caribbean. In a version from the Virgin Islands, for example, *river* is replaced by *rainbow*.

Movement for "Four White Horses" Lois Choksy/David Brummitt, 120 SINGING GAMES AND DANCES FOR ELEMENTARY SCHOOL. © 1987, p. 178. Reproduced by permission of Prentice Hall, Englewood Cliffs, New Jersey.

MOVEMENT: *Preparation for Game*

This activity prepares students for the complete game for "Four White Horses," Lesson 6, page 81, *Movement*.
Formation: partners facing, pairs in scattered formation
Game: (Verbal Cue—*clap, partner, clap, side*)
Beat 1: clap own hands;
Beat 2: clap partner's two hands;
Beat 3: clap own hands;
Beat 4: place hands palms out at shoulder height to the side, "clapping" the air.

ACROSS the

SOCIAL STUDIES

MAPS

"Roads Go Ever Ever On"

PAIR   **15–30 MIN**

MATERIALS: national or world maps; optional—reference books

Have students work in pairs to create their own imaginary routes from their hometown to other parts of the United States and the world. Each pair starts out with a possible destination and follows an imaginary route along a map. If they need to cross a Great Lake, the Gulf of Mexico, or an ocean, a boat voyage becomes part of their route.

Have each pair list the places and landforms they pass along their route. They may want to use reference books to help them decide what places they would like to visit. Pairs present their routes to the class. Award prizes for the most roundabout and interesting, the most direct, and other categories of routes presented by students.

COMPREHENSION STRATEGIES: Making decisions, sequencing

MATHEMATICS

ESTIMATING

"Trail to Mexico"

GROUP   **15–30 MIN**

MATERIALS: national maps, string

Have groups of students represent people from different cities of the United States—Seattle, Boston, Dallas, and so on. Each group is planning a trip to New Mexico, northern Texas, and Mexico. Place a map at the front of the classroom. Decide together on a common destination point.

Each group makes a list of all the cities represented, in order of trip distance—from the longest to the shortest. (Students can assume straight line distances.)

To confirm their lists, students use a string to measure the distance on the map from each city to the end point of their trip. They can mark or cut the string to show each length. Students list the order of string lengths on the board. Any group whose list matches the list on the board wins.

COMPREHENSION STRATEGIES: Estimating, compare and contrast

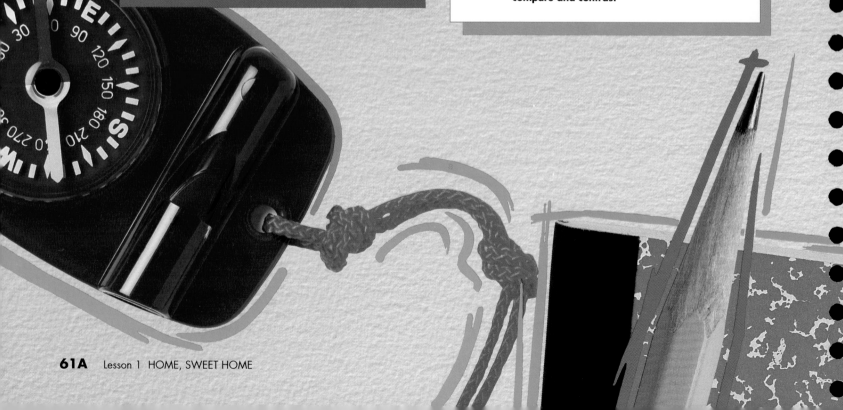

CURRICULUM

ACROSS THE CURRICULUM

ART

WORLD ART

"Trail to Mexico"

INDIVIDUAL   **30 MIN OR LONGER**

MATERIALS: art paper, scissors, glue, tissue paper, crayons, markers

Ask students if they have ever dreamed of riding a horse like the cowboy in the song. Have students paint or draw a picture of themselves driving the steers as in the song. To get an idea of setting and locale, they might want to use reference books showing pictures of Mexico, New Mexico, northern Texas (around Abilene), and other parts of the Southwest. Remind them to consider shape, line, color, symbols, and patterns. Encourage creativity and freedom of expression.

COMPREHENSION STRATEGY: Visualizing

LANGUAGE ARTS

NEW WORDS GAME

"Four White Horses"

GROUP   **15–30 MIN**

Have students work in small groups, sitting in a circle, to play a word game. The goal is to substitute three new words for *Four white horses*:

- the first word must be a number or word about quantity (*all, few*);
- the second word must be a descriptive word (adjective);
- the last word is a name of an animal, plant, or nonliving thing;
- the new words must have the same rhythm as the originals.

Choose a group to go first. When that group offers the new opening to the song, any other group responds by revising the next phrase, *on the river,* in a way to fit the new opening. That group is the next group to rewrite the opening words. Each group that rewrites the opening words correctly, following the rules, gets a point.

COMPREHENSION STRATEGY: Expressing main ideas

UNIT TWO
LESSON 2

LESSON PLANNER

FOCUS Duration, three and four sounds to a beat

OBJECTIVES
OBJECTIVE 1 Signal when a rhythm pattern with sixteenth notes is heard (tested)
OBJECTIVE 2 Match word patterns with sixteenth-note durations to rhythm pattern pictures (tested)

MATERIALS
Recordings
The Old Carrion Crow   CD2:17
Recorded Lesson: Catch Those
  Phrases   CD2:18
Listening: Karşi Bar   CD2:19
En la feria de San Juan   CD2:20
Recorded Lesson: Instruments
  for Sale   CD2:21

Resources
Resource Master 2 • 1 (practice)
Recorder Master R • 3 (pitches A B)

▶ = **BASIC PROGRAM**

A Story

Before radio and television were popular, songs like "The Old Carrion Crow" were passed from person to person. As you sing, see how the clear story, repeated melodies, and funny nonsense syllables could make this song easy to remember.

D Dorian

The Old Carrion Crow

Nova Scotian Folk Song

Verse *mf* Dm   C   Dm   Am

1. Oh, the old car-rion crow was sit-ting on an oak,
2. Hur-ry now___ bring me my cross___ and my bow,
3. Oh, the tai - lor___ shot and missed___ his___ mark,
4. The___ old sow___ died and the bells___ did___ toll,
5. Oh,___ now the___ old sow's dead___ and___ gone,

Dm   C   Dm

Fol the rid - dle, all the rid - dle hey ding
(1.) doh,
(2.) doh,
(3.) doh, And he
(4.) doh, And the
(5.) doh, And the

62

MEETING **INDIVIDUAL** NEEDS

MULTICULTURAL PERSPECTIVES: *Folk Songs*

Like folktales, songs were often part of the cultural riches brought by the peoples who settled the Americas. "The Old Carrion Crow" probably descends from an English folk song that immigrants brought to North America. Another version can be heard in Appalachia, where many people have English ancestors. The song's clear musical form made it easy to remember, while the nonsense syllables made it fun to sing. Lyrics such as *fol the riddle* link the song to traditional English folk songs, but

others such as *kimo* seem to have been added after the song reached this continent.

MOVEMENT: *Sensing Sixteenth Notes*

Divide the class in half with several students left over. Half of the class walks in a circle and steps quarter notes. The other half circles in reverse direction inside the walking students and jogs eighth notes. The several students left clap sixteenth notes, sitting inside the two circles. Lead one group at a time to move by playing its note value on a drum or other instrument then changing to another note value.

in a Song

Dm   C   Dm   Am

(1.) Watch - ing   a   tai - lor   cut - ting   out   a   coat.
(2.) That   I   may shoot   yon   car - ri - on_____ crow.
(3.) shot the   mil - ler's   sow   right   through_____ the_____ heart.
(4.) lit -tle   pigs_____   cried   and   prayed_____   for   her   soul.
(5.) lit -tle   pigs_____   play   and   wad - dle_____   on,

mp
slightly held back
Dm   in tempo

Sing he,   sing ho,   the   old car - rion crow,   Fol the rid -dle, all the rid -dle

Refrain
C   Dm   Am   G   F   slightly held back   C

hey ding doh.   Ki - me -lea - ro   kill my kea - ro,   ki - me - lea - ro   ki - mo,

in tempo
Dm   C   Dm   Am   Dm   C Dm

To me bump, bump, bump, jump Pol - ly wol - ly lee,   Lin - ko   kil - ly cum   ki - mo.

Unit 2 *Traveling On* **63**

1 GET SET

"Does your family have stories they like to tell? Sometimes stories are handed down in songs." Have students:

▶ • Listen to "The Old Carrion Crow" CD2:17 and identify the parts that tell the story and the sounds that are just fun to sing.

"Today you'll be listening for special rhythms in this song and in others."

2 DEVELOP

1. Identify similar phrases and three and four sounds to a beat in "The Old Carrion Crow." Have students:

Recorded Lesson CD2:18

▶ • Listen to "Catch Those Phrases;" echo-sing and pat *Fol the riddle, all the riddle, hey ding doh* and *linko killy cum kimo*, then discover that the phrases are similar.

• Find the similar phrases in the notation.

▶ • Sing the song.

• In two groups, determine how many sounds occur on each beat by having one group clap with the beat and the other pat *fol the riddle* four times.

• Describe *fol the riddle* as having four sounds to a beat.

• Repeat with *killy cum* and describe it as having three sounds per beat.

(Change every eight beats.) Groups rotate. To cue two groups to respond at the same time, have a student play quarter notes while you play either eighth or sixteenth notes.

CRITICAL THINKING: *Oral Tradition*

Have students compare "The Old Carrion Crow" with songs they learned through oral tradition, such as "Pat-a-cake," and discuss why they think these songs survived.

CAREERS: *Music Journalism*

Tracing the roots of folk songs is one of many possible challenges for the music journalist. Some journalists research and write about music; others review it. Have students imagine interviewing their favorite singer.

MUSIC BUILDS READING SKILLS

Phonological Awareness and **Listening**
In identifying the number of sounds to a beat, students will be identifying the number of syllables in words.

UNIT TWO
LESSON 2

continued from previous page

2. Introduce "Karşi Bar" CD2:19. **Identify a phrase by the rhythm.** Have students:

• Perform the rhythm patterns on page 64.

▶ • Listen to "Karşi Bar" (kar **shi** bar) and walk to the beat, walking straight, curved, or zigzag pathways.

OBJECTIVE 1 Informal Assessment

• Listen to "Karşi Bar" with eyes closed and raise a hand as soon as they hear the rhythm phrase. (beginning of B section)

▶ • Dance and create movement for "Karşi Bar." (See *Movement* on the bottom of page 65. This recording contains spoken dance instructions over the music. You may adjust the stereo balance control to hear the music alone.)

3 APPLY

Introduce "En la feria de San Juan" CD2:20. **Match word patterns with rhythm patterns.** Have students:

Recorded Lesson CD2:21

▶ • Listen to "Instruments for Sale" and clap each instrument's word pattern.

▶ • Listen for these patterns in "En la feria de San Juan" (en la **fe** ɾya ðe san **xwan**).

▶ • Work in four groups, one for each instrument, and determine which rhythm pattern picture on page 65 matches their assigned word patterns. (Optional: Use **Resource Master 2 · 1**, in which students match word phrases to rhythm pattern pictures.)

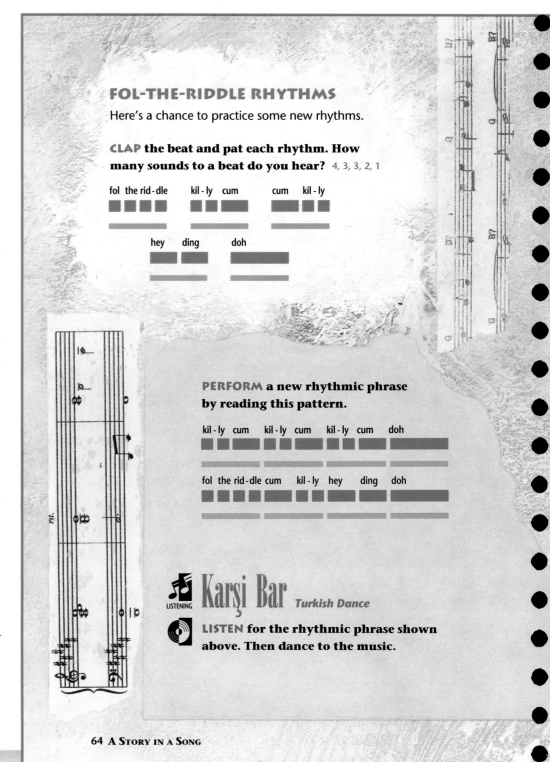

FOL-THE-RIDDLE RHYTHMS

Here's a chance to practice some new rhythms.

CLAP the beat and pat each rhythm. How many sounds to a beat do you hear? 4, 3, 3, 2, 1

fol the rid-dle   kil-ly cum   cum kil-ly

hey ding doh

PERFORM a new rhythmic phrase by reading this pattern.

kil-ly cum   kil-ly cum   kil-ly cum   doh

fol the rid-dle cum   kil-ly hey   ding   doh

Karşi Bar *Turkish Dance*
LISTENING

LISTEN for the rhythmic phrase shown above. Then dance to the music.

64 A STORY IN A SONG

MEETING **INDIVIDUAL** NEEDS

ALTERNATE TEACHING STRATEGIES

OBJECTIVE 1 Have students walk to the beat as they pat the rhythm phrase in the middle of page 64. Then have them signal each time they hear the phrase as you perform the following. Clapping or drumming, play eight beats of quarter notes, the phrase, eight beats of ♩♩ ♩, the phrase, eight beats of ♫♫ ♩, and finally the phrase.

OBJECTIVE 2 Have students pat one sound to a beat, then two, then four. Draw both rhythm patterns from "En la feria de San Juan" on the board, and have students practice switching as you point to the patterns in turn.

MULTICULTURAL PERSPECTIVES: *"Karşi Bar"*
MOVEMENT

"Karşi Bar" is a traditional folk dance from eastern Anatolia in Turkey. *Karşi* means "welcoming," and a *bar* is a line dance that usually features several distinct sections, one after another. The dance leader triggers section changes by signaling the musicians to change rhythms, then the dancers change their movements.

SING and pat the rhythm for each instrument.

piti, piti, piti, el pitío

ton, ton, ton, el tambor

tara, tara, tara, la guitarra

Which word patterns in the song match these rhythms?

pitío or guitarra

tambor or violín

lin, lin, lin, el violín

THINK IT THROUGH

What are some ways you could use the rhythm patterns or parts of the patterns to create other rhythm patterns?
Students may combine beats to create new 4-beat patterns, or they may add patterns together to create longer ones.

Unit 2 *Traveling On* **65**

▶ • After you name an instrument and speak its word pattern, signal with one or two fingers to show which rhythm pattern matches the phrase they heard.
▶ • Discuss the *Think It Through.*

4 CLOSE

"How many sounds to a beat did you listen for today?" (three and four) Have students:
• Clap the rhythm patterns from "En la feria de San Juan," and say the words that fit each pattern.

LESSON SUMMARY

Informal Assessment In this lesson, students:

OBJECTIVE 1 Signaled when they heard a rhythmic pattern with sixteenth notes in "Karşi Bar."

OBJECTIVE 2 Matched word patterns with sixteenth-note durations from "En la feria de San Juan" to rhythm pattern pictures.

National Standards for Music Education
I b Sing with appropriate dynamics, phrasing, and interpretation.
6e Respond to musical characteristics through movement.
9d Identify and describe the various roles of musicians.

MORE MUSIC: Reinforcement
More Songs to Read, page 351 (four sounds to a beat)
"When I Was a Lad," page 96 (sixteenth-note rhythms)

MOVEMENT: *Preparation for "Karşi Bar"* MOVEMENT

Review side-closes. (Left foot steps left, right foot closes and steps next to it.) In Lesson 4, page 73, *Movement,* students learn the traditional dance and compare it to movements they create for this B section.

Form: A B A B A B

A section (sixteen beats): eight side-closes, four beginning with the left foot and moving left, then four to the right. Perform every fourth side-close as a side-touch. Arms move in windshield-wiper fashion from side to side with bent elbows.

B section: Invite groups of six to eight students to create four-beat locomotor sequences that can be performed in one direction, then repeated in the opposite direction, then again in the original direction, then one last time in the opposite direction. The entire sequence will take sixteen beats. For example, walk forward four steps, backward four steps, forward four, backward four.

Final Form: Perform the A section; have each group perform its own movement for the B section simultaneously; return to the A section.

ACROSS the

LANGUAGE ARTS

DRAMATIZATION

"The Old Carrion Crow"

GROUP   **30 MIN OR LONGER**

MATERIALS: optional—objects for costumes or props

Have students work in groups to retell the story of the song in the form of a skit or short play. To create the play, group members can take on different roles:

- story consultant—outlines the events that occur in the song and organizes events into scenes
- character analyst—lists and describes the characters in the song (people and animals) and considers possibility of adding characters (tailor's wife—or husband, if the tailor is a woman)
- costume and prop specialist—lists items to use in the play
- scene designer—lists and describes possible settings

The group members combine their results and develop the script. Different group members take on the various roles, rehearse the play, and perform it. Emphasize that this is a silly song and the scene depicting the shooting of the sow can be done lightly and not as a real "tragedy."

COMPREHENSIVE STRATEGIES: Expressing main ideas, sequencing

MATHEMATICS

COORDINATE GRAPHING

"The Old Carrion Crow"

PAIR   **15–30 MIN**

MATERIALS: unlined paper, ruler, colored pencils

Have students work in pairs to draw the path of the tailor's arrow. They start by drawing a grid map:

- Using rulers, mark off 3 cm segments along each side of the sheet of paper.
- Use the marks to draw nine parallel horizontal lines and seven parallel vertical lines.

Then they label each line along the bottom and along the left side from 1 to 7. They choose three points where two lines meet to draw and label dots showing the tailor's position, the crow's position, and the sow's position. Then they use the ruler to connect the tailor and the sow. (To give the game a "happy ending," they can also show where the sow would have to be to avoid the arrow. The crow should be located just to one side of the line.)

COMPREHENSION STRATEGIES: Exploring spatial relationships, organizing information

CURRICULUM

LANGUAGE ARTS

WRITING A STORY

"The Old Carrion Crow"

INDIVIDUAL   **30 MIN OR LONGER**
MATERIALS: optional—newspapers

The story of "The Old Carrion Crow" is a single event that makes for a good news "flash" idea: Flash—Tailor misses the mark. Have students use this song and rewrite its story to give it a "happy ending," or think of a news story based on something that happened at school. Students can play the roles of interviewers at the scene, a news reporter, or a newspaper writer.

For each case, have students write:

- a headline,
- a "grabber" or opening statement that summarizes the story,
- a depiction of the place, the times, and the characters.

Students can write the story and illustrate it in the form of a newspaper article, or they can present it orally as a radio or TV news flash.

COMPREHENSION STRATEGIES: Expressing main ideas, summarizing

MATHEMATICS

MULTIPLY/DIVIDE

"The Old Carrion Crow"

PAIR   **15–30 MIN**
MATERIALS: math counters, poster board, markers

Have pairs of students draw a large, leafless tree on a sheet of poster board. The tree should be symmetrical with seven branches on each side, all about the same length. Branches should be about an inch (2.5 cm) above/below each other, to hold math counters.

Each counter represents a crow. Each partner tells the other a multiplication or division story.

Multiplication:

- Five crows were sitting on each branch. How many crows were there? (70)

Division:

- There were twenty crows. How many branches had crows if there were three on a branch? (7)

The partner models the story with the counters. Together they revise the story to fit details. (The story may not work or there may be remainders in division stories.)

COMPREHENSION STRATEGIES: Using models, revising

RELATED ARTS [MOVEMENT] [THEATER] [VISUAL ARTS]

LESSON PLANNER

FOCUS Tone color, instrument families

OBJECTIVE

OBJECTIVE 1 Following a listening map, identify families of instruments heard in an orchestral excerpt

MATERIALS

Recordings

En la feria de San Juan	CD2:20
Recorded Lesson: Pronunciation for "En la feria de San Juan"	CD2:22
En la feria de San Juan (performance mix)	CD10:11
Listening: Strings and Things	CD2:23
Recorded Lesson: Family Fusion	CD2:24
Listening: Promenade from *Pictures at an Exhibition* by M. Mussorgsky	CD2:25

Resources

Resource Master 2 • 2 (practice)
Listening Map Transparency T • 3 (Promenade)
Recorder Master R • 4 (pitches G A B)
Musical Instruments Masters—brass family, percussion family, string family, woodwind family

VOCABULARY

orchestra

▶ = **BASIC PROGRAM**

MEET THE INSTRUMENTS

You might see musical instruments among the odds and ends for sale at a flea market or fair. You will name quite a collection of instruments by singing this cumulative song!

En la feria de San Juan
In the Market of San Juan

Puerto Rican Folk Song
English Version by MMH

MEETING **INDIVIDUAL** NEEDS

BUILDING SELF-ESTEEM: *Speaking Spanish*

Invite native Spanish-speaking students to guide the class in pronouncing "En la feria de San Juan." These students may feel that their language is a hindrance in the class. They now can display their language expertise.

MULTICULTURAL PERSPECTIVES: *La feria*

Popular with children throughout Puerto Rico and Central America, "En la feria de San Juan" resembles many Spanish children's songs. A *feria*, or fair, is a place of rides and

games. As at an outdoor flea market, people may sell chickens, produce, and goods, such as the instruments in the song.

MOVEMENT: *"En la feria de San Juan"*

Use this movement to practice body-facing changes. (See *Movement*, Unit 1, Lesson 3, page 23.)

Formation: four groups, each group in a circle

Verse: Walk facing clockwise in a circle (eight beats). Stop and pat the rhythm of *piti, piti, piti, el pitío*. (Other instruments: stamp *ton, ton, ton, el tambor*; pat-clap *tara, tara, tara, la guitarra*; snap *lin, lin, lin, el violín*.)

1 GET SET

"Let's listen to 'En la feria de San Juan.'" (CD2:20 pp. 66–67) "What are the instruments that are for sale there?" Have students:

▶ • Listen to the song and name the instruments: whistle (pitío), drum (tambor), guitar (guitarra), violin (violín).

"Each instrument has its own special sound, and each belongs to a family of instruments. To which family does a guitar belong?" (strings) "Violin?" (strings) "Drum?" (percussion) "Whistle?" (woodwinds)

"Today you'll learn more about instrument families."

2 DEVELOP

1. Learn the song "En la feria de San Juan." Have students:

Recorded Lesson CD2:22

▶ • Listen to "Pronunciation for 'En la feria de San Juan.'"

▶ • Sing all the verses.

▶ • Learn the movement. (See *Movement* on the bottom of page 66.)

Song lyrics (from illustration):

2. En la feria de San Juan
yo compré un tambor.
Ton, ton, ton, el tambor, . . .

en la fe ɾya ðe san xwan
yo kom pɾe un tam boɾ
ton ton ton el tam boɾ . . .

In the market of San Juan
I bought myself a drum.
Tum, tum, tum, tum, the drum . . .

3. yo compré una guitarra,
tara, tara, tara, la guitarra . . .

yo kom pɾe una gi ta ɾa
ta ɾa ta ɾa ta ɾa la gi ta ɾa . . .

I bought a guitar,
tara, tara, tara, the guitar . . .

4. yo compré un violín,
Lin, lin, lin, el violín, . . .

yo kom pɾe un βyo lin
lin lin lin el βyo lin . . .

I bought a violin,
Lin, lin, lin, the violin, . . .

Refrain: Face center and walk four beats in and four back out. Then face out (backs toward center of circle) and walk four beats forward and four backward. Face clockwise to begin again.

PLAYING INSTRUMENTS: *Orff*

Accompany "En la feria de San Juan" on guitar and have students add any of these parts. **Maracas:** play on the instrument sound words (*piti, piti*, etc.). **Alto xylophone/ bells:** play the melody of refrain. **Bass xylophone/ contra bass bells:** play roots of guitar chords.

COOPERATIVE LEARNING: *Creating a Dance*

MOVEMENT

Have groups create dances for "En la feria de San Juan." Each chooses a formation, circle or line, and includes two body-facing changes. If they begin in a line facing north, they might end facing south. If they begin facing a partner, they might turn back to back.

PRONUNCIATION: *"En la feria de San Juan"*

a f<u>a</u>ther   e ch<u>a</u>otic   i b<u>ee</u>   o <u>o</u>bey   u m<u>oo</u>n
β b without lips touching   ð <u>the</u>
ɾ flipped r   x slightly guttural h, *Spanish* b<u>a</u>jo

continued from previous page

2. Introduce instrument families. Have students:

▶ • Read and look at pages 68–69.

• Discuss how the instruments of each family are related. (Include materials they are made of and how they produce sound.)

▶ • Identify which family had no instrument for sale at the fair (brass) and which instrument in the song is not usually part of the orchestra (guitar).

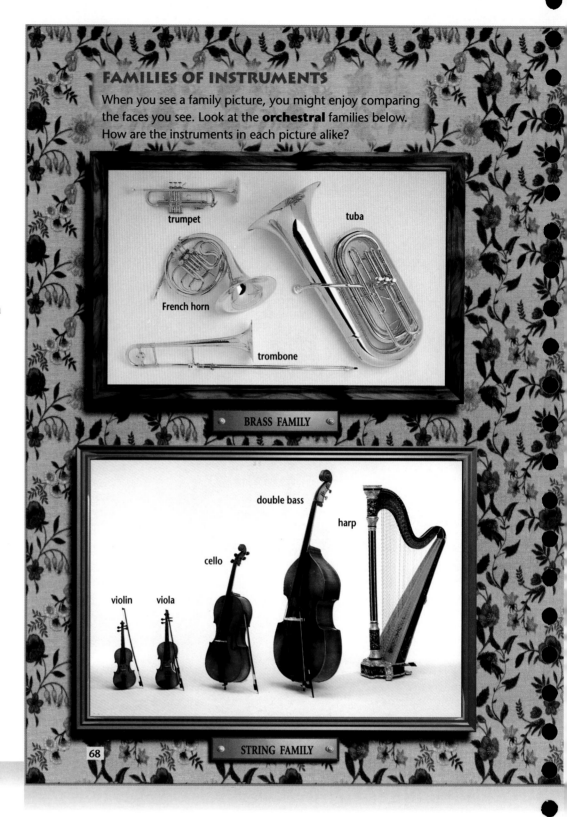

FAMILIES OF INSTRUMENTS

When you see a family picture, you might enjoy comparing the faces you see. Look at the **orchestral** families below. How are the instruments in each picture alike?

trumpet

tuba

French horn

trombone

BRASS FAMILY

double bass

harp

cello

violin   viola

STRING FAMILY

68

MEETING **INDIVIDUAL** NEEDS

EXTRA HELP: *Instrument Families*

Have students listen to recorded examples or song accompaniments that feature each family.
1. Percussion: "Michie Banjo" (Orff instruments, page 264); "Tina Singu" (African percussion, page 158)
2. Strings: "Scherzo" (string quartet, page 116) **3.** Woodwinds: Presto (piano, oboe, and bassoon, page 216) **4.** Each family: "Variations on an American Theme" (page 283)

BACKGROUND: *From the Renaissance to Today*

Many orchestral instruments were played in the Renaissance or earlier, but have undergone changes since then. Modern string instruments are larger than those of the Renaissance and may use steel strings instead of catgut. Also, the bow has become much straighter and is now held near the bottom, not the center.

Early horns and trumpets, made from a single coiled tube, could produce only a limited number of notes. Additional valves give modern brass instruments a wider range and larger role orchestrally.

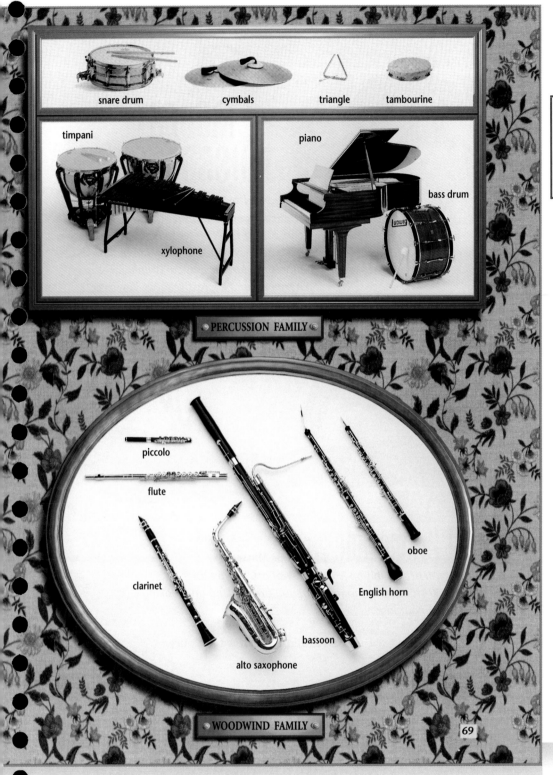

snare drum   cymbals   triangle   tambourine

timpani

piano

bass drum

xylophone

PERCUSSION FAMILY

piccolo

flute

clarinet

alto saxophone

bassoon

English horn

oboe

WOODWIND FAMILY

69

3. Introduce "Strings and Things" CD2:23
and listen for sounds of instrument families.
Have students:

▶ • Listen to "Strings and Things," in which
  they hear each family of instruments play.

Recorded Lesson CD2:24

▶ • Listen to "Family Fusion" and call out the
  names of the instrument families after they
  hear them play alone. They may imitate the
  motion of playing an instrument of their
  choice when all four families play at the same
  time.

The oboe and bassoon, double reed instruments, once had a
mouthpiece around the reed. Players found that removing
the mouthpiece and controlling the reed with their lips produces a smoother sound.

Percussion instruments have become standard in the orchestra only during the past 100 years. The inclusion of a
greater number of traditional instruments from around the
world and the special interest that many twentieth-century
composers have in rhythm and tone color have resulted in
the wide variety of percussion instruments heard in today's
orchestras.

CRITICAL THINKING: *Instrument Families*

Have pairs of students look at pictures of different instruments. (Pages 30, 42, 72–73, and 90 display instruments
from various cultures.) Ask them to create a list of similarities and differences and then to use their lists to place instruments in the appropriate families. They should compare
such characteristics as shape, size, playing technique, and
material. Challenge each pair to create a new "instrument
family" and list its characteristics.

continued from previous page

3 APPLY

Introduce "Promenade" CD2:25. Follow a listening map. Have students:

▶ • Read about the music on page 70, then listen to it with eyes closed and pat with the beat, alternating hands as if walking.

▶ • Follow the map, tapping each footprint with fingers, listening for the order in which they hear families play. (Optional: Use **Listening Map Transparency T • 3.**)

OBJECTIVE 1 Informal Assessment

▶ • Signal with one, two, three, or four fingers (for strings, woodwinds, brass, or percussion) to show which families they hear as they follow the listening map. Discuss the order in which the families were heard. (brass, strings, woodwinds, all three)

▶ • Identify the family that was not heard by itself. (percussion)

Spotlight on MODEST MUSSORGSKY

Modest Petrovich Mussorgsky (1839–1881) studied piano with his mother. He began composing short pieces in school. Then he became busy with a military career and didn't get further musical training. His rich harmony and expressive ideas, however, place him among the most talented Russian composers. Mussorgsky wrote **Pictures at an Exhibition** *to go with ten paintings by a friend.*

 Promenade from *Pictures at an Exhibition*
by **Modest Mussorgsky**

LISTENING

 An art exhibition is a display of art. As you listen to **Promenade,** *imagine that you are walking and looking at paintings.*

LISTEN for the instrument families that play this melody.

70 MEET THE INSTRUMENTS

MEETING **INDIVIDUAL** NEEDS

ALTERNATE TEACHING STRATEGY

OBJECTIVE 1 Post pictures of the instrument families around the room. As students listen to "Promenade," have them stand and "conduct" by facing each family as they hear it or by pointing to the appropriate pictures on pages 68–69. (Optional: Have students place instruments in the correct family on **Resource Master 2 • 2.**)

BIOGRAPHY: *Modest Mussorgsky*

The music of Modest Petrovich Mussorgsky (mo **dɛst** pe **tɾo** vɪch mʊ **sɔɾg** ski), 1839–1881, reflects his great

love for his Russian homeland. He often borrowed folk melodies to use as themes for his works, and other melodies he composed sound like Russian folk tunes. Bold and original, his work used changing and irregular meters long before other composers employed these techniques. After his death, Mussorgsky's music greatly influenced other composers, especially Claude Debussy (klod də bü si), 1868–1918, and Maurice Ravel (ma **ɾis** ɾɑ **vel**), 1875–1937. Ravel wrote that he would "never forget that day" he first heard Mussorgsky's work.

LISTENING MAP *Tap each footprint as you listen for the entrance of each instrument family.*

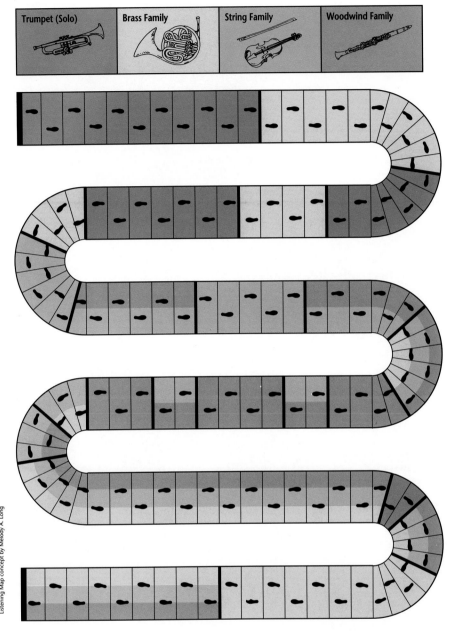

| Trumpet (Solo) | Brass Family | String Family | Woodwind Family |

Listening Map concept by Melody A. Long

Unit 2 *Traveling On* **71**

4 CLOSE

"How are the instruments of the orchestra grouped into families?" (by the way they make sound and the material they are made from) "Which family has the most members?" (Percussion; the percussion section of the orchestra also has the smallest number of players since they each play several instruments.) Have students:

▶ • Listen again to "Promenade" and "walk" with their hands on their knees, but only when they hear their assigned family, freezing when their family is not playing. (The woodwinds, brass, and string groups will "promenade.")

LESSON SUMMARY

Informal Assessment In this lesson, students:

OBJECTIVE 1 Following a listening map, identified families of instruments in "Promenade" from *Pictures at an Exhibition.*

National Standards for Music Education
2c Play repertoire from diverse genres and cultures.
6d Identify instrumental and vocal sounds from various cultures.

MORE MUSIC: Reinforcement

"Orchestra Song," page 98 (orchestral instruments)
"Singing Reeds," page 246 (orchestral instruments)
"O Tannenbaum!," page 326 (Christmas; singing in non-English language)
Symphony No. 35, ("Haffner"), First Movement (excerpt), page 385C (orchestral instruments)
"The Shrovetide Fair," page 385G (orchestral instruments)
"Island Rhythms," page 385K (orchestral instruments)

BACKGROUND: *"Promenade"*

Mussorgsky wrote *Pictures at an Exhibition* in 1874 in memory of a young artist friend, Nikolai Hartmann. After Hartmann's death, a gallery exhibit of his paintings inspired Mussorgsky to compose a collection of musical "pictures." He named each section after the painting it represented. The "Promenade" theme introduces the work and leads the listener from "picture" to "picture" as if strolling through a gallery. Composed for piano alone, the work was arranged for full orchestra by Maurice Ravel in 1922. Today the

orchestral version, with its beautiful tone colors, is more widely known.

ART CONNECTION: *An Art Exhibition*
VISUAL ARTS

Have students plan and hold an art exhibition for their families, perhaps in conjunction with a musical performance. Students should decide what type of work they will display, where and how they will display it, and how they will identify each piece of art and its maker. Students might act as guides for the exhibition.

UNIT TWO LESSON 4

RELATED ARTS | **MOVEMENT** | THEATER | VISUAL ARTS |

LESSON PLANNER

FOCUS Duration—sixteenth notes, upbeat

OBJECTIVE

OBJECTIVE 1 Perform a vocal ostinato from rhythm notation with sixteenth notes (tested)

MATERIALS

Recordings

The Old Carrion Crow	CD2:17
Listening: Karşi Bar	CD2:19
Trail to Mexico (I—with instrumental ostinato)	CD2:14
Trail to Mexico (II—with vocal ostinato)	CD2:26

Resources

Resource Master 2 • 3 (practice)
Resource Master 2 • 4 (practice)
Recorder Master R • 5 (pitches G A B)

VOCABULARY

sixteenth notes, upbeat

▶ = **BASIC PROGRAM**

Symbols and Cymbals

The musical symbols for four equal sounds to a beat can be written with four **sixteenth notes** (♪♫♫).

Fol the rid-dle, all the rid-dle hey ding doh.

Three unequal sounds to a beat can be written with two sixteenth notes and one eighth note (♫♪ or ♪♫).

Lin - ko kil-ly cum ki - mo.

MAKE UP words with three unequal sounds to a beat.
examples: diddle-dum, katy-did, hey-diddle, sing-silly, be-boppa

72

MEETING **INDIVIDUAL** NEEDS

EXTRA HELP: *Identifying Rhythms*

Divide the class into three groups. Have one group pat an ostinato of *fol the riddle*, one group snap *hey ding*, and the other clap *cum killy*. Determine on which parts of the beat the groups' sounds match each other and when they differ. Review the rhythmic patterns from page 64. Point out how the pattern for *killy cum* translates into musical notation ♫♪ Look at the pattern for *cum killy*, compare it to *killy cum* (reversed), and derive the notation ♪♫

PLAYING INSTRUMENTS: *Unpitched*

Accompany "Karşi Bar" with these ostinatos or other rhythms the class creates. **A section:** mallet or hand drum.

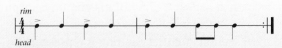

B section: tambourine

Listen for beats with three or four sounds in "Karşi Bar."

Look at the notes below. Part of the rhythmic phrase from "Karşi Bar" is missing.

| kil- ly cum | kil- ly cum | kil- ly cum | doh |

| fol the rid-dle | cum kil - ly | hey ding | doh |

POINT to the rhythm that belongs in the empty box.

How did you decide on your answer? Students may feel the rhythm as three sounds, the last two of which are quicker; or they may recognize the opposite of *killy cum* and reverse the symbols.

From left to right, the kanun, oud, tez, dumbek, and ney are heard in traditional Turkish music.

Unit 2 *Traveling On* **73**

1 GET SET

"Sing 'The Old Carrion Crow' and do as I do." CD2:17 (See pages 62–63.) Have students:

▶ • Sing "The Old Carrion Crow" and pat the rhythm of the nonsense phrases with you. "Today you'll learn how to write the rhythm of the phrases we just patted as well as rhythms from other songs you know. The more rhythms you know, the more songs you will be able to read on your own."

2 DEVELOP

1. Review "Karşi Bar" CD2:19 (p. 64). Introduce sixteenth notes. Have students:

• Say *fol the riddle* and *killy cum* while you clap one sound per beat, then read about sixteenth notes on page 72.

• Make up words to go with the two-sixteenth/one-eighth-note patterns.

▶ • Listen to "Karşi Bar" and sing the melody on *lai*, snapping with the beat during the B section.

• Pat the rhythmic phrase on page 73.

• Choose the rhythmic symbol that is missing from the phrase and discuss how they derived their answers.

▶ • Listen to "Karşi Bar" and perform the A-section movement, then learn the traditional movement for the B section. (See *Movement* below. This recording contains spoken dance instructions over the music. You may adjust the stereo balance control to hear the music alone.)

MOVEMENT: *Traditional Dance*

The traditional movement for the B section of "Karşi Bar" uses a four-beat pattern and moves in one direction and then back again. (See Lesson 2, page 65, *Movement*.)

B section preparation: (Verbal Cue—*side, cross, side, touch*) *Side*—L foot steps to L side; *cross*—R foot steps, crossing in front of L foot; *side*—L foot steps to L side; *touch*—R foot touches next to L foot, without weight transfer so the pattern can begin again in the opposite direction. When able, change the *touch* into a *stamp* (no weight transfer) (Verbal Cue—*side, cross, side, stamp*).

Final Version (A B A B A B)

Formation: broken circle (horseshoe), link little fingers with neighbors

A section: three side-closes, one side-touch moving L with "windshield wiper" arms moving L-R; three side-closes, one side-touch to R with arms moving R-L. **B section:** *side, cross, side, stamp* R; *side, cross, side, stamp* L; repeat.

Arm movement for B section: on *side*, arms go up; on *cross*, arms come down; on *side, stamp*, push hands forward and around in a small circle, palms facing out.

UNIT TWO
LESSON 4

continued from previous page

3 APPLY

Review "Trail to Mexico" (p. 59). Add an ostinato. Have students:

▶ • Sing "Trail to Mexico" (with instrumental ostinato **CD2:14**).

OBJECTIVE 1 Informal Assessment

• Read the ostinato line on page 74 and pat the rhythm.

• Learn the melodic ostinato.

• Read about upbeat, then perform "Trail to Mexico" (with vocal ostinato **CD2:26**), one group singing the song, the other the ostinato.

• Determine which part begins with an upbeat. (melody)

PAT the rhythm of the green line. Then sing the line as an ostinato.

American
Cowboy Song
Music Adapted by
Carol King

1. I made up my mind _____ in the ear - ly
2. 'Twas in the __ year _____ of __ eight - y -
3. 'Twas in the __ spring - _____ time __ of the

Vocal Ostinato

Rid - in' on the West-ern Trail.

morn _____ To leave the
three _____ That A. J.
year _____ I vol - un -

Up in the sad - dle all day.

home _____ where __ I was born, _____ To leave my
Stin - _____ son hired __ me. _____ He said,"Young
teered _____ to __ drive the steers. _____ I'll tell you,

Rid - in' on the West-ern Trail.   Up in the sad-dle all day.

74 SYMBOLS AND CYMBALS

MEETING **INDIVIDUAL** NEEDS

ALTERNATE TEACHING STRATEGY

OBJECTIVE 1 Write the rhythm of the ostinato on the board. Have students recall the nonsense syllables that match each rhythmic pattern and write them underneath the rhythm. Have them pat the rhythm, saying the nonsense syllables, then pat the rhythm, thinking the syllables. Add the ostinato text. (Optional: Use **Resource Master 2 · 3** for practice matching the syllables to musical symbols, and **Resource Master 2 · 4** for practice writing rhythms with sixteenth notes.)

EXTRA HELP: *Learning the Ostinato*

Sing the ostinato while you track the two levels on the board.

        western   *saddle all*
Ridin' on the   *trail. Up in the*   *day.*

Then have students listen to the song and sing the ostinato as you play it on resonator bells or other pitched instruments. Divide the class into two groups, one to sing the song and one to sing the ostinato. Assign a student to lead each group.

na - ... tive home for a
man, _____ I want you to
boys, _____ 'twas a long___ hard

Rid - in' on the West - ern Trail.

while, _____ And trav - el___
go, _____ And fol - low my
go, _____ As the trail rolled___

Up in the sad - dle all day.

west _____ for — man-y a mile. _____
herd _____ to — Mex - i - co." _____
on _____ in-to Mex - i - co.

Rid-in' on the West-ern Trail. Up in the sad-dle all day.

Music that begins *before* the first beat of a
measure begins on an **upbeat.** Look before
the first bar line. When a song starts with an
upbeat, there are fewer beats before the
first bar line than are shown in the meter
signature. Which part of "Trail to Mexico"
begins with an upbeat, the melody or the
ostinato?

Unit 2 Traveling On **75**

"Let's sum up what you learned about rhythm
today. What musical symbols can you use to
write four equal and three unequal sounds to a
beat in $\frac{4}{4}$?" (four sixteenth notes; one eighth,
two sixteenths; or two sixteenths, one eighth)
"What is it called when a phrase begins before
the first complete measure?" (upbeat) "How
will this help you with other songs?" Have
students:

• Switch groups (from *Apply*) to sing "Trail to
Mexico" with the ostinato.

LESSON SUMMARY

Informal Assessment In this lesson,
students:

OBJECTIVE 1 Performed the vocal ostinato for "Trail to Mexico" from notation
with sixteenth notes.

National Standards for Music Education
1d Sing ostinatos, partner songs, and rounds.
2a Play instruments with accurate pitch and rhythm.
6c Use correct terms to explain various aspects of
music.

MORE MUSIC: Reinforcement
More Songs to Read, page 352 (sixteenth-note
   rhythms)
"When I Was a Lad," page 96 (sixteenth-note
   rhythms)
"Sing a Song of Peace," page 301 (downbeat)
"A Mince Pie or Pudding," page 311 (♪♫;
   Thanksgiving)
"Haida," page 375 (sixteenth-note rhythms)
"The Shrovetide Fair," page 385G (sixteenth
   notes)

PLAYING INSTRUMENTS: *Unpitched*

Teach students to perform one of these patterns while
singing the ostinato (imitate horses' hooves). Then transfer
to unpitched percussion instruments such as woodblocks or
temple blocks.

SPECIAL LEARNERS: *Learning the Ostinato*

Students with disabilities need to experience success in
front of their peers. Adapt the ostinato for "Trail to Mexico" as necessary to allow everyone a chance at success.

MUSIC BUILDS MATH SKILLS

Number and Operations Differentiating
sixteenth notes from eighth, quarter, and half
notes reinforces students' understanding of
fractions.

ACROSS the

PROBLEM SOLVING

"The Old Carrion Crow"

INDIVIDUAL **15 MIN OR LESS**
MATERIALS: optional—calculator

Suppose the tailor wanted to chase the crow because, if he did not, more crows would perch on the tree. Every 5 seconds the number of crows would double.

How many crows would be on the tree in 30 seconds if there was one crow on the tree at the start? (64)

Have students try to find a way to solve this problem. They might use their calculators, or they might simply use pencil and paper to tally the number of birds at the end of every 5-second period in 30 seconds.

(In 30 seconds, the number would double 6 times—that is, 30 seconds divided by 5 seconds = 6. So, 1 x 2 x 2 x 2 x 2 x 2 x 2 = 64)

COMPREHENSION STRATEGIES: Making decisions, reasoning

MAP READING

"Trail to Mexico"

GROUP **30 MIN OR LONGER**
MATERIALS: maps, ruler, pins, string

Have students do map-work in groups, searching for the routes of cattle drives that were used in the 1800s to get cattle from Texas to the railroads.

- The Chisholm Trail started in San Antonio and went north to Abilene.
- Cattle from southern Texas were also driven through San Antonio along the Western Trail that led to Dodge City, Kansas, and finally to Ogallala, Nebraska.
- Cattle from San Angelo were driven southwest through Big Lake to McCamey and up along the Pecos River on the Goodnight-Loving Trail north of Denver, Colorado.

Students can lay string along these trails on maps and compare string lengths in measuring the drives. They can draw their own maps and plot and label the drives.

COMPREHENSION STRATEGY: Compare and contrast

CURRICULUM

SOCIAL STUDIES

MAP GAME

"Trail to Mexico"

PAIR   **15–30 MIN**

MATERIALS: maps showing the United States and Mexico

Have each member of a pair find two points on a map: a starting point (anywhere on continental United States) and a destination somewhere in Mexico or the southwestern United States. Each student makes a list of six places that one would pass through on an imaginary trip between the points, but not in order. (The trip should be as straight a line as possible.) Then exchange the lists.

Each student rearranges the list to put the places in order showing the straightest line possible—with the fewest detours. Students should feel free to check and revise each other's answers—or the original plans for the order.

COMPREHENSION STRATEGY: Sequencing

LANGUAGE ARTS

WRITING LETTERS

"Trail to Mexico"

INDIVIDUAL   **15–30 MIN**

Have students imagine they are narrators of the song. (Girls can imagine that A. J. Stinson addressed them as *Young lass . . .*) They should start with the idea that they are old enough to leave home, to go out on their own with their family's approval. Have them write letters back home describing their adventures and how they feel about their decision to go out into the world on their own.

Students should include in their letters any details or emotions expressed in the song.

COMPREHENSION STRATEGY: Expressing main ideas

ACROSS THE CURRICULUM

UNIT TWO
LESSON 5

LESSON PLANNER

FOCUS Pitch—low *la*, low *so*; D E G A B

OBJECTIVES
OBJECTIVE 1 Sing phrases with pitch letter names D E G A B (tested)
OBJECTIVE 2 Sing an ostinato with pitch syllables *so,* *la,* and pitch letter names D E (tested)

MATERIALS
Recordings
Down the Road (A section)   CD2:16
Down the Road (A and B
  sections)   CD2:27
Trail to Mexico (II—with vocal
  ostinato)   CD2:26

Instruments
resonator bells or other pitched
  instruments

Resources
Resource Master 2 • 5 (practice)
Resource Master 2 • 6 (practice)
Orff Orchestration O • 5 (Down the Road)
Recorder Master R • 6 (pitches G A B)

VOCABULARY
treble clef

► = **BASIC PROGRAM**

This song may bring some bounce to your steps! As you sing the melody, notice how it moves down to pitches below *do*.

DOWN THE ROAD
American Folk Song

76

MEETING **INDIVIDUAL** NEEDS

MOVEMENT: *"Down the Road"*

Formation: two lines, partners facing

A section: Both lines begin by moving to their left. (Verbal Cue—*side, close, side, touch*) *Side*—L foot steps to the L side; *close*—R foot closes next to L foot; *side*—L foot steps to L side; *touch*—R foot touches next to L with no weight transfer, allowing the pattern to begin immediately in the opposite direction, with the right foot. Repeat pattern to the right, then repeat entire sequence.

B section: Head partners improvise a "walk" down the alley. Allow time before the game starts for partners to decide on their walk. (See *Movement, Creating a "Walk."*)

MOVEMENT: *Creating a "Walk"*

To create ways to walk "Down the Road," make a list of adverbs (*happily, proudly, lazily*) and a list of verbs that are walk variations (*tip-toe, slink, stomp, saunter*). Have the students combine one word from each list, such as "tip-toe happily" or "stomp proudly."

In "Down the Road," you sang two pitches that are "down the road" from *do*.

FIND *do re mi*. Do is the tonal center of this song. Where are the new pitches? the three notes before the last note

The new pitches are called *low so* and *low la*. Recall the pitch syllables you have learned.

1 GET SET

"Sing 'Down the Road' (A section) and show the shape of the melody, touching your waist when you sing the tonal center." **CD2:16** Have students:

▶ • Sing the A section of the song (page 76), drawing the melodic shape in the air with their arms.

▶ • Sing it again, showing the shape of the melody only when they sing the words *down the road*.

"Did you notice that each time you sang *down the road* it had a different melodic shape? Today you'll learn a game and then find out how these melodies are different."

2 DEVELOP

1. Introduce "Down the Road" (A and B sections, CD2:27). Learn the movement and introduce low *so* and low *la*.

▶ • Learn the B section, then perform the song and speech.

▶ • Learn the movement. (See *Movement: "Down the Road,"* on the bottom of page 76.)

• Look at the notation and name *do* as the tonal center.

• Sing the first two phrases with pitch syllables. (*mi mi mi, mi re do*)

• Describe the new pitches in the last phrase. (two pitches; lower than *do*; close to each other; one on a line, one in a space)

• Read about low *so* and low *la*.

• Sing the last *down the road* with pitch syllables. (*so, la, do*)

Song contributed by Grace Nash.

PLAYING INSTRUMENTS: *Keyboard/Orff*

Students can practice this part to play with the A section of "Down The Road."

MUSIC BUILDS MATH SKILLS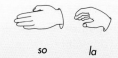

Geometry Teaching the movement to "Down the Road" reinforces students' spatial sense.

PITCH SYLLABLES: *Low So and Low La*

Use hand signs for these pitch syllables.

so   la

ORFF: *"Down the Road"*

See **O • 5** in *Orchestrations for Orff Instruments*.

UNIT TWO
LESSON 5

continued from previous page

2. Introduce pitch letter names in "Down the Road." Have students:

• Listen to you play D E G A B on resonator bells or other pitched instruments.

• Determine which bells to use for each *down the road.* (B B B, B A G, D E G)

• Read about pitch letter names on page 78.

• Tell the letter names and staff positions of the pitches in the song.

OBJECTIVE 1 Informal Assessment

• Watching the notation, sing each *down the road* with pitch letter names. (Optional: Use **Resource Master 2 • 5** for practice identifying pitch letter names, and **Resource Master 2 • 6** for practice drawing the treble clef.)

▶ • Sing the song while a few students play each *down the road* on the bells.

3 APPLY

Review "Trail to Mexico" CD2:26 (pp. 74–75). Sing the ostinato with pitch syllables and letter names. Have students:

• Review the ostinato on page 79 and then sing the song with the ostinato.

• Hum the tonal center and label it G/*do.*

OBJECTIVE 2 Informal Assessment

• Sing the ostinato with pitch syllables (*so₁ la₁*) and pitch letter names (D E).

▶ • Discuss the *Think It Through.*

The introductions are not yet over! Each pitch has a letter name as well as a pitch syllable name.

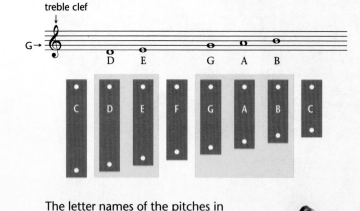

The letter names of the pitches in "Down the Road" are D E G A B.

SING "Down the Road" with letter names.

The **treble clef** is shaped like an old-fashioned letter G. It circles the second staff line, and a note on that line is called G.

78 MOVING ON

MEETING **INDIVIDUAL** NEEDS

ALTERNATE TEACHING STRATEGIES

OBJECTIVE 1 Divide the class into five groups, one for each pitch (D E G A B). Give at least one resonator bell of the assigned pitch to each group. Each group must stand to sing and play their pitch letter name when you point to their note on the staff. Exchange pitches for more practice.

OBJECTIVE 2 Have students determine that there are only two pitches in the ostinato. Have them sing the words and perform the rhythm, patting on the lower pitch and clapping

the higher. Refer to page 77 to name the pitch syllables, then sing. Repeat, using page 78 for letter names.

VOCAL DEVELOPMENT: *Harmony*

Have most of the class sing the melody while you and a few students, including at least one uncertain singer, stand off to one side singing the ostinato. This allows the uncertain singer to become secure with one part before the two groups stand closer together.

HIT THE TRAIL

Now you can sing this ostinato three different ways.

SING it with pitch syllables, letter names, and words.

Vocal Ostinato

Rid-in' on the West-ern Trail.   Up in the sad-dle all day.

THINK IT THROUGH

Listen to "Trail to Mexico" with and without the ostinato. How does the ostinato change the song? Why would a composer add an ostinato to a song?

Unit 2 *Traveling On* 79

"Let's sing the pitch syllables you used today as I point to them on the board." (*so, la, do re mi*) "Sing the same pitches, but use pitch letter names." (D E G A B) Have students:

• Sing "Trail to Mexico" in two parts.

LESSON SUMMARY

Informal Assessment In this lesson, students:

OBJECTIVE 1 Sang phrases of "Down the Road" with pitch letter names D E G A B.

OBJECTIVE 2 Sang the ostinato for "Trail to Mexico" with pitch syllables (*so, la,*) and pitch letter names (D E).

National Standards for Music Education
1d Sing ostinatos, partner songs, and rounds.
2a Play instruments with accurate pitch and rhythm.
5b Use a system to read notation in treble clef in major keys.

MORE MUSIC: Reinforcement
More Songs to Read, pages 353–354 (*so, la,*; sixteenth-note rhythms)
"Over the Sea to Skye," page 149 (*la,*)
"Winter Fantasy," page 314 (*so, la,*; winter)

ART CONNECTION: *Photographic Montage* VISUAL ARTS

Have students study the photograph of the cowboy gear. Tell them that a montage is a picture made by arranging a variety of objects or elements. To create an interesting composition, artists may overlap objects, vary the sizes and textures, and let some "bleed off," or go off the edge of the composition. Have students find examples of these techniques in this montage. Discuss whether the use of brown tones and deep shadows adds or detracts from the photo. Invite students to create photo montages using pictures about a specific theme such as a sport, a holiday, or the weather.

JAZZ: *Vocal Jazz*

Let students try some jazz-style singing in "Down the Road." On the first two *roads,* try a "fall off," letting the pitch drop off. Add a "doit," or a slide up, on the last *road.* Then reverse the pattern.

"fall off"

"doit"

ACROSS the

LANGUAGE ARTS

DESCRIPTIVE WRITING

"Down the Road"

INDIVIDUAL   **15–30 MIN**

Have students think about the best trip or vacation they have ever had or the dream trip they hope to take one day. Ask them to organize their thoughts into two or three paragraphs describing their trips:

- Name the place and describe how they traveled (or hope to travel).
- Describe what they did (or hope to do) on the trip.

Students may bring in photographs or souvenirs from a trip they took. They may illustrate their composition with hand-drawn pictures or magazine cutouts.

Tell students that one aim of their writing is to persuade other students to want to take the same trip one day. Allow students to read their writings aloud.

COMPREHENSION STRATEGIES: Expressing main ideas, organizing information

LANGUAGE ARTS

MAKING A LIST

"Down the Road"

GROUP   **15 MIN OR LESS**

Have students work in small groups. Have each group decide on two locations in the school building or on school grounds and agree upon a route or trail they would take to get from one location to the other.

Then each group member makes an imaginary trip along that route and lists everything he or she would see along the way—in the order in which the things would be seen: entrances, classrooms, water fountains, stairs, lockers, and so on.

When all group members finish, they compare lists and combine them to get the most detailed list possible describing the route between the two points.

COMPREHENSION STRATEGIES: Sequencing, compare and contrast

CURRICULUM

SOCIAL STUDIES

MAPPING A TRAIL

"Down the Road"

PAIR   **15 MIN OR LESS**
MATERIALS: drawing paper, pencils or markers; optional—graph paper

Have students work in pairs to make a simple map of a trail or route between two points. First they pick two points or locations in their neighborhood or in the area around school—two points that would take at least 15 minutes of walking time.

They draw the first location at a given point on the drawing paper. Then they draw a route they follow to get to the other location. They should clearly identify each street or road. The drawing should include directions, such as turning left or right. Students might draw a directional rosette on the map to identify north, south, east, and west.

Some students might like to use graph paper and label the coordinate lines as streets and roads.

COMPREHENSION STRATEGIES: Sequencing, organizing and displaying information

MATHEMATICS

ELAPSED TIME

"Down the Road"

PAIR   **15–30 MIN**
MATERIALS: slips of paper; optional—2 paper plates, 2 pencils per plate (one shorter than the other)

Each partner writes down a time in hours and minutes, such as 3:44. The times should span 1:00 P.M. to 6:00 P.M. They place their written times where they both can see them. Have them compare the two times. The earlier time represents the starting time of an imaginary trip. The later time is the arrival time. The partners race to find how long (in hours and minutes) the imaginary trip took.

Another way to play this activity is for each partner to use a paper-plate model of a clock. They use two pencils as clock hands (a shorter one for the hour hand and a longer one for the minute hand) to set the time.

COMPREHENSION STRATEGY: Compare and contrast

UNIT TWO
LESSON 6

LESSON PLANNER

FOCUS Pitch—*do la₁ so₁*, G E D, tonal center

OBJECTIVES
OBJECTIVE 1 Sing a melodic pattern that includes *do la₁ so₁*
OBJECTIVE 2 Sing a song with pitch sylla-bles *so₁ la₁ do re mi* and pitch letter names D E G A B (tested)

MATERIALS
Recordings
Four White Horses   CD2:15
Mongolian Night Song   CD1:15
Swapping Song   CD2:28

Instruments
resonator bells (E C# B) or other pitched instruments

Resources
Resource Master 2 • 7 (practice)
Recorder Master R • 7 (pitches G A B)

▶ = **BASIC PROGRAM**

Review a song you know.

RAISE your hand when you hear this pattern in "Four White Horses."

do   la₁   so₁

Play the game in groups of four.

Clap own hands.

Clap partner's hands.

80

MEETING **INDIVIDUAL** NEEDS

ALTERNATE TEACHING STRATEGY

OBJECTIVE 1 Sing the song one phrase at a time, drawing the contour of the *do la₁ so₁* pattern in the air and on the board. Identify the phrases that contain this contour. (1, 2, 5) Check by playing or singing the pitch pattern after each phrase is sung to hear the match. Finally, sing only those phrases aloud and think the others silently.

VOCAL DEVELOPMENT: *Singing on Pitch*

Some students sing with such a full voice that they can't tell if they are on pitch. Put a student with a pitch problem

between two strong, on-pitch singers and tell the middle student to "Listen louder than you sing." Singing more softly and listening to others who are on pitch will help the middle student correct the pitches.

ENRICHMENT: *Pitch Practice*

The opening phrase of "Promenade" from *Pictures at an Exhibition* begins and ends with *la₁ so₁*. Have students find those two places in the notation on page 70, then sing the entire phrase with pitch syllables. (*la₁ so₁ do re so mi re so mi do re la₁ so₁*)

"Four White Horses" Lois Choksy/David Brummitt, 120 SINGING GAMES AND DANCES FOR ELEMENTARY SCHOOL, © 1987, p. 178. Reproduced by permission of Prentice Hall, Englewood Cliffs, New Jersey.

Clap own hands.

Clap side partner's hands.

1 GET SET

"Listen to 'Four White Horses' and hum the tonal center at the end of the song." CD2:15 (See page 60.) Have students:

▶ • Perform a clap-snap pattern with the beat as they listen to the song, then hum. (E)

"Let's form a search party to find low *la* and low *so* and D E G A B in today's songs."

2 DEVELOP

1. Listen for melodic patterns and learn the game for "Four White Horses." Have students:

• Read page 80 and listen to you play (or sing on a neutral syllable) the pitch pattern on resonator bells or other pitched instruments. (E C♯ B)

• Listen to the song and raise a hand each time the pattern is heard. (three times)

• Check their responses in the notation on page 60.

OBJECTIVE 1 Informal Assessment

• Sing the pattern with pitch syllables. (*do la₁ so₁*)

• Identify the tonal center as *do* and E.

▶ • Sing the song.

• Play the game. (See *Movement* below.)

2. Review "Mongolian Night Song" CD1:15 (p. 19). Find the tonal center. Have students:

▶ • Sing the song.

• Sing the first four pitches with syllables and letter names.

• Identify E/*la* as the tonal center. Compare the tonal center with that of "Four White Horses." (See *Critical Thinking* below.)

PLAYING INSTRUMENTS: *Unpitched*

Select three different-sounding instruments (A, B, and C), then play a four-beat ostinato to match the form of the movement to "Four White Horses": A B A C.

CRITICAL THINKING: *Comparing Tonal Centers*

Have students compare the tonal centers of "Four White Horses" (E/*do*) and "Mongolian Night Song" (E/*la*) to find that the tonal center is not always *do*. Also, unlike letter names, pitch syllable names may be assigned to any line or space. Apply this to "Swapping Song" (G/*do*).

MOVEMENT: *"Four White Horses" Game*

For preparation see Lesson 1, page 61, *Movement*.

Formation: groups of four, partners facing across

Game: (Verbal Cue—*clap, partner, clap, side*) **Beat 1:** *clap*—Clap own hands. **Beat 2:** *partner*—Clap partner's hands. One couple will clap hands above other couple's hands. **Beat 3:** *clap*—Clap own hands. **Beat 4:** *side*—Clap side partners' hands. Repeat pattern until the song ends, alternating which couple's hands clap above and below on Beat 2.

continued from previous page

3 APPLY

Introduce "Swapping Song" CD2:28. **Name the pitches.** Have students:

▶ • Read about and listen to the song.

▶ • List all the items which were "swapped."

• Listen to Verse 1 and the refrain, then hum and name the tonal center, pointing to the last pitch (G/*do*).

OBJECTIVE 2 Informal Assessment

• Sing the pitches of the refrain, first with pitch syllables, then with pitch letter names (*so, la, do re mi* and D E G A B).

SWITCH TO SWAPPING

What does "swap" mean to you? In this song, the swapping goes on and on!

LISTEN to the song and find all the items that are swapped along the way.

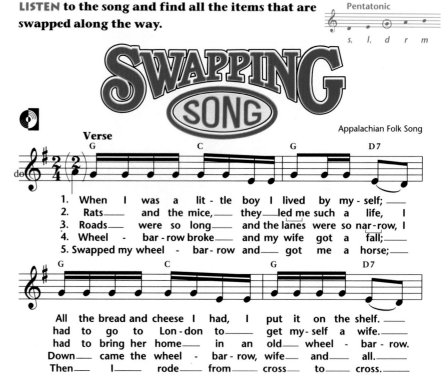

Appalachian Folk Song

Verse

1. When I was a lit-tle boy I lived by my-self; ___
2. Rats ___ and the mice, ___ they ___ led me such a life, I
3. Roads ___ were so long ___ and the lanes were so nar-row, I
4. Wheel - bar-row broke ___ and my wife got a fall; ___
5. Swapped my wheel - bar-row and ___ got me a horse; ___

All the bread and cheese I had, I put it on the shelf. ___
had to go to Lon-don to ___ get my-self a wife. ___
had to bring her home ___ in an old ___ wheel - bar - row.
Down ___ came the wheel - bar-row, wife ___ and ___ all. ___
Then ___ I ___ rode ___ from ___ cross ___ to ___ cross. ___

82 SING AND CLAP A PATTERN

MEETING INDIVIDUAL NEEDS

ALTERNATE TEACHING STRATEGY

OBJECTIVE 2 Have students hum the tonal center and label it *do*, then hum the verse and refrain slowly phrase by phrase, raising their hands when the melody goes above *do* and pointing to the floor when it goes below *do*. Have them identify the complete pitch set used (*so, la, do re mi*), then perform the melody slowly again, humming on *do* and singing pitch syllable names for pitches above and below *do*. (Optional: Use **Resource Master 2 • 7** to match pitches with pitch syllables.)

SOCIAL STUDIES CONNECTION: *Cultural Treasures*

English, Scottish, and Scotch-Irish settlers who brought songs such as "Swapping Song" to this country considered them a precious heritage. Have students explore aspects of their ethnic heritage they consider "cultural treasures," such as folktales they learned from parents or grandparents, or food, customs, and/or language. Encourage students acquiring English to participate.

"You found the tonal centers in three songs, and each was different in some way from the others. Name the tonal centers we sang today." ("Four White Horses": E/*do*, "Mongolian Night Song": E/*la*, "Swapping Song": G/*do*.)

"Now let's learn all the verses of 'Swapping Song' and sing it for fun."

LESSON SUMMARY

Informal Assessment In this lesson, students:

OBJECTIVE 1 Sang a melodic pattern from "Four White Horses" using *do la, so,*.

OBJECTIVE 2 Sang "Swapping Song" with pitch syllables *so, la, do re mi* and pitch letter names D E G A B.

National Standards for Music Education
1a Sing accurately, on pitch and in rhythm.
1b Sing with appropriate dynamics, phrasing, and interpretation.
5b Use a system to read notation in treble clef in major keys.

MORE MUSIC: Reinforcement

"For Health and Strength," page 310 (tonal center; Thanksgiving)
"Somewhere in My Memory," page 327 (*do mi so;* Christmas)

Refrain

Wing wong wad - dle, to my jack straw strad - dle, To my John - nie fair fad - dle, to my long ways home.

6. Swapped my horse and got me a mare;
   Then I rode from fair to fair.

7. Swapped my mare and got me a mule;
   Then I rode like a doggone fool.

8. Swapped my mule and got me a goat;
   When I got on him, he wouldn't tote.

9. Swapped my goat and got me a sheep;
   Then I rode myself to sleep.

10. Swapped my sheep and got me a cow;
    And in that trade I just learned how.

11. Swapped my cow and got me a calf;
    In that trade I just lost half.

12. Swapped my calf and got me a hen;
    Oh what a pretty thing I had then.

13. Swapped my hen and got me a rat;
    Put it on the haystack away from the cat.

14. Swapped my rat and got me a mouse;
    Its tail caught afire and burned up my house.

NAME and point to the tonal center of this song. G/*do*

You can read *all* the pitches and rhythms in this song!

ENRICHMENT: *Rhythmic Reading*

Show the rhythmic notation of each phrase of "Swapping Song" (Verse 1) scrambled on the board. Have students pat each phrase separately. Sing the song, then have them organize the phrases to match the song.

ENRICHMENT: *"Swapping Song" Games*

Game 1: (2 beanbags) Stand in the center of a circle of students, tossing the first beanbag to student #1 and holding the other beanbag. Then sing the song, catching the bean-

bags with the beat. Student #1 tosses the first beanbag to you as you toss the second to student #2, and you catch beanbag #1 at the same moment student #2 catches beanbag #2. Send the first beanbag to student #3, and catch the other beanbag from student #2 just when student #3 catches your toss. Try to complete the circle without a miss. Stop if a beanbag is dropped.

Game 2: (beanbag for every group of four) Partners toss the beanbag during the refrain only. Encourage groups to create their own variations.

RELATED ARTS [MOVEMENT] [THEATER] [VISUAL ARTS]

LESSON PLANNER

FOCUS Duration, sixteenth notes

OBJECTIVES

OBJECTIVE 1 Perform rhythm patterns, including sixteenth notes, using body percussion (tested)

OBJECTIVE 2 Create and perform four-measure rhythmic interludes from notated patterns that include sixteenth notes (tested)

MATERIALS

Recordings

Listening: Carrion Crow Rhythm	CD2:29
The Old Carrion Crow	CD2:17
Listening: Prelude to *Carmen* (I—first 16 measures) by G. Bizet	CD2:30
Listening: Prelude to *Carmen* (II—excerpt) by G. Bizet	CD2:31
Swapping Song	CD2:28

Resources

Recorder Master R • 8 (pitches G A B)

VOCABULARY

overture, motive, interlude

▶ = **BASIC PROGRAM**

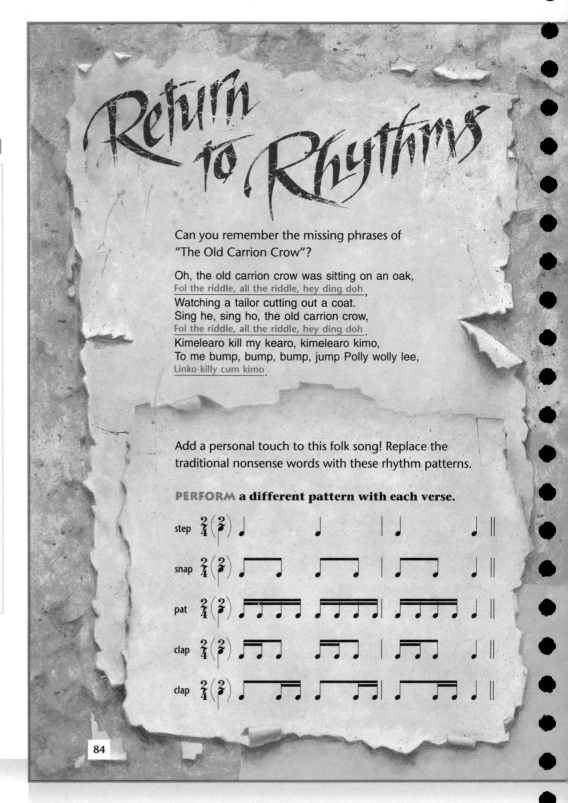

Can you remember the missing phrases of "The Old Carrion Crow"?

Oh, the old carrion crow was sitting on an oak,
Fol the riddle, all the riddle, hey ding doh,
Watching a tailor cutting out a coat.
Sing he, sing ho, the old carrion crow,
Fol the riddle, all the riddle, hey ding doh
Kimelearo kill my kearo, kimelearo kimo,
To me bump, bump, bump, jump Polly wolly lee,
Linko killy cum kimo.

Add a personal touch to this folk song! Replace the traditional nonsense words with these rhythm patterns.

PERFORM a different pattern with each verse.

84

MEETING **INDIVIDUAL** NEEDS

ALTERNATE TEACHING STRATEGY

OBJECTIVE 1 Have students use the nonsense words from page 64 and whisper them as they perform the rhythms with body percussion. Use student leaders for each verse.

EXTRA HELP: *Tempo Changes*

To help students adjust for the tempo changes in Verses 4 and 5 of "The Old Carrion Crow," have them practice clapping ♫ as you snap ♩, first at a slower tempo, then at the original tempo.

EXTRA HELP: *Identifying the Motive*

Have students use the nonsense words from page 64 to say the three patterns at the bottom of page 85, then practice identifying which one you are playing on a drum. Next, you or a musically trained student should play each pattern on various pitches on the piano, recorder, or resonator bells and ask the class to determine which pattern you were using as you created a melody.

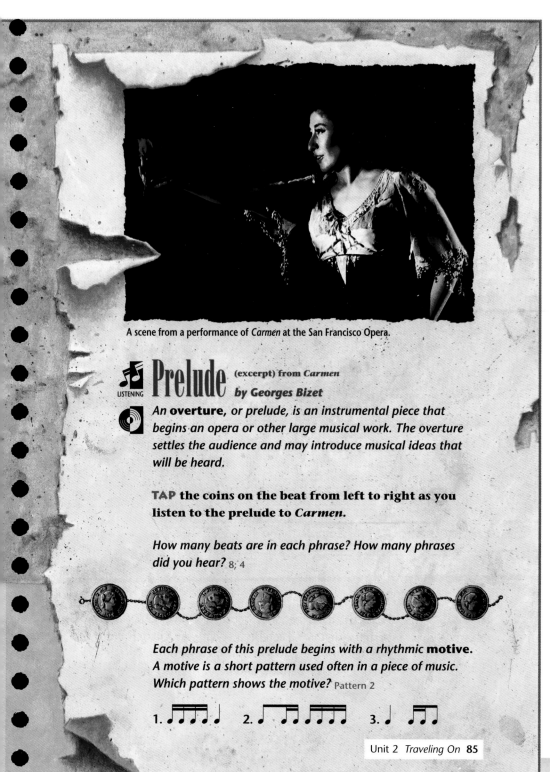

A scene from a performance of *Carmen* at the San Francisco Opera.

Prelude (excerpt) from *Carmen*
by Georges Bizet

LISTENING

*An **overture**, or prelude, is an instrumental piece that begins an opera or other large musical work. The overture settles the audience and may introduce musical ideas that will be heard.*

TAP the coins on the beat from left to right as you listen to the prelude to *Carmen*.

How many beats are in each phrase? How many phrases did you hear? 8; 4

*Each phrase of this prelude begins with a rhythmic **motive**. A motive is a short pattern used often in a piece of music. Which pattern shows the motive?* Pattern 2

1. ♩♫♫♩   2. ♩♫♫♫♪   3. ♩ ♫♫♩

"Guess this song from its rhythm." Have students:

▶ • Listen to "Carrion Crow Rhythm" **CD2:29** then name and sing "The Old Carrion Crow" **CD2:17** on page 62.

"Today you'll use some of these rhythms to make new patterns."

2 DEVELOP

1. Play a rhythm game with "The Old Carrion Crow." Have students:

• Recall the similar phrases, using page 84.

▶ • Listen to Verse 1, walking with the beat during those phrases.

▶ • Sing Verse 1, thinking those phrases silently.

• Practice the replacement rhythms on page 84, recalling the tempo changes. (Verse 4 is slower, Verse 5 is in the original tempo.)

OBJECTIVE 1 Informal Assessment

• Use body percussion to perform rhythm patterns during the similar phrases.

2. Introduce Prelude to *Carmen* CD2:30 (first 16 measures). Identify motive. Have students:

▶ • Read about overtures, then listen to the selection, tapping the beats on page 85.

• Signal the number of phrases. (4)

• Read about motives. Listen and signal—with one, two, or three fingers—which motive they hear. (two)

BACKGROUND: *Carmen* THEATER

Carmen, an opera by Georges Bizet (ʒarʒ bi **ze**), 1838–1875, is set in Spain. Don José (dɔn xo **se**), a soldier, falls in love with the beautiful gypsy, Carmen. He follows her into the mountains, where she has joined a gang of smugglers. When he discovers that she loves the bullfighter Escamillo (es ka **mi** yo), he is so jealous he wants to kill Escamillo. Instead, as the last act ends, he stabs Carmen to death as Escamillo is fighting a bull. Bizet, a French composer, wrote a score full of Spanish flavor without having been to Spain. His knowledge of Spanish music came from books at the Paris Library.

ENRICHMENT: *Prelude to* Carmen

Invite the students to enjoy a longer excerpt of the prelude to *Carmen* CD2:31. Challenge them to tap the coins or pat the motive from page 85 during the selection.

ENRICHMENT: *"The Old Carrion Crow"*

Have three students sing each nonsense phrase. On the next verse, have two students sing. For Verse 3, have soloists sing the phrases.

continued from previous page

3 APPLY

Review "Swapping Song" CD2:28 **(p. 82). Create rhythm patterns.** Have students:

▶ • Sing the song and then discuss any "swapping" done with friends.

▶ • Perform each rhythm pattern on pages 86–87 with body percussion.

▶ • With a partner, choose one pattern from each page and practice performing it, swapping the order.

▶ • Read about interludes, then listen to Verse 1 and practice performing their pair of patterns as described after the refrain.

OBJECTIVE 2 Informal Assessment

▶ • Sing the song and perform their patterns as interludes between verses. (Choose pairs of students to perform after every verse but the last one.)

RHYTHM SWAP

Have you ever swapped baseball cards or video games with a friend? In this game, you will create patterns by swapping the rhythms in the railroad cars.

Work with a partner and choose different sounds to perform the rhythms. Each partner chooses a pattern from one side. Perform the patterns one after the other. Then, swap the order of the patterns and perform them that way.

86 RETURN TO RHYTHMS

MEETING **INDIVIDUAL** NEEDS

ALTERNATE TEACHING STRATEGY

OBJECTIVE 2 Have students suggest and practice all the possible combinations of two patterns, one from each page. They should use different body percussion for each pattern in the pair, then swap the sequence of the patterns in each pair. Perform and swap a sample combination they suggest, then write that sequence on the board for all to try.

SPECIAL LEARNERS: *Swapping Rhythms*

Students with physical disabilities can still play the rhythm-swap game, even if they cannot perform the actual rhythms. Divide the class into groups of three (with no more than one disabled student per group). The activity remains the same, except that the student with disabilities, or the third member in other groups, has the fun of choosing the rhythms for the others to perform. Rotate the person choosing the rhythms as appropriate in the groups of three.

"Explain the difference between interlude and motive." (An interlude is a short musical connection between sections; a motive is a short pattern often repeated.) Have Students:

• Listen to the prelude to *Carmen* and mirror you as you pat with the music. (Pat this, alternating hands.)

An **interlude** is a short musical connection between sections or verses of a longer musical piece.

PERFORM your two patterns as an interlude between two verses of "Swapping Song."

LESSON SUMMARY

Informal Assessment In this lesson, students:

OBJECTIVE 1 Performed rhythm patterns including sixteenth notes, using body percussion during phrases of "The Old Carrion Crow."

OBJECTIVE 2 Created and performed four-measure rhythmic interludes from notated patterns that included sixteenth notes for "Swapping Song."

National Standards for Music Education
2f Play parts while others perform contrasting parts.
5a Read standard note values in duple and triple meters.

MORE MUSIC: Reinforcement
"Sourwood Mountain," page 196 (sixteenth notes, motive)
"In the Window," page 316 (motive; Hanukkah)
"Para pedir posada," page 318 (Las Posadas)
"Entren santos peregrinos," page 321 (Las Posadas)
"Dale, dale, dale!," page 322 (Las Posadas)
"The Path to the Moon," page 372 (melodic motive)
Erlkönig, page 385E (motive)
"The Dance at the Gym (Mambo)," page 385I (motive)

COOPERATIVE LEARNING: *Creating Rhythms*

Have groups of four students work, in pairs, to create rhythm patterns. One student claps a four-beat rhythm. Another group member repeats the rhythm with one change in the rhythm itself, body percussion used, or tempo. After a few rhythm patterns, partners may switch roles, then return to their group to demonstrate their variations. Each group should choose two eight-beat patterns to share with the class and tell why they were chosen. You may wish to have two students demonstrate the process to the class before assigning groups.

PLAYING INSTRUMENTS: *Unpitched*

Ostinato to *Carmen*: Form lines of four students behind six to eight drums or tambourines. Each student plays the pattern in the *Close* once, alternating hands, and then passes the drum back to the next person in line (or moves to the end of the line) during the rests at the end of the pattern.

Interlude to "Swapping Song": Have students perform their patterns from pages 86–87 on unpitched instruments, swapping as they did with the body percussion.

RELATED ARTS | MOVEMENT | THEATER | VISUAL ARTS

LESSON PLANNER

FOCUS Design—A B, A B A

OBJECTIVES
OBJECTIVE 1 Signal when they hear the A section of a piece return

OBJECTIVE 2 Create and perform eight-beat patterns as a contrasting section with a song

MATERIALS
Recordings

Listening: Karşi Bar — CD2:19
Down the Road (A and B sections) — CD2:27
Recorded Lesson: Meet the A Section — CD2:32
Listening: In a Mountain Path arranged by Han Kuo-huang — CD2:33
Four White Horses — CD2:15
Recorded Lesson: Rhythmic Clapping — CD2:34

Instruments

resonator bells or other pitched instruments

Resources

Resource Master 2 • 8 (listening map)
Listening Map Transparency T • 4 (In a Mountain Path)

▶ = **BASIC PROGRAM**

Here's a song you know. How can you figure out what song it is without hearing it? by reading the pitch or rhythm

SING the song when you recognize it. "Down the Road"

88

MEETING **INDIVIDUAL** NEEDS

PLAYING INSTRUMENTS: *Keyboards*

Have students speak the B section of "Down the Road," (p. 76) tapping the rhythm with fingers 1, 2, and 3 of either hand. Then improvise B section melodies by playing the rhythm of the first two measures of each line with the left hand (D E G) or the right hand (B A G). Play the rhythm of the rest of each line with the opposite hand. End each line with thumb on G.

THE FORM

In music, you hear repetition and contrast. Some phrases are the same. Some are different. This is also true of larger parts of musical works.

Some music is made up of two or more sections. Songs with two sections that sound the same have a form called A A. Songs with two different-sounding sections have a form called A B.

NAME the form of the song "Down the Road." Why did you choose your answer?

AB; Reasons should reflect the differences between the sections, for example, sung vs. spoken sections.

Unit 2 *Traveling On* **89**

"Let's do the dance to 'Karşi Bar' and compare its parts and movement." CD2:19 (The A section moves side to side and has a stylistic arm gesture. The B section also moves side to side, but with a foot-stamp gesture. For "Karşi Bar" dance, see Lesson 4, page 73, *Movement*.) Have students:

▶ • Describe how they knew when a new section began. (The movement changed.)

"Same and different sections can be shown through movement. Today you'll learn about sections in music."

2 DEVELOP

1. Review "Down the Road" (A and B sections CD2:27, p. 76). Identify the song from notation and introduce sectional form. Have students:

• Look at the notation on page 88 and discuss ways to determine what song it is.

• Say the letter names and listen as you play those pitches on resonator bells or other pitched instruments. (D E G A B)

• Sing the pitch syllables in order from *mi* to low *so*.

• Sing the melody's opening pitches with syllables (2 measures), then name the song.

▶ • Read about form on page 89.

• Perform the song and speech from page 76.

• Contrast the two sections and name the form A B.

▶ • Sing the song with movement. (See Lesson 5, page 76, *Movement*.)

LANGUAGE ARTS CONNECTION: *Story Form*

Draw parallels between form in music and form in literature. To prepare students for the discussion of A B A form on page 90, have them think of stories that follow a circular pattern, in which the main character begins in one place, travels to another, and then returns to the original place. Use the story of *The Wizard of Oz* as an example. Point out that Dorothy starts off and ends up in Kansas but travels to Oz in the middle. Draw the diagram (right) on the board, then discuss how musical compositions often follow a similar pattern. They begin in one musical "place" (A), travel to another (B), and then return to the original (A).

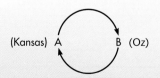

(Kansas) A   B (Oz)

LESSON 8

continued from previous page

2. Introduce "In a Mountain Path" CD2:33. Listen for form. Have students:

Recorded Lesson CD2:32

▶ • Listen to "Meet the A Section" to learn about characteristics of "In a Mountain Path," a traditional Chinese song arranged by Han Kuo-huang (hɑn kuɔ hwɑng).

▶ • Describe what they would expect to hear if the form were A B A. (A section, section of contrasting music, return to A section)

OBJECTIVE 1 Informal Assessment

▶ • Listen to the entire piece, raising a hand on the A section's return. (Optional: Use **Listening Map Transparency T · 4** or **Resource Master 2 · 8**.)

▶ • Improvise a dance to the music. (See *Movement* on the bottom of page 91.)

3 APPLY

Review "Four White Horses" CD2:15 (p. 60). Improvise a B section. Have students:

▶ • Sing "Four White Horses."

Recorded Lesson CD2:34

▶ • Listen to "Rhythmic Clapping" and echo-clap, then improvise eight-beat phrases.

▶ • Have volunteers clap solo eight-beat improvisations while the class pats with the beat.

OBJECTIVE 2 Informal Assessment

▶ • Play the game, creating a B section of improvised phrases. (See *Improvisation* below.)

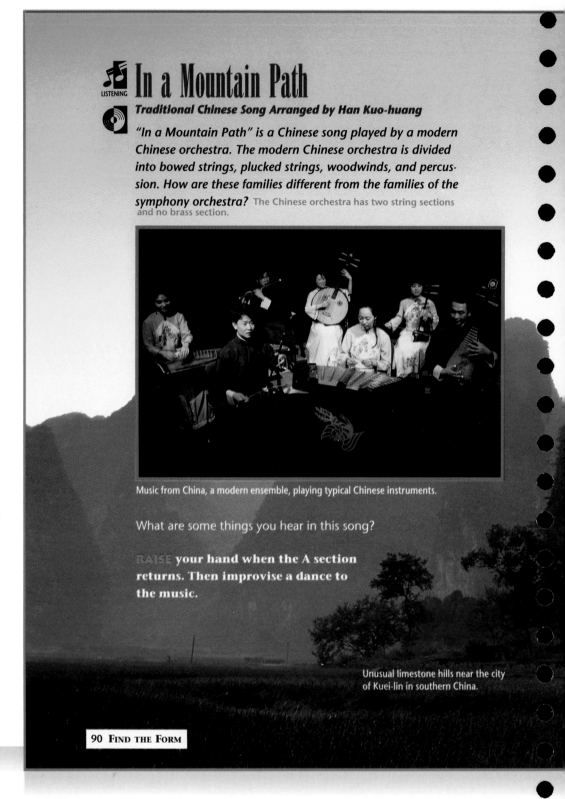

🎵 In a Mountain Path

LISTENING

Traditional Chinese Song Arranged by Han Kuo-huang

"In a Mountain Path" is a Chinese song played by a modern Chinese orchestra. The modern Chinese orchestra is divided into bowed strings, plucked strings, woodwinds, and percussion. How are these families different from the families of the symphony orchestra? The Chinese orchestra has two string sections and no brass section.

Music from China, a modern ensemble, playing typical Chinese instruments.

What are some things you hear in this song?

RAISE your hand when the A section returns. Then improvise a dance to the music.

Unusual limestone hills near the city of Kuei-lin in southern China.

90 FIND THE FORM

MEETING **INDIVIDUAL** NEEDS

ALTERNATE TEACHING STRATEGIES

OBJECTIVE 1 Have students listen only to the A section while following the map on **Transparency T · 4** or **Resource Master 2 · 8**. Ask them to discuss how the map matches what they hear. Then listen to the entire piece while following the map.

OBJECTIVE 2 Have the class improvise responses to your eight-beat phrase. Ask for solo volunteers and have the class listen for how the response was different, as well as for the eight-beat length. Then have partners improvise on each other's phrases. Help them keep track of the phrase length by drumming eight beats with a mallet followed by eight beats on the rim. Stop periodically to give students a chance to regroup.

IMPROVISATION: *"Four White Horses"*

A section: Sing and play as usual, in groups of four.

B section: Each group member, in turn, improvises an eight-beat clapping pattern.

LANDSCAPE IN THE STYLE OF DONG BEIYUAN

This Chinese scroll was painted in the time of the Ming Dynasty (1368–1644). The word *Ming* means "bright" in Chinese. Can you see how the artist, Dong Qichang, used contrasts to make his ink painting interesting and dramatic?

4 CLOSE

"Today you experienced and named the form or sections of three pieces of music." Have students:

▶ • Use letters to describe the form of each. ("Down the Road": A B, "In a Mountain Path": A B A, "Four White Horses": A B A)

▶ • Play "Four White Horses" once more with their new B section.

LESSON SUMMARY

Informal Assessment In this lesson, students:

OBJECTIVE 1 Signaled when they heard the A section of "In a Mountain Path" return.

OBJECTIVE 2 Created and performed "Four White Horses" in A B A form by improvising a B section.

National Standards for Music Education
3a Improvise "answers" to given phrases.
3c Improvise rhythmic variations and melodic embellishments.

MORE MUSIC: Reinforcement

"Powama," page 150 (sectional form)
"Dry Bones," page 308 (sectional form)
"A Holly Jolly Christmas," page 324 (Christmas)
"Dormi, dormi," page 328 (sectional form; Christmas)
"We Three Kings," page 329 (Christmas)
"The Twelve Days of Christmas," page 330 (Christmas)

MOVEMENT: *"In a Mountain Path"*

Have students experiment with nonlocomotor marcato movements for the arms (bend, straighten, lift, drop) and head (turn to sides, look up and down). Then have them use these marcato movements to improvise to the A section. When the B section occurs, they face a partner and perform legato mirror movement. (See *Movement: Mirroring Overview*.) When the A section recurs, they again improvise in place alone. Finally, discuss the similarities and differences of the movement for the A and B sections.

MOVEMENT: *Mirroring Overview*

Mirror movements help students to feel phrase-lengths and to experience moving slowly and smoothly. To start, have the leader of each pair draw a circle or a cursive letter slowly in the air. Then invite him or her to paint a picture very slowly in the air, using an imaginary brush. Students should also try moving their arms bilaterally (for example: both moving in the same way in the same direction) and independently (for example: one arm up and one out to the side). Encourage students to concentrate on their partner's movements so that an observer cannot tell who is leading.

UNIT TWO
LESSON 9

RELATED ARTS | MOVEMENT | THEATER | VISUAL ARTS

LESSON PLANNER

OBJECTIVES
To review songs, skills, and concepts learned in Unit 2 and to test students' ability to:
1. Identify sixteenth notes
2. Recognize patterns using pitches D E G A B from staff notation

MATERIALS
Recordings

Four White Horses	CD2:15
Down the Road (A and B sections)	CD2:27
Trail to Mexico (I—with instrumental ostinato)	CD2:14
Trail to Mexico (II—with vocal ostinato)	CD2:26
Unit 2 Assessment A	CD2:35–38
Unit 2 Assessment B	CD2:39–42

RESOURCES
Resource Master 2 • 9 (assessment)
Resource Master 2 • 10 (assessment)
Resource Master TA • 1 (assessment)

▶ = BASIC PROGRAM

REVIEW

GETTING THERE IS HALF THE FUN

Do you like sending postcards? Think of the song shown on one of these cards. Describe what you might see if you went to the place in the song. Then sing the song.

Choose your favorite card and write a message on a piece of paper to friends "back home." Tell them about the rhythm, pitches, or game that goes with the song on the postcard.

Trail to Mexico

92

MEETING **INDIVIDUAL** NEEDS

PROGRAM IDEA: *Getting There Is Half the Fun*

This review can be enjoyed in the classroom or presented as a simple program. Additional materials from Unit 2, *Celebrations*, or *Music Library* may be added, as well as original work from students.

"Think about a place that you have traveled to or one you would like to visit. Music can take us to faraway places and unfamiliar lands." Have students sing the Caribbean folk song "Four White Horses," tapping with the beat.

"Quite often we can take a trip without boarding a plane or a ship. We can take a walk with a friend just to enjoy ourselves." Have students sing the song and add a walk to "Down the Road."

"Taking a walk with a friend can be relaxing, but how about riding on the western trail?" Have students sing "Trail to Mexico" while pretending to be cowhands.

Down the Road

Four White Horses

1. Review the *do la, so,* pattern in "Four White Horses" CD2:15 (p. 60). Have students:

▶ • Sing the song and discuss what sights they imagine.

• Sing the song again, raising a hand each time they sing the *do la, so,* melodic pattern. (*on the river, up tomorrow, banana*)

▶ • In groups of four, play the game. (See *Movement* on the bottom of page 81.)

2. Review melodic notation in "Down the Road" CD2:27 (p. 76). Have students:

▶ • Sing the song and discuss a special road they have traveled.

• Name the pitches of the song, first with pitch syllables and then with letter names. (*so, la, do re mi* and D E G A B)

▶ • Play the game in two or three groups. (See *Movement* on the bottom of page 76.)

3. Review patterns with sixteenth notes in "Trail to Mexico." Have students:

▶ • Sing the song CD2:14 on page 59, and discuss what sights one might encounter along a western trail.

• Sing the words and clap the rhythm of the ostinato. (Review the following.)

• Sing the ostinato with pitch syllables, then letter names. (*so,* and *la,*; D and E)

• In two groups, sing the song with the ostinato CD2:26, on pages 74–75.

DRAMA CONNECTION: *Living Postcards* THEATER

As you read a folktale to the class, ask students to close their eyes and "see" the folktale. Discuss how postcards could show moments in the story, and discuss which moments of the story you read are important. Then have a volunteer "sculpt," using classmates as clay, an image of the most important moment of the story. Choose another sculptor to sculpt a second "postcard" image. Finally, ask the entire class to work together and sculpt the most important postcard of the folktale.

UNIT TWO
LESSON 9

ASSESSMENTS A AND B CD2:35–42

Different recorded examples for Assessments A and B allow for two uses of the same set of questions. When appropriate, recorded examples for Assessment A use familiar musical examples with which students have worked for the given concept. The recorded examples for Assessment B use musical selections the students have not previously worked with for the concept, encouraging the application of knowledge to new material.

The pupil page is intended for those who wish to assess quickly with the whole class or in small groups. Each assessment may be used as a pretest or as a final review before presenting the written test (**Resource Master 2 • 9**).

ANSWERS

	ASSESSMENT A	ASSESSMENT B
1.	b	a
2.	a	d
3.	c	b
4.	b	c

CHECK IT OUT

1. Which rhythm do you hear?

   a.

   b.

   c.

   d.

2. Which rhythm do you hear?

   a.

   b.

   c.

   d.

3. Which pitches do you hear?

   a.   c.

   b.   d.

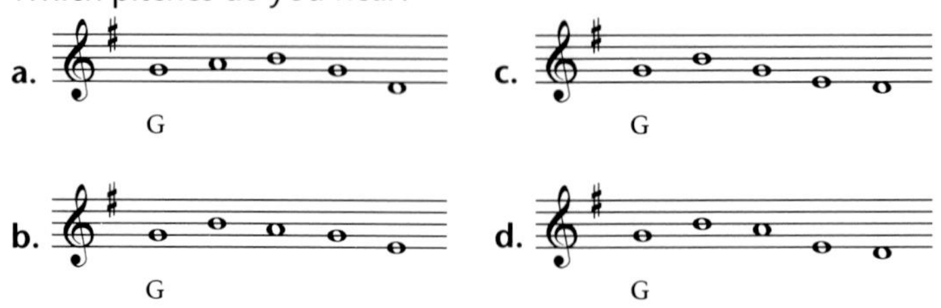

4. Which pitches do you hear?

   a.   c.

   b.   d.

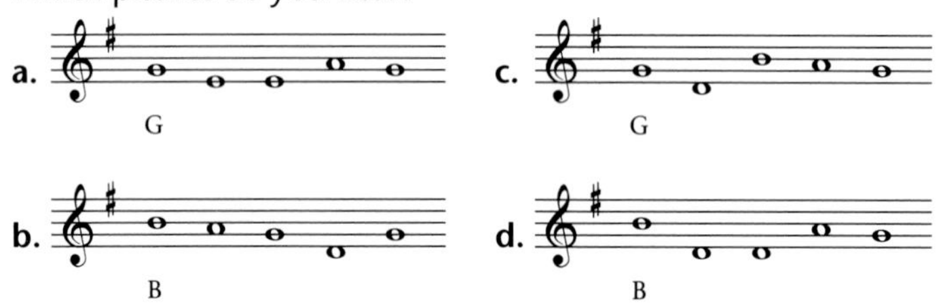

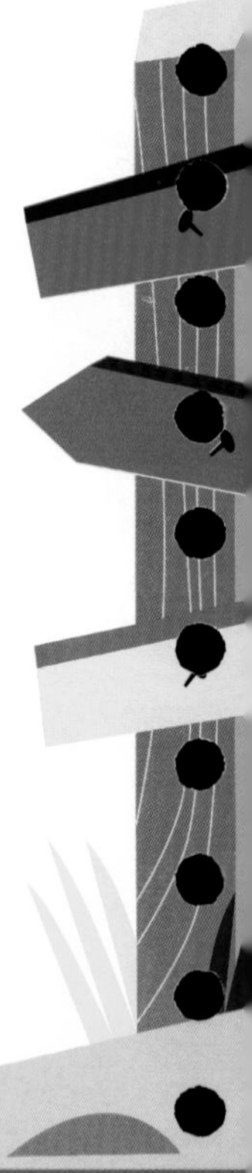

94

MEETING **INDIVIDUAL** NEEDS

PORTFOLIO ASSESSMENT

To evaluate student portfolios, use the Portfolio Assessment form on **Resource Master TA • 1**. See page 54B for a summary of Portfolio Opportunities in this unit.

SOCIAL STUDIES CONNECTION: *Travel Poster*

VISUAL ARTS

Have students work in small groups to research ways of travel used from the early 1800s to today. They might cut out pictures from magazines or draw pictures and paste them on a large piece of oaktag. Under each picture, there should be a description of what type of travel is being shown, when it was invented and by whom (if relevant), and any other information available. Have each group present its poster to the class.

CREATE

Pair Up for ABA

CREATE a melody with a partner. Use the pitches D E G A B and one of the rhythm patterns below.

PERFORM your melody as part of a B section between the verses of "Trail to Mexico."

Write

The journey to a place can be as interesting as the place you visit.

Write words for a song describing your trip to the Market of San Juan or on a cattle drive to Mexico. Describe what you see, what you think, who you meet, and what surprises or difficulties occur along the way.

1. Create melodies. Have students:

• Work in pairs and follow the instructions on page 95 to create a melody. (Optional: Use **Resource Master 2 • 10** to notate the melodies.)

• Perform their melodies in turn as a B section between verses of "Trail to Mexico."

2. Write lyrics. Have students:

▶ • Write song lyrics as described. (Ask volunteers to teach the class their song.)

National Standards for Music Education
1a Sing accurately, on pitch and in rhythm.
1b Sing with appropriate dynamics, phrasing, and interpretation.
5b Use a system to read notation in treble clef in major keys.

VISUAL ARTS
ART CONNECTION: *Patterns*

In art, pattern is the effect created by repetition of shapes, symbols, or designs. The repetition can establish a rhythm or sense of direction. Have students locate and discuss the repeated patterns in the illustrations on pages 92–93 and 95. (waves, lines on fields, bumps on road) How do the patterns create a sense of the water's movement or the road's going back in space? Often only the size of a repeated symbol is changed to create a feeling of going back into space, or perspective. (bumps on road) Invite students to create their own patterned picture using paper cutouts.

RELATED ARTS MOVEMENT THEATER VISUAL ARTS

When I Was a Lad

Unit 2 Reinforcement
sixteenth-note rhythms, *pages 65 and 75*

1. Perform four sounds to a beat CD2:43.
Have students:

• Listen to Verse 1 without looking at the notation and snap with the beat.

• Tell what they think is the occupation of the solo singer. (ruler of the Queen's Navy—an admiral)

• Chant *Now I am the ruler of the Queen's Navee* in rhythm as they snap with the beat.

• Form two groups, one group to snap with the beat, the other to pat the rhythm of the same phrase. Find the beats that have four sounds to the beat. (Beats 1 and 2)

MORE SONGS TO SING

Music by Arthur S. Sullivan
Words by William S. Gilbert

Leader

1. When I was a lad I served a term As
2. As of-fice boy I made such a mark That they
3. Now, lands-men all, who-ev-er you may be, If you

of - fice boy to an at - tor - ney's firm; I
gave me the post of a jun - ior clerk; I
want to rise to the top of the tree, If your

cleaned the win-dows and I swept the floor, And I
served the writs with a smile so bland, And I
soul is -n't fet-tered to an of - fice stool, Be

Group

pol -ished up the han - dle of the big front door. He
cop -ied all the let - ters in a big round hand; He
care -ful to be guid -ed by this gold - en rule: Be

96

MEETING **INDIVIDUAL** NEEDS

BIOGRAPHIES: *Gilbert and Sullivan*
Sir William Gilbert (1836–1911) and Sir Arthur Sullivan (1842–1900) were, respectively, the lyricist and the composer of 14 operettas. These include the most popular operettas of the English language—*H.M.S Pinafore* (1878), *The Pirates of Penzance* (1879), *Patience* (1881), *The Mikado* (1885), and *The Gondoliers* (1889). Gilbert's sharp wit was reflected in the satirical words and story lines of most of the works. He was in his own right a journalist and playwright. Sullivan was a noted composer of his time. He

wrote the music for the hymn "Onward, Christian Soldiers" and composed a full-length dramatic opera, *Ivanhoe.*

BACKGROUND: *"When I Was a Lad"*
This song is from *H.M.S. Pinafore,* an operetta that pokes fun at the British Navy of the late 1800s and, in particular, at the customs and pretensions of the admiralty. This song is sung by the Admiral, a buffo (humorous) character, who is the "playful" villain of the piece.

pol-ished up the han-dle of the big front door. I
cop-ied all the let-ters in a big round hand; I
care-ful to be guid-ed by this gold-en rule: Stick

pol-ished up the han-dle so care-ful-lee That
cop-ied all the let-ters in a hand so free That
close___ to your desks,___ and nev-er go to sea, And you

now I am the rul-er of the Queen's Na-vee. He
now I am the rul-er of the Queen's Na-vee. He
all___ may be rul-ers of the Queen's Na-vee. Stick

pol-ished up the han-dle so care-ful-lee That
cop-ied all the let-ters in a hand so free That
close___ to your desks___ and nev-er go to sea, And you

now he is the rul-er of the Queen's Na-vee.
now he is the rul-er of the Queen's Na-vee.
all___ may be rul-ers of the Queen's Na-vee.

2. Sing the song. Have students:

• Listen to the song following the notation.

• Read the words and discuss their humor, describing how the solo singer never traveled to sea, yet became an admiral.

• Listen again, this time singing the sections marked "group."

• Practice saying the words while tapping with the beat.

• Sing the entire song.

• Sing again, with one student singing the solo parts while the rest of the class sings the group part. Repeat with new soloists each time.

ENRICHMENT: *Creating a Musical* THEATER

Invite students to put on a musical by selecting favorite songs and linking them with a story or theme. Working in groups, have students think of a simple story line. They can flesh out several characters and two or three simple scenes. Have them then select at least one song for each character or scene that explains the character's personality or the mood of the scene.

Orchestra Song

Unit 2 Reinforcement
orchestral instruments, *page 71*

1. Name instruments and instrumental families CD2:44. Have students:

• Name the four instrumental families and some of the instruments in each. (You may wish to use pictures of the instruments as a reminder: see pages 68–69. Optional: Use **Musical Instruments Masters**—brass family, percussion family, woodwind family, string family.)

• Listen to the song without looking at the music, then list the instruments named and the families to which they belong.

• Listen again while following the music, then compare the sound of each instrument's line in the song.

• Learn each part of the song, then sing it through in unison, one part at a time.

Austrian Round

98

MEETING **INDIVIDUAL** NEEDS

ENRICHMENT: *Performing "Orchestra Song"*

Students may pretend to play each instrument while singing about it. They can perform their pantomime while singing the song as a canon.

CRITICAL THINKING: *Compare and Contrast*

Have students compare the instruments in this song with those in "En la feria de San Juan," page 66.

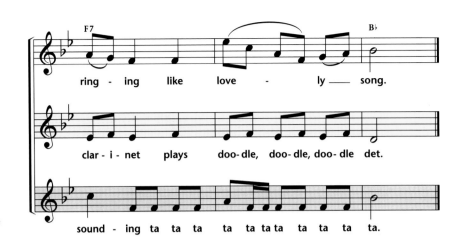

ring - ing like love - ly ___ song.

clar - i - net plays doo - dle, doo - dle, doo - dle det.

sound - ing ta ta ta ta ta ta ta ta ta ta ta.

Add these parts to the first three.

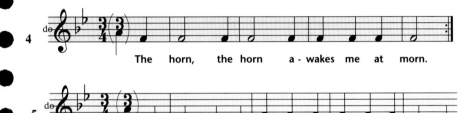

4

The horn, the horn a - wakes me at morn.

5

The drum's play - ing two tones and al - ways the same tones,

Five, one, one, five, five, five, five, five, one.

Unit 2 *Traveling On* **99**

2. Sing the song as a canon or as a cumulative song. Have students:

• Perform the canon either of two ways:
—each of five groups chooses one part and sings only that part repeatedly;
—each of five groups begins at the beginning and sings all five parts one after another.

• Perform cumulatively by adding one part each time through. (Optional: Use "Orchestra Song" Performance Mix **CD10:12**.)

ENCORE
MULTICULTURAL PERSPECTIVES
RELATED ARTS | MOVEMENT | THEATER | VISUAL ARTS

LESSON LINKS

Singin' in the Rain *(15 min)*

OBJECTIVE Sing a song that describes the feeling of being in the rain

Reinforcement melodic shape, rain, *page 111*

MATERIALS
Recordings
Singin' in the Rain   CD2:45
Singin' in the Rain
(performance mix)   CD10:13

A Kenyan Folktale *(20 min)*

OBJECTIVE Read a folktale and accompany it with instrument sounds

Reinforcement
accompaniment, *page 261*
African cultures, *page 171*

MATERIALS
Instruments pitched and unpitched

Resources
Resource Master 2 • 11 (practice)
Resource Master 2 • 12 (practice)

Rainfall *(15 min)*

OBJECTIVE Listen and move to music that sounds like rain

Reinforcement rain, *page 111*

MATERIALS
Recordings
Rainfall by L. Worsley (listening)   CD3:1
Recorded Lesson: Interview
with Cleo Parker Robinson   CD3:2

Encore BLUE SKIES

Songs, poems, and stories about rain are found in cultures all over the world. What feeling does this song express about rain? How do you feel when it rains?

SINGIN' in the RAIN

Music by Nacio Herb Brown
Words by Arthur Freed

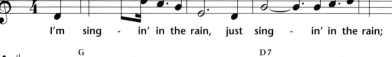

I'm sing - in' in the rain, just sing - in' in the rain;

What a glo - ri - ous feel - ing, I'm hap - py a - gain!

I'm laugh - ing at clouds so dark up a - bove.

The sun's in my heart and I'm read - y for love.

100

MEETING **INDIVIDUAL** NEEDS

BACKGROUND: *Singin' in the Rain*

The musical *Singin' in the Rain* (1952) used many songs that Nacio Herb Brown (1896–1964), composer, and Arthur Freed (1894–1973), lyricist, had written for other MGM musicals. Nacio Herb Brown was a former real-estate office manager, and Arthur Freed had at one time been in vaudeville. The two collaborated on many musicals, and Arthur Freed also produced many of them. The song "Singin' in the Rain" was originally written for a movie called *Hollywood Revue*. The movie *Singin' in the Rain* was a gentle satire that poked fun at silent films and early movies.

ART CONNECTION: *A Watercolor Wash*

Have students use watercolor in a wash or thin coat of paint to create a sky that shows rain. Students can wet the paper, apply paint near the top of the paper, and then tilt the paper so that the color bleeds down toward the horizon.

GRAY SKIES

Gene Kelly, an American actor and dancer, made the song "Singin' in the Rain" famous in the movie of the same name.

Singin' in the Rain CD2:45

Sing a song that describes the feeling of being in the rain. Have students:

• Share their feelings about rain or their memories of a rainstorm.

• Listen to the song and identify sounds in the music that imitate raindrops falling.

• Listen again, drawing the melodic contour in the air with their arms and noting the melodic movement by steps and skips.

• Learn the song.

• Compare their feelings about rain to the feelings expressed in the song.

Let the storm - y clouds chase ev' - ry - one from the place;

Come on with the rain, I've a smile on my face!

I'll walk down the lane with a hap - py re - frain,

And sing - in', just sing - in' in the rain!

Encore 101

LANGUAGE ARTS CONNECTION: *Writing a Poem*

Have students use each letter, R-A-I-N, to begin a line of a four-line poem describing the sounds of rain. The poem can also describe students' feelings about rain.

DRAMA CONNECTION: *"As If"* THEATER

Have the class create three word lists: one of words describing rain (cold, pounding, gentle); one of types of rain (drizzle, downpour); and one of emotions (happy, angry, bored). Have students use a word from each list to set up an imaginary situation and emotion (for example, cold drizzle,

bored). Ask students to close their eyes and remember the sensations of being cold and bored. "What do your fingers feel like when you are cold? Your nose?" Have students continue to "sense" the images while they sing the song "as if" they were bored in a cold drizzle. Then have them imagine a contrasting situation and sing as if happy in a warm downpour. Have the class discuss whether the concept of "as if" helped them to sing expressively and when else they might use it.

ENCORE
MULTICULTURAL PERSPECTIVES

continued from previous page

A Kenyan Folktale

1. Read a folktale about rain. Have students:

• Read the Kenyan folktale about rain, summarizing what the tale is about.

• Name things in the story that could be represented by a sound. (grass, feather, eagle, arrow, bow, cloud, thunder, rain)

• Practice the vocal call. (You may want to play it for the students on a keyboard or other melodic instrument.)

2. Accompany the story with instrument sounds. Have students:

• Choose instruments to represent the sounds of the story. (See *Playing Instruments, Percussion* below, or use **Resource Master 2 • 11.**)

• Divide into groups, with one group telling the story and the other performing on the instruments. (Optional: Begin and end with the vocal call and have students use **Resource Master 2•12** to learn the Orff accompaniment.)

Vocal call contributed by Susanne Burgess.

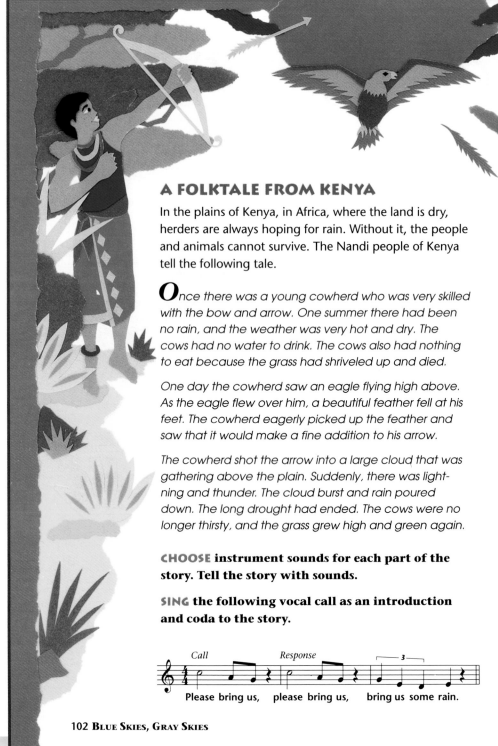

A FOLKTALE FROM KENYA

In the plains of Kenya, in Africa, where the land is dry, herders are always hoping for rain. Without it, the people and animals cannot survive. The Nandi people of Kenya tell the following tale.

Once there was a young cowherd who was very skilled with the bow and arrow. One summer there had been no rain, and the weather was very hot and dry. The cows had no water to drink. The cows also had nothing to eat because the grass had shriveled up and died.

One day the cowherd saw an eagle flying high above. As the eagle flew over him, a beautiful feather fell at his feet. The cowherd eagerly picked up the feather and saw that it would make a fine addition to his arrow.

The cowherd shot the arrow into a large cloud that was gathering above the plain. Suddenly, there was lightning and thunder. The cloud burst and rain poured down. The long drought had ended. The cows were no longer thirsty, and the grass grew high and green again.

CHOOSE instrument sounds for each part of the story. Tell the story with sounds.

SING the following vocal call as an introduction and coda to the story.

Please bring us, please bring us, bring us some rain.

102 **BLUE SKIES, GRAY SKIES**

MEETING **INDIVIDUAL** NEEDS

PLAYING INSTRUMENTS: *Percussion*

Have students use instruments each time they hear these words: *cowherd*—piccolo blocks; *bow*—kalimba; *arrow*—vibraslap; *rain*—Brazilian rainstick; *cows*—agogo (a **go** go) bell; *grass*—cabasa; *eagle*—chime tree; *feather*—brush on cymbal; *cloud*—large hand drum; *thunder*—timpani.

PLAYING INSTRUMENTS: *Orff*

Students can accompany the vocal call, using the Orff arrangement on **Resource Master 2 • 12.**

MULTICULTURAL PERSPECTIVES: *Rain Dances*

Rain, and its power to preserve life, has deep meaning for many people. Among Native American people of arid regions, rain dance ceremonies are one expression of their regard for rain. The Tohono O'odham Indians of Arizona, for example, hold rain dances before they plant their crops. The ceremony includes dancing, singing, and drinking cactus juice. The people believe that, as they become full by drinking this juice, the earth will become filled with rain.

Rainfall
LISTENING

Rainfall by Linda Worsley

People have dreamed of controlling the weather for thousands of years. Inventors have tried to make artificial rain. People living in dry areas held rain dances in the hope of rainfall.

MOVE to music that sounds like rain.

Cleo Parker Robinson, an American dancer, created her own rain dance.

Members of Cleo Parker Robinson's troupe rehearse "Raindance."

Meet CLEO PARKER ROBINSON

Cleo Parker Robinson has made her career as a choreographer, a person who creates dances. She trained in both modern dance and ballet. Robinson formed her own dance school while she was a college student. She has traveled with her dancers around the world and has received many awards for her teaching and community service. One of her goals is to make the experience of dance available to all.

LISTEN to Cleo Parker Robinson talk about her experiences performing her rain dance.

Encore 103

Rainfall CD3:1

Listen to music that sounds like rain and create movement for it. Have students:

• Discuss why rain is important. (drinking water for people and animals, survival of crops)

• Listen to "Rainfall" and tell how it sounds like rain.

Recorded Lesson CD3:2

• Listen to "Interview with Cleo Parker Robinson," and hear the choreographer talk about performing her rain dance.

• Divide into groups and create movement to go with the music.

BIOGRAPHY: *Cleo Parker Robinson* MOVEMENT

Cleo Parker Robinson grew up dancing for fun with her family and started studying dance formally only when she went to college. Originally, she wanted to be a doctor, but then decided that dance makes people feel good without any medicine. She started her Denver-based company, named after her, in 1970 and now directs the company, choreographs, performs, teaches, and tours around the world. She has found that people of all cultures and ages love, and respond to, dance and that the influences of other cultures and choreographers inspire her.

LANGUAGE ARTS CONNECTION: *Writing a Folktale*

Have students write and illustrate their own folktales about the origin of rain, then read them aloud to the class.

SOCIAL STUDIES CONNECTION: *Drought*

Have students research and report on droughts and where they are likely to occur in the world. Reports should include maps showing the locations of these areas.

*J*ust Imagine

MULTICULTURAL PERSPECTIVES

Through exposure to diverse materials, students develop an awareness of how people from many cultures create and participate in music. This unit includes:

African/African American
- **Pay Me My Money Down,** work song, 111

European/European American and Canadian
- *Canal,* by American painter Helen Frankenthaler, 123
- **Come and Sing Together,** traditional Hungarian melody and canon, 114
- *Concert Champêtre,* painting of Renaissance musicians, 126
- **The Eagle,** by American educators Hap Palmer and Martha Cheney, 118
- **Fire** (poem), by Pat Taylor of England, 122
- **I's the B'y,** Newfoundland folk song, 132
- **One More River,** college song, 112
- **Over the Hills and Far Away,** concert band music by Percy Grainger, 130
- **Volte,** Renaissance dance music by Michael Praetorius, 126

Hispanic/Hispanic American
- *Baile en Tehuantepec,* by Mexican artist Diego Rivera, 141
- **La pájara pinta,** Mexican folk song, 110
- **La raspa,** Mexican folk music, 134
- **Scherzo,** by Venezuelan-born composer Maria Teresa Carreño, 116

Native American
- **A'tsah Biyiin Sin,** traditional Laguna melody with Navajo words by Julius Chavez, 121
- **I Wonder,** by Yakima poet Earl Thompson, 105

For a complete listing of materials by culture throughout the book, see the Classified Index.

UNIT 3

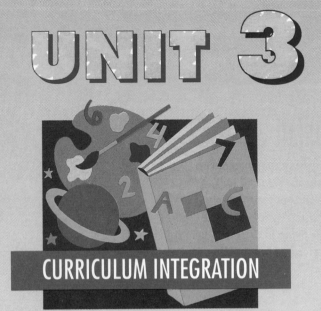

CURRICULUM INTEGRATION

Activities in this unit that promote the integration of music with other curriculum areas include:

Art
- Paint speckled birds in imitations of Mexican bark paintings, 111A
- Sketch clothing designs, 117A
- Create an endangered species mural, 131A

Math
- Role-play sales transactions, 127B
- Solve an animal word problem, 131B
- Solve rhythmic value problems, 143

Reading/Language Arts
- Write resumes for various jobs, 111B
- Write essays about change, 117B
- Create new verses to a song, 125
- Play a game of altering word phrases, 127B
- Write essays about decisions, 131A
- Write lyrics for a harmony pattern, 141
- Write poems or plays, 146

Science
- Make a graph based on raindrops, 111A
- Conduct wind-speed experiments, 111B
- Classify animals, 117B
- Study the paths of rivers, 117A
- Create a fact sheet about eagles, 119
- Make condensation models, 127A
- Research endangered species, 131A
- Keep a weather journal, 131B

Social Studies
- Role-play a conversation between people from different places, 127A

New! **UNIT OPENERS WITH THEMATIC TEACHING PROJECTS**

PLANNER

ASSESSMENT OPTIONS

Informal Performance Assessments

Informal Assessments correlated to Objectives are provided in every lesson with Alternate Strategies for reteaching. Frequent informal assessment allows for ongoing progress checks throughout the course of the unit.

Formal Assessment

An assessment form is provided on pupil page 146 and Resource Master 3•8. The questions assess student understanding of the following main unit objectives:

- Identify melodic movement by repeated notes, steps, and skips
- Identify *fa*
- Recognize patterns using C and F from staff notation
- Read rhythms (♩♪, ♫♫, ♩) in ⁶⁄₈ meter

Music Journal

Encourage students to enter thoughts about selections, projects, performances, and personal progress. Some journal opportunities include:

- Discussion of impressions of "A'tsah Biyiin Sin," TE 121
- *Think It Through,* 122, 133, 137
- Critical Thinking, TE 127
- Write, 147

Portfolio Opportunities

Update student portfolios with outcome-based materials, including written work, audiotapes, videotapes, and/or photos that represent their best work for each unit. Some portfolio opportunites in this unit include:

- Performance of Orff Orchestrations (audiotape), TE 109, 127, 131
- Marking melodic movement by steps, skips, repeated notes (Resource Master 3•1), TE 109
- Unpitched accompaniment to "Come and Sing Together" (audiotape), TE 115
- Planned performance of "Fire" with movement and dynamics (videotape), 122
- Arranging and notating pitch syllables from lowest to highest (Resource Master 3•2), TE 124
- Work with C, F (Resource Master 3•3), TE 126
- Working with rhythms in ⁶⁄₈ (Resource Masters 3•4, 3•5, 3•7), TE 130, 131, 142
- "Storm" compositions (Resource Master 3•6, audiotape, videotape), TE 137
- Check It Out (formal assessment), 146; Resource Master 3•8
- Portfolio Assessment (Resource Masters TA•1–5), 146
- Create 147; Resource Master 3•9
- Write, 147

UNIT 3

CONCEPT

		LESSON 1 CORE p.108	LESSON 2 CORE p.112	LESSON 3 p.118
FOCUS		Pitch—repeated notes, steps, skips	Duration, two and three sounds to a beat	Dynamics
SELECTIONS		I Don't Care If the Rain Comes Down La pájara pinta Pay Me My Money Down	One More River Come and Sing Together Scherzo from String Quartet in B Minor (listening)	The Eagle A'tsah Biyiin Sin (listening) Fire (poem)

MUSICAL ELEMENTS	CONCEPTS	UNIT OBJECTIVES Bold = Tested			
EXPRESSIVE QUALITIES	Dynamics	• Use and notate dynamics		• See dynamics in notation	• Notice dynamics aurally • Choose and sing various dynamics • Perform poem with dynamics
	Tempo		• *Sing phrases slowly*		
	Articulation			• Listen for pizzicato, arco	• Hear sung legato phrases
TONE COLOR	Vocal/ Instrumental Tone Color			• Hear string quartet • *Practice singing with good tone quality*	• Hear Native American singing and drumming
DURATION	Beat/Meter	• **Read rhythms in ⁶⁄₈ meter**	• See and sing in ⁶⁄₈	• **See, sing and clap ⁶⁄₈ motive (E/D)** • Distinguish between 2 and 3 equal sounds to beat • Move to show division of beat • Hear changing meter • *Conduct in 2*	• Pat with beat
	Rhythm	• **Read ♫♩, ♩ ♪, ♩ in ⁶⁄₈ meter**	• See and sing rhythms in ⁶⁄₈ meter • *Read rhythm notation in ²⁄₄*	• **See notation, sing and clap rhythms in ⁶⁄₈ (E/D)**	
PITCH	Melody	• **Identify repeated notes, steps, skips** • **Identify fa, C, F**	• Draw and describe melodic shape (E/D) • Identify and move to repeated notes, steps, skips (I/P) • **Recognize melodic movement in 2 songs (Rf)** • Sing and discuss melodies with fa, C, F (E)	• Sing C, F	
	Harmony	• Recognize harmonic changes	• *Play Orff orchestration*	• *Play Orff orchestration* • *Sing two ostinatos in harmony*	
	Tonality major/minor			• Sing songs in major and minor • Hear piece in minor	
DESIGN	Texture			• *Sing 2 ostinatos at once* • *Play unpitched accompaniment*	• Hear drumming accompaniment • *Add unpitched instruments*
	Form/ Structure		• Find same, similar, different phrases • See and sing A B song	• Listen for rhythmic motive • Sing song with 10 verses, refrain	• Sing coda
CULTURAL CONTEXT	Style/ Background	• Hear and sing music from diverse cultures • Develop understanding of musical concepts using selections from diverse cultures	• Listen to Mexican folk song • Sing African American work song	• Sing nineteenth-century American college song • Sing Hungarian melody • Listen to string quartet by Maria Teresa Carreño	• Hear Native American music

Learning Sequence: E = Explore, D = Describe, I = Identify, P = Practice, Rf = Reinforce, Rd = Read, C = Create See also *Program Scope and Sequence,* page 402.

Italic = Meeting Individual Needs

LESSON 4 CORE p.124	LESSON 5 CORE p.128	LESSON 6 p.132	LESSON 7 p.136	LESSON 8 p.140
Pitch—*fa*; C, F	Duration—§, ♫♩, ♩ ♪, ♩	Harmony	Dynamics	Duration
I Don't Care If the Rain Comes Down Volte (listening) Pay Me My Money Down	One More River Over the Hills and Far Away (listening) La pájara pinta	I's the B'y La raspa (listening) Pay Me My Money Down	I Don't Care If the Rain Comes Down Over the Hills and Far Away (listening) Come and Sing Together	I's the B'y La raspa (listening)
• *Analyze how piece's dynamics influenced impressions*	• Hear piece with varying dynamic levels		• Compose with dynamics • Compare graphic notation and standard symbols • Follow listening map and notation with dynamics	
		• *Sing phrases slowly*		
• Hear staccato, accents • *Sing jazz scat syllables with staccato accents*			• *Use tremolo, staccato, glissando*	
• Hear Renaissance instruments	• Hear concert band • Recognize instrument families in concert band	• Hear mariachi music	• Compose with varying sounds • *Explore tone colors on electronic keyboards* • *Use tremolo, staccato, glissando on keyboards*	
• Make up 4-beat motion patterns • Clap with offbeat	• **Identify and sing in § meter (I/P)** • **Read patterns in § meter (Rd)** • **Create ostinatos in § (C)**	• **Sing song in § meter (Rf)** • See graphic notation of beat • *Signal on strong beats*	• **Clap rhythm from notation in § meter (Rf/Rd)**	• **Determine meter (Rf)** • Label equal and unequal beat divisions • *Review bar lines* • *Pat on strong beats*
• Sing song with ♫, ♫♫ • *Play accompaniments with ♫, ♩, ♩, ♩*	• **Learn notation, move to rhythms in § (I/P)** • **Read patterns in § (Rd)** • **Create ostinatos (C)**	• **Sing rhythms in § (Rf)** • Sing dotted half notes	• **Clap rhythm from notation (Rf)**	• **Use ♫, ♩ ♪ (Rf)** • Recognize song from rhythm • Distinguish predominant rhythm patterns
• **Indicate melodic movement (Rf)** • **Describe, identify, and sing *fa* (D/I/P)** • **Use *do re mi fa so* (Rd)** • **Move to and play melodic motives (E/D)** • **Read C D E F G (I/P/Rd)** • *Play C, F, fa on keyboard*	• Recognize song from melody	• Recognize *do* and *so₁*		• **Sing harmony part with letter names (Rf)**
• *Play Orff accompaniment*	• *Play Orff accompaniment*	• Define harmony • Evaluate, sing, play harmony parts • Use graphic notation, move to show harmonic changes		• Sing harmonic pattern with *do* and *so₁*
• Locate *fa* in C major song		• Recognize tonal center • Define key signature • Listen for chords based on *do* and *so₁*	• Sing in minor	
• *Play keyboard accompaniment* • *Play Orff accompaniment*	• Create and play unpitched ostinatos	• Sing and play accompaniments • Hear tremolo	• Sing in unison and canon • *Play unpitched accompaniment in canon*	• Sing melody and harmony parts
• Recognize melodic motives	• Hear piece with repeated A and B sections	• Sing song with 3 verses, refrain	• Follow listening map with introduction, repeated A and B sections	• Distinguish predominant rhythm patterns in A and B sections
• Hear music by Michael Praetorius and see Renaissance instrument pictures	• Hear music by Percy Grainger	• Sing folk song of Newfoundland • Listen to Mexican folk music	• Sing Hungarian melody	• Learn Mexican folk dance

SKILLS		LESSON 1 CORE p.108	LESSON 2 CORE p.112	LESSON 3 p.118
CREATION AND PERFORMANCE	Singing	• Sing repeated notes, steps, skips • Sing call-and-response song	• *Practice good tone quality and intonation* • *Sing 2 ostinatos in harmony* • Sing songs in major and minor • *Sing phrases slowly*	• *Practice singing various dynamics* • Speak poem with dynamics • Sing dynamics
	Playing	• *Play Orff orchestration*	• *Play Orff orchestration*	• *Add unpitched instruments*
	Moving	• Draw melodic shape in air • Change range of movement to show melodic movement	• Move to show division of beat • Move with beat • *Conduct in 2*	• Pat with beat • Change body design to show crescendo • Create movement interpretation of poem
	Improvising/ Creating			• Create speech and movement interpretation of poem
NOTATION	Reading	• *Read rhythm notation* • See symbols for and sing A B sections • Use graphic notation of melodic movement	• See dynamics in notation • Follow listening map	• See dynamics in notation
	Writing			• *Devise graphic notation for dynamics*
PERCEPTION AND ANALYSIS	Listening/ Describing/ Analyzing	• Listen for melodic movement • Find same, similar, different phrases	• Listen for rhythmic motive • Distinguish between 2 and 3 equal divisions of beat • Compare pizzicato and arco	• Identify dynamics

TECHNOLOGY

SHARE THE MUSIC VIDEOS

Use videos to reinforce, extend, and enrich learning.
· Lesson 3, p. 118: Signing, Grades 3–6 (The Eagle); Musical Expression (dynamics)
· Lesson 6, pp. 132–134: Musical Expression (dynamics); Making a Music Video (harmony); The Mariachi Tradition (Mexican folk music)
· Lesson 8, p. 140: The Mariachi Tradition (Mexican folk music)

MUSIC WITH *MIDI*

MIDI technology allows students to manipulate musical elements and make musical decisions with this song:
· Lesson 6, p. 132: I's the B'y

MUSICTIME™

This notational software develops students' music reading and writing skills through activities correlated to these lessons:
· Lesson 5, Project 1 (create rhythm patterns)
· Lesson 7, Project 2 (use Latin American sounds)
· Lesson 9, Project 3 (create an interlude)

OVERVIEW

LESSON 4 CORE p.124	LESSON 5 CORE p.128	LESSON 6 p.132	LESSON 7 p.136	LESSON 8 p.140
• *Sing jazz scat syllables with staccato accents* • *Create and sing solo verses*	• *Practice singing open vowel sounds*	• Sing harmonic accompaniment pattern • *Sing phrases slowly*	• Sing familiar song with altered words • Make varying vocal sounds • Sing in unison and canon • *Practice singing various dynamics*	• Sing harmonic pattern with *do* and *so₁*
• *Play keyboard accompaniment* • *Play melodic motives* • *Play Orff accompaniment*	• *Play Orff accompaniment* • Create and play unpitched ostinatos	• *Play harmonic accompaniments*	• *Create sound effects using tremolo, staccato, glissando on keyboards* • *Play unpitched accompaniment in canon*	
• Move to melodic motives • Create motion patterns	• *Create movement for rhythms in* § • *Move to song in* § • Create 8-beat movement ostinatos • Walk pathways	• Move to show harmonic changes • *Review movement to song*	• *Design movement to reflect dynamic changes*	• Move to show rhythms • Create back and forth movements; skip, gallop, slide • Learn Mexican folk dance
• *Create and sing solo verses* • Create motion patterns	• *Create movement for rhythms in* § • Create 8-beat movement ostinatos • Create and notate unpitched ostinatos	• *Write new lyrics*	• Devise graphic notation for sounds, dynamic levels • Create composition with varying sounds and dynamics • *Create sound effects on keyboards* • *Design movement*	• *Write lyrics for harmony part* • Create back and forth movements
• Read pitches C D E F G on staff	• Identify § meter • Read patterns in § meter • Sing song from notation in § • Perform ostinato notated in §	• Identify key signature, flat • Use graphic notation of harmony and beat	• Compare graphic notation and standard dynamic symbols • Clap rhythm from notation in § • Follow listening map • Identify and follow dynamic markings in notation	• Read rhythms in § • *Review bar lines*
	• *Write* § *rhythm patterns* • Create and notate unpitched ostinatos		• Devise graphic notation for sounds, dynamic levels	• *Write bar lines in* § *meter*
• Use inner hearing for section of song • Recognize melodic motives • *Analyze how piece's dynamics influenced impressions*	• Listen for theme in §	• Evaluate harmonic accompaniments • Listen for chords based on *do* and *so₁* • Predict harmonic changes	• Listen for and evaluate dynamic changes • Compare graphic notation and standard dynamic symbols	• Identify song from rhythm • Listen for beat divisions • Distinguish predominant rhythm patterns in A and B sections

UNIT 3 PLANNER

MUSIC ACE™

Music Ace reinforces musical concepts and provides ear-training opportunities for students.
- Lesson 1, p. 104: Lesson 6 (steps, skips); Lesson 18 (steps)
- Lesson 3, p. 118: Lesson 12 (loud/soft)
- Lesson 4, p. 124: Lessons 7 & 8 (pitch names)
- Lesson 6, p. 132: Lessons 20, 21, & 22 (sharps/flats); Lesson 23 (key signature)
- Lesson 7, p. 136: Lesson 12 (loud/soft)

NEW! MUSIC ACE 2™

Music Ace 2™ introduces basic rhythm concepts and furthers the melodic and harmonic concepts covered in Music Ace.

THEME:
JUST IMAGINE

> **FOCUS** Music can help us imagine many feelings and ideas.
>
> **OBJECTIVE** To set the stage for Unit 3
>
> **MATERIALS**
> I Wonder (poem)
> Oh, Susanna — CD3:3
> Oh, Susanna
> (performance mix) — CD10:14

INTRODUCE THE THEME

1. Discuss the theme. "In this unit, you will sing and listen to music that expresses a variety of feelings. The words of a song may express feelings all by themselves but the melodies also affect how we feel when we listen to or sing the song." Have students:

• Name a song they know that expresses a feeling or helps them expand their imagination.

2. Introduce "I Wonder." "If you could be a bird, a fish, or any animal, what animal would you like to be? Listen to the poem 'I Wonder' to find out what this person is imagining." Have students:

• Listen as a volunteer reads "I Wonder" and listen for the surprise ending.

• Share what kind of animal they would like to be.

U N I T 3

Just Imagine

104

UNIT 3 THEME PROJECTS

Through the songs in this unit students will have a chance to walk in other people's shoes, so to speak. They will learn how other people feel in particular situations.

CREATE A BOOK OF FEELINGS Have students discuss the feelings expressed or implied in the songs that they sing. For example, "I Don't Care If the Rain Comes Down" (page 108) and "Come and Sing Together" (page 115) express joy; "Pay Me My Money Down" (page 111) expresses anger; "The Eagle" (page 118) expresses feelings of freedom; "I's the B'y" (page 132) expresses pride in one's accomplishments. Have them find another way to express these same feelings, such as a painting, a drawing, a poem, or a dance or movement piece. Compile a book with students' work. (If any students choose to create a dance or movement piece, you may wish to photograph it for the book.) *(Lessons 1, 2, 3, and 6)*

I WONDER

I wonder how it feels to fly
high in the sky . . .
    like a bird.
I wonder how it feels to sit
on a nest . . .
    like a bird.
I wonder how it feels to catch
a worm in the morning . . .
    like a bird.
I feel funny . . .
maybe he is wondering
    how it feels to be like a man.

—Earl Thompson (Yakima)

Meet the Poet A Native American of the Yakima (yæk ə mɔ) nation, poet Earl Thompson (b. 1950) grew up on the Yakima reservation in the state of Washington. He studied at various colleges, but his most important teacher was his grandfather, who passed along to him the oral traditions of his people. Both Yakima and non-Native culture influence his work. He compares himself to the trickster of Native American lore, Coyote, who is said to have fashioned the Yakima people out of stones. "As Coyote used stones to create," writes Thompson, "I use words to survive in harmony with my inner and outer natures."

Social Studies Link The Yakima nation brings together fourteen allied tribes living in Washington, Oregon, and Idaho. Their name may come from the word *Yaka* (meaning "bear") in the native Columbia River plateau language. Traditionally, the Yakima lived in fishing villages around the Columbia River and its tributaries, with salmon as their staple food. In 1959 they were settled on a reservation in Toppenish, Washington, that remains the seat of tribal government and home to most Yakima today. Contemporary Yakima work hard to preserve their traditions while adapting to the demands of an industrialized society.

THROUGH AN ANIMAL'S EYES Have students discuss what it would feel like to be some of the animals that they have sung about, such as an eagle, a speckled bird, or one of the animals mentioned in "One More River" (page 112). Have them think about which animal they would like to be and why. Have them research the animal and then write an essay or poem about how it would feel to be the animal of their choice. Include these pieces in the Book of Feelings. *(Lessons 1, 2, and 3)*

WHAT DO FEELINGS LOOK LIKE? Have students draw or paint an abstract design that depicts a feeling such as joy, sadness, or anger. Have them think about what colors they would use to express a particular feeling and what kind of design would help communicate it. The pictures can accompany the written pieces in the Book of Feelings. *(Lessons 1–8)*

3. Introduce "Oh, Susanna" CD3:3. "Music can help us stretch our imaginations. The song 'Oh, Susanna' tells of one person's unusual trip." Have students:

• Read page 106, then read the words of the song to locate nonsense phrases.

• Listen to the song.

• Listen again and sing along as they are able.

4. Set the stage for Unit 3. Have students:

• Think again about their responses to how music can express feelings.

• Briefly look through the unit and share what they can imagine being. (For example: an elephant in "One More River," page 112, or an eagle in "The Eagle," page 118.)

• Sing the unit theme song, "Oh, Susanna."

Have you ever read about Pecos Bill, Paul Bunyan, or John Henry? They are all characters in traditional American stories called "tall tales." These stories stretch the truth just for fun. In a similar way, the composer used his imagination to make this song entertaining.

106

UNIT 3 MUSIC PROJECT:

This project will give students further practice in creating rhythms and notating them accurately. Have the class follow these steps after the appropriate lessons. This will help them successfully complete the "Create" activity in Lesson 9.

1 WRITE A SHORT PATTERN Have partners pat or clap with the beat to create an ostinato in duple meter. Then, using the words *hippo, elephant*, and *cross*, have partners combine the words to speak 4-beat patterns alternately

over the ostinato, for a total of eight beats. Have them choose their favorite combination of words and write them down, storing the piece of paper in a folder.
(After Lesson 2)

2 EXTEND AND REST IN THE PATTERN Have partners extend their patterns from to eight beats per person, being sure each part sounds finished on the eighth beat. Encourage them to insert a rest if they feel it fits.
(After Lesson 3)

Program Idea:
A Fantastic Invention

Have students create dialogue to go with this scene of an inventor's workshop. The inventor has put together a machine that can turn a person into someone or something else, and can even transport a person to another place or time. Some ideas are given below.

• The machine transforms a sunny day into a rainy day. Song: "I Don't Care If the Rain Comes Down" (page 108)

• The machine beams them to Mexico. Song and game: "La pájara pinta" (page 110); dance "La raspa" (page 134)

• The machine transforms them into cargo ship workers. Song: "Pay Me My Money Down" (page 111)

• The machine transforms them into Newfoundland fishers. Song: "I's the B'y" (page 132)

• The machine beams them to Scotland. Song: "Over the Sea to Skye" (page 149)

• The machine transports them back in time to pioneer days. Song: "When I First Came to This Land" (page 148)

CREATE AN EIGHT-BEAT PATTERN

3 NOTATE AND PERFORM THE PATTERN Have students refer to page 147. Again using the words *hippo, elephant*, and *cross*, have partners create a new eight-beat pattern. Guide them to write the pattern in eight boxes using the notation taught on that page. Then have students perform their patterns for each other. *(After Lesson 5)*

RELATED ARTS **MOVEMENT** THEATER **VISUAL ARTS**

LESSON PLANNER

FOCUS Pitch—repeated notes, steps, skips

OBJECTIVES
OBJECTIVE 1 Draw melodic shape in the air while singing (tested)
OBJECTIVE 2 Indicate whether a melody moves mainly by repeated notes, steps, or skips (tested)

MATERIALS
Recordings
I Don't Care If the Rain Comes
  Down   **CD3:4**
Recorded Lesson: Melodic
  Movement   **CD3:5**
La pájara pinta   **CD3:6**
Pay Me My Money Down   **CD3:7**

Resources
Resource Master 3 • 1 (practice)
Orff Orchestration O • 6 (I Don't Care If
  the Rain Comes Down)
Recorder Master R • 9 (pitches G A B)

VOCABULARY
repeated notes, step, skip

    ▶ = **BASIC PROGRAM**

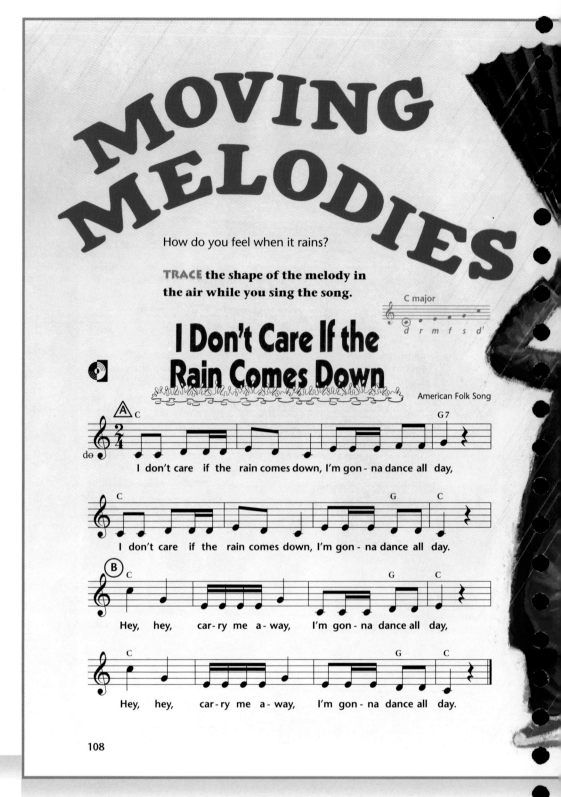

MOVING MELODIES

How do you feel when it rains?

TRACE the shape of the melody in the air while you sing the song.

C major

d r m f s d'

I Don't Care If the Rain Comes Down

American Folk Song

A C   G7

I don't care if the rain comes down, I'm gon-na dance all day,

C   G   C

I don't care if the rain comes down, I'm gon-na dance all day.

B C   G   C

Hey, hey, car-ry me a-way, I'm gon-na dance all day,

C   G   C

Hey, hey, car-ry me a-way, I'm gon-na dance all day.

108

MEETING **INDIVIDUAL** NEEDS

ALTERNATE TEACHING STRATEGY

OBJECTIVE 1 Write the lyrics of "I Don't Care If the Rain Comes Down" on the board. Have the class listen to the song and determine which phrases are the same or different melodically. Sing each phrase slowly and have students describe its melodic shape and sing it back, drawing its shape with their arms as you or a student draws the contour line above the lyrics.

ENRICHMENT: *Rhythm Reading*

"I Don't Care If the Rain Comes Down" can be read using the rhythms learned in Unit 2, Lesson 4, on page 72.

MOVEMENT: *Range of Movement* 🕴 MOVEMENT

The term *range of movement* refers to the size of a movement or to the amount of space we occupy as we move. Range can refer to locomotor movement (such as walking or skipping) or nonlocomotor movement (such as in-place twisting or arm waving).

Melodies can move in three ways.

Some move with **repeated notes,** using one pitch that is repeated.

▬	▬	▬	▬	▬	▬	▬	▬
I	don't	care	if	the	rain	comes	down

They can move by **steps.** Each note is followed by a pitch just above or below it.

I don't care if the rain comes down

When a melody moves by **skips,** each note is followed by a pitch two or more steps away.

I don't care if the rain comes down

MOVE to the repeated notes, steps, and skips in these melodies.

Unit 3 *Just Imagine* **109**

"Why is it important to think about how others are feeling?" Have students:

▶ • Discuss the importance of understanding others and treating them with respect.

"Today we'll sing songs that express a variety of feelings. A song's words may express feelings all by themselves, but the melodies also affect how we feel when we listen to or sing the song."

2 DEVELOP

1. Introduce "I Don't Care If the Rain Comes Down" CD3:4. Show melodic shape. Have students:

▶ • Read page 108 and listen to the song.

▶ • Discuss their feelings when it rains and the feelings expressed in the song, then sing the song.

▶ • Sing again and create new verses by substituting words for *dance* such as *sing, sleep, play.*

OBJECTIVE 1 Informal Assessment

▶ • Sing the song drawing the melodic shape in the air with their arms.

• Describe the contour, finding same, similar, and different phrases.

2. Identify repeated notes, steps, and skips. Have students:

▶ • Read about ways melodies move.

Recorded Lesson CD3:5

▶ • Listen to "Melodic Movement," and walk in place to a melody with repeated notes, take small steps through shared space to a stepwise melody, and take larger steps to a melody with skips. (See *Movement* on the bottom of page 108 for more practice in range of movement.)

(Optional: Use **Resource Master 3 · 1** for practice recognizing melodic skips, steps, and repeated notes.)

Increasing students' awareness of the size of their movements helps them relate themselves to the space around them. Explore range of movement by asking students to open and close just their hands and fingers. This is a small movement. Now ask them to expand their range of movement by opening and closing their arms, hands, and fingers. The same can be experienced with swinging arms from side to side, first using a small amount of space, then using more energy and space to create a larger movement. Likewise, as in *Develop 2* above, students can walk in place, walk through shared space using very small steps, and walk using very large steps.

MUSIC BUILDS MATH SKILLS 123

Geometry Tracing the shape of the melody in the air while singing "I Don't Care If the Rain Comes Down" reinforces spatial sense.

ORFF: *"I Don't Care If the Rain Comes Down"*
See **O · 6** in *Orchestrations for Orff Instruments.*

UNIT THREE
LESSON 1

continued from previous page

3. Introduce "La pájara pinta" CD3:6. Listen to the melodic movement. Have students:

▶ • Listen to the entire song on page 110.

• Listen again, this time for repeated notes, steps, and skips.

3 APPLY

Introduce "Pay Me My Money Down" CD3:7. Identify melodic movement. Have students:

▶ • Read about and listen to the song.

▶ • Discuss the possible emotions of the singer. (worried, afraid, angry, jealous)

▶ • Sing the song with the recording, noticing repeated notes, steps, and skips.

OBJECTIVE 2 Informal Assessment

▶ • With eyes closed, hold up one, two, or three fingers to show whether the melody moves mostly by repeated notes, steps, or skips. (two—steps)

Listen for repeated notes, steps, and skips in the melody of this song. G major

La pájara pinta
THE SPECKLED BIRD

Mexican Folk Song
English Version
by MMH

Spanish: Y es-ta-ba la pá-ja-ra pin-ta sen-ta-da en su ver-de li-
Pronunciation: yes ta βa la pa xa ɾa pin ta sen ta ðaen su βeɾ ðe li
English: A bright speck-led bird — was sit-ting up-on a green lem-on

món. — Con el pi-co re-co-ge las flo-res, Con el
mon kon el pi ko ɾe ko xe las flo ɾes kon el
branch. With her beak — she gath-ered flow-ers, with her

pi-co re-co-ge el a-mor. — Ay, ay, ay, ay! ¿En
pi ko ɾe ko xel a moɾ ai ai ai ai en
beak — she gath-ered love, — Ay, ay, ay, ay — Then

dón-de la en-cuen-tro yo? — Con el pi-co re-co-ge las
don de laen kwen tro yo kon el pi ko ɾe ko xe las
tell me where will it be? — With her beak — she gath-ered

flo- res, Con el pi-co re-co-ge el a- mor.
flo ɾes kon el pi ko ɾe ko xel a moɾ
flow- ers, with her beak — she gath- ered love.

110 MOVING MELODIES

MEETING **INDIVIDUAL** NEEDS

ALTERNATE TEACHING STRATEGY

OBJECTIVE 2 Stack resonator bells (C D E F G A) at the board so that students can see them, or have six students stand at the front of the class, each holding a bell in ascending order from left to right. Play each phrase of "Pay Me My Money Down," and have them describe the movement from pitch to pitch. (Phrase 1—skips; Phrases 2–4—steps)

PRONUNCIATION: *"La pájara pinta"*

ɑ f**a**ther   e ch**a**otic   i b**ee**   o **o**bey
u m**oo**n   β b without lips touching   ð **the**
ɾ flipped r   x slightly guttural h, *Spanish* ba**j**o

MULTICULTURAL PERSPECTIVES: *Circle Game*

"La pájara pinta," a traditional children's game song, holds a place in Mexican culture similar to that of "London Bridge" or "Ring-Around-a-Rosy" in Anglo-American culture. In one version, children hold hands in a circle, and one

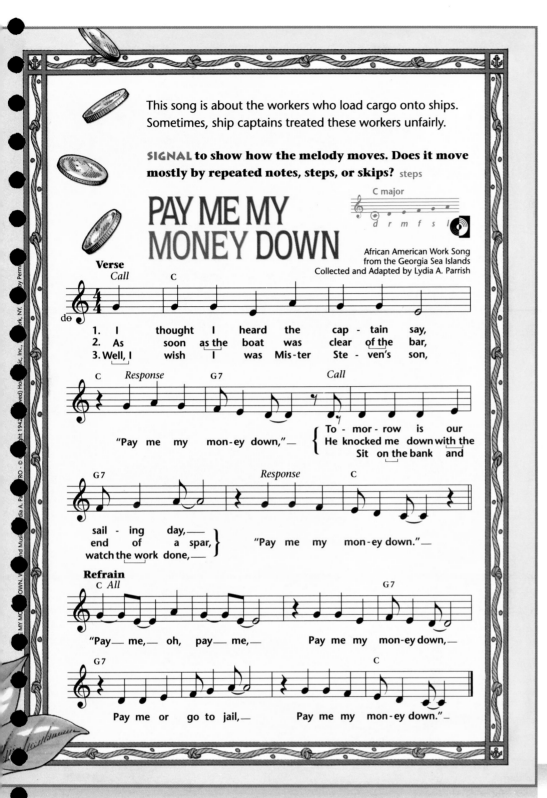

This song is about the workers who load cargo onto ships. Sometimes, ship captains treated these workers unfairly.

SIGNAL to show how the melody moves. Does it move mostly by repeated notes, steps, or skips? steps

PAY ME MY MONEY DOWN

C major

d r m f s l

African American Work Song
from the Georgia Sea Islands
Collected and Adapted by Lydia A. Parrish

Verse
Call

1. I thought I heard the cap - tain say,
2. As soon as the boat was clear of the bar,
3. Well, I wish I was Mis - ter Ste - ven's son,

Response

"Pay me my mon-ey down,"—

{ To - mor - row is our
He knocked me down with the
Sit on the bank and

Call

Response

sail - ing day,—
end of a spar,
watch the work done,—

} "Pay me my mon-ey down."—

Refrain
All

"Pay— me,— oh, pay— me,— Pay me my mon-ey down,—

Pay me or go to jail,— Pay me my mon-ey down."—

4 CLOSE

"What are three ways pitches of a melody can move?" (by repeated notes, steps, or skips) "What were some of the feelings you heard expressed in the music today?" (happiness, love, anger, and so forth) Have students:

▶ • Form two groups, and sing "Pay Me My Money Down" as a call-and-response song.

LESSON SUMMARY

Informal Assessment In this lesson, students:

OBJECTIVE 1 Drew in the air the melodic shape of "I Don't Care If the Rain Comes Down" while singing the song.

OBJECTIVE 2 Signaled to show stepwise movement in "Pay Me My Money Down."

National Standards for Music Education
Ia Sing accurately, on pitch and in rhythm.
Ib Sing with appropriate dynamics, phrasing, and interpretation.
Ic Sing memorized repertoire from diverse genres and cultures.

MORE MUSIC: Reinforcement

More Songs to Read, page 355 (melodic movement)
"Singin' in the Rain," page 100 (melodic shape; rain)
"Rainfall," page 103 (rain)
"A Tragic Story," page 197 (melodic movement by steps and skips)
"Somewhere in My Memory," page 327 (melodic movement by skips)
"Suk san wan pi mai," page 332 (melodic movement by steps; New Year)

child stands in the middle and acts as the "speckled bird." As the circle moves around, the speckled bird has to declare his/her love to one of the other children, who then becomes the speckled bird.

MULTICULTURAL PERSPECTIVES: *A Work Song*

"Pay Me My Money Down" was sung by African American stevedores (dock workers) from the Georgia Sea Islands to protest their treatment at ports in mainland Georgia. The work of the stevedores was often back breaking.

They had to load cargo using little or no machinery—only ropes and pulleys. Songs helped to pass the time and gave rhythm to the work. This song also conveyed a demand. In the Gullah dialect of the Sea Islands, the stevedores were saying "Pay me my money *now*," in hopes that the ship owners would hear and be embarrassed into giving them their pay. *Mr. Steven's son* is the boss's son, watching over the workers to make sure they did their jobs. When the Georgia Sea Island Singers perform this song, they grunt at certain points and make a rope-pulling motion, reminders of the time the song accompanied labor.

ACROSS *the*

SCIENCE

COLLECTING RAINDROPS

"I Don't Care If the Rain Comes Down"

GROUP   **15 MIN OR LESS**

MATERIALS: pie pans, flour, strainers, metric rulers, graph paper, cardboard, colored paper

Students can collect raindrops:

- Sift flour through a strainer into a pie pan. Place the pan of flour in the rain just for a second until a few drops have landed in the flour.
- Put the flour (and raindrops) into the strainer using the cardboard as a scoop.
- Shake the strainer, letting dry flour fall onto the second pie plate. Shake until all loose flour has fallen through.
- The dough balls remaining in the strainer are your raindrops. Put them on the colored paper.
- With a pencil tip, group the drops by size: 0–1 mm, 1–2 mm, 2–3 mm, etc. Use the ruler to determine the size of the drops.
- Draw a graph relating the size of raindrops to the number collected.

If you live in a dry area, use a water atomizer and squirt from a close distance and then from a farther distance into a pan.

COMPREHENSION STRATEGIES: Making observations, drawing conclusions

ART

PAINTING

"La pájara pinta"

GROUP/INDIVIDUAL   **30 MIN OR LONGER**

MATERIALS: brown paper bags, paints

Have students work in groups to discuss what the speckled bird in the song might look like. Have members of each group brainstorm ideas. One member records ideas.

Each student makes a drawing showing how he or she imagines the speckled bird. Give students a piece of brown paper torn from a grocery sack. (The brown paper is used to imitate Mexican bark painting.) Then have them use bright paints to add color to their birds.

Have students vote on the "Most Original," "Most Detailed," "Most Realistic," "Most Colorful," and any other category they wish to include.

COMPREHENSION STRATEGY: Visualizing

CURRICULUM

LANGUAGE ARTS

JOB APPLICATIONS

"Pay Me My Money Down"

INDIVIDUAL   **15–30 MIN**

Use this song to introduce the idea of qualifications for jobs. In groups, have students think of jobs that once were associated with women and jobs once associated with men. (women: nurse, secretary, house-keeper; men: doctor, lawyer, firefighter) Have each student list a number of jobs and choose one for a male and one for a female and write a resume for *each* position. Have them consider that a woman can have the necessary qualifications for a job associated with men, and vice versa.

Have each group share its viewpoints with the rest of the class.

COMPREHENSION STRATEGY: Expressing points of view

SCIENCE

WIND SPEED

"Pay Me My Money Down"

INDIVIDUAL   **30 MIN OR LONGER**
MATERIALS: string, newspaper

Ask students why the strength of the wind is essential when navigating a sailboat. On several successive days, have students go outside to perform a wind experiment.

Provide each student with a piece of string that is held at arm's length. The higher the string flies, the stronger the wind. Keep a record of the results and check a local daily newspaper to find the wind speed on each day the ob-servation is made.

One way to estimate wind speed is to use the Beaufort scale. This scale lists wind speeds (in knots—knot is about 1.15 miles or 1,852 meters per hour) that produce certain effects.

COMPREHENSION STRATEGIES: Making obser-vations, using a chart

BEAUFORT WIND SCALE

#	OBSERVATION	CONDITIONS	WIND SPEED
0	Calm	Smoke rises vertically	0 (knots)
2	Slight breeze	Wind felt on face	5
4	Moderate breeze	Dust, small branches move	12
6	Strong breeze	Large branches move	22
8	Fresh gale	Twigs broken	33
10	Whole gale	Trees uprooted	45
12	Hurricane	Widespread damage	60

UNIT THREE
LESSON 2

RELATED ARTS | MOVEMENT | THEATER | VISUAL ARTS |

LESSON PLANNER

FOCUS Duration, two and three sounds to a beat

OBJECTIVES
OBJECTIVE 1 Pat two equal sounds to a beat with a song
OBJECTIVE 2 Recognize where the division of equal sounds per beat changes from two to three and three to two (tested)

MATERIALS
Recordings
One More River   CD3:8
Come and Sing Together (unison)   CD3:9
Listening: Scherzo from String
    Quartet in B Minor (excerpt) by
    T. Carreño   CD3:10

Instrument triangle

Resources
Signing Master S • 4 • 3 (One More River)
Orff Orchestration O • 7 (One More River)
Orff Orchestration O • 8 (Come and Sing Together)
Listening Map Transparency T • 5 (Scherzo)
Recorder Master R • 10 (pitches G A B)

▶ = **BASIC PROGRAM**

AN OLD STORY

This song is based on a Biblical story. Noah saves some animals from a flood by loading them onto a boat called an ark.

PAT the rhythm of the words and sing the motive *There's one more river to cross.* Then sing the whole song and create more verses.

Pentatonic
s, d r m s l

ONE MORE RIVER

Nineteenth Century College Song

Verse F

1. Old   No-ah,   he   built   him-self an   ark;
2. The   an - i - mals went   in   one   by   one;
3. The   an - i - mals went   in   two   by   two;
4. The   an - i - mals went   in   three by three;
5. The   an - i - mals went   in   four   by four;

There's one more riv-er to

He   built   it   out   of   hick'-ry bark;
The   el - e - phant chew-ing a   car-a- way bun;
cross. The rhi - no - cer - os and the kang - a - roo;   There's
The   bear,   the   bug, and   the   bum - ble-bee;
The   hip - po - po-ta-mus stuck in the   door;

112

MEETING **INDIVIDUAL** NEEDS

VOCAL DEVELOPMENT: *Vocal Role Models*

Singing in tune and with good tone quality requires that students focus their attention and energy. Let them hear examples of fine singing voices of children, either through recordings or by having other students serve as vocal models. Ask two or three volunteers who sing well to sing "One More River" for the class, then have everyone join the singing and imitate the sound of the model students.

BACKGROUND: *"One More River"*

College songs were staples of the glee club repertory earlier in this century and in centuries past. They were well known and fun to sing. "One More River" recalls a spiritual in form and content but not in its lighthearted tone. It refers to the Biblical account of Noah and the flood (Genesis: Ch. 6–8), and to the Jordan, the chief river of Palestine, which is not in the story of Noah.

one more riv-er to cross. There's one more riv-er, And

that wide riv-er is Jor-dan, There's one more

riv-er, There's one more riv-er to cross.

6. The animals went in five by five;
   There's one more river to cross.
   "It's raining," said Noah, "so look alive!"
   There's one more river to cross.
   Refrain

7. The animals went in six by six; . . .
   The monkeys were up to monkey tricks; . . .
   Refrain

8. The animals went in sev'n by sev'n; . . .
   The rabbit said, "I wish I had driv'n."; . . .
   Refrain

9. The animals went in eight by eight; . . .
   "That's 'nuff," said Noah, and slammed
   the gate! . . .
   Refrain

10. And as they talked of this and that; . . .
    The ark, it bumped on Ararat; . . .
    Refrain

1 GET SET

"Say these words with me: *There's one more river to cross.* Let's pat the beat as we listen for these words in this song, then stop patting and raise a hand each time you hear them." (Play the first verse-refrain of "One More River" **CD3:8**. Words occur three times.) "This pattern is a motive in the song. A motive is a pattern that occurs often." Have students:

▶ • Clap the rhythm of the motive.

▶ • Listen to Verse 1 and walk through shared space with the beat, clapping the rhythm of the motive each time it occurs.

"Today you'll learn more about the rhythms in this song, and listen for them in other songs."

2 DEVELOP

1. Learn "One More River." Have students:

▶ • Read page 112, discuss the text of the song, and listen to all the verses, singing the motive each time.

• Pat the rhythm of all the words of Verse 1, and sing the motive.

▶ • Sing the entire song.

▶ • Make up their own verses for the next time they sing the song.

SIGNING: *"One More River"*

Signing Master S • 4 • 3 has sign language for this song.

MOVEMENT: *One and Two Sounds to a Beat*

1. Have students practice walking with the quarter-note beat while clapping two eighth notes to a beat. Give a signal for them to reverse, jogging eighth notes while clapping with the beat.

2. Have students walk with the beat in a clockwise circle. Invite five or six students to jog eighth notes outside the circle, going counterclockwise. Ask how their range of movement differs. (They have to take larger jogging steps to cover the larger outer circle.) Have students change circles until everyone has moved to two sounds to a beat using larger, faster steps.

3. Try this activity with three eighth notes to a beat.

ORFF: *"One More River"*

See **O • 7** in *Orchestrations for Orff Instruments.*

continued from previous page

2. Explore divisions of the beat in "One More River." Have students:

• Speak and clap the motive on page 114.

• Form two groups, one group walking with the beat through shared space, while the other group stands still and claps the motive. Then switch parts.

• Clap the motive while walking with the beat through space.

• Explore the division of the beat on page 114.

DISCOVER BEAT DIVISIONS

Clap this motive while you walk with the beat. How many sounds are there to each beat? first beat: 2; second beat: 3; third beat: 1; fourth beat: none.

| one | more | riv - | er | to | cross |

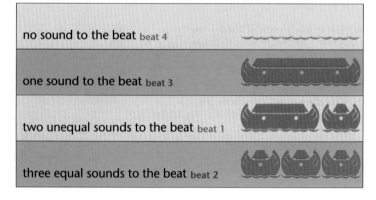

The arks show the number of sounds to each beat.

MATCH each row to one of the beats shown above.

no sound to the beat beat 4	
one sound to the beat beat 3	
two unequal sounds to the beat beat 1	
three equal sounds to the beat beat 2	

CLAP the rhythms of these words. Then match them with the patterns of arks.

caraway bun
bottom
stuck in the door
bottom

kangaroo
top
one by one
top

114

MEETING **INDIVIDUAL** NEEDS

ALTERNATE TEACHING STRATEGY

OBJECTIVE 1 Bounce-catch a ball as the students speak and pat the phrase *"river to, river to."* Have the students continue to pat as you speak "Come and Sing Together." Pat the two equal eighth-note rhythms of *"shining, shining"* as you speak. Ask which rhythm is the rhythm of this song. (*"shining"*)

MUSIC BUILDS MATH SKILLS

Number and Operations Arranging the pitch syllables in order from low to high relates to ordering numbers.

MOVEMENT: *"Come and Sing Together"*

Formation: lines or circles, standing

Measures 1–2: Move with the beat—step L, stamp R, step R, stamp L, step L, stamp R twice, rest. **Measures 3–4:** Repeat sequence, beginning with R. **Measures 5–6:** Raise hands while clapping

Measures 7–8: Lower hands, clapping the same rhythm. **Measure 9:** Kick with the beat—R, L, R, L. **Measures 10–11:** Repeat Measures 1–2.

Many beats in "Come and Sing Together" are divided into two parts.

LISTEN to discover if the beats are divided equally or unequally.

D minor

s, l, t, d r m l t

COME AND SING TOGETHER

Hungarian Melody

If you'd dance then you must have boots of shin-ing leath-er,

Mon-ey in your pock-et-book, in your hat a feath-er.

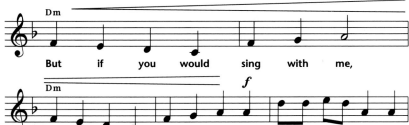

But if you would sing with me,

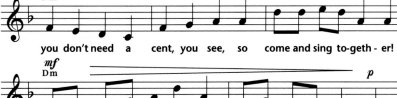

you don't need a cent, you see, so come and sing to-geth-er!

If you'd dance then you must have boots of shin-ing leath-er!

115

3. Introduce "Come and Sing Together" (unison) CD3:9. Identify two equal sounds per beat. Have students:

• Listen to "Come and Sing Together" and discuss with a partner whether the beats are divided into two equal or unequal sounds. (equal)

OBJECTIVE 1 Informal Assessment

• Listen again and pat two equal divisions of the beat on their knees using alternate hands in time with the song.

▶ • Read the text of the song and discuss what it expresses.

▶ • Sing the song.

EXTRA HELP: *Pitch Practice—Steps and Skips*

Review melodic steps and skips with "Come and Sing Together." Students sing the melody on *lai*, drawing the contour in the air. Have them locate the skips in the first two phrases. (*you must have; pocketbook*) Then divide the class into two groups. One sings *in your hat a feather* as an ostinato while the other sings *you must have* as an ostinato.

ORFF: *"Come and Sing Together"*

Practice these parts with body percussion: clap the triangle part, pat the tambourine part, and stamp the whip part. Also see **O · 8** in *Orchestrations for Orff Instruments*.

UNIT THREE
LESSON 2

continued from previous page

3 APPLY

Introduce Scherzo from String Quartet in B Minor (excerpt) CD3:10. Listen for changes in the division of the beat. Have students:

▶ • Read about the composer on page 116.

▶ • Speak *river to, river to,* patting three sounds to the beat on the left knee, then change to *shining, shining,* patting two sounds to the beat on the right knee.

▶ • Follow the listening map, listening for the change of divisions of the beat from two to three and three to two equal sounds, patting these words as needed. (Optional: Use **Listening Map Transparency T • 5**.)

OBJECTIVE 2 Informal Assessment

• With eyes closed, listen again and signal with two or three fingers to show when they hear changes of beat division from two to three and three to two. (two, three, two, three, two, three)

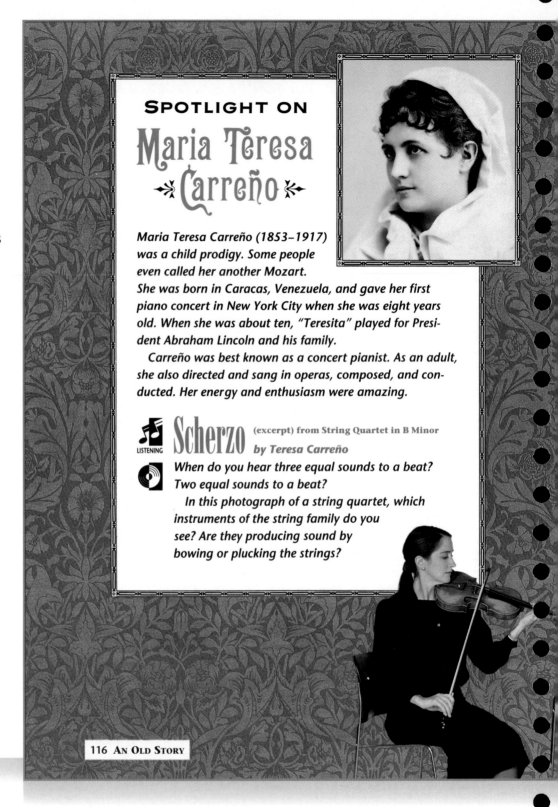

SPOTLIGHT ON
Maria Teresa
⊰ Carreño ⊱

Maria Teresa Carreño (1853–1917) was a child prodigy. Some people even called her another Mozart.

She was born in Caracas, Venezuela, and gave her first piano concert in New York City when she was eight years old. When she was about ten, "Teresita" played for President Abraham Lincoln and his family.

Carreño was best known as a concert pianist. As an adult, she also directed and sang in operas, composed, and conducted. Her energy and enthusiasm were amazing.

LISTENING ♪ **Scherzo** (excerpt) from String Quartet in B Minor
by Teresa Carreño

When do you hear three equal sounds to a beat? Two equal sounds to a beat?

In this photograph of a string quartet, which instruments of the string family do you see? Are they producing sound by bowing or plucking the strings?

116 AN OLD STORY

MEETING **INDIVIDUAL** NEEDS

ALTERNATE TEACHING STRATEGY

OBJECTIVE 2 Have students quietly pat two sounds to the beat while thinking *shining* as they listen to Scherzo. Direct them to raise a hand when they find their patting pattern no longer fits the music.

BIOGRAPHY: *Maria Teresa Carreño*

Maria Teresa Carreño (ma ɾi a   te ɾe sa   ka ɾe nyo), 1853–1917—usually called Teresa—won acclaim at a very young age as a concert pianist thanks to her dazzling tech-

nique and sensitive interpretations. Throughout her career, she displayed considerable talent as a composer as well. Full of challenging passages to perform, the music she wrote reflects her skill and experience as a performer. Her scores show the influence of composers in whose work she specialized as a performer, such as Chopin (sho pɛ̃) and Liszt (lɪst). A person of great energy and ambition, she led a rich and diverse musical life, traveled the world over, and was much in demand as a teacher.

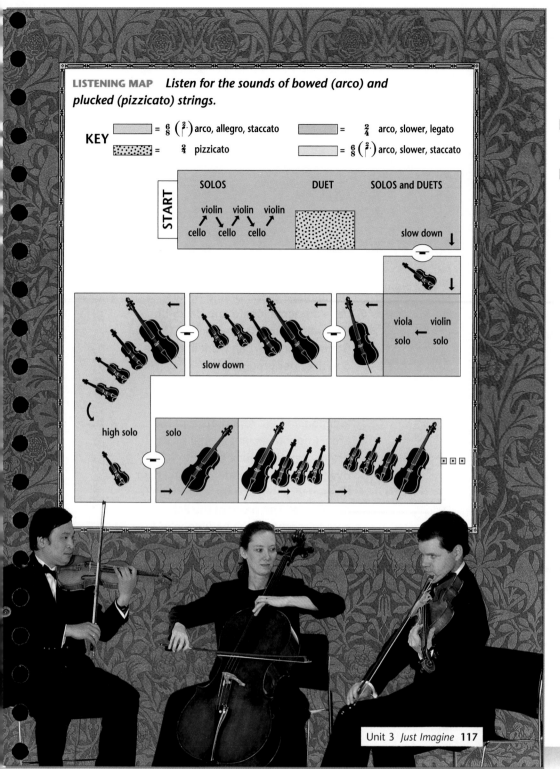

LISTENING MAP *Listen for the sounds of bowed (arco) and plucked (pizzicato) strings.*

KEY:
- ▬ = $\frac{6}{8}$ ($\frac{2}{?}$) arco, allegro, staccato
- ▦ = $\frac{2}{4}$ arco, slower, legato
- ▨ = $\frac{2}{4}$ pizzicato
- ▬ = $\frac{6}{8}$ ($\frac{2}{?}$) arco, slower, staccato

START

| SOLOS | DUET | SOLOS and DUETS |

violin violin violin
cello cello cello

slow down ↓

↓

viola violin
solo solo

slow down

high solo   solo

4 CLOSE

"In the songs you sang today, how were the rhythms different?" (Some had two equal sounds to a beat; others had three.) Have students:

▶ • Listen as a student claps the rhythm to one of the songs in the lesson, then determine which song was chosen.

▶ • Sing the song.

LESSON SUMMARY

Informal Assessment In this lesson, students:

OBJECTIVE 1 Patted two equal sounds to a beat with "Come and Sing Together."

OBJECTIVE 2 Signaled when they heard the division of equal sounds per beat change from two to three and three to two in Scherzo.

National Standards for Music Education
- **1d** Sing ostinatos, partner songs, and rounds.
- **4a** Create and arrange music to accompany dramatizations.
- **4c** Use a variety of sound sources when composing.
- **5c** Identify and interpret symbols and traditional terms.

MORE MUSIC: Reinforcement
More Songs to Read, page 356 ($\frac{6}{8}$ meter)
"Over the Sea to Skye," page 149 ($\frac{6}{8}$ rhythm patterns)
"The Wind on the Hill," page 374 ($\frac{6}{8}$ meter—aural)

ENRICHMENT: *Conducting Scherzo*

Divide the class into two groups. Assign one group the job of conducting when they hear three equal sounds to a beat; the other when they hear two equal sounds to a beat. Then have them listen to Scherzo and conduct using the two-beat conducting pattern. (See *Enrichment,* Unit 1, Lesson 1, pages 14–15.) The two groups should be conducting at different times.

ART CONNECTION: *Texture Rubbings*

VISUAL ARTS

Point out to students that arco and pizzicato affect the texture in music. In visual arts, texture is the surface quality of materials. Actual texture is felt through the sense of touch. Implied texture is seen but not felt, as in a soft velvet robe or a dog's fur in a painting. (See pages 177, 232.) Invite students to explore implied texture through crayon rubbings. Have them collect textured items such as cardboard, leaves, sponges, and woven fabric, then place the items under paper and rub crayons over them to capture the texture.

ACROSS the

ART

CLOTHES DESIGN

"Come and Sing Together"

GROUP   **15–30 MIN**
MATERIALS: art paper, drawing materials

In this song, students learn that Hungarians enjoy singing and dancing, and that they have a folk tradition of wearing shiny boots when they dance.

Ask students to think of kinds of shoes and clothes people wear today in cities or farms of the United States—for work, for play. Have students work in groups to list types of clothes: for school, for working in an office, for working on a ranch or on a farm.

They might consider specific parts of the country: clothes to wear going to school on a winter day in Alaska, to wear to play after school on a hot day in Florida or Arizona, to wear to a Hawaiian feast.

In groups, students design the clothes and make sketches of them, and display their designs.

COMPREHENSION STRATEGIES: Drawing conclusions, compare and contrast

SCIENCE

MAPS

"One More River"

GROUP   **15–30 MIN**
MATERIALS: maps of the United States

Using maps of the United States, have students locate and describe the paths of major rivers in the United States. Students can work in groups, one river per group.

Each group should try to determine where the river begins—the general location and the topography of the area. (mountains, flat plains) Each group then describes the path of its river by listing the states that the river passes through, and the cities within each state. The order of the list should represent the sequence of locations along the river's path. Finally, each group needs to mention where the river ends.

Groups then generalize a basic description about the paths of rivers. (In general, rivers start in high elevations and flow into the ocean or a large body of water such as a Great Lake or the Gulf of Mexico.)

COMPREHENSION STRATEGY: Drawing conclusions

CURRICULUM

SCIENCE

ANIMAL KINGDOM

"One More River"

WHOLE CLASS   **15–30 MIN**

Suppose Noah brought these animals onto the ark: chickens, frogs, snakes, sharks, dogs, turtles, alligators, elephants, horses, trout, ostriches. Suppose also that different sections of the ark were reserved for: Amphibians, Fish, Reptiles, Birds, Mammals.

Which animals would go into each section? Have students use this Yes-No Key to help them answer:

ANY ANIMAL WITH A BACKBONE

1) Does it have feathers?
   If Yes—Bird
   If No—go to 2
2) Does it have fins and gills?
   If Yes—Fish
   If No—go to 3
3) Does it have body hair?
   If Yes—Mammal
   If No—go to 4
4) Does it have dry scales on its body and claws on its toes?
   If Yes—Reptile
   If No—Amphibian

(Birds—chickens, ostriches; fish—sharks, trout; mammals—dogs, horses, elephants; reptiles—snakes, alligators; amphibians—frogs)

Have students think of other animals to add. They can use reference texts to check their responses.

COMPREHENSION STRATEGIES: Classifying, compare and contrast

LANGUAGE ARTS

EXPRESSING OPINIONS

Scherzo

INDIVIDUAL   **15–30 MIN**

In Scherzo, students hear changes in the rhythm of the music and the way in which the violin is played. Students create a list of things around them that are changing all the time, such as plants, weather, their feelings, buildings being built in towns and cities, fields being planted or harvested in farm country.

Students write a short essay based on the theme: How I feel about change. Ask some questions to get them started:

- How has a major event changed your life?
- What would you like to change about your life, and how could you make the change?

COMPREHENSION STRATEGY: Expressing points of view

RELATED ARTS | MOVEMENT | THEATER | VISUAL ARTS

LESSON PLANNER

FOCUS Dynamics

OBJECTIVE
OBJECTIVE 1 Perform a poem with expressive dynamics and movement, increasing and decreasing the size of the movement (range)

MATERIALS
Recordings
The Eagle   CD3:11
Recorded Lesson: Interview with
  Julius Chavez   CD3:12
Listening: A'tsah Biyiin Sin
  (Navajo words by J. Chavez)   CD3:13

Resources Signing Master S • 4 • 4 (The Eagle)

VOCABULARY
dynamics

▶ = **BASIC PROGRAM**

Flying with the Eagles

What do you think of when you see an eagle fly?

Dynamics are the levels of loudness and softness of the performance. How do the dynamics in this song help express feelings? Louder parts express pride, anger; softer parts express loss, sadness, doubt.

E major

l, d r m f s l

THE EAGLE
Music by Hap Palmer
Words by Martha Cheney

mf 1. Born   for a   west-ern sky, —   sweep-ing a cir - cle
mp 2. Brave   and a   hunt-er's son,   *f* the land was his 'til he
p 3. There   on a   moun-tain high, —   wound-ed — ea - gle
mf 4. Dream - ing of   days gone by, —   when lit - tle chil-dren

as   he flies. —
met   a gun. —
wants to die. —
watched him fly. —
} He was free — when they let him be. —

118

MEETING **INDIVIDUAL** NEEDS

VOCAL DEVELOPMENT: *Dynamics*

When asked to sing loudly, students sometimes sing with a forced, pushed sound. When they try to sing softly, their sound may become weak, breathy, and unsupported. To develop the deep breath support needed to sing at both levels, divide the class into two groups, one standing on each side of the room. Have one group cup one hand around their mouth, put the other on their waist, and call *hoo-hoo* to the other side at a loud dynamic level. Ask the group on the other side to echo back. To project their voices, students will automatically breathe deeply and will feel this as their waist expands. Making sure they maintain good posture as they call, repeat the activity at a softer dynamic level. Let students discover that the breathing process and posture are the same for both dynamic levels.

BIOGRAPHIES: *Hap Palmer and Martha Cheney*

Hap Palmer began writing children's songs when he taught students with learning disabilities and needed to develop a curriculum. Impressed by his enjoyable, movement-oriented songs, a school administrator contacted the record company that launched Palmer's music.

"Have you recently read a poem that was about feelings or emotions? If so, name one and talk about it." Have students:

▶ • Read the poem, "I Wonder," on page 105.

▶ • Recall the ideas expressed in the poem. (wondering how others might feel)

"Words by themselves express feelings. Today you will find musical ways to add to the meaning of the words you sing, hear, and speak."

2 DEVELOP

1. Introduce "The Eagle" CD3:11. **Listen for dynamics.** Have students:

▶ • Listen to the song and discuss the feelings it expresses.

▶ • Learn the song on page 118.

▶ • Read about dynamics and listen for them in the recorded performance, signaling loud and soft by moving hands apart for loud, together for soft.

▶ • Sing the song with dynamics (either those of the recorded performance or new dynamics suggested by the students).

In a land with-out a friend, — will there be an emp-ty sky — where the ea - gle used to fly — in the wind?

Verse 2 — Go back to the beginning
Verse 4 — Go to Coda

Coda

Born for a west - ern sky, — sweep-ing a cir - cle as he flies. — He was free — when they let him be.

He was free — when they let him be.

SING the song with dynamics that are different from the recording. Find another way to express the feelings of the words.

Martha Cheney is a writer, teacher, and author of many songs. She believes that combining music and language in songs may be the ultimate form of communication. She enjoys helping students develop their own writing abilities, and loves the outdoors.

SIGNING: *"The Eagle"*

Signing Master S • 4 • 4 has sign language for this song. The meaning of the text, not necessarily each word, is signed. For example, the signs for *he, they,* and *him be* mean *eagle, people,* and *live.* Sign smoothly and with dignity, in the mood of the song.

SCIENCE CONNECTION: *Eagles*

Have students create an eagle-shaped fact sheet about eagles. Start with these intriguing facts:

— The largest, most powerful eagle in the world is Steller's sea eagle. It lives on the coast of Siberia but may stray near Alaska.

— Philippine eagles eat monkeys, large birds, and reptiles.

— Most eagles live 20 to 30 years, some even as long as 50 years.

UNIT THREE
LESSON 3

continued from previous page

2. Introduce "A'tsah Biyiin Sin." Learn about the Eagle Dance. Have students:

▶ • Read about Julius Chavez (**ju** li əs **chæ** vɪs) and "A'tsah Biyiin Sin" (aˑ **tsɑ** bi **yin** sɪn) on pages 120–121.

Recorded Lesson CD3:12
▶ • Listen to "Interview with Julius Chavez," in which he describes the dance and story "A'tsah Biyiin Sin" and the importance of learning songs and dances in Native American culture.

Among many Native American cultures, the eagle is admired for its beauty, grace, and strength. The eagle is also a spiritual figure to many Native Americans, serving as a messenger between people and the Creator. The eagle has the sharpest eyes, flies the highest, and carries prayers on its feathers up to the Creator.

MEET **JULIUS CHAVEZ**

Julius Chavez is a Native American of the Navajo nation in Arizona and New Mexico. He has spent many years learning songs and dances of the Navajo people. He is also interested in learning and teaching the music of other Native American groups.
The songs and dances are passed on from performer to performer and from parents to children. One must listen carefully to learn the songs, because they are not written down. Mr. Chavez learned much of what he knows from his grandparents.

LISTEN as Julius Chavez explains the meaning of **"A'tsah Biyiin Sin."**

120 **FLYING WITH THE EAGLES**

MEETING **INDIVIDUAL** NEEDS

SPECIAL LEARNERS: *Dynamics in Everyday Speech*

Knowing when and how to use dynamics in speaking is a social skill. Discuss how dynamics express meaning in everyday speech and how that meaning can be intentional or unintentional. Have students suggest situations in which everyone is expected to talk softly (in small groups in the classroom, in the lobby of a concert hall, hospital, library). Ask them what soft talking means in each situation (feelings of respect, concern, thoughtfulness to others, and so on). Then have groups of three students practice soft talking by having two read a familiar poem together in their

softest voices while the third listens. Also encourage soft-spoken students to speak loudly within a small group of supportive friends.

MULTICULTURAL PERSPECTIVES: *The Navajo*

The Navajo (**nɑ** vɑ ho) probably arrived in the Southwest around the 1500s as wandering hunters and gatherers. Later many Navajo became sheepherders. With a ready supply of wool, they also learned to weave beautiful rugs. Other Navajo are well known for the jewelry they make of silver and a blue-colored stone called turquoise.

3. Listen for dynamics in "A'tsah Biyiin Sin" CD3:13. Have students:

▶ • Listen to the piece and discuss their impressions of it.

▶ • Identify places where they heard dynamics.

▶ • Listen to "A'tsah Biyiin Sin" again, quietly patting with the beat.

A'tsah Biyiin Sin

LISTENING

Traditional Laguna Melody
Words by Julius Chavez

In "A'tsah Biyiin Sin," (The Song that Belongs to the Eagle) Julius Chavez uses the melody from the traditional Laguna Eagle Dance Song with his own words in Navajo. The dance shows scenes in the eagle's life, which may teach people about their own lives.

LISTEN to "A'tsah Biyiin Sin."

121

Today the Navajo are one of the biggest of the Native American groups. More than 160,000 people live on the 16-million acre reservation, which is rich in oil, coal, and uranium. Their schools teach Navajo customs and language and are a model for other Native American educators. Singers like Julius Chavez keep Navajo legends and songs alive.

MULTICULTURAL PERSPECTIVES: *Eagle Dance*

MOVEMENT

The Eagle Dance is a favorite among Native Americans. Many native people regard the eagle with reverence, and it holds great symbolic importance in various Native American cultures. This song and dance attest to that fact. The Laguna people are one of the nations commonly known as the Pueblo. The Spanish gave them the name *Pueblo* in the 1500s because of their apartment-style housing. *Pueblo* means "city" or "town" in Spanish. The Laguna people still live in and near their old village of multi-storied adobe houses west of Albuquerque, New Mexico, along the Rio Paraje river. They lead modern lives, while at the same time trying to maintain their traditional culture.

UNIT THREE
LESSON 3

continued from previous page

3 APPLY

Introduce "Fire." Perform a poem with dynamics. Have students:

• In scattered formation, make themselves into as tiny a shape as possible, then "grow" larger and larger as you play a gradual crescendo on a drum until they occupy as much space as possible.

▶• Read the poem, "Fire," on page 122, discussing any unfamiliar words.

▶• Discuss the *Think It Through* questions in preparation for planning a movement interpretation of the poem.

▶• Divide into small groups and work out a movement interpretation of the poem. (See *Movement* below.)

▶• In each group, choose speakers and movers.

▶• Choose dynamics that help express the text.

OBJECTIVE 1 Informal Assessment

▶• Perform the poem with their chosen dynamics and movement, while increasing and decreasing the size of the movement (range). (The movers perform simultaneously with the speakers of the poem.)

▶• Discuss differences in interpretation.

YOUR TURN WITH DYNAMICS

Have you ever watched a fire in a fireplace, or a campfire? Fire is a very powerful natural force. Poets have written about fire as if it had a personality and feelings. This poem was written by a thirteen-year-old girl from England.

READ the poem. What is fire's enemy? water

FIRE

I am fire. You know me
For my warmth and light
For my crackling, leaping
Colored light
Which comforts all.
I am fire. You know me
For my endless moving,
Burning, destroying hunger
Which eats all.
I am fire. I have one foe
Who conquers my might,
Who quenches my thirst,
Who swallows my light.

— Pat Taylor

THINK IT THROUGH

How could you use sound and movement to show a fire? How could you show the fire growing? Dying down?

Encourage students to discuss how dynamics, range of movement, body parts, and body design can be used to show various aspects of fire.

122 FLYING WITH THE EAGLES

MEETING **INDIVIDUAL** NEEDS

ALTERNATE TEACHING STRATEGY

OBJECTIVE 1 Write "Fire" on the board (or make a chart or transparency). Work as a class to try each line with dynamic variations. Write *loud, soft,* and so on, or have students devise graphic notation to show the dynamics chosen. Perform the poem.

MOVEMENT: *"Fire" Improvisation*

Review body design (Unit 1, p. 15) and range (Unit 3, p. 108).

1. Discuss the characteristics of a campfire.

2. Make a body design to represent wood of different sizes and shapes in a fire. At first, move only fingers to imitate flames as flames start. Gradually add wrists, hands, arms, and other body parts, filling more space (increasing range of movement) as the fire grows. Add sudden, sharp movement to show shooting flames. Add twirls or other locomotor movement for crackling and sputtering.

3. Reverse the process as the fire dies down and smolders.

4. Repeat this in small groups. Begin with a group design and change range of movement as the fire grows and dies.

CHOOSE the dynamics and movement you feel would best express the meaning of the poem. Speak the poem with dynamics and perform your movement.

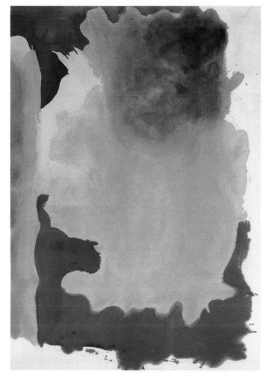

CANAL

The American artist Helen Frankenthaler often paints shapes of color that let each viewer see something different in them. What do you see in this painting?

"What are dynamics?" (loud and soft sounds and all the levels in between) "How did you experience dynamics today?" (expressing feelings, adding to the meaning in songs and speech) Have students:

▶ • Sing "The Eagle" again, with the dynamics shown.

LESSON SUMMARY

Informal Assessment In this lesson, students:

OBJECTIVE 1 Performed the poem "Fire" with expressive dynamics and movement, increasing and decreasing the size of the movement (range).

National Standards for Music Education
4a Create and arrange music to accompany dramatizations.
4c Use a variety of sound sources when composing.

MORE MUSIC: Reinforcement

"A Lakota Legend," page 152 (Native American cultures)
"For the Flute Players," page 153 (poem to perform)
"Powama," page 150 (Native American music)
"Donna, Donna," page 291 (dynamics; theme of freedom)
"Scary Music Montage," page 307 (dynamics)
"Chinese Lion Dance," page 335 (ceremonial dance and music)

PLAYING INSTRUMENTS: *Unpitched*

Have students add instrument sounds to go with images in the poem "Fire," the dynamics, and their movement.

BACKGROUND: *Miracles*

Miracles: Poems by children of the English-speaking world, the collection from which "Fire" is taken, was edited by Richard Lewis (b. 1935) and published in 1966. Convinced that even 5 year olds can write serious poetry, Lewis compiled children's writing while teaching. With the help of UNESCO, he collected over 3,000 poems by poets from the ages of 5 to 13 in 18 countries.

BIOGRAPHY: *Helen Frankenthaler*

VISUAL ARTS

Abstract expressionist painter Helen Frankenthaler (b. 1928) pours layers of thinned paint to soak into raw canvas. The color pools run into one another, sometimes overlapping, sometimes leaving parts of the canvas bare. Color and texture are thus central to her work. For her, "painting is a matter of making some kind of beautiful order out of human feeling and experience." Usually she begins without a set idea of what the finished painting will be like.

UNIT THREE
LESSON 4

RELATED ARTS MOVEMENT THEATER VISUAL ARTS

LESSON PLANNER

FOCUS Pitch—*fa*; C, F

OBJECTIVE
OBJECTIVE 1 Sing melodic phrases using pitch letter names including C and F (tested)

MATERIALS
Recordings
I Don't Care If the Rain Comes
  Down   CD3:4
Recorded Lesson: "Volte" A
  Section   CD3:14
Listening: Volte by M. Praetorius   CD3:15
Pay Me My Money Down   CD3:7

Instruments
resonator bells or other pitched
  instruments

Resources
Resource Master 3 • 2 (practice)
Resource Master 3 • 3 (practice)
Recorder Master R • 11 (pitches E G A B)

▶ = **BASIC PROGRAM**

Look closely at the pitches of "I Don't Care If the Rain Comes Down." Where is the new pitch? third measure

I don't care if the rain comes down, I'm gon-na sing all day,

I don't care if the rain comes down, I'm gon-na sing all day.

Fa is the pitch syllable between *mi* and *so*. Name these syllables from low to high, then sing the verse with pitch syllables.

so₁ la₁ do re mi fa so la

SING the two melodic motives on the next page. Try the motions!

124

MEETING **INDIVIDUAL** NEEDS

COOPERATIVE LEARNING: *Pitch Syllables*

Before writing the pitch syllables in order on the board, have students work in groups to arrange the pitch syllables in order from low to high. Assign roles and set a time limit. (Optional: Use **Resource Master 3 • 2** for practice ordering pitch syllables and relating them to notes on the staff. Then have a designated member explain their group's reasoning and report the results.)

JAZZ: *Scat Singing*

Have students replace *Hey, hey, carry me away* with scat syllables. Then let them try "scatting" with the syllables at other places in the song.

∧ —heavy accent, held less than a full count
Λ —heavy accent, held as short as possible

Motive 1

Touch shoulders.   Touch head.   Shake hands overhead.

Motive 2

Touch shoulders.   Touch waist.   Touch knees.

1 GET SET

"Listen to 'I Don't Care If the Rain Comes Down.' Each time you hear the words *I'm gonna dance all day* and the melody goes up, raise your hand. If you hear the melody of those words go down, point at the floor." Have students:

▶ • Listen to the song **CD3:4**, moving hands up (lines 1, 3) or down (lines 2, 4).

▶ • Sing the song on page 108 substituting the words *I'm gonna sing all day.*

"Today you'll learn the name of a new pitch syllable in this song and in other music."

2 DEVELOP

1. Introduce *fa* in "I Don't Care If the Rain Comes Down." Have students:

• Form four groups, each in turn singing two measures from the notation on page 124.

• Determine that groups 1, 3, and 4 sang melodies with the same pitches, *do re mi.*

• Determine that the melody of group 2 begins on *mi* and goes up by steps.

• Read about *fa,* then write the known pitch syllables, in order, on the board as they say them. (*so, la, do re mi fa so la*)

• Sing the verse silently, singing measures 3–4 and 7–8 aloud with pitch syllables. (*mi fa so; mi re do*)

▶ • Sing the song, adding the verses from Lesson 1, page 108, *Develop 1,* or create new ones.

PLAYING INSTRUMENTS: *Keyboards*

Have students sing these melodies using pitch syllables (*do re mi fa so*), letter names (C D E F G), and finger numbers (1 2 3 4 5). Play the melodies, one octave higher, with "I Don't Care If the Rain Comes Down."

PITCH SYLLABLES: *Fa*

Use this hand sign
for the new pitch syllable.   *fa*

MUSIC BUILDS MATH SKILLS

Number and Operations Arranging the pitch syllables in order from low to high relates to ordering numbers.

UNIT THREE
LESSON 4

continued from previous page

2. Introduce "Volte" CD3:15. Identify *mi fa so* and *mi re do* phrases. Have students:

• Sing the motives (page 125) with motions.

▶ • Read about "Volte" (vɔlt) and Michael Praetorius (maɪ kəl pre tɔ ri əs) on pages 126 and 127.

Recorded Lesson CD3:14

▶ • Listen to "'Volte' A Section," and identify and move to *mi fa so* and *mi re do* motives (motive order: 1, 2, 1, 2).

▶ • Listen to "Volte."

3. Play melodic patterns and introduce letter names C and F. Have students:

▶ • Listen and watch as you play C D E F G on resonator bells, and find by trial and error the bells needed to play each motive on page 125. (E F G, E D C)

▶ • Read about C and F on page 126.

▶ • Play and sing all five pitches (C D E F G) stepwise, ascending and descending.

3 APPLY

1. Review "Pay Me My Money Down" CD3:7 (p. 111). Sing with letter names. Have students:

▶ • Sing Verse 1 in call-and-response form.

• With a partner, identify the response which contains both C and F and sing it with letter names. (Response 2)

LISTENING 🎵 **Volte** *by Michael Praetorius*

🔊 *The volte was a popular dance in European courts in the early 1600s. What kind of movement does this music make you want to do?*

MOVE to the motives as you listen to "Volte." Then play each motive on resonator bells. C and F are the new letter names.

CONCERT CHAMPÊTRE
Musicians of Praetorius' time enjoyed playing various combinations of instruments. This painting shows early keyboard, string, and wind instruments.

126 SING ALL DAY

MEETING **INDIVIDUAL** NEEDS

ALTERNATE TEACHING STRATEGY

OBJECTIVE 1 Have students point to and count each C and F in "Pay Me My Money Down," then find the responses with both pitches. Have them figure out how to play the responses on resonator bells to review the other letter names. Finally, sing each response with letter names. (For practice with C and F use **Resource Master 3 · 3.**)

BACKGROUND: *"Volte"* MOVEMENT

"Volte" is from a collection of dance music of 1612 called *Terpsichore* (tərp sɪk ə ri), named after the Greek goddess of dance. Michael Praetorius arranged these dances to "entertain and delight princely tables and banquets." The music itself was composed by French dancing masters. Since dance teachers didn't have the tapes or disks available today, many played the violin or lute as they gave a dance lesson; they often wrote their own music as well.

The Volte ("the turn"), the dance for which "Volte" was written, was a court dance popular in Europe from 1550–1650. It is made up of three-quarter turns and leaps.

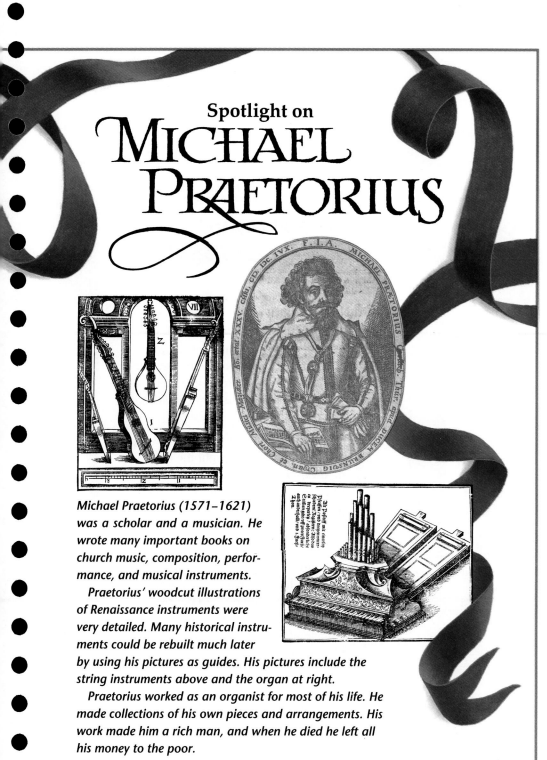

Spotlight on
MICHAEL PRAETORIUS

Michael Praetorius (1571–1621) was a scholar and a musician. He wrote many important books on church music, composition, performance, and musical instruments.

Praetorius' woodcut illustrations of Renaissance instruments were very detailed. Many historical instruments could be rebuilt much later by using his pictures as guides. His pictures include the string instruments above and the organ at right.

Praetorius worked as an organist for most of his life. He made collections of his own pieces and arrangements. His work made him a rich man, and when he died he left all his money to the poor.

Unit 3 *Just Imagine* **127**

OBJECTIVE 1 Informal Assessment
• Hum verse. Sing letters on response.

2. Perform movement. Have students:

▶ • With a partner, create simple four-beat non-locomotor motion patterns for the calls.

▶ • Perform the song with movement. (In long-ways sets, one pair of partners performs their motions twice for the first call, then all clap on Beats 2 and 4 of the response; the next pair performs the next call; all clap the response as before. Continue by phrase.

4 CLOSE

"Name and describe the new pitch syllable you learned today." (*fa*—higher than *mi* and lower than *so*) "What were the two new letter names we sang today?" (C and F) "Sing the letter names as I point to the staff." (point to G F E D C) Have students:

▶ • Sing one more verse of "Pay Me My Money Down" with motions on the calls.

LESSON SUMMARY

Informal Assessment In this lesson, students:

OBJECTIVE 1 Sang melodic phrases from "Pay Me My Money Down" using letter names including C and F.

National Standards for Music Education
1a Sing accurately, on pitch and in rhythm.
5b Use a system to read notation in treble clef in major keys.

MORE MUSIC: Reinforcement
More Songs to Read, page 357 (*fa*)
"When I First Came to This Land," page 148 (*fa*, C F)
"Martin's Cry," 336 (*fa*, C F; Martin Luther King, Jr., Day)

CRITICAL THINKING: *Dynamics* MOVEMENT

Have students tell how the dynamics of "Volte" influenced their description of the dance. Discuss how different dynamics might make one think of another style of dancing. Encourage students to compare expressive effects rather than choosing a "better" version.

PLAYING INSTRUMENTS: *Orff*

Have students play the melody of the response phrases on soprano instruments and add the Orff accompaniment (right) to "Pay Me My Money Down."

ACROSS the

SCIENCE

CONDENSATION MODEL

"I Don't Care If the Rain Comes Down"

PAIR   **30 MIN OR LONGER**

MATERIALS: round pan about (10 cm deep), small empty jar (baby-food-jar size), plastic wrap, small stones, rubber band

Working in pairs, students place a small jar in the center of a deep pan and put about 3 cm of water in the pan. (Place a stone in the jar, if needed, to keep it from floating.) Tightly cover the pan with plastic wrap, securing the wrap with a rubber band. Place a stone above the wrap over the center of the jar. Place the pan in a sunny spot.

After several hours, what do students see on the underside of the wrap and in the jar? Have them offer explanations of why this happened. How can this model explain clouds and rain? (Water evaporated from the pan and condensed into fine beads on the wrap. The beads collected and fell as drops into the jar. Water evaporates from Earth's surface and condenses in the atmosphere, forming clouds. The droplets come together and fall as rain.)

COMPREHENSION STRATEGIES: Making observations, drawing conclusions

SOCIAL STUDIES

ROLE PLAYING

"Volte"

GROUP   **15–30 MIN**

MATERIALS: reference books

During the Renaissance, most European countries had not formed yet. Instead, people identified themselves with and felt loyalty to particular regions, duchies, states, principalities, and even cities.

Have students imagine they are living in such a time. How might their state be divided? What would the citizens of different areas identify as distinguishing characteristics of their home?

Divide the class into groups and ask each group to think of a situation to role play that involves people from one place interacting with people from another. Ask them to role-play a conversation that shows different attitudes, beliefs, and values between two groups. How do they work with their differences? How are disputes resolved? Examples: traveling to exchange farm produce for tools or handicrafts; being stopped at a border and questioned about the purpose of your journey; or visiting with a relative who has moved to another country.

COMPREHENSION STRATEGY: Understanding different points of view

CURRICULUM

LANGUAGE ARTS

WORD GAME

"Volte"

GROUP   **15–30 MIN**

Volte is French and refers to turning around. This game is called "Volte" because one player "turns" to speak to the next player. A phrase is passed around a circle, each student adding one word at the end.

Divide the class into groups and select a person in each group to go first. Groups choose a topic, such as gardening or playing in an orchestra. The first person makes a phrase to start a sentence. The second person repeats the phrase and adds another word. The group that gets around the circle the most times before someone forgets part of the story or cannot think of a word gets to choose the next topic for the other groups.

COMPREHENSION STRATEGIES: Sequencing, finding supporting ideas

MATHEMATICS

BUY-SELL GAME

"Pay Me My Money Down"

GROUP   **15–30 MIN**

MATERIALS: calculator, index cards; optional—play money

One group member acts as shopkeeper and writes the name of an article for sale and its price on a card. The shopkeeper makes at least 5 cards, including such items as:

- pencil $.27
- eraser $.49
- loose-leaf binder $2.59

One student acts as salesperson. Other students act as customers. They select items (cards) for sale. The salesperson writes out a sales slip and finds the total amount of the sale. The customer then offers the shopkeeper a rounded amount of imaginary money—$5.00, $10.00. The shopkeeper determines the change.

Students change roles as they repeat the activity. If play money is available, students can use given amounts of money to make purchases.

COMPREHENSION STRATEGY: Compare and contrast

UNIT THREE
LESSON 5

LESSON PLANNER

FOCUS Duration— 6/8 , ♫♩ , ♩♪, ♩.

OBJECTIVES

OBJECTIVE 1 Speak rhythm patterns from notation in 6/8 meter (tested)

OBJECTIVE 2 Perform an ostinato in 6/8 from notation (tested)

MATERIALS

Recordings

Recorded Lesson: Pitch It!	CD3:16
One More River	CD3:8
Recorded Lesson: Grainger Theme	CD3:17
Listening: Over the Hills and Far Away (excerpt) by P. Grainger	CD3:18
La pájara pinta	CD3:6
Recorded Lesson: Pronunciation for "La pájara pinta"	CD3:19

Instruments
claves, maracas, or güiro

Resources
Resource Master 3 • 4 (practice)
Resource Master 3 • 5 (practice)
Recorder Master R • 12 (pitches E G A)
Musical Instruments Master—saxophone

VOCABULARY
dotted quarter note

▶ = BASIC PROGRAM

Step to the Ark!

In the song "One More River," the animals did the walking. Now you can "step to the ark"! Before you move, look at the notation for each rhythm.

CLAP the rhythm of each word several times.

cross
hip - po
el - e - phant

BY TWO OR BY SIX?

The meter signature of "One More River" can be written in two ways, 2/4 and 6/8. Although these two meter signatures look different, each measure lasts as long as two **dotted quarter notes** (♩. ♩.) or **six eighth notes** (♫♫ ♫♫).

FIND the meter signature and ♫♩ pattern in **"One More River" on page 112.** Learn the dance.

128

MEETING **INDIVIDUAL** NEEDS

EXTRA HELP: *Rhythms for "Step to the Ark"*

Have students try these combinations for eight beats or create others. Step the rhythm of each word; clap and step the beat while saying *cross;* clap *cross* while galloping *hippo;* clap *elephant* while stepping *cross.*

MOVEMENT: *"One More River"*   MOVEMENT

Formation: two lines facing, four couples per set

Dance: Measures 1–2: four steps toward partner

Measures 3–4: four steps back to place

Measures 5–8: do-si-do R shoulders with partner, then back to place

Measures 9–16: Head couple faces the bottom of the set and joins inside hands. All other couples face the top of the set and join inside hands, forming arches which the head couple walks under.

—Couple 2 releases hands, faces the bottom of the set, joins the opposite hands, and follows Couple 1 under the arches, followed by Couples 3 and 4.

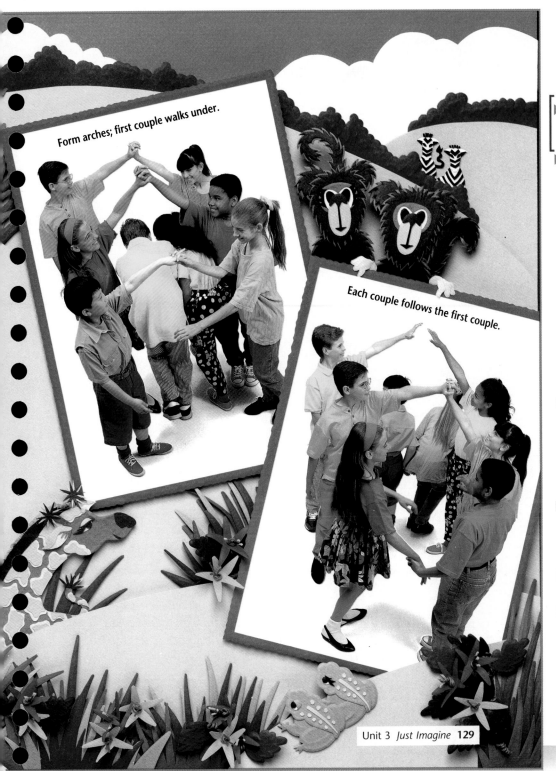

Form arches; first couple walks under.

Each couple follows the first couple.

"Listen and see if you can name this song."
Have students:

Recorded Lesson CD3:16
▶ • Listen to "Pitch It!" and hear the melody of
"One More River" sung without rhythmic
patterns.

▶ • Discuss how the song was changed. (The
rhythm was changed.)

• Listen to Verse 1 of "One More River" CD3:8
(page 112), singing and clapping only *There's
one more river to cross* and patting the other
words.

"Today you're going to learn how these
rhythms are written so you can find them in
the songs and use them in your own patterns."

2 DEVELOP

1. Introduce notation in "One More River."
Have students:

▶ • Sing Verse 1 again in two groups, one group
singing *There's one more river to cross,* the
other singing all other words.

• Study the notation on page 128.

• Perform eight-beat combinations of rhythms.
(See *Extra Help* on the bottom of page 128.)

▶ • Read about ²⁄₄· and ⁶⁄₈ meter.

• Identify the meter signature and the ♩♪♩
pattern, then sing the entire song from notation.

▶ • Sing verses they created for the song, as suggested in Lesson 2, page 113, *Develop 1.*

▶ • Learn the movement. (See *Movement* on the
bottom of page 128.)

—As Couple 1 reaches the bottom of the set, the couple releases hands, faces the top of the set, then joins opposite
hands, forming an arch for the other couples to walk under.

—All couples continue in this manner, moving forward to
their original positions by the end of each refrain.

MUSIC BUILDS MATH SKILLS

Algebra As students perform in ostinato in 6/8
from notation, they apply their knowledge of
numerical patterns.

MOVEMENT: *Assessing Movement*

Have each group (set of four couples) watch another group
do the "One More River" movement and look for ways to
help them improve their performance. Did they:

—move appropriately with the music?

—use the correct body facing?

—form the arch at the appropriate time?

—begin and end together?

UNIT THREE
LESSON 5

continued from previous page

2. Introduce "Over the Hills and Far Away"
CD3:18. Read the rhythm of the theme.
Have students:

OBJECTIVE 1 **Informal Assessment**
▶ • Read the rhythm pattern on page 130 using *cross, hippo,* and *elephant.*

▶ • Read about Percy Grainger and his music.

Recorded Lesson CD3:17
▶ • Listen to "Grainger Theme" and whisper the rhythm pattern.

▶ • Listen to "Over the Hills and Far Away" and, when they hear the rhythm pattern, walk their own pathways through shared space. (Rhythm pattern occurs in A section; form is Intro A A B B A A B B A A B B)

• Discuss how a concert band is different from an orchestra—based on what they read and heard.

3 APPLY

1. Review "La pájara pinta" CD3:6 (p. 110).
Create nonlocomotor movements. Have students:

• Listen to the song, moving to the beat with a different nonlocomotor movement of their own choosing for each eight beats (four measures). (Suggestions: move shoulders up and down, bend and straighten elbows or knees, shake hands and fingers, swivel hips)

Recorded Lesson CD3:19
▶ • Listen to "Pronunciation for 'La pájara pinta.'"

▶ • Sing the song.

CLAP and speak the rhythm pattern below. Say *cross, hippo,* and *elephant* for the three rhythms.

Hip-po hip-po cross cross el-e-phant hip-po hip-po cross

cross hip-po hip-po hip-po el-e-phant hip-po cross

U.S. Marine Band

LISTENING Over the Hills and Far Away (excerpt)
by Percy Grainger

This march was written by Percy Grainger for a military concert band in 1918. Unlike the orchestra, the concert band has only three families of instruments: woodwinds, brass, and percussion. Which family of instruments is not in a concert band? strings

LISTEN for the rhythms above in the march.

130 STEP TO THE ARK!

MEETING **INDIVIDUAL** NEEDS

ALTERNATE TEACHING STRATEGIES

OBJECTIVE 1 Write these rhythms on the board: ♩., ♩♪, and ♪♪♪ Have students copy them onto paper. Play one of the rhythms on a drum, and have students point to the correct symbol on their paper. Then, reverse the process. Point to the symbols on the board and have students say and clap the correct rhythm. (*cross, hippo,* or *elephant*)

OBJECTIVE 2 Students may use only one rhythm, or alternate between two. They may write and create 6/8 patterns on **Resource Master 3 • 5.**

BIOGRAPHY: *George Percy Aldridge Grainger*

Percy Grainger (1882–1961) experimented with rhythm and improvisation and developed a distinctive approach to orchestration. Instead of writing out specific parts for each instrument, he arranged his free-spirited music using "elastic" scoring, playable by various instrumental combinations. He also wrote multiple versions of many pieces. His expertise in writing for wind bands reflects his experience playing in such bands.

SPOTLIGHT ON
Percy Grainger

Percy Aldridge Grainger (1882–1961) was an Australian composer and pianist. His mother gave him his first piano lessons, and he began his concert career at the age of ten.

One of Grainger's favorite foods was brown-sugar sandwiches. Because he didn't like carrying things, he tied his pens, pencils, and papers to his jacket with string. He also planned his own museum, including the donation of his own skeleton!

Grainger was known as a fine pianist. He also became an important scholar of English folk music, researching and collecting English songs, many of which he wove into his own new compositions.

2. Add an ostinato to "La pájara pinta."
Have students:

• Divide into four groups and create short spoken ostinatos (four or eight beats) using the words/rhythms on page 128. (Optional: Use **Resource Master 3 • 4** in which students create ostinato rhythms for "La pájara pinta.")

• Listen to and notate each ostinato.

OBJECTIVE 2 Informal Assessment

• Sing the song, each group in turn accompanying it by clapping or playing their ostinato on claves, maracas, or güiro.

4 CLOSE

"In what meter are the rhythms you read and performed today?" (⁶⁄₈, or ²⁄)
Have students:

• Choose an ostinato that includes ♪♪♪ and accompany "La pájara pinta" on instruments.

LESSON SUMMARY

Informal Assessment In this lesson, students:

OBJECTIVE 1 Spoke rhythm patterns from notation in ⁶⁄₈ meter that included ♩. , ♩♪, and ♪♪♪

OBJECTIVE 2 Created and performed an ostinato to "La pájara pinta" in ⁶⁄₈ from notation.

National Standards for Music Education
4c Use a variety of sound sources when composing.
5d Use standard symbols to notate patterns.

MORE MUSIC: Reinforcement
More Songs to Read, pages 358–359 (low *so* and *la;* rhythms in ⁶⁄₈ meter)
"Over the Sea to Skye," page 149 (⁶⁄₈ rhythms)
"Bonhomme! Bonhomme!," page 312 (⁶⁄₈ rhythms; winter)

VOCAL DEVELOPMENT: *Vowel Sounds*

Uniform shaping of vowel sounds is needed for clear diction and for good tone quality. The Spanish language contains many open vowels. Have students listen as you demonstrate the vocalise. Model an open, relaxed jaw with the tongue forward and the tip resting against the bottom inside gum. As you change from vowel to vowel, the mouth stays open and only closes slightly on *oh* and *oo*.

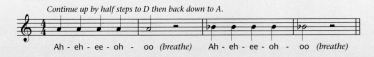

PLAYING INSTRUMENTS: *Orff*

Accompany "La pájara pinta" with Orff instruments.

ACROSS *the*

ART/SCIENCE

ANIMAL MURAL

"One More River"

WHOLE CLASS   **30 MIN OR LONGER**

MATERIALS: mural paper, paints, magazine pictures, scissors, glue, art paper, markers, crayons, reference materials

Every week, about twenty species of plants and animals become extinct. Have students research species of animals that are in danger of becoming extinct.

Students draw or cut out pictures of endangered species of animals. Have them paint a large ark on a sheet of mural paper. They place the animal pictures on the ark. Students think of a title for the mural, such as "Sailing for Point Protection" or "SS Conservation." These organizations have information:

- Defenders of Wildlife
  1101 14th St. NW #1400
  Washington, DC 20005
- The Nature Conservancy
  1245 N. Fairfax Dr., Suite 100
  Arlington, VA 22203
- Wildlife Information Center
  624 Main St.
  Slatington, PA 18080
- World Wildlife Fund
  1250 24th St. NW
  Washington, DC 20037

COMPREHENSION STRATEGIES: Organizing information, exploring spatial relationships

LANGUAGE ARTS

CREATIVE WRITING

"One More River"

WHOLE CLASS   **15–30 MIN**

Discuss choices Noah might have had to make in preparing the ark. (Examples: how much food to take; which animals to leave behind) Ask students to think about some difficult decisions and tough choices they have to make. (managing time, doing chores, getting homework done) What were the outcomes of their decisions?

Have them organize their thoughts into an essay around the theme "My Toughest Decision." Have them outline their essay:

- the problem I faced
- reasons why the problem was tough
- choices that I had available
- reasons for and against each choice
- way I made the decision
- the outcomes of my decision

COMPREHENSION STRATEGIES: Compare and contrast, expressing main ideas and supporting details

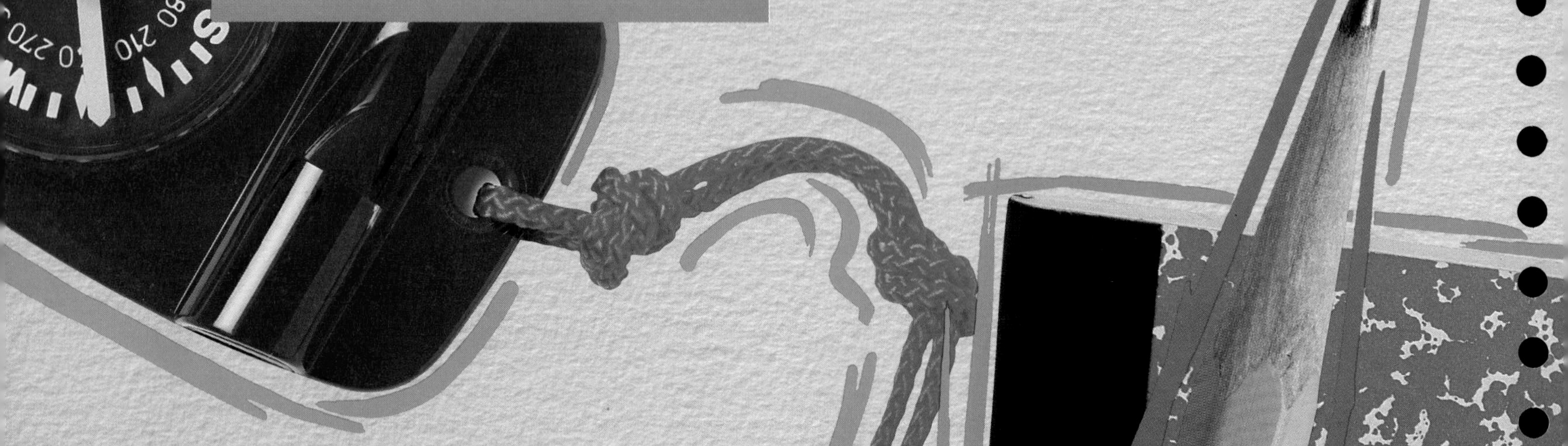

CURRICULUM

MATHEMATICS

PROBLEM SOLVING

"One More River"

GROUP **30 MIN OR LONGER**

MATERIALS: calculators (optional)

The story of Noah tells us that Noah took 2 of each animal on the ark. Well, suppose that Noah could fit only 100 animals on the ark.

Imagine that the animals on board included:

- elephants that boarded alone
- rhinos that boarded in two's
- hippos in three's
- bears in four's.

Using the above numbers, students work in groups to figure out how many of each animal the ark was able to hold. Have students compare to see how many different answers each group was able to come up with.

COMPREHENSION STRATEGY: Reasoning

SCIENCE

WEATHER JOURNAL

"One More River"

INDIVIDUAL **30 MIN OR LONGER**

Ask students to describe the weather today and discuss how weather affects people's lives and influences their choices. How might students feel after forty days and nights of rain?

Have students observe the weather and record their observations for a week. They begin by designing a table. The table can look like a calendar with the days of the week listed across the top. Along the side, students can list the daily observations they will make:

- highest/lowest temperatures
- precipitation (rain or snow—yes or no, if "yes" how much)
- cloud cover (if so, how much)
- wind speed and direction (highest during the day, direction from which wind was coming)

(They can get this information from a newspaper or a broadcast report.) Students might also note what is happening to any animals or plants around them. Have them write any ways in which the weather influenced their plans or affected them in any way during the week.

COMPREHENSION STRATEGIES: Recording information in a table, making observations

UNIT THREE
LESSON 6

RELATED ARTS MOVEMENT | THEATER | VISUAL ARTS

LESSON PLANNER

FOCUS Harmony

OBJECTIVES
OBJECTIVE 1 Change level in response to harmonic changes
OBJECTIVE 2 Signal when harmonic changes occur in a song

MATERIALS
Recordings
Listening: B'y with Harmony   CD3:20
I's the B'y   CD3:21
Recorded Lesson: Singing
  Harmony   CD3:22
Recorded Lesson: Harmony Hop   CD3:23
Listening: La raspa   CD3:24
Pay Me My Money Down   CD3:7

Instruments
resonator bells or other pitched instruments

Resources Recorder Master R • 13 (pitches E G A B)

Technology Music with MIDI: I's the B'y

VOCABULARY
key signature, flat, harmony

▶ = **BASIC PROGRAM**

ADD A LITTLE HARMONY

In this song the b'y, or boy, is a busy young fisherman from Newfoundland, an island off the east coast of Canada.

I's the B'y

F major

s, t, d r m f s

Newfoundland Folk Song

Verse
1. I's the b'y that builds the boat, And I's the b'y that sails her!
2. Sods and rinds to cov-er your flake,— Cakes and tea for sup-per,
3. I don't want your mag-got-y fish,— That's no good for win-ter,

I's the b'y that catch-es the fish, And brings them home to Liz-er.
Cod-fish in the spring o' the year,— Fried in mag-got-y but-ter.
I could buy as good— as that— Down in Bon - a - vis-ta.

Refrain
Hip your part-ner, Sal - ly Tib - bo, Hip your part-ner, Sal - ly Brown!

Fo - go, Twil - lin-gate, Mor - ton's Har-bour, All a-round the cir - cle.

132

MEETING **INDIVIDUAL** NEEDS

BUILDING SELF-ESTEEM: *Writing Lyrics*
Encourage students to write new lyrics to "I's the B'y" about things they can do well or have accomplished. Suggest they begin with "I'm the boy/girl who . . ."

EXTRA HELP: *Singing Harmony*
Have some students play the *do so,* pitches on resonator bells or other pitched instruments to reinforce the singers.

MULTICULTURAL PERSPECTIVES: *"I's the B'y"*
MOVEMENT
Most Newfoundlanders love to dance, and this lively sea chantey is a favorite dance tune. Like many folk songs, it has many variations. Because of Newfoundland's coastal location, fishing has been an important industry there. Fogo, Twillingate, Morton's Harbour, and Bonavista are fishing villages and ports. *Maggots* are the wormlike larvae of flies; they can infest improperly preserved food. *Sods* and *rinds* are the dirt and bark used to cover the *flake,* a platform or rack on which fish are dried.

In "I's the B'y," *do* appears in the first space. What is the letter name for *do*? F

The **key signature** comes before the meter signature at the beginning of a song. When *do* is F, the key signature has a **flat** (♭) on the third line.

Harmony is created when two or more different pitches are sung or played at the same time. Try singing *do* in harmony with "I's the B'y."

CREATE another harmony by singing this pattern with the song. Clap lightly with each *do*, pat with each low *so*.

THINK IT THROUGH
Which do you prefer for this song, harmony with pitches that stay the same or harmony with pitches that change? Why?

Unit 3 *Just Imagine* 133

1 GET SET

"Singing in harmony means singing two or more pitches at the same time. Listen to hear if this song is sung in harmony." Have students:

▶ • Listen to and discuss "B'y with Harmony" CD3:20, in which they hear the melody of "I's the B'y" sung alone, then with an added harmony part.

"Adding harmony to a melody makes it more interesting. Today you're going to be singing, playing, and listening for harmony in several songs."

2 DEVELOP

1. Introduce "I's the B'y" CD3:21. Sing an unchanging harmony and a changing harmony. Have students:

▶ • Listen to Verse 1 on page 132, and discuss the text and feelings it expresses.

• Listen again and hum the tonal center. (*do*, the last pitch)

• Sing dotted half notes on that pitch with the syllable *do* to accompany Verse 1.

• Describe how the accompaniment sounded and suggest improvements. (Sometimes it fit; at other times it needed to change.)

Recorded Lesson CD3:22
▶ • Listen to "Singing Harmony," and learn the pattern on page 133.

• Sing the pattern with each verse, clapping and patting as directed, and sing the melody and words of each refrain.

▶ • Discuss the *Think It Through.*

PLAYING INSTRUMENTS: *Keyboards*

Have one student perform the harmony pattern (Part 2) from page 133 with "I's the B'y." Have a second student add Part 1, playing with one finger of each hand.

ART CONNECTION: *Creating a Seascape* VISUAL ARTS

Tell students that seascapes show ocean scenery. In seascapes and landscapes, artists use the concept of foreground, middle ground, and background. Have students discuss the illustration on these pages: Which fish are in the foreground or closer to the viewer? Which are in the middle ground? Where is the boat? As things go back into space they get smaller and less detailed. Invite students to use this concept in creating a seascape. Suggest using crayons for fish, shells, and seaweed and using a wash of blue paint for the water.

continued from previous page

2. Introduce "La raspa" CD3:24. Recognize the harmonic pattern. Have students:

Recorded Lesson CD3:23
▶ • Listen to "Harmony Hop," then hop and freeze to show harmony changes between chords based on *do* and *so₁*.

▶ • Listen for the harmonic patterns, pictured on page 134, in "La raspa." (la **ras** pa) (Each block represents a strong beat, or measure.)

OBJECTIVE 1 Informal Assessment
• Listen again and show which harmonic pattern they hear by changing level—standing on *do* and sitting on low *so* (Pattern 1).

3 APPLY

Review "Pay Me My Money Down" (p. 111) CD3:7. Identify harmonic changes. Have students:

• Sing the song unaccompanied, then predict how it will sound with no harmony changes.

OBJECTIVE 2 Informal Assessment
• Sing the song as they hear a tremolo played on *do* (C), silently tapping their hands on a desk top or knee to indicate when a harmony change is needed. Identify the words sung on each signal as *money down*. (To play a tremolo, rapidly alternate mallets on the C resonator bell.)

• Sing to check their answers as you play C or G as indicated on page 135.

La raspa *Mexican Folk Music*

"La raspa" (The Rasp) is a popular Mexican folk dance.

MATCH the harmonic pattern you hear in this dance with one of the patterns below. *first pattern*

134 ADD A LITTLE HARMONY

MEETING **INDIVIDUAL** NEEDS

ALTERNATE TEACHING STRATEGIES

OBJECTIVE 1 Draw bar lines for eight measures on the board. Write a G (or *do*) over the first measure. Have students listen to "La raspa" while you tap the strong beat in each measure. (Note that "La raspa" is in ⁶₈.) Ask them to signal on which strong beats a chord change occurs. (Measures 4 and 8) Then write G (*do*) or D (*so₁*) over each measure. (G G G D D D D G) Play the pattern indicated on resonator bells or use G and D chords on the autoharp, piano, or guitar to let them check their answer.

OBJECTIVE 2 Write the text to Verse 1 and the refrain of "Pay Me My Money Down" on the board. Slowly sing each phrase while playing the C tremolo. Stop after each phrase to allow students to evaluate the sound. If the students think a harmony change would be appropriate, have them identify the words where the change should occur. Try each suggestion by singing with G instead of C.

HEARING HARMONY

Find your favorite harmony for "Pay Me My Money Down."
As you hear harmony that stays on the same pitch, predict
where harmony changes would sound better.

**COMPARE these harmony changes with your
predictions.**

How many times would you need to play this harmonic
pattern to accompany the song? Which other piece in this
lesson has similar harmony changes? once per verse, once
per refrain; "La raspa"

Dancers of the
Ballet Folklórico
of Mexico City.

Unit 3 *Just Imagine* 135

"How do you create harmony?" (play or sing
two or more pitches at the same time: the
melody pitches and another set of pitches) "In
today's songs, what syllable did you sing when
you wanted to change the harmony part from
do? (low *so*) Have students:

▶ • Sing "Pay Me My Money Down" with the
harmony on page 135.

LESSON SUMMARY

Informal Assessment In this lesson,
students:

OBJECTIVE 1 Changed level to show the
harmonic changes in "La raspa."

OBJECTIVE 2 Signaled when harmonic
changes occurred in "Pay Me My
Money Down."

National Standards for Music Education
1d Sing ostinatos, partner songs, and rounds.
6d Identify instrumental and vocal sounds from
various cultures.
7b Explain musical preferences, using appropriate
musical terms.

MORE MUSIC: Reinforcement

"Down by the Riverside," page 338 (harmonic
changes—I V; Martin Luther King, Jr., Day)

MULTICULTURAL PERSPECTIVES: *"La raspa"* MOVEMENT

Since European colonists first came to North and South
America, many cultural traditions have been so well ab-
sorbed that they now seem to come from the new culture
rather than the old. "La raspa" was brought to Mexico by European settlers many years ago. It probably originated in
Italy, since *raspa* is an Italian noun meaning "file." The same
Italian word, as a verb, means "to scratch the ground like a
chicken." The dance has two contrasting sections; the second
one sounds like an Italian tarantella.

PLAYING INSTRUMENTS: *Timpani/Orff*

Have students transfer the "Pay Me My Money Down" accompaniment to timpani or pitched instruments.

ENRICHMENT: *Harmony and Movement*

Have one group of students play the harmony to "Pay Me
My Money Down" as another group performs the movement in Lesson 4, page 127, *Apply 2.*

LESSON PLANNER

FOCUS Dynamics

OBJECTIVE
OBJECTIVE 1 Sing a song following dynamic markings in the notation

MATERIALS
Recordings
I Don't Care If the Rain Comes
  Down   CD3:4
Listening: Over the Hills and Far
  Away (excerpt) by P. Grainger   CD3:18
Come and Sing Together (unison)   CD3:9
Come and Sing Together (canon)   CD3:25
Come and Sing Together (canon)
  (performance mix)   CD10:15

Resources
Resource Master 3 • 6 (practice)
Listening Map Transparency T • 6 (Over
  the Hills and Far Away)

VOCABULARY
forte, mezzo forte, mezzo piano, piano,
crescendo, decrescendo

▶ = **BASIC PROGRAM**

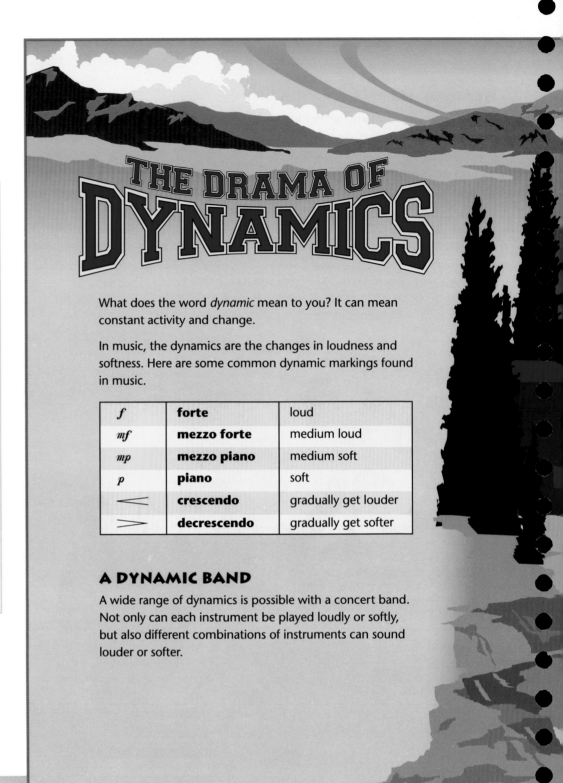

THE DRAMA OF DYNAMICS

What does the word *dynamic* mean to you? It can mean constant activity and change.

In music, the dynamics are the changes in loudness and softness. Here are some common dynamic markings found in music.

f	**forte**	loud
mf	**mezzo forte**	medium loud
mp	**mezzo piano**	medium soft
p	**piano**	soft
<	**crescendo**	gradually get louder
>	**decrescendo**	gradually get softer

A DYNAMIC BAND

A wide range of dynamics is possible with a concert band. Not only can each instrument be played loudly or softly, but also different combinations of instruments can sound louder or softer.

MEETING **INDIVIDUAL** NEEDS

COOPERATIVE LEARNING: *"Storm" Compositions*
Have small groups each create a "storm" within a five- or ten-minute period. Appoint a recorder to write down the group's choices of sounds and notation. Ask a reporter to present the choices to the class. Then have the group perform its composition. Ask students to compare how each group's choices vary.

EXTRA HELP: *Performing "Storm" Compositions*
To set up the visual representation at the board, list each sound—thunder, lightning, and so on—on the left. Draw the graphics horizontally after each sound. Use your arm or a yardstick held vertically to "conduct" by moving slowly across the chart (or ask a student volunteer to conduct).

MOVEMENT: *Showing Dynamics with Range*
Have each of the groups design nonlocomotor movement to represent their storm elements. Discuss changing the range (size) of movement to reflect changes in dynamics. (Examples: When wind is quiet, turn one arm in a circle; when it's louder, turn the whole body. For lightning and thunder, go from a small shape to a large shape.) Guide students to see

LISTENING MAP *Listen for the dynamics in "Over the Hills and Far Away." The markings show you what to expect.*

1 Introduction *mp*

2 A *pp*

3 A *pp*

4 B *pp* <

5 B *p*

6 A *mp*

7 A *mp* <

8 B *mf*

9 B *f* <

10 A *mf* <

11 A *f* <

12 B *ff* <

13 B *fff*

THINK IT THROUGH

If *f* (forte) means loud, what do you think *ff* and *fff* mean? How do the dynamic changes affect the way you feel?

ff - fortissimo, very loud; *fff* - fortissississimo, as loud as possible

Unit 3 *Just Imagine* **137**

"What do you hear at the beginning of a storm?" (distant thunder, light rain, wind speeding up) Have students:

▶ • Sing "I Don't Care If the Rain Comes Down" CD3:4 a few times, substituting a new word for *dance* each time. (See page 108.)

▶ • Describe more details of storm sounds.

"Today you'll create a 'storm' with sound and make up a way to write your music."

2 **DEVELOP**

1. Create a "storm" composition and introduce dynamic markings. Have students:

▶ • Suggest vocal and body percussion sounds which imitate those of a storm.

▶ • Devise graphic notation for each sound. (Optional: Use **Resource Master 3 • 6** for graphic notation.) Draw it on the board.

▶ • Devise notation for dynamic variations.

▶ • Experiment with putting the sounds together to create a "storm," then draw the sequence on the board.

▶ • Divide into groups, one for each storm sound, and perform "Storm," following the notation. (See *Extra Help* on the bottom of page 136.)

▶ • Read page 136 about dynamics and compare markings with their own graphic notation.

2. Review "Over the Hills and Far Away" CD3:18 **(p. 130). Follow a listening map with dynamic markings.** Have students:

• Clap the rhythm of the theme on page 130.

▶ • Follow the map, page 137. (Optional: Use **Listening Map Transparency T • 6.**)

▶ • Discuss the *Think It Through*.

---

that larger movements, which involve more body parts and/or more space, can represent louder sounds; smaller movements, which use fewer body parts and/or less space, can represent quieter sounds. Have each group perform their sound and movement alone as you lead them across the "notation." Have others suggest changes in the notation or the performance.

PLAYING INSTRUMENTS: *Percussion/Keyboards*

Percussion: Transfer "Storm" to unpitched percussion.

Keyboards: Incorporate the following effects into

"Storm." Create other effects, and if using an electronic keyboard, explore a variety of tone colors.

With sustain pedal: octave tremolo, low register; palm/hand cluster, low register; single slow glissando up, high register; continuous glissando up and down, middle register.

Without sustain pedal: slow, staccato two-finger clusters, alternating hands; four random staccato pitches, high register.

Unit 3 JUST IMAGINE **137**

continued from previous page

3 APPLY

Review "Come and Sing Together" (unison, p. 115). Sing it with dynamics and as a two-part canon. Have students:

▶ • Sing the song (unison) **CD3:9**.

▶ • Sing again, following the top part of the notation on pages 138–139.

▶ • With a partner, discuss the dynamic markings and how they should be sung.

OBJECTIVE 1 Informal Assessment

▶ • Sing the song, following the dynamic markings.

• Sing it as a two-part canon after they are secure singing it in unison **CD3:25**.

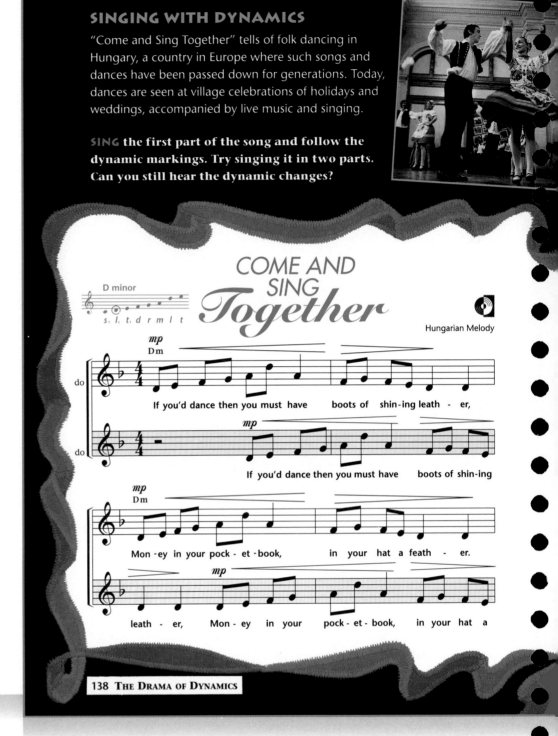

SINGING WITH DYNAMICS

"Come and Sing Together" tells of folk dancing in Hungary, a country in Europe where such songs and dances have been passed down for generations. Today, dances are seen at village celebrations of holidays and weddings, accompanied by live music and singing.

SING the first part of the song and follow the dynamic markings. Try singing it in two parts. Can you still hear the dynamic changes?

138 THE DRAMA OF DYNAMICS

MEETING **INDIVIDUAL** NEEDS

ALTERNATE TEACHING STRATEGY

OBJECTIVE 1 List the dynamic markings on the board. Point to each marking as the students chant or sing the first phrase with that dynamic. Sing each phrase from the notation one by one, following the dynamics marked.

SPECIAL LEARNERS: *Work with Dynamics*

Beginning a sound at the correct dynamic level—either softly or loudly enough—is both an important social and music performance skill. Students who have not yet learned

to control the dynamics of their speaking voices will benefit from additional work with dynamics. Demonstrate your conducting gesture for forte, give a pitch, and then have all students sing and hold the pitch on cue. Repeat with piano. Continue to practice entrances to familiar songs at different dynamic levels, including mezzo forte and mezzo piano.

MULTICULTURAL PERSPECTIVES: *Folk Music*

Hungarians take great pride in their folk music and dancing. Songs such as "Come and Sing Together" have been passed down through the generations for hundreds of years.

"As you name the dynamics you used in today's music, (student's name) can write the markings for each one on the board." (loud—forte, soft—piano, medium loud, or soft—mezzo forte or mezzo piano, crescendo and decrescendo). Have students:

▶ • Suggest the dynamics for each phrase of "Come and Sing Together." (Write on the board the order of dynamic markings suggested by the class before singing the song.)

▶ • Sing the song, using the dynamics chosen.

LESSON SUMMARY

Informal Assessment In this lesson, students:

OBJECTIVE 1 Demonstrated understanding of traditional dynamic markings by singing "Come and Sing Together" with the dynamics marked in the notation.

National Standards for Music Education
4b Create and arrange short songs and instrumental pieces.
4c Use a variety of sound sources when composing.
5c Identify and interpret symbols and traditional terms.

MORE MUSIC: Reinforcement

"A Tragic Story," page 197 (dynamic markings in notation)
"Dormi, dormi," page 328 (dynamics)
"Lincoln Portrait," page 340 (dynamics; Presidents' Day)
"To Meet Mr. Lincoln," page 341 (dynamics; Presidents' Day)
"Haida," page 375 (canon)
Symphony No. 35 ("Haffner"), page 385C (dynamics)

Because traditional Hungarian songs and dances retain the styles of the regions from which they came, they reflect the wide variety within Hungarian culture. Circle and line dances are especially popular. They are mainly girls' dances and are often danced at weddings and village holidays, accompanied by live instrumental music and singing. Other popular dances are the csárdás (**char** dash), a couples dance, and the verbunko (**ver** bun ko), a military-style dance. Professional folk-dance companies also perform in a more athletic style using war-like movements and sword-twirling.

ENRICHMENT: *Singing with Dynamics*

Have students sing "The Eagle" following the dynamics on page 118.

PLAYING INSTRUMENTS: *Orff*

Have two sets of instrumentalists play the accompaniment from Lesson 2, page 115, each set beginning with one group of singers as they perform "Come and Sing Together" in canon.

LESSON 8

LESSON PLANNER

FOCUS Duration

OBJECTIVES
OBJECTIVE 1 Signal to identify the meter of a song (tested)
OBJECTIVE 2 Signal to identify the predominant rhythmic motive in each section of a piece (tested)

MATERIALS
Recordings
Recorded Lesson: Rhythm Riddle   CD3:26
I's the B'y   CD3:21
Listening: La raspa   CD3:24

Resources
Resource Master 3 • 7 (practice)
Recorder Master R • 14 (pitches E G A)

▶ = BASIC PROGRAM

A METER MYSTERY

The meter signature is missing from the music below.

LISTEN and follow the music. Think about how you can tell what the meter signature should be.

The rhythm has many clues. Clues: How many beats do you feel in a set, or measure? How many sounds to each beat do you hear? Are the beats divided equally or unequally?

What is the meter signature of this song? ⁶₈

WHICH RHYTHM?

"La raspa" has rhythms made for dancing! The music shifts back and forth between two sections, A and B. In each section you hear one rhythmic motive more than any other.

In which section do you hear ♫♫ many times? In which do you hear ♩ ♪ ? Try the motions to each motive, then listen for them again. B section; A section

140

MEETING **INDIVIDUAL** NEEDS

ALTERNATE TEACHING STRATEGIES

OBJECTIVE 1 Sing the verse, patting only on the strong beats, then determine that the beats are felt in sets of two. Review the contrasting feeling of two and three sounds per beat, and of equal and unequal divisions of the beat, by having the students switch between jogging ♫ and galloping ♩ ♪ as you drum to the beat. Divide the students into two groups and sing "I's the B'y," one group patting each beat, the other clapping the rhythm. Determine that the rhythm may include either three equal eighth notes or a quarter and eighth, which make two unequal sounds to a beat.

Check the notation for confirmation. Remind students that ⁶₈ has these characteristic rhythms with beats felt in sets of two. (Note: Students are not expected to know rhythms written with triplet eighth notes in ²₄ or ⁴₄ .)

OBJECTIVE 2 Describe each motive's sound: ♩ ♪ has two unequal sounds to a beat, and ♫♫ has three equal sounds to a beat. Listen to the A section of "La raspa" only, then have each group perform their motive several times. Decide which motive most closely resembles the music (♩ ♪). Do the same with the B section (♫♫). Each section has other rhythms but one motive is heard more often.

BAILE EN TEHUANTEPEC

When Mexican artist Diego Rivera traveled to the Tehuantepec region of Mexico, he sketched hundreds of scenes, some of which he turned into paintings years later. In this painting, the people are dancing to lively Mexican folk music.

Los Angeles County Museum of Art

1 GET SET

"Raise your hand when you recognize this song from its rhythm." Have students:

Recorded Lesson CD3:26

▶ • Listen to "Rhythm Riddle" to hear only the rhythm of "I's the B'y," then identify the song.

"Let's sing Verse 1. The rhythm in today's music gives each song its own special quality."

2 DEVELOP

1. Review "I's the B'y" CD3:21 **(p. 132). Identify the meter and review the harmony.** Have students:

• Read page 140 (top) and listen to Verse 1.

OBJECTIVE 1 Informal Assessment

• Tell the meter on page 140 and signal with hands on knees for $\frac{2}{4}$, arms folded for $\frac{6}{8}$, hands behind back for $\frac{4}{4}$. ($\frac{6}{8}$)

• Share strategies for determining meter.

• Look on page 132 to see the meter signature.

• Review the harmony pattern on page 133 and sing it with letter names F (*do*) and C (*so,*).

• Sing the song and divide into two groups during the refrain. (melody, harmony)

2. Review "La raspa" CD3:24 **(p. 134). Identify rhythmic motives.** Have students:

• Read page 140 (bottom) and listen to the music. (A and B sections, once through)

• Practice each motive with body percussion. (♩♪♪—clap-pat(R)-pat(L); ♩ ♪—clap-snap)

• Divide into two groups, one for each motive, and perform their motive only when you point to it on the board.

OBJECTIVE 2 Informal Assessment

• Listen to the song, each group standing only during the section in which theirs is the predominant rhythm. (A: ♩ ♪, B: ♪♪♩)

ENRICHMENT: *Writing Lyrics*

Have students write lyrics for the "I's the B'y" harmony pattern on page 133.

BIOGRAPHY: *Diego Rivera*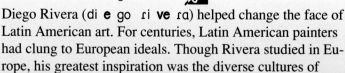

Diego Rivera (di **e** go ɾi **ve** ɾa) helped change the face of Latin American art. For centuries, Latin American painters had clung to European ideals. Though Rivera studied in Europe, his greatest inspiration was the diverse cultures of Mexico. He painted vibrant scenes celebrating the common people and folk traditions of his nation.

BACKGROUND: *"Baile en Tehuantepec"*

This painting portrays a popular folk dance, the zandunga (zɑn **dung** ɑ) of the Tehuantepec (tə **wan** tə pɛk) people. Bold colors, fluid lines, and a lively sense of movement contrast with the people's stony faces. Rivera is affirming both the vitality of traditional culture and the hard lot faced by the ordinary men and women of his country. Rivera had painted Tehuantepec dances before, in a series of frescoes two stories high and three blocks long, for the Mexican Ministry of Education's courtyard.

continued from previous page

3 APPLY

Learn the dance to "La raspa." Have students:

▶ • Prepare to dance to "La raspa" by exploring ways to make a sawing motion. (hand up and down side, toe back and forth across floor)

▶ • Work in pairs to create "sawing machines" to fit with the A section. Each pair must show a large and a small sawing movement. Saw on dotted quarter notes only:

$\frac{6}{8}$ ♩. ♩. | ♩ 𝄾 | ♩ ♩. ♩. | ♩. 𝄾 ‖

▶ • Perform sawing with the A section, then skip, gallop, or slide through space during the B section, returning to partner for A section.

▶ • Learn the dance to "La raspa." (See *Movement* below.)

DANCE TO LA RASPA!

La raspa means "the rasp," a tool used to smooth the rough places on metal. In the dance for "La raspa," the hands and feet move back and forth like a rasp. The dance is sometimes known as the Mexican Hat Dance because it can be danced around a hat placed on the floor.

1 Find a partner.

2 Move to the music.

142

MEETING **INDIVIDUAL** NEEDS

MOVEMENT: *"La raspa"*

This is sometimes mistakenly called the "Mexican Hat Dance" in the United States.

Formation: scattered partners

A section: Partners hold each other's hands and pump arms back and forth in contrary motion to the rhythm of the A section preparation. Feet move in the same rhythm, using a kick-leap motion (alternate extending right heel to right front while landing on the left, then extending left heel to left front while landing on right). **B section:** Partners swing each other's right elbows (8 beats) then left elbows (8 beats). Repeat, or skip, gallop, or slide through shared space to find a new partner. (16 beats)

Point out that in this dance it matters which foot goes first. To avoid kicking his or her partner, each student should kick the *same* heel forward. (left/left) Since they are facing each other, their feet will move alongside each other rather than on top of each other.

④ Skip, gallop, or slide and find a new partner.

③ Swing your partner.

Unit 3 *Just Imagine* 143

"What was the meter for both of today's songs?" (§) "What were the rhythms that gave each section of 'La raspa' its special character?" (A section: ♩ ♪ ; B section: ♫♪) "Let's dance to 'La raspa' once more."

LESSON SUMMARY

Informal Assessment In this lesson, students:

OBJECTIVE 1 Signaled to indicate § as the meter of "I's the B'y."

OBJECTIVE 2 Signaled to identify the prominent rhythmic motive in each section of "La raspa."

National Standards for Music Education
6a Identify simple musical forms by ear.
6b Describe, in words or movement, music from diverse cultures.
8b Describe how other school disciplines are related to music.

MORE MUSIC: Reinforcement

"Over the Sea to Skye," page 149 (§ rhythm patterns)
"The Path to the Moon," page 372 (§ rhythm-patterns)

MATHEMATICS CONNECTION: *Equivalent Notes*

Pose the following questions to students, encouraging them to explain their reasoning. If an eighth note equals 1, what does a quarter note equal? (2) a dotted quarter note? (3) What combinations of notes are equivalent to ♩ or 𝄽 ? (Possible answers: ♫♪ , ♩♪ , ♪ 𝄾 ♪ , ♩ 𝄾) Have students work in pairs to see who can think of the most combinations in five minutes.

CRITICAL THINKING: *Bar Lines in* §

Review how bar lines divide music into measures (Unit 1, page 26). Ask students how they would divide songs in § time into measures. Then have them draw in the missing bar lines on **Resource Master 3 • 7**.

UNIT THREE
LESSON 9

RELATED ARTS MOVEMENT | THEATER | VISUAL ARTS

LESSON PLANNER

OBJECTIVES
To review songs, skills, and concepts learned in Unit 3 and to test students' ability to:
1. Identify melodic movement by repeated notes, steps, and skips
2. Identify *fa*
3. Recognize patterns using C and F from staff notation
4. Read rhythms (♩ ♪, ♫, ♩.) in ⅜ meter

MATERIALS
Recordings
Pay Me My Money Down	CD3:7
One More River	CD3:8
La pájara pinta	CD3:6
I Don't Care If the Rain Comes Down	CD3:4
Unit 3 Assessment A	CD3:27–30
Unit 3 Assessment B	CD3:31–34

RESOURCES
Resource Master 3 • 8 (assessment)
Resource Master 3 • 9 (assessment)
Resource Master TA • 1 (assessment)

▶ = **BASIC PROGRAM**

REVIEW

EXPRESSIVE MOMENTS

Music can express the way a singer or songwriter feels about something, from calm to angry, from amused to serious.

What are some feelings expressed by the songs pictured here?

SING your favorite song from the unit. Sing it expressively.

I Don't Care If the Rain Comes Down

144

MEETING **INDIVIDUAL** NEEDS

PROGRAM IDEA: *Expressive Moments* 🎭 THEATER

This review can be enjoyed in the classroom or presented as a simple program. Additional materials from Unit 3, *Celebrations,* or the *Music Library* may be added as well as original work from the students.

"Think about your favorite song and how it makes you feel. Is it a happy song or a sad song? Imagine what the songwriter was thinking about when he or she wrote that song." Students sing "I Don't Care If the Rain Comes Down" CD3:4, page 108, patting with the beat and having different soloists end each phrase.

"Express yourself as you sing your favorite song from the unit." Students may work in pairs to change the words, tempo, or dynamics and come up with their own expressive rendition of their favorite unit song.

"There are many other ways to be expressive besides singing. Acting is a very popular form of expression." Using their favorite unit song, have students act out the words to the song in a group.

La pájara pinta

Pay Me My Money Down

1. Review melodic concepts in "Pay Me My Money Down" CD3:7 (p. 111). Have students:

▶ • Sing the song, drawing the melodic shape in the air.

• Find examples of repeated pitches, steps, and skips in the melody.

• Sing the last response of the verse with pitch syllables and letter names. (*so so fa mi re do* and G G F E D C)

▶ • Sing the song and perform the movement. (See *Apply 2,* page 127.)

2. Review "One More River" CD3:8 (p. 112). Review rhythms in ⅜. (♩.) **Have students:**

▶ • Sing Verse 1 and the refrain, performing a pat-clap pattern to emphasize the feeling of beats in sets of two.

• Review the rhythmic notation on page 128.

• Sing the song from notation, clapping the rhythm.

▶ • Sing some of the verses they created to add to the song. (See *Develop 1,* page 113.)

3. Sing "La pájara pinta" CD3:6 (p. 110) for fun. Have students:

▶ • Find the related picture on the page and discuss the feelings the song expresses.

▶ • Sing the song.

DRAMA CONNECTION: *Define a Setting*

As students choose songs to perform, have them consider giving their song a specific place or setting. Ask them to imagine, as the character or singer, where they are and what they "see" that makes them want to sing. "Where are you? On a street in the rain? What street? Is it night or day? How does the rain feel? Taste?" Encourage students to imagine the details, then to write and draw the details. Ask students to use class furniture to define their setting and then to perform their song in this setting.

SPECIAL LEARNERS: *Music and Feelings*

Students who feel unhappy, angry, lonely, or without adult support can use music as an outlet for these emotions. Discuss the link between music and feelings. Ask students to name situations in which music is used to evoke a specific mood—for example, parades, graduation ceremonies, and religious services. Then have students think about how they themselves can turn to music when they are feeling angry or sad. Guide them to see that by finding an outlet for their emotions they can stop their feelings from getting worse. They can express their feelings.

UNIT THREE
LESSON 9

ASSESSMENTS A AND B CD3:27–34

Different recorded examples for Assessments A and B allow for two uses of the same set of questions. When appropriate, recorded examples for Assessment A use familiar musical examples with which students have worked for the given concept. The recorded examples for Assessment B use musical selections the students have not previously worked with for the concept, encouraging the application of knowledge to new material.

The pupil page is intended for those who wish to assess quickly with the whole class or in small groups. Each assessment may be used as a pretest or as a final review before presenting the written test (**Resource Master 3 · 8**).

ANSWERS		
	ASSESSMENT A	**ASSESSMENT B**
1.	d	c
2.	a	c
3.	b	a
4.	b	d

CHECK IT OUT

1. How does this melody move?

   a. steps and skips
   c. repeated notes, steps, and skips
   b. mostly skips
   d. repeated notes and steps

2. Which example do you hear?

   a.
   c.

   b.
   d.

3. Which melody do you hear?

   a.
   c.

   b.
   d.

4. Which rhythm do you hear?

146

MEETING **INDIVIDUAL** NEEDS

PORTFOLIO ASSESSMENT

To evaluate student portfolios, use the Portfolio Assessment form on **Resource Master TA · 1**. See page 104B for a summary of Portfolio Opportunities in this unit.

LANGUAGE ARTS CONNECTION: *Poetry or Play* THEATER

Have students choose their favorite song in the unit and write a poem about how it makes them feel. Alternatively, they can work in small groups to write a short play that focuses on the feelings they experienced while singing their favorite song. Students may read their poems to the class or act out their short plays.

CREATE

Snappy Interludes

CREATE an eight-beat pattern. Use each word and rhythm at least once. On a piece of paper, write your pattern.

cross

hip - po

el - e- phant

The boxes below will help you plan your patterns.

cross

PERFORM the pattern twice through as an interlude between the verses of "One More River."

Write

Choose a person, bird, or animal from one of the songs in this unit.

Write a diary entry describing how the person, bird, or animal you chose feels about what happens in the song.

Unit 3 *Just Imagine* 147

CREATE AND WRITE

1. Create and perform interludes. Have students:

• Follow the instructions on page 147 to create and perform interludes to "One More River." (Optional: Use **Resource Master 3 • 9** to fill in rhythm boxes.)

2. Write diary entries. Have students:

▶ • Write diary entries as described. (Read selected entries to the class and sing the corresponding songs.)

> **National Standards for Music Education**
> **5d** Use standard symbols to notate patterns.
> **8b** Describe how other school disciplines are related to music.
> **9c** Identify and describe various daily uses of music.

ART CONNECTION: *Silhouettes* VISUAL ARTS

Have students notice the black and white pictures on these pages. Tell them that these are called silhouettes, which are like shadows—solid shapes without many interior details. Silhouette art is usually one color, often black. At the turn of the century, it was popular to have portraits cut from paper by silhouette artists. Ask students if they have ever created a silhouette by projecting shadows of their hands to create animals on a wall, or if they have noticed their shadows on sunny days. Invite them to create silhouette pictures by cutting shapes out of black paper and pasting them on a white background.

When I First Came to This Land

Unit 3 Reinforcement
fa; C F, *page 127*

More Reinforcement
♪, ♩, *page 27*
I IV V chords, *page 183*

1. Introduce the song CD3:35. Have students:

• Listen to the song and imagine the various emotions the singer might be feeling. Describe what it might be like to build a farm.

• Clap the rhythm of the refrain, reading it from the notation.

• Sing the refrain.

• List key words in each verse (*shack, cow, horse, wife, son*) and tell why the singer might have given each person or thing on the list its "nickname."

• Identify the song as being a cumulative song. (Each verse gets longer by adding a phrase to the verses before it.)

• Sing the song.

2. Sing with solo parts. Have students:

• Sing the song with a different soloist singing the first part of each verse.

• Create new verses with "nicknames" and sing them with new soloists.

MORE SONGS TO SING

When I
First Came
to This
Land

Words and Music by Oscar Brand

148

TRO - © Copyright 1957 (renewed) and 1965 Ludlow Music, Inc., New York, NY. Used by Permission.

MEETING **INDIVIDUAL** NEEDS

ENRICHMENT: *Reading Pitches*

After students have learned *fa*, C, and F (Unit 3, Lesson 4, page 124), have them sing the third line of "When I First Came to This Land" with pitch syllables and pitch letter names, then play it on a melodic instrument each time it occurs.

PLAYING INSTRUMENTS: *Pitched*

Point out the chord symbols above the staff in "When I First Came to This Land." Review that these chord names

are based on the chord roots, then help students find the pitches for each chord. (C E G, F A C, G B D) Have some students practice a chordal accompaniment to the song and perform it as the rest of the class sings.

IMPROVISATION: *Creating an Interlude*

Have students improvise interludes between verses of "When I First Came to This Land." Prepare for this by singing the song and silently counting to eight between the verses. Then improvise for eight beats on resonator bells, using pitches C D E G A.

Over the Sea to Skye

Music by Annie MacLeod
Words by Sir Harold Boulton

Pentatonic

"Speed, bon - nie boat, like a bird on the wing:
"Car - ry the lad that's— born to be king

On - ward! the sail - ors cry!___ Skye!"
O - ver the sea to

Verse

1. Loud the winds howl, loud the waves roar,
2. Tho the waves leap, soft shall ye sleep,
3. Man - y's the lad fought on that day,
4. Burned are our homes, ex - ile and death

Thun - der clouds rend the air;___ Baf - fled our foes,
O - cean's a roy - al bed;___ Rocked in the deep,
Well the clay more could wield,___ When the night came,
Scat - ter the loy - al men;___ Yet ere the sword

Last time, go back to
the beginning and sing to the end
(Da Capo al Fine)

stand on the shore, Fol - low they will not dare.___
flo - ra will keep Watch by your wea - ry head.___
si - lent - ly lay Dead on Cul - lo - den's field.___
cool in the sheath, Char - lie will come a - gain.___

Unit 3 *Just Imagine* 149

Over the Sea to Skye

Unit 3 Reinforcement
§ rhythm patterns, *pages 117, 131, 143*
More Reinforcement
la, page 79

1. Introduce the song CD3:36. Have students:

• Listen to the song and identify the tempo and form. (slow; A B A)

• Clap this rhythm from the verse (notate it on the board):

• Listen to the refrain and Verse 1 of the song and signal when they hear the rhythm on the board.

• Listen to the song while following the notation.

• Have students describe the emotions evoked by the lyrics and style of the song. (Grief, pride, hope, and so on; discuss the song's background and the meanings of the difficult words.)

• Sing the song. (Optional: Use "Over the Sea to Skye" Performance Mix CD10:16.)

2. Read pitches and change dynamics. Have students:

• Practice singing patterns from the pitch set of the verse: *la, do re mi.*

• Sing the pitches of the verse with syllables.

• Choose dynamics for each verse, then sing the song with those dynamics.

BACKGROUND: *"Over the Sea to Skye"*

The words to this song were originally written by Scottish poet Robert Louis Stevenson (1850–1894). The poem is about Bonnie Prince Charlie, a descendant of the Stuart British monarchs, who tried to recapture the British throne for his family. After losing a battle in 1745, he took refuge in the Isle of Skye in Scotland. Annie MacLeod composed the melody for the poem.

CRITICAL THINKING: *Compare and Contrast*

Have students compare "Over the Sea to Skye" with other songs about war and national pride, such as "The Star-Spangled Banner," and contrast the style and effect.

ENCORE
MULTICULTURAL PERSPECTIVES
RELATED ARTS MOVEMENT THEATER VISUAL ARTS

Traditionally, most Native American music is sung, accompanied by rattles and drums. Flutes were also popular among Indians in North and South America. Today, the flute is still used among many Native Americans such as the Cahuilla, the Andean, and the Lakota.

Western flute

Look at the pictures of the two flutes. How are these flutes the same? How are they different?

Native American flute

LISTENING ♫ **Powama** *Cahuilla Song*

The words of the Cahuilla song "Powama" are "powama powama yawe." This means "these feathers move when you dance." Listen to Ernest Siva, a member of the Cahuilla Nation, play "Powama."

150

MEETING **INDIVIDUAL** NEEDS

BACKGROUND: *Wiirer*

Flutes of many sizes, shapes, and materials were common among Native American peoples. They were played as solo instruments in courtship and for personal entertainment at quiet times. *Wiirer* is the Serrano name for a flute made of elderberry cane and blown through a whistle-type end.

BIOGRAPHY: *Ernest Siva*

Ernest Siva (**sι** vɑ) is a Native American of Cahuilla (kə **wi** ə) and Serrano (Maringá´) (sɛ **rɑ** no ma **rιng** ɑ)

ancestry. He was born and raised on the Morongo Reservation in California and learned music in the traditional way, from the elders of his tribe. Siva is one of the few remaining people who know these songs. He performs at traditional events and also works in music education and ethnomusicology.

MULTICULTURAL PERSPECTIVES: *Powama*

Powama (po **wɑ** ma) is a traditional bird song of the Cahuilla Nation. Bird songs are a very old type of song that are usually sung and danced. They tell stories about the

in Flight

El condor pasa *Andean Song*
LISTENING

The Indians of South America also have flute songs about birds. "El condor pasa" is a popular folk song which describes the majesty of the condor as it flies over the Andes mountains.

Edgar Zurita playing the quena.

Powama CD3:37

Listen to a Cahuilla song played on the wiirer and identify its form. Have students:

• Read about Native American flutes, comparing the two flutes shown. (Western flute—made of metal, has keys over holes, played sideways; Native American flute—made of wood or cane, no keys, played vertically)

• Listen to the song played on the wiirer (**wɪɾ** əɾ).

• Listen again, and describe the form of Powama. (A A B A)

El condor pasa CD3:38

Listen to an Andean Indian flute song and compare the quena and wiirer. Have students:

• Read about the Andean song and look at the picture of the quena player.

• Share what they know about condors. (largest bird of North and South America, very endangered)

• Locate the Andes Mountains on a map and identify which countries they cross.

• Listen to "El condor pasa" played on the quena (**ke** nɑ) by Edgar Zurita (**ɛd** gər zu **ɾi** tɑ).

• Compare the sounds of the two flutes, the wiirer and quena. (They are similar in tone color and in pitch.)

beginnings of things on earth and have been passed down among the Cahuilla people for many generations.

BIOGRAPHY: *Edgar Zurita*

Edgar Zurita is a Bolivian of Andean Indian heritage. While growing up in Bolivia, he learned the traditional music of his country at La Scuela Jkhrkas (lɑ **skwe** lɑ **kɑɾ** kɑs), a school where folk music traditions are taught.

SCIENCE CONNECTION: *The Condor*

Have students research and illustrate reports about condors, including the California condor and Andean condor. They can learn about the condors' size, environment, and potential imminent extinction.

ART CONNECTION: *A Collage of Birds*
VISUAL ARTS

Have students make a collage of birds. Students can draw pictures of the birds mentioned in the lesson or cut out pictures from magazines, and then decorate the collage with natural finds such as twigs, grass, small pebbles, or sand.

ENCORE

MULTICULTURAL PERSPECTIVES

continued from previous page

A Lakota Legend CD3:39

Illustrate a Lakota legend. Have students:

• Listen to the legend as told by Gary Fields.

• Illustrate the part of the story they liked best.

• Place finished pictures in the front of the room in the sequence of the story.

• Listen to the story again, checking the pictures to find any missing sections.

Among many Native Americans, the flute was the instrument that a young man used to court a young woman. Each day, he played beautiful melodies for her. According to Lakota legend, the first flute was created to win the heart of an important chieftain's daughter. Here is the story:

During a time when food was difficult to find, a young man from a certain village goes hunting. As he is walking, he spots some elk tracks. He begins to follow the tracks and soon loses his way in the forest. Because it is too dark to return home, he decides to spend the night there. He begins to make his bed for the night, but he is stopped by a strange sound. He listens more closely. After a time, he falls asleep. He dreams. In his dream, he meets a red-headed woodpecker, "woknooka."

The next morning, the young man wakes up to the sight of the woodpecker sitting in a tree. As the bird flies from tree to tree, the young man follows him. Finally, the bird lands on a hollow branch. The wind blows through the branch. Suddenly, the young man remembers the sound of the wind blowing through the branch as the strange sound he heard the night before. He takes the branch and returns to his home.

Once he is back, he tries to make the beautiful sound he remembers. Nothing happens. After many failures, he goes back out to the forest by himself. Once again, he falls asleep. In his dream, the woodpecker reappears as a man who shows him how to make a flute from the hollow branch. When the young man wakes up, he goes home. Once there, he makes a flute. When he learns about the chieftain's daughter who will not fall in love with anyone, he decides that he will win her heart by making up special flute songs for her.

 LISTEN to Gary Fields, a member of the Lakota and Cree Nations, tell the story about the first flute.

152 MELODIES IN FLIGHT

MEETING **INDIVIDUAL** NEEDS

MULTICULTURAL PERSPECTIVES: *The Lakota*

The Lakota (la **ko** ta) are one of several groups that make up what is commonly called the Sioux (**su**) nation. They were among the great Native American cultures that thrived on the northern Plains region of North America. The Lakota people once hunted buffalo and lived in tipis (**ti** piz). They were moved to reservations in North and South Dakota as a result of treaties with the United States government in the 1800s. They are very active in maintaining their traditional cultures.

BIOGRAPHY: *Gary Fields*

Gary Fields is a member of the Lakota (Sioux) and Cree tribes. He is the leader of Morning Star, a group that performs Native American songs and dances throughout the United States and Europe. Fields believes in the importance of sharing Native American traditions in order to educate people accurately and to promote better understanding of Native American cultures among people everywhere.

This poem expresses the importance of flutes in Native American cultures.

FOR THE FLUTE PLAYERS

Theirs is the sound of wood
whispering Creator's breath
through branches hollowed
with sacred instruction

Theirs is the sound of breezes
dancing timeless songs
of passionate hearts
in circles around the Earth

Theirs is the sound of birds
sending meadow voices
on feathered wings
to all directions

Theirs is the sound of echoes
shaping red rock walls
in long canyon spaces
that remember forever

—Edwin Schupman
Muscogee (Creek)

Encore 153

For the Flute Players

Read a poem about flutes in Native American cultures. Have students:

• Read the poem aloud.

• Describe in their own words what the sound of the flute is being compared to in each stanza. (wood whispering, breezes dancing, birds singing, echoes in canyons)

• Divide into small groups and perform each stanza, adding vocal expression, movement, and sound effects.

BIOGRAPHY: *Edwin Schupman*

Edwin Schupman, a member of the Muscogee (Creek) Nation of Oklahoma, works in American Indian education. He is also an ethnomusicologist who believes in the importance of accurately understanding the music and cultures of Native Americans. Schupman wrote the poem to express his respect for the traditions associated with the flute and for the work of the many flute-makers and players who keep those traditions alive.

LANGUAGE ARTS CONNECTION: *Legends*

Have students look up the definition of *legend*, then research legends from other cultures. They might look for other legends related to musical instruments.

ART CONNECTION: *Illustrating the Poem*

Have students use art materials or clay to illustrate the imagery of "For the Flute Players."

CONNECTIONS

MULTICULTURAL PERSPECTIVES

Through exposure to diverse materials, students develop an awareness of how people from many cultures create and participate in music. This unit includes:

African/African American, Caribbean, and Middle Eastern

- **Ayazein,** Egyptian folk song, 174
- Dumbek (African/Middle Eastern drum), 174
- **Hosanna, Me Build a House,** calypso, 164
- **I Missed the Bus,** rap by Kris Kross, 186
- **Little David, Play on Your Harp,** spiritual, 168
- **Nathaniel's Rap,** by poet Eloise Greenfield, 184
- **Stone Pounding,** Jamaican folk song, 160
- **Things Ain't What They Used to Be,** by Mercer Ellington, 191
- **Tina Singu,** folk song from Lesotho, 158

Asian/Asian American

- **Hoe Ana Te Vaka,** Tahitian folk song, 181

European/European American

- *Anna Codde,* by Dutch painter Maerten van Heemskerck, 177
- **Hoedown,** by Aaron Copland, 178
- **Sarasponda,** Dutch spinning song, 167
- **Things Ain't What They Used to Be,** jazz improvisation by pianist Marian McPartland, 191

Hispanic/Hispanic American

- **Guadalquivir,** Andean Indian/Spanish carnival music, 163

Native American

- **Guadalquivir,** Andean Indian/Spanish carnival music, 163

For a complete listing of materials by culture throughout the book, see the Classified Index.

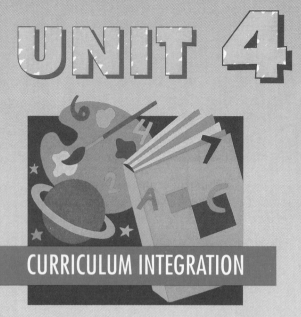

UNIT 4

CURRICULUM INTEGRATION

Activities in this unit that promote the integration of music with other curriculum areas include:

Art

- Create fire-safety posters, 163A
- Use geometric shapes to draw houses, 167B
- Draw spinning wheels, 167B
- Make stone sculptures, 175A
- Build models of their dream houses, 183

Math

- Play a number game with stones, 163B
- Draw room diagrams, find areas, 167A
- Use geometric shapes to draw houses, 167B
- Draw wheels using a compass, 167B
- Create units of measurement, 175A
- Test predictions of probability, 179A
- Find the area and perimeter of squares, 179B

Reading/Language Arts

- Write or outline a dialogue, 163A
- Develop a picture code language, 175B
- Create party invitations, 179A
- Write a rap, 187

Science

- Create fire-safety posters, 163A
- Explore the weathering of stone, 163B
- Create erosion models, 167A

Social Studies

- Draw a map of the Nile river, 175B
- Research folk dancing, 179B
- Research the origins of calypso music, 194

New! **UNIT OPENERS WITH THEMATIC TEACHING PROJECTS**

PLANNER

ASSESSMENT OPTIONS

Informal Performance Assessments

Informal Assessments correlated to Objectives are provided in every lesson with Alternate Strategies for reteaching. Frequent informal assessment allows for ongoing progress checks throughout the course of the unit.

Formal Assessment

An assessment form is provided on pupil page 194 and Resource Master 4•9. The questions assess student understanding of the following main unit objectives:

- Recognize Patterns using octaves with C and C'
- Read the *short long short* (♪ ♩ ♪) rhythm pattern

Music Journal

Encourage students to enter thoughts about selections, projects, performances, and personal progress. Some journal opportunities include:

- *Think It Through,* 171, 187
- Description of imagined rap, 185
- Write, 185

Portfolio Opportunities

Update student portfolios with outcome-based materials, including written work, audiotapes, videotapes, and/or photos that represent their best work for each unit. Some portfolio opportunities in this unit include:

- Work with rhythm notation, ties, ♪ ♩ ♪ (Resource Masters 4•1, 4•3, 4•4), TE 160, 173, 174
- Two-part singing (audiotape), TE 159
- Playing Orff Orchestrations (audiotape), TE 164, 169
- Playing ostinatos (audiotape), TE 174, 181
- Composing and notating ostinato (audiotape/Resource Master 4•5), TE 176
- Pitch syllable labeling (Resource Master 4•6), TE 178
- Circling chord roots; naming chords (Resource Master 4•7), TE 182
- Cooperative Learning: performing rap (audiotape/Resource Master 4•8), TE 186
- Playing melodic, chordal, rhythmic accompaniments (audiotape), TE 188
- Check It Out (formal assessment), 194; Resource Master 4•9
- Portfolio Assessment (Resource Masters TA•1–5), 194
- Create 195; Resource Master 4•10
- Write, 195

MY MUSIC NOTEBOOK

UNIT 4

CONCEPT

			LESSON 1 CORE p.158	**LESSON 2 CORE** p.164	**LESSON 3** p.168
		FOCUS	Duration, ♪ ♩ ♪ (*short long short*)	Pitch, octave	Timbre
		SELECTIONS	Tina Singu Stone Pounding Guadalquivir (listening)	Hosanna, Me Build a House Tina Singu Sarasponda	Little David, Play on Your Harp Hosanna, Me Build a House

MUSICAL ELEMENTS	CONCEPTS	UNIT OBJECTIVES Bold = Tested			
EXPRESSIVE QUALITIES	Dynamics			• Choose and sing dynamics	
	Tempo			• Sing song in two tempos • *Listen to slow phrases*	
	Articulation		• Hear staccato		
TONE COLOR	Vocal/ Instrumental Tone Color	• Identify changed voices	• Hear Andean quena	• Define vocables	• Recognize changed voices • *Hear varied vocal tone colors, including falsetto*
DURATION	Beat/Meter		• Pat and clap with beat • Move with half-note beat • See graphic notation of beat	• Dance with beat	• Perform step-clap with beat
	Rhythm	• **Read ♪ ♩ ♪** • Identify syncopation	• **Clap rhythm of words (E)** • **Perform and describe ♪ ♩ ♪ pattern (E/D)** • **Recognize ♪ ♩ ♪ rhythm aurally (P)** • **See graphic notation of ♪ ♩ ♪ (I)** • *Review ♫, ♩, ♩, ♩*	• Sing syncopated rhythms	• **Sing ♪ ♩ ♪ (Rf)** • Compare rhythms • *Play rhythm of words*
PITCH	Melody	• **Recognize octaves, C, C¹** • Use do¹	• Sing octaves • Hear melodic ornamentation	• **Draw and describe melodic shape (E/D)** • **Identify and sing octave motive (I/P)** • *Play patterns with C, C¹ (E)*	• **Recognize octaves (Rf)** • Compare melodies • *Echo-sing melodic patterns for intonation*
	Harmony	• Identify I IV V chords		• Sing song in two parts • *Play Orff orchestration* • *Play patterns with C, C¹*	• *Play Orff orchestration*
	Tonality major/minor		• Observe key signature of D major		
DESIGN	Texture		• *Play drum accompaniment*		• *Play Latin percussion*
	Form/ Structure		• Recognize and sing call-and-response • See symbols for and sing A, A¹ sections	• See symbols for A, B, C sections and coda	• Sing B and C sections of song • See *Da capo al Fine*
CULTURAL CONTEXT	Style/ Background	• Hear and sing music from diverse cultures • Develop understanding of musical concepts using selections from diverse cultures	• Sing song from Lesotho • Sing Jamaican folk song • Listen to Bolivian carnivalito	• Sing Jamaican calypso song	• Sing spiritual • See African and Haitian drums

Learning Sequence: E = Explore, D = Describe, I = Identify, P = Practice, Rf = Reinforce, Rd = Read, C = Create   See also *Program Scope and Sequence,* page 402.

OVERVIEW

LESSON 4 CORE p.172	LESSON 5 CORE p.176	LESSON 6 p.180	LESSON 7 p.184	LESSON 8 p.188
Duration, ♪ ♩ ♪ (*short long short*)	Pitch—high *do*, C¹	Harmony, I-IV-V chord changes	Duration, syncopation	Pitch/Improvisation
Guadalquivir (listening) Stone Pounding Ayazein (listening)	Sarasponda Hoedown (listening)	Tina Singu Hoe Ana Te Vaka Hosanna, Me Build a House	Stone Pounding I Missed the Bus (listening) Nathaniel's Rap (listening)	What's New? (listening) Hosanna, Me Build a House Things Ain't What They Used to Be (listening) Little David, Play on Your Harp
	• Hear dynamic contrasts		• *Choose dynamics for performance*	
	• Hear presto tempo		• *Choose tempos, tempo changes for performance*	
	• Hear staccato		• Define accents • *Choose use of accents for performance*	• Hear legato phrasing
• Hear Egyptian music and dumbek	• Hear orchestral music		• Listen to and compose rap	• Hear steel drums • Hear jazz piano
• Move with beat • Locate measures with ♪ ♩ ♪ • *Pound with beat*	• Make up 16-beat movement • *Move with beat*	• Perform traditional movement with half-note beat	• Tap with beat of syncopated music	• Pat-clap with beat
• **Clap, read, and write tied rhythms and ♪ ♩ ♪ (Rd/Rf)** • **Sing from notation including ♪ ♩ ♪ (Rd/Rf)** • **Perform ostinato with ♪ ♩ ♪ (Rd/Rf)** • Distinguish 2-beat rhythm patterns	• Compose melody to given rhythm	• ***Accompany song with ostinatos including ♫, ♩, ♩, ♪ ♩ ♪ (Rf)*** • *Chant rhythm pattern*	• Step with rhythm • Define syncopation • Perform poem with syncopation • *Read poem with ♫, ♩, ♩* • *Improvise syncopated B section*	• Define and perform rhythmic improvisation • *Improvise syncopated B section*
	• **See octaves notated (Rd)** • **Move with octave motive (Rf)** • **Label C, C¹ on staff (I/P/Rd)** • **Create and notate melody with C, C¹ (C/Rf)** • Sing *do* and *do¹* • *Use pitch syllables do re mi fa so la do¹*	• Name pitches of C, F, G chords and chord roots		• **Recognize octave (Rf)** • **Use C, C¹ (Rf)** • Discuss and perform melodic improvisation • Name pitches of melodic motives
	• Perform pitched ostinato	• Define chord, chord root, chord names, chord changes • Play I, IV, V chords		• Play I, IV, V chords
• Hear modal Egyptian music	• Hear *do/do¹* octaves in C, D, and G major	• Define and play I, IV, V chords in C major		• Locate and play motives in C major • Recognize tonal center
• Perform syncopated ostinato	• Perform ostinato	• *Accompany song with ostinatos*	• Use recorded rap accompaniment	• *Play unpitched and pitched accompaniments*
	• Devise B section movement • *Recognize phrases*	• Learn harmonic pattern of B section	• Recognize refrains • *Improvise syncopated B section*	• *Vary accompaniment by section (A B C)* • *Improvise syncopated B section*
• Hear Egyptian folk song • See dumbek	• Hear music by Aaron Copland	• Learn Tahitian canoe song and movements	• Hear rap by Kris Kross	• Hear jazz improvisation

UNIT 4 PLANNER

UNIT 4

SKILLS

SKILLS		LESSON 1 CORE p.158	LESSON 2 CORE p.164	LESSON 3 p.168
CREATION AND PERFORMANCE	Singing	• Sing in Sotho • Sing octaves	• Sing in 2 parts • Sing syncopated rhythms, octave motive, dynamics • *Practice downward and upward octave skips*	• *Practice intonation by echo-singing melodic patterns*
	Playing	• *Play drums*	• *Play Orff orchestration* • *Play patterns with C, C¹*	• *Play Orff orchestration* • *Play rhythm of words on Latin percussion*
	Moving	• Pat and clap with beat • Move with half-note beat • Step rhythmically • *Identify various group movement formations*	• Dance with beat	• Perform step-clap with beat
	Improvising/ Creating			
NOTATION	Reading	• Read graphic notation of beat and rhythm • See symbols for and sing A and A¹ sections • Observe key signature of D major • *Review ♫, ♩, 𝄽, 𝅗𝅥*	• See symbols for A, B, C sections and coda	• See ♪♩♪ • See *Da capo al Fine*
	Writing	• *Write patterns with ♫, ♩, 𝄽, 𝅗𝅥*		
PERCEPTION AND ANALYSIS	Listening/ Describing/ Analyzing	• Identify ♪♩♪	• Compare meanings of two verses • Identify octaves	• Identify changed voices • Compare rhythms, melodies, ideas expressed

 TECHNOLOGY

SHARE THE MUSIC VIDEOS

Use videos to reinforce, extend, and enrich learning.
- Lesson 1, p. 163: Blending Musical Styles (fusion of South American Indian and Spanish styles)
- Lesson 2, p. 167: Making a Music Video (two-part singing)
- Lesson 3, p. 171: Sounds of Percussion (drums)
- Lesson 4, p. 174: Sounds of Percussion (dumbek)
- Lesson 5, p. 178: Blending Musical Styles (fusion of square dance and 20th-century styles)
- Lesson 7, pp. 184–187: Making a Music Video (rap); Introduction to Computers in Music (sampler)

- Lesson 8, pp. 188–191: Sounds of Percussion (steel drum band); Musical Expression (improvise, jazz); Blending Musical Styles (jazz)
- Encore, pp. 198–200: Musical Expression (improvise, jazz); Introduction to Computers in Music (saxophone)

MUSIC WITH *MIDI*

MIDI technology allows students to manipulate musical elements and make musical decisions with this song:
- Lesson 2, p. 167: Sarasponda

OVERVIEW

Italic = Meeting Individual Needs

LESSON 4 CORE p.172	LESSON 5 CORE p.176	LESSON 6 p.180	LESSON 7 p.184	LESSON 8 p.188
• Sing from notation including ♪ ♩ ♪	• Sing pitch syllables including *do¹* • Sing motive with octave	• Sing in Tahitian	• Perform rap	• Sing motives from notation
• Play syncopated drumming ostinato	• Perform ostinato on C, C¹	• Play I, IV, V chords • *Accompany song with ostinatos*		• Play motives from notation • *Play unpitched and pitched accompaniments* • *Play keyboards*
• Move with beat • *Pound on ground with beat*	• Move with octave motive • *Move with beat*	• Perform traditional movement with half-note beat • *Move to show harmony changes*	• Step with rhythm • Do "rap walk" to show refrains	
	• Create movement • Create melody to given rhythm		• Create "rap walks" • Create rap-style performance of poem • *Improvise syncopated B section*	• Improvise melodically and rhythmically • *Improvise syncopated B section* • *Create new lyrics*
• Read notation of ♪ ♩ ♪, tie • Sing from notation including ♪ ♩ ♪ • Read various 2-beat rhythm patterns	• Label C, C¹ on staff • Follow listening map	• Identify chord roots, chord names on notation • Read graphic notation for chord changes		• See notation of melodic theme of improvisation
• *Write tied and syncopated rhythms*	• *Notate ostinato with C, C¹*		• *Notate rap graphically*	
• Compare and contrast rhythm patterns • Listen for rhythm pattern	• Identify octaves, octave motive	• Identify chord changes	• Compare rap performances	• Listen for rhythmic, melodic improvisation • Listen for octaves, syncopation

MUSICTIME™

This notational software develops students' music reading and writing skills through activities correlated to these lessons:
- **Lesson 4, Project 1 (create a syncopated rhythm pattern)**
- **Lesson 5, Project 2 (use high *do*)**
- **Lesson 9, Project 3 (compose a pentatonic melody)**

- **Lesson 5, p. 176: Lesson 19 (C major scale, octave); Lesson 24 (major scales)**
- **Lesson 8, p. 188: Lesson 19 (C major scale, octave); Lessons 2, 4, & 5 (piano keyboard)**

MUSIC ACE™

Music Ace reinforces musical concepts and provides ear-training opportunities for students.
- Lesson 1, p. 154: Lesson 20, 21 & 22 (sharps/flats)
- Lesson 2, p. 164: Lessons 4, 5, & 6 (octave)

NEW! MUSIC ACE 2™

Music Ace 2™ introduces basic rhythm concepts and furthers the melodic and harmonic concepts covered in Music Ace.

UNIT 4 THEME: CONNECTIONS

FOCUS Music connects us to many different people and cultures.

OBJECTIVE To prepare for Unit 4

MATERIALS
Finding a Way (poem)
It's a Lovely Day Today   CD4:1
It's a Lovely Day Today
  (performance mix)   CD10:17

INTRODUCE THE THEME

1. Discuss the theme. "Music is able to connect us to many different people and cultures. Music can help us learn about and understand others who are different from us." Have students:

• Name the people to whom they feel closely connected (family, classmates, teammates) and identify what connects them. (They share the same parents, classrooms, or interests.)

• Consider individuals or groups to whom they feel less connected. (people who live in another part of town, or even another country)

• List all of the similarities instead of differences between themselves and those who are not connected to them. Lead them to see that there are numerous characteristics we share, even with those who are different.

• Recall songs, listening selections, or movement activities they have done this year that came from a place or group of people that was new for them, and discuss ways that music can connect us. (enjoying music from a wide variety of cultures; comparing words, movements, styles of singing, rhythms, pitches, and harmonies)

UNIT 4

CONNEC

Finding A Way

I'd like you for a friend.
I'd like to find the way
Of asking you to be my friend.
I don't know what to say.

What would you like to hear?
What is it I can do?
There has to be some word, some look
Connecting me to you.

—*Myra Cohn Livingston*

154

UNIT 4 THEME PROJECTS

Ask students what they think the phrase "we're all connected" means. Through the songs in this unit, students will find connections between peoples from all over the world as well as people in the same town.

BE A GOOD FRIEND Have students discuss what makes a person a good friend. The outcome of this discussion will be a list of characteristics that make someone a good friend. Put this list in the center of a "Friendship" bulletin

board. Attach a box to the bulletin board (or put the box next to the bulletin board). Have each student put an index card with his or her name in the box. Whenever partners or small groups are needed for an activity, have students pick names from this "Friendship" box. The list of what makes a good friend on the bulletin board will remind students of ways to be a good friend to the others in their group. (*Lesson 1*)

154

2. Introduce "Finding a Way." "We all have connections to the people and places in the world around us. As you read the poem 'Finding a Way,' think of something you have in common with a friend." Have students:

• Listen as you read the poem.

• Share something that they have in common with a friend.

Meet the Poet How people become friends is a favorite topic of Myra Cohn Livingston (b. 1926), who has written or edited over 30 collections of poems. In her verse she tries to capture the everyday world of children, their "early daily experiences of feelings, sights, and sounds," she says. Having worked with children all across the country, she believes that their surroundings matter less than the "humanness" they bring to the simple things in life. She loves poems that make people laugh and has put together several books of humorous verse. Her work has won her many honors.

155

EXPLORE CONNECTIONS Whether building a house ("Hosanna, Me Build a House," page 164) or paddling a canoe ("Hoe Ana Te Vaka," page 181), people need to work together. After discussing how people need to get along in order to work together effectively, have each student pick a name from the "Friendship" box. Have partners talk with each other to find out something that they have in common and something that they each like about each other. Then have them work together to put their conclusions in writing. Put these essays on the "Friendship" bulletin board. *(Lessons 2 and 6)*

CREATE A CALYPSO Have students work in small groups to create new words to "Hosanna, Me Build a House" (page 164). For example: "Hosanna, me did my homework…." Have each group share its calypso lyrics with the class. *(Lesson 2)*

3. Introduce "It's a Lovely Day Today" CD4:1.
"Listen to the song 'It's a Lovely Day Today' and discover what is more fun when it's shared with a friend." Have students:

• Listen to the song and sum up the wish that is being expressed in the words. (Days and experiences are made more special when you can share them with someone.)

• Listen again, tracing the outline of the melody in the air.

• *Optional challenge*: Draw shapes on the board to represent a melody with 1) a smooth narrow range, 2) a stepwise ascending melody, 3) a stepwise descending melody, 4) a melody with many skips and a wide range. Name the drawing that characterizes the type of melody they traced. (4; Tell the class they will be learning about wide distances between pitches in melodies in this unit.)

4. Set the stage for Unit 4. Have students:

• Think again about their responses to how music connects us to others.

• Plan a group performance of the theme song.

• Read the poem "Finding a Way" as an introduction.

• Form two groups and sing "It's a Lovely Day." Alternate phrases between the two groups.

UNIT 4 THEME SONG

It's a Lovely Day Today

Words and Music
by Irving Berlin

156

UNIT 4 MUSIC PROJECT:

Having students write down the music they create helps them gain confidence in dealing with notation and a sense of ownership of their creative work.

1 WRITE THE OSTINATO ON A STAFF Have students write the melodic ostinato they created for "Sarasponda" (page 167) on staff paper. Have them first notate the rhythm pattern from page 167, then write the letter names C or C' below the rhythm notation. Finally, have them transfer the melody to staff paper. *(After Lesson 5)*

Have students cut strips of construction paper for making links in a paper chain. On the back of each strip, have them write a clue to a song in the unit. Clues might include "work song," "game song," "song about people," "working together," "playing together," "meeting people." (More specific clues could also be created.) Select songs to fit each category and determine in advance the order the songs will be sung in the program. Connect the chain to reflect that order. Begin the program by singing the unit theme song, "It's a Lovely Day Today" (page 156). Have students tear off a link of the chain and read the clue. Then the class sings a song that fits that category. For example:

• Work songs: "Tina Singu," "Hosanna, Me Build a House," "Sarasponda," "Hoe Ana Te Vaka" (pages 158, 164, 167, 181)

• Game songs: "Stone Pounding" (page 160)

• Songs about people: "Little David, Play on your Harp," "Nathaniel's Rap," "A Tragic Story," "Sourwood Mountain" (pages 168, 184, 197, 196)

Unit 4 *Connections* 157

WRITING ON A STAFF

2 PLAY AN OSTINATO Invite students to add more pitches to the ostinato from the previous activity. Have them use resonator bells or Orff instruments with the pitches C D E G. Encourage them to begin and end each ostinato on C as they practice. When they are pleased with their melodic patterns, have them again write the letter names under the rhythm notation. Then have them divide into pairs and play each other's ostinatos. For an extra challenge, have students play the ostinatos in canon: start the second ostinato two beats after the first. *(After Lesson 6)*

3 NOTATE THE PATTERN Have students review the ostinatos created in the previous activity by clapping the rhythm and singing or playing the pitches. Then have them write the ostinatos in staff notation. *(After Lesson 8)*

UNIT FOUR
LESSON 1

LESSON PLANNER

FOCUS Duration, ♪ ♩ ♪ (*short long short*)

OBJECTIVES

OBJECTIVE 1 Pat and clap with the beat and rhythm of the words of a song that includes the *short long short* pattern (tested)

OBJECTIVE 2 Clap the rhythm of a phrase including the *short long short* pattern (tested)

MATERIALS

Recordings

Tina Singu	CD4:2
Tina Singu (performance mix)	CD10:18
Recorded Lesson: Pronunciation for "Tina Singu"	CD4:3
Stone Pounding	CD4:4
Recorded Lesson: Switch	CD4:5
Recorded Lesson: Bolivian Rhythm	CD4:6
Listening: Guadalquivir (A section)	CD4:7
Listening: Guadalquivir (entire)	CD4:8

Resources
Resource Master 4 • 1 (practice)
Recorder Master R • 15 (pitches E G A)

VOCABULARY
sharp

▶ = **BASIC PROGRAM**

RHYTHM ALL AROUND

This song from southern Africa is about letting fire burn the bush, or wilderness area. Fire naturally clears the land of old shrub and allows space and sunlight for new growth. *Watsha* means "burn," and the song says "We are the burning fire; we burn, we burn."

SING this call-and-response song and pat with the beat.

Tina Singu

Song from Lesotho
As Sung by Kathleen Hill

158

MEETING **INDIVIDUAL** NEEDS

MULTICULTURAL PERSPECTIVES: *"Tina Singu"*

Lesotho is an African country about the size of the state of Maryland. It is totally surrounded by the Republic of South Africa. The people of Lesotho enjoy the sounds of both folk and modern music. Sankomota, a rock band of Lesotho, is internationally famous. "Tina Singu" is a folk song in call-and-response form, a form often found in cultures in which musical heritage is passed down orally. "Tina Singu" was made popular in the United States in the 1950s by a folk group, The Weavers, whose best-known member is Pete Seeger. The words passed down in the

United States were altered from the original Sotho, the primary language of Lesotho. For example, in correct Sotho *tima* is "blow out," *seng* means "not," and *hocha* is "burn."

MUSIC BUILDS MATH SKILLS

Algebra Clapping to the *short-long-short* rhythm pattern, students strengthen the skill of identifying numerical patterns.

"What are some of the songs, listening selections, or movement activities that you've done this year that come from a place or group of people that was new to you?" Have students:

▶ • List some songs or activities that come to mind and name where they are from.

"Let's continue to explore how the music of different cultures is connected as we learn new songs and a new rhythm pattern."

2 DEVELOP

1. Introduce "Tina Singu" CD4:2. Identify call-and-response form. Have students:

▶ • Read about and listen to the song, noting the call-and-response form.

Recorded Lesson CD4:3

▶ • Listen to "Pronunciation for 'Tina Singu.'"

2. Sing "Tina Singu" as a call-and-response song. Have students:

▶ • Learn the first section and Part 1 of the two-part section. (To listen to Part 1 without Part 2, adjust the stereo balance control.)

▶ • Sing the song and pat with the quarter note beat, alternating hands.

▶ • In two groups, sing the song in call-and-response form and add a dance pattern with their feet. (See *Movement* below.)

Unit 4 *Connections* 159

MOVEMENT: *"Tina Singu"*

Formation: two lines, partners facing, or two concentric circles, partners facing

Step with the half note beat (Verbal Cue: *side, close, side, touch*). *Side*—step right with right foot; *close*—step with left foot, closing next to right foot; *side*—step right again; *touch*—touch left foot next to right foot.

Repeat sequence moving to the left. Reverse right and left every two measures.

Have students assess their performances by watching for precision of movement:

—Did the movement begin on the same foot?

—Were the steps with the beat?

—Did the formations remain clear?

PRONUNCIATION: *"Tina Singu"*

| a f<u>a</u>ther | e ch<u>ao</u>tic | ɛ p<u>e</u>t | i b<u>ee</u> |
| o <u>o</u>bey | u m<u>oo</u>n | | |

UNIT FOUR
LESSON 1

continued from previous page

3. Introduce "Stone Pounding" CD4:4. **Perform the rhythm.** Have students:

▶ • Read about and listen to the song.

▶ • Practice the words, then learn the song.

▶ • Sing the song twice, first moving with the beat by making pounding motions with a fist on the floor or in other palm. Then, the second time, clap the rhythm of the words.

OBJECTIVE 1 Informal Assessment
Recorded Lesson CD4:5

▶ • Listen to "Switch," and switch between clapping the rhythm of the words and patting with the beat when they hear a cue.

• Speak the words *three stone a stone* and perform the following body percussion in the same rhythm: *clap, clap, clap, pat (upper chest near collarbone with one hand)* while you perform the pounding motion with the beat.

• Describe the rhythm pattern of the claps (*three stone a*) as three sounds, *short long short*, occuring over the time of two beats.

"Stone Pounding" was sung years ago by road workers, mostly women, as they broke large stones into smaller pieces. Now children play a game as they sing this song.

SWITCH between clapping the rhythm of the words and patting with the beat.

D major

t, d r m f s l t d'

Jamaican Folk Song
Transcribed by Helen H. Roberts

STONE POUNDING

Three stone a stone, then a three stone a stone, then a
three stone a stone say tam-boo-lay and no quar-rel. You no
hear-e what me yer-ry? You no hear-e what me yer-ry? You no
hear-e what me hear, say tam-boo-lay and no quar-rel.

160 RHYTHM ALL AROUND

MEETING **INDIVIDUAL** NEEDS

ALTERNATE TEACHING STRATEGIES

OBJECTIVE 1 Have students watch as you sing and walk first with the beat of "Stone Pounding," then the rhythm of the words. Ask them when you were walking with the beat and how they could tell. (Rhythm is made of long and short sounds that match the words.) Have them listen and walk with the beat, then sing and walk the rhythm. Then have them listen, switching between patting with the beat and clapping the rhythm as you point to a visual cue (a card marked *beat* or *rhythm*). It may help to start by switching at the end of each phrase.

OBJECTIVE 2 Play eight-beat rhythmic phrases with ♩, ♫, 𝄽, and ♩ on a drum. Play each phrase twice. Separate each pair of phrases with four beats on the rim. Play the *short long short* pattern only as part of the phrase from page 161. Include this phrase regularly as you drum. Students walk with the beat during all phrases but freeze upon hearing the phrase with the *short long short* pattern, then clap the rhythm with you on its repeat.

EXTRA HELP: *Rhythm Review*

Use **Resource Master 4•1** for students requiring a review of half notes, quarter notes, eighth notes, and quarter rests.

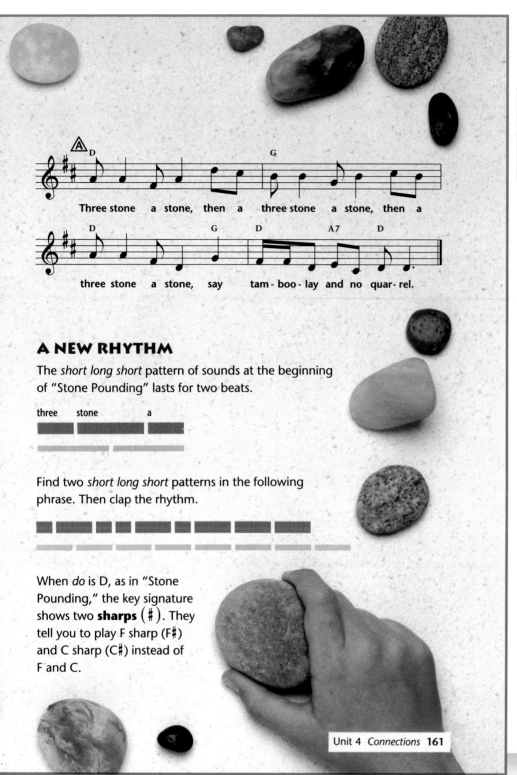

4. Introduce the *short long short* rhythm pattern. Have students:

▶ • Read page 161 about the new rhythm pattern.

Recorded Lesson CD4:6

▶ • Listen to "Bolivian Rhythm" and clap to the rhythmic phrase shown on page 161.

OBJECTIVE 2 Informal Assessment

▶ • Listen to the phrase again, then clap the rhythm pattern.

Three stone a stone, then a three stone a stone, then a

three stone a stone, say tam-boo-lay and no quar-rel.

A NEW RHYTHM

The *short long short* pattern of sounds at the beginning of "Stone Pounding" lasts for two beats.

three   stone   a

Find two *short long short* patterns in the following phrase. Then clap the rhythm.

When *do* is D, as in "Stone Pounding," the key signature shows two **sharps** (♯). They tell you to play F sharp (F♯) and C sharp (C♯) instead of F and C.

Unit 4 *Connections* **161**

MULTICULTURAL PERSPECTIVES: *A Work Song*

The Jamaican folk song "Stone Pounding," was sung by laborers as they crushed rocks to make cobblestone roads. Such work songs were sung at social gatherings and also became children's game songs. The "Stone Pounding" game is for three players, who kneel in a circle and beat the ground rhythmically with stones as they sing. In informal Jamaican English, *You no heare what me yerry?* means "Haven't you heard what I've heard?" The words *say tamboolay and no quarrel* mean: if your fingers get hurt by the stones, remember that "it's a game, so don't make a fuss, don't take it seriously."

ENRICHMENT: *Drum Game for "Stone Pounding"*

Have students sit in a circle, then distribute drums.

A section: Perform this pattern three times, then pass drums to the left unless every student has one.

drum   *pat chest*

A' section: Brush the drum or alternate thumb and finger strokes in even eighth notes, then pass the drum to the left on *say tamboolay and no quarrel*.

UNIT FOUR
LESSON 1

continued from previous page

3 APPLY

Introduce "Guadalquivir." Listen for the *short long short* rhythm pattern. Have students:

• Listen to "Guadalquivir" (**gwa** ðal ki **vir**) (A section **CD4:7**) and raise a hand each time they hear the rhythmic phrase with the *short long short* pattern. (Phrases 1–4, 8)

▶ • Read about and listen to the entire selection **CD4:8** on page 163.

▶ • Learn the folk dance step for the A section. (See *Movement* on the bottom of page 163.)

These scenes show the festive costumes and traditional instruments of Andean carnivals. A Peruvian man plays a large flute (middle right) and the Bolivian marchers (middle left) play panpipes and drums. Bolivian and Peruvian musicians (opposite page) show two types of Andean flutes called quenas.

162 RHYTHM ALL AROUND

MEETING **INDIVIDUAL** NEEDS

MULTICULTURAL PERSPECTIVES: *Andean flutes*

For centuries the Inca (**ing** kə), Quechua (**kɛch** wə), and other native peoples of Bolivia and Peru have fashioned flutes from wood, clay, or bone. These flutes, including panpipes and quenas (**ke** nɑs), can create haunting melodies that linger in the mind. The song "El condor pasa" is a good example. As the festive "Guadalquivir" makes clear, however, Andean flutes can express far more than one emotion. Just after Peru was conquered, Spanish church officials recognized this. They tried to ban the quena because it could stir up so many feelings. Fortunately, their efforts failed.

Guadalquivir *Andean Dance Song*

LISTEN to "Guadalquivir" and raise your hand each time you hear the phrase with the *short long short* pattern. How many times do you hear the phrase? 5

"Guadalquivir" is a carnavalito. Carnavalitos blend South American Indian and Spanish musical traditions. They are usually sung and danced during festivals called carnivals.

Village carnivals may celebrate weddings, holy days, or anniversaries special to the village. People wear masks and fancy costumes, and enjoy singing, dancing, feasting, and parades.

PERFORM this step with the A section of "Guadalquivir."

right   left   right left right   left   right   left right left

Unit 4 *Connections* **163**

4 CLOSE

"Describe the rhythm pattern we worked with today." (*short long short* over two beats) Have students:

- Clap the opening phrase of "Guadalquivir," which has the *short long short* pattern in it.
▶ • Listen to "Guadalquivir" again and move through shared space, performing the stepping pattern from the dance.

LESSON SUMMARY

Informal Assessment In this lesson, students:

OBJECTIVE 1 On cue, switched between patting with the beat to clapping the rhythm of the words "Stone Pounding."
OBJECTIVE 2 Clapped the rhythm of a phrase including the *short long short* pattern from "Guadalquivir."

National Standards for Music Education
2b Perform easy patterns on various classroom instruments.
6b Describe, in words or movement, music from diverse cultures.
6d Identify instrumental and vocal sounds from various cultures.
6e Respond to musical characteristics through movement.

MORE MUSIC: Reinforcement
More Songs to Read, page 360 (*short long short* pattern)
"Carnival Time in Puerto Rico," page 50 (carnival)
"El condor pasa," page 151 (Andean quena music)

MOVEMENT: *"Guadalquivir" Preparation*

Have students practice the following stepping pattern for the A section first in self space, then traveling through shared space. Tell students that in a later lesson they will discover what two group formations this dance uses.

$\frac{2}{2}$ ♩   ♩ | ♩ ♩ ♩ | ♩   ♩ | ♩ ♩ ♩ ‖
   R   L   R L R   L   R   L R L

DRAMA: *Andean Carnival*

Have the class create an Andean carnival. Students may make festive costumes using available materials. If possible, help students choose an Andean folktale to dramatize. Then have them begin with a parade to show the costumes, perform the folktale, and culminate with the dance to "Guadalquivir." (See *Movement,* page 172.) Invite other villages (classes) to attend and teach them the dance and song.

ACROSS the

LANGUAGE ARTS

WRITING A SCENE

"Finding a Way"

GROUP   **15–30 MIN**

Have students work in groups to write a short scene about two students who are sitting next to each other but do not know each other. The scene should show how the two characters "break the ice" and start a friendship.

Group members can suggest ways they might start talking to a new student at school or a new boy or girl in their neighborhood. They can use these ideas in the script. The scene should be preceded by descriptions of the setting and the two characters. Each character might be allowed to talk to the audience without the other character hearing. Other characters might be in the scene to help reach the happy ending.

Students can write out dialogue or may just write notes for the actors to use when they improvise dialogue. Group members can practice and perform their scripts.

COMPREHENSION STRATEGY: Expressing main ideas

SCIENCE/ART

HEALTH-SAFETY

"Tina Singu"

GROUP   **15–30 MIN**
MATERIALS: poster board, markers, crayons, reference materials

Have students work in groups to create posters showing how to prevent fires and how to act during a fire or fire drill. Suggestions:

- a series of posters on prevention—scenes of overloaded electrical sockets, oil-soaked rags in confined spaces, lit matches carelessly discarded—each with a red X through the center;
- a floor plan of each level of the school showing exits and routes to take during a fire drill;
- scenes showing people crouched low to avoid inhaling smoke during a fire.

The posters can be used for a fire-safety class presentation, which could include a visit from an official of the local fire department.

COMPREHENSION STRATEGIES: Visualizing, displaying information

CURRICULUM

MATHEMATICS

STONE GAME

"Stone Pounding"

PAIR   15–30 MIN

MATERIALS: 25 pieces of gravel (substitutes—math counters or buttons)

Simple stones can be used as playing pieces in games that require reasoning and decisions. Here's a modern stone game to test a player's ability to decide.

Two players each get 5 stones (or substitutes). They place a pile of 15 stones between them. The goal is to group stones into sets of three. One player starts by making any one of three possible moves:

- take two stones from the pile;
- take one stone from the opponent (whether or not it is in a set of three);
- group any of his/her own stones into a set of three.

A player carries out only one move in a turn. The game alternates between players, ending when the last stone is taken from the center pile. The player with the most grouped stones wins.

As an added move, at any point after doing one task, a player may group any two of his/her piles of three into a pile of six and draw an extra stone from the pile.

COMPREHENSION STRATEGIES: Reasoning, making decisions

SCIENCE

WEATHERING

"Stone Pounding"

PAIR   30 MIN OR LONGER

MATERIALS: piece of chalk, two jars, vinegar or lemon, plastic spoon, goggles, plastic sandwich wrap

Stones can be crumbled by pounding them, but chemicals can also be used to crumble stones. Have students represent the stone by a piece of chalk and the chemical by a very weak acid, such as vinegar or lemon juice. (CAUTION: Although they are common substances, students should handle them with care and wear goggles.)

They break the chalk into two equal halves. Then they break one half into several smaller pieces. They fill two jars with equal amounts of vinegar or juice. They put the half-piece of chalk into one jar and put the smaller pieces into the other. They may cover the jars loosely with plastic wrap.

Have students observe and compare results in the two jars, observing several times over twenty minutes. (In both jars, the chalk crumbles—more so when smaller pieces expose more surface to the vinegar.)

COMPREHENSION STRATEGIES: Compare and contrast, drawing conclusions

UNIT FOUR
LESSON 2

RELATED ARTS MOVEMENT THEATER VISUAL ARTS

LESSON PLANNER

FOCUS Pitch, octave

OBJECTIVES
OBJECTIVE 1 Sing a two-note octave motive in a call-and-response song (tested)
OBJECTIVE 2 Signal to show recognition of octaves in a song (tested)

MATERIALS
Recordings
Hosanna, Me Build a House   CD4:9
Tina Singu   CD4:2
Recorded Lesson: Octaves
    Demonstration   CD4:10
Sarasponda   CD4:11

Resources
Resource Master 4 • 2 (practice)
Orff Orchestration O • 9 (Hosanna, Me
    Build a House)
Recorder Master R • 16 (pitches E G A)

Technology Music with MIDI: Sarasponda

VOCABULARY
vibrations, octave, vocables

▶ = **BASIC PROGRAM**

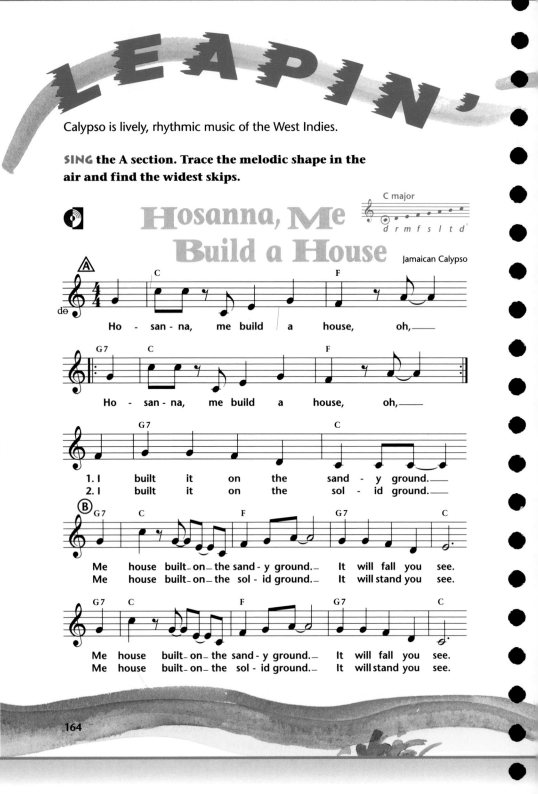

Calypso is lively, rhythmic music of the West Indies.

SING the A section. Trace the melodic shape in the air and find the widest skips.

Hosanna, Me Build a House

Jamaican Calypso

C major

d r m f s l t d'

Ho - san - na, me build a house, oh,—

Ho - san - na, me build a house, oh,—

1. I built it on the sand - y ground.—
2. I built it on the sol - id ground.—

Me house built on the sand - y ground.— It will fall you see.
Me house built on the sol - id ground.— It will stand you see.

Me house built - on — the sand - y ground.— It will fall you see.
Me house built - on — the sol - id ground.— It will stand you see.

164

MEETING **INDIVIDUAL** NEEDS

VOCAL DEVELOPMENT: *Downward Octave Skips*
This vocalise will help students to sing downward octave skips without "sinking" into the lower pitch and also to maintain a uniform tone quality between the lighter and heavier vocal registers.

Continue up by half steps to F.

Ha Ha (breathe) Ha Ha (breathe) Ha Ha (breathe)

Beat 1: Stand with feet flat on the floor. **Beat 2:** Stand on tiptoe. **Beat 3:** Come back to standing position. **Beat 4:** Breathe and prepare to repeat vocalise a half-step higher.

As students sing downward octave skips in "Hosanna, Me Build a House," have them stand on tiptoe for the lower pitch until they sing without sinking into it.

ORFF: *"Hosanna, Me Build a House"*
See **O • 9** in *Orchestrations for Orff Instruments.*

LINKS

The rain will wet it up, ha! ha!
The rain can't wet it up, ha! ha!

The sun will burn it up, ha! ha!
The sun can't burn it up, ha! ha!

The breeze will shake it up, ha! ha!
The breeze can't shake it up, ha! ha!

Da Capo after Verse 1
Coda after Verse 2

The storm will bring it to the ground, ha! ha!
The storm can't bring it to the ground, ha! ha!

Coda *Sing 3 times*

Ho - san-na, me build a house, oh,— Ho - san-na!

Unit 4 *Connections* **165**

1 GET SET

"Listen to this song from Jamaica, 'Hosanna, Me Build a House.' Many of the words are the same in both verses, but some are different. As you listen, find the main differences between the two verses." Have students:

▶ • Listen to the song **CD4:9**.

▶ • Discuss differences of meaning in the lyrics of the verses. (building on sandy or solid ground with different consequences)

"The rhythm of this song is similar to that of songs you have learned, and its melody has something in common with new songs in this lesson. We'll be listening for a melodic connection today."

2 DEVELOP

1. Draw the melodic shape of "Hosanna, Me Build a House." Have students:

▶ • Learn the A section.

▶ • Sing the A section and draw the melodic shape in the air.

▶ • Discuss the melodic movement and note the widest skips.

MUSIC BUILDS READING SKILLS

Comprehension In discussing how the lyrics in the first and second verses of a song differ in meaning, students will be contrasting ideas and details.

MULTICULTURAL PERSPECTIVES: *Calypso*

Calypso, a lively rhythmic music with African roots, began in the West Indies as a way for enslaved Africans to communicate. They used it to make fun of the slave owners and to pass on news. Today lyrics remain the primary focus of calypso songs. Singers comment on social and political issues. Many calypso singers pride themselves on their ability to think up new rhymes off the top of their head.

BACKGROUND: *"Hosanna, Me Build a House"*

"Hosanna, Me Build a House" probably developed out of an old work song sung by men of the building trade. The lyrics allude to a Biblical parable about faith (*Matthew*), which teaches that the wise build their houses on rock (solid faith) while the foolish build theirs on sand (shifting faith). *Hosanna* comes from a Hebrew word meaning "pray" or "save us." In this song it means "Thanks to God."

Unit 4 CONNECTIONS **165**

UNIT FOUR
LESSON 2

continued from previous page

2. Review "Tina Singu" CD4:2 (p. 158). Introduce octaves. Have students:

▶ • Sing "Tina Singu."

▶ • Read about the octave on page 166.

Recorded Lesson CD4:10

▶ • Listen to "Octaves Demonstration" to hear examples of octave skips.

(Optional: Use **Resource Master 4 · 2** to explore words with the prefix *oct*.)

▶ • Listen for the octave in the first section of the song. (second *Tina*)

OBJECTIVE 1 Informal Assessment

• Sing the first section silently inside their heads, except for the octave, which should be sung aloud.

• Compare the melodic movement of the first and second *Tina*. (repeated notes vs. skip)

• Learn Part 2 and, when secure singing each part separately, sing both parts together.

3 APPLY

Introduce "Sarasponda" CD4:11. Identify the octave. Have students:

▶ • Listen to "Sarasponda" (sæ ra **spän** da) and discuss the vocables.

OBJECTIVE 2 Informal Assessment

▶ • Listen, with eyes closed, and raise a hand when they hear the octaves. (four times in B section, *ah-do*)

▶ • Learn the song.

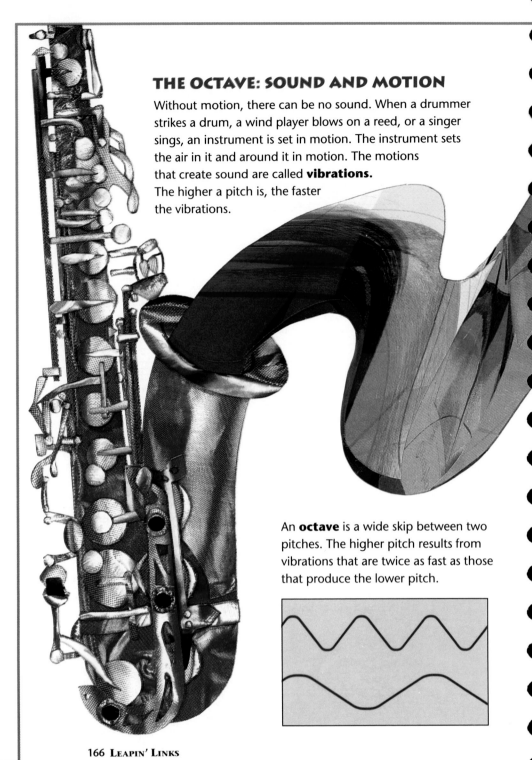

THE OCTAVE: SOUND AND MOTION

Without motion, there can be no sound. When a drummer strikes a drum, a wind player blows on a reed, or a singer sings, an instrument is set in motion. The instrument sets the air in it and around it in motion. The motions that create sound are called **vibrations.** The higher a pitch is, the faster the vibrations.

An **octave** is a wide skip between two pitches. The higher pitch results from vibrations that are twice as fast as those that produce the lower pitch.

166 LEAPIN' LINKS

MEETING **INDIVIDUAL** NEEDS

ALTERNATE TEACHING STRATEGIES

OBJECTIVE 1 Draw the melodic shape in the air as you sing "Tina Singu" and have a student draw the contour on the board. Have students find the wide skip. (second *Tina*) If they have trouble, review repeated notes, steps, and skips on page 109. Divide the class into two groups. One group should sing the first syllable (*Ti-*) and sustain it. The other group should sing the entire word and sustain the second syllable (*-na*). Have students listen for how the two pitches sound "the same" but the second pitch is at a lower level.

OBJECTIVE 2 Place resonator bells for "Sarasponda" on stacks of books, or have students hold them, so that the heights of the bells reflect the relation of the pitches. Play each phrase of the song slowly so that students can watch for the vertical change with each pitch. Isolate short patterns that move by steps (Measure 2) or by small skips (Measure 6) to compare with the octave skips.

VOCAL DEVELOPMENT: *Wide Upward Skips*

Singing wide upward skips requires more breath support. As students sing this vocalise, have them bend their knees and raise their hands above their heads to "touch" the top

In this folk song, nonsense words called **vocables** are used to imitate the sound of a spinning wheel.

RAISE your hand when you hear an octave.

SARASPONDA

Dutch Spinning Song

A C | G7 | C
Sa - ra - spon - da, Sa - ra - spon - da, Sa - ra - spon - da, Ret - set - set!

C | G7 | C
Sa - ra - spon - da, Sa - ra - spon - da, Sa - ra - spon - da, Ret - set - set!

B F | C | F | C
Ah - do - ray - oh! Ah - do - ray - boom - day - oh!

G7 | C | G7 | C
Ah - do - ray - boom - day, Ret - set - set! Ah - say - pa - say - oh!

Unit 4 *Connections* **167**

• Sing the song with a chosen sequence of dynamic levels (one level per phrase).
• Learn the movement for the A section. (See *Movement* below.)
• Sing the song, with chosen dynamics, performing the movement with the A section and singing in place for the B section.

4 CLOSE

"Name and describe the wide melodic skip we learned about." (Octave; two pitches sound alike, but one is higher, produced by twice as many vibrations.) Have students:

• Sing "Sarasponda," touching their hips on the first pitch and their shoulders on the second pitch of each octave.

LESSON SUMMARY

Informal Assessment In this lesson, students:

OBJECTIVE 1 Sang a two-note octave motive in the call-and-response song "Tina Singu."
OBJECTIVE 2 Signaled upon hearing the octaves in "Sarasponda."

National Standards for Music Education
2c Play repertoire from diverse genres and cultures.
2d Echo short rhythmic and melodic patterns on instruments.

MORE MUSIC: Reinforcement
More Songs to Read, page 361 (octave)
"A Tragic Story," page 197 (octave)
"The Path to the Moon," page 372 (octave)

---

pitch. Have them do the same as they sing the wide upward skips in "Sarasponda."

Continue up by half steps to E or F.

Ha Ha (breathe) Ha Ha (breathe)

PLAYING INSTRUMENTS: *Orff Instruments*

Have students imitate on Orff instruments one-measure patterns on low and high C that you sing with the letter name C. Then have them identify which patterns moved by repeated pitches and which contained octave skips.

MOVEMENT: *"Sarasponda" A Section*

Formation: groups of four

Measures 1–2: Have each group form a small circle, with everyone facing clockwise. Perform a right-hand star by having everyone place their right hand into the center of the circle, palms down, and stacking one on top of the next. The circle walks clockwise for eight steps.

Measures 3–4: Reverse, performing a left-hand star. Tell students that in Lesson 5, they will create movement that uses a different formation for the B section.

ACROSS the

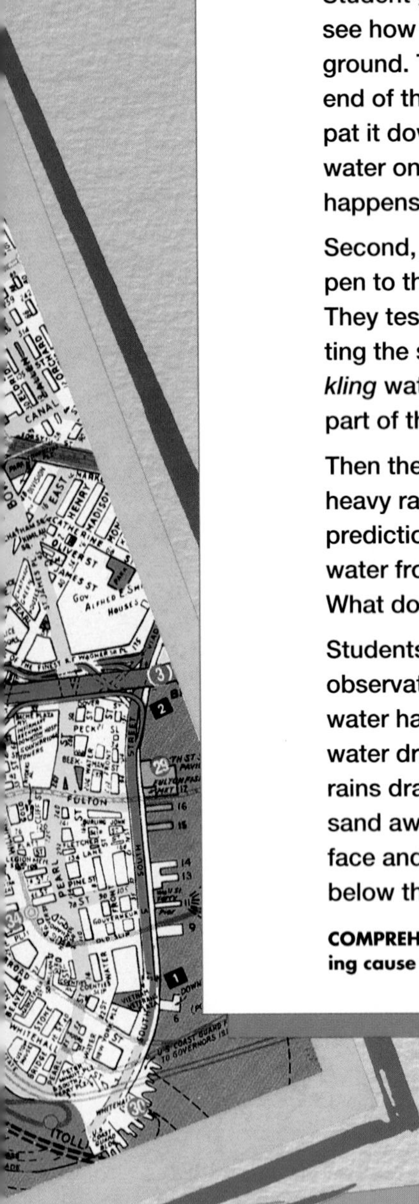

SCIENCE

EROSION MODEL

"Hosanna, Me Build a House"

GROUP   **15–30 MIN**

MATERIALS: rectangular baking pan (about 33 cm x 23 cm x 5 cm), sand or soil, pitcher of water, bucket

Student groups can build models to see how water changes sandy ground. Their first step is to fill one end of the pan with sand or soil and pat it down. They gently *sprinkle* water on top and observe what happens.

Second, they predict what might happen to the sandy area when it rains. They test the prediction by first patting the sand down again and *sprinkling* water from the pitcher to one part of the sand.

Then they can predict the effect of a heavy rainfall. Before they test the prediction, they need to pour runoff water from the pan into the bucket. What do they notice in the runoff?

Students record their predictions and observations, and describe the effect water has on the land. (Sprinkled water drains into the sand. Heavier rains drain in and run off, carrying sand away—wearing down the surface and wearing away the land from below the surface.)

COMPREHENSION STRATEGIES: Understanding cause and effect, using a model

MATHEMATICS

AREA

"Hosanna, Me Build a House"

PAIR   **15–30 MIN**

MATERIALS: centimeter graph paper per pair, metric rulers

Have students work in pairs to draw a rectangle on graph paper as a diagram of a room. The students must decide how many graph-squares long and wide the room will be and must make sure that opposite sides of the room are equally long.

Their task is to decide how many tiles it would take to cover the floor. Each square in the diagram represents one tile. Have them find the number of tiles by telling them to count the rows of tiles and the number of tiles in each row. (For the total number of tiles, they multiply the two numbers.)

Each partner then draws a floor plan made of four connected square or rectangular rooms. They exchange drawings and find the number of tiles needed to cover the floor.

COMPREHENSION STRATEGIES: Compare and contrast, using a diagram

CURRICULUM

MATHEMATICS/ART

HOUSE DRAWINGS

"Hosanna, Me Build a House"

INDIVIDUAL   **15 MIN OR LESS**

MATERIALS: drawing paper, pencils, erasers, cutout shapes of plane figures—triangles, squares, rectangles, parallelograms

Have students make pictures of houses by tracing, from the cutout, the shapes that make up their houses. They can trace many squares or rectangles touching side by side or stack the shapes vertically to create a tall building. Then they can erase the interior lines where the shapes connected.

They can use squares to make windows and can make a large triangular roof by using the triangle.

Once they have completed a simple design, let them experiment with making more elaborate buildings.

COMPREHENSION STRATEGY: Exploring spatial relationships

MATHEMATICS/ART

CIRCLES

"Sarasponda"

INDIVIDUAL   **15 MIN OR LESS**

MATERIALS: string, compass, drawing paper, pencil, ruler; optional—peg-board tacks, string, heavy notepad

Students can use a compass to draw a spinning wheel for "Sarasponda." They start by plotting a dot at the center of a sheet of drawing paper. They put the compass point on the dot and open the compass carefully so that it does not extend beyond the edge of the paper. They draw a circle by turning the pencil around the dot.

Then they draw spokes of the wheel. They use a straightedge to draw a line from one side of the circle to another side, going through the center. (As an option, they can mount the circle on heavy cardboard and put pairs of tacks on opposite sides of the circle's circumference. Instead of drawing a line, they can connect the tacks with tautly fitted loops of string.)

They repeat in several directions to make spokes. In addition, they can adjust the compass-setting to make circles of various sizes.

COMPREHENSION STRATEGIES: Exploring spatial relationships, following directions

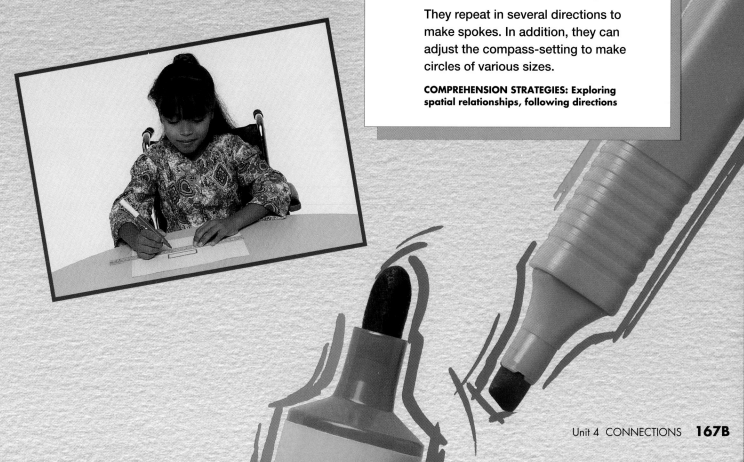

CULTURAL

LESSON PLANNER

FOCUS Timbre

OBJECTIVE

OBJECTIVE 1 Signal when they hear changed voices singing

MATERIALS
Recordings
Little David, Play on Your Harp   CD4:12
Recorded Lesson: Interview with
    Joseph Shabalala   CD4:13
Hosanna, Me Build a House   CD4:9

Resources
Orff Orchestration O • 10 (Little David,
Play on Your Harp)

VOCABULARY
spiritual

▶ = **BASIC PROGRAM**

Spirituals were created by African Americans, who combined African rhythms with melodies they created and heard in America. Many spirituals, such as this one about David and Goliath, are based on Biblical stories.

LITTLE DAVID, PLAY ON YOUR HARP

African American Spiritual

Pentatonic

Refrain
Lit - tle Da - vid, play on your harp, Hal - le - lu! Hal - le - lu!
Lit - tle Da - vid, play on your harp, Hal - le - lu!

Verse
1. Lit - tle Da - vid was a shep - herd boy, He
2. Old Da - vid was a might - y king, and

slew Go - li - ath and shout - ed for joy.
all the peo - ple came to sing.

Go back to the beginning and sing to the end (Da Capo al Fine)

168

MEETING **INDIVIDUAL** NEEDS

VOCAL DEVELOPMENT: *Matching Pitch*

Encourage a student who sings below pitch to think "higher" and to point to the ceiling while singing. Use a "listening tube" (Tone Tube), a three-foot cylindrical hose sold in toy stores. Sing a familiar pattern into one end of the tube while the student holds the other end to his or her ear. Then put your end of the tube to the student's mouth so s/he can hear him/herself echo-sing the pattern. Instruct others to signal whether the student is above, below, or on pitch when echoing the pattern. You may need to lower the pitch to the point where the student can succeed.

MULTICULTURAL PERSPECTIVES: *Spirituals*

Enslaved Africans were not allowed to speak their own language, practice their own religion, or play their own music. After converting to Christianity, they combined African musical traditions with Protestant hymns, creating spirituals. Sometimes called "sorrow songs," the hymns expressed both pain and hope. At times spirituals also served as a way to communicate secretly, even to plan escapes. The hymn "Deep River," for example, could signal a meeting at the river. The influence of spirituals lives on in music today, from blues to pop, folk, rock, soul, and gospel.

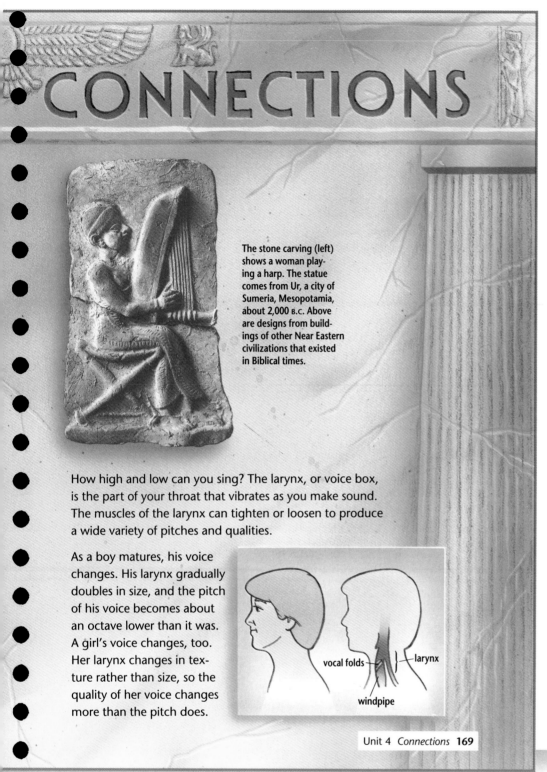

CONNECTIONS

The stone carving (left) shows a woman playing a harp. The statue comes from Ur, a city of Sumeria, Mesopotamia, about 2,000 B.C. Above are designs from buildings of other Near Eastern civilizations that existed in Biblical times.

How high and low can you sing? The larynx, or voice box, is the part of your throat that vibrates as you make sound. The muscles of the larynx can tighten or loosen to produce a wide variety of pitches and qualities.

As a boy matures, his voice changes. His larynx gradually doubles in size, and the pitch of his voice becomes about an octave lower than it was. A girl's voice changes, too. Her larynx changes in texture rather than size, so the quality of her voice changes more than the pitch does.

vocal folds — larynx

windpipe

Unit 4 *Connections* 169

"Listen to 'Little David, Play on Your Harp,' and see if you can describe the singers." Have students:

▶ • Listen to the song **CD4:12**.

▶ • Identify the singers as children and men.

"How were you able to identify the types of people singing?" (The men had low voices; the children had high voices.) "Today we will learn more about voices and how they change as you grow."

2 DEVELOP

1. Learn "Little David, Play on Your Harp" and learn about changing voices. Have students:

▶ • Read about and learn the song.

▶ • Read about voices on page 169 and discuss examples of changed and unchanged voices. (Students might listen to how different teachers and students talk and then report how the voices vary.)

▶ • Sing the song, adding a step-clap pattern during the refrain.

BACKGROUND: *"Little David, Play on Your Harp"*

This spiritual was often sung by nineteenth-century choirs giving benefit concerts for early African American colleges such as Fisk and Hampton. The lyrics refer to the second king of Israel, a mighty warrior who in his youth slew the giant Goliath with one stone. David played the harp so well that he won the favor of his predecessor King Saul. Tradition credits David with writing much of the Book of Psalms. This Biblical text consists of sacred poems meant to be sung. The word *psalm* comes from the Greek *psalmos*

(**sa** mos), meaning "plucking of the harp" (or "song accompanied by harp").

ENRICHMENT: *Vocal Timbre*

Have students close their eyes and listen as each student says a phrase (perhaps from a poem). See if they can identify who is speaking.

ORFF: *"Little David, Play on Your Harp"*

See **O · 10** in *Orchestrations for Orff Instruments.*

UNIT FOUR
LESSON 3

continued from previous page

2. Learn about the leader of a South African singing group and discuss cultural connections. Have students:

▶ • Read about Joseph Shabalala (sha **ba** la la) and Ladysmith Black Mambazo (mam **ba** zo).

Recorded Lesson CD4:13

▶ • Listen to "Interview with Joseph Shabalala," and hear him talk about his work with Ladysmith Black Mambazo.

▶ • Read page 171 and look at the drums featured.

• Discuss the *Think It Through*.

3 APPLY

Review "Hosanna, Me Build a House" CD4:9 (p. 164). Listen for changed and unchanged voices. Have students:

▶ • Sing the A section.

OBJECTIVE 1 Informal Assessment

▶ • Listen to the song and raise a hand when they hear changed voices. (B section; form is A B C A B C)

▶ • Learn the B and C sections.

MEET JOSEPH SHABALALA

Have you ever dreamed of taking your own special music to friends, neighbors, and beyond to the far corners of the earth? This is what Joseph Shabalala, founder of Ladysmith Black Mambazo, did. Starting with his own relatives, he developed a group that shares the musical traditions of the Zulu with people all over the world.

LISTEN to Joseph Shabalala talk about his career as a composer and leader of a musical group.

170 CULTURAL CONNECTIONS

MEETING **INDIVIDUAL** NEEDS

ALTERNATE TEACHING STRATEGY

OBJECTIVE 1 Have students sing all of "Hosanna, Me Build a House." Divide the class into two groups, singers and listeners. Have the singers sing the song along with the recording, and have the listeners identify when the singers on the recording have dropped an octave below the student singers. (B section) Have the groups switch parts.

BACKGROUND: *Ladysmith Black Mambazo*

This a cappella group gained fame in the United States after collaborating with Paul Simon on his smash 1985 album

Graceland. The group had started 20 years earlier as a church choir in Ladysmith, South Africa, with members drawn from the Shabalala (sha ba la la) and Mazibuko (ma zi **bu** ko) families. Joseph Shabalala, the group's lead singer and composer, picked their name, which means "black ax of Ladysmith," in 1973. Former farmers, they soon became the best-selling group in South Africa and have sold over four million records there. Though their songs often focus on everyday concerns, their singing is joyful and delicately balanced. Their harmonies live up to a Zulu saying that Joseph Shabalala has quoted: "Singing makes all people happy because it is the voice of happiness."

CONNECTING CULTURES

Many of the songs you sang in this unit were created by people of African origin. Some of the people live there now. Others have ancestors who came from Africa.

THINK IT THROUGH

Compare the rhythms, melodies, and ideas expressed in the songs you sang. Find similarities and differences.

Students may find that rhythms are similarly active, melodies are different.

Drums play an important part in the music of Africa, including Zaire (top). In Haiti, people of African descent carry on the tradition of drumming (left), and in the United States, Chick Webb, an African American drummer, put together the first standard trap set (right).

Unit 4 *Connections* 171

"What happens to a boy's voice when it changes?" (The larynx grows, and the pitch becomes lower.) Have students:

▶ • Sing '"Hosanna, Me Build a House" once more.

LESSON SUMMARY

Informal Assessment In this lesson, students:

OBJECTIVE 1 Signaled when they heard singing by changed voices in "Hosanna, Me Build a House."

National Standards for Music Education
2c Play repertoire from diverse genres and cultures.
6d Identify instrumental and vocal sounds from various cultures.

MORE MUSIC: Reinforcement
"A Folktale from Kenya," page 102 (African cultures)
"Macnamara's Band," page 342 (St. Patrick's Day, C', changed voices)
"Hallelujah Chorus," page 385A (changed voices)
"Erlkönig," page 385E (changed voices)
"Allundé, Alluia," page 376 (performing with percussion)

PLAYING INSTRUMENTS: *Unpitched Percussion*

Have students play the rhythm of the words with the B section of "Hosanna, Me Build a House" to indicate when they hear changed voices singing. You may divide the rhythm of the words of the C section between two Latin percussion instruments, playing *ha ha* on one (güiro) and all other words on the other (claves).

ENRICHMENT: *"Mañana Iguana"*

Review "Mañana Iguana" (page 20) to hear the expanded range of a male voice. Discuss falsetto.

UNIT FOUR
LESSON 4

RELATED ARTS | MOVEMENT | THEATER | VISUAL ARTS

LESSON PLANNER

FOCUS Duration, ♪ ♩ ♪ (*short long short*)

OBJECTIVES
OBJECTIVE 1 Identify the measures in which the *short long short* pattern occurs in notation (tested)
OBJECTIVE 2 Perform a percussion ostinato that includes the *short long short* pattern (tested)

MATERIALS
Recordings
Listening: Guadalquivir (A section)   CD4:7
Listening: Guadalquivir (entire)   CD4:8
Stone Pounding   CD4:4
Listening: Ayazein   CD4:14

Instruments hand drums

Other
stones, beanbags, or paper wadded into balls

Resources
Resource Master 4 • 3 (practice)
Resource Master 4 • 4 (practice)
Recorder Master R • 17 (pitches E G A B)

VOCABULARY
tie

▶ = **BASIC PROGRAM**

COME TO

Join the festive dancing! You've danced to the A section of "Guadalquivir." Here's the formation for the B section.

DANCE to "Guadalquivir."

172

MEETING **INDIVIDUAL** NEEDS

MOVEMENT: *"Guadalquivir"*

A section
Formation: lines of six, leader at front, holding hands
Review the stepping pattern from Lesson 1, page 159, *Movement*. Add a slight bow on the first step of the pattern, straightening up on the second step. Perform the pattern, moving forward in the pathways the leaders choose:

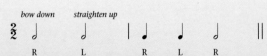

Repeat with opposite foot.

B section
Formation: circles of six, holding hands
Each leader brings his or her line around into a circle or the entire group can form one large circle or two concentric circles. All perform step-hops in this pattern:

$\frac{2}{2}$ ♩ ♩ | ♩ ♩ ||
step R   hop R   step L   hop L

CARNIVAL!

CONNECTING SOUND AND SYMBOL

The *short long short* pattern can be heard in both "Guadalquivir" and "Stone Pounding."

PAT and clap these two patterns from "Stone Pounding." How are they alike? How are they different? Alike–last for two beats; different–different rhythm and number of sounds.

Pat: Clap:

hear - e   what   me   three   stone   a

Hear-e what me can be written this way.

Three stone a can be written two ways. A **tie** connects the two eighth notes that sound as one quarter note.

or

FIND this rhythm pattern in the music for "Stone Pounding" on page 160.

Unit 4 *Connections* 173

1 GET SET

"Listen to 'Guadalquivir' and pat with the beat." Have students:

▶ • Listen to the A section CD4:7 and pat with the beat, alternating hands.

▶ • Clap the rhythm of Phrase 1 and recall that it contains the *short long short* pattern.

"Today we will learn how to write this pattern and find it in other songs."

2 DEVELOP

1. Learn the dance for "Guadalquivir." (entire CD4:8) Have students:

▶ • Recall the movement for the A section.

▶ • Look at page 172 to see the traditional formation for the B section.

▶ • Learn the complete dance. (See *Movement* on the bottom of page 172.)

2. Review "Stone Pounding" CD4:4 (p. 160). Introduce notation for the *short long short* pattern. Have students:

▶ • Sing the song, referring to page 160.

• Form two groups, one group clapping the rhythm of the first pattern while the other pats the rhythm of the second pattern on page 173.

• Compare the rhythms of the two patterns.

• Read about notation on page 173. (Optional: Use **Resource Master 4 • 3** to practice rewriting tied rhythms with the *short long short* pattern.)

▶ • In groups of three, sing and play the game. (See *Enrichment* below.)

ENRICHMENT: *"Stone Pounding" Game*

Formation: circle of three, kneeling, stone in each student's right hand (Beanbags or wadded-up paper can be used in place of stones.)

Game: Pound the stone on the ground in this pattern— 4 beats in front, 4 beats to the right, 4 in front, 4 to the left. Repeat until the song ends.

MUSIC BUILDS MATH SKILLS

Algebra and Geometry The "Stone Pounding Game" supports the concept of numerical patterns and reinforces spatial sense.

continued from previous page

3. Sing "Stone Pounding" from notation (p. 160). Have students:

OBJECTIVE 1 Informal Assessment
• Identify where the *short long short* pattern occurs in the notation by signaling with thumbs up as you count off the measures. (Measures 1, 2, 3, 9, 10, 11) (For more practice use **Resource Master 4 • 4.**)

• Sing, clapping the rhythm from the notation.

3 APPLY

Introduce "Ayazein" CD4:14. Perform the ostinato. Have students:

▶ • Read about the dumbek (**dum** bɛk) and the drumming pattern.

OBJECTIVE 2 Informal Assessment
• Perform the pattern on page 174, playing it on a drum or with body percussion.

▶ • Listen to "Ayazein" (α ya **zeɪn**).

• Watch as several students play the pattern as an ostinato to "Ayazein" on drums. (To play the dumbek, hold the drum under the left arm and strike it with both hands. One palm plays the *dum* or low tone in the center of the drum. The other hand, open and palm down, strikes the rim with the fingertips, playing the *tak,* or high-pitched tone.)

CARRY ON THE CARNIVAL RHYTHM

The  rhythm can be found in the music of many parts of the world. In Egypt, you might hear this pattern played on a clay or metal hand drum called a dumbek.

PERFORM the pattern below as if you were playing a dumbek. Use one palm on *dum* and the fingertips of the other hand on *tak*. Say the words as you drum.

dum   tak   tak   dum   tak

 LISTENING Ayazein   *Egyptian Folk Song*

LISTEN for the dumbek pattern in "Ayazein." Try to play along as you listen again!

Dumbeks are widely used in Middle Eastern countries, Turkey, and Greece. A floral pattern has been hammered into this metal dumbek from Turkey.

174 COME TO CARNIVAL!

MEETING **INDIVIDUAL** NEEDS

ALTERNATE TEACHING STRATEGIES

OBJECTIVE 1 Make flashcards of (or draw on the board) the two-beat combinations of half, quarter, and eighth notes students have learned to read.

Have students clap only when you display the *short long short* pattern. Shuffle and repeat. Have students clap each pattern softly, clapping only the *short long short* pattern loudly.

OBJECTIVE 2 Have students clap the drumming pattern, first saying *three stone a stone stone,* then saying the *dum-tak* word pattern. If alternating hands is difficult, have them pat with both hands on *dum* and clap on *tak*.

MULTICULTURAL PERSPECTIVES: *"Ayazein"*

This Egyptian hymn of praise (here heard as an instrumental) is a very famous Arabic folk song. *Zein* (zeɪn) means not only "beautiful" (or "good") but is also a man's name. The prefix *Aya* (α ya) may be translated as "Oh." The lyrics begin "Oh, Zein," and address him directly, then poetically praise the beauty of his faith.

The dumbek is often played with other instruments. In this scene from Egypt, it is played with two rababas.

4 CLOSE

"Let's clap each of these two-beat rhythm patterns." Write these on the board:

$$\quad \downarrow \; \sqcap \, , \qquad \downarrow \; \downarrow \; \downarrow \, , \qquad \sqcap \; \downarrow$$

"Which one shows the *short long short* rhythm pattern you worked with today?" Have students:

▶ • Listen to "Ayazein" once more and perform the ostinato with body percussion as some students play it on a drum.

LESSON SUMMARY

Informal Assessment In this lesson, students:

OBJECTIVE 1 Identified the measures in which the *short long short* pattern occurs in the notation of "Stone Pounding."

OBJECTIVE 2 Performed a percussion ostinato pattern for "Ayazein" that includes the *short long short* pattern.

National Standards for Music Education
2c Play repertoire from diverse genres and cultures.
6a Identify simple musical forms by ear.

MORE MUSIC: Reinforcement

More Songs to Read, page 362 (reading rhythms—$\sqcap\!\sqcap$, $\downarrow \downarrow \downarrow$)
"Down by the Riverside," page 338 ($\downarrow \downarrow \downarrow$)

SPECIAL LEARNERS: *"Ayazein" Ostinato*

Students with disabilities need opportunities to perform as part of a select group. Assign a small group to develop an accompaniment to "Ayazein" with additional unpitched instruments. Include the disabled student in a group of friendly, nondisabled students who are able to perform the ostinato. Allow the group time to choose unpitched instruments and to rehearse. When the group feels prepared, have them accompany the class singing "Ayazein."

MULTICULTURAL PERSPECTIVES: *Dumbek*

The dumbek is a single-headed drum shaped like a goblet. Its body can be made of wood, metal, or clay, and some makers adorn it with pictures or elaborate designs. Played primarily in the Middle East and North Africa, the dumbek has two tones—high and low. In Iran, it is known as a *zarb* (zɑrb) and has an unusual function: It is played in gymnasiums to provide a steady beat for exercising.

ACROSS the

MATHEMATICS

MEASURING

"Stone Pounding"

GROUP   **15–30 MIN**
MATERIALS: stones (or modeling clay)

Have each student find oblong-shaped stones to use as units of length. (Students can "make" stones by molding clay into a ball, squeezing it in their hands, and stretching it out into an oblong shape.) Students should use "stones" of different sizes, some longer than others, and name or number each measuring stone.

Have students use their stones to measure the lengths of tabletops, books, and other objects in the classroom. To do so, they tell how many times the stone could fit along the edge of an object, recording the number with the name of the object.

Then group members place their stones on a table for comparison—longest to shortest. They compare their recorded measurements, those taken with the longest stones to those with shorter stones.

COMPREHENSION STRATEGY: Compare and contrast

ART

STONE SCULPTURE

"Stone Pounding"

INDIVIDUAL   **15 MIN OR LESS**
MATERIALS: stones of various sizes, tempera paint, brushes; optional—modeling clay, buttons

Have students collect stones of various sizes. They should wash them to remove soil and let them dry a day before starting to "sculpt."

The stone sculpture should be based on each student's imagination. Students can study the stones in their collection to find shapes that resemble parts of animals, people's faces, and so on. They can choose a large stone as a trunk of a body and smaller ones as heads, eyes, and limbs. Then they glue together parts to make the sculpture, using pieces of clay or buttons as needed.

They may finish their creations by painting details on them.

COMPREHENSION STRATEGIES: Visualizing, exploring space and shape

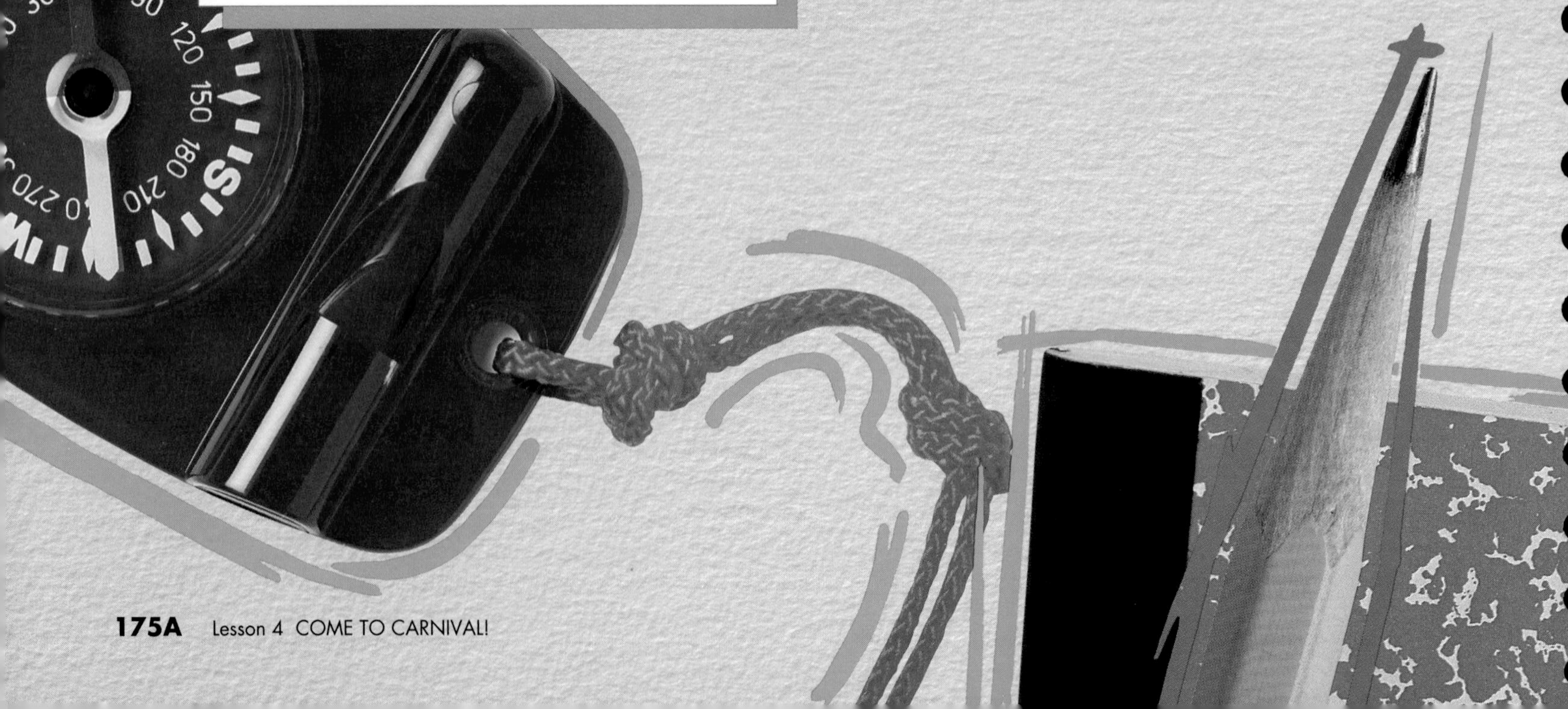

CURRICULUM

LANGUAGE ARTS

PICTURE MESSAGES

"Ayazein"

PAIR   **15–30 MIN**

MATERIALS: paper, markers; optional—pictures of hieroglyphs

Ancient Egyptians used a system of writing in which pictures symbolized the words or letters of their language. In the excavated tombs and monuments of ancient Egypt, we find messages written in these picture symbols, called hieroglyphs.

Have each pair of students work together to come up with a way of writing messages, using simple pictures to represent people, animals, or objects, as well as action words or ideas. Part of their task is to use the pictures as a code. Each time a particular picture is used, it has the same meaning—unless it has coded markings that change the meaning.

Have pairs exchange their picture messages and see if they can "crack" each other's code.

COMPREHENSION STRATEGY: Expressing main ideas

SOCIAL STUDIES

RIVERS OF THE WORLD

"Ayazein"

GROUP   **15–30 MIN**

MATERIALS: world maps, globe, drawing paper, colored pencils, string

Have students, working in groups, find the Nile River on a map or globe. Have them follow the course of the river, from its source—Lake Victoria in Uganda—to Egypt, where it reaches the Nile Delta and the Mediterranean Sea. Have students draw a map of the course of the river, labeling nations the river flows through and cities and land areas (Libyan Desert, for example) along the way.

Have students use a globe to measure the length of the Nile. First they lay a string along its course. Then they can compare its length with other long rivers—the Mississippi, the Amazon in Brazil, and the Chang in China. Have them rank the rivers by length. (The Nile is longest, followed by the Amazon, the Chang, and the Mississippi rivers.)

COMPREHENSION STRATEGY: Compare and contrast

UNIT FOUR
LESSON 5

RELATED ARTS MOVEMENT | THEATER | VISUAL ARTS

LESSON PLANNER

FOCUS Pitch—high *do*, C'

OBJECTIVES

OBJECTIVE 1 Play an original ostinato on pitched percussion using low and high C (tested)

OBJECTIVE 2 Using pitch syllables, sing a melodic motive that includes an octave skip (tested)

MATERIALS
Recordings
Sarasponda   CD4:11
Listening: Hoedown (excerpt)
   from *Rodeo* by A. Copland   CD4:15
Recorded Lesson: "Hoedown" B
   Theme   CD4:16

Instruments
resonator bells or other pitched instruments

Resources
Resource Master 4 • 5 (practice)
Resource Master 4 • 6 (practice)
Listening Map Transparency T • 7 (Hoedown)

▶ = **BASIC PROGRAM**

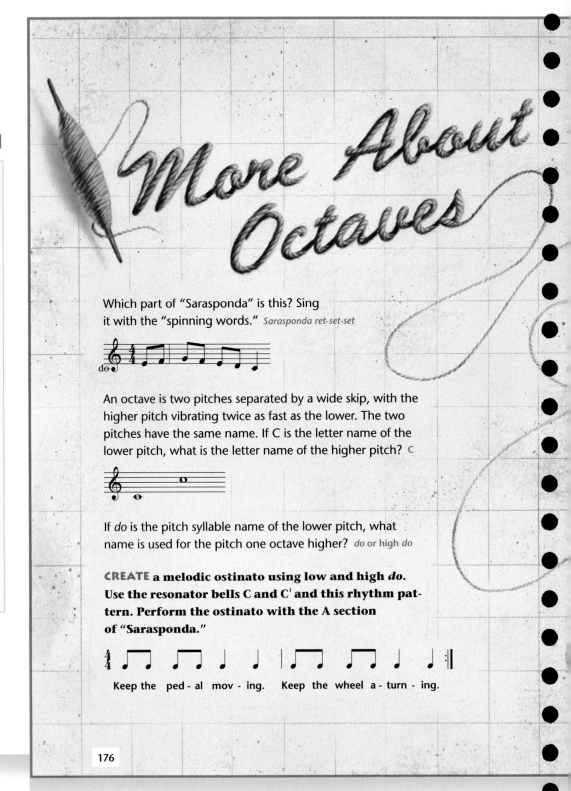

Which part of "Sarasponda" is this? Sing it with the "spinning words." *Sarasponda ret-set-set*

An octave is two pitches separated by a wide skip, with the higher pitch vibrating twice as fast as the lower. The two pitches have the same name. If C is the letter name of the lower pitch, what is the letter name of the higher pitch? C

If *do* is the pitch syllable name of the lower pitch, what name is used for the pitch one octave higher? *do or high do*

CREATE a melodic ostinato using low and high *do*. Use the resonator bells C and C' and this rhythm pattern. Perform the ostinato with the A section of "Sarasponda."

Keep the ped - al mov - ing.   Keep the wheel a - turn - ing.

176

MEETING **INDIVIDUAL** NEEDS

ALTERNATE TEACHING STRATEGY

OBJECTIVE 1 Have students pat the ostinato with the left hand only, then the right hand, then alternating hands. Encourage them to vary their hand patterns, then transfer the patterns to resonator bells C and C'. (Optional: Have students notate the ostinatos they create on **Resource Master 4 • 5.**)

COOPERATIVE LEARNING: *Phrasing*

Have students work in groups of four to figure out the phrasing of "Sarasponda." Tell them that as "Phrase Detectives," their tools are resonator bells and other pitched in-

struments. Encourage group members to share the tasks in their detective agency. Tasks might include keeping the beat, playing the bells, checking that the notes and rhythm are played correctly, and determining what words go with each phrase. Choose one member at random to whisper their results to you.

PITCH SYLLABLES: *"Sarasponda"*

Have the class figure out and sing "Sarasponda" with pitch syllables. They may also use the hand signs (pages 31 and 125) as they sing.

ANNA CODDE

Maerten van Heemskerck's portrait shows a woman with her spinning wheel. The glowing light and calm domestic scene are typical of Dutch paintings from the 1500s. Imagine the turning posts, spools, and wheel making rhythmic sounds such as *ret set set* as they spin fleece into wool.

1 GET SET

"What do the words of 'Sarasponda' imitate?" (spinning wheel) "The movement for the A section also imitates the wheel." (See *Movement* on the bottom of page 167.) "Let's sing the A section with the movement, then stand in place and listen for octave skips in the B section." Have students:

▶ • Sing and move to the song **CD4:11**.

▶ • Name the vocables that were sung with octave skips. (first two *Ah-do*s of each B section)

"In this lesson you'll learn how octave skips are written and use a new pitch."

2 DEVELOP

1. Review pitch syllable and letter names in "Sarasponda." Have students:

• Read page 176 and identify the lyrics of the notated phrase, sharing strategies used. (Provide resonator bells or other pitched instruments.)

• Sing the phrase with pitch syllables, then sing it with pitch letter names. (*mi fa so fa mi re do*; E F G F E D C)

2. Create an ostinato using low and high C. Have students:

• Read about octaves, then find them in the notation of "Sarasponda" on page 167.

• Name the pitches in those octaves. (C and high C; *do* and high *do*)

• Speak and pat the ostinato on page 176.

OBJECTIVE 1 Informal Assessment

• Use low and high C to create a melody on bells for the rhythmic ostinato.

• Perform the ostinato with the A section.

• Create movement for the B section. (See *Movement* below.) Then perform the entire song with movement, while some students play the ostinato.

SPECIAL LEARNERS: *Performing the Ostinato*

Students who have problems patting even eighth notes at the correct tempo may use a simpler ostinato.

Mov - ing, turn - ing.

Have all students speak and pat both patterns, but when using instruments, have students who need to play the simpler one. They may use one pitch instead of both.

MOVEMENT: *"Sarasponda" B Section*

Have each group of four follow these parameters in creating a B section movement. Since the A section is performed in circles, the B section should use a different formation, such as a line. Not everyone in the line needs to have the same body facing. Lines can travel through shared space or stay in place. The dance should be sixteen beats long, and after the repeat, each group must again form a circle, ready for the right-hand star.

UNIT FOUR
LESSON 5

continued from previous page

3 APPLY

Introduce "Hoedown" CD4:15. **Sing a motive containing an octave.** Have students:

▶ • Read about Aaron Copland and "Hoedown."

▶ • Listen to "Hoedown."

OBJECTIVE 2 **Informal Assessment**

• Sing the motive on page 178 with pitch syllables. (*mi re do do'*)

• Sing it again, adding a stamp on the *do* and a clap on the *do'*.

Recorded Lesson CD4:16

▶ • Listen to "'Hoedown' B Theme" to hear an octave motive, and perform a stamp-clap movement with it.

▶ • Listen to "Hoedown" again and follow the listening map. (Optional: Use **Listening Map Transparency T • 7.**) The motive has been transposed to a lower key in the informal assessment to fit students' vocal range.

Hoedown (excerpt) from *Rodeo*
by Aaron Copland

"Hoedown" borrows musical ideas from square dances and rodeos.

SING this motive with pitch syllables. Stamp on low *do* and clap on high *do*.

LISTENING MAP *Listen to "Hoedown" and follow the map.*

178

MEETING **INDIVIDUAL** NEEDS

ALTERNATE TEACHING STRATEGY

OBJECTIVE 2 Identify the first three pitches of the motive on page 178 as the familiar *mi re do*. Play them, then sing *do'*. Have students sing the pattern back and identify the syllables (*mi re do do'*). (Optional: Use **Resource Master 4 • 6** to reinforce relative staff positions of pitch syllables.)

PITCH SYLLABLES: *Review*

Read "I Don't Care If the Rain Comes Down" on page 108 with pitch syllables and letter names.

BIOGRAPHY: *Aaron Copland*

Aaron Copland didn't study music until he was in his teens. His first symphony was performed when he was 24. Copland won a Pulitzer prize for the ballet *Appalachian Spring*.

MUSIC BUILDS MATH SKILLS

Algebra and Connection Singing with pitch syllables reinforces students' understanding of variables in a number sentence.

"Describe how the names of the pitches in an octave are related." (They have the same pitch syllable names and letter names.)

▶ • Listen again to "Hoedown," stamping on low *do* and clapping on high *do* of the octave motive.

LESSON SUMMARY

Informal Assessment In this lesson, students:

OBJECTIVE 1 Played an original ostinato on pitched percussion using low and high C to accompany "Sarasponda."

OBJECTIVE 2 Using pitch syllables, sang a melodic motive from "Hoedown" that includes an octave skip.

National Standards for Music Education

1a Sing accurately, on pitch and in rhythm.

5a Read standard note values in duple and triple meters.

5b Use a system to read notation in treble clef in major keys.

MORE MUSIC: Reinforcement

More Songs to Read, page 363 (octaves)
"Sourwood Mountain," page 196 (*so, la, do re mi so la do'*)
"Somewhere in My Memory," page 327 (*do mi so do'*)
"Macnamara's Band," page 342 (octave; C')
"The Tree Song," page 345 (octave; spring)
Symphony No. 35 ("Haffner"), page 385C (octaves)

SPOTLIGHT ON AARON COPLAND

Aaron Copland (1900–1990) was born in Brooklyn, N.Y. His first contact with music came from listening to his older sister practice the piano. By age 8, he was composing songs. As an adult, he became one of the first American composers to have his work known all over the world.

Copland's use of jazz and American folk tunes gave his music a sound all its own. Besides composing for concerts, the ballet, opera, radio, theater, and movies, he was a pianist and conductor. He also lectured and wrote books to help people understand and appreciate modern music.

Unit 4 *Connections* 179

MOVEMENT: *"Hoedown"*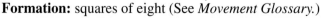

Formation: squares of eight (See *Movement Glossary.*)

A section: Circling theme—square joins hands and walks or slides counterclockwise, then clockwise (8 beats each). Face corner and allemande left (holding L hands, walk once around and back to place) (8 beats); face partner and allemande right (8 beats). Repeat circling theme (16 beats). Head couples walk 4 beats in toward center, then out 4 beats; side couples walk in and out (8 beats). Do-si-do corner; do-si-do partner (8 beats each). Repeat circling theme (16 beats). Step in place (22 beats).

B section: Couple 1 performs a "Rip and Snort" (16 beats). All hold hands; couple 1 walks across the set and stands directly in front of couple 3. Couple 3 raises their inside hands and forms an arch. Couple 1 walks through the arch, leading the others through by the hands. Once through, couples drop hands and separate—students on right go right, students on left go left—and walk outside the set back to place. As the last dancers pass through the arch, couple 3 turns under their own arms, or "wrings the dishrag," facing the center once again. This figure is repeated by couples 2, 3, and 4. (16 beats each) Then repeat circling theme (16 beats). Finally, all walk in to the center (4 beats) and out (4 beats), throwing arms up at end.

Unit 4 CONNECTIONS **179**

ACROSS the

MATHEMATICS

SPINNING PROBABILITY

"Sarasponda"

PAIR   **15–30 MIN**

MATERIALS: index cards, math compass (or plastic cup), ruler, crayons, pencil, scissors

Each pair of students traces a circle on an index card—using a compass or tracing around the rim of a plastic cup. They cut out the circle and use a ruler to draw a line to divide the circle in half. (They can fold the circle in half, open it, and draw along the crease.) They repeat to create four equal quarters and color each section: red, blue, yellow, green.

They make a hole through the center, using a pencil point. One partner then holds the pencil upright and places the hole of the circle over the point, checking to make sure that the circle spins freely. That partner holds up the thumb of the same hand. The other partner spins the circle 20 times, recording how many times each color stops beside the thumb.

They repeat with another circle, coloring two sections red, one blue, and one yellow. Have them predict how results may differ from the first test. Why? Have them test their predictions.

COMPREHENSION STRATEGY: Compare and contrast

LANGUAGE ARTS

WRITING INVITATIONS

"Hoedown"

INDIVIDUAL   **15 MIN OR LESS**

MATERIALS: drawing paper, markers or crayons, stickers

Have students think of a reason for giving a party, such as a birthday, a holiday, a celebration of a school event. Then each student thinks of an appropriate message for an announcement or invitation card for the party. The message should refer to the kind of dancing that the party might have, including square dancing.

Have students write out their messages on drawing paper and decorate their messages to make appealing party invitations.

COMPREHENSION STRATEGY: Expressing main ideas

CURRICULUM

SOCIAL STUDIES

DANCE IN AMERICA

"Hoedown"

GROUP   **30 MIN OR LONGER**

Have students work in groups to research the popular form of American folk dancing, square dancing. Have them describe why it is called "square," describe different formations (running set, longways), the role of the "caller," and the meanings of some of the calls. Students may describe the origins of this type of dancing as well as explain why there are many variations in different communities. Students might present their findings with a demonstration of the moves.

Some groups of students might research the life of Martha Graham, who choreographed *Appalachian Spring* in 1944 and became one of the greatest names of modern dance. What were her achievements? How did she affect the style of dance?

COMPREHENSION STRATEGY: Organizing information

MATHEMATICS

SQUARES

"Hoedown"

PAIR   **15–30 MIN**

MATERIALS: centimeter graph paper, ruler, pencil

Have students work in pairs. Each partner draws a square on graph paper, careful to note that all sides of a square are equal in length. They can use the small graph squares to guide their drawings, deciding how many graph-squares the four sides of their figures should be. To make sure their figures are different, partners should announce their decisions to each other before drawing their squares.

They exchange graphs. Each partner finds the area and perimeter of the square. The area is the number of little graph-squares inside the figure. The perimeter is the number of sides of little graph-squares along the four sides of the figure.

Students compare results. Have them try to think of a faster way of finding the areas and perimeters other than counting. (Area = side x side; perimeter = side x 4)

COMPREHENSION STRATEGIES: Drawing conclusions, using diagrams and models

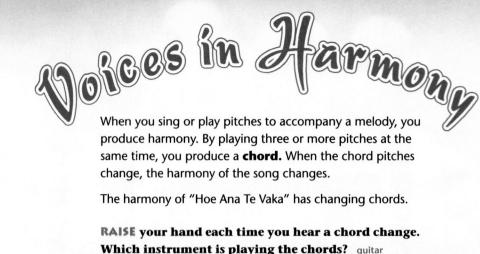

Voices in Harmony

When you sing or play pitches to accompany a melody, you produce harmony. By playing three or more pitches at the same time, you produce a **chord.** When the chord pitches change, the harmony of the song changes.

The harmony of "Hoe Ana Te Vaka" has changing chords.

RAISE your hand each time you hear a chord change. Which instrument is playing the chords? guitar

In the South Pacific, the canoe has long been an important form of transportation. "Hoe Ana Te Vaka" describes paddling a canoe and sighting the islands of Tahiti and Mo'orea.

LESSON PLANNER

FOCUS Harmony, I-IV-V chord changes

OBJECTIVES
OBJECTIVE 1 Signal when a chord change occurs in a song's accompaniment
OBJECTIVE 2 Play a chordal accompaniment to a song

MATERIALS
Recordings
Tina Singu	CD4:2
Hoe Ana Te Vaka	CD4:17
Recorded Lesson: Pronunciation for "Hoe Ana Te Vaka"	CD4:18
Recorded Lesson: Chord Change	CD4:19
Hosanna, Me Build a House	CD4:9

Instruments
resonator bells, autoharps, ukuleles, or guitars

Resources
Resource Master 4 • 7 (practice)
Recorder Master R • 18 (pitches E A B)

VOCABULARY
chord, chord root

▶ = **BASIC PROGRAM**

MEETING **INDIVIDUAL** NEEDS

ALTERNATE TEACHING STRATEGY

OBJECTIVE 1 Have students start in scattered formation; their eyes may be closed. Strum a chord repeatedly (A, D, or E chord). On each chord change, students change body shape/design and freeze until the next chord change. At first, strum each chord for at least 8 beats, changing regularly. Continue, changing irregularly.

MOVEMENT: *"Hoe Ana Te Vaka"* MOVEMENT
Formation: lines of 6–8, standing or squatting in rows or "canoes." **Motions:** (perform on the half-note beat)

A section: *Hoe ana te vaka*—Paddle twice on R, twice on L. *Hoe ana*—Paddle once R, L, R, L. *I Tahiti*—Put L hand on hip and point R index finger up to Tahiti. *Mo'orea*—Put R hand on hip and point L index finger down to Mo'orea. *Hoe ana te vaka*—Paddle twice on R, twice on L. **B section:** *Tiai mai*—With both hands palms down, push out in front of body four times. *Tae atu vau*—Both hands (palms facing) sweep towards one another in front of body four times. *Ia oe*—Both hands above head wave towards self four times, as though beckoning. *Ta'u he*—Tap chest twice, *-re,* cross arms over chest and tap upper arms twice.

Hoe Ana Te Vaka
PADDLE THE CANOE

Tahitian Folk Song
Collected and Transcribed
by Kathy B. Sorensen

Tahitian: Ho-e a-na te va-ka, Ho-e a-na,
Pronunciation: ho e a na te va ka ho e a na

I Ta-hi-ti, Mo-'o-re-a, Ho-e a-na te va-ka.
i ta hi ti mo 'o re a ho e a na te va ka

Ti-a-i mai, Tae a-tu vau,
ti a i mai tae a tu vau

I-a o-e Ta-'u he-re.
i a o e ta 'u he re

Ho-e a-na te va-ka, Ho-e a-na,
ho e a na te va ka ho e a na

I Ta-hi-ti, Mo-'o-re-a, Ho-e a-na te va-ka.
i ta hi ti mo 'o re a ho e a na te va ka

A major

Unit 4 *Connections* **181**

"When you sang 'Tina Singu,' how many different pitches did you sing at one time?" (two) "Singing or playing two or more pitches at one time is called adding harmony." Have students:

▶ • Listen to "Tina Singu" **CD4:2** and raise their hands when they hear the two vocal parts together.

"Adding harmony to a melody can make music more interesting. Today we'll learn about and play harmony that uses three or more pitches at one time."

2 DEVELOP

1. Introduce "Hoe Ana Te Vaka" CD4:17 Introduce chords. Have students:

▶ • Read about chords on page 180.

▶ • Read about and listen to the song.

Recorded Lesson CD4:18
▶ • Listen to "Pronunciation for 'Hoe Ana Te Vaka.'"

2. Listen to the chordal accompaniment in "Hoe Ana Te Vaka." Have students:

Recorded Lesson CD4:19
OBJECTIVE 1 Informal Assessment
▶ • Listen to "Chord Change" to hear the A section of "Hoe Ana Te Vaka" without, then with, the melody, and signal each time they hear a chord change. (Measures 1, 2, 4, 5, 8)

▶ • Sing the song and learn the movement by mirroring. (See *Movement* on the bottom of page 180.)

PLAYING INSTRUMENTS: *Unpitched Percussion*

Large woodblocks, slit drums, or log drums: accompany "Hoe Ana Te Vaka" with this ostinato: ♩ ♩ ♩ ♩ **Lummi or rhythm sticks:** Have partners play the rhythm of the words, using these three patterns in the order necessary.

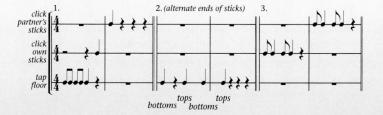

click partner's sticks
click own sticks
tap floor

1. 2. (alternate ends of sticks) 3.

bottoms tops bottoms tops

MULTICULTURAL PERSPECTIVES: *'Aparima* MOVEMENT

"Hoe Ana Te Vaka" is a Tahitian *'aparima* (ɑ pɑ ɾi mɑ), a group dance in which hand and arm motions reflect the words. The motions are as important as the words and are always performed with the song. Traditional canoe songs are still quite popular and are performed by people of all ages at schools, parties, weddings, and other social occasions.

PRONUNCIATION: *"Hoe Ana Te Vaka"*

ɑ f<u>a</u>ther	e ch<u>a</u>otic	i b<u>ee</u>	o <u>o</u>bey
u m<u>oo</u>n	ɾ flipped r	' glottal stop, as in 'uh 'oh!	

continued from previous page

3 APPLY

Review "Hosanna, Me Build a House" CD4:9 **(pp. 164–165). Play chordal harmony.** Have students:

▶ • Sing the song, page 164.

▶ • Read about chord roots on page 182 and find the chord names above the music.

• Sing the B section, page 182, adding body percussion: clap on green, stamp on blue, and pat on orange.

• Practice playing the chords on page 182.

OBJECTIVE 2 Informal Assessment

• Sing the B section, playing resonator bells or other pitched instruments and changing chords on the downbeats.

NAME THAT CHORD!

Each chord has a letter name based on a pitch called the **chord root.** Usually when the pitches of a chord are arranged close to each other on the staff, the lowest pitch is the chord root and gives the chord its name.

FIND the chord names above the music.

182 VOICES IN HARMONY

MEETING **INDIVIDUAL** NEEDS

ALTERNATE TEACHING STRATEGY

OBJECTIVE 2 Display large colored pieces of paper on the board: green, blue, orange. Assign students to three groups, one for each chord. Have them perform the body percussion sound for their assigned chord as you point to each color. Have them transfer this to playing the resonator bells or other pitched instruments as you point to the colors in time with the harmonic pattern.

EXTRA HELP: *Playing Chordal Harmony*

Make a transparency of **Resource Master 4 • 7** to guide the class through the harmonic pattern studied.

SPECIAL LEARNERS: *Music for Leisure*

Although students with disabilities will enjoy playing the resonator bells, give them many keyboard experiences as well, since keyboards are more common outside of school. In class, the students could play chord roots at the keyboard with a friend. Code the keys to match chord letter names.

HOSANNA! WE BUILD A CHORD!

The colors show the harmonic pattern for the B section of "Hosanna, Me Build a House."

PLAY the harmonic pattern for "Hosanna, Me Build a House" with these three chords.

C E G   F A C   G B D

Unit 4 *Connections* 183

"What is a chord?" (three or more pitches sounded at the same time) "What happens when the harmony changes?" (The pitches in the chord change.)

"Let's sing 'Hosanna, Me Build a House' all the way through, and each time we sing the B section, play the harmony."

LESSON SUMMARY

Informal Assessment In this lesson, students:

OBJECTIVE 1 Signaled to identify chord changes in the accompaniment to "Hoe Ana Te Vaka."

OBJECTIVE 2 Played a chordal accompaniment for "Hosanna, Me Build a House."

National Standards for Music Education
2a Play instruments with accurate pitch and rhythm.
2f Play parts while others perform contrasting parts.
8b Describe how other school disciplines are related to music.

MORE MUSIC: Reinforcement

"When I First Came to This Land," page 148 (harmony—I IV V chords, C F G chords)

"Dale, dale, dale!," page 322 (I IV V chords, C F G chords)

"We Three Kings," page 329 (I IV V chords)

PLAYING INSTRUMENTS: *Keyboards/Orff*

Have students sing the letter and pitch syllable names of the chord roots (bass line), then play this accompaniment to the B section of "Hosanna, Me Build a House." Students may chant the harmonic pattern's rhythm before adding it to the bass line: *"Build a house, Sing Hosanna!"*

ART CONNECTION: *Building a House*

VISUAL ARTS

In the spirit of "Hosanna, Me Build a House," students may wish to design their own houses and build models. First, have students work in small groups to dream up a house and create informal "blueprints." Encourage students to be imaginative—even outlandish—in their designs and to describe where they would like their houses to be. Then group members can collaborate to build a model of their dream house. Suggest they use everyday materials such as pencils, twigs, ice cream sticks, cardboard, and paper for their "building supplies."

LESSON PLANNER

FOCUS Duration, syncopation

OBJECTIVE
OBJECTIVE 1 Perform a poem with syncopation, in rap style (tested)

MATERIALS
Recordings
Listening: Stone Pounding
(instrumental)   CD4:20
Stone Pounding   CD4:4
Listening: I Missed the Bus   CD4:21
Listening: Nathaniel's Rap   CD4:22

Resources
Resource Master 4 • 8 (practice)
Recorder Master R • 19 (pitches E G A B)

VOCABULARY
accented, syncopated

▶ = **BASIC PROGRAM**

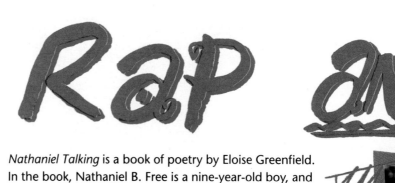

Nathaniel Talking is a book of poetry by Eloise Greenfield. In the book, Nathaniel B. Free is a nine-year-old boy, and this is his rap.

Nathaniel's RAP

It's Nathaniel talking
and Nathaniel's me
I'm talking about
My philosophy
About the things I do
And the people I see
All told in the words
Of Nathaniel B. Free
That's me
And I can rap
I can rap
I can rap, rap, rap
Till your earflaps flap
I can talk that talk
Till you go for a walk
I can run it on down
Till you get out of town
I can rap
I can rap
Rested, dressed and feeling fine
I've got something on my mind

184

MEETING **INDIVIDUAL** NEEDS

BIOGRAPHY: *Eloise Greenfield*

When Eloise Greenfield (b. 1929) was in her early twenties, she discovered that writing gave her great satisfaction. Since childhood she had loved to read, but there seemed to be far too few books about African Americans. She wanted to help change that. She started by writing three short stories, which no one wanted to publish. That almost made her give up. She realized, though, that writing takes more than talent—it takes practice. Her first poem was not published until 1963, when she was 34, and it was 1972 before her first book came out. Since then about 20 books for children

have followed, including fiction, biographies, and poetry. Her aim has been simple yet ambitious: to give young readers "words to love, to grow on." *Nathaniel Talking* won the prestigious Coretta Scott King Award in 1990.

MULTICULTURAL PERSPECTIVES: *Rap*

Rap music is a brand-new art form, dating back only to the 1970s. Its roots, however, go back centuries—to African boasting and praise songs and to African American oral tradition. Once an underground music, rap has become an important medium for African Americans to share ideas and

Rhythm

Friends and kin and neighborhood
Listen now and listen good
Nathaniel's talking
Nathaniel B. Free
Talking about
My philosophy
Been thinking all day
I got a lot to say
Gotta run it on down
Nathaniel's way
Okay!
I gotta rap
Gotta rap
Gotta rap, rap, rap
Till your earflaps flap
Gotta talk that talk
Till you go for a walk
Gotta run it on down
Till you get out of town
Gotta rap
Gotta rap
Rested, dressed and feeling fine
I've got something on my mind
Friends and kin and neighborhood
Listen now and listen good
I'm gonna rap, hey!
Gonna rap, hey!
I'm gonna rap!

—Eloise Greenfield

What can you tell about Nathaniel from this poem? Possible answers: He likes to rap; he feels good today; he loves his friends, family, and neighborhood.

DESCRIBE how the poem could sound when it is performed aloud as a rap.

"When you recognize this song, tap lightly with the rhythm of the melody." Have students:

▶ • Listen to "Stone Pounding" (instrumental) CD4:20 and identify the song.

▶ • Sing "Stone Pounding" CD4:4 (p. 160), moving through shared space as they step with the rhythm of the words.

• Compare the rhythms of sections A and A'. (A: some rhythms uneven, not on the beats; A': even, correspond with beats)

"These rhythms which sound 'off' the beat can be found in all types of music. We'll hear and create some of those rhythms today."

2 DEVELOP

1. Introduce the poem "Nathaniel's Rap." Have students:

▶ • Read about the poem in the book.

▶ • Read and discuss the content of the poem.

▶ • Describe how they would expect this poem to sound if it were performed aloud. (Write the comments on the board.)

experiences. Early groups such as Grandmaster Flash and the Furious Five blazed the trail with hard-hitting, socially conscious lyrics. A wide spectrum of styles continues to emerge. These styles range from tough-talking "gangsta" rap, which has at times stirred controversy, to feminist rap, humorous rap, and rap with jazz, funk, and blues influences. "Hardcore" rap, one of the major styles, often carries timely social or political messages. Other rap is about having a good time and dancing.

ENRICHMENT: *Syncopation*

In place of the A' section of "Stone Pounding," have students create a new B section of rhythmic improvisation which incorporates syncopation, or sounds that are off the beat. Students can tap stones or stamp their feet to make the sounds.

UNIT FOUR
LESSON 7

continued from previous page

2. Introduce "I Missed the Bus" CD4:21. Listen to an example of rap. Have students:

▶ • Read about Kris Kross.

▶ • Listen to the rap and tap lightly with the beat.

• Describe the performance characteristics and add them to the list created for "Nathaniel's Rap." (instrumental and spoken ostinatos, verses spoken as a solo)

▶ • Listen again and identify the refrains by doing a "rap walk" of their own creation.

3 APPLY

Interpret the poem "Nathaniel's Rap" in rap style. Have students:

▶ • Read about accents and syncopation.

▶ • In small groups, take a section of the poem and decide how to perform it using syncopated rhythms and accents. (Optional: Use **Resource Master 4 • 8.**)

OBJECTIVE 1 Informal Assessment

▶ • Perform their section of the poem in rap style. (Adjust the stereo balance control to "Nathaniel's Rap" **CD4:22** to provide a rap track, without vocals, to accompany students.)

▶ • Listen to "Nathaniel's Rap" and compare the interpretation to their own.

🎵 I Missed the Bus *by Jermaine Dupri*
LISTENING

In 1992 the rap duo Kris Kross recorded "I Missed the Bus." They were 13 years old. Their special style is wearing everything–hat, shirt, and jeans–backwards. But their music, with its fresh rhythms and appealing rhymes, is what made them successful. They've had a triple-platinum album, Totally Krossed Out, from which "I Missed the Bus" is taken.

Rap sprang up in African American communities during the 1970s. Rappers put together fast, catchy phrases over rhythm tracks. Some rap is pure entertainment. Other rappers' words turn to serious themes such as politics, poverty, and racism.

LISTEN to "I Missed the Bus" and describe what you hear. Possible answers: rhythmic speech; repeated phrases; rhymes; sudden dynamics; rhythmic background; solo versus group rapping

Chris Smith and Chris Kelly of Kris Kross

186 RAP AND RHYTHM

MEETING **INDIVIDUAL** NEEDS

ALTERNATE TEACHING STRATEGY

OBJECTIVE 1 Read the poem aloud with "straight" rhythms (all ♩'s, ♪ ♪'s, 𝄽's) as the class pats with the beat. Have students compare the reading with the rhythmic style of "I Missed the Bus" and discuss the use of syncopation. Clap some eight-beat rhythm patterns over a drum beat, some syncopated, some not. Repeat, having students raise hands when they hear syncopation.

COOPERATIVE LEARNING: *"Nathaniel's Rap"*

Assign each group of four a section of the poem to perform. Give groups ten minutes to plan and rehearse quietly. Encourage them to use syncopation. (Optional: Use **Resource Master 4 • 8** to plan and notate the rap.)

BIOGRAPHY: *Kris Kross*

The rappers in Kris Kross, Chris Smith and Chris Kelly, were born in 1979 and grew up listening to hip-hop music. Friends since first grade, they were already sporting their trademark backwards fashions when they were discovered

In some music, stressed or **accented** sounds come between the beats instead of on the beat. Rhythm patterns with sounds between the beats are called **syncopated**.

Syncopation can be found in many kinds of music. The *short long short* pattern in "Stone Pounding" is an example of syncopation. The rhythms of rap are also very syncopated.

CREATE your own syncopated rap version of "Nathaniel's Rap."

THINK IT THROUGH
How would "Nathaniel's Rap" sound if every syllable were unaccented and on the beat? Try saying it that way. How does it compare with the recording?

Unit 4 *Connections* **187**

"Name and describe the musical style we worked with today." (rap; lyrics spoken rapidly with intense sound, rhythms highly syncopated with strong accents, instrumental and spoken rhythmic ostinatos)

"Now let's perform our own version of 'Nathaniel's Rap,' putting all the sections of the poem together."

LESSON SUMMARY

Informal Assessment In this lesson, students:

OBJECTIVE 1 Performed the poem "Nathaniel's Rap" in rap style with syncopated rhythms.

National Standards for Music Education
1a Sing accurately, on pitch and in rhythm.
3c Improvise rhythmic variations and melodic embellishments.
3d Improvise using sound sources available in the classroom.

MORE MUSIC: Reinforcement
"Martin's Cry," page 336 (syncopation)
"Hambone," page 200 (syncopation)
"Don't Let the Music Stop," page 380 (syncopation)
"The Dance at the Gym," page 385I (syncopation)

---

by their producer, Jermaine Dupri, at an Atlanta shopping mall. Dupri, himself only six years older, shaped the act. With input from the two boys, he wrote all of the songs on their triple-platinum album, *Totally Krossed Out.*

TECHNOLOGY IN MUSIC: *Sampling*

Pioneering hip-hop "MCs" rapped to rhythm tracks created by splicing together bits and pieces of earlier records. This approach took a big step forward around 1980 with electronic "samplers." Samplers turn a sound into digital codes which allow it to be reproduced exactly. Samplers can easily lift a drumbeat off of an old song or record the screech

of a car's brakes. With a sampler, musicians can treat chunks of sound as building blocks and put them together in various ways to create fresh rhythms and melodies. Most samplers look like cassette decks but work more like computers, using floppy disks, not tape. Musical instruments can also be equipped with samplers.

LANGUAGE ARTS CONNECTION: *Write a Rap*

Have students write a rap about a problem (losing homework, having an argument) or about something good (winning a contest, having a friend).

MAKE YOUR OWN MELODY

Steel drums are tuned instruments made from oil drums and steel barrels. One drum can play up to thirty pitches, so a steel drum band can play both melody and harmony.

Steel drums accompany parades during Carnival. Steel drum bands, also called pan orchestras, are popular throughout the Caribbean and in other places with large numbers of West Indian people.

LISTEN to "Hosanna, Me Build a House" with steel drums playing the melody. When do the musicians make up new melodies in place of the melody of the song? Section C (form: ABBC)

188

MEETING **INDIVIDUAL** NEEDS

ALTERNATE TEACHING STRATEGY

OBJECTIVE 1 Have students sing the A section, adding body percussion as they sing each motive: clap-snap-snap on each *Hosanna,* and pat the rhythm of the words *sandy ground* with alternating hands on one leg. Have a set of resonator bells displayed horizontally for the students to see. Play each motive and have them match what you played with the words from the text.

PLAYING INSTRUMENTS: *Pitched/Unpitched*

Divide students into three groups, one for each section of "Hosanna, Me Build a House." Sing the song with each group performing during its section: the melodic motives for the A section of the song, the chord changes for the B section (see Lesson 6, pages 182–183), and the rhythm of the words of the C section on unpitched Latin percussion (see Lesson 3, pages 170–171).

Steel drum band playing during Carnival in St. George's, Grenada. Opposite page: musicians playing steel drums on St. Lucia, a Caribbean island.

ADD SOME HIGHLIGHTS

Another way to change "Hosanna, Me Build a House" is to highlight parts of the melody by playing them on instruments. Find the pitches needed to play the tinted motives.

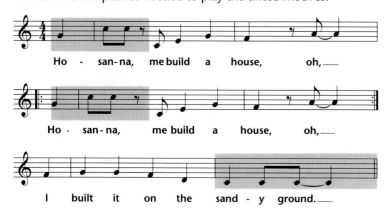

Ho - san - na,   me build   a   house,   oh, ——

Ho - san - na,   me build   a   house,   oh, ——

I   built   it   on   the   sand - y   ground. ——

PLAY the motives as you sing the song.
G = *ho*, high C = *sanna*, low C = *sandy ground*

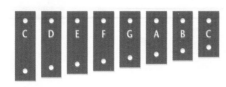

What is the skip between the lowest and highest pitches called? octave

"There are many ways to change how a song is performed. One way is to play it instead of singing it. Listen to this version of a song you know. Raise a hand when you hear the musicians change part of the melody." (C section) Have students:

▶ • Listen to and discuss "What's New?" **CD4:23**, in which they hear "Hosanna, Me Build a House" played on steel drums, with improvisation in the C section.

▶ • Read about steel drum bands on page 188.

"Today you will be using what you've learned about pitch and rhythm to create your own versions of songs."

2 DEVELOP

1. Review "Hosanna, Me Build a House" CD4:9. Play motives on resonator bells or other barred instruments. Have students:

▶ • Sing the song (p. 164).

• Read page 189, then identify the pitches of the tinted motives. (*so do' do'* and *do do do*; G C'C' and C C C)

• Describe the relationship of the two C's (octave), then hum the A section, singing the two motives with letter names.

OBJECTIVE 1 Informal Assessment
• Sing the song, playing the two motives on resonator bells or other pitched instruments.

IMPROVISATION: *Create a B Section*

For further instrumental enrichment, have students create a B section for "Hosanna, Me Build a House" and practice the *short long short* pattern. They can practice the rhythms suggested below, then combine several.

cabasa—

claves—

bongos—

conga—

maracas—

agogo bells—

UNIT FOUR
LESSON 8

continued from previous page

2. Introduce "Things Ain't What They Used to Be" CD4:25. Listen to an example of improvisation. Have students:

▶ • Read about jazz on page 190.

Recorded Lesson CD4:24

▶ • Listen to "Interview with Marian McPartland," in which they hear the artist demonstrate jazz in improvisation.

▶ • Listen to "Things Ain't What They Used to Be" and describe what they heard in the improvisation. (different pitches, rhythms, "extra notes" added)

3 APPLY

Review "Little David, Play on Your Harp" CD4:12 (p. 168). Improvise melodies. Have students:

▶ • Sing the song and identify the tonal center as F/*do*.

• Name the pitches shown on the bottom of page 191, then find them on resonator bells or other pitched instruments. (C D F G A C')

Recorded Lesson CD4:26

▶ • Listen to "Improvising," in which rhythmic and melodic improvisation is demonstrated.

▶ • Sing the song, patting improvised rhythms in place of the verses.

OBJECTIVE 2 Informal Assessment
• Sing the song, pat-clapping to the beat during the refrain, with groups of four students improvising melodies on the prescribed pitches during each verse.

THE JAZZ CONNECTION

The syncopated rhythms and melodies of **jazz** grew from the spirituals, work songs, and blues of African Americans. The roots of jazz go back to rhythms from western Africa, which African Americans mixed with harmony from classical and folk music they learned in America. Jazz appeals to people of all cultures and many play this music.

Many jazz musicians are known for their ability to **improvise**, or find new ways to play melodies and rhythm patterns each time they perform.

meet
MARIAN McPARTLAND

Marian McPartland is a pianist and a songwriter who also improvises on other compositions, interpreting them her own way. She hosts a radio show, "Piano Jazz," on which she talks to and performs with other jazz pianists.

LISTEN to Marian McPartland as she discusses and demonstrates jazz improvisation.

190

MEETING **INDIVIDUAL** NEEDS

ALTERNATE TEACHING STRATEGY

OBJECTIVE 2 Have students create new verses and play the rhythms of the words on the low C resonator bell, alternate between low and high C, then use three or more of the prescribed pitches. (For practice, have students echo-clap phrases such as these and transfer them to bells.)

COOPERATIVE LEARNING: *Writing Verses*

Have groups of four choose modern heroes/heroines and create and perform new verses for "Little David, Play on Your Harp." Assign roles such as encourager, who makes sure each member contributes.

EXTRA HELP: *Improvising*

Demonstrate improvising during the verse of "Little David, Play on Your Harp" on the resonator bells. Arrange four sets of bells so students can form lines behind them. Direct a new set of four players to improvise during each verse.

LISTENING

Things Ain't What They Used to Be
by Mercer Ellington

LISTEN to Marian McPartland improvise on this jazz melody.

IMPROVISE melodies on these pitches during the verses of "Little David, Play on Your Harp."

Unit 4 *Connections* **191**

4 CLOSE

"Describe the ways you used pitches to change how you performed two songs." (played some of the motives as well as singing them, played new melodies as verses) Have students:

• Perform "Little David, Play on Your Harp" once more with a soloist improvising on bells.

• Listen for octaves and syncopated rhythms in the soloist's improvised melody.

LESSON SUMMARY

Informal Assessment In this lesson, students:

OBJECTIVE 1 Played and sang motives from notation of "Hosanna, Me Build a House."

OBJECTIVE 2 Improvised new melodies for the verse of "Little David, Play on Your Harp."

National Standards for Music Education
2c Play repertoire from diverse genres and cultures.
3c Improvise rhythmic variations and melodic embellishments.
3d Improvise using sound sources available in the classroom.

MORE MUSIC: Reinforcement
"Now's the Time," page 199 (improvisation)
"Hambone," page 200 (improvisation)

BIOGRAPHY: *Marian McPartland*

British-born Marian McPartland (b. 1920) has won praise for her elegant piano-playing and her wide-ranging musical curiosity. She gained attention after she moved to the United States in 1946 and began playing in the Dixieland band of her husband, trumpeter Jimmy McPartland. Duke Ellington once told her, "You play so many notes." Months later she realized, "He was telling me to edit myself. And of course he was right." Today McPartland is best known for her award-winning radio show, *Piano Jazz,* on which she interviews and plays duets with a different keyboard player each week.

PLAYING INSTRUMENTS: *Keyboards*

To improvise melodies to "Little David, Play on Your Harp," students can play the rhythms of their verses or use this ostinato. Help them position their hands as shown and encourage them to end on F.

Play on your harp, play on your harp, play on your harp, sing Hal-le-lu!

UNIT FOUR
LESSON 9

RELATED ARTS   MOVEMENT   THEATER   VISUAL ARTS

LESSON PLANNER

OBJECTIVES
To review songs, skills, and concepts learned in Unit 4 and to test students' ability to:
1. Recognize patterns using octaves with C and C'
2. Read the *short long short* (♪ ♩ ♪) rhythm pattern

MATERIALS
Recordings

Stone Pounding	CD4:4
Sarasponda	CD4:11
Hosanna, Me Build a House	CD4:9
Tina Singu	CD4:2
Unit 4 Assessment A	CD4:27–30
Unit 4 Assessment B	CD4:31–34

Resources
Resource Master 4 • 9 (assessment)
Resource Master 4 • 10 (assessment)
Resource Master TA • 1 (assessment)

▶ = BASIC PROGRAM

REVIEW

MAKING CONNECTIONS

When you meet someone new, you may first notice how that person is different from you. When you find something that is the same between you, such as an activity that you both enjoy, you have made a connection. You are on your way to being friends.

192

MEETING **INDIVIDUAL** NEEDS

PROGRAM IDEA: *Rhythmic Connections*

This review can be enjoyed in the classroom or presented as a simple program. Additional materials from Unit 4, *Celebrations,* or the *Music Library* may be added as well as original work from the students.

"Let's travel to two different parts of the world. Instead of an airplane connection, we'll make a 'rhythmic connection' by singing some of the music that comes from these places." Have some students locate the general area where they live on a globe.

"Let's head first to the Caribbean Sea where we'll visit the island of Jamaica." Help students to locate Jamaica on the globe (18°N, 77°W) and point out the location to the class. "Perhaps some of you have visited a Caribbean island. Think about what may be different about an island compared to where you live." Students sing the Jamaican folk song "Stone Pounding," switching between patting with the beat and clapping the rhythm of the words.

1. Review the *short long short* rhythm in "Stone Pounding" CD4:4 **(p. 160).** Have students:

▶ • Sing the song and recall other singing games for small groups. (Possible answer: "Four White Horses")

• Review the *short long short* rhythm pattern, then sing the song from notation, clapping the rhythm.

• Name a unit song from a different country with the *short long short* rhythm. ("Guadalquivir")

▶ • Play the stone-pounding game. (See Lesson 4, *Enrichment,* page 173.)

2. Review "Sarasponda" CD4:11 **(p. 167). Review octave, *do,* and C¹.** Have students:

▶ • Sing the song and discuss why people might enjoy a spinning song.

• Review octaves and pitch names, page 176.

• Sing *Ah-do-ray-oh* with pitch syllables, then letter names.

• Name a unit song from a different country with an octave skip. ("Tina Singu")

▶ • Sing "Sarasponda" with the movement. (See Lesson 2, page 167, and Lesson 5, page 177, *Movement.*)

People everywhere enjoy playing together. "Stone Pounding" is a singing game from Jamaica.

Singing while you work can make the job easier. "Sarasponda" is a work song from Holland, and "Tina Singu" is one from Lesotho.

What other singing games do you know? What other work songs do you know?

Unit 4 *Connections* **193**

"Singing can be even more fun when there is action to go along with it. Let's sing another song from Jamaica and move to it." Students sing "Hosanna, Me Build a House" CD4:9, page 164, and improvise house-building motions with the beat.

"Now let's travel all the way across the Atlantic Ocean to southern Africa. We're headed for the small country of Lesotho." Help students locate Lesotho (approximately 10°S, 30°E). Have them show the class on the globe the transatlantic route they take to get from Jamaica to Lesotho.

"In southern Africa, people often sing in call-and-response form." Students divide into two groups and sing "Tina Singu" CD4:2 page 158, patting with the beat with alternating hands.

Have students trace their routes on a map or globe—from their hometown to each of the countries in the program—and back home again.

UNIT FOUR
LESSON 9

ASSESSMENTS A AND B CD4:27–34

Different recorded examples for Assessments A and B allow for two uses of the same set of questions. When appropriate, recorded examples for Assessment A use familiar musical examples with which students have worked for the given concept. The recorded examples for Assessment B use musical selections the students have not previously worked with for the concept, encouraging the application of knowledge to new material.

The pupil page is intended for those who wish to assess quickly with the whole class or in small groups. Each assessment may be used as a pretest or as a final review before presenting the written test (**Resource Master 4 · 9**).

ANSWERS		
	ASSESSMENT A	ASSESSMENT B
1.	b	a
2.	b	c
3.	a	b
4.	c	a

CHECK IT OUT

1. How many times do you hear the *short long short* rhythm (♪ ♩ ♪) ?

   a. two times   **b.** three times   **c.** four times

2. Which rhythm do you hear?

   a.

   b.

   c.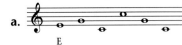

   d.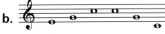

3. Which pitches do you hear?

   a.   **c.**   **b.**   **d.**

4. Which pitches do you hear?

   a.   **c.**   **b.**   **d.**

194

MEETING **INDIVIDUAL** NEEDS

PORTFOLIO ASSESSMENT

To evaluate student portfolios, use the Portfolio Assessment form on **Resource Master TA · 1.** See page 154B for a summary of Portfolio Opportunities in this unit.

SOCIAL STUDIES CONNECTION: *Research*

Have students do research to discover where calypso music originated. After they discover the country, have them chart their discoveries about that country under headings such as name of country, food, climate, music, or other headings they think of. Have students share their charts with the class.

CREATE

Syncopation in C

CREATE a melody using the pitches C D E G C'. Use this rhythm pattern.

Write your melody on a staff. Where does it move by steps? by skips? Mark the steps with 1 and the skips with 2.

C is *do*. Sing your pattern with pitch syllable names.

PLAY your melody as an introduction to "Sarasponda."

Write

Explore your connections to the musical experiences of your family or neighbors.

Interview an older person to find out about his or her musical experiences. Ask about the person's favorite songs from school, or the musicians and groups that he or she enjoyed. Write a newspaper article about what you learn.

CREATE AND WRITE

1. Create an introduction. Have students:

• Work in small groups and follow the instructions on page 195 to create an introduction to "Sarasponda." (Optional: Use **Resource Master 4 • 10** to notate the melodies and mark melodic movement.)

2. Write newspaper articles. Have students:

▶ • Conduct interviews and write articles as described. (Put articles together to create a special-edition newspaper for students to enjoy.)

National Standards for Music Education

4b Create and arrange short songs and instrumental pieces.

4c Use a variety of sound sources when composing.

5a Read standard note values in duple and triple meters.

5b Using a system, read notation in treble clef in major keys.

DRAMA CONNECTION: *Word Rhythms* THEATER

Discuss with students that the rhythm of a work song such as "Sarasponda" can come from the rhythm of the actual work. Have groups of five each pick an occupation, such as carpenter, farmer, or weaver. Ask groups to create a repeatable gesture that could be used in their chosen occupation (for example, hammering a nail). Instruct all group members to repeat the gesture simultaneously and to find the rhythm of the movement. Then they should add a sound to

their gesture and present the routine to the class. Ask students what types of work are done in Jamaica (see p. 160) and Holland (see p. 167), and invite them to create rhythms for these types of work.

RELATED ARTS | MOVEMENT | THEATER | VISUAL ARTS

Sourwood Mountain

Unit 4 Reinforcement
so, la, do re mi so la do', page 179

More Reinforcement
sixteenth notes, motive, *page 87*

1. Identify pitch syllables CD4:35. Have students:

• Listen to the song and compare the melodic material of each *Hey de-ing…ally day* motive. (All four end with *mi re do;* the first two begin on *do* and ascend, the last two begin with *so* and *la.*)

• Listen to the song again, showing the melodic shape with their arms and singing along with each *Hey de-ing…* motive.

• Analyze the pitches of Measures 1–2 and 9–10. (*mi do re do la, so,; so la do' so mi*)

• Sing the song with pitch syllables on all the measures except the *Hey de-ing…* motives, when the words should be sung.

• Sing the entire song with the words.

• (Optional: **Technology**—Use Music with MIDI.)

2. Create rhythmic ostinatos with sixteenth notes. Have students:

• Pat the rhythm of the song from the notation, noticing the sixteenth-note patterns.

• Create rhythmic body percussion ostinatos using ♫♫, ♩♫, and ♫♩

196

MEETING **INDIVIDUAL** NEEDS

ORFF: *"Sourwood Mountain"*
See **O•11** in *Orchestrations for Orff Instruments.*

PLAYING INSTRUMENTS: *Unpitched/Pitched*
Add this accompaniment to "Sourwood Mountain" with body percussion and voices; then transfer to unpitched percussion and melodic instruments.

MOVEMENT: *"Sourwood Mountain"* MOVEMENT

Formation: single circle (Partners are 1s and 2s, 2s on the left.) **Meas. 1–4:** 1s clap with beat and take 4 steps into, then out of circle. **Meas. 5–8:** All clap with beat, 2s take 4 steps into circle, then turn to face partners, creating a double circle. **Meas. 9–12:** Partners swing R elbows once around. **Meas. 13–16:** Partners join hands, all face counterclockwise and promenade around circle. On final *diddle ally day,* 2s move to right of partners, forming a single circle again. 2s now have new 1s to their right, and they progress to a new partner each time the dance is done.

A Tragic Story

Music by Benjamin Britten
Words by William M. Thackeray

D minor

Start slowly *p* 1. There liv'd a sage in days of yore, And
p 2. He mus'd up-on this cu-rious case, And
More movement *mf* 3. Says he, "The mys-ter-y I've found, I'll
Getting faster *f* 4. Then 'round and 'round, and out and in, All
Faster & louder 5. And right and left, and 'round a-bout, And

he a hand-some pig-tail wore, But won-der'd much and
swore he'd change the pig-tail's place, And have it hang-ing
turn me 'round," He turn'd him 'round, He turn'd him 'round, he
day the puz-zled sage did spin; In vain it mat-ter'd
up and down, and in and out, he turn'd, But still the

sor-row'd more, Be-cause it hung be-hind him.
at his face, Not dan-gling there be-hind him.
turn'd him 'round, But still it hung be-hind him.
not a pin, The pig-tail hung be-hind him.
pig-tail stout hung stead-i-ly be-hind him.

ff
Very fast 6. And though his ef-forts nev-er slack, And though he twist, and

f slow
twirl, and tack, A-las! still faith-ful

f resolutely
to his back, The pig-tail hangs be-hind him.

Unit 4 *Connections* 197

---

3. Sing in call-and-response form. Have students:

• Divide into two groups, one singing the first phrase of each pair, the other singing the *Hey de-ing…* motives in response.

• Alternatively, the class sings the calls and assigned soloists each sing a response.

A Tragic Story

Unit 4 Reinforcement
octave, *page 167*

More Reinforcement
melodic movement, *page 111*
dynamic markings, *page 139*
changing dynamics and tempo, *page 257*

1. Listen for dynamics and tempo CD4:36. Have students:

• Look at the title and define *tragic*.

• Predict what feelings might be expressed in the song.

• Listen to the song and discuss whether or not the predictions were realized.

• Listen again to determine what makes the verses different from each other. (different dynamics and tempos)

• Discuss why they think the composer chose the tempo and dynamic markings that he did, and how those markings create dramatic effect.

• Sing the song.

2. Compare verses and phrases. Have students:

• Listen to the song and determine which verses have the same rhythm and melody. (They are all the same except Verse 6.)

• Describe how the melody of the song moves. (primarily stepwise with a skip at the beginning of each phrase, and an octave skip between the first two phrases)

BIOGRAPHY: *Benjamin Britten*

Benjamin Britten (1913–1976) studied piano and viola from an early age and began his training in musical composition at the age of 13, eventually attending the Royal College of Music in London. Britten is best known for his vocal music, including the *War Requiem* and operas such as *Peter Grimes* and *Billy Budd*. He also wrote a children's opera based on the medieval English play, *Noye's Fludde*. His most famous work for children is *The Young Person's Guide to the Orchestra*. In the last year of his life,

Queen Elizabeth II made him a Lord, the first composer in England's history to be knighted.

ENCORE
MULTICULTURAL PERSPECTIVES
RELATED ARTS | MOVEMENT | THEATER | VISUAL ARTS |

LESSON LINKS

Now's the Time *(20 min)*

OBJECTIVE Learn about Charlie Parker, move to the music, and compare the versions

Reinforcement jazz improvisation, *page 191*

MATERIALS
Recording Now's the Time
(Versions 1 and 2) by
C. Parker (listening) CD4:37–38

Resources Musical Instruments Master—saxophone

Hambone *(20 min)*

OBJECTIVE Improvise using body percussion and handjive

Reinforcement
syncopation, *page 187*
jazz improvisation, *pages 191, 237*

MATERIALS
Recording Hambone CD4:39

Resources Orff Orchestration O•12
(Hambone)

Irene Bankhead: Quiltmaker *(5 min)*

OBJECTIVE Learn how artists improvise as part of the creative process

ENCORE
improvise!

Jazz musicians have always enjoyed the freedom of improvising. This allows them to change a piece of music as they play. Performing in this way did not start with jazz musicians. Performers have always improvised. Classical musicians such as Bach, Mozart, and Beethoven were masters of improvising at the keyboard.

SPOTLIGHT ON
CHARLIE PARKER

Charlie Parker, one of the all-time great saxophone players, was famous for his improvisations. Born in Kansas City in 1920, he began playing the alto saxophone when he was thirteen years old. During the 1940s, Parker's way of playing changed the style of jazz. His free style earned Parker the nickname "Bird."

MEETING **INDIVIDUAL** NEEDS

BACKGROUND: *Saxophone*

The saxophone was invented around 1840 by a Belgian instrument maker, Antoine "Adolphe" Sax (ã **twä** ɑ **dɔlf** sɑks). He wanted to make a woodwind instrument that could be heard outdoors. He created an unusual woodwind—made of brass with a single-reed mouthpiece. Some instrument-makers scoffed at the new instrument, others tried to steal the credit, but none could duplicate it. Sax intended the saxophone primarily for military bands. He was so enthusiastic about its use in bands that he convinced the French composer Hector Berlioz (ɛk tɛr **bɛr** lyoz) to

transcribe one of his marches to feature the saxophone. Today saxophonists play many styles of music, from jazz to salsa to classical to rock.

BIOGRAPHY: *Charlie Parker*

Charlie Parker (1920–1955) was born in Kansas City and left school at fifteen to play alto saxophone in Chicago jazz clubs. He moved to New York, where he played in many bands. Parker is remembered for his style of playing, in which he ornamented melodies and changed rhythms with tempos so fast they were described as "breakneck."

The Charlie Parker combo in 1947, with Miles Davis playing trumpet.

LISTENING

Now's the Time (Versions 1 and 2)
by Charlie Parker

Listen to a twelve-bar blues piece composed by Charlie Parker. You will hear two versions. The first version was made for Bird, a movie about Charlie Parker. Using an old recording, engineers erased the drum, bass, and piano parts. Only the saxophone parts played by Charlie Parker were kept. New musicians were hired to play the other parts. The second version is the original recording of "Now's the Time."

DESCRIBE the differences you hear between the two recordings.

Encore 199

Now's the Time CD4:37–38

1. Learn about Charlie Parker. Have students:

• Read page 198 and identify the instrument Charlie Parker plays in the pictures.

• Think of a question about Charlie Parker and discuss how to research the answers. (Ask parents, read encyclopedias, read record or CD jackets, interview a jazz musician, look at CD-ROM, search internet.)

2. Move to a listening selection. Have students:

• In scattered formation, move in place in time with the music **CD4:37**, bouncing lightly with beats 1–3 and clapping with beat 4. (bounce-bounce-bounce-clap pattern)

• Mime motions from daily life, clapping every fourth beat and moving appropriately in place. (See *Movement* below.)

3. Compare the two versions. Have students:

• Read about the two versions of the song and summarize the information. (One is the movie version; the other is the original.)

• Listen to the original version **CD4:38**, identifying how it differs from the movie version. (faster tempo, melody stated twice, different improvisation)

MOVEMENT: *"Now's the Time"* THEATER

Have students mime daily activities, performing motions to the first three beats and clapping with the fourth beat of each set. For example, to mime waking up in the morning, students could stretch-stretch-stretch-clap, then wash-wash-wash-clap. You may either model or call out each activity. Motions for a typical day might include stretch, wash face, dry hands, brush teeth, comb hair, get dressed, pour juice, eat breakfast, wash dishes, say good-bye to parents, walk or ride to school, wave hello to friends, read a book, write name (in the air), raise hand, play recess games (hopscotch-soccer-jump rope), go to music class, and so forth.

ENRICHMENT: *Nicknames*

Jazz musicians' nicknames reveal something about their personalities. Have students research reasons for these nicknames: King (King Oliver), Duke (Duke Ellington), Count (Count Basie), Empress of the Blues (Bessie Smith), Lady Day (Billie Holiday), Prez (Lester Young), Satchmo (Louis Armstrong), Bird (Charlie Parker), Diz (Dizzy Gillespie), Fats (Fats Waller).

MULTICULTURAL PERSPECTIVES

continued from previous page

Hambone CD4:39

1. Learn a song with syncopation. Have students:

• Look at the song on page 200 and discover the two measures of rest that end each line.

• Listen to the song, doing a pat-snap pattern with the beat during the measures of rest.

• Read about the rhythm of the song on page 200 and find the syncopation. (*heard, bird*)

• Form two groups, one clapping the rhythm of the words and the other pat-snapping with the beat during the measures of rest.

• Sing the song, with the two groups clapping or pat-snapping as practiced.

2. Improvise patterns with body percussion and handjive. Have students:

• Explain what improvise means. (to make up and perform on the spot)

• Pair off and practice improvising in question-and-answer style with body percussion and handjive. (Suggest using at least two different body percussion sounds: snap, clap, pat chest, pat front of thighs, stamp, tap fists one on top of the other.)

• Practice the improvisation over eight beats, the question and answer each lasting four beats. (Clap or drum a steady beat in the song's tempo.)

• Perform the song with partners taking turns creating body percussion improvisations during the measures of rest. (To give volunteers opportunities to "solo," have the class divide into groups of six, with each member improvising in turn as they sing the song.)

MEETING **INDIVIDUAL** NEEDS

IMPROVISATION: *"Hambone"*

Rhythmic Improvisation: Use unpitched instruments for the rhythmic improvisations during the two measures of rest.
Melodic Improvisation: Have pairs use pitched percussion instruments to take turns improvising on pitches E G A B♭ C D. They should improvise during the rests, while the class performs the following movement.
Movement Improvisation: Form two lines; walk 8 beats toward partner, perform a simple handjive with partner for 8 beats, walk 8 beats away from partner, perform a handjive with a neighbor.

ORFF: *"Hambone"*

See **O•12** in *Orchestrations for Orff Instruments.*

ART CONNECTION: *Making a Quilt*

Provide students with scrap fabric or paper, glue, scissors, and construction paper. Have students cut out pieces of fabric or paper and glue them to a construction-paper background to create one square for a quilt design. Then glue the squares together into a class quilt.

200 Encore IMPROVISE!

Other artists also improvise in the way they use materials. Irene Bankhead, a quiltmaker, sews together beautiful pieces of cloth to make colorful designs. Bankhead, who started quilting when she was thirteen, can often finish a quilt in three days.

String by **Irene Bankhead**

Irene Bankhead: Quiltmaker

Learn how artists improvise as part of the creative process. Have students:

• Discuss what quilts are and how they are made. (coverings made from pieces of materials that are sewn together in a pattern)

• Suggest ways a quiltmaker could improvise. (move the fabric around to change the visual patterns; vary the shapes or materials)

• Suggest reasons why Irene Bankhead named the quilt shown *String*.

BIOGRAPHY: *Irene Bankhead*

Irene Bankhead (b. 1925) started sewing at age 13. She remembers quilting with five families of neighbors in Louisiana; together they would finish a quilt in a day. Bankhead described her improvisatory creative process: "I'll sew two [blocks] together . . . and then I'll lay them aside and I'll make two more . . . Whatever it comes out when I put the four together . . . then if that give me an idea of doin' somethin' different, then I'll just work from that."

BACKGROUND: *African American Quiltmaking*

Improvisation is an important part of African American music, art, and dance. In African American quiltmaking, there is no such thing as a mistake: instead, the "mistake" is an opportunity for the quiltmaker to create something new. Quiltmaker Wanda Jones of California says that when she made a mistake her mother would say, "It's nothin' about makin' it a little different. It's still the same pattern. You just added somethin' of your own to it."

Music with a Message

MULTICULTURAL PERSPECTIVES

Through exposure to diverse materials, students develop an awareness of how people from many cultures create and participate in music. This unit includes:

African/African American

- *Down by the Riverside,* wood carving by Daniel Pressley, 228
- **Take Time in Life,** Liberian folk song, 206
- **Wade in the Water,** spiritual, 229

Asian/Asian American, Pacific Islands, and Israeli

- **Aquaqua,** Israeli game, 219
- **Hei Tama Tu Tama,** Maori counting game, 212

European/European American

- *Boy Playing Flute,* by Dutch painter Judith Leyster, 232
- **Calypso,** by John Denver, 208
- **D'Hammerschmiedsgesellen,** Bavarian folk dance, 207
- **Galliard,** by German Renaissance composer Tielman Susato, 232
- **Music Alone Shall Live,** German round, 231
- **Presto,** by French composer Francis Poulenc, 216
- **Proverbs** by Aesop, 203
- **Slavonic Dance Op. 46, No. 8,** by Czech composer Antonin Dvořák, 226
- **Tum-Balalaika,** Russian Yiddish folk song, 210

Native American

- **Canoe Song and Dance,** Eastern Woodlands social dance music, 222

For a complete listing of materials by culture throughout the book, see the Classified Index.

CURRICULUM INTEGRATION

Activities in this unit that promote the integration of music with other curriculum areas include:

Art

- Create numbered geometrical drawings, 221A

Math

- Schedule a Saturday afternoon get-together, 209A
- Make a bar-graph profile map of a model ocean floor, 209B
- Graph average temperatures, 213A
- Create numbered geometrical drawings, 221A
- Figure out months between present and future events, 225A

Reading/Language Arts

- Write a personal narrative, 209A
- Create riddles, 213A
- Learn to use the Maori alphabet, 213B
- Write camp stories, 221B
- Write paragraphs using poetic imagery, 225B
- Write poems or songs about a favorite day, 240

Science

- Map an ocean route, 209B
- Make a model ocean floor, 209B
- Create floating models, 225A

Social Studies

- Map an ocean route, 209B
- Map a route to New Zealand, 213B
- Play a longitude-latitude game, 221B
- Record and present stories heard from others, 222
- Plan a "dream" trip, 225B
- Create an Underground Railroad fact sheet, 235

New! **UNIT OPENERS WITH THEMATIC TEACHING PROJECTS**

PLANNER

ASSESSMENT OPTIONS

Informal Performance Assessments

Informal Assessments correlated to Objectives are provided in every lesson with Alternate Strategies for reteaching. Frequent informal assessment allows for ongoing progress checks throughout the course of the unit.

Formal Assessment

An assessment form is provided on pupil page 240 and Resource Master 5•8. The questions assess student understanding of the following main unit objectives:

- Identify ¾ meter
- Read rhythms including the dotted quarter-eighth pattern (♩ ♪) in meter

Music Journal

Encourage students to enter thoughts about selections, projects, performances, and personal progress. Some journal opportunities include:

- Discussion of expressive musical elements, TE 211
- *Think It Through,* 225
- Write, 241

Portfolio Opportunities

Update student portfolios with outcome-based materials, including written work, audiotapes, videotapes, and/or photos that represent their best work for each unit. Some portfolio opportunities in this unit include:

- Working with meter (Resource Masters 5•1, 5•2), TE 206, 208
- Unpitched percussion performance of riddle rondo composition (audiotape), TE 211
- Conducting in ¾ (videotape), TE 214
- Writing and identifying *la ti do'* in different keys (Resource Master 5•3), TE 218
- Identifying C major scales (Resource Master 5•4), TE 221
- Working with ties, dotted quarter notes (Resource Master 5•5), TE 224
- Playing keyboard (audiotape), TE 225
- Playing Orff accompaniments (audiotape), TE 229, 230
- Improvise measures in "Wade in the Water" and then notate (Resource Master 5•7), TE 236
- Part-singing with ostinato (audiotape), 236
- Check It Out (formal assessment), 240; Resource Master 5•8
- Portfolio Assessment (Resource Masters TA•1–5), 240
- Create 241; Resource Master 5•9
- Write, 241

UNIT 5

CONCEPT

			LESSON 1 CORE p.206	LESSON 2 CORE p.210	LESSON 3 p.214
		FOCUS	3/4 meter	Pitch, major and minor	Expresssive qualities/ Tempo
		SELECTIONS	Take Time in Life D'Hammerschmiedsgesellen (listening) Calypso	Tum-Balalaika Hei Tama Tu Tama Calypso	D'Hammerschmiedsgesellen (listening) Presto (listening) Hei Tama Tu Tama

MUSICAL ELEMENTS	CONCEPTS	UNIT OBJECTIVES Bold = Tested	LESSON 1 CORE	LESSON 2 CORE	LESSON 3
EXPRESSIVE QUALITIES	Dynamics			• Notice soft dynamic level	• Hear varying dynamics
	Tempo	• Identify standard tempos and tempo changes	• Move to tempo changes	• Notice moderately slow tempo	• Recognize tempo change • Define adagio, moderato, allegro, presto, accelerando, ritardando • Sing, perform, follow map with tempo changes
	Articulation				• Hear staccato, legato, accents
TONE COLOR	Vocal/ Instrumental Tone Color		• Hear Bavarian folk band	• Recognize strings • *Play unpitched instruments to show rondo sections*	• Recognize oboe, bassoon, piano
DURATION	Beat/Meter	• **Identify 3/4 meter**	• **Listen for meter, match to graphic representation and 3/4 meter signature (E/D/I)** • **Make up and perform 3-beat pattern in 3/4 (P)** • **Distinguish meter (3/4) (Rf)** • Pat with strong beat • Recognize 4/4 aurally • Make up and perform 4-beat pattern in 4/4	• **Recognize and move to show 3/4 (Rf)** • Perform body percussion with beat • See notation in 3/4 and 4/4	• **Move with beat in 3/4 (Rf)** • **Conduct in 3/4 (Rf)** • Hear music with changing meter • *Toss beanbag with strong beat*
	Rhythm	• **Read ♩ ♪**	• **Sing, see dotted rhythms (E)** • *Improvise rhythmically*	• **Sing, see dotted rhythms (E)** • *Play rhythms on unpitched instruments*	
PITCH	Melody	• Identify *ti*	• *Improvise melodically*	• Hum melody • Draw melodic contour in air • Hear and sing *ti*	
	Harmony				
	Tonality major/minor	• Identify major, minor		• Compare sound of major and minor • Identify shifts between major, minor • Sing in major, minor	
DESIGN	Texture		• *Play unpitched accompaniment*		• Hear instrumental trio
	Form/ Structure		• Move to show A B sections • *Play A B sections*	• *Compose rondo*	• Recognize A B A¹ sections, bridge
CULTURAL CONTEXT	Style/ Background	• Hear and sing music from diverse cultures • Develop understanding of musical concepts using selections from diverse cultures	• Sing Liberian folk song • Hear Bavarian folk music	• Sing Russian Yiddish folk song	• Hear music by Francis Poulenc • Sing Maori counting song

Learning Sequence: E = Explore, D = Describe, I = Identify, P = Practice, Rf = Reinforce, Rd = Read, C = Create   See also *Program Scope and Sequence,* page 402.

OVERVIEW

Italic = Meeting Individual Needs

LESSON 4 CORE p.218	LESSON 5 CORE p.222	LESSON 6 p.226	LESSON 7 p.230	LESSON 8 p.234
Pitch, *ti*	Duration, dotted quarter-eighth rhythm (♩ ♪)	Pitch, major and minor	Duration, dotted quarter-eighth rhythm (♩ ♪)	Pitch—*ti*, major, minor
Take Time in Life Hei Tama Tu Tama Aquaqua	Canoe Song and Dance (listening) Take Time in Life Tum-Balalaika Calypso	Aquaqua Slavonic Dance (listening) Wade in the Water	Calypso Take Time in Life Tum-Balalaika Music Alone Shall Live Galliard (listening)	Hei Tama Tu Tama Wade in the Water
	• *Drum with crescendo*	• Follow listening map with dynamics		
	• *Play drum to keep tempo steady*	• Recognize allegro		• *Sing in tempo*
	• *Drum with accents*	• Hear staccato and legato		
	• Hear Native American singing and playing • *Use different sounds*	• Hear orchestral music • *Play Orff instruments with different tone colors*	• Learn about recorders, Renaissance double-reeds • *Play Orff instruments*	
• Perform body percussion pattern with beat	• **Recognize ¾ and read notation (Rf/Rd)**	• Follow listening map with number of beats shown	• **Read notation in ¾ (Rd)** • *Step with beat*	• Perform body percussion with beat
• Identify ⸒	• **Clap ♩ ♪, match to graphic representation (E/D)** • **Learn notation, locate and sing ♩ ♪ in notation (I/P)** • **Match rhythm notation to familiar melodies (Rd)** • Perform and use graphic notation for ♫, ♩ • Work with ties	• *Improvise melodically on given rhythm*	• **Recognize and clap ♩ ♪ (Rf)** • **Perform dotted rhythms from notation (Rd/Rf)** • **Create rondo with rhythmic speech patterns (Rf)** • **Dance dotted rhythm (Rf)** • *Play ♩ ♪ (Rf)* • *List rhythms (Rf)*	• *Improvise rhythmically with ♩ ♪ (C)* • Play half-note accompaniment • *Improvise rhythmically with ♪♩♪ patterns*
• Define *do* and *ti* • Find *la ti do¹* in notation • Sing C major scale with pitch syllables • *Draw melodic contour in air*	• Match familiar melodies to rhythm notation	• *Improvise melodically on given rhythm*	• Match familiar melody to rhythm	• Sing syllables *ti₁ do re mi* • Sing F major scale with pitch syllables and letter names • Sing minor pitch set • Play octave accompaniment
	• *Play keyboard accompaniment*	• *Play major and minor chords on keyboard*		• Sing harmonic vocal ostinato
• Name tonal center • Compare two key signatures • Learn major scale	• Recognize minor	• Recognize major, minor, and changes between tonality • Follow map of tonality • Sing in minor • *Move to show major, minor* • *Play major, minor chords*		• Recognize major, minor • Sing improvised phrases in minor • Name tonal centers as *do* and *la*
	• Hear singing and percussion • *Play drum accompaniment*	• *Play Orff accompaniment*	• Sing round • *Play Orff accompaniment*	• Add vocal ostinato
	• Sing responses of call-and-response music	• Follow listening map with A B C sections, coda	• Create rondo • Clap theme of A section	• Sing introduction, refrain, verses • *Improvise in call-and-response form*
• Sing and play Israeli camp game	• Learn Native American song and dance	• Hear music by Antonin Dvořák • Sing spiritual	• Sing German round • Hear music by Tielman Susato • See Renaissance and Baroque instruments	• Sing spiritual

UNIT 5 PLANNER

UNIT 5

SKILLS

SKILLS		LESSON 1 CORE p.206	LESSON 2 CORE p.210	LESSON 3 p.214
CREATION AND PERFORMANCE	Singing	• Sing in 2/4 and 6/8	• *Practice singing vowel sounds and descending passages* • Hum melodies • Sing in major and minor • *Sing solos*	• Sing different tempos, increasing tempo
	Playing	• *Play unpitched accompaniment that shows A B sections*	• *Play different unpitched instruments to show rondo sections*	
	Moving	• Pat with strong beat • Create and perform 3- and 4-beat movement patterns in 3/4 and 4/4 • Move to show A B sections and tempo changes	• Draw melodic contour in air • Move to show 6/8 • Perform body percussion with beat	• *Conduct in 6/8* • Move with beat in 6/8 • *Toss beanbag with strong beat*
	Improvising/ Creating	• Create and perform 3- and 4-beat movement patterns in 3/4 and 4/4 • *Improvise melodically and rhythmically*	• *Create rondo*	
NOTATION	Reading	• Identify 4/4 meter signature in notation • Read graphic notation of meters	• See notation in 3/4 and 4/4 • See notation with dotted rhythms	• Follow listening map with tempo changes
	Writing	• *Practice writing meter signatures*		
PERCEPTION AND ANALYSIS	Listening/ Describing/ Analyzing	• Determine meter by trying 2 movement patterns	• Describe music as soft, moderately slow, played by strings • Compare sound of major and minor • Describe effect of change from major to minor	• Identify tempo changes

TECHNOLOGY

SHARE THE MUSIC VIDEOS

Use videos to reinforce, extend, and enrich learning.
- Lesson 1, p. 208: Making a Music Video (pop song)
- Lesson 3, p. 215: Musical Expression (tempo)
- Lesson 6, p. 229: Making a Music Video (two-part singing)

MUSIC WITH *MIDI*

MIDI technology allows students to manipulate musical elements and make musical decisions with this song:
- Lesson 6, p. 229: Wade in the Water

MUSICTIME™

Use MusicTime to develop students' music reading and writing skills in this unit.

OVERVIEW

Italic = Meeting Individual Needs

LESSON 4 CORE p.218	LESSON 5 CORE p.222	LESSON 6 p.226	LESSON 7 p.230	LESSON 8 p.234
• Sing C major scale with pitch syllables • Sing nonsense song from Israel	• Sing Native American vocable responses learned aurally	• Sing in major and minor	• Sing German round	• Sing F major scale with pitch syllables, letter names • Sing harmonic vocal ostinato • *Sing C, F, G major scales* • Sing improvised phrases in minor
• Play *la ti do¹* on bells • *Play melodic motives with ti*	• *Drum with accents, crescendo* • *Use different percussion instrument sounds* • *Play keyboard accompaniment*	• *Play major and minor chords on keyboard* • *Play Orff accompaniment*	• *Play Orff accompaniment*	• Play C, F, G major scales • *Contrast F major, D minor scales on keyboards* • *Play ostinato* • Play octave ♩ accompaniment • *Improvise rhythmically on instruments*
• *Draw melodic contour in air* • Perform circle movement	• Perform Native American canoe dance • Step dotted rhythms	• *Move to show major, minor*	• *Step with beat* • Dance to dotted rhythm • Move to show instruments heard	• Perform body percussion with beat • *Choreograph 3-part movement*
		• *Improvise melodically on given rhythm*	• Create rondo	• Sing improvised phrases • *Improvise rhythmically on instruments* • *Choreograph 3-part movement*
• Identify *la ti do¹* in notation • Compare two key signatures • Identify ⅞ • *Distinguish C major scales*	• Read graphic notation of ♩, ♫, ♩ ♪ • Read notation with ties • Identify dotted rhythm in notation • Match rhythm notation to familiar melodies	• Follow listening map with tempo, section, beats, dynamic markings, and graphic notation of tonality	• Read and perform from notation in ⅜ with ♩ ♪	• Identify key signatures and scales in F major, D minor • Identify B♭ in notation • *Read C, F, G major scales*
• *Write* la ti do¹ *pattern*	• *Write dotted and tied rhythms*		• *List rhythms of selection*	
• *Practice inner hearing* • Describe *ti* as lower than *do*	• Learn song aurally • Compare rhythmic durations	• Listen for major, minor	• Identify number of times rhythm pattern occurs • Distinguish recorders and Renaissance double-reed instruments	• Compare pitch sets, key signatures of F major, D minor scales

MUSIC ACE™

Music Ace reinforces musical concepts and provides ear-training opportunities for students.
- **Lesson 2, p. 210: Lesson 24 (major scales)**
- **Lesson 4, p. 218: Lessons 4, 5, 6, & 9 (piano keyboard/pitch names); Lesson 19 (C major scale); Lesson 23 (key signatures); Lesson 24 (major scales)**
- **Lesson 6, p. 226: Lesson 12 (loud/soft)**
- **Lesson 8, p. 234: Lessons 2, 4, 5, 6, & 9 (piano keyboard/pitch names); Lesson 23 (key signature); Lesson 24 (major scales)**

NEW! MUSIC ACE 2™

Music Ace 2™ introduces basic rhythm concepts and furthers the melodic and harmonic concepts covered in Music Ace.

UNIT 5 PLANNER

THEME: MUSIC WITH A MESSAGE

FOCUS Music can communicate messages and ideas.

OBJECTIVE To set the stage for Unit 5

MATERIALS
Proverbs by Aesop (poem)
The Song of the World's Last Whale   CD5:1
The Song of the World's Last Whale
   (performance mix)   CD10:19
Pawdawe (story)   CD5:2

INTRODUCE THE THEME

1. Discuss the theme. "In this unit, we will learn how music can be used to communicate important messages and ideas." Have students:

• Recall a time they received a message from someone. Ask them if they ever received a message from someone in any way other than through words. (for example, through body language such as raising your eyebrows, nodding, or shaking your head)

• Share what other ways they have received messages. (Draw a happy face to encourage them to see symbols or pictures as a means of communicating.)

2. Introduce "Proverbs by Aesop." "Proverbs are wise sayings that are passed along from generation to generation. They are messages that have a bit of advice in them. Aesop wrote his proverbs many years ago. Do you think they are still good advice for today?" Have students:

• Read each proverb and talk about the advice given.

202

UNIT 5 THEME PROJECTS

The songs in this unit can be used as a point of departure for exploring and comparing the many ways that people can communicate important messages, ideas, and lessons.

WRITE A MAGAZINE ARTICLE Have students discuss the messages of "The Song of the World's Last Whale" (page 205) and "Calypso" (page 208). Using these songs as a basis, discuss endangered species and the importance of protecting animals from becoming extinct. Have students choose an animal that is endangered and write an article about it. Collect the articles in a class magazine. *(After Unit Opener and Lesson 1)*

a Message

PROVERBS BY AESOP

Slow and steady wins the race.
— *The Hare and the Tortoise*

**Don't count your chickens
before they are hatched.**
— *The Milkmaid and Her Pail*

Appearances are often deceiving.
— *The Wolf in Sheep's Clothing*

**No act of kindness, however small,
is wasted.**
— *The Lion and the Mouse*

203

Meet the Author Aesop (ĭ sŏp), c. 620–560 B.C., was probably a Greek slave who was later freed. Legend has it that he became an ambassador for King Croesus (krē səs) and used his fables to teach and to make political points at a time when free speech was dangerous. Most characters in Aesop's tales are talking animals, yet his subject was always human virtue and vice. Aesop did not invent all the fables himself— he drew on ancient tales from India, Egypt, and Sumeria—nor did he put them in writing. For centuries they were passed on orally by Athenians, who loved his humor and wisdom.

Language Arts Link Encourage students to share proverbs or sayings spoken in their homes—or to make up their own. This will provide a good opportunity for non-English speakers to "show off" their knowledge. The class may discover that some languages have similar sayings. For example, in Spanish, *Mas vale un pájaro en la mano que cien volando* means "Better to have one bird in your hand than one hundred flying around." In English the saying is, "A bird in the hand is worth two in the bush."

WRITE AN ADVICE COLUMN Have the class talk about the importance of slowing down to enjoy life, the message conveyed in "Take Time in Life" (page 206). Discuss other advice that would make life more enjoyable and more meaningful. (For example, do unto others as you would have them do unto you, practice random acts of kindness, see the glass as half full rather than half empty.) Have students select one piece of advice, then think of a problem that would fit the advice. Write a letter asking for advice and a response to the letter. Combine the letters into an advice column, and add it to the class magazine. *(Lesson 1)*

PLAY CHARADES Have a class discussion about ways of communicating without words or music (gestures, facial expression, sign language, Braille). Play charades, using the songs in the unit as the topics. *(Lessons 1–8)*

3. Introduce "The Song of the World's Last Whale." CD5:1. "The words of music carry messages, but sounds without words can express things that words cannot. Listen to our theme song for this unit, 'The Song of the World's Last Whale.' What message does this song bring?" Have students:

• Read page 204.

• Listen to the song, following the words in their books.

• Identify the message of the song. (Whales need to be protected because they are an endangered species. If we can't protect the whales, all other living things are at risk.)

• Discuss how some people traditionally depended on the sea's resources.

• Listen to the story "Pawdawe" CD5:2 told by Elizabeth Haile, a member of the Shinnecock Nation. (The Shinnecock people were among those who needed the sea to survive. During the 1800's, Shinnecock men were famous for rescuing boaters who were in trouble. Now the people of the Shinnecock Nation live on a reservation on the southeastern end of Long Island, N.Y.)

• Listen to the song again, singing along as they are able.

4. Set the stage for Unit 5. Have students:

• Look through the unit and find what message several of the songs are trying to teach.

• Form four groups, each to read one of Aesop's proverbs aloud.

• Sing "The Song of the World's Last Whale," with attention to correct singing posture.

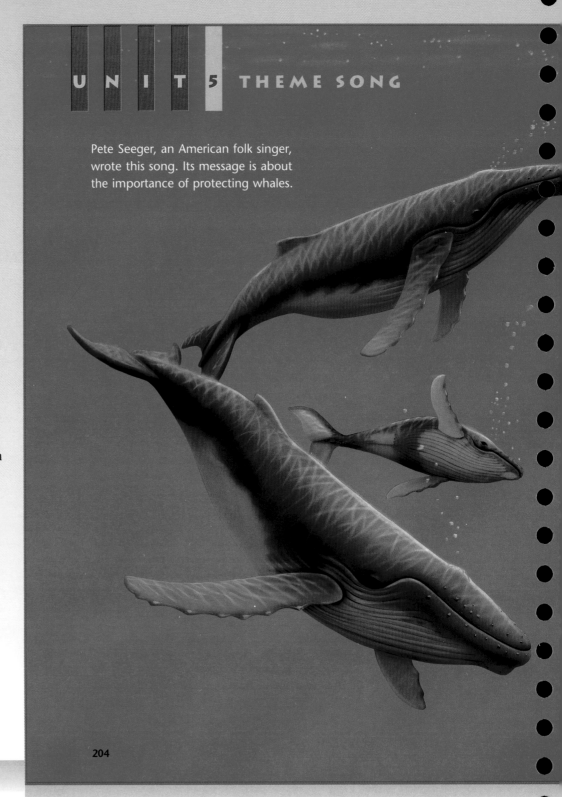

UNIT 5 THEME SONG

Pete Seeger, an American folk singer, wrote this song. Its message is about the importance of protecting whales.

204

UNIT 5 MUSIC PROJECT:

Students should keep a folder to save their work as they complete various stages of this project. As they complete these activities, students will grow in understanding of rhythms in $\frac{3}{4}$. Completion of this project will help students achieve success in the end-of-unit "Create" activity, Lesson 9.

1 CLAP IN $\frac{3}{4}$ METER Have students listen to "Calypso" (page 208) and perform a clap-snap-snap pattern with the beat, clapping on the strong beat. Then have the class form two groups, one continuing the body percussion with the beat and the other patting the rhythm of the words. Switch parts and repeat. *(After Lesson 1)*

The Song of the World's Last Whale

Words and Music by Peter Seeger

1. and 6. I heard the song___ of the world's last
2. It was down off Ber-mu-da___ Ear-ly last
whale,___ As I rocked in the moon-light___
spring,___ Near an un-der-wa-ter moun-tain___
___ and reefed the sail,___ It-'ll hap-pen to
___ Where the hump-backs sing.___ I___ low-ered the
you al-so with-out fail, if it hap-pens to
mi-cro-phone A quar-ter mile___ down, Switched___ on the re-
me___ sang the world's last whale.___
cor-der___ And let the tape spin round.___

3. I didn't just hear grunting, I didn't just hear squeaks,
I didn't just hear bellows, I didn't just hear shrieks.
It was the musical singing and the passionate wail,
That came from the heart of the world's last whale.

D minor
s, l, d r m s l t

4. Down in the Antarctic the harpoons wait,
But it's upon the land they decide my fate.
In London Town they'll be telling the tale,
If it's life or death for the world's last whale.

5. So here's a little test to see how you feel,
Here's a little test for this age of the automobile.
If we can save our singers in the sea,
Perhaps there's a chance to save you and me.

Unit 5 *Music with a Message* 205

Program Idea: Reporting the News

Have students develop a program based on a scene at the editorial offices of a newspaper. Students are reporters trying to get important stories into the next edition. Each story has a message, and each message is related to a song in the unit:

• Message: We must all take responsibility for protecting wildlife. Song: "The Song of the World's Last Whale" (page 205)

• Message: If you rush through life you'll miss a lot. Song: "Take Time in Life" (page 206)

• Message: Remember Jacques Cousteau and the important work he did to protect ocean life. Song: "Calypso" (page 208)

• Message: Music is important and enduring. Song: "Music Alone Shall Live" (page 231)

• Message: Learning can be fun. Song: "Hei Tama Tu Tama" (page 212)

• Message: It is important to do things just for fun. Songs: "Aquaqua," "Push the Business On" (pages 219, 245)

CREATE AN ACCOMPANIMENT

2 CLAP A DOTTED RHYTHM Write on the board the two dotted-rhythm patterns from the two-part keyboard activity on page 225. Have the class read and brush the rhythms on their thighs or desktops. Then have two groups brush these rhythms simultaneously with one group taking part A and the other part B. Guide them to notice that one part is brushing shorter durations while the other is brushing longer durations. *(After Lesson 5)*

3 ACCOMPANY A SONG Write on the board the three rhythm patterns from "Create," page 241. Have students use these patterns to create a two-part, 12-beat pattern in which the parts are active at opposite times, as they were in the previous activity. The rhythms should not duplicate the rhythm of "Music Alone Shall Live" at any point. Have students play their 12-beat pattern through 3 times as the class sings the song. *(After Lesson 7)*

UNIT FIVE
LESSON 1

RELATED ARTS [MOVEMENT] | THEATER | VISUAL ARTS

LESSON PLANNER

FOCUS ⅜ Meter

OBJECTIVES

OBJECTIVE 1 Sing a song while repeating four-beat movement patterns

OBJECTIVE 2 Perform a three-beat body-percussion pattern with a song in ⅜ meter (tested)

MATERIALS

Recordings

Take Time in Life	CD5:3
Recorded Lesson: Beat Groupings	CD5:4
Listening: D'Hammerschmiedsgesellen	CD5:5
Calypso	CD5:6
Calypso (performance mix)	CD10:20

Resources

Resource Master 5 • 1 (practice)
Resource Master 5 • 2 (practice)
Signing Master S • 4 • 5 (Take Time in Life)

▶ = **BASIC PROGRAM**

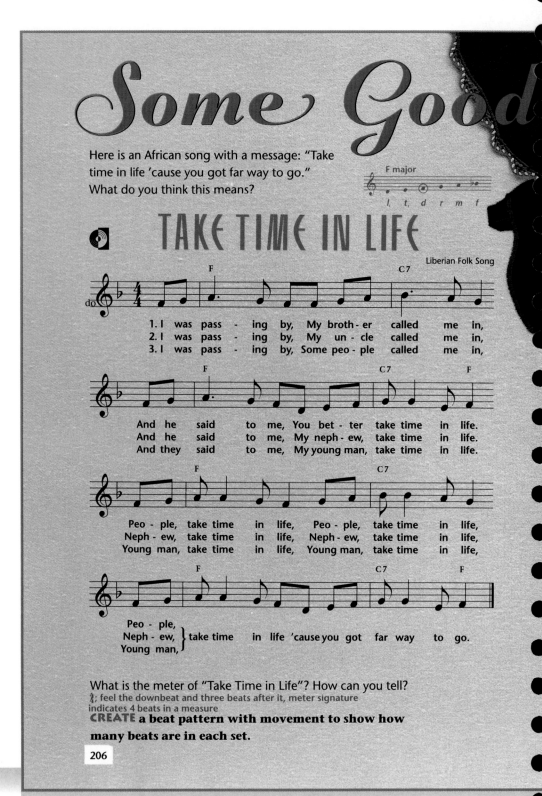

Some Good

Here is an African song with a message: "Take time in life 'cause you got far way to go." What do you think this means?

F major

l t d r m f

TAKE TIME IN LIFE

Liberian Folk Song

1. I was pass - ing by, My broth - er called me in,
2. I was pass - ing by, My un - cle called me in,
3. I was pass - ing by, Some peo - ple called me in,

And he said to me, You bet - ter take time in life.
And he said to me, My neph - ew, take time in life.
And they said to me, My young man, take time in life.

Peo - ple, take time in life, Peo - ple, take time in life,
Neph - ew, take time in life, Neph - ew, take time in life,
Young man, take time in life, Young man, take time in life,

Peo - ple,
Neph - ew, } take time in life 'cause you got far way to go.
Young man,

What is the meter of "Take Time in Life"? How can you tell?
⁴⁄₄; feel the downbeat and three beats after it, meter signature indicates 4 beats in a measure
CREATE a beat pattern with movement to show how many beats are in each set.

206

MEETING **INDIVIDUAL** NEEDS

ALTERNATE TEACHING STRATEGY

OBJECTIVE 1 Use **Resource Master 5 • 1** to guide students through finding the strong beat, counting the number of beats in a set, and identifying each four-beat set. Review upbeat if necessary (page 75).

EXTRA HELP: *Sample Four-Beat Pattern*

Tell students the movement on the first beat should be different so that it stands out. For example, Beat 1: step to the right with right foot; Beats 2–4: tap left toe three times. Reverse for next four beats.

MUSIC BUILDS MATH SKILLS

Algebra Creating a pattern that shows beats in sets of four is related to extending number patterns according to a rule.

PLAYING INSTRUMENTS: *Unpitched*

"D'Hammerschmiedgesellen"—A section: Play each strong beat with triangles or two large metal spoons.

B section: Play with all beats using three woodblocks.

D'Hammerschmiedsgesellen

Bavarian Folk Dance

The name of this dance means "The Journeyman Blacksmith." A journeyman was a young man learning a trade. Blacksmiths made horseshoes and other metal objects.
Listen to "D'Hammerschmiedsgesellen" to find the meter. Which meter signature fits the music? ⅜

| 2/4 | 3/4 | 4/4 |

CREATE a movement pattern to show how many beats are in each set.

Unit 5 *Music with a Message* **207**

"List ways people communicate messages or ideas to each other." Have students:

▶ • Suggest ideas for the list. (books, teachers, doing something new, TV, reading, talking)

"As you listen for ideas in the words you sing today, listen also for how the music helps to express them. In particular, listen for the meter."

2 DEVELOP

1. Introduce "Take Time in Life" CD5:3. **Identify meter.** Have students:

▶ • Read about and listen to the song, then discuss the advice given.

▶ • Learn the song, then sing it, patting a neighbor's hand with a "high five" gesture on each downbeat, alternating right and left hands.

▶ • Identify the meter as ⁴⁄₄ and find the meter signature in the music.

• With a partner, create a beat pattern which shows beats in sets of four. (See *Extra Help* on the bottom of page 206.)

OBJECTIVE 1 Informal Assessment

• Sing the song, performing the four-beat movement patterns with their partners.

▶ • Learn the dance. (See *Movement,* below.)

2. Introduce "D'Hammerschmiedsgesellen" CD5:5. **Identify** ⅜ **meter.** Have students:

Recorded Lesson CD5:4

▶ • Listen to "Beat Groupings" to find beats in sets of three in "D'Hammerschmiedsgesellen" (də **ha** məɾ **shmit** gɛ **sɛ** lən).

▶ • Read page 207 and match the meter signatures to the pictures representing sets of beats.

▶ • Listen to the complete selection and identify its meter. (Adjust the stereo balance control to hear the music without dance instructions.)

• Create beat patterns to reflect the meter.

▶ • Learn the movement and perform it with the music. (See *Movement,* below.)

MOVEMENT: *"D'Hammerschmiedsgesellen"*

Formation: partners, in scattered formation

A section: (Verbal Cue—*own, two, three; partner, two, three*) Pat own legs for three beats, then clap partner's hands three beats. Repeat throughout the A section.

B section: Walk own pathways through shared space, stepping only with strong beats. (Note: B section is faster.) Find a new partner in time for next A section.

SIGNING: *"Take Time in Life"*

Signing Master S · 4 · 5 has sign language for this song.

MOVEMENT: *"Take Time in Life"*

Formation: double circle, partners standing shoulder to shoulder; inside circle facing clockwise, outside circle facing counterclockwise

Measures 1–4: Both circles walk forward four steps, stand still while clapping four beats, walk backward four steps, clap four beats. **Measures 5–8:** Face partner, high five on each *take time in life,* alternating right and left hands. On *far way to go,* both partners take one side step to the left to be in front of a new partner, then turn to original facing and begin again.

UNIT FIVE
LESSON 1

continued from previous page

3 APPLY

Introduce "Calypso" CD5:6. Identify the meter. Have students:

▶ • Read about and listen to the song.

▶ • Discuss the message of the lyrics.

• With a partner, listen again and determine the meter by trying the beat patterns they created for ¾ and ¼ meter. (Optional: use **Resource Master 5 • 2** for more practice in identifying meter.)

OBJECTIVE 2 Informal Assessment
• With the song, perform the beat pattern which represents the meter. (¾ pattern, either their own or the one from the A section of "D'Hammerschmiedsgesellen.")

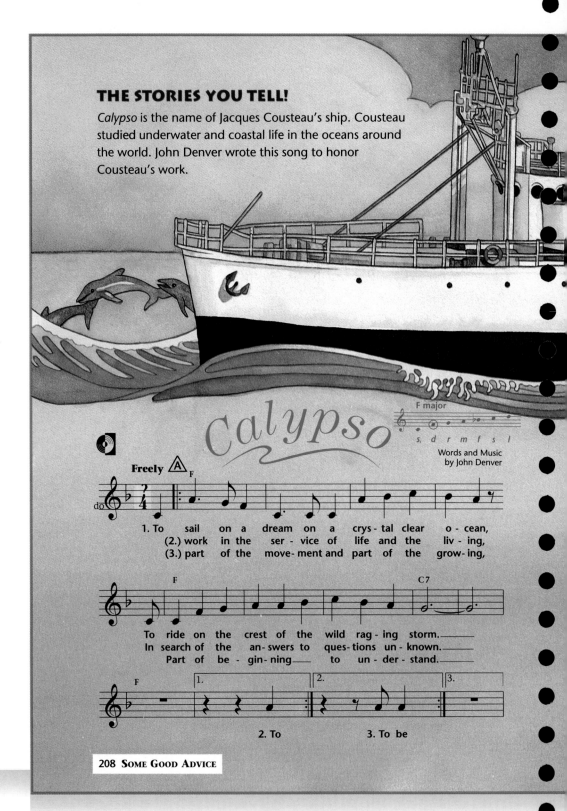

THE STORIES YOU TELL!
Calypso is the name of Jacques Cousteau's ship. Cousteau studied underwater and coastal life in the oceans around the world. John Denver wrote this song to honor Cousteau's work.

Calypso

F major

Words and Music by John Denver

Freely **A** F

1. To sail on a dream on a crys-tal clear o-cean,
(2.) work in the ser-vice of life and the liv-ing,
(3.) part of the move-ment and part of the grow-ing,

F   C7

To ride on the crest of the wild rag-ing storm.
In search of the an-swers to ques-tions un-known.
Part of be-gin-ning to un-der-stand.

F   1.   2.   3.

2. To   3. To be

208 SOME GOOD ADVICE

MEETING **INDIVIDUAL** NEEDS

ALTERNATE TEACHING STRATEGY

OBJECTIVE 2 Have partners work together, one seated, one standing behind. Play "Calypso" and have the standing partner tap the strong beats on the shoulders of the seated partner, who pats all beats. When they are comfortable with this, have them count one on each tapped beat, then determine how many beats there are in each set. (3) Finally, have them face each other and perform the pattern for the A section of "D'Hammerschmiedsgesellen."

BIOGRAPHY: *John Denver*

John Denver (1943–1997) was an activist as well as a singer and songwriter. When his grandmother gave him a guitar, he was not very interested in it. As a teenager, though, he was so excited by the new sound of Elvis Presley's music that he practiced hard. In college he studied architecture, but began earning money by performing, and decided to pursue music. "Rocky Mountain High," "Leaving on a Jet Plane," and "Take Me Home, Country Roads" (page 12) are some of his hits. Denver also concentrated on efforts to stop world hunger and pollution.

"What was the meter signature of each song in today's lesson?" ("Take Time in Life"— 4/4 ; "D'Hammerschmiedsgesellen" and "Calypso"— 3/4)

"What were the lessons for living you sang about today?" (take time in life, and work in the service of life) "Let's end by singing 'Calypso.'"

MORE MUSIC: Reinforcement

More Songs to Read, page 364 (6/8, 3/4, and 4/4 meters)

"Waltzing with Bears," page 242 (3/4 meter)

"Para pedir posada," page 318 (3/4 meter)

"Entren santos peregrinos," page 320 (3/4 and 4/4 meters)

Aye,—— Ca - lyp - so, the plac - es you've been to, The
Aye,—— Ca - lyp - so, I sing to your spir - it, To

things that you've shown us, the sto - ries you tell! well. Hi - dee -
those who have served you so long and so

ay ee oo——— oh - dle - oh oo——— Hi - dee - oo—

Which meter signature goes at the beginning of "Calypso"? 2/4   3/4   4/4   3/8

BACKGROUND: *"Calypso"*

John Denver wrote this song in honor of the great explorer-oceanographer Jacques Cousteau (ʒɑk kus **to**). Cousteau named his research ship after Calypso, a sea creature from Greek mythology. Born in France in 1910, Cousteau has helped bring global attention to the fascinating worlds beneath the ocean's surface. His crusades to preserve those worlds have had a major impact. Cousteau's many documentaries continue to appear on television and have won him several awards.

IMPROVISATION: *"Take Time in Life"*

Set up barred instruments or resonator bells for pitches F G A C' D'. Have students clap the following 4/4 pattern:

Then play the pattern on 1, then 2, 3, and finally all 5 of the pitches, in any order. Repeat the pattern to match a verse's length. Experiment with changing the order of the measures or with adding B♭ or E, then perform as an additional verse to "Take Time in Life."

ACROSS the

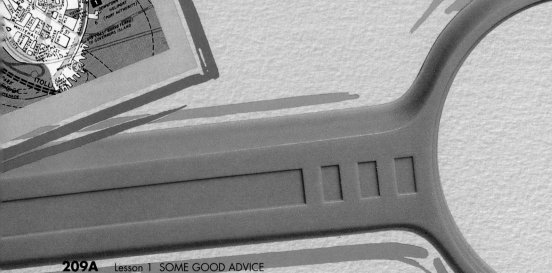

LANGUAGE ARTS

PERSONAL NARRATIVE

"Take Time in Life"

INDIVIDUAL   **15–30 MIN**

Have students read the proverbs on page 203 and then the words to the song on page 206. Ask them to think about the best advice they have ever gotten from a friend or relative.

Have each student choose one memorable event to tell about when they received valuable advice. They should describe:

- why they needed some advice;
- who offered the advice;
- what the outcome was—Did the student follow the advice or not, and what happened? Students who did follow the advice might speculate about what might have happened if they had not followed the advice.

Students might end their writing by explaining why they would or would not offer the same advice to anyone else.

COMPREHENSION STRATEGY: Expressing main ideas

MATHEMATICS

MAKING PLANS

"Take Time in Life"

PAIR   **15 MIN OR LESS**

MATERIALS: paper plate, two pencils (one shorter than the other) to use as clock hands

Have students work in pairs to plan a Saturday afternoon get-together with some friends. They meet at noon and have four hours to do some homework and have some fun.

Each partner writes out a list of things they will do, in the order in which they will do them. The partners exchange lists and make a time schedule, giving a time limit of 15, 30, or 45 minutes for each activity. The sum of the time spent on all the activities must equal four hours. Have partners check their schedules.

As a help, students can use a model clock, which they make by drawing a clock face on a paper plate and using two pencils, with eraser ends at the center of the clock face, as clock hands.

COMPREHENSION STRATEGY: Sequencing

CURRICULUM

SCIENCE/SOCIAL STUDIES

OCEAN ROUTES

"Calypso"

PAIR   **30 MIN OR LONGER**

MATERIALS: globe

Have students suppose they are on the *Calypso* in the middle of an ocean. Have pairs of students locate the Atlantic, Pacific, Arctic, Antarctic, and Indian oceans on a globe. One partner places a finger at a point in any of them and then, using the finger as the *Calypso*, "sails" through all the other oceans without ever crossing land or lifting the finger until they get back to the starting point. Can they do it?

Have each pair describe their ocean voyage. Which continents and islands do they pass by? What direction do they take to sail around each landmass they encounter? (Students will find that all the oceans are interconnected even when the oceans appear to be separated by land.)

COMPREHENSION STRATEGY: Sequencing

SCIENCE/MATHEMATICS

MAPPING

"Calypso"

PAIR   **30 MIN OR LONGER**

MATERIALS: clay, shoebox with lid, straw, metric ruler, marker

Students, in pairs, use clay and the bottom of a shoebox to create a model landscape of the ocean floor—mountains and hills, with valleys in between. Then they draw a straight centered line across the length of the box top. Next, using a pencil, they pierce a hole every 3 centimeters along this line. (CAUTION: They should point the pencil away from themselves and others.) They letter the holes, starting with A at one end, and then cover the box.

Each pair will use the covered model to make a map of the ocean floor. First, they use a ruler to make a mark every cm along a straw. Then they number these marks, starting with 1 cm. Next, they lower the straw (the 1-cm end) into each hole in the box lid until it touches bottom. They read and record the depth from the straw.

They can plot the findings on graph paper to make a bar-graph profile map of their model ocean floor.

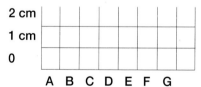

2 cm / 1 cm / 0 — A B C D E F G

COMPREHENSION STRATEGY: Recording and displaying information

UNIT FIVE
LESSON 2

LESSON PLANNER

FOCUS Pitch, major and minor

OBJECTIVE

OBJECTIVE 1 Signal to indicate when music shifts between major and minor

MATERIALS
Recordings

Tum-Balalaika	CD5:7
Hei Tama Tu Tama (steady tempo)	CD5:8
Recorded Lesson: Major and Minor	CD5:9
Calypso	CD5:6
Listening: Calypso (major/minor)	CD5:10

Resources
Recorder Master R • 21 (pitches D E)
Musical Instruments Master—balalaika

VOCABULARY
major, minor

▶ = **BASIC PROGRAM**

SONGS FOR

What riddles do you know? Riddles make you think about things in new ways. Find the riddles in "Tum-Balalaika."

Tum-Balalaika

Russian Yiddish Folk Song

Verse

1. Maid - en, maid - en, can you ex - plain,
2. Fool - ish boy, I can ex - plain, A

What can grow with - out an - y rain?
stone can grow with - out an - y rain.

What can burn for man - y a year?
True love can burn for man - y a year. A

What can cry, and shed not a tear?
sad heart can cry, and shed not a tear.

210

MEETING **INDIVIDUAL** NEEDS

EXTRA HELP: *Riddles*

If students can't think of any riddles, read these: *What's black and white and read all over?* (a newspaper) or *What comes in at every window and every door crack, runs around and around the house, but never leaves a track?* (the wind)

MUSIC BUILDS MATH SKILLS

Algebra Singing and performing the pattern to "Hei Tama Tu Tama" reinforces the skill of pattern recognition.

VOCAL DEVELOPMENT: *Vowel Sounds*

The refrain of "Tum-Balalaika" uses two of the pure vowel sounds, *oo* and *ah*. As students sing this vocalise, remind them of correct singing posture and breathing. They should maintain an openness in the back of the throat, as in the beginning of a yawn, and round their lips to form the *oo*, making certain lips are not too tense. Sing the refrain of "Tum-Balalaika" with the same openness.

Continue up by half steps to F.

Oo - ah - oo - ah - oo (breathe)   Oo - ah - oo - ah - oo (breathe)

THINKING

Refrain

Tum - ba - la, Tum - ba - la, Tum - ba - la - lai - ka,
tum ba la tum ba la tum ba la lai ka

Tum - ba - la, Tum - ba - la, Tum - ba - la - lai - ka,
tum ba la tum ba la tum ba la lai ka

Tum - ba - la - lai - ka, Tum - ba - la - lai - ka,
tum ba la lai ka tum ba la lai ka

Tum - ba - la - lai - ka, Tum - ba - la, tum!
tum ba la lai ka tum ba la tum

The balalaika is a popular Russian instrument that is played
by rapidly plucking its three strings. Balalaikas of different
sizes are played together in balalaika orchestras.

Unit 5 *Music with a Message* **211**

1 GET SET

"Who has a riddle to share?" Have students:

▶ • Share a few riddles. (See *Extra Help* on the bottom of page 210.)

▶ • Read about "Tum-Balalaika" (**tum** ba la **lai** ka), find the riddles, and imagine how the music might help express the riddles. For example, will it be fast or slow? Loud or soft? Use more brass or strings? (Answers may vary; explore all opinions.)

▶ • Listen to "Tum-Balalaika" **CD5:7** and compare their answers with what they hear. (not too fast, rather soft, strings)

"Today you'll learn how the set of pitches of a song can also help to express the meaning of the words."

2 DEVELOP

1. Learn "Tum-Balalaika." Have students:

▶ • Hum the melody and draw its contour in the air with one arm.

▶ • Identify the meter as ¾, then learn the song.

• Sing the song, showing the sets of beats during the refrain by patting knees on beat one, tapping chests with arms crossed on beat two, and clapping hands on beat three. (This pattern prepares students to do the hand-clap pattern for "D'Hammerschmiedsgesellen" in Lesson 3. See *Movement* on the bottom of page 214.)

MULTICULTURAL PERSPECTIVES: *"Tum-Balalaika"*

This popular folk song was originally written in Yiddish, the language of Jews in Eastern Europe. The song has many variations. In one version, the song asks a few more questions: *What is higher than a house?* (a chimney) *What is faster than a mouse?* (a cat) *What is deeper than a well?* (the mind) Another version changes the basic situation. Instead of a young man questioning a prospective bride, it features a police officer being made fun of by a Jewish man he was trying to harass.

PLAYING INSTRUMENTS: *Unpitched Percussion*

Have students choose three riddles (A, B, C) that can be said rhythmically, then play the rhythm of each with a different type of unpitched instrument. Have them create a riddle rondo, A B A C A form, by playing riddle A's rhythm on metal instruments (triangles, cymbals), B's on wooden instruments (woodblocks, claves), and C's on drums.

PRONUNCIATION: *"Tum-Balalaika"*

a f<u>a</u>ther   ι <u>i</u>t   u m<u>oo</u>n

UNIT FIVE
LESSON 2

continued from previous page

2. Introduce "Hei Tama Tu Tama" CD5:8
Learn a hand pattern. Have students:

▶ • Read about and listen to the song.

▶ • Listen again, singing *Hei tama tu tama* each time it occurs.

▶ • Practice a body-percussion pattern with the beat: pat knees, clap, snap, clap, pat knees.

▶ • Listen to the song, performing the pattern each time they sing *Hei tama tu tama*. (The last phrase requires extending the pattern with two more repetitions.)

▶ • With a partner, sing and perform the pattern, clapping partners' hands in place of the snaps.

▶ • Hum the melody and draw its contour.

3. Introduce major and minor. Have students:

▶ • Read page 213 and compare the sounds of "Tum-Balalaika" and "Hei Tama Tu Tama."

Recorded Lesson CD5:9
▶ • Listen to "Major and Minor," hear the pitch sets of the two songs, and identify them as major or minor.

COUNTING IN MAORI

Children everywhere sing alphabet and counting songs. In New Zealand, Maori children count with this chant. Try counting from one to ten in Maori.

🔊 HEI TAMA TU TAMA

Sing three times counting 1 - 9   Traditional Maori Children's Counting Game

Maori: **Ka   ta — hi,   Hei   ta — ma tu   ta — ma___**
Pronunciation: ka   ta   hi   heι   ta   ma tu   ta   ma

Ka   ru — a,   Hei   ta — ma tu   ta — ma___
ka   ɾu   a   heι   ta   ma tu   ta   ma

Start here 4th time to count 10

Ka   to — ru,   Hei   ta — ma tu   ta — ma,
ka   to   ɾu   heι   ta   ma tu   ta   ma

After 3rd time go to

Hei   ta — ma tu   ta — ma, Hei   ta — ma tu   ta — ma.___
heι   ta   ma tu   ta   ma heι   ta   ma tu   ta   ma

Tahi, rua, toru are the words for "one, two, three."
Wha, rima, ono are "four, five, six."
Whitu, waru, iwa are "seven, eight, nine."
Tekau is "ten" and *tama* means "young boy."

Four-tone

t,   d   r   m

212 SONGS FOR THINKING

MEETING **INDIVIDUAL** NEEDS

ALTERNATE TEACHING STRATEGY

OBJECTIVE 1 Have each student choose two different-colored markers, one for major and one for minor. Give each student two sheets of white paper, one for each color. Have them write *major* and *minor* in the chosen colors. Listen again to "Calypso" (major/minor) and have them hold up *minor* when it comes to the second verse.

PRONUNCIATION: *"Hei Tama Tu Tama"*

a f<u>a</u>ther   e ch<u>a</u>otic   i b<u>ee</u>   ι <u>i</u>t
o <u>o</u>bey   u m<u>oo</u>n   ɾ flipped r

MULTICULTURAL PERSPECTIVES: *A Maori Song*

"Hei Tama Tu Tama" is a Maori (**mɑo** ɾi) children's counting song which traditionally went to nine but now is generally sung through ten. The syllables *ka, tu,* and *hei* are vocables used as filler, much as a bandleader might say, "a-one, a-two, a-one, two, three, four." There are many possible variants of the song; some Maoris chant it with a game of arm movements that is played like the familiar "paper, scissors, stone" game.

MAJOR AND MINOR

The melodies of "Tum-Balalaika" and "Hei Tama Tu Tama" have different sounds. One reason is that they use different sets of pitches. The set of pitches heard in "Tum-Balalaika" is called **minor**. The set of pitches in "Hei Tama Tu Tama" is called **major**.

Unit 5 *Music with a Message* **213**

3 APPLY

Review "Calypso" (pp. 208–209). Identify shifts between major and minor. Have students:

▶ • Sing "Calypso" **CD5:6**.

OBJECTIVE 1 Informal Assessment
• Listen to "Calypso" (major/minor **CD5:10**) with eyes closed and raise a hand each time they hear the song shift from major to minor, or vice versa. (Verse 1—major; Verse 2—minor; Verse 3—major)

▶ • Describe how the shift to minor changed the feeling of the second verse.

4 CLOSE

"The pitch set can make music expressive. Of the three songs you sang, which were major and which was minor?" Have students:

▶ • Choose one of the songs to sing again.

LESSON SUMMARY

Informal Assessment In this lesson, students:

OBJECTIVE 1 Signaled to show shifts between major and minor as they listened to "Calypso."

National Standards for Music Education
1a Sing accurately, on pitch and in rhythm.
9a Identify musical examples from various eras and cultures.

MORE MUSIC: Reinforcement

More Songs to Read, page 365 (major and minor)
"We Three Kings," page 329 (minor/major)

VOCAL DEVELOPMENT: *Descending Passages*

Review correct singing posture and breathing (Unit 1, Lesson 1, page 13, *Vocal Development*), then have students: Put one hand on their chests and the other just below their waists to monitor the deep inhalation of breath. Inhale and feel an openness in the back of the throat, as in the beginning of a yawn. Beginning at the top of their vocal registers, glissando down to the bottom of their registers. They should maintain a steady supply of air throughout the glissando and should keep the singing posture without collapsing. Have them sing the vocalise with the same open throat

and breath support, then apply this to the descending *oo*'s in the coda of "Calypso."

Continue up to E and F.

oo———— (breathe) oo———— (breathe)oo———— (breathe)

ENRICHMENT: *Singing "Calypso"*

Have soloists sing each verse of "Calypso" and the whole group sing the refrain.

ACROSS the

LANGUAGE ARTS

RIDDLES

"Tum-Balalaika"

PAIR   **15–30 MIN**

MATERIALS: "hideable" objects, like an eraser or paperback book

Have students work in pairs. Each has a small hideable object and must think of some place within the classroom (or in the schoolyard, if this is played outdoors) in which to hide it. The partners work together to write two riddles that would help someone else find the objects. Point out that the riddle is in the form of a question. The question does not seem to make sense. But the answer reveals the hiding place. For example:

● What's the farthest place you can get to, without ever leaving the room? (The object is hidden behind a globe or map.)
● What makes the room feel like summer on a cold winter day? (The object is hidden near the radiator—but rule out the radiator as a hiding place if it is giving off heat.)

Partners read their riddles to the class to give everyone a chance to find the objects.

COMPREHENSION STRATEGY: Expressing main ideas

MATHEMATICS

NUMBER PATTERNS

"Hei Tama Tu Tama"

GROUP   **15–30 MIN**

MATERIALS: optional—centimeter graph paper

Write this list of average monthly high temperatures for Auckland, New Zealand, on the board:

JAN.	79°F	JULY	62°F
FEB.	79°F	AUG.	63°F
MAR.	77°F	SEPT.	65°F
APR.	73°F	OCT.	68°F
MAY	67°F	NOV.	73°F
JUNE	63°F	DEC.	76°F

Have students describe how the high temperatures change throughout the year in Auckland. When are they the highest? The lowest? How does this general change compare with the way temperatures change at home?

Students can make a line graph to show the data. Label the bottom of the graph by the months of the year and label the vertical axis with a broken scale to show a range of 60°F to 80°F in units of 1 degree.

COMPREHENSION STRATEGIES: Compare and contrast, making generalizations, displaying information

213A Lesson 2 SONGS FOR THINKING

CURRICULUM

SOCIAL STUDIES

MAPS

"Hei Tama Tu Tama"

PAIR   **15 MIN OR LESS**

MATERIALS: maps, globes

Help students find the two islands that make up New Zealand by locating them on a map. They are to the southeast of Australia, about 172°E and 40°S.

Have students work in pairs to make an imaginary trip to New Zealand from their hometown. They might decide to plot a flight route across major cities of North America, then across the Pacific Ocean to the Hawaiian Islands and beyond.

Have students list land areas (land forms, countries, cities) and bodies of water that they would pass along the way. Students should present their itineraries to the class.

COMPREHENSION STRATEGY: Sequencing

LANGUAGE ARTS

WRITING SENTENCES

"Hei Tama Tu Tama"

INDIVIDUAL   **15–30 MIN**

The Maori language first came to be written down when European settlers devised combinations of English letters to represent the sounds of spoken Maori. The resulting Maori alphabet uses 15 letters of the English alphabet; the following letters are absent: *b, c, d, f, j, l, q, s, v, y, z.*

Ask students to write the Maori alphabet out of the remaining 15 letters. Then ask them to write a sentence in English using only these 15 letters. Have them share their work. Which letters were the hardest to avoid using?

COMPREHENSION STRATEGY: Compare and contrast

LESSON PLANNER

FOCUS Expressive qualities/Tempo

OBJECTIVES
OBJECTIVE 1 Signal to indicate the tempos heard in a listening selection
OBJECTIVE 2 Sing and perform a body-percussion pattern that includes several tempo changes

MATERIALS
Recordings

Listening: D'Hammerschmieds-gesellen	CD5:5
Listening: D'Hammerschmieds-gesellen (A section)	CD5:11
Listening: Presto (excerpt) from Trio for Piano, Oboe, and Bassoon by F. Poulenc	CD5:12
Recorded Lesson: Pronunciation for "Hei Tama Tu Tama"	CD5:13
Hei Tama Tu Tama (steady tempo)	CD5:8
Hei Tama Tu Tama (changing tempo)	CD5:14

Resources
Listening Map Transparency T • 8 (Presto)
Musical Instruments Masters—bassoon, oboe, piano
Recorder Master R • 22 (pitches D E G A B)

VOCABULARY
tempo, adagio, moderato, allegro, presto, accelerando, ritardando, bassoon, oboe, double reed

▶ = BASIC PROGRAM

Tempo Terms

Folk dancers dance to both slow and lively music. Sometimes the music changes speed, challenging the dancers to go slower or faster.

clap

cross

legs

DANCE to "D'Hammer-schmiedsgesellen," a folk dance from the Bavarian region of Germany.

214

MEETING **INDIVIDUAL** NEEDS

ENRICHMENT: *Conducting in ¾*

Have students learn the conducting pattern for ¾ , then conduct with the "D'Hammerschmiedsgesellen" A section.

SPECIAL LEARNERS: *Conducting*

To help all students conduct, adapt patterns as needed. Have them use only downward arm movements with a somewhat larger movement on the first beat, or use only hand movements on the first—or all—beats.

MOVEMENT: *Hand-Clap Pattern and Step-Hops*

For preparation, see Lesson 1, page 207, *Movement: "D'Hammerschmiedsgesellen."*

A section: (Verbal Cue—*legs, cross, clap, right, left, both*) Pat own knees with two hands, cross arms and pat chest, and clap own hands, then clap right hands with partner, left hands, and both hands (six beats). (Do this eight times.)

B section: Perform step-hops with this rhythm (in ¾ it will feel more like a slow skip).

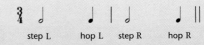

step L   hop L   step R   hop R

right

left

both

SPEED LIMIT AHEAD!

The **tempo** is the speed of the beat of a song. Here are some Italian words used to describe the tempo of music.

adagio	slow
moderato	medium
allegro	fast
presto	very fast

Music can begin at any tempo and then change. When the music speeds up, the change is called an **accelerando**, and when it slows down, the change is called a **ritardando**. Tempo changes can take you by surprise and make the music more interesting or expressive.

LISTEN for the tempos in "D'Hammerschmiedsgesellen."

Unit 5 *Music with a Message* **215**

1 GET SET

"Listen to 'D'Hammerschmiedsgesellen.' Listen carefully for what happens to the beat." (Play the A and B sections once from the complete version **CD5:5**.) Have students:

▶ • With a partner, perform the hand-clap pattern during the A section, and step in place with the strong beats during the B section. (See Lesson 1, page 207, *Movement: "D'Hammer-schmiedsgesellen."*)

• Determine that the beats in the B section are faster than those in the A section.

"Today, we'll listen to and perform music that has changes in the speed of the beat, and you'll learn how to describe these changes."

2 DEVELOP

1. Learn the dance to "D'Hammerschmieds-gesellen." Have students:

▶ • Learn the new hand-clap pattern. (See *Movement* on the bottom of page 214.)

▶ • Perform the new hand-clap pattern for the A sections, and the step-hop pattern during the B sections, moving to find a new partner. (See *Movement* below. This recording and the slower A section recording contain spoken dance instructions over the music. You may adjust the stereo balance control to hear the music alone.)

▶ • Read about tempo markings—adagio (ɑ **dɑ** jo), moderato (mo de **rɑ** to), allegro (ɑl **le** gɾo), presto (**pɾɛs** to), accelerando (ɑt che le **rɑn** do), ritardando (ɾi tɑr **dɑn** do) —and listen for tempos in the music.

MOVEMENT: *"D'Hammerschmiedsgesellen" Dance*

This dance is traditionally performed by men.

Formation: groups of four, partners facing each other across square

```
    1
3 ←─┼─→ 4
    2
```

A section: Have students try the A section hand-clap pattern (left) and discover that in groups of four, their hands will bump into each other. Try possible solutions. (One pair changes level of hands or starts later.) In the traditional dance, one couple performs the pattern as practiced and the other begins on beat 1 with the beat 4 movement (*R, L,*

both, legs, cross, clap). Allow groups to practice with the A section (**CD5:11**), which is recorded at a slower tempo.

B section: First time—circles of four join hands and circle clockwise for eight measures, using step-hops beginning with left foot. Repeat, moving counterclockwise. Second time—feet move as before, but instead of joining hands, circles form a right-hand star as they move clockwise, and a left-hand star as they move counterclockwise. Third time—circles of four open up to form a circle of the entire group. All join hands and move as in first B section.

continued from previous page

2. Introduce Presto (excerpt) CD5:12. Follow a listening map with tempo changes. Have students:

▶ • Read about the instruments.

▶ • Locate the A, Bridge, B, and A' sections on the listening map.

▶ • Listen for the tempo changes in the music while following the map. (Point out that the hill, second row of map, is not a melodic contour but influences the bicyclist's speed.) (Optional: Use **Listening Map Transparency T · 8.**)

OBJECTIVE 1 Informal Assessment

• Listen again, patting with the beat with eyes shut, and hold up one finger to signal slower tempos (adagio, moderato) and two for faster tempos (allegro, presto) as they hear them in A, B, and A' sections. (two, one, two)

3 APPLY

Review "Hei Tama Tu Tama" (p. 212). Perform a body-percussion pattern with changing tempo. Have students:

Recorded Lesson CD5:13

▶ • Listen to "Pronunciation for 'Hei Tama Tu Tama,'" and learn the Maori numbers, then sing the song.

▶ • With a partner, practice the body-percussion pattern from Lesson 2, page 212, *Develop 2.*

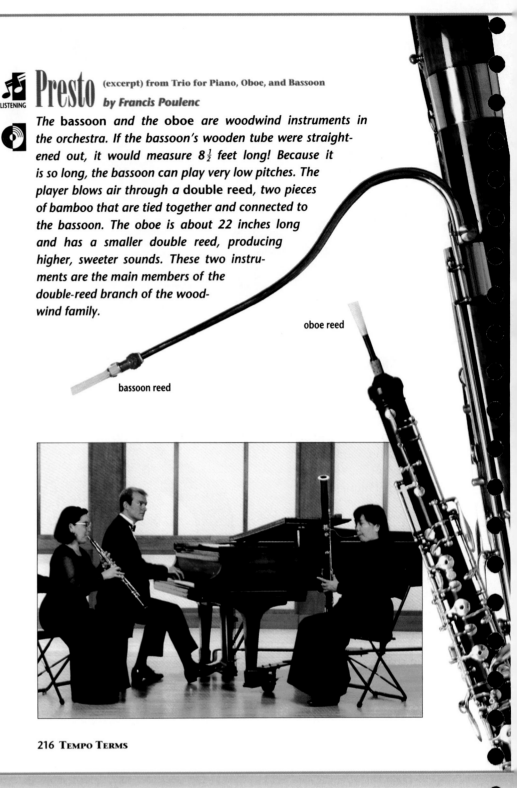

Presto (excerpt) from Trio for Piano, Oboe, and Bassoon
by Francis Poulenc

*The **bassoon** and the **oboe** are woodwind instruments in the orchestra. If the bassoon's wooden tube were straightened out, it would measure 8½ feet long! Because it is so long, the bassoon can play very low pitches. The player blows air through a **double reed**, two pieces of bamboo that are tied together and connected to the bassoon. The oboe is about 22 inches long and has a smaller double reed, producing higher, sweeter sounds. These two instruments are the main members of the double-reed branch of the woodwind family.*

oboe reed

bassoon reed

216 TEMPO TERMS

MEETING **INDIVIDUAL** NEEDS

ALTERNATE TEACHING STRATEGIES

OBJECTIVE 1 List the four tempo words from page 215 on the board. Have students pat steadily and adjust their tempo as you point to each term. To help them sense tempo changes in Presto, draw two dots on the board and have a student tap the dots back and forth in tempo as the class listens to the piece. (You may introduce a metronome also.)

OBJECTIVE 2 Label verses *adagio, moderato,* and *allegro.* Students listen to "Hei Tama Tu Tama" (changing tempo) and watch as two toss a beanbag back and forth on each strong beat. All sing as you point to the tempo words.

SPECIAL LEARNERS: *Movements in Control* MOVEMENT

Since speeding up music can make it more exciting, it will be important for students to learn to control their movements. Excitable students may need to practice stopping their movements, particularly at faster tempos. They may also benefit from audible cues or reminders to keep movements in control. Since students will maintain control if they hear and move with the beat, provide an extra cue by playing a drum with the beat as students sing and move.

Unit 5 *Music with a Message* **217**

• Sing the song (steady tempo **CD5:8**) and perform the pattern.

• Listen to "Hei Tama Tu Tama" (changing tempo **CD5:14**) and tell what happens to the beat.

OBJECTIVE 2 Informal Assessment

• Sing and perform the pattern, increasing the tempo with each verse.

4 CLOSE

"As I call out words to describe tempo, you tell me which of our new words matches what I say." (slow—adagio; medium—moderato; fast—allegro; very fast—presto; speed up—accelerando; slow down—ritardando)

"Let's have someone stand at the board and point to the tempos as we sing 'Hei Tama Tu Tama.' We will try to sing in the tempo that our 'conductor' points to."

LESSON SUMMARY

Informal Assessment In this lesson, students:

OBJECTIVE 1 Signaled to indicate the tempos they heard in Presto.

OBJECTIVE 2 Sang and performed a body-percussion pattern with "Hei Tama Tu Tama" that included several tempo changes.

National Standards for Music Education
6a Identify simple musical forms by ear.
6e Respond to musical characteristics through movement.

MORE MUSIC: Reinforcement

"Sounds of the Oboe," page 247 (oboe)
"Sounds of the Bassoon, page 248 (bassoon)
"The Shrovetide Fair," page 385G (tempo)
"Island Rhythms," page 385K (tempo)

BIOGRAPHY: *Francis Poulenc*

Francis Poulenc (frä sis pu lɛ̄k), 1899–1963, lived in Paris, France. First taught piano by his mother, he became a highly praised pianist, organist, and composer. He wrote many works in various genres: piano music, operas, ballets, choral works, chamber music (mostly for winds and piano), film music, and songs. The trio which includes this Presto movement was written by Poulenc at age 27, and showcases each instrument with important solos.

BACKGROUND: *Oboe and Bassoon*

The oboe and bassoon are both woodwind instruments with double reeds. While the oboe is a soprano instrument, the bassoon is a bass. Oboes are usually made of an African black wood called *grenadilla* (grɛn ə dɪl lə) or of rosewood. The bassoon's body is usually made of maple or beech. Since the right thumb alone has 13 keys to operate, playing the bassoon takes excellent coordination. Having big hands helps, too! The oboe is smaller and easier to handle. It has a clear, colorful sound and often plays beautiful solo parts in orchestral pieces.

LESSON PLANNER

FOCUS Pitch, *ti*

OBJECTIVE

OBJECTIVE 1 Signal when they hear the melodic pattern *la ti do'*

MATERIALS
Recordings
Take Time in Life   CD5:3
Hei Tama Tu Tama (steady
    tempo)   CD5:8
Aquaqua   CD5:15
Recorded Lesson: Pronunciation
    for "Aquaqua"   CD5:16

Instruments resonator bells

Resources
Resource Master 5 • 3 (practice)
Resource Master 5 • 4 (practice)
Recorder Master R • 23 (pitches D E G)

VOCABULARY
eighth rest, major scale

▶ = **BASIC PROGRAM**

Listen as you sing
the last phrase from
"Hei Tama Tu Tama."
You only sing *do* and a
lower pitch. That pitch, just
below *do*, is called *ti*.

The letter name for *do* in "Hei Tama
Tu Tama" is F. What is the letter name for *ti*? E

PLAY this phrase on an instrument.

Hei   ta - ma tu   ta - ma,   Hei   ta - ma tu   ta - ma,

Hei   ta - ma tu   ta - ma._____

NAME the pitch syllables in this pattern.
Clue: The pattern ends on high *do* (*do'*). *la ti do'*

do'

Raise your hand when you hear the pattern in "Aquaqua."

218

MEETING **INDIVIDUAL** NEEDS

ALTERNATE TEACHING STRATEGY

OBJECTIVE 1 Have the class sing the *la ti do'* motive, drawing the melodic shape of the motive in the air. Working in pairs, have students listen to "Aquaqua" as one partner traces the melodic shape of each phrase and the other watches to identify the shape of the *la ti do'* motive. Then have each pair complete **Resource Master 5 • 3**, on which they practice writing *la, ti,* and *do'* and identify the motive in notation.

VOCAL DEVELOPMENT: *Inner Hearing*

Accurate inner hearing contributes to singing on pitch. Students must be able to "think" the correct pitch before singing it. After they can sing "Take Time in Life" very well, explain that when you give the starting pitch of the song and clap, they are to sing until you clap again. They should then "listen" to the pitches inside their heads until you clap a third time, when they can resume singing out loud. Use this procedure with other songs students know well. Tip: Have them audibly tap with the beat during the entire song.

C major

m s l t d'

Aquaqua

Israeli Children's Game
Collected by Rita Klinger

C   F   C   F   G   C

do

Nonsense: A - qua qua del - la   o - mar   qua   qua   qua
Pronunciation: a kwa kwa de la   o mar   kwa   kwa   kwa

C   F   C   F   G   C

del si - ma tri - co   tri - co   tri - co tra
del si ma tri   ko   tri ko   tri ko tra

C   G   C

va - lo   va - lo   va - lo va-lo va-lo va - lo 1 2 3   4 5
va lo   va lo   va   lo va lo va lo va lo

In "Hei Tama Tu Tama," *do* is F. The key signature has a flat
(♭) on the third line. In "Aquaqua," *do* is C. How does its
key signature differ from the one in "Hei Tama Tu Tama"?

Look at the song again. A silence the length of an eighth
note is shown with an **eighth rest** (𝄾).

Unit 5 *Music with a Message* 219

"Let's sing 'Take Time in Life.'" CD5:3 Have
students:

▶ • Sing the song. (See page 206.)

• Hum the last pitch and identify it as the tonal
center, *do*. Think the final phrase silently except for singing aloud the last two words, *to go*,
and describe the pitch of *to*. (lower than *do*)

"Today you'll learn about this pitch that is just
below *do*."

2 DEVELOP

1. Review "Hei Tama Tu Tama" CD5:8
(p. 212). Introduce *ti*. Have students:

▶ • Sing the song and review the body percussion pattern first without a partner, then seated
on the floor with a partner. (Lesson 2, page
212, *Develop 2*)

• Identify the last pitch as *do*.

• Sing the *hei tama tu tama* patterns aloud and
think all other words, moving hands from
knees to floor when the pattern moves to the
lower pitch. (next to last pattern)

• Read about *ti* and identify its letter name as E.

• Sing the last three *hei tama tu tama* patterns
with pitch syllables. (*do ti, do*)

• Sing the song, playing the patterns on bells.

2. Introduce "Aquaqua" CD5:15. Find
la ti do'. Have students:

• Study the pitch pattern at the bottom of page
218 and name the pitch syllables. (*la ti do'*)

• Play the *la ti do'* pattern on resonator bells,
A B C'.

OBJECTIVE 1 Informal Assessment

• Watch the notation and listen to the song,
signaling when they hear the *la ti do'* pattern.
(Measures 2 and 4)

• Compare the two key signatures.

PITCH SYLLABLES: *ti*

Teach students the hand sign for *ti*.

ti

PRONUNCIATION: *"Aquaqua"*

a f<u>a</u>ther   e ch<u>a</u>otic   i b<u>ee</u>   o <u>o</u>bey   ɾ flipped r

MUSIC BUILDS READING SKILLS

Listening In signaling when they hear the
melodic pattern *la ti do*, students will be
listening critically and responsively.

UNIT FIVE
LESSON 4

continued from previous page

3. Learn the major scale. Have students:

• Look at page 220 and listen as one student plays the C major scale on resonator bells, using all the pitch syllables between *do* and high *do*.

• Sing the C major scale using pitch syllables, then try descending from high to low *do*.

3 APPLY

Learn the game for "Aquaqua." Have students:

Recorded Lesson CD5:16
▶ • Listen to "Pronunciation for 'Aquaqua.'"
▶ • Sing the song once.
▶ • Read about the game, then play it as they sing the song again. (See *Enrichment* below.)

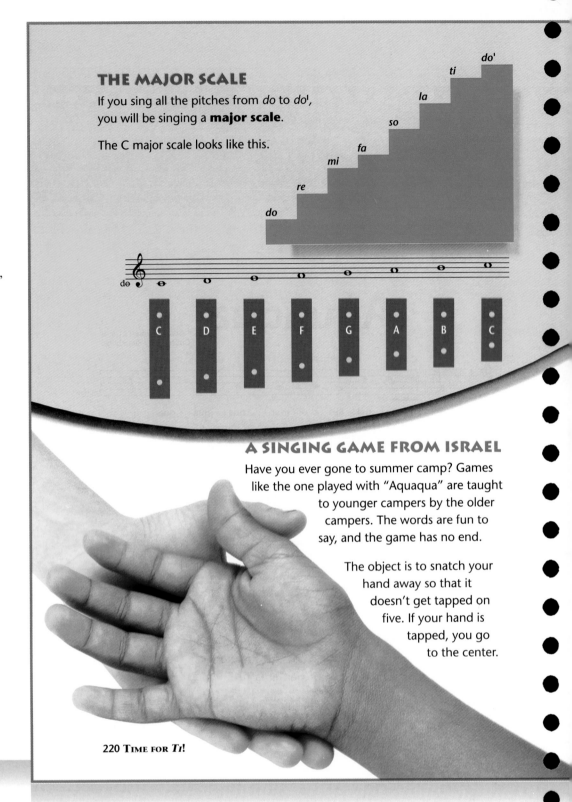

THE MAJOR SCALE

If you sing all the pitches from *do* to *do'*, you will be singing a **major scale**.

The C major scale looks like this.

do re mi fa so la ti do'

A SINGING GAME FROM ISRAEL

Have you ever gone to summer camp? Games like the one played with "Aquaqua" are taught to younger campers by the older campers. The words are fun to say, and the game has no end.

The object is to snatch your hand away so that it doesn't get tapped on five. If your hand is tapped, you go to the center.

220 Time for Ti!

MEETING **INDIVIDUAL** NEEDS

ENRICHMENT: *Game for "Aquaqua"*

Formation: circle, all hands held palms up, with right hand resting on top of right-hand neighbor's left hand

Designate someone to be student 1.

Phrases 1–2: All face and walk clockwise.

Phrase 3: Stand and face center until the first number. Student 1 calls out *one* and brings her/his right hand over to lightly tap the left-hand neighbor's right palm. That person then calls out *two,* making the same motion. Continue to

five. If student 5 taps the neighbor's hand, the neighbor must go into the center, but if the neighbor snatches her/his hand away in time, student 5 goes into the center.

The song and game then resume with a new student 1. When five or six students are in the center, they begin their own game. The game can go on indefinitely, with more and more concentric circles forming. As the original circle has fewer and fewer members, the challenge is to stretch and keep going.

Count out and tap hands.

Continue to five.

4 CLOSE

"In this lesson, we found *ti* in two songs and a scale. Tell me where to look for *ti* in "Hei Tama Tu Tama." (pitch below *do,* E) "How about in 'Aquaqua'?" (in *la ti do'* motive) "Where is *ti* in the C major scale?" (between *la* and *do'*, B) Have students:

▶ • Sing "Aquaqua."

• Sing the pitch syllables of the major scale (sing in C major).

LESSON SUMMARY

Informal Assessment In this lesson, students:

OBJECTIVE 1 Signaled to show recognition of the *la ti do'* pattern in "Aquaqua."

National Standards for Music Education
1a Sing accurately, on pitch and in rhythm.
1b Sing with appropriate dynamics, phrasing, and interpretation.
1c Sing memorized repertoire from diverse genres and cultures.
1e Sing in groups, responding to the conductor.
6b Describe, in words or movement, music from diverse cultures.
6e Respond to musical characteristics through movement.

MORE MUSIC: Reinforcement
More Songs to Read, page 366 (*ti*)
"Push the Business On," page 245 (reading pitches including low *ti*)
"A Holly Jolly Christmas," page 324 (*ti*)

MOVEMENT: *Parallel and Contrary Motion*

Help students to understand parallel motion and contrary motion. Parallel motion involves two lines of motion that go along together. Point out that having the inside circle walk and tap hands in the same direction as the outside circle shows parallel motion. Encourage students to discover what happens if the inside circle walks and taps hands counterclockwise. (Hands need to be set up in reverse—left hands rest on right hands, left hands tap by moving left to right.) This produces contrary motion.

PLAYING INSTRUMENTS: *Keyboard*

Have students sing the *do ti, do* and *la ti do'* motives from this lesson with letter names, then find them on the keyboard. (F E F, A B C') Have them play the motives when they occur in "Hei Tama Tu Tama" or "Aquaqua."

ENRICHMENT: *C Major Scale*

Have students list characteristics of the C major scale. (Possible list: no flats, no sharps, 8 notes, C = *do,* major key) Then have them look at the scales on **Resource Master 5 · 4** and decide whether or not they are C major scales and why.

ACROSS *the*

MATHEMATICS

NUMBER GAME

"Hei Tama Tu Tama"

PAIR   **15 MIN OR LESS**

MATERIALS: index cards, scissors, markers, timer or watch with second hand, paper and pencil

Students work in pairs. Each partner cuts an index card into 9 small rectangles, all about the same size. Have both partners label the cards from 1 to 9.

Round 1: The partners set a time limit, such as 2 or 3 minutes. Then, in that period, each partner arranges the 9 cards to make as many different 7-digit numbers (numbers to the millions place value) as possible. When they finish, they compare lists, crossing off any number that appears on both lists or is duplicated on the same list. Each player gets a point for any remaining number on his or her list.

Round 2: Repeat, building 8-digit numbers (to ten millions place).

Round 3: Repeat, building 9-digit numbers (to hundred millions place).

COMPREHENSION STRATEGY: Compare and contrast

MATHEMATICS/ART

NUMBERS & FIGURES

"Hei Tama Tu Tama"

INDIVIDUAL   **15–30 MIN**

MATERIALS: drawing paper, cutouts of the three plane figures—circle, square, equilateral triangle; optional—crayons

Students start by tracing one of the figures on drawing paper. Then they trace another figure that overlaps the first figure and results in a three-area drawing: one area where the two figures overlap, and two areas where the figures do not overlap.

Then they trace the third figure to overlap one or both of the other two. The goal is to create drawings with 4, 5, 6, or more distinct areas.

For each drawing, students should use numbers to label the parts, and might color the parts to make them more visible.

COMPREHENSION STRATEGIES: Cause and effect, explore spatial relationships

CURRICULUM

SOCIAL STUDIES

LONGITUDE/LATITUDE

"Aquaqua"

PAIR   **15–30 MIN**

MATERIALS: world maps, globes, timer or watch with second hand

Help students locate Israel on a globe or world map. It is located at about 35°E longitude and about 32°N latitude. The numerical values of these coordinates are close. Have students play a globe game based on the idea of coordinates that have the same numerical value.

Have students work in pairs. Each student thinks of a number from 0 to 90 and two directions: "East or West" and "North or South"—for example, 85°E and 85°N. Partners write their coordinates and exchange them face-down. They take turns turning up the coordinates and hunting on the globe for the given location. The student who finds the location in less time wins.

COMPREHENSION STRATEGY: Compare and contrast

LANGUAGE ARTS

CAMP STORIES

"Aquaqua"

INDIVIDUAL   **15–30 MIN**

"Aquaqua" is a camp game. Have students imagine that they are at summer camp (day camp or sleep-away camp) or on a camping trip. Have them write about one day at camp:

- where they are;
- what time they get up;
- activities played during the day;
- fun shared with friends or family.

Students who have been at camp or have gone camping can describe actual experiences. Students who have never gone camping or been at camp can use their imaginations to describe what they think camp would be like. In either case, their writings can end with reasons why they would (or would not) like to go camping or go to camp the coming summer.

COMPREHENSION STRATEGIES: Expressing main ideas, expressing point of view

UNIT FIVE
LESSON 5

RELATED ARTS | **MOVEMENT** | THEATER | VISUAL ARTS |

LESSON PLANNER

FOCUS Duration, dotted quarter-eighth rhythm (♩. ♪)

OBJECTIVES

OBJECTIVE 1 In three groups, perform contrasting rhythms: ♩♩, ♫, and rhythm of a song including ♩. ♪ (tested)

OBJECTIVE 2 Identify the correct rhythmic notation for song phrases including the dotted quarter-eighth rhythm (tested)

MATERIALS

Recordings
Take Time in Life   CD5:3
Listening: Canoe Song and
  Dance   CD5:17
Tum-Balalaika   CD5:7
Calypso   CD5:6

Resources
Resource Master 5 • 5 (practice)
Signing Master S • 4 • 4 (Take Time in
  Life)
Recorder Master R • 24 (pitches D E G A B)

▶ = **BASIC PROGRAM**

Music That

Music can carry a personal message, and it can also pass on the knowledge and traditions of a group of people.

LISTENING ♫ Canoe Song and Dance

As Performed by Members of the Haliwa-Saponi Nation

Throughout their history, Native Americans have used songs and dances to teach life skills, such as hunting, and to tell stories. This Eastern Woodlands social dance tells the following story.

The women of the village are paddling canoes down the river to do the washing. They see the men of the village paddling upstream. The men are tired from the hard work of hunting. At first the men pass the women, but they are so happy to see each other that the men turn around and they all paddle downstream together.

Songs such as "Canoe Song and Dance" are learned by hearing someone sing them.

Eastern Woodlands canoe

Eastern Woodlands woven belt

222

MEETING **INDIVIDUAL** NEEDS

BACKGROUND: *"Canoe Song and Dance"*   MOVEMENT

The exact origins of this music are unknown. Arnold Richardson, a cultural leader of the Haliwa-Saponi (**ha** lı wa sa **po** ni) nation of North Carolina, revived the "Canoe Song and Dance" for his people. The syllables sung are vocables, not words.

MUSIC BUILDS MATH SKILLS   123

Number and Operations When performing the dotted quarter-eighth patterns, students reinforce their knowledge of fractions.

PLAYING INSTRUMENTS: *Drums*

Nondancers may accompany "Canoe Song and Dance" by drumming steady eighth notes. Drum the last measure with accents.

Repeat as needed   *last measure*

ENRICHMENT: *Oral History Project*

Have students record and present stories that an older relative, friend, or neighbor tells them.

Teaches Tradition

LEARN to sing "Canoe Song and Dance" by listening to these members of the Haliwa-Saponi Nation.

Canoe Dance performed by Haliwa-Saponi people of North Carolina.

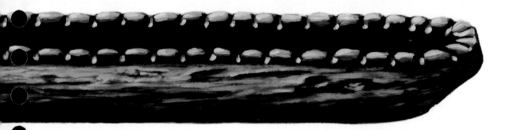

Unit 5 *Music with a Message* **223**

1 GET SET

"Echo-clap the rhythm you hear." Have students:

▶ • Listen to the first phrase of "Take Time in Life" **CD5:3**, then clap its rhythm. (See page 206.)

"You'll learn more about this rhythm pattern in today's lesson."

2 DEVELOP

1. Learn the dance for "Canoe Song and Dance" **CD5:17**. Have students:

▶ • Read about and listen to the song.

▶ • Learn to sing the response by listening to the song.

▶ • Learn the dance. (See *Movement* below.)

▶ • Listen and perform the dance, singing the response.

Contributing research by Dr. Bryan Burton.

MOVEMENT: *Canoe Dance*

Basic Step: Have students chant this verbal cue: (Note that these words are for learning the movement pattern, and do not represent the vocables sung.)

L R L R L R L   R L R L R L R
Mov-ing for-ward in a line,   Mov-ing for-ward in a line.

1. Step to the rhythm of the words. When the pattern begins with the left foot, it travels forward and slightly to the left; the left foot leads and the right foot drags or slides to

close behind it. Reverse when the pattern begins with the right foot. **2. Move in lines.** In this dance it is important that the girls and boys form separate lines of four to five students. The leader of each line bends her/his elbows. All others hold on to the elbows of the person in front of them. **Final Form:** All the "girls' canoes" enter first, paddling "downstream." The "boys' canoes" then enter, paddling "upstream" (moving in contrary motion to the "girls' canoes"). The boys' canoes pass behind the girls', turn, and arrive next to the girls'. Now they are moving in parallel motion with the girls' canoes, and they paddle downstream in unison.

UNIT FIVE LESSON 5

continued from previous page

2. Introduce the dotted quarter-eighth rhythm of "Take Time in Life." Have students:

▶ • Sing the song without the notation.

• Clap the rhythm of Verse 1, then of the first phrase only (first eight beats).

OBJECTIVE 1 Informal Assessment

• Form three groups, one group patting quarter notes, one snapping eighth notes, one clapping the rhythm of Phrase 1.

• Identify and compare the iconic notation for each group's rhythm on the top of page 224, then read about the rhythmic notation.

• Sing the song (page 206) and locate the three dotted quarter-eighth patterns, identifying the words sung each time. (*passing, called me, said to*)

3 APPLY

Review "Tum-Balalaika" CD5:7 (p. 210) and "Calypso" CD5:6 (p. 208). Identify rhythmic notation. Have students:

▶ • Sing Verse 1 and the refrain of "Tum-Balalaika," recalling that the song is minor.

• Identify the meter as ¾, then sing the refrain while performing a pat-clap-snap pattern with the beat.

• Sing the refrain's first phrase and step the rhythm, finding the longer durations.

TAKE TIME FOR A NEW RHYTHM

Which line shows the rhythm you performed with the first phrase of "Take Time in Life"? Line 3

The rhythm of the first phrase could be written like this.

SING the song on page 206 and find all the ♩. ♪ patterns.

A dot following a note adds half of the note's rhythmic value. A dot after a quarter note makes it an eighth note longer.

MEETING **INDIVIDUAL** NEEDS

ALTERNATE TEACHING STRATEGIES

OBJECTIVE 1 Have three large cards at the board, one with the word *pat,* one with the words *snap snap,* and one with the words *I was passing by, my brother called me in.* Have each group perform their rhythm only while you are pointing to their card. Have one or two students play a beat on the drum to keep a steady tempo. When each group is secure, try two groups together at a time, then three. For more aural distinction between parts, add a different unpitched percussion sound to each group (for example, let ♩ = drum, ♫ = woodblock, rhythm = güiro).

OBJECTIVE 2 Draw six eighth notes on the board. Have a student tap the eighth notes repeatedly from left to right as the class sings *tumbala, tumbala* slowly in the rhythm of the refrain. Then have the class help the student at the board determine on which eighth notes they sang the syllables, tie the eighth notes together under longer syllables, and finally rewrite the rhythm using quarters and dotted quarters. (Optional: Use **Resource Master 5 · 5** for practice with ties.)

SIGNING: *"Take Time in Life"*
Signing Master S · 4 · 4 has sign language for this song.

A RHYTHM RIDDLE

Which pattern below shows the correct notation for the first phrase of the refrain of "Tum-Balalaika"? For the first phrase of "Calypso"? *Pattern 3; Pattern 1*

After you've solved the riddle, sing "Tum-Balalaika" with a soloist on each verse.

THINK IT THROUGH

How long would a dotted half note sound? A dotted eighth note? *a quarter note longer; a sixteenth note longer*

225

OBJECTIVE 2 Informal Assessment
• Indicate with number of fingers which example on page 225 shows the rhythmic notation for the first phrase of the refrain. (3)
• Check their answers on page 211.
• Repeat with phrase 1 of "Calypso," showing one finger for the first example on page 225 check answers on page 208.

4 CLOSE

"What is the new rhythm pattern we learned today?" (♩. ♪) "How long does a pitch written as ♩. sound?" (same as 3 eighth notes) Have students:

▶ • Sing "Tum-Balalaika," (page 210).

LESSON SUMMARY

Informal Assessment In this lesson, students:

OBJECTIVE 1 In three groups, performed contrasting rhythm patterns including the rhythm of the words of "Take Time in Life."

OBJECTIVE 2 Signaled to identify the correct rhythmic notation for phrases from "Tum-Balalaika" and "Calypso."

National Standards for Music Education
5d Use standard symbols to notate patterns.
6b Describe, in words or movement, music from diverse cultures.

MORE MUSIC: Reinforcement

More Songs to Read, page 367 (syncopation).
"Powama," page 150 (Native American music)
"A Lakota Legend," page 152 (Native American cultures)
"America, the Beautiful," page 300 (dotted quarter-eighth rhythm; patriotic)
"And Where is Home?," page 378 (♩. ♪)
"Don't Let the Music Stop," page 380 (♩. ♪)

MOVEMENT: *Exploring Parallel and Contrary Motion*

Review the A section movement for "Take Time in Life" (Lesson 1, page 207, *Movement*). Have a pair of students draw the pathway of each partner on the board, then discuss whether their motion was parallel or contrary. (contrary) Ask another pair to draw possible parallel pathways.

contrary: parallel:

⟵ and ⟶   ⟶ or ⟵

Ask partners to develop ways to move in parallel motion during the A section. (Partners face the same way and move the same direction at the same time, or partners keep

original facing and one moves forward, the other backward.) Have students perform a solution.

PLAYING INSTRUMENTS: *Keyboards*

Have students play this to accompany "Take Time in Life."

Across the

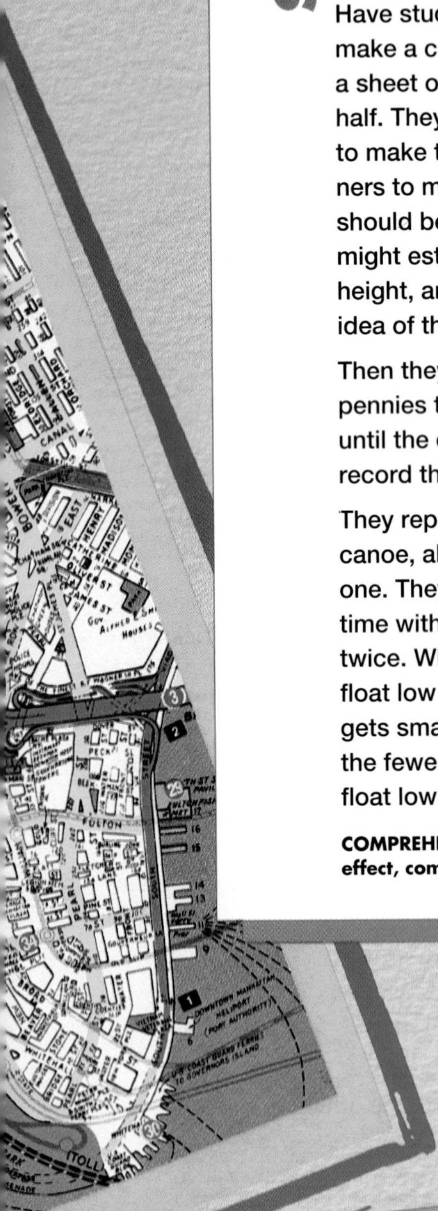

SCIENCE

FLOATING MODEL

"Canoe Song and Dance"

GROUP   **15–30 MIN**

MATERIALS: sheet of aluminum foil (10 in. x 12 in.—22 cm x 30 cm), pennies, basin of water; optional—ruler, calculator

Have students work in groups to make a canoe model. They start with a sheet of aluminum foil folded in half. They fold up ends and corners to make the sides, overlapping corners to make it leak-proof. The canoe should be wide and long. (Students might estimate the length, width, and height, and multiply to get a rough idea of the volume.)

Then they float the canoe and add pennies to it, as many as they can until the canoe floats very low. They record the number of pennies.

They repeat the activity with a smaller canoe, about half the size of the first one. They use the same sheet, this time with the sheet folded in half twice. What happens to its ability to float low with pennies as the canoe gets smaller? (The smaller the canoe, the fewer pennies it takes to make it float low.)

COMPREHENSION STRATEGIES: Cause and effect, compare and contrast

MATHEMATICS

TIME

"Take Time in Life"

PAIR   **15 MIN OR LESS**

MATERIALS: optional—calculator

Have students work in pairs to find out how much time—in months—there is between the present and:

- their next birthday,
- the next major holiday,
- their next vacation from school,
- their graduation from elementary school, middle school, high school.

Have students think of other possibilities, based on things they might look forward to: "How many months until my family's trip to___?" "How many months until I'm old enough to get a driver's license?" "How many months until I'm old enough to vote?"

COMPREHENSION STRATEGY: Sequencing

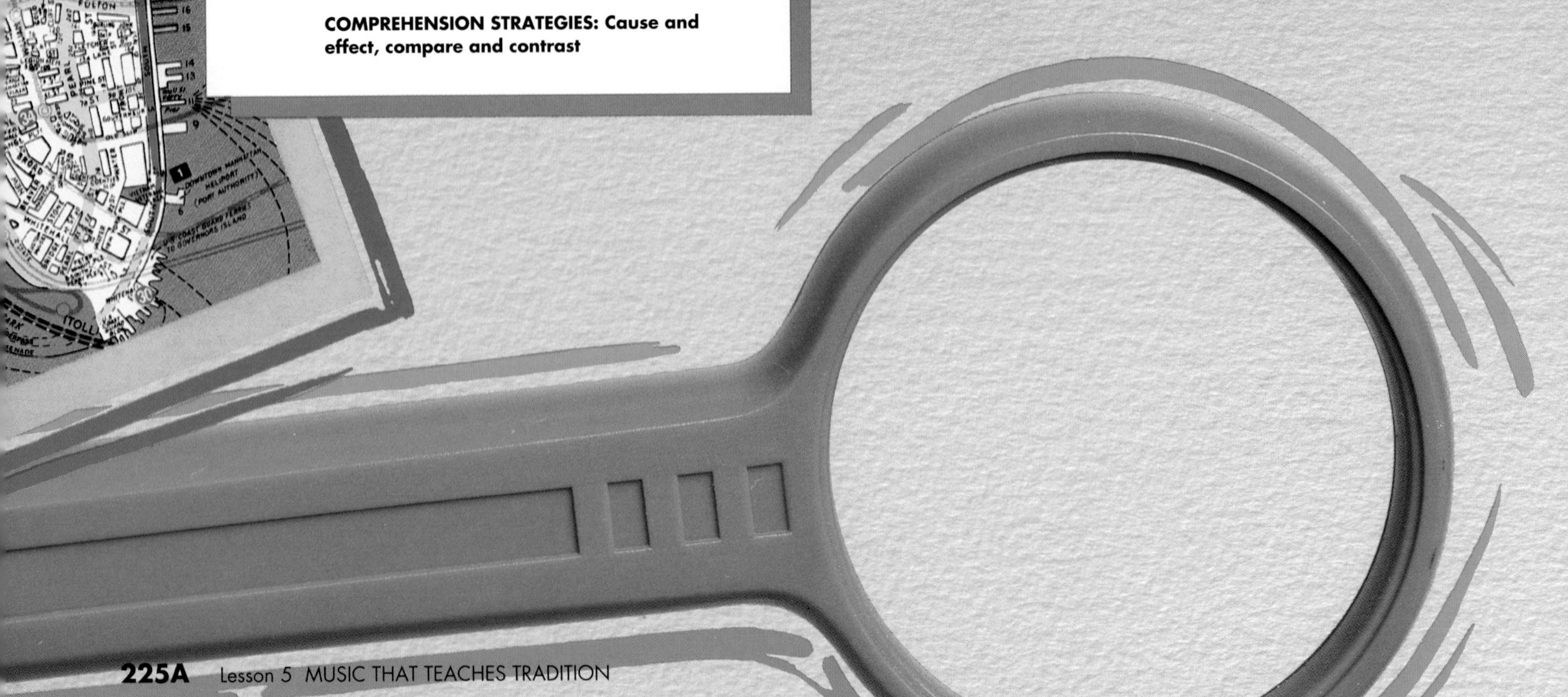

CURRICULUM

SOCIAL STUDIES

A DREAM TRIP

"Calypso"

INDIVIDUAL   **15–30 MIN**

MATERIALS: world map, globe; optional—reference books

Have students think about a "dream" trip, where in the world they would want most to visit if they had the *Calypso*, a plane, or any other means of transportation to take them there.

Have them use a map or globe to determine their route from their hometown to their destination. (By plane, they may need to change flights at a hub—such as, Chicago, Dallas, New York, or Boston.) As part of their "dream trip," they might want to visit places along the way. They might want to use reference texts to help them find sites of interest based on the places they will pass on the routes.

Have students write a description of their dream trip, including the details of the route they are taking. Have them explain why this trip is important to them.

COMPREHENSION STRATEGIES: Sequencing, expressing points of view

LANGUAGE ARTS

IMAGERY

"Tum-Balalaika"

INDIVIDUAL   **15–30 MIN**

The words to this song are filled with poetic images: *True love can burn, A sad heart can cry*. In less poetic terms, these images mean simply that a person is in love or is sad. Here are some other poetic images:

- My grades soared like an eagle.
- The movie was like lead.
- The TV show lasted an eternity.
- I have golden memories of that trip.

Ask students what these images mean in simple words. Then have them write a short paragraph about a favorite holiday, celebrity, family member, or a memorable day that they just spent. Ask them to add poetic images to make their descriptions come alive for the reader.

COMPREHENSION STRATEGIES: Expressing main ideas, visualizing

LESSON PLANNER

FOCUS Pitch, major and minor

OBJECTIVES

OBJECTIVE 1 Signal upon hearing music change from minor to major

OBJECTIVE 2 Signal to indicate if a song is major or minor

MATERIALS

Recordings
Aquaqua	CD5:15
Recorded Lesson: "Slavonic Dance No. 8" Theme	CD5:18
Listening: Slavonic Dance Op. 46, No. 8 (excerpt) by A. Dvořák	CD5:19
Wade in the Water	CD5:20

Resources
Listening Map Transparency T • 9 (Slavonic Dance No. 8)
Recorder Master R • 25 (pitches D E G A B)

Technology Music with MIDI: Wade in the Water

▶ = **BASIC PROGRAM**

Dancing to Major and Minor

Most music is in either major or minor. Sometimes it's interesting to hear both in one piece.

SPOTLIGHT ON
Antonin Dvořák

Antonin Dvořák (1841–1904) was the son of a Czech innkeeper and butcher, who had hoped his son would stay in the business. Antonin played violin at the inn, and at 16 began to study music seriously. He learned to sing and to play violin, viola, organ, and piano. He later worked as a church organist and composer. Dvořák included Czech folk melodies in his pieces, and his tuneful, rhythmic music is still very popular.

LISTENING
Slavonic Dance Op. 46, No. 8
(excerpt)

by Antonin Dvořák

SIGNAL with your hand each time you hear a shift between minor and major.

226

MEETING **INDIVIDUAL** NEEDS

ALTERNATE TEACHING STRATEGY

OBJECTIVE 1 Play the pattern G' D B♭ G on the resonator bells, labeling it minor, then play G' D B♮ G and label it major. Divide the class into two sides, one for major, one for minor. Switch between repeating the minor pattern and repeating the major pattern, and have students stand only when they hear their assigned pattern.

BIOGRAPHY: *Antonin Dvořák*

The first Czech (chɛk) composer to become internationally famous, Antonin Dvořák (**an** tɔn in **dvɔr** ʒak),

1841–1904, loved Czech dance and folk melodies, and he infused them into his music. Dvořák was one of the founders of the Czech nationalist movement, which combined universal musical elements with Czech melodies and rhythms. Dvořák also loved the music of the United States. From 1892 to 1895, he lived and taught in New York. There he wrote one of his greatest works, *The New World Symphony.* While Dvořák continued using Slavic melodies, parts of the symphony also show the influence of African American spirituals and Native American music.

LISTENING MAP *What does the tempo marking tell you?*
The speed of the beat will be fast.

A Allegro
f
4 beats

f
4 beats

B :||
p
16 beats

A
f

C
p
16 beats

B
$fpfpfpfp$
16 beats

D
$p \longrightarrow f$
24 beats

CODA

A
$f \longrightarrow pp$
12 beats

Unit 5 *Music with a Message* **227**

1 GET SET

"Let's sing 'Aquaqua.'" **CD5:15** (page 219)
Have students:

▶ • Tell if the song is in major or minor. (major)

"We will play the game for 'Aquaqua' at the end of the lesson after we listen for major and minor in other songs."

2 DEVELOP

1. Introduce Slavonic Dance Op. 46, No. 8 (excerpt). Identify major and minor phrases. Have students:

▶ • Read page 226.

**OBJECTIVE 1 Informal Assessment
Recorded Lesson** CD5:18

▶ • Listen to "'Slavonic Dance No. 8' Theme," and use an open hand to signal hearing minor and a closed fist for major. (minor/major/minor/major)

▶ • Listen to a longer excerpt **CD5:19** and follow the listening map. (Optional: Use **Listening Map Transparency T • 9.**)

PLAYING INSTRUMENTS: *Keyboards*

Identify G major and G minor chords at the keyboard. (G B D, G B♭ D) Have a student choose and play a sequence of four chords and have others signal, name, or write the sequence.

MOVEMENT: *Slavonic Dance Op. 46, No. 8* 🎵

Have students hold their hands several inches apart, and experiment with ways to move their hands and arms as if they were painting train tracks in the air. The air pathways of the two hands must be parallel. Next have them experiment

with contrary ways to move their hands and arms. (For example, one arm moves up while the other moves down, or arms move toward and away from each other.) The contrary motions must in some way be opposite of each other, not just different from one another.

Now have each student decide on one way to show parallel and one way to show contrary motion. As Slavonic Dance plays, they should move arms in parallel motion during minor, then in contrary motion during major. For further practice, have partners work together to show parallel and contrary arm movements.

Unit 5 MUSIC WITH A MESSAGE **227**

continued from previous page

3 APPLY

Introduce "Wade in the Water" CD5:20.
Identify major or minor. Have students:

▶ • Read about the song, then listen to it.

OBJECTIVE 2 Informal Assessment
• Listen again and signal whether the song is major or minor by showing the corresponding hand gesture (minor, open hand).

▶ • Learn the song.

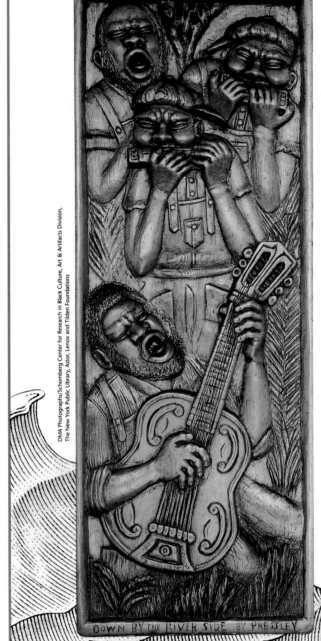

DMA Photographs/Schomburg Center for Research in Black Culture, Art & Artifacts Division, The New York Public Library, Astor, Lenox and Tilden Foundations

228 DANCING TO MAJOR AND MINOR

A SPIRITUAL
The words of the song "Wade in the Water" refer to a Biblical story about the Pool of Bethesda, a pond in Jerusalem. Sometimes the water's surface ripples and moves, and this was called "troubling the waters."

People believed that the pool was brushed by the wing of an angel, and that the first person to step into the water after it moved would be healed of diseases and ailments. Many who were in poor health gathered there to wait for the water to be "troubled."

DOWN BY THE RIVERSIDE
The musicians in this 1966 wood carving by Daniel Pressley are singing and playing traditional instruments, the guitar and the harmonica. The texture and depth of the carving add to the sense of energy and feeling in their music.

MEETING **INDIVIDUAL** NEEDS

ALTERNATE TEACHING STRATEGY

OBJECTIVE 2 Play phrases of songs students know, and help them label each example major or minor. ("Take Time in Life," "I Don't Care If the Rain Comes Down"—major; "Tum-Balalaika," "Mongolian Night Song"—minor.) Then play the phrases again in a different order, and have students signal major or minor (closed or open hand).

IMPROVISATION: *"Wade in the Water"*

Set up barred instruments or resonator bells in *la* pentatonic: D F G A C D' (Note: *la* pentatonic looks exactly like

F pentatonic on the instruments. The minor sound results when the improvisation begins and ends on *la*, or D in this case.) Have students:

1. Find the song's solo sections. (Measures 9–10, 13–14)

2. Substitute the words and melodies in these measures with the rhythm of the words played (or sung with neutral syllables) on any of the pitches provided, ending on D or D'. (In Lesson 8, students will sing improvised melodies with the words.)

LISTEN to the song. Does it sound major or minor?

Pentatonic

m, s, l, d r m s l

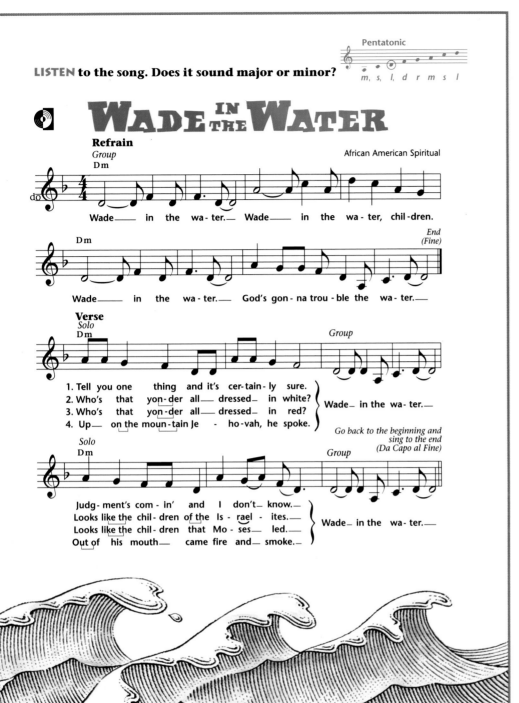

WADE IN THE WATER

Refrain
Group

African American Spiritual

Dm

do

Wade— in the wa-ter.— Wade— in the wa-ter, chil-dren.

Dm

End (Fine)

Wade— in the wa-ter.— God's gon-na trou-ble the wa-ter.—

Verse
Solo
Dm

Group

1. Tell you one thing and it's cer-tain-ly sure.
2. Who's that yon-der all— dressed— in white?
3. Who's that yon-der all— dressed— in red?
4. Up— on the moun-tain Je - ho-vah, he spoke.

Wade— in the wa-ter.—

Go back to the beginning and sing to the end (Da Capo al Fine)

Solo
Dm

Group

Judg-ment's com-in' and I don't— know.—
Looks like the chil-dren of the Is - rael - ites.—
Looks like the chil-dren that Mo - ses led.—
Out of his mouth— came fire and— smoke.—

Wade— in the wa-ter.—

Unit 5 *Music with a Message* 229

PLAYING INSTRUMENTS: *Orff*

Accompany the refrain of "Wade in the Water" with these ostinatos.

tambourine

clap

conga

rim   bass tone

AM   AX

BIOGRAPHY: *Daniel Pressley*

VISUAL ARTS

Born in Wasamasaw, South Carolina, Daniel Pressley (1918–1971) was the son of a farmer. He became interested in art at a very young age. By the time he was seven he had begun to whittle wood, like his grandfather, whom he had never known. He never studied art of any kind and called his work folk art. His carvings frequently feature music and musicians.

---

4 CLOSE

"Let's recall the songs we sang today, and whether they were in major or minor." ("Aquaqua," major; "Wade in the Water," minor) "Now let's sing 'Aquaqua' and play the game." Have students:

▸ • Play the game for "Aquaqua" on page 220.

LESSON SUMMARY

Informal Assessment In this lesson, students:

OBJECTIVE 1 Changed hand motions to signal shifts between minor and major while listening to Slavonic Dance Op. 46, No. 8.

OBJECTIVE 2 Signaled to indicate that "Wade in the Water" is in minor.

National Standards for Music Education
2a Play instruments with accurate pitch and rhythm.
2b Perform easy patterns on various classroom instruments.
2e Perform in instrumental groups, responding to the conductor.
3a Improvise "answers" to given phrases.

MORE MUSIC: Reinforcement

"Down by the Riverside," page 338 (African American spiritual)

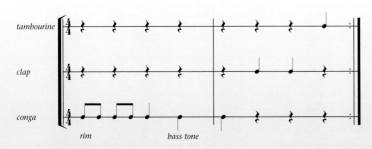

RELATED ARTS MOVEMENT THEATER VISUAL ARTS

LESSON PLANNER

FOCUS Duration, dotted quarter-eighth
rhythm (♩. ♪)

OBJECTIVES
OBJECTIVE 1 Clap a pattern including the
dotted quarter-eighth rhythm when it
occurs in a song (tested)

OBJECTIVE 2 Clap a phrase from notation
that includes dotted rhythm patterns
(tested)

MATERIALS
Recordings

Recorded Lesson: Dotted Rhythms	CD5:21
Calypso	CD5:6
Take Time in Life	CD5:3
Tum-Balalaika	CD5:7
Music Alone Shall Live (Himmel und Erde)	CD5:22
Recorded Lesson: Pronunciation for "Music Alone Shall Live"	CD5:23
Listening: Galliard by T. Susato	CD5:24

Instruments unpitched instruments

Resources
Recorder Master R • 26 (pitches
D E G A B)
Musical Instruments Master—recorders

▶ = **BASIC PROGRAM**

D·O·T·T·E·D
Rhythms Return

Name a song you know for each picture.

CLAP the rhythm and match it to a phrase from one
of the songs. *Calypso*

Take Time in Life

Tum-Balalaika

MEETING **INDIVIDUAL** NEEDS

ALTERNATE TEACHING STRATEGY

OBJECTIVE 1 Play three-beat rhythm patterns in ¾ on a
hand drum. Play one measure, repeat it, then play three
quarter notes on the rim before continuing with another
rhythm pattern. Vary the rhythms and include the dotted
rhythm pattern ♩ ♪ ♩ often. Have students step with
the beat. When they hear the dotted rhythm pattern, they
should freeze, then clap the rhythm with the drum on its
repeat.

PLAYING INSTRUMENTS: *Orff*

Add this ostinato to "Music Alone Shall Live." When performing in unison, add a triangle playing the dotted rhythm
pattern on each *musica*. Use different unpitched instruments on *musica* with each voice of the canon.

Singing is an important part of German culture, and songs such as this canon are traditional favorites.

Find the rhythm that is always sung with the word *Musica*.

TAP or play this rhythm each time you sing it.

Music Alone Shall Live

Himmel und Erde

German Round
Words Adapted by MMH

German: Him - mel und Er - de müss - en ver - gehn;
Pronunciation: hɪ mǝl ʊnt ɛr dǝ mü sǝn fɛr gen
English: All things will per - ish be - neath the sky;

a - ber die Mu - si - ca, a - ber die Mu - si - ca,
a bǝr di mu zi ka a bǝr di mu zi ka
Mu - sic a - lone shall live, Mu - sic a - lone shall live,

a - ber die Mu - si - ca blei - bet be - stehn.
a bǝr di mu zi ka blaɪ bǝt bǝ shten
Mu - sic a - lone shall live, nev - er to die.

F major

s, l, t, d r m f s l

Calypso

"Echo these rhythms with the dotted quarter and eighth note pattern." Have students:

Recorded Lesson CD5:21
▶ • Listen to "Dotted Rhythms," and pat and clap four-measure phrases in ¾ that include the dotted quarter and eighth pattern.

"Today you'll learn more about the dotted quarter and eighth note rhythm pattern."

2 DEVELOP

1. Review "Calypso" CD5:16 (p. 208), "Take Time in Life" CD5:3 (p. 206), and "Tum-Balalaika" CD5:7 (p. 210). Identify a song from rhythm notation. Have students:

▶ • Name the songs suggested by the pictures on page 230. Clap the first phrase of each song.

• Clap the pattern shown and identify it as a rhythm from "Calypso." Turn to page 208 and confirm their answers.

• Sing the song, clapping the rhythm of the first phrase.

2. Introduce "Music Alone Shall Live" CD5:22. Identify words with the dotted rhythm pattern ♩. ♪ ♩
Have students:

▶ • Read about the song.

Recorded Lesson CD5:23
▶ • Listen to "Pronunciation for 'Music Alone Shall Live.'"

• Determine that *musica* is sung with the dotted rhythm pattern.

OBJECTIVE 1 Informal Assessment
• Sing the song, clapping or playing unpitched instruments each time the dotted rhythm pattern occurs. (*Erde, musica*)

• Add B and C sections, naming places where music "lives." (See *Enrichment* below.)

• Review the places and tell which, if any, were spoken with the dotted rhythm pattern.

ENRICHMENT: *B and C Sections*

1. Have students list places on the board (for example, Africa, Germany, Sweden, Minnesota, Iowa, Canada) and identify which can be spoken with the dotted rhythm pattern.

2. Have the class perform an ostinato of pat-pat-pat, clap-clap-clap with the beat in ¾ and practice saying a place-name of their choice, fitting the word into the time span of three beats as they pat and clap.

3. Form a circle, then create a rondo (A B A C A): A section—sing the song, maintaining the body-percussion pattern throughout. B section—students 1–6 each take turns performing their chosen places on the three pats, resting during the three claps. A section—sing the song again. C section—six new students perform their chosen places in the same way. A section—sing the song. (The rondo may continue until all students have had a turn.)

PRONUNCIATION: *"Music Alone Shall Live"*

ɑ f<u>a</u>ther	e ch<u>a</u>otic	ɛ p<u>e</u>t	i b<u>ee</u>	ɪ <u>i</u>t
u m<u>oo</u>n	ʊ p<u>u</u>t	ǝ <u>a</u>go	ɾ flipped r
ü lips form [u] and say [i]	ʊ̈ lips form [ʊ] and say [ɪ]

continued from previous page

3 APPLY

Introduce "Galliard" CD5:24. Read the rhythm of the theme. Have students:

▶ • Read about the galliard (gǽl yərd).

OBJECTIVE 2 Informal Assessment
• Clap the theme of the A section.

▶ • Listen to the piece and count the number of times the two-measure notated pattern is heard. (six)

▶ • Read about the instrumentation.

▶ • Listen again and perform the basic galliard step. (See *Movement* on the bottom of page 233.)

 Galliard *by Tielman Susato*

LISTENING

The galliard, an athletic and energetic dance, was one of the most popular dances in European courts during the 1500s. It was the only court dance for which the men removed their hats–which otherwise would have fallen off!

CLAP the rhythm of the A section of "Galliard." Which part is the same as the rhythm of the words *aber die Musica?* Measures 1–2

LISTEN to all of "Galliard" to hear how many times this rhythm is played in the melody: six times

Boy Playing Flute by Judith Leyster. Statens Konstmuseer, Stockholm, Sweden

BOY PLAYING FLUTE
Judith Leyster painted this around 1630. The boy is playing a kind of flute which was played either to the right or to the left. On the wall are a Baroque violin and bow and a recorder.

232 DOTTED RHYTHMS RETURN

MEETING **INDIVIDUAL** NEEDS

ALTERNATE TEACHING STRATEGY

OBJECTIVE 2 Have students identify and list each one-measure rhythm pattern that occurs in the "Galliard" A section. Speak *aber die* for ♩ ♩ ♩, *musica* for ♩ ♪ ♩, and *Erde* for ♩ ♩ Practice saying each word-rhythm pattern as you point back and forth among the examples. Then say and clap the rhythmic theme of "Galliard."

BIOGRAPHY: *Tielman Susato*

The German composer Tielman Susato (**til** mɑn su **zɑ** to) lived from about 1500 to 1563. When he was around 30, he moved to Antwerp (**æn** twərp), where he served as a town trumpeter for 20 years. Besides composing and performing, he established a successful music-printing business. The firm published over 50 volumes of church music, songs, and other compositions.

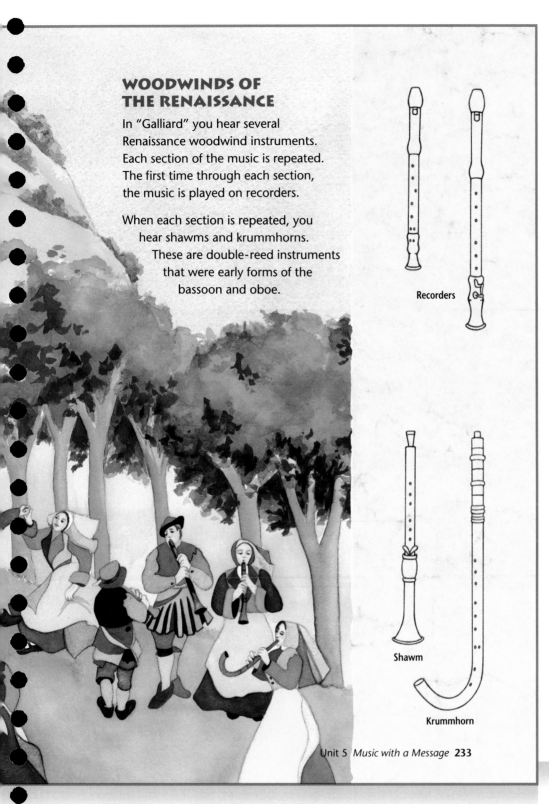

WOODWINDS OF THE RENAISSANCE

In "Galliard" you hear several Renaissance woodwind instruments. Each section of the music is repeated. The first time through each section, the music is played on recorders.

When each section is repeated, you hear shawms and krummhorns. These are double-reed instruments that were early forms of the bassoon and oboe.

Recorders

Shawm

Krummhorn

Unit 5 *Music with a Message* **233**

4 CLOSE

"What was the rhythm pattern we found in all of the music today?" (♩. ♪ ♪) Have students:

▶ • Divide into two groups and listen to "Galliard" again.

▶ • Perform the dance step only when they hear the recorders.

▶ • Perform it only when they hear the double reeds.

MORE MUSIC: Reinforcement

"Waltzing with Bears," page 242 (dotted-rhythm pattern)

"Las mañanitas," page 244 (¾ meter and dotted rhythms)

"America," page 302 (¾ meter and dotted rhythms; patriotic)

MOVEMENT: *"Galliard"*

The galliard originated in Italy, spread throughout Europe, and became a leading court dance of the Renaissance. When dancing the galliard solo, men improvised to show off their athletic abilities. They did jumps, pirouettes, and double turns that only professional dancers perform today. Queen Elizabeth I of England is said to have danced several galliards every morning as a wake-up exercise. This would have been a healthy habit, since the energetic kicks and leaps would have provided good aerobic exercise and increased both flexibility and strength of feet and legs. Dancing can be healthy exercise today as well.

Have students perform this rhythm with their hands first:

Now have students try the step, moving through shared space. (In the final form, dancers kick the free leg forward with each step so that they actually leap off the ground in scissors-kick fashion.)

LESSON PLANNER

FOCUS Pitch—*ti*, major, minor

OBJECTIVE
OBJECTIVE 1 Sing improvised melodic phrases

MATERIALS
Recordings
Hei Tama Tu Tama (steady tempo)　CD5:8
Hei Tama Tu Tama (changing tempo)　CD5:14
Wade in the Water　CD5:20
Wade in the Water (improvisation)　CD5:25

Instruments resonator bells and/or keyboard

Resources
Resource Master 5 • 6 (practice)
Resource Master 5 • 7 (practice)

VOCABULARY
minor scale

▶ = **BASIC PROGRAM**

A MAJOR

"Hei Tama Tu Tama" sounds major. What is its tonal center?
do, F
When a song has *do* as its tonal center, it is in major. "Hei Tama Tu Tama" is in F major. The pitches in this song come from the F major scale.

PLAY and sing a major scale, beginning on F.

do re mi fa so la ti do'

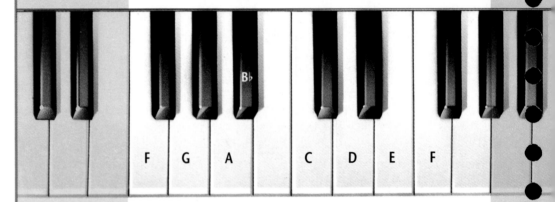

When F is *do*, there is a flat on the B line of the staff. This flat tells you to use B flat (B♭) instead of B in this song. Notice the black key (B♭) that is used in the F major scale.

234

MEETING **INDIVIDUAL** NEEDS

SPECIAL LEARNERS: *Keyboard*

To help students accompany, play solo, and improvise at the keyboard, use as many cues as necessary to identify the keyboard notes. Have students accompany by playing the same notes (possibly using quarter notes) as those for the solo sections of the verse. (A G F D) Have them use right-hand fingering (5, 4, 3, 1) and keep the hand in position, ready to play each repetition. If successful, have the student play this as a solo, or with a partner who plays the same pattern in a different octave. Students may improvise different melodies with the pitches, using the same rhythm.

MULTICULTURAL PERSPECTIVES: *Messages*

Enslaved Africans sent hidden messages through songs. The spiritual "Wade in the Water" sometimes functioned as a warning. If enslaved people were trying to escape and their absence had been detected, their friends sang "Wade in the Water" loud enough so that enslaved people on other plantations could hear. These people then passed the song along, so that the runaways might hear it and know that they were being tracked by bloodhounds. *Wade in the water* was good advice, because then the dogs could not track their scent.

EVENT

ADD MINOR HARMONY

When a song has *la* as its tonal center, it is in minor. "Wade in the Water" is in D minor. The pitches you sing come from the D **minor scale**.

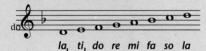

la, ti, do re mi fa so la

A scale in D minor has the same key signature as one in F major. The scale in F major begins and ends on *do*. The scale in D minor begins and ends on *la*.

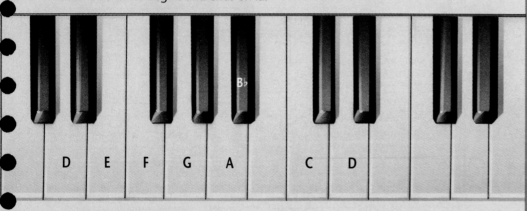

D E F G A C D

SING this harmony part with the refrain of "Wade in the Water."

Wade on chil-dren, wade_ in the wa-ter. Wade, chil - dren,   Wade on.

PLAY a minor scale beginning on D. Remember to play a B♭.

Unit 5 *Music with a Message* **235**

---

1 GET SET

"Who can remember how to count in the Maori language?" Have students:

▶ • Recall counting from 1–10 in Maori.

▶ • Sing "Hei Tama Tu Tama," page 212 (steady tempo CD5:8).

▶ • Recall that the song is major.

"Today you will find another way to tell if a song is major or minor."

2 DEVELOP

1. Learn about major with *do* as tonal center in "Hei Tama Tu Tama." Have students:

• Determine that the pitch syllables for the song are *ti, do re mi,* ending on *do*.

• Form two groups and sing the song with pitch syllables: one group sings only on *mi* and *re,* the other only on *do* and *ti,*.

• Name the tonal center of the song as *do,* then read page 234.

• Play and sing an F major scale, first with pitch syllables, then with letter names.

• Read about the key signature in F major.

• Sing the song with the body percussion pattern. (See Lesson 2, page 212, *Develop 2.* Allow students to choose whether to perform with the steady tempo or the changing tempo of the song CD5:14.)

2. Review "Wade in the Water" CD5:20 (p. 229). Learn about minor with *la* as tonal center. Have students:

▶ • Sing the song (melody only) and recall that the song is minor, then name the tonal center as *la*.

• Read about songs based on minor scales and key signatures for F major and D minor.

PLAYING INSTRUMENTS: *Pitched Instruments*

Provide students with pitched instruments and **Resource Master 5 • 6** for practice reading, singing, and playing scales in C major, F major, and G major.

SOCIAL STUDIES CONNECTION: *Fact-Finding*

When enslaved people were escaping, they often followed a secret trail of hiding places known as the Underground Railroad. Have students use encyclopedias or textbooks to create a fact sheet of interesting information about it.

ENRICHMENT: *Ostinato Pitches*

Have students work in small groups with resonator bells or other pitched instruments to derive the pitches for the ostinato. Then have them sing and play the ostinato with pitch syllables and/or letter names.

PLAYING INSTRUMENTS: *Keyboard*

Teach students to play a D minor scale and F major scale on a keyboard. Ask them to compare the pitch sets and key signatures. (They use the same pitches and key signature, but begin and end on different pitches.)

continued from previous page

3. Add a vocal ostinato. Have students:

- Learn the harmony part for the refrain. (Adjust the stereo balance control to hear the ostinato sung without the song.)

- Sing the refrain in two parts.

- Sing the entire song, adding the vocal ostinato during the refrain.

3 APPLY

Improvise with a minor pitch set in "Wade in the Water." Have students:

- Listen to "Wade in the Water" (improvisation, **CD5:25**), following the notation, thinking and tapping the rhythm of the words in Measures 1–2, 5–6 of the verses. (Note: This recording has no vocal line during Measures 1–2, 5–6 of verses.)

- Sing the texts of those measures to prepare for improvising, first all on *la,* then all on *do,* then switching back and forth between *do* and *la,* using resonator bells if needed to support the pitch.

- Listen to, then sing, the pitch set.

- Practice singing the text of the empty measures, improvising melodies using that pitch set, over D–D' (octave) half-note accompaniment (played by you or a student).

OBJECTIVE 1 Informal Assessment
- Sing the song with soloists improvising during Measures 1–2 and 5–6 of the verses.

African American Spiritual

Intro.

Dm · C · Dm

All

Wade on chil-dren, wade— in the wa-ter. Wade, chil-dren, Wade on.

Refrain

Part 1 Dm

Wade___ in the wa-ter.___ Wade___ in the

Part 2

Wade on chil-dren, wade— in the wa-ter. Wade, chil-dren,

Dm

wa-ter, chil-dren. Wade___ in the wa-ter.

Wade on. Wade on chil-dren, wade— in the wa-ter.

Dm · C · Dm · *End (Fine)*

God's gon-na trou-ble the wa-ter.___

Wade, chil - dren, Wade on.

236 A MAJOR EVENT

MEETING **INDIVIDUAL** NEEDS

ALTERNATE TEACHING STRATEGY

OBJECTIVE 1 To help students improvise, have them gradually increase the number of pitches they use from two to the complete set, adding a pitch with each verse. You and the students who are successfully improvising may model the activity and lead small groups through it. (Optional: Use **Resource Master 5 · 7** as a guide.) If necessary, sing several notes for a student to echo and alter in a call-and-response-style continuation. Not all pitches must be used, and students may support their singing with resonator bells or rhythmic clapping if they find it difficult to stay on pitch or in tempo.

PLAYING INSTRUMENTS: *Unpitched Instruments*

Have students vary the performance of "Wade in the Water" by substituting *rhythmic* improvisations on unpitched instruments in Measures 1–2 and 5–6. Encourage them to include the dotted quarter-eighth and the *short long short* rhythms they have studied.

"How can looking at the notation of a song help you decide whether or not it is major or minor?" (major if *do* is tonal center, minor if *la* is tonal center) Have students:

▶ • Sing the refrain of "Wade in the Water."

• Add the ostinato and continue it several times after the refrain is over, ending with a decrescendo.

LESSON SUMMARY

Informal Assessment In this lesson, students:

OBJECTIVE 1 Sang improvised melodic phrases with "Wade in the Water."

National Standards for Music Education
1d Sing ostinatos, partner songs, and rounds.
3c Improvise rhythmic variations and melodic embellishments.
5a Read standard note values in duple and triple meters.

MORE MUSIC: Reinforcement
"Push the Business On," page 245 (*ti*)
"Hambone," page 200 (improvisation)
"Donna, Donna," page 291 (minor)

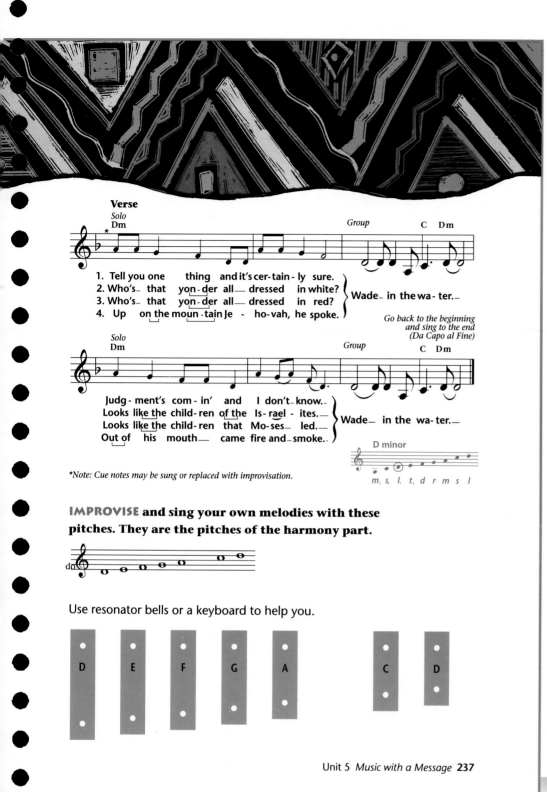

Verse

Solo
Dm

1. Tell you one thing and it's cer-tain-ly sure.
2. Who's_ that yon-der all__ dressed in white?
3. Who's_ that yon-der all__ dressed in red?
4. Up on the moun-tain Je - ho-vah, he spoke.

Group C Dm

} Wade_ in the wa-ter._

Go back to the beginning and sing to the end (Da Capo al Fine)

Solo
Dm

Judg-ment's com-in' and I don't_ know._
Looks like the child-ren of the Is-ra-el - ites._
Looks like the child-ren that Mo-ses_ led._
Out of his mouth__ came fire and_ smoke._

Group C Dm

} Wade_ in the wa-ter._

D minor

m, s, l, t, d r m s l

*Note: Cue notes may be sung or replaced with improvisation.

IMPROVISE and sing your own melodies with these pitches. They are the pitches of the harmony part.

do

Use resonator bells or a keyboard to help you.

D E F G A C D

MOVEMENT: *Choreographing "Wade in the Water"*
Students will enjoy using their knowledge of contrary and parallel motion, and images of waves and water, in choreographing this song.

1. Discuss the characteristics of waves—forward-and-back motion, surging and ebbing, repetitive, curling in and out. Have each student experiment with a movement that can be repeated over and over, simulating the motion of waves.

2. Divide the class into three groups. Group 1 will be the "waders." They develop a simple step to use to travel "through" the other groups (such as *side, close* or *forward,*

touch). Group 2 represents part of the water. They find one movement to do as a group that shows parallel motion and reflects the qualities of the water/waves. Group 3 follows the same directions as Group 2, but their movement in some way shows contrary motion.

3. When all groups have had sufficient time to practice, play "Wade in the Water" and have groups 2 and 3 begin moving when the music starts. When the singing starts, have the "waders" travel through the other two groups. For a final performance you might add silk scarves or long pieces of fabric to enhance the effect.

UNIT FIVE
LESSON 9

LESSON PLANNER

OBJECTIVES
To review songs, skills, and concepts learned in Unit 5 and to test students' ability to:
1. Identify $\frac{3}{4}$ meter
2. Read rhythms, including the dotted quarter-eighth pattern (♩. ♪) in $\frac{3}{4}$ meter

MATERIALS
Recordings
Hei Tama Tu Tama (steady tempo)	CD5:8
Tum-Balalaika	CD5:7
Take Time in Life	CD5:3
Calypso	CD5:6
Aquaqua	CD5:15
Unit 5 Assessment A	CD5:26–29
Unit 5 Assessment B	CD5:30–33

Resources
Resource Master 5 • 8 (assessment)
Resource Master 5 • 9 (assessment)
Resource Master TA • 1 (assessment)

▶ = BASIC PROGRAM

REVIEW

SONGS THAT TEACH

Think of something you learned today and how you learned it. Share that information with your neighbor.

SING the song that goes with each picture. What can each song teach you?

Hei Tama Tu Tama

238

MEETING **INDIVIDUAL** NEEDS

PROGRAM IDEA: *Some Good Advice*

This review can be enjoyed in the classroom or presented as a simple program. Additional materials from Unit 5, *Celebrations,* or the *Music Library* may be added, as well as original work from the students.

"We are often so busy with daily activities that we don't get a chance to sit back and relax or do what we want for a change." Students sing the Liberian folk song "Take Time in Life" and switch between patting with the beat and clapping the rhythm of the words.

"What could be more relaxing than to go sailing in the crystal-clear ocean?" Students close their eyes and imagine that they are out in the ocean as they sing "Calypso" CD5:6, page 208.

"Spending the day alone can be relaxing, but it's always fun to play with good friends." Students sing "Aquaqua" CD5:15, page 219, and play the circle game.

Which songs are in minor? Major?
Which songs are in ⅜ ? ¼ ?

MAKE up your own question about one
of the songs to ask your neighbor.

Tum-Balalaika

Take Time in Life

Unit 5 *Music with a Message* 239

1. Review ¼ meter, major, and *ti* with "Hei Tama Tu Tama" CD5:8 **(p. 212).** Have students:

▶ • Sing the song, patting with the strong beats, then identify the meter as ¼.

• Describe where *ti* is in relation to *do* (just below *do*) and sing the last three measures with pitch syllables.

• Determine that the song is in major.

▶ • Tell what the message of the song is. (counting in Maori)

2. Review ⅜ meter, minor, and ♩. ♪ in "Tum-Balalaika" CD5:7 **(p. 210).** Have students:

• Sing Verse 1, patting only with strong beats, then identify the meter as ⅜.

• Sing the refrain in two groups, one group patting with the beat and the other clapping the rhythm, and review the dotted quarter-eighth rhythmic pattern.

• Recall that the song is in minor.

▶ • Tell what the message of the song is. (riddles)

▶ • Sing the song with a different soloist on each phrase of the verse.

3. Review ¼ meter and ♩. ♪ in "Take Time in Life" CD5:3 **(p. 206).** Have students:

• Sing Verse 1 of the song and determine that the meter is ¼.

• Review the dotted quarter-eighth rhythm in ¼ and sing the verse while clapping the rhythm.

▶ • List some of the things the song teaches. (philosophy of life)

▶ • Perform movement as they sing the song. (See Lesson 1, page 207, *Movement: "Take Time in Life."*)

UNIT FIVE
LESSON 9

ASSESSMENTS A AND B CD5:26–33

Different recorded examples for Assessments A and B allow for two uses of the same set of questions. When appropriate, recorded examples for Assessment A use familiar musical examples with which students have worked for the given concept. The recorded examples for Assessment B use musical selections the students have not previously worked with for the concept, encouraging the application of knowledge to new material.

The pupil page is intended for those who wish to assess quickly with the whole class or in small groups. Each assessment may be used as a pretest or as a final review before presenting the written test (**Resource Master 5 • 8**).

ANSWERS		
	ASSESSMENT A	**ASSESSMENT B**
1.	a	b
2.	b	a
3.	c	a
4.	b	c

CHECK IT OUT

1. Which example is in $\frac{6}{8}$?

   a. Example 1   **b.** Example 2

2. Which example is in $\frac{3}{4}$?

   a. Example 1   **b.** Example 2

3. Which rhythm do you hear?

4. Which rhythm do you hear?

MEETING **INDIVIDUAL** NEEDS

PORTFOLIO ASSESSMENT

To evaluate student portfolios, use the Portfolio Assessment form on **Resource Master TA • 1.** See page 202B for a summary of Portfolio Opportunities in this unit.

LANGUAGE ARTS CONNECTION: *Taking Time*

Have students choose their favorite day of the week. Then have them write a short poem or song describing what they would do on that day if they could do whatever they wished.

CREATE

Playing with Threes

CREATE an accompaniment of four measures for "Tum-Balalaika." Use these rhythm patterns.

EXPERIMENT with different combinations of the rhythm patterns. Play them on tambourines or other percussion instruments.

Which combination of rhythms do you like with the song? Why?

Write

Which message from the songs in this unit meant the most to you?

Write several sentences explaining the message and what it means to you.

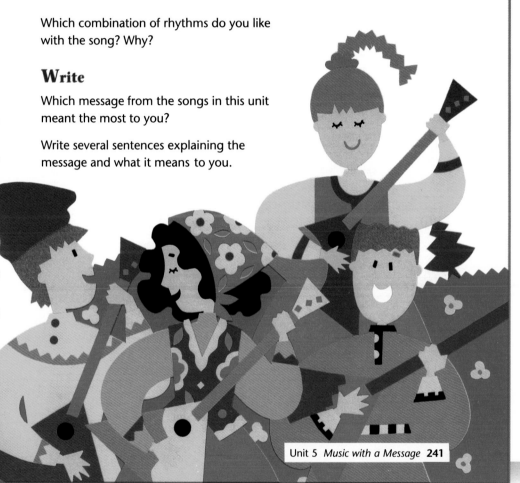

Unit 5 *Music with a Message* 241

1. Create an accompaniment. Have students:

• Follow the instructions on page 241 to create percussion accompaniments to "Tum-Balalaika." (Optional: Use **Resource Master 5 • 9** to notate accompaniment rhythms.)

2. Write an explanation. Have students:

▶ • Write several sentences as described. (Read a selected explanation to the class and sing the corresponding song.)

National Standards for Music Education
4b Create and arrange short songs and instrumental pieces.
4c Use a variety of sound sources when composing.
5d Use standard symbols to notate patterns.

RELATED ARTS MOVEMENT THEATER VISUAL ARTS

Waltzing with Bears

Unit 5 Reinforcement
⅜ meter, page 209
♩. ♪ ♩, page 233

1. Discuss the lyrics and identify ⅜ meter
CD5:34. Have students:

• Read the lyrics and describe the point of view of the narrator. (How does the narrator see Uncle Walter in Verses 1–4? How does he or she feel about Uncle Walter waltzing with bears? How does this point of view change in Verse 5?)

• Listen to the refrain, patting with the strong beats. Then describe how the beats are grouped and how this meter adds to the feeling of the song. (grouped in sets of 3, or ⅜ meter; feels like a dance, or waltz in ⅜)

• Listen to the entire song, joining in on the refrain and using their own movements to keep time with the ⅜ meter.

2. Practice dotted rhythms. Have students:

• Look at the notation and find the measures with dotted quarter-eighth rhythm patterns.

• Divide into two groups, one patting with the beat and the other softly clapping the rhythm of the refrain. Switch roles and repeat.

• Sing the entire song. (Optional: Use "Waltzing with Bears" Performance Mix **CD10:21**.)

242

MEETING **INDIVIDUAL** NEEDS

ART CONNECTION: *Illustrating Created Verses* VISUAL ARTS

Have students illustrate the scenes they imagined when they created their own verses. They may show their animal(s), relatives, and themselves. Suggest that they show how each character feels, in addition to what they are doing.

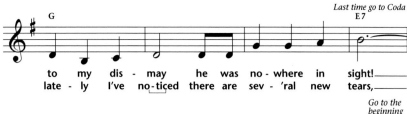

Last time go to Coda
E7

to my dis - may he was no - where in sight!____
late - ly I've no - ticed there are sev - 'ral new tears,____

Go to the
beginning
(Da Capo)

My un - cle Wal - ter goes waltz-ing at night.
My un - cle Wal - ter goes waltz-ing with bears.

Coda

____ Well, it all feels like fly - ing, there____ is no de -

Go to the beginning
and sing to the end
(Da Capo al Fine)

ny- ing, And____ now my pa - ja - mas are cov- ered with hair!

3. We told Uncle Walter that he should be good.
   And do all the things we say that he should,
   But I know he'd rather be off in the wood,
   We're afraid we will lose him, we'll lose him for good.
   Refrain

4. We said, "Uncle Walter, oh, please won't you stay,"
   And managed to keep him at home for a day,
   But the bears all barged in and they took him away,
   For the pandas demand at least one waltz a day!
   Refrain

5. Last night when the moon rose we crept down the stairs,
   He took me to dance where the bears have their lairs,
   We danced in a bear hug with nary a care, *(to Coda)*

Unit 5 *Music with a Message* **243**

3. Create lyrics. Have students:

• Form pairs or small groups.

• Choose one of their favorite animals, bear or otherwise, and create a verse for their animal after they answer these questions. Would their animal waltz, or move in a different way? Would their animal barge into their house to take an uncle or other relative away?

• Have groups share their verses as the class sings the refrain.

Las mañanitas

Unit 5 Reinforcement
¾ meter, dotted rhythms, *page 233*

1. Sing a Spanish song with dotted rhythms
CD5:35. Have students:

• Sing the traditional birthday song ("Happy Birthday") from the United States.

• Listen to "Las mañanitas," a birthday song from Latin America.

• Compare the two songs. (Both are in ¾, "Las mañanitas" has no words specifically naming the birthday or person.)

• Listen again, signaling each time the ¾ rhythm is sung.

Recorded Lesson CD5:36

• Listen to "Pronunciation for "'Las mañanitas.'"

• Sing the song. (Optional: Use "Las mañaitas" Performance Mix CD10:22.)

Las mañanitas
The Morning Song

Mexican Folk Song
English Version by MMH

Spanish: És - tas son las ma - ña - ni - tas
Pronunciation: es tas son las ma nya ni tas
English: Now we sing *las ma - ña - ni - tas,*

que can - ta - ba el Rey Da - vid,
ke kan ta βael rei ða βið
as King Da - vid long a - go

a las mu - cha - chas bo - ni - tas
a las mu cha chaz βo ni tas
sang a song to greet the morn - ing,

se las can - ta - mos a - sí:
se las kan ta mos a si
to greet the sun - light's first glow.

Des - pier - ta, mi bien, des - pier - ta,
des pyeɾ ta mi βyen des pyeɾ ta
A - wak - en, dear one, a - wak - en

mi - ra que ya a - ma - ne - ció,
mi ɾa ke ya ma ne syo
and wel - come the ros - y dawn.

244

MEETING **INDIVIDUAL** NEEDS

PRONUNCIATION: *"Las mañanitas"*

ɑ father	e chaotic	i bee	o obey
u moon	β b without lips touching		ð the
ɾ flipped r	x slightly guttural h, *Spanish* bajo		

BACKGROUND: *"Las mañanitas"*

This traditional birthday song is popular in Mexico as well as in many other Latin American countries. In the past this song was sung early in the morning to serenade whoever was celebrating a birthday. Today it is sung at birthday parties for children, as well as older people.

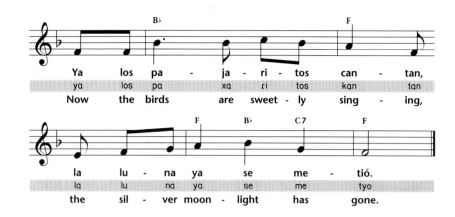

Ya los pa - ja - ri - tos can - tan,
ya los pa xa ri tos kan tan
Now the birds are sweet - ly sing - ing,

la lu - na ya se me - tió.
la lu na ya se me tyo
the sil - ver moon - light has gone.

Push the Business On

G major

s, l, t, d r m f

English Singing Game

We'll hire a horse and grab a rig; And all the world will dance a jig;

And we will do what - ev - er we can to push the busi-ness on.

To push the busi- ness on. To push the busi- ness on.

And we will do what - ev- er we can to push the busi-ness on.

Unit 5 *Music with a Message* **245**

Push the Business On

Unit 5 Reinforcement
reading pitches including low *ti, page 221*

1. Introduce the song CD5:37. Have students:

• Echo-clap eight-beat phrases in § that reflect the song's rhythmic phrases.

• Listen to the song, singing along with the motives for *push the business on.*

• Look at the notation and describe the phrase form of the song. (Phrases 2 and 4 are the same.)

• Whisper the words in rhythm while showing the melodic shape in the air with their arms.

2. Read pitches. Have students:

• Name the pitch set with syllables and notate it, then sing pitches as you point to them.

• Sing the *push the business on* motives with pitch syllables.

• Perform the song, thinking the pitch syllables silently and singing the motives aloud.

• Sing the song with pitch syllables, then with the words.

MOVEMENT: *"Push the Business On"*

Formation: partners side by side in a single circle, entire circle holding hands

Measures 1–8: Circle slides (side-gallop) counterclockwise. **Measures 9–10:** Face partner and clap partner's hands on *push, bus-, on.* **Measures 11–12:** Repeat, facing and clapping with corner. **Measures 13–16:** Swing R elbows one and a half times around, trading places with partner. This game is a progressive mixer: Everyone will have a new partner each time.

Unit 5 MUSIC WITH A MESSAGE **245**

ENCORE

LESSON LINKS

Sounds of the Oboe (15 min)

OBJECTIVE Listen to the tone color of the oboe

Reinforcement oboe, *page 217*

MATERIALS
Recording Sounds of the Oboe (listening)   CD5:38
Other
drinking straws, classroom scissors

Sounds of the Bassoon (15 min)

OBJECTIVE Listen to the tone color of the bassoon

Reinforcement bassoon, *page 217*

MATERIALS
Recording Sounds of the Bassoon (listening)   CD5:39

Singing Reeds (20 min)

OBJECTIVE Listen to excerpts from *The Nutcracker* to compare the oboe, bassoon, and English horn

Reinforcement orchestral instruments *page 71*

MATERIALS
Recording Recorded Lesson: Singing Reeds (excerpts from "Arabian Dance" from *The Nutcracker*)   CD5:40
Resources Musical Instruments Masters— oboe, bassoon, English horn

encore Singing Reeds

Have you ever held two blades of grass together with your thumbs, and blown between them? You might have heard the same sound early musicians heard thousands of years ago when they tried this.

A double-reed instrument is a wind instrument with two blades, or reeds, that vibrate together when air passes between them. These reeds may be made of cane, metal, or even plastic.

The two double-reed instruments that are the most familiar to us today are the oboe, a higher-pitched instrument, and the bassoon, a larger, lower-pitched instrument.

246

MEETING **INDIVIDUAL** NEEDS

BACKGROUND: *Oboe*

Early oboes, known as shawms, were used outdoors for sports events or military battles. They were the equivalent of modern-day loudspeakers, announcing the starting and ending of events or battles. The oboe was developed in the late 1600s in France to be used indoors by court musicians. Three sizes of the oboe were established in Europe, especially in Germany, during the 1700s, and were used in music written by composers such as Johann Sebastian Bach.

ENRICHMENT: *Making a Double-Reed Instrument*

Have students experiment with how a reed produces sounds by using a plastic beverage straw. Have students crease and flatten the top section of the straw to make a "reed." They may cut the top of the straw at an angle to create a wedge shape, then blow through it to create buzzing sounds. Have students experiment with raising the pitch by cutting off small sections at the other end of the straw. Explain that an oboist raises the pitch by uncovering holes along the tube, making the length of the uninterrupted tube shorter.

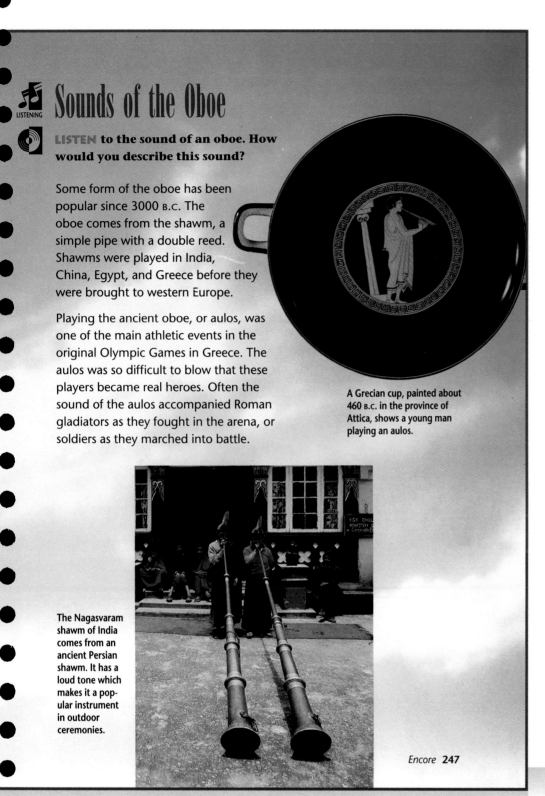

Sounds of the Oboe

LISTENING

LISTEN to the sound of an oboe. How would you describe this sound?

Some form of the oboe has been popular since 3000 B.C. The oboe comes from the shawm, a simple pipe with a double reed. Shawms were played in India, China, Egypt, and Greece before they were brought to western Europe.

Playing the ancient oboe, or aulos, was one of the main athletic events in the original Olympic Games in Greece. The aulos was so difficult to blow that these players became real heroes. Often the sound of the aulos accompanied Roman gladiators as they fought in the arena, or soldiers as they marched into battle.

A Grecian cup, painted about 460 B.C. in the province of Attica, shows a young man playing an aulos.

The Nagasvaram shawm of India comes from an ancient Persian shawm. It has a loud tone which makes it a popular instrument in outdoor ceremonies.

Encore 247

Sounds of the Oboe CD5:38

Listen to the tone color of the oboe. Have students:

• Share what they know about the oboe, then read about oboes on pages 246–247.

• Study the pictures of oboes on pages 246–249, naming the instruments and pointing to the reeds—shawms (shɔmz), aulos (aʊ los), baroque oboe, modern oboe.

• Experiment with making sounds through a double thickness of material by using a drinking straw. (See *Enrichment* on the bottom of page 246.)

• Listen to "Sounds of the Oboe" and describe the tone color of an oboe.

Use their results to predict which instruments would have a higher pitch—flute or piccolo, trumpet or trombone. (piccolo, trumpet; the shorter the length of the air column, the higher the pitch)

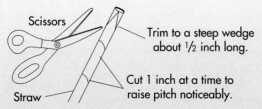

Scissors

Trim to a steep wedge about ½ inch long.

Cut 1 inch at a time to raise pitch noticeably.

Straw

ART CONNECTION: *Ancient Greek Ceramics* VISUAL ARTS

Tell students that the ancient Greeks created many vases and pots and painted them with scenes from sports, mythology, everyday life, or history. Point out the delicate lines of the drawing in this cup, and how the painted figure fits perfectly into the cup's bottom. Tell students that Greek artists idealized the human figure, drawing perfectly formed rather than realistic people. Discuss whether the person in the cup looks real or idealized. Have students cut out brown paper vase shapes and decorate them with scenes in black marker.

ENCORE

continued from previous page

Sounds of the Bassoon CD5:39

Learn about the bassoon. Have students:

• Examine the pictures of the bassoons, pointing out the reeds.

• Compare the bassoon's features with those of the oboe. (bassoon is bigger; reed placement is in central area of instrument)

• Listen to "Sounds of the Bassoon" and describe the tone color of the bassoon.

Sounds of the Bassoon

One early name for the bassoon was dulcian. Dulcian is from the Latin word dulcis, which means "soft" or "sweet." In the 1500s, the dulcian developed into the early bassoon.

LISTEN to the bassoon. Why do you think it is related to the dulcian?

248

MEETING **INDIVIDUAL** NEEDS

BACKGROUND: *Bassoon*

The bassoon is a double-reed instrument that produces low sounds. The reeds are made from thread, wire, and cane, and fit onto a special curved tube called a bocal (**bo** kəl). Like the oboe, bassoons are related to the shawm, but they are also related to two other Renaissance instruments, the curtal and dulcian (**kər** təl, **dʌl** siən). The first bassoon dates from the 1650s. Many of the early improvements made to the bassoon came from the Heckel family of Germany; modern bassoons are still made by the Heckel Company.

BACKGROUND: *English Horn*

The English horn is not English at all. The instrument is actually a big oboe with a pear-shaped bell. It is also known by the name *cor anglais* (kɔr ɑn **glē**), which means "English horn" in French. The word *anglée*, meaning "angled" or curved, was misunderstood to be *anglais* meaning "English." Most modern orchestras have one English horn player. The English horn often plays solo parts, adding a rich, deep tone color that is likely to have a haunting or plaintive effect.

The oboe and bassoon have changed many times during the past three hundred years. Extra keys have been added to make them easier to play.

COMPARE the number of keys on each instrument below.

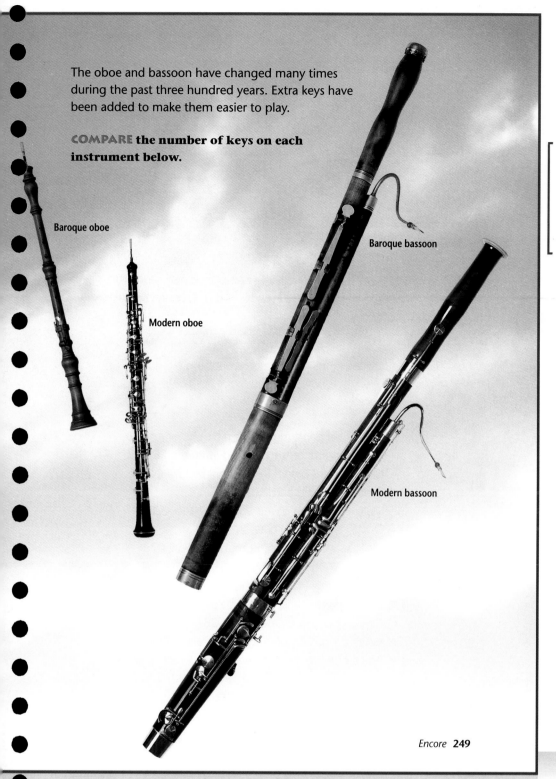

Baroque oboe

Modern oboe

Baroque bassoon

Modern bassoon

Encore **249**

Singing Reeds

Listen to excerpts from *The Nutcracker* to compare the oboe, bassoon, and English horn. Have students:

• Summarize what they have learned about the oboe and bassoon. (Both are double-reed woodwind instruments.)

Recorded Lesson CD5:40

• Listen to "Singing Reeds" and hear excerpts of "Arabian Dance" from *The Nutcracker*.

• Compare the sounds of the solo oboe and bassoon with the way they sound in the orchestra.

• Compare the tone colors of the English horn, oboe, and bassoon.

A WORLD OF CHANGE

MULTICULTURAL PERSPECTIVES

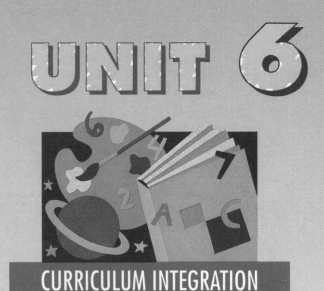

UNIT 6

CURRICULUM INTEGRATION

Through exposure to diverse materials, students develop an awareness of how people from many cultures create and participate in music. This unit includes:

African/African American
- **I Can Be,** by Anthony Q. Richardson, 254
- **Michie Banjo,** Creole Bamboula, 264
- **Vocal Ornamentation Montage,** including African American blues singer, 280

Asian/Asian American and Middle Eastern
- **Vocal Ornamentation Montage,** including Indian and Palestinian singers, 280

European/European American
- *Appalachian Spring,* by Aaron Copland, 272
- **The Cat Came Back,** American folk song, 258
- **Chiotikos,** Greek fold dance, TE 284
- **Clickbeetle,** by poet Mary Ann Hoberman, 271
- **The Court of King Carraticus,** American song, 263
- **Korobushka,** Russian folk dance, 257
- *Off Franklin or Nolensville Pike, Nashville,* by Appalachian painter Mayna Treanor Avent, 272
- **Old Joe Clark,** American folk song, 260
- **Rocks,** by writer Florence Parry Heide, 251
- **Simple Gifts,** Shaker song, 269
- **This Pretty Planet,** by Americans John Foster and Tom Chapin, 257
- *Untitled,* by American artist Keith Haring, 277
- *Variations on a American Theme,* by American composer Linda Worsley, 283

Native American
- **Vocal Ornamentation Montage,** including Hopi singer, 280

For a complete listing of materials by culture throughout the book, see the Classified Index.

Activities in this unit that promote the integration of music with other curriculum areas include:

Art
- Make clay earth models, 257B
- Make a mural of the cat's adventures, 261B
- Use different colors in identical pictures, 264
- Create greeting cards, 269B
- Make a diagram or model of a beetle, 273B
- Create a spring display, 273B
- Discuss and work with ornamentation, 278

Math
- Create paper "grid globes," 257B
- Play a grid coordinate game, 261A
- Solve a word problem using a table, 269B
- Solve and create word problems, 273A

Reading/Language Arts
- Write future autobiographies, 257A
- Write new "tall tale" verses to a song, 261B
- Write personal narratives, 269A
- Play a word clues game, 269A
- Create greeting cards with simple verses, 269B
- Use listing technique in writing a poem, 273B
- Outline and create spring displays including a poem or skit, 273B
- Discuss and write about changes, 288

Science
- Make clay earth models, 257B
- Make a diagram or model of a beetle, 273A

Social Studies
- Follow longitudinal lines around the globe, 257B

New! **UNIT OPENERS WITH THEMATIC TEACHING PROJECTS**

PLANNER

ASSESSMENT OPTIONS

Informal Performance Assessments

Informal Assessments correlated to Objectives are provided in every lesson with Alternate Strategies for reteaching. Frequent informal assessment allows for ongoing progress checks throughout the course of the unit.

Formal Assessment

An assessment form is provided on pupil page 288 and Resource Master 6•8. The questions assess student understanding of the following main unit objectives:

- Identify rhythmic augmentation
- Identify phrases in minor
- Describe changes in tempo and dynamics
- Describe how a melody is accompanied

Music Journal

Encourage students to enter thoughts about selections, projects, performances, and personal progress. Some journal opportunities include:

- Effects of dynamic changes, 256
- Expressive effects of accompaniments, TE 259
- Journal of weekly goals, TE 266
- Effects of augmentation 271
- *Think It Through,* 276
- Write, 289

Portfolio Opportunities

Update student portfolios with outcome-based materials, including written work, audiotapes, videotapes, and/or photos that represent their best work for each unit. Some portfolio opportunities in this unit include:

- Performance with chosen dynamics (audiotape, Resource Master 6•1), 256
- Cooperative Learning: planned accompaniment (audiotape), TE 259
- Sing in 3-part canon (audiotape), TE 260
- Create and perform 4-beat speech ostinatos to "Old Joe Clark" (audiotape), 261
- Performance of Orff Orchestrations (audiotape), TE 261, 265
- Playing keyboard (audiotape), TE 265, 279
- Perform Orff ostinato (audiotape), TE 266
- Write augmentations of rhythms (Resource Master 6•5), TE 270
- Create and perform unpitched version of "Clickbeetle" to show augmentation, TE 271
- Create and perform variations (audiotape, notation, Resource Master 6•7), 284
- Check It Out (formal assessment), 288; Resource Master 6•8
- Portfolio Assessment (Resource Masters TA•1–5), 288
- Create 289; Resource Master 6•9
- Write, 289

UNIT 6

CONCEPT

			LESSON 1 CORE p.254	LESSON 2 CORE p.258	LESSON 3 p.262
		FOCUS	Expressive qualities— tempo, dynamics	Texture, accompaniment	Tone color
		SELECTIONS	I Can Be This Pretty Planet Korobushka (listening)	The Cat Came Back This Pretty Planet Old Joe Clark	The Court of King Carraticus Michie Banjo American Theme (listening) Strings and Things (listening)
MUSICAL ELEMENTS	**CONCEPTS**	**UNIT OBJECTIVES** Bold = Tested			
EXPRESSIVE QUALITIES	Dynamics	· **Describe dynamic changes**	· **Choose, sing, and describe dynamics (Rf)** · **Identify dynamic changes (Rf)**		
	Tempo	· **Describe changes in tempo**	· **Move to beat that changes tempo (Rf)** · **Identify tempo changes (Rf)**	· Hear tempo changes	
	Articulation		· Sing legato phrases		
TONE COLOR	**Vocal/ Instrumental Tone Color**	· Identify tone color changes	· Hear Russian folk music	· Play "found" instruments · *Experiment with keyboard sound effects*	· Gesture to show 6 different tone colors · Recognize Orff instruments and orchestral families · *Play 6 tone colors*
DURATION	Beat/Meter		· Move to beat that changes tempo	· Compose and perform 4-beat ostinatos in ⅞ · *Snap, walk, make up movement to beat*	· Pat with beat · Sing song with changing meters
	Rhythm	· **Identify augmentation**	· Sing sixteenth-note patterns	· Read and make up rhythmic ostinatos	· Sing ♫♫ , ♫ , ♪ ♪
PITCH	Melody			· Accompany melody with speech ostinatos	
	Harmony		· Hear 2- and 3-part vocal harmony	· Sing 2-part vocal harmony · Sing 3-part canon · *Play Orff orchestration*	· *Play Orff orchestration and keyboard accompaniment*
	Tonality major/minor	· **Identify minor**	· Hear music in major and minor	· Sing in minor and mixolydian	
DESIGN	Texture	· **Identify types of accompaniment**		· **Identify accompaniment changes (I)** · **Accompany melody with speech ostinatos (P)** · *Plan and record song accompaniment (Rf)* · Sing 3-part canon · *Play Orff orchestration*	· **Identify tone colors of accompaniment (Rf)**
	Form/ Structure	· Identify theme and variations	· Follow notation with introduction, repeats, coda	· Sing verse, refrain, interlude, coda	· Sing cumulative song · Sing *Da Capo al Fine* · *Make up new verses to cumulative song*
CULTURAL CONTEXT	Style/ Background	· Hear and sing music from diverse cultures · Develop understanding of musical concepts using selections from diverse cultures	· Sing songs composed by Anthony Richardson, John Forster, Tom Chapin · Hear Russian folk music	· Sing American folk songs	· Sing American nonsense song · Sing Creole Bamboula · See Orff instruments

Learning Sequence: E = Explore, D = Describe, I = Identify, P = Practice, Rf = Reinforce, Rd = Read, C = Create   See also *Program Scope and Sequence*, page 402.

OVERVIEW

Italic = Meeting Individual Needs

LESSON 4 CORE p.266	LESSON 5 CORE p.270	LESSON 6 p.274	LESSON 7 p.278	LESSON 8 p.282
Pitch, major and minor	Rhythm, augmentation	Duration, meter	Pitch, ornamentation	Design, theme and variations
I Can Be Korobushka (listening) Simple Gifts	Clickbeetle (speech piece) Simple Gifts Appalachian Spring (listening)	This Pretty Planet The Court of King Carraticus	Music Alone Shall Live Fancy Musica (listening) Vocal Ornamentation Montage (listening) Old Joe Clark	The Cat Came Back American Theme (listening) Variations on an American Theme (listening) Music Alone Shall Live Chiotikos
• Sing and move to music with dynamic changes (Rf)				**• Review, choose, and sing dynamic changes (Rf)**
• Move to music with tempo changes (Rf)		• Hear ritardando		**• Review, choose, and sing tempo changes (Rf)**
• *Sing legato*	• Hear legato phrases	• Sing legato phrases		• Hear contrasting articulation
	• Learn about clarinet • Hear orchestral music • *Choose and play unpitched instruments to sound like beetles*		• Hear vocal ornamentation from various cultures	• Review tone color changes • Follow listening map with changing orchestral families • Change tone color • *Choose sound effects*
• Move with beat to show A B sections	• Tap with beat • Use rhythms in 4/4	• Move with beat in 4/4 • Compare notation, sing same song in 4/4, 6/8 • Recognize meter changes		• Review changing meters • Change meter of song • *Move with beat in 4/4 and 6/8*
• Sing ♫♫, ♫	**• Perform, read, and describe rhythmic differences (E/D)** **• Identify, perform augmented rhythm (I/P)** **• See, sing augmented phrase (Rd/Rf)** **• Move to show augmentation (Rf)** **• *Hum, write augmented rhythms (Rf)***	• Move to ♩, ♩ • *Jog ♫ and skip ♩ ♪ to show meter*	• Read graphic notation of rhythm • *Play dotted rhythms* • *Move to rhythm pattern*	**• Review augmentation (Rf)** • Change rhythm of words • *Play half-note ostinato*
• Echo-sing E major and minor scales • Sing major and minor melodies with pitch syllables	• Listen for melody and variations on it	• Sing and move to same melody in different meters	• Use graphic notation of melodic ornamentation • Sing vocal ornamentation	• Review ornamentation • Sing vocal ornamentation
• Sing in 3 parts • *Play Orff ostinato*		• Sing in 2- and 3-part canon	• *Play descant*	• Review accompaniment • Sing in 2- or 3-part canon • *Perform harmonic ostinato*
• Sing minor melodies with pitch syllables (Rf) • Recognize tonal center • Echo-sing E major and minor scales		• Sing in major	• Ornament mixolydian song	**• Review minor (Rf)** • Review major
• *Play Orff ostinato*	• *Perform in 2 groups, one augmenting rhythm*	• Sing in 2- and 3-part canon • Perform 2- and 3-part movement canon		**• Review accompaniment changes (Rf)** • Sing in 2- or 3-part canon • *Play, speak, or sing half-note ostinato*
• Move with beat to show A B sections	• Hear canon, theme and variations	• Sing in canon	• Sing refrain with ornamentation • *Perform rondo*	• Define, follow map of theme and variations • Create and perform variations on familiar song • *Dance with variations*
• Sing Shaker song	• Hear music by Aaron Copland		• Hear vocal ornamentation from various cultures	• Hear music by Linda Worsley • *Perform Greek folk dance*

UNIT 6 PLANNER

UNIT 6

SKILLS

SKILLS		LESSON 1 CORE p.254	LESSON 2 CORE p.258	LESSON 3 p.262
CREATION AND PERFORMANCE	Singing	• Choose and sing with dynamics • *Practice breath support for dynamic changes* • Sing legato phrases	• Sing 2-part vocal harmony • Sing 3-part canon • Accompany melody with speech ostinatos • *Practice articulation*	
	Playing		• *Explore keyboard sound effects* • Play "found" instruments • *Play Orff orchestration*	• *Play sound cues* • *Play metallophones, xylophones* • *Play Orff orchestration and keyboard accompaniment*
	Moving	• Move to beat that changes tempo • Learn schottische step	• *Walk and create movement to beat*	• Gesture to show 6 different tone colors
	Improvising/ Creating		• *Plan and record accompaniment to song* • Create and perform 4-beat speech ostinatos • *Create movement to beat*	• *Create new verses*
NOTATION	Reading	• Follow notation with introduction, repeats, coda	• See notation with verse, refrain, interlude, coda • Read rhythmic ostinatos	• See notation with changing meter signatures, ♫♫, ♫♪, ♪♪♪ • See *Da Capo al Fine*
	Writing		• Write new verses	
PERCEPTION AND ANALYSIS	Listening/ Describing/ Analyzing	• Identify dynamic and tempo changes • Describe expressive effects of dynamics	• Identify accompaniment changes • Compare accompaniment styles	• Distinguish 6 different tone colors • Aurally identify wooden and metallic Orff instruments

 TECHNOLOGY

SHARE THE MUSIC VIDEOS

Use videos to reinforce, extend, and enrich learning.
- Lesson 1, p. 254: Making a Music Video (pop song)
- Lesson 2, pp. 258–259: Making a Music Video (two-part singing); Creating Musical Moods (movie music)
- Lesson 3, p. 265: Sounds of Percussion (Orff instruments)
- Lesson 4, pp. 266–267: Making a Music Video (pop music composer)
- Lesson 5, p. 272 Blending Musical Styles (fusion of Shaker and 20th-century styles)
- Lesson 8, pp. 284–285: Musical Expression (expressive elements); Creating Musical Moods (musical choices)

MUSIC WITH *MIDI*

MIDI technology allows students to manipulate musical elements and make musical decisions with this song:
- Lesson 4, p. 269: Simple Gifts

MUSICTIME™

Use MusicTime to develop students' music reading and writing skills in this unit.

OVERVIEW

Italic = Meeting Individual Needs

LESSON 4 CORE p.266	LESSON 5 CORE p.270	LESSON 6 p.274	LESSON 7 p.278	LESSON 8 p.282
• Sing in 3 parts • Echo-sing E major and minor scales • Sing dynamic changes • Sing major and minor melodies with pitch syllables • *Practice singing legato*	• Chant augmented rhythm • *Hum in augmentation* • Sing phrase in augmentation	• Sing in 2- and 3-part canon • Sing same song in ¢ and 8	• Sing vocal ornamentation	• *Speak or sing half-note ostinato* • Sing in 2 parts • Sing 2- or 3-part canon • Ornament melody vocally • Change vocal tone color • Change meter and rhythm of song • Choose and sing dynamic and tempo changes
• *Play Orff ostinato* • *Play major and minor on keyboard*	• *Choose and play unpitched instruments*		• *Play descant with dotted rhythms*	• *Choose and play instrumental sound effects* • *Play half-note ostinato* • Change instrumental tone color
• Move with beat to show A B sections • Move to music with dynamic and tempo changes • *Draw curved pathways in air*	• Move to show augmentation	• Move to beat, ♩, and ♪ in ¢ • Perform 2- and 3-part movement canon • *Jog ♫ and skip ♩ ♪ to show meter*	• *Create ornamented movement patterns*	• *Move with beat* • *Perform folk dance with variations*
			• *Create ornamented movement patterns*	• Create and perform variations on familiar song
• Identify accidentals in notation • Read E major and E minor scales • *Identify songs in major, minor*	• Perform and read ♬♬, ♫, ♩, ♩ • Identify whole note	• Compare same song written in different meters • Identify meter changes in notation	• Read graphic notation of rhythm, melodic ornmentation	• Follow listening map of theme and variations with expressive qualities, orchestral families
	• *Write rhythms in augmentation*			• *Write down changes in meter, rhythm, dynamics, tempo, ornamentation, instrumentation*
• Identify tonal center, major, minor	• Describe effects of augmentation • Listen for melody and variations on it • Identify augmentation • Identify clarinet	• Identify meter, meter changes	• Distinguish 3 types of ornamentation	• Listen for variations on theme • Identify orchestral families

UNIT 6 PLANNER

MUSIC ACE™

Music Ace reinforces musical concepts and provides ear-training opportunities for students.
· Lesson 4, p. 266: Lessons 2, 4, 5, 6, & 9 (piano keyboard/pitch names); Lesson 20, 21, & 22 (sharps/flats); Lesson 24 (major scales)

NEW! MUSIC ACE 2™

Music Ace 2™ introduces basic rhythm concepts and furthers the melodic and harmonic concepts covered in Music Ace.

**UNIT
6**
THEME:
A WORLD OF CHANGE

FOCUS Music helps us experience change in many ways.

OBJECTIVE To prepare for Unit 6

MATERIALS
Rocks (poem)
Comes Once in a Lifetime   CD6:1
Comes Once in a Lifetime
(performance mix)   CD10:23

INTRODUCE THE THEME

1. Discuss the theme. "We experience changes all through our lives. As you move towards the end of the school year, you will be getting ready for a change of grade. Our unit theme, 'A World of Change,' focuses on ways the world around us can be changed, and the ways that music can change." Have students:

• Share things that never change and things that seem to change constantly. (Discuss their responses, pointing out both subtle and remarkable changes in the examples they cite.)

2. Introduce "Rocks." "Sometimes changes are small, and sometimes they are big. The poem 'Rocks' talks about a big change that happens because of many small changes over a long period of time." Have students:

• Listen as one student reads "Rocks" out loud.

• Discuss the change described in the poem.

• Listen as the same student reads the poem again and changes something about the way he or she reads it.

• Discuss the change, then try out other ways to change it. (Read it slower or faster, accent a different word.)

U N I T 6

A WORLD

250

UNIT 6 THEME PROJECTS

Through the songs in this unit, students will explore change—how we ourselves change, how things around us change, and how we can create change. Create an interactive bulletin board with the caption "The Challenge of Change." Have students add these projects to the board as they are completed.

CREATE A PERSONAL TIME LINE Discuss with the class the ideas expressed in "Comes Once in a Lifetime." (It is important to appreciate what you are experiencing in the present moment, because the past is over and the future doesn't exist yet.) Also discuss the message of "I Can Be" (page 254). (We are in charge of ourselves.) Talk about how the two songs are related: we can influence the future by what we do in the present. Have students create a time line of their lives and add a "future" section in which they write in their timeline where they would like to be in ten years. *(Lesson 1)*

ROCKS

Big rocks into pebbles
Pebbles into sand.
I really hold a million million rocks here in my hand.

— *Florence Parry Heide*

OF CHANGE

251

Meet the Poet   Florence Parry Heide (hīd), b. 1919, became a writer because of music—some of her very first writings were lyrics to go with music composed by a friend. She and her friend Sylvia Van Clief were Wisconsin homemakers who wanted to start a business. After giving up on a fudge sauce enterprise, they decided, without previous experience, to write music. Famous performers returned their first songs unopened, but they wrote some children's songs and immediately sold the first ten. Encouraged, Heide started writing children's stories, but again had no luck at first. One story was rejected 17 times before it became her first published book. Heide went on to write over 50 books, including mysteries, novels, and picture books.

PROTECT THE EARTH   With the words of "This Pretty Planet" (page 257), "Simple Gifts" (page 269), and "Garden Song" (page 290) as points of departure, discuss with students how the earth has changed as technology has developed, and what we can do about protecting the earth and keeping it clean and beautiful. Have students choose a topic related to ecology and research it through books, magazine articles, or newspapers, then create a list of suggestions for keeping the earth "green." *(Lessons 1 and 4, More Songs to Sing)*

CREATE VARIATIONS ON A VISUAL THEME   Have the class decide on a visual theme, such as a letter of the alphabet or a number; a square, circle, or other shape; a familiar object like a car; or an animal. Discuss the ways in which their "theme" can be varied, for instance in size, thickness, color, style of drawing, use of ornaments, and so on. Then have each student draw a variation on the chosen theme. *(Lessons 7 and 8)*

3. Introduce "Comes Once in a Lifetime" CD6:1.
"Listen to see if you can discover the message in the song 'Comes Once in a Lifetime.'" Have students:

• Listen to the song, following the words on pages 252–253.

• Tell what message about change is expressed. (Everyday brings something new and it is important to treasure each day for what it has to offer.)

• Listen again, singing along as they are able.

4. Set the stage for Unit 6. Have students:

• Look through the unit to find the musical changes they will be learning about. (List them on the board as they name them.)

• Sing the theme song "Comes Once in a Lifetime" again.

UNIT **6** THEME SONG

Comes Once in a Lifetime

Music by Jule Styne
Words by Betty Comden and Adolph Green

252

UNIT 6 MUSIC PROJECT:

In this project, students use tonality, augmentation, and ornamentation to demonstrate an understanding of how music can be changed. Working on each of these steps at the end of the appropriate lessons will prepare students for the "Create" activity in Lesson 9.

1 MATCH A MELODY TO RHYTHM Have students choose one of the six patterns from page 270 and clap it twice to make an eight-beat pattern. Then have them use pitches A B C D E to make up a melody for their eight-beat pattern. They should begin on A, move away from A

by using the other pitches, and return to A at the end of the eight beats. Have them notate the eight-beat rhythm on a sheet of paper, then write the letter names underneath. *(After Lesson 4)*

2 CHANGE FROM MAJOR TO MINOR Have students play their melody from the previous activity again. Then substitute C♯ for C. Have students play their melody with the changed pitch, which will make the melody major instead of minor. Talk about how this changes their melody. *(After Lesson 4)*

Who knows what it brings?_____ While the

fu-ture waits,_____ the pres-ent swings_____ from

day to day_____ In Brook - lyn or

Chi - na cross the bay._____ On - ly

once comes this par - tic - u - lar sky, On - ly
once these pre - cious hou - rs will fly, On - ly

once in a life - time to - day comes by,_____ So

Da Capo al Coda

live, live, live, to - day._____

Coda ⊕

day._____ Let's live to - day._____

B♭ major

Program Idea: Graduation Day

Have students create a simple narrative about the end of the school year, summer opportunities, and the change to Grade 5. Have them incorporate highlights from the past year in the narrative to personalize it. Suggest the following examples of topics and songs related to change:

• The world changes everyday: "Comes Once in a Lifetime" (page 252)

• You can change your life: "I Can Be" (page 254)

• The earth is ever changing: "This Pretty Planet" (page 257)

• Sometimes, change is resisted: "The Cat Came Back," "Old Joe Clark" (pages 258, 260)

• Sometimes it's better to keep things simple: "Simple Gifts" (page 269)

• One way we can change our environment is to grow a garden: "Garden Song" (page 290)

• Freedom is a change for the better: "Donna, Donna" (page 291)

CREATE AND CHANGE A MELODY

3 CREATE IN AUGMENTATION Have students review the melody they created in the previous activity. Then have them look again at the patterns on page 270, find the pattern they chose originally, and clap the other pattern on the same line. (If they chose a at first, now they clap b. If they chose b, now they clap a.) Have them identify whether they are clapping in augmentation or diminution, then have them play the new pattern. (*After Lesson 5*)

4 DISCOVER ORNAMENTATION Using the augmented version of the melody they created, have students add pitches to make the melody "fancy." They can move to a

neighboring pitch, as in the trill, or incorporate a turn using the pitches above and below a particular pitch. Have them refer to the diagrams on page 279. (*After Lesson 7*)

5 VARY THE MELODY Have students review the melody they wrote after Lesson 4 and choose one part of the rhythm to change. Then have them play their melody in both major and minor with this new rhythm. Next have them play the melody again, augmenting the new rhythm. Finally, have them play the new rhythm using pitches A B C D E F G A'. They should make sure their melody ends on the tonal center A and feels finished. (*After Lesson 8*)

UNIT SIX
LESSON 1

RELATED ARTS MOVEMENT THEATER VISUAL ARTS

LESSON PLANNER

FOCUS Expressive qualities—tempo, dynamics

OBJECTIVES
OBJECTIVE 1 Sing a song with varied dynamics to create an expressive effect (tested)
OBJECTIVE 2 Move to the beat of music that changes tempo (tested)

MATERIALS
Recordings
I Can Be   CD6:2
This Pretty Planet (4/4 unison)   CD6:3
Listening: *Korobushka*   CD6:4

Resources
Resource Master 6 • 1 (practice)
Resource Master 6 • 2 (practice)
Recorder Master R • 27 (pitches
  D E G A B)

▶ = BASIC PROGRAM

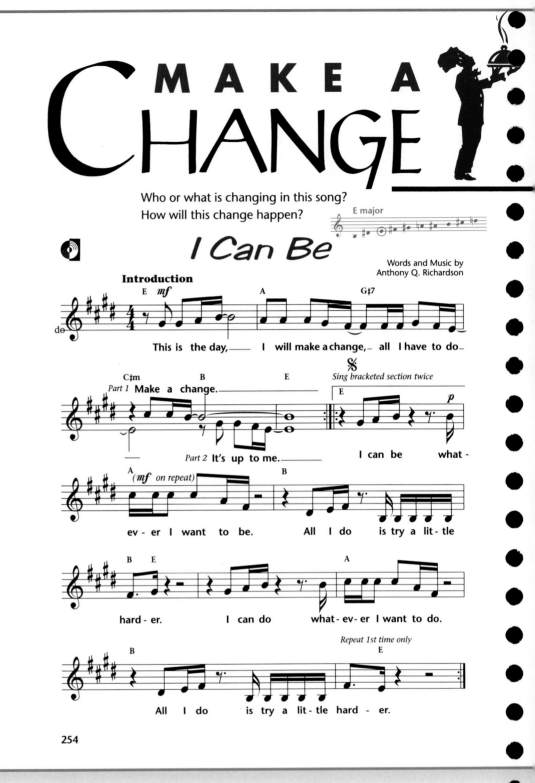

MAKE A CHANGE

Who or what is changing in this song?
How will this change happen?

E major

I Can Be

Words and Music by
Anthony Q. Richardson

254

MEETING INDIVIDUAL NEEDS

BUILDING SELF-ESTEEM: *"I Can Be"*

This song strongly suggests that a positive attitude toward education can help us achieve our goals. Use this message to begin discussing self-esteem. Encourage students to name things education can help them achieve. (interesting work, ability to understand and discuss ideas, knowledge of cultures) Then point out that nobody can expect to get the best grade or win every game all the time. What each of us can do is concentrate on what really matters to us and learn to do it as well as we can.

VOCAL DEVELOPMENT: *Dynamic Changes*

Review breath management for singing at various dynamic levels in Unit 3, page 98, *Vocal Development*. Have students maintain correct singing posture, hold an imaginary straw to their lips with one hand, and place the other hand on the abdomen below the waist. Have them sip air through the straw to a count of three and notice the abdominal muscles expanding. Exhale to the count of five, making the hissing sound: *s-s-s-s*. Repeat, sipping to the count of four and exhaling to six. Remind students to maintain this breath support as they sing dynamic changes in this unit.

1 GET SET

"How am I different today from the last time you saw me?" Have students:

▶ • Determine what is different about your appearance. (clothes, shoes)

"During this unit, you'll get to experiment with some of the ways you can make musical changes. Today, we'll study changes in tempo and dynamics."

2 DEVELOP

1. Introduce "I Can Be" CD6:2. Learn the first page. Have students:

▶ • Listen to "I Can Be" while following the notation (follow highlighted part, page 255).

▶ • Discuss the changes described in the lyrics.

▶ • Learn the first page.

2. Focus on the dynamics in "I Can Be" and sing with the change in dynamics. Have students:

▶ • Listen to the song through the repetition at the end of the first page, identify the change in dynamics, and discuss the effect of the change. (soft to loud, gives stronger emphasis to those words, brings out the feelings in the song)

▶ • Sing the first page with the change in dynamics.

Unit 6 *A World of Change* **255**

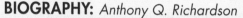

MUSIC BUILDS MATH SKILLS

Problem Solving Moving with the beat to show tempo changes reinforces the "act it out" strategy in solving a problem.

BIOGRAPHY: *Anthony Q. Richardson*

Anthony Q. Richardson (b. 1959), Memphis, Tennessee, music educator and composer needed a song about self-esteem for a school program. About six o'clock the morning of the program he had the idea for "I Can Be." Later that day he taught the song to his students and they performed it for the program.

SPECIAL LEARNERS: *Identifying Changes*

Identifying changes is difficult for many students with disabilities. Present brief, simple examples of change for each of the elements in this unit. Focus students' attention on one element at a time. For example, before students listen to the dynamic changes in "I Can Be," sing short phrases from familiar songs demonstrating the same dynamic changes that you want students to hear (for example, soft to loud). For those unable to transfer the idea to new material, present simple examples from the lesson material as well. (Sing only the section of "I Can Be" that changes from soft to loud.)

Unit 6 A WORLD OF CHANGE **255**

continued from previous page

3. Introduce "This Pretty Planet" CD6:3.
Sing with dynamics. Have students:

▶ • Listen to "This Pretty Planet" (4/4 unison) without looking at the book and discuss the meaning of the text.

▶ • Learn the song.

▶ • List ways to make the song more expressive by varying the dynamics.

OBJECTIVE 1 Informal Assessment

▶ • Try out suggestions, then choose dynamics and perform the song with them. (Optional: Mark the dynamics chosen on a transparency of **Resource Master 6 · 1.** Small groups can prepare their dynamics and perform their version for the class.)

▶ • Discuss the effect of their dynamic choices. (Singing louder makes it sound like we really mean it. Singing softer sounds sweeter.)

3 APPLY

Introduce "Korobushka" CD6:4. **Identify changes in dynamics and tempo.** Have students:

▶ • Listen to "Korobushka" and describe the dynamic changes. (Verse 1/refrain—mezzo forte throughout; Verse 2—piano on verse, crescendo first time through on refrain, decrescendo on repeat; Verse 3—same as 2)

▶ • Read about the music, then listen again to find another aspect which changes. (tempo)

▶ • Describe what happened to the tempo. (second and third time, gradual accelerando)

SING the first page with the dynamics as marked.

How do you think the change in dynamics brings out the meaning of the words?

256 MAKE A CHANGE

MEETING **INDIVIDUAL** NEEDS

ALTERNATE TEACHING STRATEGIES

OBJECTIVE 1 Review dynamics terms and markings (page 136). Discuss the lyrics and ideas of "This Pretty Planet." Have students compare the way the song sounds with dynamic changes and with only one dynamic level. (Optional: Use **Resource Master 6 · 2.**)

OBJECTIVE 2 Have students pretend to toss a beanbag from one hand to the other with the beat of "Korobushka," imitating as you or another student perform with a real beanbag, showing the tempo changes. Repeat without a leader to see if students sense the changes, then have them prac-

tice the movement for "Korobushka" as you play with the beat on a drum.

MOVEMENT

MOVEMENT: *Preparation for "Korobushka"*

Preparation: Teach the *schottische* (**shät** ɪsh) step: (Verbal Cue—*step, two, three, hop*) Step R, step L, step R, hop R, step L, step R, step L, hop L. (eight beats)

The final version is in Lesson 4, page 266.

CHOOSE dynamics that help to express the feelings in this song.

F major

s, l, t, d r m f s

THIS PRETTY PLANET

Words and Music by
John Forster and Tom Chapin

do

1
F   Gm

This pret-ty plan - et spin-ning through space.— You're a

C7   F   **2**

gar-den. You're a har-bor. You're a ho - ly place.— Gold - en

Gm   C7   F

sun go-ing down.— Gen-tle blue gi - ant, spin us a-round.—

3
F   Gm   C7   F

All through the night. Safe 'til the morn-ing light.—

LISTENING

Korobushka *Russian Folk Song*

In Russia, a korobushka is a trunk in which a peddler carries all sorts of items for sale.

LISTEN for musical changes in "Korobushka." Move to the music.

Unit 6 *A World of Change* **257**

▶ • Learn the movement. (See *Movement* on the bottom of page 256.)

OBJECTIVE 2 Informal Assessment

▶ • Perform the movement with the music, showing the changes in tempo.

4 CLOSE

"What was changed in each song today?" ("I Can Be" and "This Pretty Planet"—dynamics; "Korobushka"—dynamics and tempo) Have students:

▶ • Listen to "Korobushka" once more and show the tempo changes with movement.

LESSON SUMMARY

Informal Assessment In this lesson, students:

OBJECTIVE 1 Sang "This Pretty Planet" with varied dynamics to create an expressive effect.

OBJECTIVE 2 Moved with the beat to show tempo changes in "Korobushka."

National Standards for Music Education
5c Identify and interpret symbols and traditional terms.
6e Respond to musical characteristics through movement.

MORE MUSIC: Reinforcement
More Songs to Read, page 368 (tempo, dynamics)
"A Tragic Story," page 197 (changing dynamics and tempo)
"Garden Song," page 290 (changing dynamics)
"Erlkönig," page 385E (dynamics)

Formation: double circle of partners, inside circle facing out, outside circle facing in

A section: (Verbal Cue—*step, two, three, hop*) **Beats 1–4**—Beginning with R foot, schottische step away from the center of the circle. (Inside circle moves forward; outside circle moves backward.) **Beats 5–8**—Beginning with left foot, schottische step toward the center of the circle. (Inside circle now moves backward; outside circle moves forward.) **Beats 9–16**—Repeat Beats 1–4, then do three jumps in place.

B section: Beats 1–8—(Verbal Cue—*side, close, side, touch, side, close, side, touch*) Each partner moves R with a side R, close L, side R, touch L. Clap hands once on *touch.* Reverse. **Beats 9–16**—(Verbal Cue—*in, touch, out, touch, change places with partner*) With R foot, partners take one step toward each other, touch the L foot next to the R, then step away from each other with L foot, touching the R foot beside L. Then take four steps to exchange places (pass R shoulders). Partners will now be in the opposite circle.

Repeat of B section: Repeat entire sequence, with partners finishing in their original positions.

ACROSS the

LANGUAGE ARTS

AUTOBIOGRAPHIES

"I Can Be"

INDIVIDUAL   **15–30 MIN**

Have students write short autobiographies describing themselves in the future. Have them include the kinds of careers they would like to pursue. Have them describe how they "worked" to achieve their career goals. They should include the role that education played in achieving their goals.

Give students a chance to outline their autobiographies before writing them. Review the strategies of sorting out main ideas and building paragraphs from them.

Students can put their finished writings together in a booklet called: Our Class—Tomorrow.

COMPREHENSION STRATEGIES: Expressing main ideas, expressing points of view

MATHEMATICS

CIRCLES

"This Pretty Planet"

PAIR   **15–30 MIN**

MATERIALS: globe, strips of paper (½-inch thick), tape, string, scissors

Students cut strips of paper about ½-inch thick. They tape the strips end to end to make a strip long enough to fit around a globe at the equator. Then, taking the strip away from the globe, label it *Equator*, and tape the ends of the strip together to create a circle the size of the equator.

They repeat this procedure to create circles representing meridians of longitude. For example, they can tape strips together to match the size of the prime meridian and its corresponding 180° meridian. They repeat to create at least four circles—pairs of meridians—labeling each meridian with its degree measure and direction.

Then they create "grid globes" by fitting the meridian circles one into another and wrapping the equator around the outside. They can tape string to the North Pole of their globes and hang them as displays.

COMPREHENSION STRATEGIES: Following directions, making a model

CURRICULUM

SOCIAL STUDIES

LONGITUDE

"This Pretty Planet"

PAIR   **30 MIN OR LONGER**
MATERIALS: globe, notepad

Each pair of students "travels around the globe." First, they find their location on the globe. Then they look for (and identify the measure of) the nearest line of longitude on the globe east or west of their location. They follow that line going north—listing all the cities, landforms, bodies of water that they pass. At the North Pole, they find the corresponding line of longitude in the Eastern Hemisphere (for example, they go from 60°W to 120°E) and travel south. At the South Pole, they return to the original longitude to get "home."

They repeat their journey on other lines of longitude and compare trips. Which lines crossed more ocean than land? Which lines crossed major mountain ranges?

COMPREHENSION STRATEGIES: Compare and contrast, sequencing

ART/SCIENCE

EARTH MODEL

"This Pretty Planet"

PAIR   **30 MIN OR LONGER**
MATERIALS: clay or modeling compound of various colors, plastic knives, glue or tape; optional—cotton

Ask students to think about how Earth looks from space. Have maps and globes available so they can see positions of the continents. Have them notice that the oceans are interconnected. Have students work in pairs to make models of their planet:

- Make a ball—the size of two cupped hands—from blue clay or modeling compound.
- "Carve" and shape pieces of clay to represent the continents. The shapes need not be exact, but should show the relative size and positions of the continents. (For example, North and South America should meet at a narrow point—the Isthmus of Panama.)
- Glue or use rubber bands to attach the continents to appropriate sides of the globe.
- To create the effect of a cloud cover, students can glue puffs of cotton around the globe.

COMPREHENSION STRATEGIES: Following directions, making a model

UNIT SIX
LESSON 2

RELATED ARTS MOVEMENT THEATER VISUAL ARTS

LESSON PLANNER

FOCUS Texture, accompaniment

OBJECTIVE

OBJECTIVE 1 Sing a song with some students singing the melody and others accompanying with speech ostinatos (tested)

MATERIALS
Recordings

The Cat Came Back	CD6:5
The Cat Came Back (performance mix)	CD10:24
This Pretty Planet ($\frac{4}{4}$, unison)	CD6:3
This Pretty Planet ($\frac{4}{4}$, canon)	CD6:6
Old Joe Clark	CD6:7
Recorded Lesson: Ostinato Samples	CD6:8

Resources

Orff Orchestration O • 13 (Old Joe Clark)
Signing Master S • 4 • 6 (The Cat Came Back)

▶ = **BASIC PROGRAM**

Read the lyrics. How would you change the accompaniment with each verse?

G minor

THE CAT CAME BACK

American Folk Song
Arranged by Mary Goetze

Verse Freely

1. Old Farm-er John-son had trou-bles all his own. He
2. Farm-er John-son's neigh-bor swore he'd chase him out of sight. He

had a lit-tle cat that would-n't leave his home. He
donned his fast-est shoes and he ran with all his might. The

tried and he tried to give that cat a-way! He
cat was quick, he ran a-way and John-son's neigh-bor fell.

Refrain

gave it to a man go-ing far, far a-way.—— But the
Peo-ple came from miles a-way be-cause they heard him yell.—— But the

Part 1 Gm

cat came back—— the ver-y next day.—— The

Part 2

cat came back! We thought he was a gon-er. The

258

MEETING **INDIVIDUAL** NEEDS

PLAYING INSTRUMENTS: *Keyboards*

Use electronic keyboards to explore "sound effects" for "The Cat Came Back." Ask each student or small group to find an appropriate sound to accompany selected words or phrases (for example: ran, fell, going up in a balloon, tornado) or to go with the character or mood of each verse.

ENRICHMENT: *Music Careers*

Have students name some of their favorite television shows and hum the theme songs. Tell them to check the credits of TV shows for the music credits. Explain that writing background music and scores is an exciting career for some composers. Have them discuss favorite films and recall any of the songs or themes that were in the films. They might also discuss favorite scores and then make up Oscar winners for best score and best song.

COMPANIMENT

Gm   F   E♭   D7

cat came back!___ We thought he was a gon-er, but the

cat came back!___ We thought he was a gon-er. The

Gm   F   E♭   D7   Gm   F

cat came back,___ He just would-n't stay a-way.

cat came back,___ He would-n't stay a-way.___

Interlude *(Sing after 1st, 2nd, and 4th Refrain)*

E♭   D7   Gm   F   E♭   D7   Gm   F

Part 1

Part 2

Du- du- du-doop! Me-ow!___ Du- wa,- du-du-du-doop! Me-ow!___

Go to Coda after 4th Refrain   **Coda**

E♭   D7   Gm   F   E♭   D7   Gm

Du- wa!___ He just would-n't stay a-way. Du-du- du-doop! Yeah!

3. He gave it to a man
   going up in a balloon.
   Told him to give it
   to the man up in the moon.
   The balloon came down
   about ninety miles away.
   What happened to the man?
   I really couldn't say. *Refrain*

4. A great tornado came
   just the other day.
   The wind began to blow,
   the trees began to sway.
   Thunder struck, lightning flashed,
   darkness took the day.
   The people were so frightened,
   they knelt right down to pray. *Refrain*

259

COOPERATIVE LEARNING: *Accompaniment*

Have small groups plan and record their accompaniment
for "The Cat Came Back."

SIGNING: *"The Cat Came Back"*

Signing Master S • 4 • 6 has sign language for the refrain
of this song.

---

1 GET SET

"When you watch a movie, how do you know
that something scary or funny is going to happen?" (clues such as how the background
music sounds, how the people are acting,
where the action takes place) "Let's think of
ways that background music can affect how
you feel at a movie. For example, how does
fast music make you feel?" Have students:

▶ • List different tempos, dynamics, and other
changes and how they might be used in a
movie. (fast and loud—excited, scared; slow
and soft—sad, romantic)

"The accompaniment to a song is like background music in a movie—it can help you to
better imagine the ideas expressed in the song.
Today you're going to learn more about
accompaniments."

2 DEVELOP

1. Introduce "The Cat Came Back" CD6:5.
Focus on accompaniment. Have students:

▶ • Listen to Part I of "The Cat Came Back" to
learn the refrain melody.

▶ • Read the verses of the song and suggest
accompaniment ideas based on the lyrics of
each verse. (for example, for Verse 2—quicker
tempo, to go with running, chasing)

▶ • Listen to the song, singing Part 1 of each
refrain.

• Listen for a place where the recorded accompaniment changes. (Verse 4)

---

continued from previous page

2. Review "This Pretty Planet" (p. 257). Compare accompaniment styles and perform in canon. Have students:

▶ • Sing "This Pretty Planet." (⁴⁄₄, unison CD6:3)

▶ • Listen to the song in three-part canon (⁴⁄₄, canon CD6:6) without instrumental accompaniment and then with accompaniment.

▶ • Describe the different effect of the two accompaniment styles, instrumental and vocal canon. (Sounds more complex, richer when there are more parts; point out that in a canon the song itself can be an accompaniment.)

• Sing the song three times through in canon without instrumental accompaniment.

3 APPLY

Introduce "Old Joe Clark" CD6:7. Learn the song and create a rhythmic accompaniment. Have students:

▶ • Read about "Old Joe Clark," then listen to and learn the song.

▶ • Think of other verses for the song.

Recorded Lesson CD6:8
▶ • Listen to "Ostinato Samples," hear the examples of speech ostinatos on page 261, and perform one with Verse 1.

• Identify words or ideas in the other verses which could be used to create speech ostinatos, then create and perform a four-beat speech ostinato for each verse.

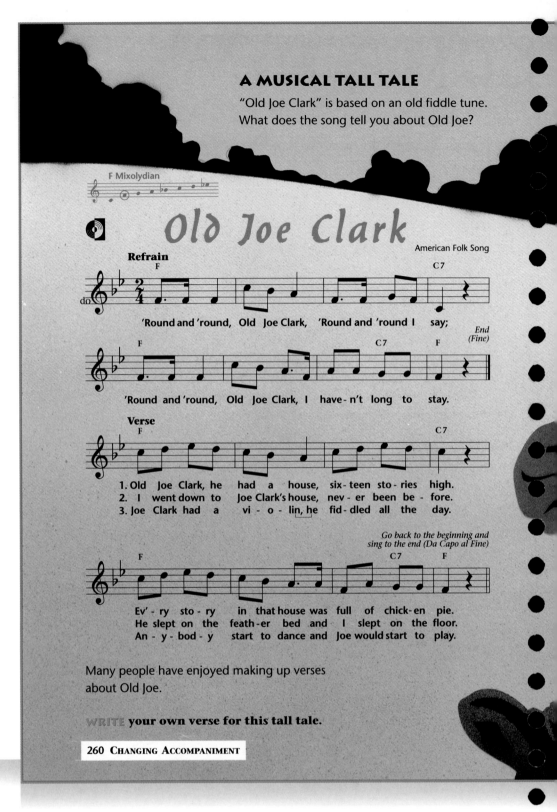

A MUSICAL TALL TALE

"Old Joe Clark" is based on an old fiddle tune. What does the song tell you about Old Joe?

Old Joe Clark

American Folk Song

Refrain

'Round and 'round, Old Joe Clark, 'Round and 'round I say;

'Round and 'round, Old Joe Clark, I have-n't long to stay.

Verse

1. Old Joe Clark, he had a house, six-teen sto-ries high.
2. I went down to Joe Clark's house, nev-er been be-fore.
3. Joe Clark had a vi-o-lin, he fid-dled all the day.

Go back to the beginning and sing to the end (Da Capo al Fine)

Ev'-ry sto-ry in that house was full of chick-en pie.
He slept on the feath-er bed and I slept on the floor.
An-y-bod-y start to dance and Joe would start to play.

Many people have enjoyed making up verses about Old Joe.

WRITE **your own verse for this tall tale.**

260 CHANGING ACCOMPANIMENT

MEETING **INDIVIDUAL** NEEDS

ALTERNATE TEACHING STRATEGY

OBJECTIVE 1 Say each ostinato while the class snaps with the beat, then write the words in four beat boxes on the board to show the duration of each sound. Have each group practice its ostinato one at a time. You might play the song without the accompaniment and have them perform the ostinato twice before each verse begins.

VOCAL DEVELOPMENT: *Diction*

Develop the use of the articulators—lips, teeth, and tip of the tongue. Have students maintain correct singing posture and breathing, then echo you as you sing the vocalise. It is important to keep the mouth in a vertical—not horizontal—oval and to avoid "chewing" the words. Sing the entire three-measure vocalise on one breath. Then sing "Old Joe Clark" with crisp, clear diction.

Repeat words with each measure. Continue up by half steps to D.

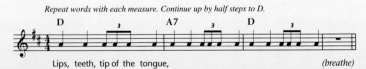

Lips, teeth, tip of the tongue, *(breathe)*

CREATE A RHYTHMIC ACCOMPANIMENT

Choose a word or idea from each verse. Create a four-beat rhythmic ostinato to accompany that verse. Here are some examples for the first verse.

$\frac{2}{4}$ Chick,   chick,   chick-en chick-en

$\frac{2}{4}$ How   high? _____ Oh my!

$\frac{2}{4}$ Bring me   some pie.

PLAY an ostinato with each verse using different combinations of sounds.

- Divide into groups. (Assign a different ostinato to each group.) Sing the song, accompanying each verse with the appropriate ostinato.
- Transfer the speech ostinato rhythms to a variety of body-percussion sounds and perform them with the song.

4 CLOSE

"Describe how we changed the songs today." (Added accompaniments—canon to "This Pretty Planet"; rhythmic speech ostinato to "Old Joe Clark") "What did you think about to create an effective accompaniment?" (the ideas in the words) Have students:

▶ • Sing "Old Joe Clark" again, transferring their speech ostinatos to make rhythmic accompaniments with sticks, pencils, or spoons.

LESSON SUMMARY

Informal Assessment In this lesson, students:

OBJECTIVE 1 Sang "Old Joe Clark" with some students singing the melody while others accompanied with speech ostinatos.

National Standards for Music Education
9b Describe how musical elements are used in world cultures.
9c Identify and describe various daily uses of music.

MORE MUSIC: Reinforcement

More Songs to Read, page 369 (accompaniment)
"A Folktale from Kenya," page 102 (accompaniment)

PLAYING INSTRUMENTS: *Unpitched*

Have students bring "found" instruments from home such as pots, pans, and spoons. Have them decide how to play each instrument and listen to its sound. Then have them find the rhyming words in "Old Joe Clark." Sing the song one time, clapping on the first set of rhyming words and patting on the second set. Transfer the first set of rhyming words to metal instruments that can be hit or tapped, transfer the second set to instruments that are scraped or plucked, and play all other words on wooden instruments.

MOVEMENT: *"Old Joe Clark"*

Formation: circles of 6–8, holding hands

Refrain: Measures 1–4—Walk with the beat, circling clockwise. **Measures 5–8**—Reverse to counterclockwise.

Verse: Have each circle create a simple dance that lasts sixteen beats. It should use only walking steps (♩ ♩) without divisions of the beat such as ♫ (Note: In Lesson 7, students will ornament their dances.)

ORFF: *"Old Joe Clark"*

See **O · 13** in *Orchestrations for Orff Instruments.*

Across the

MATHEMATICS

COORDINATE GAME

"The Cat Came Back"

PAIR   **15–30 MIN**

MATERIALS: drawing paper (or graph paper), rulers, crayons or markers

Here is a game of trying to "lose the cat." Have students prepare a game-board: draw a systematic map of a city-block area. Each block is a square, one inch by one inch. The city area is made up of 20 blocks: five rows of four blocks per row. Students should leave space between the blocks for "city streets." The map should have six "horizontal" streets: four between the rows of city blocks, one above the top row, and one below the bottom row. There should be five "vertical" streets: three between the four blocks in each row, one to the left of the first block in each row, one to the right of the last block in each row.

Students should label the vertical streets—Street 1, Street 2, etc. with numbers increasing to the right. The horizontal streets are labeled by letter— Street A, Street B, etc.—from the bottom to the top.

They label the bottom of the map *south,* the top *north,* the left edge *west,* and the right edge *east.*

The "cat" starts out at the intersection of Streets A and 1. Each player writes out four steps in which Farmer Johnson carried the cat in order to lose the cat. For example, starting at the intersection of Streets A and 1, Farmer Johnson walked:

- two blocks north,
- four blocks east,
- one block west, and
- one block north.

The two players swap directions and must locate the cat based on them. They cannot touch the map with a pencil. The first one to locate the cat wins the round. (If the directions carry the cat off the limits of the map, the player who wrote them loses the round by default.) Students can play round after round. In each case, they start at the location where the cat was found in the previous round.

COMPREHENSION STRATEGY: Using a model

CURRICULUM

ART

MURALS

"The Cat Came Back"

GROUP   **15–30 MIN**
MATERIALS: mural paper, crayons, markers

On the board or chart paper, have students list all the ways the cat came back in the song. For example, the cat:

- ran away from a man going far;
- escaped from Farmer Johnson's neighbor.

Then divide the class into groups. Give each group a large piece of mural paper. Explain to the groups that they are going to make a mural that portrays the cat's adventures.

Under each picture, they should write a caption. When the murals are finished, display them in the classroom. Have each group describe the mural.

COMPREHENSION STRATEGY: Visualizing

LANGUAGE ARTS

WRITING VERSES

"Old Joe Clark"

PAIR   **15 MIN OR LESS**
MATERIALS: drawing paper, crayons, markers

Ask students to relate the song to tall tales they may have read, such as tales of Paul Bunyan—tales filled with exaggerations and hyperboles. Have students team up in pairs to write and illustrate a tall-tale verse themselves. Example:

Old Sue Lynn, she liked to swim
Then lie in the shade.
She swam so much that she became
A beautiful mermaid.

Members of each pair can bounce ideas off each other. One student might write basic ideas down, while the other might rework the ideas to fit the rhythm of the song verse—making words rhyme at the end of each line, with one syllable per note (although several syllables can be spoken on a note if they can be spoken quickly). One member might choose to be the verse "illustrator."

When students have completed their verses, they share them with the rest of the class.

COMPREHENSION STRATEGY: Distinguishing between fact and fantasy

UNIT SIX
LESSON **3**

LESSON PLANNER

FOCUS Tone color

OBJECTIVES
OBJECTIVE 1 Signal upon hearing changes in tone color in the recorded accompaniment of the song
OBJECTIVE 2 Signal to show recognition of timbres of instrumental families in a recorded example

MATERIALS
Recordings
Recorded Lesson: Sound Cues   CD6:9
The Court of King Carraticus   CD6:10
The Court of King Carraticus
  (with sound cues)   CD6:11
Michie Banjo   CD6:12
Listening: American Theme   CD6:13

Other blank paper, 1 sheet per student

Resources
Resource Master 6 • 3 (practice)
Recorder Master R • 28 (pitches
  D E G A B)
Orff Orchestration O • 14 (Michie Banjo)
Musical Instruments Masters—glocken-
  spiel, gong, güiro/maracas, hand drum,
  tambourine, triangle, xylophone,
  strings, bass, woodwinds, percussion

▶ = **BASIC PROGRAM**

CHANGING COLORS

Each instrument pictured here
has its own special sound, or tone color.
As you listen to "The Court of King Carraticus,"
each instrument's sound will cue you to move differently. The pictures show you the motions.

PLAY the sound cue game!

vibraslap   court   drum   faces

gong   palace   triangle   noses

claves   ladies   maracas   powder

262

MEETING **INDIVIDUAL** NEEDS

EXTRA HELP: *Gestures for Sound Cues*

When each of the words below are sung, one of the instrument sounds will also be heard (on the recording with
sound cues). Have students stand up and respond to the
cues with these gestures:

court (vibraslap): sit down and stand up quickly

palace (gong): touch fingertips over head to make a "roof"

ladies (claves): brush hands down and out from hips to
show a "skirt"

faces (drum): touch palms to sides of face

noses (triangle): touch one finger to tip of nose

powder (maracas): slap hands together as if hitting a powder
puff to make the dust come out

SPECIAL LEARNERS: *Choosing Gestures*

If students have trouble matching a sound to a gesture in
"The Court of King Carraticus," give them a choice between using the gestures in their books or showing how the
instrument is played (imitate playing the vibraslap, gong,
and so on).

PERFORM the motion that goes with each tone color as you hear it.

The Court of King Carraticus

American Nonsense Song

1. Oh, the court of King Car-ra-ti-cus } is just pass-ing by;
2. Oh, the pal-ace of the court of King Car-ra-ti-cus }

Oh, the court of King Car-ra-ti-cus } is just pass-ing by;
Oh, the pal-ace of the court of King Car-ra-ti-cus }

Oh, the court of King Car-ra-ti-cus } is just pass-ing by;
Oh, the pal-ace of the court of King Car-ra-ti-cus }

Oh, the court of King Car-ra-ti-cus } is just pass-ing by.
Oh, the pal-ace of the court of King Car-ra-ti-cus }

C major
d r m s l t d'

Add one phrase on each repetition of the song.

3. ladies of the palace of the court of King Carraticus are just passing by.
4. faces of the...
5. noses of the...
6. powder on the...
7. If you want to take a photo of the...
(spoken at end)
It's too late! They just passed by!

From FIRESIDE BOOK OF FUN & GAME SONGS by Marie Winn and Alan Miller. © 1974. Reprinted by permission of the publisher, Simon & Schuster, Inc., New York.

Unit 6 *A World of Change* **263**

1 GET SET

"Listen for the different instruments on the recording." Have students:

Recorded Lesson CD6:9

▶ • Listen to "Sound Cues," and identify six different percussion sounds, then respond to each sound with the gestures shown on page 262.

"Today we'll become familiar with how a piece of music sounds when instrumental tone colors are added or changed."

2 DEVELOP

1. Introduce "The Court of King Carraticus." Learn the song and respond to tone-color cues. Have students:

▶ • Read about and listen to the song CD6:10.

▶ • Learn the song.

▶ • Listen to the song with sound cues added to each verse CD6:11.

▶ • Sing the song, performing the correct gesture each time a percussion sound is heard. (See *Extra Help* on the bottom of page 262.)

COOPERATIVE LEARNING: *Writing New Verses*

"The Court of King Carraticus" is a cumulative song. Ask students to recall other examples of cumulative songs. ("Hi! Ho! The Rattlin' Bog," "En la feria de San Juan") Then have them work in small groups to create as many new verses as they can in ten minutes. Each group then sings its verses (or, to save time, its longest verse) to the class. For fun, all the verses from each group can be added on to each other to create the "World's Longest Song."

PLAYING INSTRUMENTS: *Unpitched*

Have students play the sound cues with "The Court of King Carraticus." They may use the instruments in the book, if available, or choose others.

UNIT SIX
LESSON 3

continued from previous page

2. Introduce "Michie Banjo" CD6:12.
Explore tone colors. Have students:

▶ • Review the definition of tone color as the special sound each voice or instrument makes.

▶ • Discuss how different tone colors helped them recognize the six sound cues of "The Court of King Carraticus."

▶ • Listen to "Michie Banjo," patting with the beat and noting the tone colors of the accompaniment.

OBJECTIVE 1 Informal Assessment

▶ • Listen to the song with eyes shut and raise a hand when the tone color of the accompaniment changes. (Four times—verses and refrains alternate metallic and wooden tones.)

▶ • Look at the photograph and read about the Orff instruments, identifying which ones were played with "Michie Banjo."

▶ • Learn the song.

3 APPLY

Introduce "American Theme" CD6:13
Identify sequence of orchestral families.
Have students:

▶ • Review the families of instruments and look at the pictures of each family's members on pages 68–69. (brass, strings, percussion, woodwinds)

A RAINBOW OF PERCUSSION INSTRUMENTS

This song teases Michie Banjo for his fancy clothes. Listen for the tone colors in the accompaniment of this song.

Michie Banjo

Creole Bamboula
English Words by
Margaret Marks

Refrain

Look at Mich-ie Ban-jo, (mi shi) Fan-cy Mich-ie Ban-jo,

Strut-tin' down the street.

Verse

1. Cha-peau cocked on one side, (sha po) Mich-ie Ban-jo,
2. Dia-mond pin in his tie, Mich-ie Ban-jo,

High but-ton shoes that squeak.
Bright yel-low gloves so neat.

Walk-in' stick a-swing-in' wide, Mich-ie Ban-jo,
Trou-sers pleat-ed way up high, Mich-ie Ban-jo,

Go back to the beginning and sing to the end
(Da Capo al Fine)

Ev'-ry-thing's all com-plete.
Ev'-ry-thing's all com-plete.

264 CHANGING COLORS

MEETING **INDIVIDUAL** NEEDS

ALTERNATE TEACHING STRATEGIES

OBJECTIVE 1 To help students hear the tone colors of "Michie Banjo," adjust the stereo balance control to hear the accompaniment alone. Have some students play four F chords (F A C) on metallophones, and then have others alternate playing the same on xylophones. Have the rest of the class sit when they hear one set of tone colors and stand when they hear the other.

OBJECTIVE 2 Have students listen to "Strings and Things" to practice identifying the sound of each instrument family. Then as they listen to "Variations on an American Theme"

again, have them stand and "conduct" by facing a picture of each family or by pointing to the pictures on pages 68–69.

PRONUNCIATION: *"Michie Banjo"*

a f<u>a</u>ther   i b<u>ee</u>   o <u>o</u>bey

ART CONNECTION: *Different Colors*

Just as different tone colors change the way a melody sounds, so can different colors change a drawing. Have students use **Resource Master 6 • 3** to create their own two drawings, identical except in color.

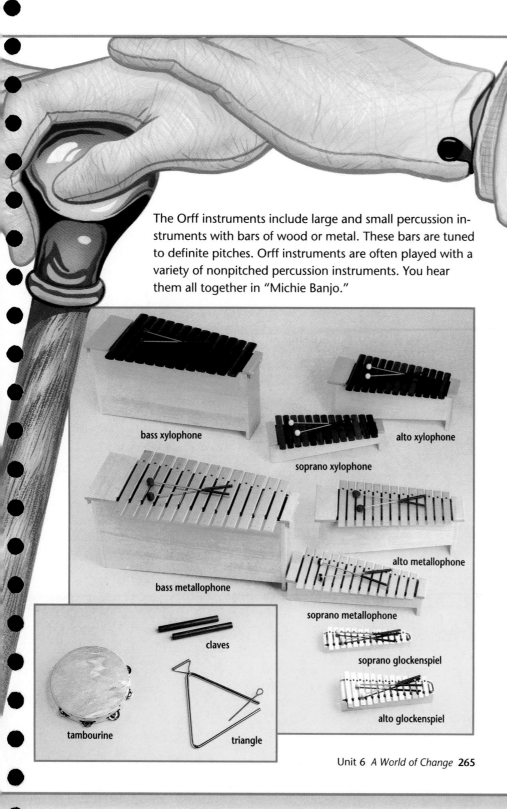

The Orff instruments include large and small percussion instruments with bars of wood or metal. These bars are tuned to definite pitches. Orff instruments are often played with a variety of nonpitched percussion instruments. You hear them all together in "Michie Banjo."

bass xylophone

alto xylophone

soprano xylophone

alto metallophone

bass metallophone

soprano metallophone

claves

soprano glockenspiel

tambourine

triangle

alto glockenspiel

Unit 6 *A World of Change* 265

▶ • Listen for the variety of instruments in "American Theme." (This is an excerpt from the introduction and theme of "Variations on an American Theme" on page 283. Point out that students will hear more than one instrument at a time.)

OBJECTIVE 2 Informal Assessment

▶ • With eyes closed, listen again to "American Theme" and pretend to play instruments they hear. (Featured instruments are, in order, flute, snare drum, trumpet, strings; strings play throughout.)

4 CLOSE

"What kind of changes were made in the music today?" (adding or changing tone colors) Have students:

• Choose and sing either "The Court of King Carraticus" or "Michie Banjo."

LESSON SUMMARY

Informal Assessment In this lesson, students:

OBJECTIVE 1 Signaled upon hearing changes in tone color in the recorded accompaniment of "Michie Banjo."

OBJECTIVE 2 Signaled to show recognition of timbres of instrumental families in "American Theme."

National Standards for Music Education
6a Identify simple musical forms by ear.
6d Identify instrumental and vocal sounds from various cultures.

MORE MUSIC: Reinforcement

"Tree Rhyme," page 345 (tone color; spring)
"Allundé, Alluia," page 376 (Orff accompaniment)
"The Shrovetide Fair," page 385G (orchestral instruments)

SPECIAL LEARNERS: *Matching Sound to Pictures*

Some students may need to identify instrument families with pictures instead of signals or names. When matching sound to pictures, the more visually different the instruments, the easier it will be. Use pictures of a violin, clarinet, trumpet, and drum, rather than entire instrumental families, or allow students to choose between two families.

ORFF: *"Michie Banjo"*

See **O · 14** in *Orchestrations for Orff Instruments*.

PLAYING INSTRUMENTS: *Keyboard*

Have two students accompany "Michie Banjo." Explore tone colors with an electronic keyboard.

*End here last time

UNIT SIX
LESSON 4

RELATED ARTS **MOVEMENT** THEATER **VISUAL ARTS**

LESSON PLANNER

FOCUS Pitch, major and minor

OBJECTIVE

OBJECTIVE 1 Sing the first seven pitches of a melody in major and minor modes, using pitch syllables (tested)

MATERIALS
Recordings
Recorded Lesson: Interview with
  Anthony Richardson   CD6:15
I Can Be   CD6:2
Recorded Lesson: "I Can Be" in
  Three   CD6:16
Korobushka   CD6:4
Recorded Lesson: Singing Scales   CD6:17
Simple Gifts   CD6:18
Recorded Lesson: Simple Shifts   CD6:19

Resources
Resource Master 6 • 4 (practice)
Recorder Master R • 29 (pitches
  E G A B C′)

Technology
Music with MIDI: Simple Gifts

VOCABULARY
natural, accidental

▶ = **BASIC PROGRAM**

A MINOR CHANGE

meet
Anthony Richardson

The composer of "I Can Be," Anthony Richardson, wrote this song for his music students at an elementary school in Memphis, Tennessee.

LISTEN as Anthony Richardson talks about why he wrote this song. Then sing "I Can Be" on page 254. Sing in three parts as shown in the score.

266

MEETING **INDIVIDUAL** NESTS

MUSIC BUILDS READING SKILLS

Listening In singing an E major and an E minor scale with pitch syllables, students will be listening critically to follow directions.

BUILDING SELF-ESTEEM: *Setting Goals*
Review the message of "I Can Be" (Lesson 1, page 255, Building Self-Esteem). Ask each student to write down a goal they can achieve in one week. When they achieve their goals, students should congratulate themselves.

PLAYING INSTRUMENTS: *Orff*
Add this ostinato to "Korobushka."

MOVEMENT: *"Korobushka"*
Review the preparation in Lesson 1, pages 256–257, *Movement*. Then add any or all of the following variations.

A sharp (♯), a flat (♭), or a **natural** (♮) sign that appears next to a pitch and is not in the key signature is called an **accidental.** The accidental changes how the pitch should be sung.

G♭ sounds a little lower than G.

G♯ sounds a little higher than G.

G♮ reminds you to sing G.

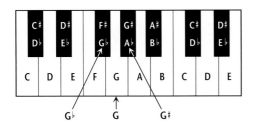

MAJOR OR MINOR?

Listen to a major scale beginning on E, then to a minor scale beginning on E.

SING each scale with the correct pitch syllables.

do re mi fa so la ti do'
E major scale

la, ti, do re mi fa so la
E minor scale

Look at "Korobushka" as you listen to it. Does its melody use the pitches of a major scale or a minor scale? How do you know? Sounds minor; tonal center is *la*; notation uses pitches from E minor scale above.

"The song 'I Can Be' was written by a music teacher for his students. Listen to find out what motivated him to write it." Have students:

▶ • Read about Anthony Richardson.

Recorded Lesson CD6:15
▶ • Listen to "Interview with Anthony Richardson" and learn about why he wrote the song.

▶ • Sing the song. **CD6:2** (See page 254.)

"Today you'll learn ways to change the pitch set of a song."

2 **DEVELOP**

1. Identify "I Can Be" as major. Have students:

• Identify *do* as the tonal center and the song as being in major.

Recorded Lesson CD6:16
• Listen to "'I Can Be' in Three," and learn the three-part section. (See page 255.)

• Read about accidentals, then locate and name accidentals in "I Can Be." (Line 7—A♯; Part 3—D♮; Coda—A♮)

• Sing the song in three parts. (Students may sing parts together when they are secure singing them separately.)

2. Label "Korobushka" CD6:4 (p. 257) as being minor. Have students:

▶ • Read about E major and minor scales.

Recorded Lesson CD6:17
▶ • Listen to "Singing Scales," and echo-sing an E major and an E minor scale with pitch syllables.

▶ • Listen to "Korobushka," then sing along with the melody with the syllable *nai*.

• Determine that it is *la*-centered and therefore a song built from a minor scale.

▶ • Perform the final version of the Russian folk dance. (See *Movement* below.)

1. A section: Partners hold hands and pump arms (alternate bending elbows) back and forth during the schottisches.

2. B section: Change each *side, close, side, touch* into *turn, two, three, touch.* Turn once around over R shoulder with a three-step turn, then touch L foot with a clap (as in preparation). Reverse to the left.

3. B section: Change to a fancier *in, touch, out, touch.* (Verbal Cue—*leap, step, step, leap, step, step*)

moving toward partner   moving away from partner

R   L R   L   R L

Final version (includes variations listed)

Formation: double circle of partners, inside circle facing out, outside circle facing in

A section: three schottische steps moving away, then toward, then away from center; three jumps in place (sixteen beats).

B section: three-step turn to the right, touch; three-step turn to the left, touch; *leap, step, step, leap, step, step;* change places with partner. Repeat.

UNIT SIX
LESSON 4

continued from previous page

3 APPLY

Introduce "Simple Gifts" CD6:18. **Experience the song in both major and minor.** Have students:

▶ • Read about the Shakers and listen to the song.

▶ • Learn the song.

• Identify the song as major with F/*do* as the tonal center.

• Sing the first seven pitches with pitch syllables.

Recorded Lesson CD6:19

▶ • Listen to "Simple Shifts" and practice singing the first seven pitches in major and in minor. (major: *so, so, do do re mi do*; minor: *mi, mi, la, la, ti, do la,*)

OBJECTIVE 1 Informal Assessment
• Listen as the first measure of the song is performed three times, singing the corresponding pitch syllable phrase to identify the mode each time. (major, minor, major)

(Optional—Use **Resource Master 6 • 4** for visual identification of songs in major and minor.)

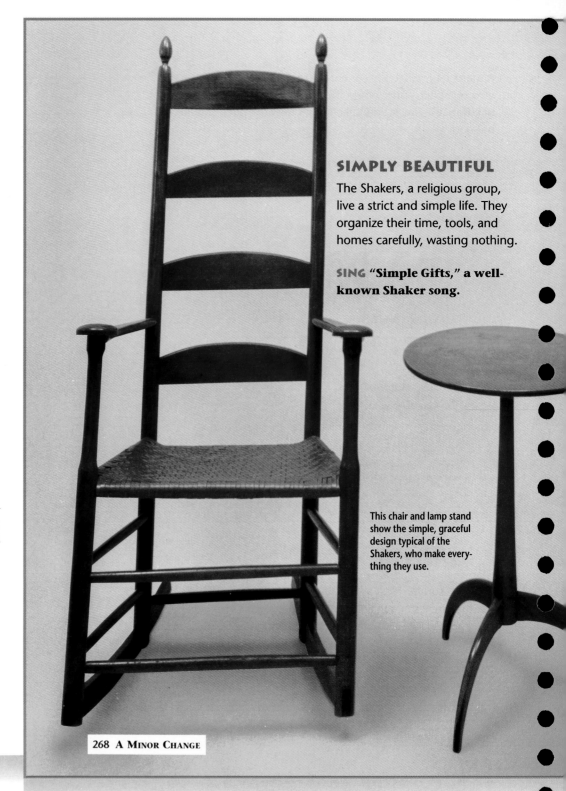

SIMPLY BEAUTIFUL

The Shakers, a religious group, live a strict and simple life. They organize their time, tools, and homes carefully, wasting nothing.

SING "Simple Gifts," a well-known Shaker song.

This chair and lamp stand show the simple, graceful design typical of the Shakers, who make everything they use.

268 A MINOR CHANGE

MEETING **INDIVIDUAL** NEEDS

ALTERNATE TEACHING STRATEGY

OBJECTIVE 1 Have students choose markers of different colors, one for major and one for minor. On a card, using one marker, they write *major* and *so so do do re mi do*. On another card, using the other marker, they write *minor* and *mi mi la la ti do la*. Have them practice singing the pitches on the cards as you play an F major or F minor chord on the autoharp or keyboard. Play the recorded lesson "Simple Shifts," stopping after each example so they can hold the appropriate card, then sing the corresponding pitch syllables with accompaniment.

VOCAL DEVELOPMENT: *Legato Style*

This vocalise will help students sing in a legato style, moving from pitch to pitch in a smooth manner.

1. Maintain correct posture and breathe deeply for singing.

2. Sustain the sound *s-s-s-s* for four beats while you play and sing the melody of each two bars of "Simple Gifts."

3. Sing each two-bar phrase of "Simple Gifts" while keeping the air flow constant as they did in Step 2.

4. Reinforce the legato movement by drawing a curved pathway in the air with their arms with each phrase.

SIMPLE GIFTS

Shaker Song

Verse

'Tis the gift to be sim-ple, 'tis the gift to be free,

'Tis the gift to come down where we ought to be.

And when we find our-selves in the place just right,

'Twill be in the val-ley of love and de-light.

Refrain

When true sim-pli-ci-ty is gained,

To bow and to bend we shan't be a-shamed.

To turn, turn will be our de-light,

Till by turn-ing, turn-ing we come 'round right.

Unit 6 *A World of Change* **269**

4 CLOSE

"What were the ways you determined whether a song was in major or minor?" (listening, singing, studying the pitches, finding the tonal center) "Let's sing 'Simple Gifts' and enjoy it once more in major."

LESSON SUMMARY

Informal Assessment In this lesson, students:

OBJECTIVE 1 Sang the first seven pitches of "Simple Gifts" in major and minor, using pitch syllables.

National Standards for Music Education
1a Sing accurately, on pitch and in rhythm.
1b Sing with appropriate dynamics, phrasing, and interpretation.
5a Read standard note values in duple and triple meters.
5b Using system, read notation in treble clef in major keys.
5c Identify and interpret symbols and traditional terms.

MORE MUSIC: Reinforcement
More Songs to Read, page 370 (minor)
"Donna, Donna," page 291 (minor)
"A Mince Pie or Pudding," page 311 (Shaker song)

MULTICULTURAL PERSPECTIVES: *Shakers* 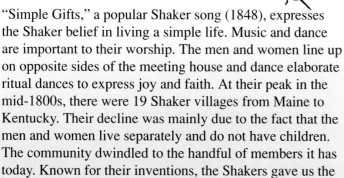 MOVEMENT

"Simple Gifts," a popular Shaker song (1848), expresses the Shaker belief in living a simple life. Music and dance are important to their worship. The men and women line up on opposite sides of the meeting house and dance elaborate ritual dances to express joy and faith. At their peak in the mid-1800s, there were 19 Shaker villages from Maine to Kentucky. Their decline was mainly due to the fact that the men and women live separately and do not have children. The community dwindled to the handful of members it has today. Known for their inventions, the Shakers gave us the first commercial washing machine. They created a short-hand way to notate music and invented a pen with a five-point nib for drawing a staff.

PLAYING INSTRUMENTS: *Keyboards*

To reinforce "Simple Gifts" in major and minor, help students play the first seven notes. Identify A♭ and play again, using A♭ instead of A. Label the two phrases as major and minor, repeat, and sing with pitch syllables.

Unit 6 A WORLD OF CHANGE **269**

ACROSS the

LANGUAGE ARTS

WORD CLUES

"Simple Gifts"

GROUP   15 MIN OR LESS

Have students play a "mystery gift" game. Working in groups, each student thinks of a "simple gift" to give to the class—either a concrete object or a wish, such as "joy." Group members write the names of their gifts on slips of paper and exchange them with members of another group.

Each student receiving a gift uses word clues to describe the gift to his/her group. The student can give four word clues, in two formats:

● "Sounds like _____"
● "It's another word for _____"

If group members name the gift on the first clue, the student gets four points—on the second clue, three points; on the third clue, two points; on the last clue, one point. Members of each group add up their points to get a group score.

COMPREHENSION STRATEGIES: Using word clues, expressing main ideas

LANGUAGE ARTS

PERSONAL NARRATIVE

"Simple Gifts"

INDIVIDUAL   15–30 MIN

The theme of this song might be summed up as: "The best things in life are free." Even the most expensive gifts may be forgotten. However, some things are beyond any price—in effect, they are free.

Have students write a paragraph on "The Best Gift I Could Ever Get," or "The Best Gift I Ever Received," or "The Best Gift I Ever Gave." The paragraph should emphasize the gift of simplicity and freedom, and the idea that the most valuable gifts are beyond any price.

Have students share their ideas by reading their finished paragraphs and/or binding them in a class book called *Simple Gifts.*

COMPREHENSION STRATEGY: Expressing points of view

CURRICULUM

LANGUAGE ARTS/ART

GREETING CARDS

"Simple Gifts"

INDIVIDUAL   **15-30 MIN**

MATERIALS: drawing paper, crayons, markers

Have students send to each other their own, personal "greetings" based on the theme of "Simple Gifts." The greetings can include wishes for happiness, joy, delight, or whatever "simple gift" one student may wish to give another. The cards can also be addressed to members of a student's family.

Have students write "simple" verses to express the gifts. Students can decorate their cards with "simple" patterns or designs.

COMPREHENSION STRATEGY: Visualizing

MATHEMATICS

PROBLEM SOLVING

"I Can Be"

GROUP   **15–30 MIN**

Have students solve a problem about a boy who is trying to be the best swimmer he can possibly be:

Sam was trying out for the swim team. He had to swim 30 laps by the end of the second week. On the first day he swam one lap; on the second day, five laps; on the third day, nine laps. He did not swim on weekends. If he kept improving as much each day, was he able to make the team at the end of two weeks? (yes)

Have groups solve the problem by making a table (with days of the week as headings) and looking for a pattern. Have groups explain their solution and write similar problems of their own for others to solve.

COMPREHENSION STRATEGY: Making a table

ACROSS THE CURRICULUM

UNIT SIX
LESSON 5

RELATED ARTS | MOVEMENT | THEATER | VISUAL ARTS |

LESSON PLANNER

FOCUS Rhythm, augmentation

OBJECTIVES
OBJECTIVE 1 Chant a speech piece, augmenting its rhythm (tested)
OBJECTIVE 2 Move to show rhythmic augmentation of the theme of a recorded example (tested)

MATERIALS
Recordings
Recorded Lesson: Augmentation   CD6:20
Speech Piece: Clickbeetle by
   M. A. Hoberman   CD6:21
Simple Gifts   CD6:18
Listening: *Appalachian Spring*
   (excerpt) by A. Copland   CD6:22

Resources
Resource Master 6 • 5 (practice)
Recorder Master R • 30 (pitches D E G A
   B C' D')
Musical Instruments Master—clarinet

VOCABULARY
whole note, augmentation, clarinet, reed

▶ = **BASIC PROGRAM**

FIND the connection between the two patterns on each line. The second pattern on each line is the first pattern with each rhythmic value doubled.

A **whole note** (o) shows a sound that lasts for four beats in $\frac{4}{4}$.

When you change a rhythm by making it twice as long, you **augment** it. To augment means to make larger. For example, when you augment a sound one beat long, it becomes a sound two beats long. In $\frac{4}{4}$, each quarter note will become a half note.

If you augment a rhythm in $\frac{4}{4}$, what would a half note become? whole note

270

MEETING **INDIVIDUAL** NEEDS

ALTERNATE TEACHING STRATEGY

OBJECTIVE 1 List on the board the note-value symbols students know (in $\frac{2}{4}$ or $\frac{4}{4}$), then across from each one write the doubled note value (for example, ♩ - ♪). Write the first three lines of the poem in a row with the rhythm notation underneath. Have students chant the words while patting with a beat. Next, underneath each rhythmic note value, have students write the augmented rhythm symbol. Have students chant six words with the new rhythm while tapping with the beat in the original tempo. Use **Resource Master 6 • 5** for further augmentation practice.

BIOGRAPHY: *Mary Ann Hoberman*

The poet Mary Ann Hoberman (b. 1930) likes to garden and to play tennis. She doesn't *look* at all unusual; it's her imagination that sets her apart. She dreams up "raucous auks" and a "backward town" where people sleep under their beds, not on top of them. Writing poetry comes naturally to her. "*Not* writing a poem would be more difficult," she thinks. Interesting names or facts stick in her mind until they come out in a poem. "Only then can I be free of them and turn my attention to something else," says Hoberman. "Usually another poem."

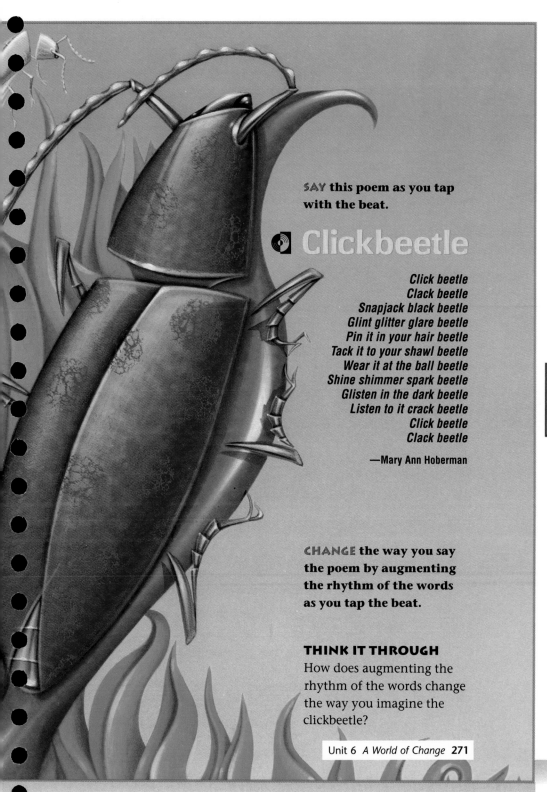

SAY this poem as you tap with the beat.

Clickbeetle

Click beetle
Clack beetle
Snapjack black beetle
Glint glitter glare beetle
Pin it in your hair beetle
Tack it to your shawl beetle
Wear it at the ball beetle
Shine shimmer spark beetle
Glisten in the dark beetle
Listen to it crack beetle
Click beetle
Clack beetle

—Mary Ann Hoberman

CHANGE the way you say the poem by augmenting the rhythm of the words as you tap the beat.

THINK IT THROUGH

How does augmenting the rhythm of the words change the way you imagine the clickbeetle?

Unit 6 *A World of Change* 271

"Let's play a rhythm game." Have students:

▶ • Divide into four groups, each adding one of the following body percussion sounds as you review each note value. (sixteenth—pat; eighth—clap; quarter—snap; half—brush) "Group 1 is patting sixteenth notes. What note lasts as long as two sixteenth notes?" (eighth note) "What note lasts as long as two eighth notes?" (quarter) "What note lasts as long as two quarter notes?" (half)

"Today you'll learn a way to change the rhythm of a song based on how these note values are related to each other."

2 DEVELOP

1. Discover augmentation. Have students:

Recorded Lesson CD6:20

▶ • Listen to "Augmentation" and hear the rhythm patterns on page 270. Determine that each duration in the second pattern of a line lasts twice as long as in the first pattern.

• In two groups, perform each pair of patterns. One group taps with a beat, the other pats the rhythms for each line. Switch parts.

• Discover that the second rhythm takes twice as many beats to complete as the first.

▶ • Read about the whole note on page 270.

2. Introduce "Clickbeetle" CD6:21. **Perform the rhythm in augmentation.** Have students:

▶ • Read about augmentation, then chant "Clickbeetle" while tapping with the beat.

• With a partner, work out how the poem would sound if the rhythms were augmented.

OBJECTIVE 1 Informal Assessment
• Chant the speech piece with the rhythm in augmentation, tapping with the beat.

▶ • Discuss the text of the poem.

PLAYING INSTRUMENTS: *Unpitched Instruments*

Have students perform the rhythm of the words of the poem with two levels of body percussion, clapping all *beetles*, and patting all other words. Then have two groups perform the poem, one with the original rhythm, one with augmented rhythm. Finally, have students choose unpitched sounds and transfer the body percussion to these, thinking the words silently and playing the rhythm. (For example, they might change pats to larger wooden unpitched instruments, such as log drums or large temple blocks, and claps to smaller wooden unpitched instruments, such as sticks, to make lots of "clicky-clacky" sounds.)

MUSIC BUILDS MATH SKILLS

Number and Operations When students augment a rhythm, they apply the concept of making doubles in addition.

UNIT SIX
LESSON 5

continued from previous page

3 APPLY

1. Review "Simple Gifts" CD6:18 (p. 269). Learn a movement ostinato. Have students:

▶ • Sing "Simple Gifts."

▶ • Learn a movement ostinato to perform with the song. (See *Movement* on the bottom of page 273.)

2. Introduce *Appalachian Spring* (excerpt) CD6:22. Listen for augmentation as well as tone color (clarinet). Have students:

▶ • Read about *Appalachian Spring* and listen to the excerpt.

• Sing the first phrase of "Simple Gifts" twice, the second time in augmentation, patting with the beat both times.

OBJECTIVE 2 Informal Assessment
• Listen to the excerpt from *Appalachian Spring* and perform the movement,

♪♪ ♩ doubling the duration of the movement ♩ ♩ ♩ when the melodic rhythm is

heard in augmentation. (Variation 2—See *Movement* on the bottom of page 273.)

🎵 Appalachian Spring (excerpt)
LISTENING   *by Aaron Copland*

*The ballet **Appalachian Spring** is about a pioneer couple's wedding day. Copland's music for the ballet includes the melody of "Simple Gifts." The melody is repeated and changed in a variety of ways. You will hear its rhythm augmented and also hear the melody played as a canon.*

OFF FRANKLIN OR NOLENSVILLE PIKE, NASHVILLE
Mayna Treanor Avent's painting shows the sunny rural beauty that may have inspired *Appalachian Spring.*

PAT with the beat and sing this phrase of "Simple Gifts."

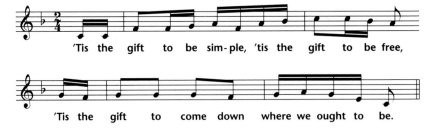

'Tis the gift to be sim-ple, 'tis the gift to be free,

'Tis the gift to come down where we ought to be.

272 DOUBLE THE FUN!

MEETING **INDIVIDUAL** NEEDS

ALTERNATE TEACHING STRATEGY

OBJECTIVE 2 Have students divide into two groups. One group claps with a beat and hums "Simple Gifts." (Have them clap at the tempo of the listening selection.) The other practices the movement. As the first continues to clap at the same tempo but hums in augmentation, the second augments the movement. Switch roles.

BACKGROUND: *Appalachian Spring*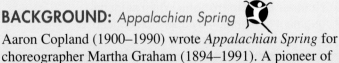

Aaron Copland (1900–1990) wrote *Appalachian Spring* for choreographer Martha Graham (1894–1991). A pioneer of

modern dance, Graham herself danced the lead at the 1944 premiere. Copland's score won the 1945 Pulitzer Prize for composition. He later drew a suite from the dance music to be played as a concert piece; it is from the suite that this excerpt is taken. The theme of the excerpt is a variation on "Simple Gifts." It features the clarinet. The first variation features the oboe and bassoon, the second variation (theme in augmentation), the trombone and viola. About halfway through the second variation, the trumpets and violins enter to play the augmented melody in canon with the trombones and violas.

PAT with the beat and sing the same phrase, this time augmenting the rhythm.

'Tis the gift to be sim-ple, 'tis the gift to be free,

'Tis the gift to come down where we ought to be.

Listen for the augmentation of "Simple Gifts" in *Appalachian Spring.*

THE CLARINET

The **clarinet** is a woodwind instrument that comes in a variety of sizes. A musician blows on a single **reed,** a piece of cane attached to the mouthpiece, to make the air inside the instrument vibrate and produce sound. Listen as the clarinet begins the music from *Appalachian Spring.*

clarinet

single reed

273

4 CLOSE

"How did you change the rhythm in the music and poetry today?" (with augmentation: doubled the rhythmic values) Have students:

• Listen to *Appalachian Spring* again and perform the movement ostinato alone, then during the augmented variation, perform the augmented ostinato facing a partner.

LESSON SUMMARY

Informal Assessment In this lesson, students:

OBJECTIVE 1 Chanted "Clickbeetle," augmenting the rhythm.
OBJECTIVE 2 Moved to show augmentation of the rhythm of a theme from *Appalachian Spring.*

National Standards for Music Education
1a Sing accurately, on pitch and in rhythm.
1b Sing with appropriate dynamics, phrasing, and interpretation.
2b Perform easy patterns on various classroom instruments.
2f Play parts while others perform contrasting parts.

MORE MUSIC: Reinforcement
More Songs to Read, page 371 (rhythmic augmentation)
"The Shrovetide Fair," page 385G (clarinet)

BACKGROUND: *Clarinet*

The clarinet was invented in Germany about 1700. The most common clarinet is pitched in B-flat. At slightly over two feet in length, the B-flat clarinet is a medium-sized member in a family that ranges from the small, shrieking E-flat clarinet to the large, growling B-flat contrabass clarinet. All clarinets use a single reed, which vibrates against the mouthpiece, and change pitches by using a combination of tone holes and keys. Their bodies are made of grenadilla wood (for professional models) or plastic (for students). The clarinet's adaptable sound has made it a favorite in styles from classical to jazz.

MOVEMENT: *Ostinato for "Simple Gifts"*

MOVEMENT

The ostinato rhythm is ♪♪ ♩ Students take two steps on the eighth notes and draw a circle in the air with both hands for the quarter note (hands moving in parallel motion like train tracks). The movement can be done in augmentation (to the *Appalachian Spring* excerpt, Variation 2) by taking bigger steps and drawing a bigger circle to demonstrate the longer durations. ♩ ♩ ♩

ACROSS the

DIAGRAMS/MODELS

"Clickbeetle"

INDIVIDUAL   **15 MIN OR LESS**

MATERIALS: crayons, markers or colored pencils, drawing paper—or clay, pipe cleaners, toothpicks

Have students draw or make models of what they think a beetle looks like from this description.

- A beetle's body is made up of three parts, connected, one part behind another—like three lumps of clay, one larger than the next.
- The front body part is a head. The head has a mouth in the front, an eye on each side, and two feelers (antennae), one on each side.
- The middle body part has three pairs of legs, one leg from each pair on each side. The legs have joints that allow them to bend. The middle part also has wings.
- The back body part, the largest, has eight pairs of tiny holes along the bottom for air.

Have students compare their drawings or models with pictures in reference books to see how close they came.

COMPREHENSION STRATEGIES: Following directions, visualizing, making a model

PROBLEM SOLVING

"Clickbeetle"

PAIR   **15 MIN OR LESS**

MATERIALS: drawing paper, markers

A beetle is trapped in a jar that is nine inches tall. Each hour the beetle crawls up three inches, but then stops for a rest and slides back one inch. How many hours will it take the beetle to crawl out?

Have students work in pairs to solve the problem. To guide them, ask questions such as: "How tall is the jar? How far does the beetle crawl in an hour? How far does the beetle slide back?" Students should draw and label the jar to visualize the problem.

(four hours: 2 inches+2 inches+2 inches+3 inches =9 inches—In the fourth hour, the beetle will make it out of the jar before stopping for a rest and sliding back.)

Have students make up similar problems for each other to solve.

COMPREHENSION STRATEGY: Reasoning

CURRICULUM

LANGUAGE ARTS

CREATIVE WRITING

"Clickbeetle"

INDIVIDUAL　　　　**30 MIN OR LONGER**

Using the chalkboard or chart paper, have students list how the beetle is used in the poem. (*pinned to hair, tacked to a shawl,* and so on) Explain that listing is a way to organize information before writing a story, poem, or paper.

Read some of the items listed below. Ask students to choose one of the items, make a list, and write a short poem about their chosen topic.

- silent things
- things that glow
- things pleasing to hear
- things you treasure
- things that stretch
- things that smell good
- things that squeak
- infinite things
- unmovable things
- things that hurt

COMPREHENSION STRATEGIES: Making a list, organizing information

ART/LANGUAGE ARTS

CREATIVE WRITING

"Appalachian Spring"

GROUP　　　　**15–30 MIN**

MATERIALS: drawing paper, crayons, markers

Have students form groups to plan a spring display. In each group, students take on various tasks. One student can write a spring poem. Others can plan a mural or bulletin-board collage. As part of the display, they can plan to show a spring wedding.

Each group should begin by listing basic ideas about spring that they want to use as the main ideas of their display. Some groups may plan to write a skit about spring, taking on the characters of animals "waking up" after a long winter or people at a wedding scene.

When they have outlined their display, have them submit their plans in writing for a review. Then, have them revise their plan based on any comments you might make. Finally, have them assemble their displays.

COMPREHENSION STRATEGIES: Organizing ideas, finding main ideas

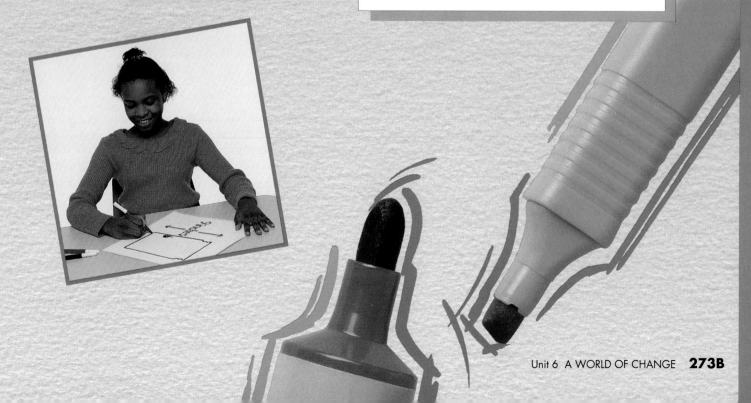

LESSON PLANNER

FOCUS Duration, meter

OBJECTIVES
OBJECTIVE 1 Perform a movement canon with a song in ⁴₄ meter
OBJECTIVE 2 Signal to identify meter changes in a recorded song

MATERIALS
Recordings
This Pretty Planet (⁴₄ , canon)	CD6:6
This Pretty Planet (⁴₄ , unison)	CD6:3
This Pretty Planet (⁶₈)	CD6:23
The Court of King Carraticus	CD6:10
The Court of King Carraticus (with sound cues)	CD6:11

Resources Recorder Master R • 31 (pitches D E G A B D')

▶ = **BASIC PROGRAM**

CHANGING

Sing "This Pretty Planet." As you sing, pat with the beats that feel strongest and clap with the other beats. How are the beats grouped?

MOVE to "This Pretty Planet" in ⁴₄.

1. Walk clockwise, then counterclockwise.

2. Face the center of the circle and raise your arms, then lower your arms.

274

MEETING **INDIVIDUAL** NEEDS

ALTERNATE TEACHING STRATEGY

MOVEMENT

OBJECTIVE 1 Have each circle practice the movement to the recording of the song in unison. Then practice with the song in canon, each circle taking a turn at performing the movement with its part of the canon. The first time through, the first circle should begin moving when the first part of the canon begins. The second time through, the second circle should begin moving when the second part of the canon begins. Finish with the two circles side-by-side and performing the movement in canon. When students are secure, they may try this movement in a three-part canon.

METER

3. Turn in place.

4. Walk toward the center of the circle, then walk back out.

1 GET SET

"Sing 'This Pretty Planet' in canon." **CD6:6** (See page 257 for notation.) Have students:

▶ • Form two or three groups and sing "This Pretty Planet" in two- or three-part canon.

"Today you're going to learn how to do movement in canon as well."

2 DEVELOP

1. Identify strong beats in "This Pretty Planet" and learn the movement. Have students:

▶ • Sing the song ($\frac{4}{4}$, unison **CD6:3**), patting knees on the strong beats, clapping on the weak beats. (See page 257.)

▶ • Learn a circular movement. (See *Movement* below.)

OBJECTIVE 1 Informal Assessment
• Perform the movement in canon.

MOVEMENT: *"This Pretty Planet"* in $\frac{4}{4}$

Formation: single circle, all students facing clockwise

Measures 1–4: Walk ♩   ♩   ♩ ♩   ♩ clockwise, then repeat counterclockwise.

Measures 5–8: On *golden sun . . .* , face center of circle, raise arms (four beats), lower arms (four beats), turn in place, following right elbow (eight beats).

Measures 9–12: Walk into center, ♩   ♩   ♩ ♩ ♩ then walk back out in the same rhythm.

When students are comfortable with the movement, have them form two side-by-side circles and sing and move to "This Pretty Planet" ($\frac{4}{4}$, canon) in two-part canon.

Have groups assess each other's performances:
—Were beginnings and endings of each step clear?
—Did each dancer make the arm circles in unison with the group?
—Were the body facings the same within each group, especially in the individual turns?

LESSON 6

continued from previous page

2. Sing "This Pretty Planet" in a different meter (§) CD6:23. Have students:

▶ • Listen to "This Pretty Planet" in ¾ and § meter.

▶ • Listen to the song in § and describe what has changed from the song in ¾. (meter)

▶ • Sing the song in §.

3 APPLY

Review "The Court of King Carraticus" CD6:10 (p. 263). Find meter changes. Have students:

▶ • Listen for and pat with the strong beats, then tell what happens. (The strong beat does not occur regularly. Point out that this means the meter changes.)

OBJECTIVE 2 Informal Assessment

• Listen again with eyes closed and raise a hand whenever a meter change is heard.

• Look at the notation on page 263 and identify the measures with meter changes.

NEW PLANET

Changing the meter of a song gives a new feeling to the music. Here is "This Pretty Planet" in §. Compare it with the same song in ¾ on page 257.

SING the song with two different meters.

This Pretty Planet

Words and Music by
John Forster and Tom Chapin
Adapted by MMH

This pret-ty plan-et spin-ning through space. You're a gar-den. You're a har-bor. You're a ho-ly place. Gold-en sun go-ing down. Gen-tle blue gi-ant, spin us a-round. All through the night. Safe 'til the morn-ing light.

THINK IT THROUGH

What happens to the sets of beats when the meter changes? Which meter do you prefer, and why? In ¾ meter they are felt in sets of four; in § meter they are felt in sets of 2 or 6.

276 CHANGING METER

MEETING **INDIVIDUAL** NEEDS

ALTERNATE TEACHING STRATEGY

OBJECTIVE 2 Have students work in groups of three or more and listen to "The Court of King Carraticus." One student claps with the strong beats, one pats with all beats, and one records how many beats occur in each set. Alternatively, draw a row of fourteen dots on the board, and as you point to one for each beat in the first two phrases, have students determine which dots represent strong beats and how many beats are in each set.

CRITICAL THINKING: *Meter Changes*

Encourage students to discover what happens to the meter with each additional verse of "The Court of King Carraticus." Tell them to pat on the strong beats and clap on the other beats, then discuss what happens. (The number of beats in the cumulative measures increases by one beat with each verse.) Ask them how they could show the meter changes. (Add 1 to the top number of the meter signature of the cumulative measures—¾, ⁴⁄₄, ⁵⁄₄, and so on.)

Some songs stay in the same meter; others change meter.

PAT with the beats that feel strongest as you listen to "The Court of King Carraticus." What happens?
Strong beat does not occur regularly.

© 1993 The Estate of Keith Haring

UNTITLED
Keith Haring's artwork expresses his wish for people to join together to enjoy and take care of the planet Earth.

4 CLOSE

"How does changing a song's meter affect the music?" (gives it a different feeling, the beats are felt in different groupings) Have students:

▶ • Sing "The Court of King Carraticus" with the gestures from page 262 (with sound cues **CD6:11**).

LESSON SUMMARY

Informal Assessment In this lesson, students:

OBJECTIVE 1 Performed a movement canon to "This Pretty Planet" in $\frac{4}{4}$ meter.

OBJECTIVE 2 Signaled to identify meter changes in a recorded song.

National Standards for Music Education
1d Sing ostinatos, partner songs, and rounds.
5a Read standard note values in duple and triple meters.
5b Using system, read notation in treble clef in major keys.
6b Describe, in words or movement, music from diverse cultures.
6e Respond to musical characteristics through movement.

MORE MUSIC: Reinforcement
"Garden Song," page 290 (environmental concern)
"Tree Rhyme," page 344 (changing meter; spring)

EXTRA HELP: $\frac{4}{4}$ *and* $\frac{6}{8}$
Review the differences in rhythmic feeling between $\frac{4}{4}$ and $\frac{6}{8}$ by having students alternately jog eighth notes for eight beats and skip ♩ ♪ for eight beats.

BIOGRAPHY: *Keith Haring*
VISUAL ARTS

Keith Haring (1958–1990) was born in Kutztown, Pennsylvania, and began drawing with his father when he was a child. He loved to draw animals and invent figures and was influenced by Walt Disney, Dr. Seuss, and the *Batman* cartoons that he watched on television in the late 1960s. He started out wanting to be a cartoonist, and early in his career he wrote and illustrated children's books. After moving to New York City, Haring began drawing in chalk on empty black panels in the subway system. Because of these drawings and his later wall murals, he was often called a graffiti artist. He wanted his art to be part of everyday life—to celebrate and communicate through his improvisatory and symbolic style. He taught and worked with children in many ethnic neighborhoods and was a political activist. His last works included graphic art, often for T-shirts, and big, colorful, outdoor sculptures.

LESSON PLANNER

FOCUS Pitch, ornamentation

OBJECTIVE
OBJECTIVE 1 Sing a familiar folk song with vocal ornamentation

MATERIALS
Recordings
Music Alone Shall Live (Himmel
  und Erde)   CD5:22
Listening: Fancy Musica   CD6:24
Listening: Vocal Ornamentation
  Montage   CD6:25
Old Joe Clark   CD6:7
Recorded Lesson: Fancy Joe   CD6:26

Other Optional—overhead projector

Resources
Resource Master 6 • 6 (practice)
Recorder Master R • 32 (pitches
  D G A B C' D')

VOCABULARY
ornamentation

▶ = **BASIC PROGRAM**

PLAIN and FANCY

Compare each pair of objects. How are they different?

One of each pair is simple and the other is ornate, or decorated. Music can be ornate also. A song can be decorated by adding pitches to the melody. This is called **ornamentation.**

COMPARE the pictures in the frames below.

This shows the original melody of "Music Alone Shall Live."

Him - mel   und   Er -   de
                                          müss- en   ver - gehn;

278

MEETING **INDIVIDUAL** NEEDS

ART CONNECTION: *Ornamentation* VISUAL ARTS

Objects, as well as music, can be decorated. Have students look at classroom objects or pictures and discuss how ornamentation changes the look of an object. You might also show students a variety of art styles, discussing how the styles may be described as plain or ornamented. (Optional: Have them complete **Resource Master 6 • 6**, decorating Picture 2 of each pair while leaving Picture 1 plain.)

ENRICHMENT: *B and C Sections*

Review the place-name activity in Unit 5, Lesson 7, page 231, *Enrichment.* Then sing "Music Alone Shall Live," using one to all three of the ways to ornament the melody when singing, and add B and C sections with place names.

"When you make a birthday cake for someone, what do you do to make it look special?" Have students:

▶ • Discuss ornaments and decorations.

▶ • Read page 278 and discuss other things that can be decorated—clothing, hair, furniture, and so on.

"Decorations change how things look. There are also ways to decorate the music you sing. Today you will learn about how to decorate a melody."

2 DEVELOP

1. Review "Music Alone Shall Live" CD5:22 **(p. 231). Introduce ornamentation and "Fancy Musica"** CD6:24. Have students:

▶ • Sing "Music Alone Shall Live."

▶ • Look at the visual representations of three types of ornamentation.

▶ • Listen to "Fancy Musica" to hear an example of each type of ornamentation, then an ornamented version of the entire song.

Here is the same melody with three types of ornamentation.

trill   turn   slide

Him - mel und Er - de müss- en ver- gehn;

Unit 6 *A World of Change* 279

PLAYING INSTRUMENTS: *Keyboards*

Play this descant to accompany "Music Alone Shall Live" and to review the dotted rhythm pattern.

ART CONNECTION: *Ornamentation*

Have students look at the clocks and pitchers on pages 278–279 and discuss how craftspeople use ornamentation, embellishing their works with intricate designs. These designs might use geometric or free-form shapes, floral patterns, or animal motifs. The designs can be symmetrical, a balance in which one side mirrors the other, or asymmetrical, where balance in achieved through the use of unlike parts or elements. Invite students to create a picture frame using ornamentation with a repeated element, or motif.

continued from previous page

2. Introduce "Vocal Ornamentation Montage" CD6:25. Listen to examples of vocal ornamentation from different cultures. Have students:

▶ • Read about vocal ornamentation in songs from around the world.

▶ • Listen to the montage while looking at the photographs on pages 280–281.

3 APPLY

Review "Old Joe Clark" CD6:7 (p. 260). Sing the refrain with ornamentation. Have students:

▶ • Sing "Old Joe Clark."

Recorded Lesson CD6:26
• Listen to "Fancy Joe" and echo examples (from page 281) of the first measure of the refrain with each type of ornamentation added.

• Choose which ornaments to sing with each refrain and list them on the board.

OBJECTIVE 1 Informal Assessment
• Sing "Old Joe Clark" (a cappella or with stereo balance control adjusted to hear accompaniment alone), adding ornamentation to the first and fifth measure of each refrain.

ORNAMENTS FROM AROUND THE WORLD

Vocal ornamentation is practiced by singers from all over the world. In some styles of music, the composer suggests how to ornament the melody. In others, the performers are creative in adding pitches to the song.

LISTENING
Vocal Ornamentation Montage

Listen to how these singers use ornamentation.

African American– turns, slides

Indian– trills, slides

280 PLAIN AND FANCY

MEETING **INDIVIDUAL** NEEDS

ALTERNATE TEACHING STRATEGY

OBJECTIVE 1 On the board, draw a picture representing each type of ornamentation (as on page 281). Point to the pictures as students echo the ornamentation from the recorded lesson "Fancy Joe." Then divide the class into three groups, one for each type of ornamentation. Have the class sing the refrain three times, one with each type of ornamentation. Each group should take turns singing Measures 1 and 5, with its ornamentation, as you point to the picture. The rest of the class sings Measures 2–4 and 6–8.

BACKGROUND: *"Vocal Ornamentation Montage"*

Students will hear these excerpts of ornamented music:

1. "Black Woman" by Vera Hall: Slides, swoops, glides, and other melodic ornaments are expressive additions to African American blues singing.

2. Prelude to "Kathakali" (ka ta **ka** li): Kathakali is a dance-drama form of Southwestern India. Performers tell ancient stories through mime, dance, hand sign language, music, and song. The example heard shows the typical Indian emphasis on ornamentation.

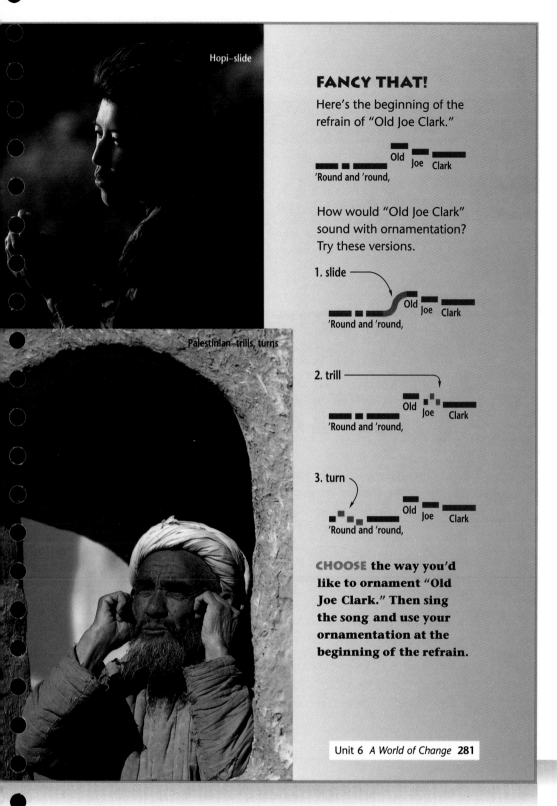

Hopi–slide

Palestinian–trills, turns

FANCY THAT!

Here's the beginning of the refrain of "Old Joe Clark."

'Round and 'round, Old Joe Clark

How would "Old Joe Clark" sound with ornamentation? Try these versions.

1. slide

'Round and 'round, Old Joe Clark

2. trill

'Round and 'round, Old Joe Clark

3. turn

'Round and 'round, Old Joe Clark

CHOOSE the way you'd like to ornament "Old Joe Clark." Then sing the song and use your ornamentation at the beginning of the refrain.

4 CLOSE

"What does it mean to ornament something?" (to change by adding something, to decorate) "How did we ornament our songs today?" (slide, trill, turn) Have students:

• Sing "Old Joe Clark," adding ornamentation on each refrain and any new verses they may have created (Lesson 2, *Apply*).

LESSON SUMMARY

Informal Assessment In this lesson, students:

OBJECTIVE 1 Sang "Old Joe Clark" with vocal ornamentation.

National Standards for Music Education
2a Play instruments with accurate pitch and rhythm.
2b Perform easy patterns on various classroom instruments.
6a Identify simple musical forms by ear.

MORE MUSIC: Reinforcement
"You're Invited: Choral Concert," page 382 (vocal styles)

---

3. Palestinian Call to Prayer: Ornamentation is important in Arabic music. The Muslim call to prayer is broadcast from a tower five times a day, performed live or recorded.

4. "Mongwa, Mongwa" (məŋ wə   məŋ wə) (The Owls Are Coming): This excerpt from a Hopi lullaby demonstrates a vocal slide, often heard in Native American music.

MOVEMENT: *"Old Joe Clark"* MOVEMENT
Discuss ways to ornament movement: Add more complicated steps, use more complicated formations, add stylized arm movements, add a solo dancer.

Students should get into the same circle as in Lesson 2, page 261, *Movement*, and review the dances they created for the verse.

Ornament the refrain movement: Change from walking with the beat to walking this rhythm pattern:

Ornament the verse movement: Have each group use an idea from the list.

LESSON PLANNER

FOCUS Design, theme and variations

OBJECTIVE

OBJECTIVE 1 Sing several variations on a familiar song, working in small groups

MATERIALS

Recordings
The Cat Came Back	CD6:5
Listening: American Theme	CD6:13
Listening: Variations on an American Theme by L. Worsley	CD6:14
Music Alone Shall Live (Himmel und Erde)	CD5:22
Listening: Chiotikos	CD6:27

Instruments unpitched percussion

Other Optional—overhead projector, tape recording equipment

Resources
Resource Master 6 • 7 (practice)
Listening Map Transparency T • 10 (Variations on an American Theme)
Recorder Master R • 33 (pitches D G A B C' D')
Recorder Master R • 34 (pitches D G A B C' D')

VOCABULARY
theme and variations

▶ = **BASIC PROGRAM**

Change= Variation

One of the many ways to change or vary a piece of music is to change the melody. A composer writes music based on a melody. Different treatments of that melody follow. The form of the music is called **theme and variations.** The original melody is the theme, and each changed version of the melody is called a variation. The theme sounds different in each variation, but you can still recognize it.

Look at these seven ways to vary a melody. Name the songs that were varied in these ways.

- dynamics
- tempo
- tone color
- rhythm
- meter
- pitch
- accompaniment

282

MEETING **INDIVIDUAL** NEEDS

PLAYING INSTRUMENTS: *Unpitched*

Have students suggest classroom instrument "sound effects" to add to each verse of "The Cat Came Back." Discuss which words and ideas suggest special sounds, then let students experiment with what, when, and how much sound should occur. Have the class listen to the sounds suggested and decide which ones to play as they sing the song.

SPECIAL LEARNERS: *Ostinato Accompaniment*

For practice with articulation and a simple rhythm, have students with keyboard experience play and speak or sing this ostinato to "The Cat Came Back" with other students.

The   cat   came   back.

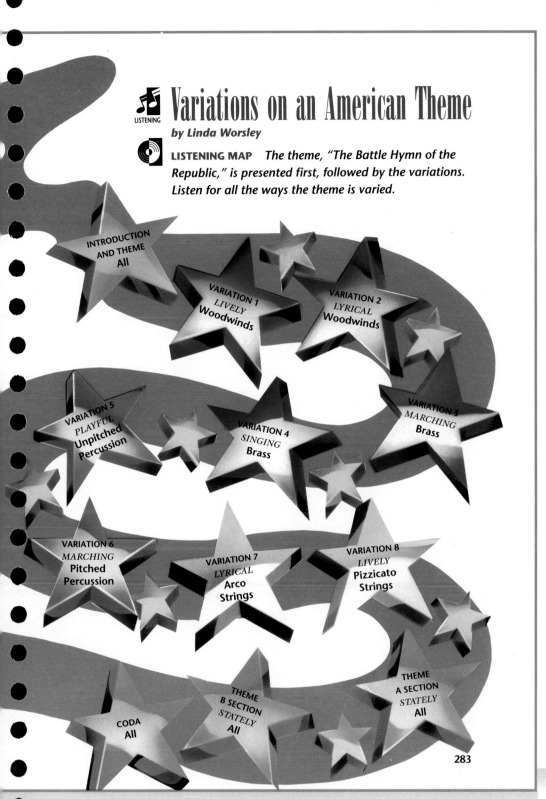

♪ LISTENING **Variations on an American Theme**

by Linda Worsley

🔊 **LISTENING MAP**   The theme, "The Battle Hymn of the Republic," is presented first, followed by the variations. Listen for all the ways the theme is varied.

INTRODUCTION AND THEME
All

VARIATION 1
LIVELY
Woodwinds

VARIATION 2
LYRICAL
Woodwinds

VARIATION 3
MARCHING
Brass

VARIATION 5
PLAYFUL
Unpitched Percussion

VARIATION 4
SINGING
Brass

VARIATION 6
MARCHING
Pitched Percussion

VARIATION 7
LYRICAL
Arco Strings

VARIATION 8
LIVELY
Pizzicato Strings

THEME A SECTION
STATELY
All

THEME B SECTION
STATELY
All

CODA
All

283

"Let's sing 'The Cat Came Back' and remember some of the changes we can make to the song." Have students:

▸ • Sing "The Cat Came Back" on pages 258–259 **CD6:5**.

▸ • Recall changes discussed in the unit. (dynamics, tempo, tone colors)

"Today you'll use all of these ways to vary or make changes in your own music. This will help you to find changes in the music you listen to or make."

2 DEVELOP

1. Learn Part 2 in "The Cat Came Back." Have students:

▸ • Listen to Vocal Part 2 of the refrain of "The Cat Came Back" on pages 258–259.

• Sing the song, dividing into two parts on the refrain.

▸ • Identify this as another way to change the accompaniment.

2. Introduce "Variations on an American Theme" CD6:14. Introduce theme and variation. Have students:

▸ • Read about theme and variations and review ways musical elements were changed in this unit. (See *Extra Help* below.)

▸ • Review "American Theme" **CD6:13** to hear the theme and recall instruments featured. (flute, snare drum, trumpet, strings)

▸ • Listen to "Variations on an American Theme" while following the listening map. (Optional: Use **Listening Map Transparency T • 10**.)

▸ • Discuss the order and kinds of variations.

EXTRA HELP: *Summing Up Variations*

dynamics: "I Can Be," "This Pretty Planet," "Korobushka"

tempo: "Korobushka," "The Cat Came Back"

tone color: "King Carraticus," "Michie Banjo," "American Theme"

rhythm (augmentation): "Simple Gifts," "Clickbeetle"

meter: "This Pretty Planet"

pitch (major/minor): "Simple Gifts;" (ornamentation): "Music Alone Shall Live," "Old Joe Clark"

accompaniment: "This Pretty Planet," "The Cat Came Back," "Old Joe Clark"

continued from previous page

3 APPLY

Review "Music Alone Shall Live" CD5:22 **(p. 231). Create a set of variations.** Have students:

▶ • Sing the song, then read about ways to vary the song on pages 284–285.

• Divide into small groups, then choose one type of variation. (You may wish to have each group choose a slip of paper with one variation listed on it. Optional: Use **Resource Master 6 • 7.**)

• Plan and practice their variation.

OBJECTIVE 1 Informal Assessment

• With their group, perform a variation.

• Identify the type of variation used by each group by raising a hand when you point to the correct variation name on the board.

284 CHANGE = VARIATION

VARIATIONS ON "MUSIC ALONE SHALL LIVE"

Now it's your turn to be the composer!

CREATE a set of variations using "Music Alone Shall Live" as your theme. Divide into groups and choose one of these ideas to change the theme.

Rhythm and Meter

Change the meter from $\frac{3}{4}$ to $\frac{4}{4}$. For example, change the rhythm of the words *aber die Musica*.

a - ber die Mu - si - ca

Tone Color

Change the vocal tone color by whispering or speaking. Or play the song on percussion instruments.

MEETING **INDIVIDUAL** NEEDS

ALTERNATE TEACHING STRATEGY

OBJECTIVE 1: Divide the class into six groups. Have students assign roles within each group: a conductor, a recorder, and so on. Have each group draw a slip with a variation and performance suggestions from **Resource Master 6 • 7.** Each group should design, write down, and practice its variation.

MOVEMENT: *"Chiotikos"*

This Greek dance, Chiotikos (xi ɔ ti kəs) CD6:27, is a theme and variations: the B and C sections elaborate on the A

section. (This recording contains spoken dance instructions over the music. Adjust the stereo balance control to hear the music alone.)

A section: 4 measures of six beats each

Formation: broken circle, holding hands, facing counter-clockwise

(Verbal Cue—*step, step, side, lift, side, lift*) Facing counter-clockwise, take two steps beginning with the R foot. Then turn to face center of circle, side step on R leg, lift L leg up slightly off the floor, knee bent and slightly turned out, side step on L leg and repeat lift with R leg. Repeat this pattern 4 times.

Accompaniment

Decide whether to perform the song as a two- or three-part canon. Decide when each part will start.

Dynamics

Use any or all of these markings to change dynamics.

f, p, mf, mp, 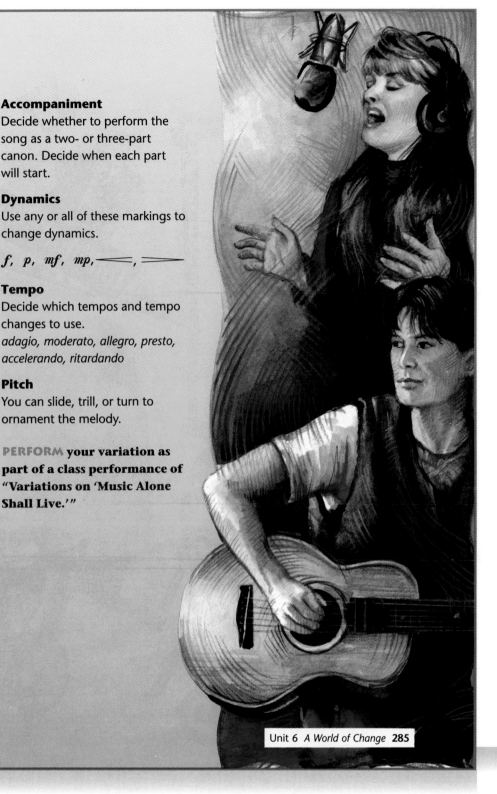,

Tempo

Decide which tempos and tempo changes to use.

adagio, moderato, allegro, presto, accelerando, ritardando

Pitch

You can slide, trill, or turn to ornament the melody.

PERFORM your variation as part of a class performance of "Variations on 'Music Alone Shall Live.'"

Unit 6 *A World of Change* **285**

4 CLOSE

"Let's have each group stand and name the type of variation it performed." (dynamics, tempo, rhythm and meter, tone color, accompaniment, ornamentation) "Now let's choose an order in which to perform your variations for a 'recording session.' We'll all perform the original theme 'Music Alone Shall Live,' then each group will perform its variation." Have students:

• Choose the order of performance of their variations.

• Perform "Variations on 'Music Alone Shall Live.'"

• Conduct a mock recording session and record the performance, if possible.

LESSON SUMMARY

Informal Assessment In this lesson, students:

OBJECTIVE 1 Sang several variations on "Music Alone Shall Live," working in small groups.

National Standards for Music Education
1a Sing accurately, on pitch and in rhythm.
5c Identify and interpret symbols and traditional terms.
6d Identify instrumental and vocal sounds from various cultures.

MORE MUSIC: Reinforcement

"Donna, Donna," page 291 (changing dynamics, rhythm, meter, tempo)
"Variations on 'America'" (excerpts), page 303 (theme and variations)

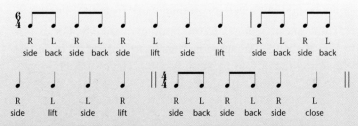

step R   step L   side R   lift L   side L   lift R

B section: 4 measures of six beats

Formation: facing center

(Verbal Cue—*turn, two, side, lift, side, lift*) The same as the A section, except replace the first two *steps* with a two-step turn over the right shoulder (one complete turn done in two steps). Immediately after the turn, hands are placed on both neighbors' shoulders for the side lifts.

C section: 2 measures of six beats, 1 measure of four
Formation: facing center, hands rejoined after B section

Take four fast steps on the balls of the feet, moving to the right side. The L foot always steps in back of the R foot.

R L R L R   L   L   R   R L R L
side back side back side   lift   side   lift   side back side back

R L L R
side lift side lift

R L R L R L
side back side back side close

UNIT SIX
LESSON 9

RELATED ARTS MOVEMENT THEATER VISUAL ARTS

LESSON PLANNER

OBJECTIVES
To review songs, skills, and concepts learned in Unit 6 and to test students' ability to:
1. Identify rhythmic augmentation
2. Identify phrases in minor
3. Describe changes in tempo and dynamics
4. Describe how a melody is accompanied

MATERIALS
Recordings
Simple Gifts	CD6:18
The Cat Came Back	CD6:5
I Can Be	CD6:2
This Pretty Planet	CD6:3
Unit 6 Assessment A	CD7:1–5
Unit 6 Assessment B	CD7:6–10

Resources
Resource Master 6 • 8 (assessment)
Resource Master 6 • 9 (assessment)
Resource Master TA • 1 (assessment)

▶ = BASIC PROGRAM

REVIEW

ALL KINDS OF CHANGES

Describe the musical changes you see. What other ways can you make changes?

Make some changes as you sing "Simple Gifts," "The Cat Came Back," and "I Can Be."

286

MEETING **INDIVIDUAL** NEEDS

PROGRAM IDEA: *Positive Changes*

This review can be enjoyed in the classroom or presented as a simple program. Additional materials from Unit 6, *Celebrations, More Songs to Sing,* or the *Music Library* may be added as well as original work from the students.

"Think about changes we go through every day. For example, we change our surroundings from waking up in bed, to boarding the bus, to being in school." Have students sing "I Can Be," patting with the beat.

"Besides making changes in our lives, we all need to pitch in together to help improve and protect the environment." Students sing "This Pretty Planet" **CD6:3**, page 257.

"What could be a more perfect gift than to keep the environment clean for one another? It would make the world a better home for all of us." Students sing "Simple Gifts," clapping with the beat.

1. Review "Simple Gifts" CD6:18 **(p. 269). Review major and rhythmic augmentation.** Have students:

• Sing the song, then identify it as being major.

• Read page 270 to review augmentation.

• Sing the song again, augmenting the rhythm and patting with the beat.

▶ • With a partner, perform the song with the movement. (See Lesson 5, *Movement* on the bottom of page 273.)

2. Review "The Cat Came Back" CD6:5 **(p. 258). Review minor and changing tempo and dynamics.** Have students:

▶ • Sing Verse 1 through the Interlude.

▶ • Identify the song as being minor and contrast its sound with the major sound of "Simple Gifts."

▶ • Choose tempo and dynamic changes for each line, then perform the verse again, adding the chosen changes.

3. Review "I Can Be" CD6:2 **(p. 254). Change the accompaniment.** Have students:

▶ • Sing the three-part section and review that one way to vary a melody is to add another vocal line.

• Sing the song, changing the accompaniment by having some students speak and clap a rhythmic ostinato during the B sections.

change   I   can   change   /   I   can

Unit 6 *A World of Changes* **287**

ASSESSMENTS A AND B CD7:1–10

Different recorded examples for Assessments A and B allow for two uses of the same set of questions. When appropriate, recorded examples for Assessment A use familiar musical examples with which students have worked for the given concept. The recorded examples for Assessment B use musical selections the students have not previously worked with for the concept, encouraging the application of knowledge to new material.

The pupil page is intended for those who wish to assess quickly with the whole class or in small groups. Each assessment may be used as a pretest or as a final review before presenting the written test (**Resource Master 6 • 8**).

ANSWERS		
	ASSESSMENT A	**ASSESSMENT B**
1.	a	a
2.	a	b
3.	b	d
4.	b	d
5.	c	b

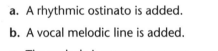

CHECK IT OUT

1. Listen to two examples. Is the second rhythm an augmentation of the first?

   a. Yes **b.** No

2. Listen to two examples. Is the second rhythm an augmentation of the first?

   a. Yes **b.** No

3. Which phrase is in minor?

   a. Phrase 1 **b.** Phrase 2 **c.** Phrase 3 **d.** Phrase 4

4. Listen to two examples. How do the dynamics and tempo change in the second example?

   a. faster and louder **c.** slower and louder

   b. faster and softer **d.** slower and softer

5. Listen to two examples. How does the accompaniment change in the second example?

   a. A rhythmic ostinato is added.

   b. A vocal melodic line is added.

   c. The melody is sung as a canon.

   d. There is no change.

288

MEETING **INDIVIDUAL** NEEDS

PORTFOLIO ASSESSMENT

To evaluate student portfolios, use the Portfolio Assessment form on **Resource Master TA • 1**. See page 250B for a summary of Portfolio Opportunities in this unit.

LANGUAGE ARTS CONNECTION: *Changes*

World Events: Review the changes that have occurred in the students' city, country, and around the world. Have them write about what changes they would like to see happen in the world next year and how they personally could help to make those changes happen.

Personal: Have students draw a picture of how they looked at the beginning of the year and how they look now, then have them draw what they imagine they will (or would like to) look like next year. Write about how they have experienced change over the year and what changes they would like to have happen over the course of the next year.

Literature: Discuss characters in literature who have undergone major changes during the course of a story, such as a change in appearance, in ability, or in knowledge.

CREATE

Melody in Minor

CREATE a melody for part of the poem "Clickbeetle."

Every time you and your partner have the word "beetle," play the pitch A. Choose the rest of your pitches from the minor scale that starts on A.

A   B   C   D   E   F   G   A

Write the pitch letter names you choose on a sheet of paper. Play your part in a performance of the whole poem.

Write

What do you like most about music class? What would you like most to change? What would you like to learn more about?

Write a letter to your teacher explaining your favorite and least favorite music class, and what musical activities you look forward to in the future.

Unit 6 *A World of Changes* 289

1. Compose and perform melodies. Have students:

• Work with partners and follow the instructions on page 289 to compose and perform melodies for "Clickbeetle." (Optional: Use **Resource Master 6 • 9** to notate the melodies.)

2. Write letters. Have students:

▶ • Write letters as described.

National Standards for Music Education

4b Create and arrange short songs and instrumental pieces.

4c Use a variety of sound sources when composing.

5d Use standard symbols to notate patterns.

RELATED ARTS | MOVEMENT | THEATER | **VISUAL ARTS**

Garden Song

Unit 6 Reinforcement
changing dynamics, *page 257*
environmental concern, *page 277*

More Reinforcement
phrase form, *page 35*

1. Introduce the song CD7:11. Have students:

• Listen to the song, following the notation, then discuss the meaning of the words.

• Label the first phrase a and listen again to determine which other phrases sound the same. (Phrase form is a b a b'.)

• Listen and sing along on each phrase.

• Sing the entire song. (Optional: Use "Garden Song" Performance Mix CD10:25.)

2. Explore use of dynamics. Have students:

• Choose different dynamics for different phrases of the song, then sing the song with the new dynamics.

• Discuss the effect of the dynamic changes they made.

MEETING **INDIVIDUAL** NEEDS

CRITICAL THINKING: *Compare and Contrast*

Have students sing "This Pretty Planet" (page 257) and compare its message with that of "Garden Song."

SCIENCE CONNECTION: *Plant Life*

Have students choose a plant that might be grown in a garden, such as strawberry, pumpkin, or iris. Have them research and illustrate its various stages of growth from seedling to mature plant.

Donna, Donna

Music by Sholom Secunda
Words by Aaron Zeitlin

E minor

l, t, d r m f s

Verse *mp*

1. On a wag - on bound for mar - ket,
2. "Stop com - plain - ing," said the farm - er,
3. Calves are eas - i - ly bound and slaugh - tered,

there's a calf with a mourn - ful eye, High a - bove— him
"who told you a— calf to be, Why don't you— have
nev - er know - ing the rea - son why, But who - ev - er

there's a swal - low wing - ing swift - ly— through the sky.
wings to fly— with, like the swal - low so proud and free?"
treas - ures free - dom, like the swal - low has learned to fly.

Refrain *f*

How the winds are laugh - ing, they laugh with all their might,

Laugh and laugh the whole day through, and half the sum - mer's night.

mf Don - na, don - na, don-na, don - na, *f* Don - na, don-na, don-na,— don.

mf Don - na, don - na, don-na, don - na, Don - na, don - na, don-na, don.

Donna, Donna

Unit 6 Reinforcement
minor, *pages 237, 269*
changing dynamics, rhythm, meter,
tempo, *page 285*

More Reinforcement
♩, ♫, ♩, ♪, *page 27*
dynamics; theme of freedom, *page 123*

1. Introduce the song CD7:12. Have students:

• Clap the rhythm of the verse and determine that the first three lines consist of two phrases that are rhythmically the same. (Review ♩, ♫, ♩, ♪)

• Listen to the song, focusing on the theme of the lyrics. (freedom)

• Decide whether the song is in major or minor. (Begins and ends in minor, but the first two lines of the refrain are major.)

• Discuss how this change from minor to major adds to the expressiveness of the song. (The contrast highlights the meaning of words, or message: minor verses have images of longing, imprisonment; the lyrics in the refrain that sound major are about laughter and the wind's freedom.)

2. Sing with dynamics. Have students:

• Listen to the song again, paying attention to dynamic changes and identifying the dynamic markings in the notation.

• Sing the refrain with expressive dynamic changes.

• Choose dynamics with which to sing the verses.

• Sing the entire song with expressive dynamic changes.

• Discuss and experiment with other changes they could make to the song. (rhythm, meter, tempo)

ART CONNECTION: *Expressive Art* VISUAL ARTS

Have students create drawings, paintings, or collages that reflect the images and themes of the words to "Donna, Donna."

ENCORE

LESSON LINKS

Thomas Edison and the Phonograph *(10 min)*

OBJECTIVE Learn about Thomas Edison and the phonograph

MATERIALS
Other paper or waxed paper

Records *(15 min)*

OBJECTIVE Learn about the development of records

MATERIALS
Other sample of a record (any type)

Recorded Sound and Technology *(15 min)*

OBJECTIVE Learn about later developments in recorded sound and technology

MATERIALS
Other samples of cassette tapes and compact discs

FOR THE RECORD

The Granger Collection

When Thomas Edison shouted "Mary had a little lamb" into the mouthpiece of his invention, in 1877, he recorded the first sounds on the first phonograph.

Edison's first "record" was a small metal cylinder. The recorded sound was very weak. After many improvements, people could listen to their favorite music on discs played on the gramophone.

292

MEETING **INDIVIDUAL** NEEDS

BIOGRAPHY: *Thomas Edison*

When Thomas Alva Edison (1847–1931) entered school at the age of seven, he asked too many questions, irritating his teachers. His mother removed him from school and taught him herself, letting him explore and experiment to his delight. As a young man, Edison worked for the railroads and became a telegrapher, then invented for himself an automatically timed telegraph that allowed him to sleep on the job—until his boss found out. The first invention he tried to sell was an electric vote-counter, but the politicians preferred to have time to talk while votes came in rather than

have efficiency. Edison resolved to improve life in ways that would be appreciated, and went on to patent 1,093 inventions in medicine, farming, and other practical areas. His work did indeed bring a lot to many people—his inventions include the electric light bulb, the phonograph, and the first duplicating machine. He also improved earlier inventions, such as the typewriter and the telephone.

BACKGROUND: *The Phonograph*

The early phonograph invented by Edison was made of a cylinder wrapped in tin foil. To record sound, a person

Tune it in...

By 1925, phonograph records were developed. Early records were large and easily broken. Each side held about six minutes of sound. By the late 1940s, long-playing records that held about thirty minutes of sound on each side began to replace the older records.

...or let 'em spin

The phonograph at left is a very early model. Radio/record players such as the one above were used for long-playing records.

Thomas Edison and the Phonograph

Learn about Thomas Edison and the phonograph. Have students:

• Experiment with making sound by using lip vibrations on a piece of paper or wax paper. (Explain that vibrations hitting a surface is the basis of producing sounds from a phonograph record. See the bottom of page 292.)

• Find the picture of Edison and suggest how the first record may have worked. (See below.)

spoke into a mouthpiece. The vibrations of the person's voice were "recorded" on the cylinder by a needle that made dents in the tin foil. The same principle is used to make records. A record's grooves are dented in response to vibrations. Then, a needle called a stylus is placed in the groove and, as the record turns, the dents cause the stylus to vibrate and produce sound, which is amplified by speakers.

BACKGROUND: *The Photograph*

The photograph of Edison and his phonograph was taken at Matthew Brady's studios in 1878. Brady (1823–1896) was

one of the first great historical photographers, and was famed for photographing the Civil War and President Lincoln.

ENRICHMENT: *Making an Invention*

In small groups, have students try to invent something, using various supplies such as paper cups, straws, tape, string, pencil, and paper. Encourage students to brainstorm, then share their ideas with the class.

ENCORE

continued from previous page

Records

Learn about the development of records.
Have students:

• Use the pictures on pages 293–294 to discuss the kinds of records shown and their differences. (dimension of record, size of hole, stereophonic sound)

• Explain what jukeboxes are. (coin-operated record or CD players where a person picks from a pre-selected set of songs)

• Examine a record to see what it's made of. (plastic, has grooves and a center hole)

• Tell the class if they have a stereo at home, explaining when it's used and who uses it.

By the 1950s, the sound quality of records was improved. Through stereophonic sound, two separate tracks of sound, one on the left and one on the right, give the impression of a live performance. When the two tracks are combined, the sound seems to surround the listener.

Left to right: records called 45s, a record player insert for playing 45s, jukebox, cassette tape, portable tape player, CDs.

294 FOR THE RECORD

MEETING **INDIVIDUAL** NEEDS

BACKGROUND: *Tape Recordings*

The first tape recordings were made in 1898 by a Danish engineer named Valdemar Poulsen (**væl** də mɑr **pɑl** sən). The popularity of records overshadowed his invention, and it wasn't until the 1950s that tape recorders became widely used. In the tape-recording process, the thin plastic ribbon of tape receives sound from a microphone in the form of electrical signals. The tape is magnetized and stores these signals as magnetic patterns. In analog recording, the signals are stored in wave form, the form of the original sound. In digital recording, the signals are converted to and stored as numerical codes. Digital audiotapes (DATs) are smaller and lighter than cassette tapes, and they produce a better sound quality. Digital technology is also used in compact discs.

BACKGROUND: *Compact Discs*

Compact discs were first introduced in Japan in 1982 and in the United States and Europe in 1983. The discs are made of plastic and coated with a thin layer of metal. Sound is recorded on the disc in digital, or numerical, codes. To play the sounds, a compact disc player uses a laser beam to

At one time, music stores were filled with rows of record albums. But today, the racks are filled with tapes and CDs. Cassette tapes became popular when small tape recorders were developed. A tape player can be easily carried to the beach or park.

The CD, or compact disc, is much smaller than the record. The sound is very clear. There are no slight hissing noises which records sometimes pick up.

A CD player uses laser technology. When a laser beam passes over one side of the disc, it crosses many pits, which contain the information that will become the music you hear. Now, you can enjoy eighty minutes of music on one CD.

New types of CDs and tapes are still being developed. The CDs and tapes of the future will be even smaller and lighter than those popular today.

Encore 295

Recorded Sound and Technology

Learn about developments in recorded sound and technology. Have students:

• Use the pictures to discuss cassette tapes and compact discs.

• Observe samples of cassette tapes and compact discs.

• Listen as you explain how tapes and CDs store sound. (See *Background* on the bottom of page 294.)

• Discuss their use of tapes and CDs.

retrieve the coded information. CDs that measure 12 centimeters can store up to 74 minutes of sound.

CAREERS: *Recording Engineer*

Recording engineers reproduce sounds for television, films, and recordings. Their challenge is to record a full range of pitches of an orchestra, voices, and other sounds at changing dynamic levels. Becoming a recording engineer requires special two- to four-year college programs, with continual training while working in an actual studio.

SOCIAL STUDIES CONNECTION: *Time Line*

Have students create a time line, using information from the lesson on the history of recording technology. Encourage students to illustrate their time lines.

SCIENCE CONNECTION: *Recorded Sound*

In small groups, have students research one aspect of recorded sound—records, tapes, or CDs. Have students play or show samples as part of their report.

CELEBRATIONS

CELEBRATIONS!

The *Celebrations* section provides music and lessons for patriotic, seasonal, and holiday celebrations from a wide variety of cultures. These materials are collected in a separate section for integration at the appropriate time, providing flexibility, depending on:
- calendar schedules, standard or year-round
- school guidelines about holiday observance
- special interests of students

INTEGRATED LESSONS FOR CONCEPT AND SKILL REINFORCEMENT

Reinforcement references in *Celebrations* lesson suggestions point out key concepts, skills, and themes for the selections, and provide page references to unit lessons that cover the same ideas.

FLEXIBLE LESSON PLANS

Celebrations lessons include separate activity suggestions for each selection, allowing you to use parts or all of a lesson as time permits.

CONTENTS

PLANNER

MULTICULTURAL PERSPECTIVES

Through exposure to diverse materials, students develop an awareness of how people from many cultures create and participate in music. This unit includes:

For a complete listing of songs by culture in this section and throughout the book, see the Classified Index.

		PATRIOTIC DAYS p.298	HALLOWEEN p.304	AUTUMN p.310
	SELECTIONS	The Star-Spangled Banner • America, the Beautiful • Sing a Song of Peace • America • Variations on "America" (listening)	The Boogie Woogie Ghost • The Ghost of John • Scary Music Montage (listening) • Theme in Yellow (poem) • Dry Bones	For Health and Strength • A Mince Pie or Pudding
CONCEPTS	**Expressive Qualities**		**Mood:** • Whisper ostinato to fit mood of song • Recite poem expressively **Dynamics:** Use dynamic changes **Tempo:** Hear accelerando	
	Tone Color	**Vocal:** Sing in heavier or lighter vocal register	**Vocal:** • Whisper phrase as ostinato • Use heavier and lighter registers **Instrumental:** Accompany poem with unpitched instruments	**Vocal:** Notice unison singing
	Duration	**Beat:** • Perform pat-snap-clap pattern with beat • Tap and pat on strong and weak beats in ¾ **Meter:** Conduct in ¾, ⁴⁄₄ **Rhythm:** Clap rhythm with ♩, ♩, ♩.	**Beat:** • Bounce puppets to beat in ⁴⁄₄ • Tap with beat **Meter:** Recognize ⁴⁄₄	**Rhythm:** Clap ♫ from notation
	Pitch	**Melody:** • Find phrases with highest pitch		**Tonality:** Recognize tonal center
	Design	**Form/Structure:** Listen to variation with interlude and coda	**Form/Structure:** Move to show A B C sections **Texture:** • Sing in canon • Whisper ostinato with song	**Texture:** Sing in canon
	Cultural Context	• *Learn about patriotic holidays* • *Learn about the National Anthem* • *Learn about "America, the Beautiful"* • *Learn about "Variations on 'America'"* • *Composer: Charles Ives*	• *Learn about Halloween* • *Learn about excerpts in "Scary Music Montage"* • *Poet: Carl Sandburg* • *Learn about "Dry Bones"*	• *Learn about the Shakers* • *Learn about Thanksgiving*
SKILLS	**Creation and Performance**	**Creating:** Create conducting patterns **Singing:** *Sing partner songs*	**Moving:** Move to show A B C sections **Creating:** Create listening maps	**Moving:** • Perform line dance in unison and in canon • Perform Shaker dance
	Notation	**Reading:** • Find highest pitch from notation • Read ♩, ♪, ♩. from notation		**Reading:** Read ♫ from notation
	Perception and Analysis	**Listening:** • Hear change from ¾ to ⁶⁄₈ • Note style and rhythm change of polonaise • Identify original melody **Analyzing:** Contrast sounds of minor and major	**Listening:** Identify elements that create scary or suspenseful music **Describing:** Describe mood of poem sections **Analyzing:** Compare and contrast elements for listening maps	**Listening:** Identify unaccompanied unison singing

SKILLS OVERVIEW

Italic = Meeting Individual Needs

WINTER p. 312	HANUKKAH p. 316	CHRISTMAS p. 318
Bonhomme! Bonhomme! • Winter Fantasy	In the Window	Para pedir posada • Entren santos peregrinos • Dale, dale, dale!
		Mood: • Use appropriate gestures and expression • Dramatize song with gestures
	Vocal: Hum melodic motive	**Instrumental:** • Play pitched ostinato • Accompany song with chord roots or chords
Beat: Perform pat-clap pattern with beat in ⁶⁄₈ **Meter:** Recognize meter as ⁶⁄₈ **Rhythm:** Clap rhythm in ⁶⁄₈ from notation		**Beat:** Clap with beat
Melody: Recognize so₁ and la₁ **Harmony:** Sing partner songs **Tonality:** Label tonal center, *do*	**Melody:** Recognize melodic motive **Harmony:** Sing in 3-part harmony	**Melody:** Sing ostinato using pitch letter names **Harmony:** • Recognize chord roots • Find pitches for 3 chords • Accompany song with chord roots or chords
Texture: Sing partner songs	**Texture:** Add countermelodies	**Texture:** Accompany song with chord roots or chords
• Learn about Québec Winter Carnival *• Learn about "Jingle Bells"*	*• Learn about Hanukkah* *• Learn about the menorah*	*• Learn about Las Posadas* *• Learn about piñatas*
Singing: Sing partner songs	**Singing:** Sing in 3-part harmony	**Creating:** Dramatize song with gestures and movements
Reading: • Read ⁶⁄₈ rhythms from notation • Identify so₁ and la₁ from notation		**Reading:** Sing pitch letter names from notation
Analyzing: Discuss divisions of beat in ⁶⁄₈	**Listening:** Identify 2- and 3-part harmony	**Listening:** Decide on number of groups of singers **Analyzing:** Share reasons for groups of singers

CELEBRATIONS PLANNER

		CHRISTMAS p. 324	**NEW YEAR** p. 332	**MARTIN LUTHER KING, JR., DAY** p. 336
	SELECTIONS	A Holly Jolly Christmas • O Tannenbaum!: Somewhere in My Memory: The Twelve Days of Christmas	Suk san wan pi mai • Chinese Lion Dance (listening)	Martin's Cry • Down by the Riverside
CONCEPTS	**Expressive Qualities**	**Dynamics:** • Review symbols *pp, p, mp, mf, f,* *<, >* • Plan dynamics for B section **Tempo:** Discuss fermata	**Dynamics:** Play drums softly to accompany song	
	Tone Color	**Instrumental:** • Play introduction, coda on unpitched metal instruments • Add chordal autoharp accompaniment	**Instrumental:** • Accompany song with high-pitched drums • Play finger cymbals • Transfer rhythm patterns to drums and cymbals	
	Duration	**Rhythm:** Clap rhythm pattern of familiar words	**Beat:** • Play drums with beat • Play finger cymbals on first beat of each measure **Rhythm:** Pat and clap ♫, ♪, ♩	**Beat:** Clap with second beat in ⅜
	Pitch	**Melody:** • Sing using pitch syllable names • Explore melodic patterns with *do mi so do¹* **Tonality:** Recognize change from minor to major	**Melody:** • Draw melodic contour in the air • Recognize stepwise movement	**Melody:** • Sing with letter names C, F • Sing with pitch syllable *fa* **Harmony:** • Define harmony • Move to show harmonic changes in accompaniment • Label G chord as based on *do* and D7 chord as based on *so*₁
	Design	**Form/Structure:** • Play introduction and coda • Sing A B form • Sing cumulative song		**Texture:** Sing chordal accompaniment **Form/Structure:** Determine same and different phrases
	Cultural Context	• Sing a song in German • *Learn about Christmas* • *Learn traditional Italian carol* • *Learn about "We Three Kings"* • *Learn traditional English carol*	• *Learn about Laotian New Year* • *Learn about Vietnamese Tet festival* • *Learn about Chinese Lion Dance*	• *Learn about Martin Luther King, Jr.* • *Learn about "Martin's Cry"* • *Learn about spiritual that advocates peace*
SKILLS	**Creation and Performance**	**Playing:** • Play introduction and coda on unpitched metal instruments • Accompany B section on autoharp **Creating/Writing:** Create visuals for sequence of cumulative song	**Playing:** Perform Lion Dance music **Moving:** Learn adapted Chinese Lion Dance **Creating/Moving:** Improvise movement for Chinese Lion Dance	**Moving:** Jump and freeze to show harmonic changes
	Notation	**Reading:** Sing pitch syllables from notation	**Reading:** Read ♫, ♪, ♩ from notation	**Reading:** Sing letter names and pitch syllables from notation
	Perception and Analysis	**Analyzing:** Contrast A and B sections	**Describing:** Describe New Year celebrations and music	**Describing:** Discuss song lyrics

SKILLS OVERVIEW

PRESIDENTS' DAY p. 340	ST. PATRICK'S DAY p. 342	SPRING p. 344
Lincoln Portrait (listening) • To Meet Mr. Lincoln (poem)	Macnamara's Band	Tree Song
Mood: Recognize expressive effects of changes in dynamics and tempo **Dynamics:** • Recognize dynamic changes • Choose dynamic levels		
	Vocal: Recognize changed and unchanged voices **Instrumental:** *Accompany song with unpitched instruments*	**Instrumental:** *Play 4 wood instruments with different tone colors*
Beat: • Recognize longer durations aurally • Perform pat-clap pattern with beat	**Beat:** • *Perform body percussion with beat* • *Play drums with beat* **Rhythm:** *Play rhythmic ostinato with song*	**Meter:** • Choose meters for speech pattern • Change meters
	Melody: • Sing with pitch syllables • Label distance between *so*₁ and *so* as octave • Name *so*₁ and *so* with letter names (C, high C)	**Melody:** • Sing major scale with pitch syllables • Recognize octave leap
Form/Structure: Perform speech piece with introduction and coda	**Texture:** *Accompany song with unpitched instruments* **Form/Structure:** *Show verse and refrain with movement*	
• *Learn about* Lincoln Portrait	• *Learn about St. Patrick's Day* • *Learn about bagpipes*	• *Learn about Arbor Day*
Creating: Create speech piece with dynamic changes	**Playing:** *Accompany song with unpitched instruments* **Moving:** *Perform line dance with partners*	**Playing:** *Accompany poem with wood unpitched instruments* **Creating:** • Create rhythmic speech pattern • *Create musical sounds with environmental objects*
	Reading: • Identify *so*₁ and *so* from notation • Name *so*₁ and *so* with letter names (C, high C)	
Describing: • Discuss how longer durations make music sound slower • Describe tempo, dynamics, and tone color changes • Describe how dynamic changes are used expressively		

CELEBRATIONS PLANNER

CELEBRATIONS

INTRODUCTION

LESSONLINKS

Festival *(15 min)*

OBJECTIVE Read a poem, recognize beat and rhythm of the words, and discuss festivals and celebrations

Reinforcement beat/rhythm of words, *page 15*

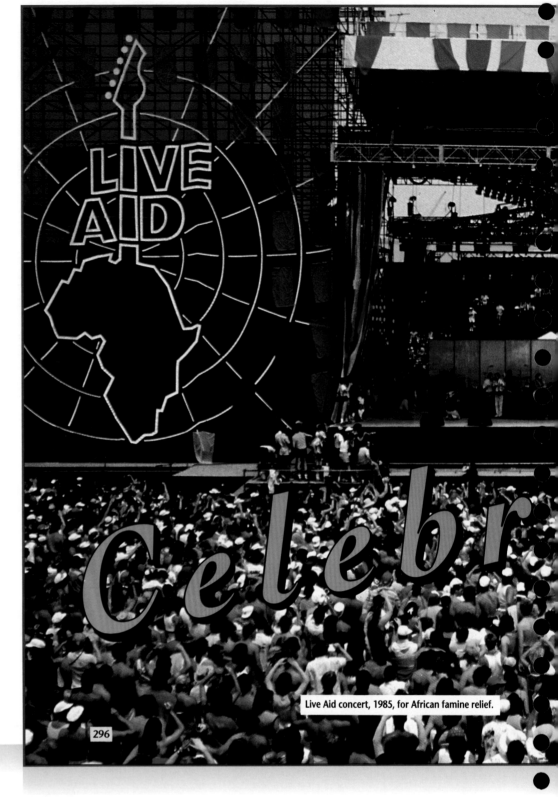

Live Aid concert, 1985, for African famine relief.

MEETING **INDIVIDUAL** NEEDS

BACKGROUND: *Live Aid*

In 1984 Irish rock musician Bob Geldof observed the famine occuring in Ethiopia and set out to use music to bring the world's attention to the problem and raise money for relief. After successfully organizing the recordings *Do They Know It's Christmas?* and *We Are the World*, he thought up a concert unprecedented in the history of rock music. With video linkup, Live Aid took place simultaneously in Philadelphia and London on July 13, 1985. Worldwide television coverage brought participation to over one and a half billion people. The event lasted a full day and in-

cluded performances by rock stars such as Tina Turner, U2, David Bowie, Phil Collins, Paul McCartney, Mick Jagger, Sting, and Madonna. The concert generated over $150 million to help starving people of the world, using rock and roll music as a powerful tool to aid humanity.

BACKGROUND: *Festivals*

Festivals are held for a variety of reasons. Arts festivals have become increasingly popular in recent years. In the early 1700s, one of the first festivals was the "Three Choirs Festival," which moved each year between several cathedral

Festival

Read a poem, recognize beat and rhythm of the words, and discuss seasonal festivals and celebrations. Have students:

• Take turns reading each line of "Festival."

• Read it again, patting steadily with a beat.

• Divide into two groups. One group keeps patting with the beat and the other claps the rhythm of the words of the poem.

• Label the actions of the two groups as "patting with the beat" and "clapping the rhythm of the words."

• Talk about festivals and celebrations, the role of music at such times, and when their favorite holidays occur during the year.

• Work in groups to make a list of songs that they enjoy singing for different celebrations.

FESTIVAL

First of all
Fast of all,
Feast of all—
Festival

—John Kitching

297

cities in England. In the 1800s, choral music was emphasized, as with the Handel Festival. Over time, as more festivals were established, they began to emphasize one composer or type of music. In the last fifty years, music festivals have become a major part of tourism as many visitors are attracted to such locations as Tanglewood in the Berkshire Hills of Massachusetts, Ravinia Park near Chicago, Illinois, and the Hollywood Bowl in Los Angeles.

LANGUAGE ARTS CONNECTION: *Repetition*

Ask students to identify the repeated letter at the beginning of each line of "Festival." (*f*) Students may not be familiar with calling repetition of consonant sounds *alliteration*, but they have encountered it. Use the example of *Peter Piper picked a peck of pickled peppers,* or another tongue twister to illustrate the repetition of an initial consonant. Ask students to think of other repeated sounds in words (rhymes), pointing out that this repetition occurs at the ends of words. Encourage them to notice repetition in all elements (lyrics, pitch, rhythm) of music.

CELEBRATIONS
PATRIOTIC DAYS

RELATED ARTS | MOVEMENT | THEATER | VISUAL ARTS

LESSON LINKS

The Star-Spangled Banner *(25 min)*

OBJECTIVE Sing the national anthem using heavier and lighter vocal registers

Reinforcement vocal registers, *page 23*

MATERIALS
Recordings
The Star-Spangled Banner   CD7:13
The Star-Spangled Banner
(performance mix)   CD10:26

People play and sing the national anthem of their country on official occasions, at athletic events, and to honor the country's leader.

"The Star-Spangled Banner" is the national anthem of the United States. The words of the song recall an important event in the history of the country.

THE STAR-SPANGLED BANNER

Music Attributed to J. S. Smith
Words by Francis Scott Key

1. Oh, — say! can you see, by the dawn's ear-ly light,
2. On the shore, dim-ly seen through the mists of the deep,
3. Oh, — thus be it ev-er when — free men shall stand

What so proud-ly we hailed at the twi-light's last gleam-ing?
Where the foe's haugh-ty host in dread si-lence re - pos-es,
Be - tween their loved homes and the war's des-o - la-tion!

298

MEETING **INDIVIDUAL** NEEDS

BACKGROUND: *Patriotic Holidays*

Patriotism is "love for or devotion to one's country." The celebration of important historical events and persons is one way of demonstrating an appreciation for one's country, just as celebrating a loved one's birthday or anniversary is a way to show care.

BACKGROUND: *The National Anthem*

The music for "The Star-Spangled Banner," a tune from the 1700s called *To Anacreon in Heaven*, was probably written

by John Stafford Smith. The words were written by Francis Scott Key, a prominent American lawyer, who was aboard a captured American ship on September 14, 1814. As he looked out over the water at dawn and saw the American flag flying over Fort McHenry, he was inspired to write the lyrics. The song was played by the Army and Navy bands in the 1890s whenever a national anthem was required. It was made the official national anthem by President Herbert Hoover in 1931.

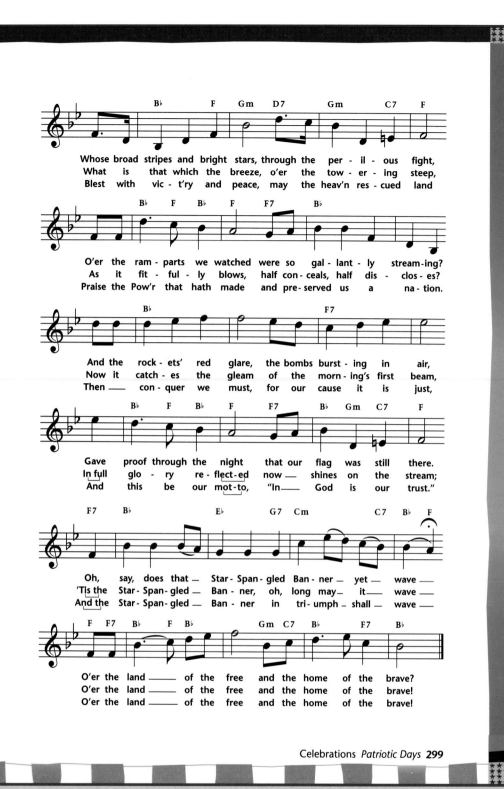

The Star-Spangled Banner
CD7:13

Sing the national anthem using heavier and lighter vocal registers. Have students:

• Listen to "The Star-Spangled Banner," paying particular attention to the words of the second and third verses.

• Identify and discuss the meaning of difficult vocabulary words.

• Look at the pitches in the first two lines of the notation and suggest measures that may be easier to sing in the heavier or in the lighter vocal register.

• Sing the first phrase in the heavier, then in the lighter register. Discuss which register is better and why. (Many students will find it easier to reach the higher pitches if they sing the lower pitches in a lighter or blended voice, rather than in the heavier register, because it does not require a register change.)

• Locate the phrases of the song that include the highest pitch (high F) and practice singing these phrases in the lighter register. (See *Vocal Development* suggestions: Unit 1, Lesson 1, page 8G; Unit 1, Lesson 3, page 22; Unit 2, Lesson 1, page 58.)

• Sing the song.

ENRICHMENT: *Discussing Patriotic Songs*

Ask the students to name the titles of all the patriotic songs that they know. Then have students discuss the places they have heard those songs: sporting events, the Olympics, movies about America, the fireworks at a park, and so forth. Have students discuss their reactions to the songs at the events as well.

SOCIAL STUDIES CONNECTION: *Cooperative Report*

Most patriotic holidays are associated with an historical event or person. Divide the class into cooperative groups. Provide a list of patriotic holidays: Independence Day, Labor Day, Inauguration Day, Pan American Day, Flag Day, Citizenship Day, United Nations Day, Bill of Rights Day, Columbus Day, Memorial Day, Veteran's Day, Armed Forces Day. Have each group choose one to research and give a report on what or who the holiday represents and how the day is typically celebrated.

CELEBRATIONS

PATRIOTIC DAYS

continued from previous page

continued from previous page

LESSON LINKS

America, the Beautiful *(30 min)*

OBJECTIVE Sing a song with dotted rhythms and create drawings to accompany some phrases

Reinforcement
phrase, *page 19*
dotted rhythms, *page 225*

MATERIALS
Recordings
America, the Beautiful   **CD7:14**
America, the Beautiful
    (performance mix)   **CD10:27**

Resources Signing Master S • 4 • 7

Sing a Song of Peace

OBJECTIVE Sing a song with downbeat rests

Reinforcement
4/4 meter, *page 43*
downbeat, *page 75*

MATERIALS
Recording Sing a Song of Peace   **CD7:15**

America, the Beautiful CD7:14

1. Sing a song with dotted rhythms. Have students:

• Listen to the first verse of the song, then clap the rhythm of the first phrase. (Note that each phrase has the same rhythm.)

Katharine Lee Bates traveled across the United States about a hundred years ago. Her trip inspired the poem that became "America, the Beautiful." The words capture not only the beauty of the American landscape, but also the pride Bates felt for her country.

300 CHEER FOR THE U.S.A.

MEETING **INDIVIDUAL** NEEDS

BACKGROUND: *"America, the Beautiful"*

The words to the song were written in 1893 by a college professor, Katharine Lee Bates, during a visit to Colorado. As she looked at Pike's Peak, she was inspired to write a poem. The poem was eventually set to the hymn "Materna," written in 1882 by Samuel Augustus Ward. The music and lyrics were published together in 1910.

LANGUAGE ARTS CONNECTION: *Poetry*

The most popular patriotic songs of the United States use poetic language to express the beauty of the countryside and loyalty to its principles. Have students jot down places, people, ideas, and descriptions that represent America to them. Then have them put the words together to make a poem about the United States.

SIGNING: *"America, the Beautiful"*
Signing Master S • 4 • 7 has sign language for this song.

Although people across the world have different languages and cultures, we can all share a desire for peace, as expressed in this song.

Sing a Song of Peace

Words and Music by Jill Gallina

Sing a song of peace through the world,
'til ev-'ry land is sing-ing._____
Sound the bells of peace through the world,
with ev-'ry na-tion ring-ing._____
Land by land 'cross moun-tain and plain, Hand in hand one
long, lov-ing chain; Un-til peace and
free-dom_____reign from sea_____ to_____ shin-ing sea.

Celebrations *Patriotic Days* **301**

• Look at the notation. Point out dotted quarter-eighth patterns and dotted half notes.

2. Create drawings to accompany some phrases. Have students:

• Listen to the whole song and name places where they may have observed the sight described in each phrase. (You may wish to display photos from books and magazines that capture the essence of each scene for students.)

• Sing the song, imagining each scene.

• Draw personal interpretations of each phrase.

Sing a Song of Peace CD7:15

Sing a song with rests on the downbeats. Have students:

• Conduct in $\frac{4}{4}$ and say *sing* on each downbeat.

• Conduct again, this time saying *sing* on the beat after the downbeat (Beat 2 of every four beats).

• Conduct for a third time, saying *and sing* immediately after each downbeat so that *sing* comes on Beat 2. (Say *and* on the and of Beat 1 and *sing* on Beat 2.)

• Describe the differences of the three conducting activities.

• Listen to the song while conducting and identify the beat each phrase starts on. (Phrase 1—Beat 2; Phrase 2—and of Beat 1; Phrase 3—Beat 2; Phrase 4—and of Beat 1; Phrases 5–7—Beat 2; Phrase 8—and of Beat 4)

• Sing the entire song, conducting in $\frac{4}{4}$.

DRAMA CONNECTION: *Poetic Gestures*

Invite students to perform "America, the Beautiful" as a poem. Have groups of 5–8 form circles and assign each group member a phrase or line of the song lyrics. Tell groups to go around the circle and speak the poem. They should then find the descriptive words or phrases (for example, spacious, amber waves) and create gestures to describe those words. Have them expand the gestures and perform the poem with words and gestures. Finally have them perform the poem with gestures only. Have groups observe each other's performances, noticing how their choices of gestures varied for the same words.

EXTRA HELP: *Conducting in $\frac{4}{4}$*

Have students use the verbal cue *down cross out up* to learn and remember the conducting pattern for $\frac{4}{4}$ meter. For a diagram, refer to page 346.

ENRICHMENT: *Partner Songs*

"Sing a Song of Peace" was written as a partner song to "This Is My Country," page 7. When students are secure in singing each song, they may perform the two songs together. Have them sing "This Is My Country" in the key of D or "Sing a Song of Peace" in C, as appropriate to the group.

Celebrations PATRIOTIC DAYS **301**

CELEBRATIONS

PATRIOTIC DAYS

continued from previous page

LESSONLINKS

America *(20 min)*

OBJECTIVE Sing a song with dotted rhythms and conduct in three

Reinforcement ¾ meter and dotted rhythms, *page 233*

MATERIALS
Recording America   **CD7:16**

Resources Recorder Master R • 35 (pitches A C' D')

Technology Music with MIDI: America

Variations on "America" *(20 min)*

OBJECTIVE Listen to variations on a theme, and follow a listening map

Reinforcement theme and variations, *page 285*

MATERIALS
Recording Variations on "America" (excerpts) by C. Ives (listening)   **CD7:17**

Resources Listening Map Transparency T • 11

The words to "America" were first recited at a children's Fourth of July picnic in Boston in the 1800s. Later, Reverend Smith, the man who wrote the words, chose a hymnlike tune from a collection of German melodies to set the words to music.

302 CHEER FOR THE U.S.A.

MEETING **INDIVIDUAL** NEEDS

BACKGROUND: *"Variations on 'America'"*

When Charles Ives was 13 years old, he began playing the organ for church services. It was in this setting that he began to improvise on the keyboard without following standard musical rules. Partly for fun, he played music in more than one key at the same time, finding an alternative to the traditional music he usually heard and played. The simultaneous use of two keys, called bitonality, produces a dissonant sound. At the age of 17, Ives used bitonality to compose "Variations on 'America.'" The piece has five main variations, as well as some interludes and a coda.

BACKGROUND: *Charles Ives*

Charles Ives (1874–1954) was born in Danbury, Connecticut and graduated from Yale University. For most of his adult life, he worked as an insurance executive. He wrote his music in the evenings and on weekends. Most of his music shows his love of American folk music, New England, baseball, and patriotic themes. Although he gained some recognition for his music toward the end of his life, most of his music was not played in public until after he died. Today he is recognized as a highly innovative composer who was way ahead of his time.

Variations on "America" (excerpts)
by Charles Ives

Musical variations are different versions of the same tune. Ives wrote these variations as a teenager. The music is humorous and somewhat outrageous. One section of the music is in two different keys at the same time–one key in the right hand and another in the left.

LISTENING MAP *You will hear the basic theme, followed by variations. Listen for the dramatic changes and playful surprises.*

Celebrations *Patriotic Days* **303**

America CD7:16

Sing a song with dotted rhythms and conduct in three. Have students:

• Listen to Verse 1 of the song, counting the times they hear and see this dotted rhythm pattern. (4)

$$\frac{3}{4} \quad \textrm{♩} \quad \textrm{♩} \quad \textrm{♩} \quad | \quad \textrm{♩.} \quad \textrm{♪} \quad \textrm{♩} \quad ||$$

• Listen again while quietly performing a pat-clap-snap pattern with the beat.

• Create their own conducting pattern in three by using motions in place.

• Sing the entire song, performing their own conducting patterns with the beat.

Variations on "America"
CD7:17

Listen to variations on a theme and follow a listening map. Have students:

• Listen to the theme, tapping shoulders on the strong beats (1) and patting knees on the other beats (2–3).

• Talk about what a calliope is, how it works, and where one might be heard. Listen to the second excerpt, patting ¾ patterns. Discover that the meter has changed to ⅝.

• Discuss the contrasting sounds of minor and major. Listen to the next excerpt (polonaise), noting the dance style and rhythm change. Try singing the melody (unaccompanied) in the minor key.

• Listen to the next excerpt (interlude), then suggest descriptive words to interpret the sounds they heard.

• Listen to the last excerpt (coda), raising hands each time they recognize the original melody.

• Listen to the piece again, following the listening map. (Optional: Use **Listening Map Transparency T · 11**.)

ENRICHMENT: *Program Ideas*

Create a program in honor of the United States. Begin by having the audience join the students in singing the National Anthem. Have students perform the Preamble to the Constitution as a choral reading, then sing "America." Choose some of the best patriotic poems in the class *(Language Arts Connection,* page 300*)* and have those students read the poems, with the class softly humming "America, the Beautiful" in the background. When the poems are finished, have students begin to sing "America, the Beautiful" while showing slides of their drawings (or photographs of the United States). Finish by performing "America, the Beautiful" in American Sign Language.

CELEBRATIONS

HALLOWEEN

RELATED ARTS | MOVEMENT | THEATER | VISUAL ARTS |

SELECTIONS

LESSON LINKS

The Boogie Woogie Ghost *(30 min)*

OBJECTIVE Move puppets in eight-beat patterns with music in $\frac{4}{4}$ meter

Reinforcement eight-beat patterns in $\frac{4}{4}$ meter, *page 43*

MATERIALS
Recordings
The Boogie Woogie Ghost   CD7:18
The Boogie Woogie Ghost
(performance mix)   CD10:28

Other paper napkins, string, pencil

FRIGHT NIGHT

The fun of fright and "things that go bump in the night" makes Halloween a playful holiday.

THE BOOGIE WOOGIE GHOST

Words and Music by
Nadine M. Peglar

1. There was a ghost on Hal-low-een, He real-ly made the ghost-ie scene,
2. He'd go out spook-ing late at night, And giv-ing ev'-ry-one a fright,

He was the Boo-gie-Woo-gie Ghost, He was the ghost-ie with the most,
He knew some wit-ches, two or three, And they would all go on a spree,

And when the kid-dies came a-round, He'd give out with a ghost-ly sound,
And when the morn-ing came a-round, He'd give one last mys-te-rious sound,

He'd go,— "Boo-oo-oo-oo-ooo."   ooo."

304

MEETING **INDIVIDUAL** NEEDS

MULTICULTURAL PERSPECTIVES: *Halloween*

Halloween falls on October 31, the eve of All Saints' Day. Many of the customs celebrated in the United States come from Ireland and Great Britain. For example, people hollowed out turnips, beets, and potatoes, placing a lit candle inside, for a Halloween lantern. Americans changed this custom by using pumpkins for their decorations. The Irish were responsible for the trick-or-treat custom. Farmers would go door-to-door to get food for their village, giving tricks or treats, depending on the generosity of the donors.

LANGUAGE ARTS CONNECTION: *Creative Writing*

"The Boogie Woogie Ghost" provides introductory material for a myriad of creative stories about this "cool" ghost. Have students silently read the words of the song, imagining what the Boogie Woogie Ghost might be like. Then have each student write a short story based on one sentence from the song.

The Boogie Woogie Ghost
CD7:18

Move puppets in eight-beat patterns with music in ¼ meter. Have students:

• Listen to the song while tapping with the beat with fingers on the back of other hand.

• Note that the meter signature of the song is ¼ and discuss that this means there are four beats to a set.

• Construct puppets. (See *Extra Help* below.)

• Practice bouncing their puppets to the beat, changing where they bounce the puppets with every two sets of beats. (eight beats on the desk, eight on the back of hand, eight on head, shoulder, knee, foot, and so on)

• Sing "The Boogie Woogie Ghost," bouncing the puppets with the beat as practiced. (During each long *Boo-oo-oo-oo-ooo* hold all puppets high in the air.)

G7   C
Though he real - ly was - n't ver - y spook - y, —

G7   C
Kids all thought that he was rath - er cool.

D7   G
E - ven though he was a lit - tle kook - y, —

Am   D   G7
He was just a spe - cial — ghoul. When you're

C
out on Hal - low - een And he ap - pears up - on the scene,

      F   C
Don't give a scream and run a - way, Just ask him if he'll stay and play.

      G   F
You'll like the Boo - gie - Woo - gie Ghost, He'll be the one you dig the most,

     C F C F   C
You'll love his Boo - oo - oo - oo - ooo.

Celebrations Halloween **305**

EXTRA HELP: *Paper-Napkin Ghosts*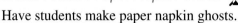

Have students make paper napkin ghosts.

1. Unfold large napkin to its full size.

2. Crumple a piece of paper (8 ½ x 11 inch) into a small ball.

3. Place paper ball in the center of unfolded napkin.

4. Wrap napkin around the paper ball and allow the ends to hang down, forming the head of the ghost.

5. Tie string or yarn around "neck" of the ghost, leaving a slight opening for the stick.

6. Place pencil (eraser out) or dowel through the neck and into the head to create a handle for the puppet.

7. Draw eyes and mouth in appropriate places.

MOVEMENT: *"The Boogie Woogie Ghost"*

Students may enjoy performing eight-beat movement ostinatos with this song. Have them use the rhythm patterns on page 43. (See *Movement*, Unit 1, Lesson 8, the bottom of page 43.)

CELEBRATIONS

HALLOWEEN

continued from previous page

LESSONLINKS

Ghost of John (20 min)

OBJECTIVE Sing a song with whispered ostinato

Reinforcement ostinato, *page 43*
phrase, *page 35*

MATERIALS
Recording The Ghost of John   CD7:19

Resources
Orff Orchestration O • 15
Recorder Master R • 36 (pitches E G A B)

Theme in Yellow (15 min)

OBJECTIVE Accompany an autumn poem with unpitched instruments

Reinforcement accompaniment to a poem, *page 39*

MATERIALS
Instruments unpitched instruments

Scary Music Montage (30 min)

OBJECTIVE Listen to a Halloween montage and create a listening map

Reinforcement Halloween, *page 43*
dynamics, *page 123*

MATERIALS
Recording Scary Music Montage (listening)   CD7:20

Whisper a spooky vocal ostinato to help express the chilling message of this song.

The Ghost of JOHN

Words and Music
by Martha Grubb

E minor

m, f, s, l, t, d r m f s

Em — Am — Em
Have you seen the ghost of John?

Em — Am — Em
Long white bones with the skin all gone, Oo, oo,

Am — Em — Am — Em
Would-n't it be chil-ly with no skin on!

306 FRIGHT NIGHT

MEETING **INDIVIDUAL** NEEDS

BACKGROUND: *"Scary Music Montage"*

"Scary Music Montage" consists of excerpts from seven pieces. **1.** "The Hut on Fowl's Legs" from *Pictures at an Exhibition* by Modest Mussorgsky (mo **dest** mu **sɔrg** ski) evokes the witch Baba-Yaga from Russian fairy tales. For more information about Mussorgsky, see Unit 2, Lesson 3, pages 70–71. **2.** Overture to *William Tell* by Gioachino (or Gioacchino) Rossini (jo a **ki** no **rɔs si** ni) is from Rossini's last opera. The section heard describes an Alpine storm. **3.** "What the Monster Saw" by Libby Larsen is from a musical drama titled *Frankenstein*. During the instrumental interlude, dancers portray what the monster feels and thinks. **4.** "Dies Irae" is from the *Requiem* Giuseppe Verdi (ju **zɛp** pɛ **ver** di) wrote to honor the Italian poet and novelist Manzoni, whom Verdi considered a great artist and patriot. **5.** *Don Quixote* (don ki **xo** te) by Richard Strauss is a tone poem about Don Quixote, the famous knight in literature who saw windmills and imagined that they were menacing giants. **6.** *The Miraculous Mandarin* by Béla Bartók (**be** la **bar** tɔk) is a one-act ballet about the ambush of a wealthy state official of Imperial China. **7.** *Atmospheres* by György Ligeti (**gyor** gi **lɪ get** i) was written in memory of a friend

Theme in YELLOW

I spot the hills
With yellow balls in autumn.
I light the prairie cornfields
Orange and tawny gold clusters
And I am called pumpkins.
On the last of October
When dusk is fallen
Children join hands
And circle round me
Singing ghost songs
And love to the harvest moon;
I am a jack-o'-lantern
With terrible teeth
And the children know
I am fooling.

—Carl Sandburg

LISTENING — Scary Music Montage

A suspense film or television program uses scary music to heighten the effect of what is happening on the screen. The frightening effect of music, however, is not only used in television and film. For a long time, composers have used minor keys, crescendos, and surprises to build tension and startle their listeners. As you listen to the "Scary Music Montage," you will hear music that makes you feel uneasy. Determine why the music might have an unsettling effect.

Celebrations *Halloween* **307**

The Ghost of John CD7:19

Sing a song with whispered ostinato. Have students:

• Listen to the song without the notation. Recall the four phrases in order.

• Say the text in rhythm.

• Sing the song, then form four groups and sing in canon.

• Dramatically whisper the phrase *Have you seen the ghost of John?* in rhythm.

• Group by group, whisper *Have you seen the ghost of John?* as an ostinato while others sing the song. (Sing the song four times so that each group performs the ostinato.)

Theme in Yellow

Accompany an autumn poem with un-pitched instruments. Have students:

• Read the poem and decide how it could be divided into three logical sections.

• Describe the mood of each section, then select unpitched instruments with tone colors that enhance each section.

• Take turns expressively reciting one or two lines as others play the chosen instruments.

Scary Music Montage CD7:20

Listen to a Halloween montage and create a listening map. Have students:

• Listen to the montage and identify musical elements that create suspense. (minor keys, crescendos, surprises)

• Listen again, writing down at least one descriptive word for each excerpt.

• Listen a third time, making up simple visual representations for what they hear.

• Create listening maps to share with the class. Compare and contrast their chosen elements and visual representations.

who was killed in a car accident. The composer says the piece contains "uninhabited, imaginary musical space."

BACKGROUND: *Carl Sandburg*

Carl Sandburg (1878–1967) was an American poet who wrote about the spirit of the American Midwest and the ordinary people who lived there. His writing style was influenced by Walt Whitman. He also wrote a six-volume biography of Abraham Lincoln and some children's books.

EXTRA HELP: *Listening Map* VISUAL ARTS

If students have difficulty making maps for "Scary Music Montage," have them look at other listening maps in the book. Encourage them to work with whatever images or words come into their minds as they listen. Relate the brief background notes to help them. Students may also divide into seven groups and together develop an image for their assigned excerpt. Use the groups' images to complete a class map.

ORFF: *"The Ghost of John"*

See **O · 15** in *Orchestrations for Orff Instruments.*

CELEBRATIONS

HALLOWEEN

continued from previous page

LESSON LINKS

Dry Bones *(20 min)*

OBJECTIVE Sing a Halloween song, showing the form with changing movement

Reinforcement
movement ostinato, *page 43*
sectional form, *page 91*

MATERIALS
Recordings
Dry Bones   **CD7:21**
Dry Bones (performance mix)   **CD11:1**

Resources Recorder Master R • 37
(pitches G A B)

Technology Music with MIDI: Dry Bones

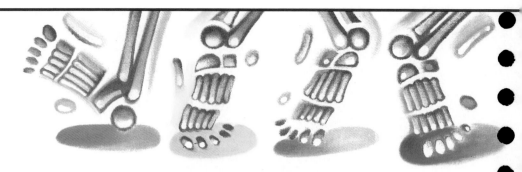

The rhythm of this song may get your skeleton moving!

DRY BONES

African American Spiritual

Freely

E - ze - kiel cried, "Them dry bones!" E - ze - kiel cried, "Them dry bones!"

E - ze - kiel cried, "Them dry bones, Now hear the Word of the Lord!" E -

gradually getting faster

Lord!" The foot bone con - nect - ed to the leg bone,

The leg bone con - nect - ed to the knee bone,

The knee bone con - nect - ed to the hip - bone,

The hip - bone con - nect - ed to the back - bone,

308 FRIGHT NIGHT

MEETING **INDIVIDUAL** NEEDS

BACKGROUND: *"Dry Bones"*

Although "Dry Bones" does not appear among collected and studied African American spirituals, the lyrics have Biblical sources. ". . . O dry bones, hear the word of the Lord. Thus says the Lord God to these bones: Behold, I will cause breath to enter you, and you shall live . . . and as I prophesied, there was a noise, and behold, a rattling; and the bones came together, bone to its bone" (from Ezekiel 37). The song's joyful rhythm and its use of the prophetic words of Ezekiel communicate the traditional spirituals' message of hope for a better life.

SCIENCE CONNECTION: *The Human Skeleton*

MOVEMENT

Have students look up the human skeleton in a science book or encyclopedia to find out about bones and how they are connected. Have them draw a picture of a skeleton and label the bones.

Have students identify on their bodies the joints, or points of movement, described in the song. (for example, "the foot bone connected to the leg bone," or ankle) Then have them explore the movement possible at each joint. Knowledge of the body and how it works can help students move sensibly and safely in work, play, and dance.

Dry Bones CD7:21

1. Practice movement. Have students:

- Describe the movement qualities that a skeleton might have. (loose, shaky, disjointed, uncoordinated)

- Walk around the room like skeletons.

- Listen to the recording and follow the notation.

- Listen again, tapping with the beat on each body part as it comes up in the lyrics. (For example, when singing *The foot bone connected to the leg bone*, students should tap on their foot and then their leg.)

2. Sing the song, showing the form with a changing movement. Have students:

- Sing the entire song, performing different movement with each section. (**A section:** clap hands with beats 2 and 4; **B section:** tap with the beat on each body part, as practiced; **C section:** walk around the room like skeletons, as rehearsed at the beginning of the lesson.)

Celebrations *Halloween* **309**

ENRICHMENT: *Halloween Party*

Have a Halloween party with costumes and goodies. Perform "The Boogie Woogie Ghost," "The Ghost of John," and "Dry Bones" as part of the celebration.

CELEBRATIONS
AUTUMN

RELATED ARTS [MOVEMENT] [THEATER] [VISUAL ARTS]

SELECTIONS
FOR HEALTH AND STRENGTH, *page 310*
A MINCE PIE OR PUDDING, *page 311*

LESSONLINKS

For Health and Strength *(20 min)*
OBJECTIVE Sing an Old English round, identify the tonal center, and perform a double-line movement

Reinforcement tonal center, *page 83*

MATERIALS
Recording For Health and Strength   CD7:22

Resources Orff Orchestration O • 16

A Mince Pie or Pudding *(20 min)*
OBJECTIVE Sing a Shaker welcome song with ♫ and perform a simple Shaker dance

Reinforcement
♫, *page 75*
Shaker song, *page 269*

MATERIALS
Recording A Mince Pie or Pudding   CD7:23

Resources Recorder Master R • 38 (pitches D E)

Every day of the year, crops are gathered somewhere in the world. Whenever and wherever the harvest comes, it is a time for celebration and thanksgiving.

F major

s, t, d r m f s

For Health and Strength
Old English Round

For health and strength and dai-ly food

We praise Thy name, Oh, Lord.

310

MEETING **INDIVIDUAL** NEEDS

MULTICULTURAL PERSPECTIVES: *The Shakers*

The Shakers were an early American religious sect that started in England about 1706. Called "The United Society of Believers in Christ's Second Appearing," they got the name "Shakers" by the way they worshiped with dancing and shaking. Like others, they came to the United States for religious freedom. The Shakers lived in self-contained communities with unusual equality between sexes and races for that time. They built prized furniture, produced the first commercial seed in the U.S., and invented such things as flat brooms, a washing machine, and the circular saw.

BACKGROUND: *Thanksgiving*

The first Thanksgiving in New England took place in Plymouth, Massachusetts, in 1621 after the Pilgrims' first successful harvest. To show their gratitude, they invited nearby Native Americans to a three-day feast. In 1863 President Lincoln designated the last Thursday in November as Thanksgiving Day; in 1941 President Franklin D. Roosevelt and Congress decreed that Thanksgiving be observed as a federal holiday on the fourth Thursday in November.

ORFF: *"For Health and Strength"*
See **O • 16** in *Orchestrations for Orff Instruments.*

During the 1800s, there were many Shaker villages in the eastern part of the United States. Kathy Jakobsen's painting, shown below, depicts the simple life-style of Shaker communities. This Shaker song welcomes visitors.

A Mince Pie or Pudding

Shaker Song

Wel - come here! Wel - come here!
All be a - live and be of good cheer!
I've got a pie all baked com - plete with

Go back to the beginning and sing to the end
(Da Capo al Fine)

pud - ding, too, that's ver - y sweet.

North Union, Shaker Village, Kathy Jakobsen, 1984

Celebrations *Autumn* **311**

For Health and Strength
CD7:22

1. Learn the song and identify the tonal center. Have students:

• Listen to the song, singing along when they know the melody.

• Hum the tonal center. (F/*do*)

• Divide into two groups and sing in canon.

2. Learn the movement. Have students:

• Practice a basic step, then perform the movement while singing the song. (See *Movement* below.)

A Mince Pie or Pudding CD7:23

1. Learn the song. Have students:

• Listen to the recording and describe what they hear. (no instruments; singing in unison)

• Clap the rhythm of the first two lines from the notation.

• Tell how many times ♩♫ occurs. (2)

• Sing the song.

2. Learn the dance. Have students:

• Sing the song again with hand gestures: pretend to shake someone's hand on Beat 1 and clap their own hands on Beat 2. (The pattern is shake-clap throughout the song.)

• Sing the song, performing hand gestures with a partner.

• Practice the dance, saying *shake, clap, shake, clap* slowly and evenly. (See *Movement* below. The formation is illustrated here.)

Girls   Boys

• Perform the song and dance.

MOVEMENT: *"For Health and Strength"*

Formation: two lines facing

Verbal Cue—*forward, close, backward, close; turn, 2, 3, 4.* Step R foot forward on *health,* close L foot beside R on *strength,* step R foot backward on *daily,* close L foot next to R on *food.* Turn once in place on *We praise thy name,* stopping on *Lord.*

Final Form: Decide which line will start in the canon, then perform the step while singing, first in unison, then in canon. (The unison and canon floor patterns will differ.)

MOVEMENT: *"A Mince Pie or Pudding"*

Formation: two continuous horseshoes, facing in direction of arrows (One horseshoe should be only boys, the other only girls, because the Shakers did not mix the men and women.)

Dance: *Shake*—shake hands with adjacent partner (always to left in girls' horseshoe, to right in boys', and walking in opposite direction) *Clap*—clap and take a small step forward, coming abreast of next partner. Continue to shake and clap with each new partner.

CELEBRATIONS
WINTER

RELATED ARTS | MOVEMENT | THEATER | VISUAL ARTS

SELECTIONS
BONHOMME! BONHOMME! *page 313*
WINTER FANTASY, *page 314*

LESSONLINKS

Bonhomme! Bonhomme! *(15 min)*

OBJECTIVE Sing a song in ⅜ about the Québec Winter Carnival

Reinforcement ⅜ rhythms, *page 131*

MATERIALS
Recordings
Bonhomme! Bonhomme!   CD7:24
Recorded Lesson: Pronunciation for
  "Bonhomme! Bonhomme!"   CD7:25

Winters are very cold in Canada. Each year, however, Canadians of all ages gather to "discover the warmth of winter" at the Quebec Carnival. Parades, fireworks, snow sculpture competitions, sporting events, and concerts are all part of the winter celebration. The festivities are led by Bonhomme Carnaval, a smiling snowman.

Bonhomme! Bonhomme!

Canadian Folk Song
English Version by MMH

B♭ major

French: Bon-homme, Bon-homme, sais-tu jou-er? Bon-homme, Bon-
Pronunciation: bɔ nɔm bɔ nɔm sɛ tü ʒu e bɔ nɔm bɔ
English: 1.-3. Bon-homme, Bon-homme, can you play this? Bon-homme, Bon-

homme, sais-tu jou-er? Sais-tu jou-er de ce vi-o-lon-
nɔm sɛ tü ʒu e sɛ tü ʒu e də sə vi o lɔ̃
homme, can you play this? { Can you play this on the vi - o -
                            Can you play this on the ti - ny
                            Can you play this on the big—— bass

312

MEETING **INDIVIDUAL** NEEDS

MULTICULTURAL PERSPECTIVES: *Winter Carnival*

Québec City, often called "The World's Snow Capital," held its first winter carnival in 1894 as a way of helping its citizens forget the harshness of the weather. The festival became an annual event in 1954 and is now an international event, welcoming thousands of visitors each year. The carnival's official symbol is Bonhomme Carnaval (bə **nɔm** kaɾ nə **val**), a smiling snowman. He wears a traditional red tuque (tŭk), or stocking cap, and a hand-woven belt like those worn by French Canadian fur traders of the late

1600s and early 1700s. Bonhomme Carnaval's official residence is a magnificent Snow Palace, built each year of nearly 9,000 metric tons of snow.

SOCIAL STUDIES CONNECTION: *Québec Province*

Have students work in pairs to research one aspect of the province of Québec and its unique history. Topics might include the St. Lawrence Seaway, natural resources, the cities of Montréal and Québec, and the government of the province. Have students summarize their findings in class, using pictures or maps if possible.

Bonhomme! Bonhomme!
CD7:24

Sing a song in § about the Québec Winter Carnival. Have students:

• Read about the Québec (ke **bɛk**) Winter Carnival.

• Listen to the song and perform a pat-clap pattern with the beat.

• Discuss the divisions of the beats they heard and look at the notation to confirm their answers. (♪♪♪, ♩♪, ♩.)

• Identify the meter signature as being § and clap the rhythm of the first three lines from the notation.

Recorded Lesson CD7:25

• Listen to "Pronunciation for 'Bonhomme! Bonhomme!'"

• Sing the song.

Bonhomme Carnaval is the official ambassador of the Quebec Carnival.

là? Sais - tu jou - er de ce vi - o - lon - **là?**
la sɛ tü ʒu e də sə vi ɔ lɔ̃ la
lin? Can you play this on the vi - o - lin?
flute? Can you play this on the ti - ny flute?
drum? Can you play this on the big___ bass drum?

verses accumulate

Zing, zing, zing de ce vi - o - lon - **là.** Bon - homme! Bon -
ʒɛ̃ ʒɛ̃ ʒɛ̃ də sə vi ɔ lɔ̃ la bɔ nɔm bɔ
Zing, zing, zing on the vi - o - lin. Bon - homme! Bon -
Toot, toot, toot on the ti - ny flute,
Boom, boom, boom on the big___ bass drum,

homme! Tu n'es pas maîtr' dans ta mai -
nɔm tü ne pa mɛtr dã ta mɛ
homme! You are not boss in your own

son Quand nous y som - mes!___
ʒɔ̃ kã nu zi sɔ mə
home When we come here to play!___

4. Can you play this on the great big horn?
Ta-ta-ra on the great big horn, . . .

PRONUNCIATION: *"Bonhomme! Bonhomme!"*

a f<u>a</u>ther   e ch<u>a</u>otic   ɛ p<u>e</u>t   i b<u>ee</u>   o <u>o</u>bey
ɔ p<u>aw</u>   u m<u>oo</u>n   ə <u>a</u>go   ɾ flipped r
ü lips form [u] and say [i]   ʒ plea<u>s</u>ure
~ nasalized vowel

DRAMA CONNECTION: *Building a Story*

Have students build a story about Bonhomme, one word at a time. Form a circle, then choose a student to begin by saying one word. Go around the circle, the other students adding a word each by responding quickly, without thinking, to the previous word. Allow the story to build past the point of absurdity. When students have finished, ask them to recount the story. Repeat the exercise, then ask students to write and reshape the story individually. Have them discuss whether this method of building a story was effective and what other methods they could use.

CELEBRATIONS
WINTER

continued from previous page

LESSON LINKS

Winter Fantasy *(30 min)*

OBJECTIVE Sing partner songs and use pitch syllables including low *so*, low *la*

Reinforcement low *so*, low *la*, *page 79*

MATERIALS
Recordings
Winter Fantasy   **CD7:26**
Winter Fantasy (performance mix)   **CD11:2**

Winter Fantasy CD7:26

1. Learn each song in unison. Have students:

• Listen to each song, following the words.

• Echo-speak the words of each song in rhythm.

• Sing each song in unison.

Add a partner song to "Jingle Bells" to create harmony.

WINTER FANTASY

Words and Music
by Jill Gallina

Snow - flakes fall - ing all o - ver town,

Dash - ing through the snow in a one - horse o - pen sleigh,

Slip - ping, slid - ing ev' - ry - bod - y rush - in' 'round.

O'er the fields we go, laugh - ing all the way.

There's an i - cy chill in the air,

Bells on bob - tails ring, mak - ing spir - its bright. What

Tell - ing us that win - ter's real - ly here. Oh!

fun it is to laugh and sing a sleigh - ing song to - night. Oh!

314 WINTER CARNIVAL

MEETING **INDIVIDUAL** NEEDS

BACKGROUND: *"Jingle Bells"*

People usually think of "Jingle Bells" as a Christmas song, but James Pierpoint actually wrote it in 1857 for a Thanksgiving program for a large Boston church he attended. No matter when it is sung, "Jingle Bells" captures the spirit of winter fun.

ART CONNECTION: *Creating a Winter Scene*   VISUAL ARTS

Have students draw or paint pictures with a winter theme. If you live in a part of the country where there is no snow, have students either look in encyclopedias for pictures and information about winter in other parts of the nation or draw pictures of the subtle differences winter brings to their own area.

F major

f

I'm so glad that win-ter is here.

f

Jin - gle bells, jin - gle bells, jin - gle all the way.

Grab your sled and let out a hap-py cheer Be -cause it's

Oh, what fun it is to ride in a one -horse o - pen sleigh.

snow - ing, blow - ing, all through the day.

Jin - gle bells, jin - gle bells, jin - gle all the way.

ff

Win - ter winds will sure-ly blow all your cares a - way. Hey!

ff

Oh, what fun it is to ride in a one - horse o - pen sleigh! Hey!

Celebrations *Winter* **315**

2. Review pitch syllables including low *so* and low *la*. Have students:

• Hum the tonal center of the songs and label it *do*.

• Locate *do* to the left of the first staff in the notation.

• Identify, then sing, the pitch syllables for the first and fifth lines of both songs. (Starting with the fifth line may be easier. Sing as slowly as necessary; use hand signs if desired.)

• Say the words of the first line where low *so* and low *la* occur. (*fall-, dash-, snow in a one-, sleigh*)

3. Sing "Winter Fantasy" in parts. Have students:

• Listen to the partner songs sung together and create a definition of partner songs. (two songs that can be sung together because they have the same harmony)

• Sing each song several times.

• Divide into two groups, one group singing each song. Switch roles and repeat. (Students should sing the songs together only when they are secure singing each one separately.)

ENRICHMENT: *Letter Exchange*

Start a letter-writing project with a fourth-grade class in another part of the country where winter is very different from where you live. Have all of the students in the class write a letter describing what winter is like in your area and asking what winter is like in the other region. Have them ask their pen pals what songs they sing in winter. You can find the address of a school or school district office by using telephone directories in a public library or exchanging letters with a colleague who lives in another part of the country. You can also simply choose a small town on the map and address your letter to:

A Fourth Grade Classroom
Town Name, State Name, Zip Code

CELEBRATIONS
HANUKKAH

SELECTION
IN THE WINDOW, *page 317*

LESSONLINKS

In the Window *(30 min)*

OBJECTIVE Identify a melodic motive and sing in three-part harmony

Reinforcement motive, *page 87*

MATERIALS
Recordings
In the Window   **CD7:27**
In the Window (performance mix)   **CD11:3**

Resources Recorder Master R • 39 (pitches D G A)

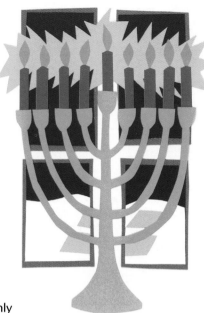

The Miracle of Lights

Lighting candles for Hanukkah honors a special event in Jewish history. Long ago, the people of Jerusalem wanted to relight their holy lamp, but there was only enough oil for one day. Miraculously, the small amount of oil lasted for eight days.

G minor

IN THE WINDOW

Hebrew Folk Song
Arranged by Mary Goetze

Slowly

In the win-dow where you can see the glow of my me-no-rah on new-ly fall-en snow, I will set you one* lit-tle can-dle(s) on this, the { first* } { last } night of Ha-nuk-kah.

*On each of the nights of Hanukkah, sing the correct number.
On the eighth verse, sing the word "last."

316

MEETING **INDIVIDUAL** NEEDS

MULTICULTURAL PERSPECTIVES: *Hanukkah*

Hanukkah celebrates the recovery and cleansing of the Jerusalem temple in 164 B.C. by Judah Maccabee (**ju** də **mæ** kə bì), also called Maccabaeus, from the Syrian ruler Antiochus IV (ɑn **ti** ə kəs). According to the story, when the people relit the lamp in the temple, there was only enough oil for one night. To their surprise, the oil lasted eight days. Years later, after the temple had been restored, there was a declaration that candles should burn for eight days of celebration in memory of the triumph. Hanukkah is also called the "festival of lights."

MULTICULTURAL PERSPECTIVES: *The Menorah*

A menorah (mɛ **nor** ɑ) is a Hanukkah candelabra with holders for nine candles. Eight of the candles represent the eight days that the miraculous oil burned in the temple; the ninth candle is used to light the other eight. A new candle is lit every night of Hanukkah until all eight candles are lit.

Add this part to some of the verses.

In the win - dow, see the glow, _____ my me - no - rah can - dles this night of Ha - nuk - kah.

Add this part to some other verses. Try singing all three parts together.

In the win - dow where you can see the glow, my me - no - rah on the fal - len snow. I will set ___ my lit - tle can - dles on this ___ night of Ha - nuk - kah.

Celebrations *Hanukkah* 317

In the Window CD7:27

1. Identify a melodic motive. Have students:

• Discuss the tradition of lighting the menorah, a lamp with nine candles. (See *Multicultural Perspectives: The Menorah* on the bottom of page 316.)

• Listen to the first two verses, then hum the first three pitches of the song.

• Review the definition of motive and label the three pitches they hummed as a melodic motive.

• Listen again to the first two verses, humming along each time they hear the motive.

2. Sing the song in three-part harmony. Have students:

• Listen to the recording and raise their hands when the singers on the recording add or sing a tune other than what they hear in Verse 1. (The first countermelody is heard with Verses 3, 5, and 8; the second is heard with Verses 7 and 8.)

• Form three groups. One learns the melody, another learns the first countermelody, and the third learns the second countermelody.

• Decide on which verses to sing one or both countermelodies, then sing the song in three-part harmony. (When students are secure singing the parts separately, have them sing the parts together.)

ENRICHMENT: *Lighting a Menorah*

As the class sings each verse of the song, have two students (under your supervision) light the candles of a menorah, one candle for each verse of the song.

CELEBRATIONS

CHRISTMAS

RELATED ARTS MOVEMENT THEATER VISUAL ARTS

SELECTIONS
PARA PEDIR POSADA, *page 318*
ENTREN SANTOS PEREGRINOS, *page 321*
DALE, DALE, DALE! *page 322*

LESSONLINKS

Para pedir posada *(30 min)*

OBJECTIVE Sing a song for Las Posadas with gestures and expression

Reinforcement
Las Posadas, *page 87*
¾ meter, *page 209*

MATERIALS
Recordings
Para pedir posada   CD7:28
Recorded Lesson: Pronunciation
  for "Para pedir posada"   CD7:29

MEXICAN CHRISTMAS SEASON

In Mexico and the southwestern United States, *Las Posadas* is a highlight of the Christmas season. The celebration begins on December 16 and lasts nine nights until Christmas Eve. Songs tell the story of Mary and Joseph's trip to Bethlehem.

There are two parts to "Para pedir posada." The first part of the song is a question, the second an answer. As the song begins, Joseph asks for shelter. The answer is that there is no room.

Para pedir posada

Mexican Folk Song
English Version by MMH

Spanish: En nom-bre del cie - lo, Os pi-
Pronunciation: en nom bre ðel sye lo os pi
English: In the name of Heav - en, Hear my

do— po-sa - da, Pues no pue-de an -
ðo po sa ða pwes no pwe ðe an
plea— for shel - ter, My— poor wife is wea -

318

MEETING **INDIVIDUAL** NEEDS

MULTICULTURAL PERSPECTIVES: *Las Posadas* THEATER

The ritual of Las Posadas has become one of the most important traditions of a Mexican Christmas. Beginning on December 16 and continuing through the next eight evenings, Mexicans and Mexican-Americans reenact the Biblical story of Mary and Joseph's search for a place to spend the night. *Posadas* literally means "inns." The story is acted out in many parts of the country by guests visiting friends and family, asking the traditional question: "Who will give shelter?" The ritual ends on Christmas Eve, with song, celebration, and a piñata.

dar, Mi es-po-sa a-ma - - da.
dar, mi es po sa a ma ða
ry, Do— not send us a-way, We— can-not go_____ on.

D *Response* A7
A - quí no— es me - són, si - gan a - de -
a ki no es me son si gan a ðe
No,— I have— no room for—you here! You must go on,— you

lan - te, yo— no pue-do a - brir,
lan te yo no pwe ðo a brir
can - not stay, I have no room for you— to - day!

No— sea al - gún tu - nan - te.
no sea al gun tu nan te
I do not know who you are, you— must— go a - way.

Celebrations *Christmas* **319**

Para pedir posada CD7:28

Sing a song for Las Posadas with gestures and expression. Have students:

• Read about Las Posadas and the song.

• Listen to the song and decide how many different groups of singers there are. (two)

• Share their ideas about why there might be two groups. (The two groups are part of the Las Posadas [lɑs po **sɑ** ðɑs] celebration. The "outside" group walks from home to home. The "inside" group consists of the people at home. The song is repeated at each house visited.)

Recorded Lesson CD7:29

• Listen to "Pronunciation for 'Para pedir posada.'"

• Divide into two groups and sing the two parts of the song using appropriate gestures and expression.

PRONUNCIATION: *"Para pedir posada"*
a f<u>a</u>ther   e ch<u>a</u>otic   i b<u>ee</u>   o <u>o</u>bey
u m<u>oo</u>n   ð <u>the</u>   ɾ flipped r

CELEBRATIONS
CHRISTMAS

continued from previous page

LESSON LINKS

Entren santos peregrinos *(15 min)*

OBJECTIVE Sing and dramatize a song for Las Posadas

Reinforcement
Las Posadas, *page 87*
$\frac{3}{4}$ and $\frac{4}{4}$ meter, *page 209*

MATERIALS
Recordings
Entren santos peregrinos (Enter, Holy Pilgrims)   **CD7:30**
Recorded Lesson: Pronunciation for "Entren santos peregrinos"   **CD7:31**

Resources Orff Orchestration O • 17

Each evening of *Las Posadas*, groups of friends walk from home to home, stopping to sing. Mary and Joseph are tired and need a place to rest. The word posada actually means "inn or shelter." The people at home answer, but the travelers are not allowed to come in.

320 **MEXICAN CHRISTMAS SEASON**

MEETING **INDIVIDUAL** NEEDS

ENRICHMENT: *Meter*

MOVEMENT

"Para pedir posada" and "Entren santos peregrinos" are in different meters. ($\frac{3}{4}$ and $\frac{4}{4}$) Have the students make up motions, in place, to show the meters of the two songs. For instance, they could pat-clap-snap or step (R foot)-tap (L toe)-tap (L toe) with the beat to show $\frac{3}{4}$. To show $\frac{4}{4}$, they could twist upper body left-center-right-center or pat head-shoulder-hips-thighs with the beat.

EXTRA HELP: *Dramatizing Las Posadas*

THEATER

Talk with students about how they might dramatize the two groups in the Las Posadas songs. For "Para pedir posada," have students suggest that the group outside is cold, hungry, tired, pleading. Gestures should match text. The group inside is suspicious, rude, and disinterested. In "Entren santos peregrinos," the attitude of the inside group changes and they welcome the outside group in. By the end, all are boisterous and happy in anticipation of the party.

At last, after being turned away again and again,
Mary and Joseph are welcomed.

D major

m, f, s, l, d

Entren santos peregrinos

Enter, Holy Pilgrims

Mexican Folk Song
English Version by MMH

Spanish: En - tren san - tos pe - re - gri - nos, pe - re - gri - nos,— Re - ci -
Pronunciation: en tren san tos pe ɾe gɾi nos pe ɾe gɾi nos ĩe si
English: En - ter in, all ho - ly pil - grims, ho - ly pil - grims.— Wel - come

ban es - te rin - cón, que aun - que es po - bre la mo - ra - da, la mo -
βan es te ɾin koen keaun kes po βɾe la mo ɾa ða la mo
to our hum - ble grove. There is lit - tle we can give you, we can

ra - da,— Os la doy de co - ra - zón.
ɾa ða os la ðoi ðe ko ɾa son
give you,— Still we wel - come you with love.

Celebrations *Christmas* **321**

Entren santos peregrinos
CD7:30

1. Learn a song for Las Posadas. Have students:

• Listen to the song as they follow the lyrics in their books.

Recorded Lesson CD7:31

• Listen to "Pronunciation for 'Entren santos peregrinos.'"

• Sing the song.

2. Sing and dramatize with gestures. Have students:

• Name words from the song they could dramatize. (suggestions: *enter in, welcome, give, love*)

• Sing the song again with dramatic gestures.

• Sing "Para pedir posada" and "Entren santos peregrinos" in a dramatization of Las Posadas. (See *Extra Help* on the bottom of page 322.)

ORFF: *"Entren santos peregrinos"*
See **O • 17** in *Orchestrations for Orff Instruments.*

PRONUNCIATION: *"Entren santos peregrinos"*

ɑ f<u>a</u>ther	e ch<u>a</u>otic	i b<u>ee</u>	o <u>o</u>bey
u m<u>oo</u>n	β b without lips touching		ð <u>the</u>
ɾ flipped r	ĩ rolled r		

CELEBRATIONS

CHRISTMAS

continued from previous page

LESSONLINKS

Dale, dale, dale! *(30 min)*

OBJECTIVE Sing and accompany a Mexican folk song for Las Posadas

Reinforcement
Las Posadas, *page 87*
I IV V chords, C F G chords, *page 183*

MATERIALS
Recordings
Dale, dale, dale!   **CD7:32**
Recorded Lesson: Pronunciation
   for "Dale, dale, dale!"   **CD7:33**
Dale, dale, dale!
   (performance mix)   **CD11:4**

Resources
Recorder Master R • 40 (pitches D E G A
   B C')
Resource Master C • 1 (practice)
Resource Master C • 2 (practice)

Instruments
resonator bells or other pitched instruments

When the posadas procession ends, the owner of the home opens the door, and everyone comes in for a festive party that includes breaking a piñata.

322 MEXICAN CHRISTMAS SEASON

MEETING **INDIVIDUAL** NEEDS

MULTICULTURAL PERSPECTIVES: *Piñatas*

A popular tradition of children in Mexico and other Latin-American countries during holiday time is breaking a piñata (pi **nya** ta), a paper or clay figure filled with candy and small gifts that can resemble any shape, such as an animal or person. It is hung from the ceiling, and the children take turns trying to break it with a stick while blindfolded. The piñata can be raised and lowered to make the task more difficult.

ENRICHMENT: *Piñata Game*

Have students play the piñata game as follows: One student is blindfolded and spun around three times. All sing the song while the student tries to hit the piñata. The turn is over when the song ends. When the piñata breaks, the one who broke it distributes the treats equally. If no piñata is available, hang a wiffle ball from a string and play a pretend version. (Optional: Use **Resource Master C • 1** to make a piñata.)

Refrain

Da-le, da-le, da-le, no pier-das el ti-no,
ða le ða le ða le no pyer ðas el ti no
Da-le, da-le, da-le, do not lose el ti-no,

Mi-de la dis-tan-cia, que hay en el ca-mi-no.
mi ðe la ðis tan sya keɑi en el kɑ mi no
Turn a-round and find it on___ el ca-mi-no.

Que si no le das de un pa-lo-te pi-no,
ke si no le ðas ðeun pa lo te pi no
For if you should miss it with pa-lo-te pi-no,

Por-que tie-nes ca-ra, de pu-ro pe - pi-no.___
poɾ ke tye nes kɑ ɾa ðe pu ɾo pe pi no
You will feel as fool-ish as pu-ro pe - pi-no.___

Celebrations *Christmas* **323**

Dale, dale, dale! CD7:32

1. Learn the song. Have students:

• Read the words to the song and figure out what the song is about. (breaking open the piñata; Spanish words in the refrain can be translated roughly as follows:

dale—hit it; *el tino*—aim; *el camino*—the distance to the piñata; *palote pino*—pine stick; *puro pepino*—pure cucumber, here, a friendly insult about the face of one who misses the piñata.)

• Listen to the recording and sing along on the vocable *la.*

Recorded Lesson CD7:33

• Listen to "Pronunciation for 'Dale, dale, dale!' "

• Clap with the beat while singing the song.

2. Accompany the song. Have students:

• Sing the following melodic ostinato using the pitch letter names.

• Transfer to resonator bells or other pitched instruments to accompany the refrain of the song.

• Note that these pitches are chord roots, and find pitches for the three chords.
(C E G, F A C, G B D)

• Divide into groups, with one singing the song and the other accompanying, either with chord roots or chords.

ENRICHMENT: *Recreate a Posada*

Divide the two groups so one starts outside the classroom and the other inside. Prepare food ahead of time and have a party. Sing "Dale, dale, dale!" while playing the piñata game. Use **Resource Master C • 2** for a recipe for buñue-los, a Mexican dessert.

PRONUNCIATION: *"Dale, dale, dale!"*

ɑ f<u>a</u>ther   e ch<u>a</u>otic   i b<u>ee</u>   o <u>o</u>bey
u m<u>oo</u>n   ß b without lips touching   ð <u>the</u>
ɾ flipped r   x slightly guttural h, *Spanish* ba<u>j</u>o

EXTRA HELP: *Adapting a Piñata for School*

A piñata is usually filled with treats, such as candy. You may want to use alternatives such as boxed raisins, bagged nuts, or tickets to be redeemed for items that don't fit in the piñata. The piñata should be suspended by a rope or hung from a long pole. You control the rope, moving the piñata as students try to hit it. Traditionally, children scramble to gather as many treats as they can for themselves. Be clear beforehand that all treats gathered from the floor will be put into a basket and distributed by the student who broke the piñata.

CELEBRATIONS

CHRISTMAS

RELATED ARTS MOVEMENT | THEATER | VISUAL ARTS

SELECTIONS

LESSON LINKS

A Holly Jolly Christmas (15 min)

OBJECTIVE Sing a Christmas song with an unpitched instrumental introduction and coda

Reinforcement
Christmas, *page 91*
ti, *page 221*

MATERIALS
Recordings
A Holly Jolly Christmas   CD7:34
A Holly Jolly Christmas
  (performance mix)   CD11:5

Instruments metal instruments, such as jingle bells

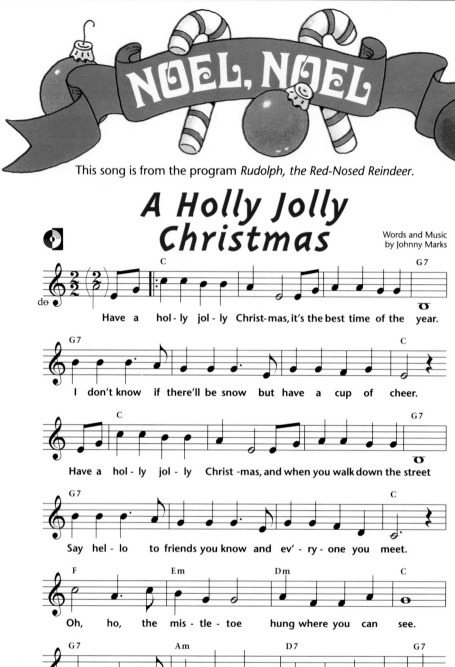

This song is from the program *Rudolph, the Red-Nosed Reindeer.*

A Holly Jolly Christmas

Words and Music
by Johnny Marks

Have a hol-ly jol-ly Christ-mas, it's the best time of the year.

I don't know if there'll be snow but have a cup of cheer.

Have a hol-ly jol-ly Christ-mas, and when you walk down the street

Say hel-lo to friends you know and ev'-ry-one you meet.

Oh, ho, the mis-tle-toe hung where you can see.

Some-bod-y waits for you, kiss her once for me.

324

MEETING **INDIVIDUAL** NEEDS

MULTICULTURAL PERSPECTIVES: *Christmas*

Christmas is a Christian holiday that celebrates the birth of Jesus Christ. December 25 was first used in Rome to celebrate the holiday, about 300 years after Christ's birth. The season was also a time when Romans celebrated the harvest. In their celebrations, they used greeneries, which eventually became part of the Christmas tradition. In the United States, celebrations are as varied as the many different cultures that have formed the country. Most people decorate their homes with greens and trees. Exchanging Christmas cards began in the 1800s.

LANGUAGE ARTS CONNECTION: *Christmas Poems*

Have students write poems about what would make them have "a holly jolly Christmas." Choose some of the best poems and have those students read the poems, with the class softly humming "A Holly Jolly Christmas" in the background.

Have a hol-ly jol-ly Christ-mas, and in case you did-n't hear,

Oh, by gol-ly, have a hol-ly jol-ly Christ-mas this year. Have a

Christ - mas_____ this year.

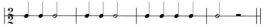

C major

325

A Holly Jolly Christmas CD7:34

Sing a Christmas song with an unpitched instrumental introduction and coda. Have students:

• Listen to the song once through, counting how many times its title is heard in the lyrics. (four times)

• Figure out and sing the pitch syllable names of the first eight notes. (*mi so do' do' ti ti la mi*)

• Practice clapping the rhythm pattern for these familiar words: *Jingle bells, jingle bells, jingle all the way.*

• Transfer this pattern to jingle bells or other metal instruments, then perform it as an introduction and coda as they sing the song.

CELEBRATIONS
CHRISTMAS

continued from previous page

LESSONLINKS

O Tannenbaum! *(15 min)*

OBJECTIVE Sing a song with English and German words

Reinforcement
singing in a non-English language,
page 71

MATERIALS
Recordings
O Tannenbaum! (O Christmas Tree!)
CD7:35

Recorded Lesson: Pronunciation
for "O Tannenbaum!"
CD7:36

Somewhere In My Memory *(25 min)*

OBJECTIVE Explore melodic patterns with
do mi so do'

Reinforcement
melodic movement by skips, *page 111*
do mi so do', *pages 83, 179*

MATERIALS
Recordings
Somewhere in My Memory
CD7:37
Somewhere in My Memory
(performance mix)
CD11:6

This German carol reminds us that decorating an evergreen tree is a favorite Christmas tradition. Sometimes we create our own traditions for celebrating a holiday, as expressed in the song on the next page. What are your unique holiday traditions?

O Tannenbaum!
O Christmas Tree!

German Carol
English Version by MMH

German: O Tan - nen - baum, O Tan - nen - baum, wie
Pronunciation: o ta nən baum o ta nən baum vi
English: O Tan - nen - baum, O Tan - nen - baum, your

treu sind dei - ne Blät - ter! Du grünst nicht nur zur
trɔt zɪnt daɪ nə blɛ tər du grünst nɪçt nur tsur
leaves are ev - er faith - ful! Not on - ly green when

Som - mers - zeit, Nein, auch im Win - ter,
zɔ mər tsaɪt naɪn aʊx ɪm vɪn tər
sum - mer glows, But in the win - ter

wenn es schneit. O Tan - nen - baum, O
vɛn ɛs shnaɪt o ta nən baʊm o
when it snows, O Tan - nen - baum, O

Tan - nen - baum, wie treu sind dei - ne Blät - ter!
ta nən baʊm vi trɔt zɪnt daɪ nə blɛ tər
Tan - nen - baum, your leaves are ev - er faith - ful!

326 NOEL, NOEL

MEETING **INDIVIDUAL** NEEDS

BACKGROUND: *Christmas Trees* VISUAL ARTS

The idea of the decorated tree as part of winter celebrations goes back to the Saturnalia Festival of early Roman times. The custom of the Christmas tree began in Germany when Martin Luther adopted it as a symbol of life everlasting. Trees were sometimes hung upside down from rafters and decorated with fruit, nuts, and pieces of colored paper. By the mid-1500s, the trees were decorated on the floor, right side up.

BACKGROUND: *"O Tannenbaum!"*

The melody to "O Tannenbaum!" was adopted for the official state song of Maryland—"Maryland, My Maryland."

PRONUNCIATION: *"O Tannenbaum!"*

ɑ f<u>a</u>ther	ɛ p<u>e</u>t	i b<u>ee</u>	ɪ <u>i</u>t	o <u>o</u>bey
ɔ p<u>aw</u>	u m<u>oo</u>n	ʊ p<u>u</u>t	ə <u>ago</u>	ç <u>h</u>ue
ɾ flipped r	ü lips form [u] and say [i]			
x guttural h, *German* Ba<u>ch</u>				

Somewhere in My Memory

D major

Music by John Williams
Words by Leslie Bricusse

do

Can - dles in the win - dow,
shad - ows paint - ing the ceil - ing, gaz - ing at the
fire glow, feel - ing that "gin - ger - bread" feel - ing.
Pre - cious mo - ments, spe - cial peo - ple, hap - py fac - es
I can see. Some - where in my mem - 'ry,
Christ - mas joys all a - round me, liv - ing in my
mem - 'ry, all of the mu - sic, all of the mag - ic,
all of the fam - 'ly home here with me._____

Celebrations *Christmas* **327**

O Tannenbaum! CD7:35

Sing a song with English and German words. Have students:

• Listen to the song and sing along only on the German words *O Tannenbaum.*

• Raise their hand when they think they hear the German words for summer and winter. (*sommer, winter*)

Recorded Lesson CD7:36

• Listen to "Recorded Lesson: Pronunciation for 'O Tannenbaum!'"

• Listen again to you or the recording and echo a whole phrase, Measures 5–8, in German.

• Practice this phrase until they have memorized the words.

• Sing the song, resting on Measures 3–4 and 11–12.

• Learn the final German phrase (*wie treu sind deine Blätter*).

• Sing the entire song in German, then English.

Somewhere In My Memory

CD7:37

Explore melodic patterns with *do mi so do'.* Have students:

• Listen to the song, tracing the melodic contour on the notation and observing that the melodic movement is mostly by skips.

• Sing a D major triad (D F♯ A) using pitch syllables. (*do mi so*)

• Create variations by changing the order of the notes. (*mi so do; mi do so*)

• Create similar variations using *mi so do'.*

• Practice the places in the song where similar variations occur. (*In the window—so mi do' so; gingerbread—mi so do; the music, the magic, the family—do' so mi*)

• Practice the melodic patterns with other sets of pitches for phrases: *feeling that—mi so do; special peo-, happy fac- —mi do so*)

• Sing the whole song.

BIOGRAPHY: *John Williams*

American composer John Williams (b. 1932) has written over 75 hit movie soundtracks, including *Jaws* (1975) and *Superman* (1979). In 1977 he composed the music for both *Star Wars* and *Close Encounters of the Third Kind.* When both scores were nominated for an Academy Award (Best Original Score), Williams was forced to compete against himself! *Star Wars* won, giving him one of the Oscars he has taken home over the years. "Somewhere in My Memory" comes from the film score to *Home Alone* (1990). Williams is also a well-known conductor, having conducted the Boston Pops Orchestra from 1980–1993. He has com-posed two symphonies and various concertos as well as TV show and Olympic Games' theme music.

LANGUAGE ARTS CONNECTION: *New Verses*

Have students write a list of events and images they associate with the winter holidays and compare them with those in the song. Have them notice what might be the same if they substituted another holiday for the word Christmas. Have the class write a second verse based on ideas not mentioned in the song, following the rhythm of the phrases and paying attention to rhyme.

CELEBRATIONS
CHRISTMAS

continued from previous page

LESSONLINKS

Dormi, dormi *(15 min)*

OBJECTIVE Sing a Christmas song in A B form using dynamic changes for emphasis

Reinforcement
Christmas; sectional form, *page 91*
dynamics, *page 139*

MATERIALS
Recordings
Dormi, dormi (Sleep, Sleep)   CD7:38
Recorded Lesson: Pronunciation
  for "Dormi, dormi"   CD7:39

We Three Kings *(15 min)*

OBJECTIVE Sing a Christmas song with a chordal accompaniment

Reinforcement
Christmas, *page 91*
minor/major, *page 213*
I IV V chords, *page 183*

MATERIALS
Recordings
We Three Kings   CD7:40
We Three Kings
  (performance mix)   CD11:7

Resources Recorder Master R • 41
(pitches D E G A B C')

Instruments autoharps

MEETING **INDIVIDUAL** NEEDS

MULTICULTURAL PERSPECTIVES: *"Natale"*

"Dormi, dormi," a traditional Italian carol, combines the tenderness and spirited happiness of the holiday season, reflecting the Italian Christmas celebration, Natale (nɑ **ta** le). Preceding Christmas Day, there are many public festivities with plenty of singing, processions, and fireworks. Christmas Eve, by contrast, includes the candlelit ceremony of passing the Baby Jesus from hand to hand to be placed in the waiting manger of the crèche, or nativity display.

PRONUNCIATION: *"Dormi, dormi"*

ɑ f<u>a</u>ther   e ch<u>a</u>otic   i b<u>ee</u>   o <u>o</u>bey
ɾ flipped r

According to the Christmas story, three wise men, or kings, brought gifts to the newborn child on January 6. In Latin American countries, this day is known as Three Kings Day. It is the day that children receive gifts.

We Three Kings

Words and Music
by John Henry Hopkins

Verse

We three kings of O - ri - ent are,
Bear - ing gifts we trav - erse a - far,

Field and foun - tain, moor and moun - tain,

Fol - low - ing yon - der star.

Refrain

O_____ Star of won - der, star of night,
Star with roy - al beau - ty bright,

West - ward lead - ing, still pro - ceed - ing,

Guide us to thy per - fect light.

Celebrations *Christmas* **329**

Dormi, dormi CD7:38

Sing a Christmas song in A B form using dynamic changes for emphasis. Have students:

• Review these symbols for dynamic markings: *pp, p, mp, mf, f,* < >

• Listen to the song, identifying the form as A B, with the A section (verse) as a lullaby and the B section as a joyous refrain.

• Find the measures in the A section where a melodic pattern is sung, then repeated softly. (mm. 5–6, 7–8 and 13–14, 15–16)

• Plan dynamic levels for the four parts of the B section. (for example: mm. 22–25 *mf* then repeat at *mp*; mm. 26–29 *p*, then repeat at *f*)

Recorded Lesson CD7:39

• Listen to "Pronunciation for 'Dormi, dormi.' "

• Sing the song with the dynamics as notated in the A section and as planned in the B section.

We Three Kings CD7:40

Sing a Christmas song with a chordal accompaniment. Have students:

• Read the text of the song as a poem, defining unfamiliar words.

• Listen to the song, noting the importance of the fermata which separates the two sections and signals the change from minor to major tonality.

• Find these chords on an autoharp or other appropriate instrument: G, C, D7.

• Practice the chord pattern of the first four measures of the refrain (after fermata). (G G C G; one student could push the buttons as another strums with the first beats).

• Practice the chord pattern for the second to last phrase. (G D C D)

• Sing the song, adding chordal autoharp accompaniment to the refrain as practiced.

BACKGROUND: *"We Three Kings"*

The American Rev. John Henry Hopkins wrote the words and music to this carol around 1857. Sometimes the carol is mistakenly thought to be much older because of its use of the major and minor modes. The song poetically celebrates the three men who first brought gifts to the Baby Jesus, but it does little to explain the identities of the three. Some people call them Magi, Wise Men, or astrologers. The song also describes the "Star of Wonder," guiding the three men to the "perfect light," a symbol for the child Jesus.

ART CONNECTION: *Three Wise Men* VISUAL ARTS

Have students make puppets, dioramas, or their own Wise Men costumes. Students may work in groups if they like. Have students present their projects in class, then sing "We Three Kings."

CELEBRATIONS

CHRISTMAS

continued from previous page

LESSONLINKS

The Twelve Days of Christmas
(15 min)

OBJECTIVE Learn a cumulative Christmas
song using visual aids

Reinforcement
Christmas, *page 91*
cumulative song, *page 23*

MATERIALS
Recordings
The Twelve Days of Christmas   CD7:41
The Twelve Days of Christmas
(performance mix)   CD11:8

There are twelve days between Christmas and Epiphany,
the day when the three kings arrived with their gifts.

The Twelve Days of
Christmas

F major

English Carol

1. On the first day of Christ-mas my true love sent to me: A
par-tridge— in a pear tree. 2. On the sec-ond day of Christ-mas my
true love sent to me: Two tur-tle doves, and a par-tridge— in a pear tree.
3. On the third day of Christ-mas my true love sent to me:
Three French—hens, two tur-tle doves, and a par-tridge— in a pear
tree. 4. On the fourth day of Christ-mas my true love sent to me:

MEETING **INDIVIDUAL** NEEDS

BACKGROUND: *"The Twelve Days of Christmas"*

This is a traditional English carol, although the tune has
variants. It celebrates the twelve days between December
25 and January 6. January 6 is the traditional date of
Epiphany, the feast commemorating the visit of the Magi
and their offering the first Christmas presents to the Baby
Jesus.

SOCIAL STUDIES CONNECTION: *Christmas*

Have students share the Christmas traditions of their families, or do some research on how Christmas is celebrated in
other countries. Discuss the stories, songs, food, decorations, and other customs of Christmas.

Four col-ly birds, two tur-tle doves, and a par-tridge— in a pear
three French— hens,

tree. 5. On the fifth day of Christ-mas my true love sent to me:

Five gold-en rings, four— col-ly birds, three French hens,

two— tur-tle doves, and a par-tridge— in a pear tree.

6.-12. On the sixth day of Christ-mas my true love sent to me:
(seventh, etc.)

Go back to the sign and sing to the end
(Del Segno al Fine)

6. Six geese a - lay - ing,

7. Seven swans a-swimming,
8. Eight maids a-milking,
9. Nine drummers drumming,
10. Ten pipers piping,

11. Eleven ladies dancing,
12. Twelve lords a-leaping,

Celebrations *Christmas* 331

The Twelve Days of Christmas CD7:41

Learn a cumulative Christmas song using visual aids. Have students:

• Divide into twelve pairs or groups, each taking a number which corresponds to a verse.

• Listen to the song, singing as they are able on repeated, cumulative verses.

• List the twelve gift items on the board: partridge, doves, hens, birds, rings, geese, swans, maids, drummers, pipers, ladies, and lords.

• Work in pairs or groups and create visual aids which prominently feature the assigned number and an illustration of the appropriate gift item.

• Display the finished projects to provide cues for singing the song in correct sequence.

DRAMA CONNECTION: *Holiday Story Sculptures* THEATER

Have students collect traditional or family holiday stories that have a beginning, a middle, and an end. Ask one student to tell a story to the class. After the story is told, divide the class into three groups. Have the first group create a human sculpture representing the beginning of the story. The second and third groups create sculptures to represent the middle and end of the story. Have one member of each group present the sculptures to the class. Continue the activity, using a different student's story each time.

*C*ELEBRATIONS

NEW YEAR

SELECTIONS
SUK SAN WAN PI MAI, *page 333*
CHINESE LION DANCE *(listening), page 334*

LESSON LINKS

Suk san wan pi mai *(10 min)*

OBJECTIVE Identify stepwise melodic movement and accompany a song with unpitched instruments

Reinforcement melodic movement (steps), *page 111*

MATERIALS
Recordings
Suk san wan pi mai (New
 Year's Song)   **CD8:1**
Recorded Lesson: Pronunciation
 for "Suk san wan pi mai"   **CD8:2**

Instruments drums, cymbals

Other map that includes Laos

*A*SIAN NEW

For Asians and Asian Americans, celebrating the new year may last for several weeks. The exact date of the holiday depends upon each country's traditions.

In Vietnam and China, the Kitchen God goes to the heavens and reports on the family at the end of the old year. After cleaning and decorating the house, families send the Kitchen God off with firecrackers, food, and gifts in hopes of a good report.

In Vietnam, the new year celebration is called Tet. During the first days of the new year everyone tries to be happy. To be angry could bring bad luck.

**Buying mume blossoms is
part of preparing for Tet.**

332

MEETING **INDIVIDUAL** NEEDS

MULTICULTURAL PERSPECTIVES: *Laotian New Year*

According to the Laotian lunar calendar, the new year begins in December. The people of Laos do not consider this a fortunate time, so they celebrate in April instead. Spring is a time of light, which means good fortune and prosperity. The New Year festivities last three days. On the first day, the goddess of the old year departs. The second day is considered dangerous since there is no protective goddess, and people pass the time by throwing water to wash away the past. When the New Year begins on the third day, there is much celebration. Special prayers are offered, children ask forgiveness of their parents and promise to be good for the rest of the year, fish and birds are released to honor Buddha's compassion for animals, and there is feasting and dancing.

MULTICULTURAL PERSPECTIVES: *Tet*

Although January 1 has been declared the official government holiday, Vietnamese people celebrate the Tet festival as their new year, carrying out the tradition of thousands of years. The festival occurs during the full moon prior to spring planting, which falls in late January or early Febru-

YEAR CELEBRATIONS

In Laos, the new year usually begins in April. In preparation, houses and temples are washed. Splashing and throwing water becomes a festive part of the celebration. People are joyful because they believe that the happier you are, the happier the year to come will be.

E♭ major

d r m f s l d'

Suk san wan pi mai
New Year's Song

Laotian Song
Collected and Transcribed by
Kathy B. Sorensen
English Version by MMH

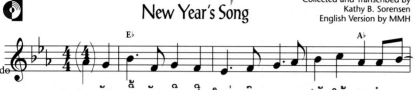

Laotian: ອັນ ນີ ອັນ ດີ ປີ ໃໝ່ ເຮົາ ມາ ອວຍ ໄຊ ໃຫ້ ສຶກ ສຳ ລານ
Pronunciation: wan ni wan di pi mai hau ma 'vai sai hai sŭk sam lan
English: To-day, to-day good New Year's Day, We wish you luck to-day!

ຊ່ວຍ ສ້າງ ອັນ ນີ ໃຫ້ ເປັນ ແດນ ສະ ຫວັນ ຊ່ວຍ
sɔi sang wan ni hai pen dɛn sa wan sɔi
— Come cel - e - brate— with us,———— Come

ສ້າງ ອັນ ນີ ໃຫ້ ເປັນ ແດນ ສະ ຫວັນ ມາ
sang wan ni hai pen dɛn sa wan ma
cel - e - brate— with us,———— Come

ຟ້ອນ ລຳ ກັນ ສະ ຫລອງ ອັນ ປີ ໃໝ່
fɔn lam kan sa lɔng wan pi mai
cel - e - brate a Hap-py New Year.

Celebrations *New Year* 333

Identify stepwise melodic movement and accompany a song with unpitched instruments. Have students:

• Describe how the New Year is celebrated in various countries represented by students in the class.

• Find the country of Laos on a map or globe and read about the Laotian celebration of the New Year.

• Listen to the song, drawing the melodic contour in the air.

• Discuss whether the melody moves by repeated notes, steps, or skips. (mostly steps)

Recorded Lesson CD8:2

• Listen to "Pronunciation for 'Suk san wan pi mai.' "

• Sing the song.

• Accompany the song by playing softly with the beat on small, high-pitched drums.

• Add finger cymbals on the first beat of each measure as they sing the song.

---

ary. It is an important time for families as they gather and honor their ancestors. There are many symbols and customs of Tet. Delicate flower blossoms represent the new beginning of spring. Long strips of red paper inscribed with new year's greetings are hung on front doors, firecrackers ward off evil, and a colorful dragon parades through the streets. The feeling of celebration continues for almost a week, but offices and schools reopen after three days.

PRONUNCIATION: *"Suk san wan pi mai"*

α f<u>a</u>ther ɛ p<u>e</u>t i b<u>ee</u> ɪ <u>i</u>t
ɔ p<u>aw</u> ʊ p<u>u</u>t

CELEBRATIONS

NEW YEAR

LESSON LINKS

Chinese Lion Dance *(40 min)*

OBJECTIVE Learn adapted drum and cymbal patterns and a beginner's version of the Chinese Lion Dance

Reinforcement ceremonial dance and music, *page 123*

MATERIALS
Recordings
Chinese Lion Dance (listening)   CD8:3
Recorded Lesson: Drum and
    Cymbal Rhythm Patterns   CD8:4

Instruments drums, cymbals

Resources
Resource Master C • 3 (practice)
Resource Master C • 4 (background)
Resource Master C • 5 (pattern)

Chinese Lion Dance CD8:3

1. Learn about the dance, then learn adapted drum and cymbal patterns. Have students:

• Listen to the piece, looking at the pictures.

Recorded Lesson CD8:4
• Listen to "Drum and Cymbal Rhythm Patterns."

• Practice using the notation on page 335 and on **Resource Master C • 3.** (See *Extra Help* on the bottom of page 335.)

• Perform their own Lion Dance music.

Preparation for the Chinese New Year begins at least a month in advance. In addition to cleaning the house, families paint their front doors red–the color red means happiness. When the new year actually arrives, the celebration lasts for fifteen days.

334

MEETING **INDIVIDUAL** NEEDS

MULTICULTURAL PERSPECTIVES: *Lion Dance*

The Lion Dance comes from an ancient tradition and is one of the favorite Chinese dances of the New Year. The lion is a Buddhist symbol of courage, majesty, and constancy, and it is also believed to bring good luck. During the dance, people entice the "lion" to dance in front of their homes and businesses to bring them luck in the New Year. Traditional Chinese Lion Dances are highly developed performance pieces. The movements are sharp and sudden, and are derived from the martial arts. One dancer is inside the lion's head, and another controls the tail. Children and

adults take classes at martial arts studios and train all year in preparation for the dance, which is performed many times during the New Year festivities. (For more information use **Resource Master C • 4.**)

MOVEMENT: *Preparing to Dance*

Have students choose motions that *thrust, stab, freeze, attack,* or *twist,* while changing levels and directions. Their knees should be bent in an athletic ready position. The lion's head should twist, shake, and stab the air aggressively. The dancer with the tail remains bent over and steps, twists, and flaps arms.

LISTENING

Chinese Lion Dance *Chinese Folk Music*

On the third to fifth days of the Chinese New Year, the Chinese Lion dances through the crowds in the streets. Martial-arts students perform the lion dance. Listen to the rhythm of the Chinese drum and cymbal.

Lion Dance Drum Pattern

Lion Dance Cymbal Pattern

The lion asleep.

The lion awakening.

The lion bowing.

The Chinese Lion, danced by students of the Wan Chi Ming Hung Gar Institute in New York City.

Celebrations *New Year* **335**

2. Learn a beginner's version of the Chinese Lion Dance. Have students:

• Follow this performance sequence.

Formation: pairs, one student holding an imaginary lion's head and the other the body

Opening/Waking Up—Roll 1: *roll, first two crashes:* both sit cross-legged or with knees tucked into chest, hidden under lion; *third crash:* suddenly lift lion's head (shoot legs out) **Roll 2:** *roll, two crashes:* hold still; *third crash:* lift head higher and shake sharply **Roll 3** *roll, two crashes:* hold still; *third crash:* stand up suddenly.

Bows in Three Directions—Rolldown 1: Lion steps forward to diagonal right and performs three bows while backing up. To bow, drop head sharply down, then lift high and shake while raising knee. To end, drum stops suddenly when head drops and knees bend to crouch. **Rolldowns 2–3:** Repeat to diagonal left and to center.

Center Floor Improvisation—Main drum and cymbal pattern: Lion improvises with kicks, jumps, walks, and strong head motions. (Begin less forcefully, build to very energetic.)

Full Turn—Turning pattern: Lion turns head from side to side. Then, with tail leading, lion turns all the way around once, freezing in place.

Meeting the Audience—Main patterns: Lion approaches and frightens audience, turning head from side to side. Lion retreats, repeats full turn.

Search for the Lettuce—Drum and cymbal roll with dynamics: Lion searches in all directions for a head of lettuce, beginning tentatively. With crescendo, lion finds the lettuce, (hands through mouth of mask) shreds it, then scatters it toward audience.

Joyful Dance and Exit—Main patterns, turning pattern: Lion improvises a short, energetic dance using jumps, kicks, and twists, then exits. (See *Improvisation* below.)

Dance contributed by Susan Kennedy.

ART CONNECTION: *Chinese Lion Costume* VISUAL ARTS

Use **Resource Master C • 5** to make a lion costume.

IMPROVISATION: *A Joyful Dance* MOVEMENT

One possible improvisation is to drop down and come up again suddenly with the drum and cymbal pattern.

Beat one: head drops down, legs are in a deep knee-bent position, head turns sharply to the right; **Beat two:** hold; **Beat three:** stand suddenly, legs straight; **Beat four:** hold.

EXTRA HELP: *Drum and Cymbal Patterns*

Roll with three crashes: practice by patting drum part, brushing and clapping cymbal part. Together, each instrument performs a roll followed by three strong strokes/crashes. **Rolldown:** drop a rubber ball and watch the bounce pattern until it stops, observing as each bounce gets smaller. Follow the bouncing motion with the arms, patting one knee each time the ball hits the floor. Transfer to drums. **Main patterns, turning pattern:** first pat drum rhythm, clap cymbal rhythm. Transfer to instruments and practice both parts together.

CELEBRATIONS

MARTIN LUTHER KING, JR., DAY

SELECTIONS
MARTIN'S CRY, *page 336*
DOWN BY THE RIVERSIDE, *page 338*

Dr. King's DREAM

The powerful speeches of Dr. Martin Luther King, Jr., inspired many people to work for equal rights. His words still give people hope and encouragement.

Martin's Cry

Words and Music by Vernon Clark

1. There was a man— named Mar - tin Lu - ther King, who said,
2. King took a stand— for civ - il rights a - cross the land,
3. King led a march— to Wash - ing - ton and said a - gain,

"Let free - dom— ring!—
Let free - dom— ring!—
"Let free - dom— ring!"—

I have a dream— that one day this na - tion will
No mat - ter where— his foot - steps led him, he would
He gave his life— so one day all peo - ple could

336

MEETING **INDIVIDUAL** NEEDS

BIOGRAPHY: *Martin Luther King, Jr.*

Martin Luther King, Jr. (1929–1968), was born in Atlanta, Georgia. He became an internationally known leader and speaker of the civil rights movement in the 1950s and 1960s. His message of eliminating inequality through non-violence came from studying the teachings of Mahatma Gandhi (ma **hat** ma **gan** di), a leader in India who advocated nonviolent resistance as the way to protest injustice. King received the Nobel Peace Prize in 1964 for his contributions. He was assassinated in 1968 in Memphis, Ten-

nessee. In 1983, Congress declared the third Monday in January a federal holiday in honor of King.

BACKGROUND: *"Martin's Cry"*

At a march and rally in Washington, D.C., in 1963, King made an inspiring speech about his wish for people of all races and religions to live peacefully together. His speech includes the phrases "I have a dream" and "Let freedom ring."

Celebrations *Martin Luther King, Jr., Day* **337**

Martin's Cry CD8:5

Sing phrases with letter names, including C and F and pitch syllable names, including *fa.* Have students:

• Listen to the song and discuss the meaning of the words.

• Listen again to the first verse and refrain, sing along with each phrase *let freedom ring,* and count how many times the phrase occurs. (6)

• Determine if any of the above phrases are the same. (2 and 6)

• Tell how the other phrases are different. (different pitches, syncopation of *ring*)

• Sing the first two of the phrases with letter names. (G C D E; F E D C)

• Sing the first two of the phrases with pitch syllable names. (*so do re mi; fa mi re do*)

• Sing the entire song.

SIGNING: *"Martin's Cry"*

Signing Master S • 4 • 8 has sign language for this song.

CELEBRATIONS
MARTIN LUTHER KING, JR., DAY

continued from previous page

LESSONLINKS

Down by the Riverside *(20 min)*

OBJECTIVE Identify harmonic changes in a song's accompaniment

Reinforcement
harmony, *page 135*
♪ ♪ ♪, *page 175*
spiritual, *page 229*

MATERIALS
Recordings
Down by the Riverside   CD8:6
Down by the Riverside
   (performance mix)   CD11:10

Resources Recorder Master R • 42
   (pitches D E G A B C')

Technology Music with MIDI: Down by the Riverside

In 1983, the birthday of Martin Luther King, Jr., became a national holiday. It is a day to celebrate his dream of equality for all people. People sing songs like this African American spiritual to honor Dr. King's belief in peace and freedom.

DOWN BY THE RIVERSIDE

African American Spiritual

338 DR. KING'S DREAM

MEETING **INDIVIDUAL** NEEDS

BACKGROUND: *"Down by the Riverside"*

Also known as "Study War No More," this spiritual's theme of peace evolved in the aftermath of the Civil War. Not only does it advocate the laying down of weapons, but it also says people must change how they think, or what they study, so that peace is possible. The lyrics imply that the way to peace involves changing thought and education so that people can turn their thoughts and actions away from war. The opening idea of sword and shield may have come from the Biblical imagery—*Isaiah 2:4*: ". . . and they shall beat their swords into plowshares, and their spears into pruning hooks:

nation shall not lift up sword against nation, neither shall they learn war any more."

EXTRA HELP: *Clapping Offbeats*

To assist students in clapping with beat 2, have them begin patting with beat 1 (alternating pats and claps). Have them pat more and more lightly, and finally just make the motion without touching their legs.

Ain't gon - na stud - y war no more,

1.
D7   **G**
Ain't gon - na stud - y war no more,

2.
D7   **G**
stud - y____ war no more.____

The Civil Rights Memorial in Montgomery, Alabama, was designed by Maya Lin. Ms. Lin also designed the Vietnam Memorial in Washington, D.C.

...UNTIL JUSTICE ROLLS DOWN LIKE WATERS AND RIGHTEOUSNESS LIKE A MIGHTY STREAM

MARTIN LUTHER KING, JR.

Down by the Riverside CD8:6

Identify harmonic changes in a song's accompaniment. Have students:

• Discuss the concept of nonviolence.

• Listen to the song and sing along on the phrase *down by the riverside*.

• Review the definition of harmony.

• Listen as you play four G chords and four D7 chords, then label the G chord as being based on *do* and the D7 chord as being based on low *so*.

• Jump in place when they hear you play G chords and freeze when you play D7 chords. (Alternate playing four of each chord.)

• Listen again to the first verse, and jump and freeze with the harmonic changes as practiced.

• Sing the song, clapping with the second beat of each measure. (See *Extra Help* on the bottom of page 338.)

CELEBRATIONS
PRESIDENTS' DAY

RELATED ARTS MOVEMENT THEATER **VISUAL ARTS**

SELECTIONS
LINCOLN PORTRAIT *(listening), page 340*
TO MEET MR. LINCOLN *(poem), page 341*

LESSON LINKS

Lincoln Portrait *(20 min)*

OBJECTIVE Listen for dynamic changes in excerpts of an orchestral piece about Abraham Lincoln

Reinforcement dynamics, *page 139*

MATERIALS
Recording Lincoln Portrait (excerpts 1 and 2) by A. Copland (listening)   CD8:7

To Meet Mr. Lincoln *(30 min)*

OBJECTIVE Read a poem and create a speech piece with dynamic changes

Reinforcement dynamics, *page 139*

A Great President

Abraham Lincoln was the sixteenth president of the United States. During the Civil War, his leadership freed the slaves and reunited the country. The wisdom and understanding of Abraham Lincoln were expressed in his speeches.

340

MEETING **INDIVIDUAL** NEEDS

BACKGROUND: *Presidents' Day*

Presidents' Day is a patriotic holiday celebrated on the third Monday in February to honor Abraham Lincoln, born February 12, 1809, and our first president, George Washington, born February 22, 1732.

EXTRA HELP: *Speech-Piece Phrases*

Have students write down adjectives and brief descriptive phrases about Abraham Lincoln. They should add the dynamic markings of their choice, then practice saying the phrases at their dynamic levels in time with four beats. (two

pat-claps) Examples: *Student 1:* (*mf*) Jet-black hair, *Student 2:* (*p*) Sixteenth President, *Student 3:* (*f*) Born in Kentucky, *Student 4:* (*pp*) Studied by firelight.

SOCIAL STUDIES CONNECTION: *Gettysburg*

Gettysburg, Pennsylvania, was the site of a great victory by the Union army over the Confederate army. Many lives were lost, and Lincoln delivered his famous speech while dedicating a cemetery on the battlefield. Have students look up "The Gettysburg Address" in a textbook or an encyclopedia and find the part of the speech used in *Lincoln Portrait.* (the closing lines) Read along with the recording.

Lincoln Portrait

(excerpts) *by Aaron Copland*

Lincoln Portrait *was the result of Aaron Copland's being asked to write a musical portrait of a great American. When he started, he was concerned that it would be difficult for his music to express the greatness of Abraham Lincoln. He solved the problem by using Lincoln's letters and speeches as the text. Copland's music frames Abraham Lincoln's own words. You will hear a full orchestra and a soloist who speaks those words.*

To Meet MR. LINCOLN

If I lived at the time
That Mr. Lincoln did,
And I met Mr. Lincoln
With his stovepipe lid

And his coalblack cape
And his thundercloud beard,
And worn and sad-eyed
He appeared:

"Don't worry, Mr. Lincoln,"
I'd reach up and pat his hand,
"We've got a fine President
For this land;

And the Union will be saved,
And the slaves will go free;
And you will live forever
In our nation's memory."

— *Eve Merriam*

Celebrations *Presidents' Day* **341**

Lincoln Portrait CD8:7

Listen for dynamic changes in excerpts of an orchestral piece about Abraham Lincoln. Have students:

• Listen to the first excerpt, tapping various body parts to the beat.

• Discuss what makes the music sound slower during the brass melody "On Springfield Mountain." (Longer durations make it sound slower.)

• Describe what happens at the end of the excerpt. (The music slows and gets softer, someone speaks.)

• Listen to the second excerpt and describe how dynamic changes are used expressively. (piano—Lincoln's quiet nature; cresc., forte—beliefs, strength; fortissimo—determination)

• Discuss the phrase about slavery and the Gettysburg Address.

• Listen to both excerpts again.

To Meet Mr. Lincoln

Read a poem and create a speech piece with dynamic changes. Have students:

• Perform an alternating pat-clap pattern with the beat while reading "To Meet Mr. Lincoln" aloud.

• Think of brief descriptions of Lincoln, and choose dynamic levels for each.

• Sit or stand in a circle and perform the pat-clap pattern. Each student in turn speaks their descriptive phrase in four beats at the chosen dynamic level. (See *Extra Help* on the bottom of page 340.)

• Perform the speech piece using the poem as an introduction and coda.

BACKGROUND: *Lincoln Portrait*

Aaron Copland used Lincoln's own words in his *Lincoln Portrait* and said: "I was after the most universal aspects of Lincoln's character, not physical resemblance. The challenge was to compose something simple, yet interesting enough to fit Lincoln . . ." Copland included two folk songs popular in Lincoln's lifetime, namely "Camptown Races" and "On Springfield Mountain." In the excerpts presented, students will hear "On Springfield Mountain."

ART CONNECTION: *Visual Art*

Abraham Lincoln was President at a time when photography was making tremendous advances. He was the first President to be the subject of so many photographs. Locate photos of Lincoln in books in the library.

Have students look at photographs of the Lincoln Memorial and discuss the purpose of such a monument. Create a class memorial in the room using drawings, poems, or other projects about Lincoln.

RELATED ARTS MOVEMENT | THEATER | VISUAL ARTS

SELECTION
MACNAMARA'S BAND, *page 342*

LESSON LINKS

Macnamara's Band *(15 min)*

OBJECTIVE Listen for changed voices and sing a song that includes C'

Reinforcement
changed voice, *page 171*
octave; high C, *page 179*

MATERIALS
Recording Macnamara's Band   CD8:8

MARCHING ON

Macnamara's Band

Music by Shamus O'Connor
Words by John J. Stamford

Verse

1. Oh! me name is Mac-na-mar-a, I'm the lead-er of the band,—
2. Right— now we are re-hears-in', for a ver-y swell af-fair,—
3. Oh! my name is Un-cle Yul-ius and from Swe-den I have come,—
4. Oh! I wear a bunch of sham-rocks and a un-i-form of green,—

Al-though we're few in num-bers we're the fin-est in the land.
The an-nual cel-e-bra-tion, all the gen-try will be there.
To play with Mac-na-mar-a's band and beat the big bass drum,
And I'm the fun-niest look-ing Swede that you have ev-er seen.

We play at wakes and wed-dings and at
When Gen-'ral Grant to Ire-land came he
And when I march a-long the street the
There's O'-Bri-ens and Ry-ans and Shee-hans and Mee-hans, they

ev'-ry fan-cy ball,— And when we play to
took me by the hand,— Says he, "I nev-er
la-dies think I'm grand,— They shout, "There's Un-cle
come from Ire-land,— But by Yim-min-y I'm the

342

MEETING **INDIVIDUAL** NEEDS

MULTICULTURAL PERSPECTIVES: *St. Patrick's Day*

Saint Patrick was born in Britain, but he was taken to Ireland as a slave in the early 400s. After six years of slavery, he escaped to France where he studied for the priesthood. He returned to Ireland as a Christian missionary in A.D. 432. Many of the Irish accepted Christianity and came to regard Patrick as their patron saint. Today his feast day, March 17, is a national holiday in Ireland and is celebrated in many other parts of the world.

BACKGROUND: *Bagpipes*

Known in ancient Rome, bagpipes are reed instruments found in various forms in Europe, North Africa, and Asia. The bag inflates with air from the piper's mouth or by a bellows action of the arm. Air from the bag makes the reeds sound. Unlike players of orchestral wind instruments, pipers can inhale without interrupting the sound. The pipes usually include a chanter or melody pipe that is fingered, and one or more drone pipes that accompany the melody with one pitch or a chord. Bagpipes may have either single or double reeds, which are found at the upper ends of the pipes where they go into the bag.

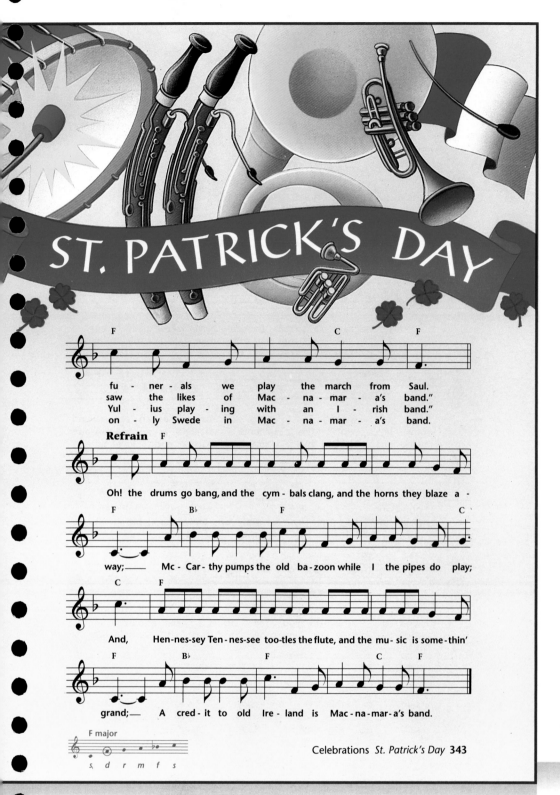

Macnamara's Band CD8:8

Listen for changed voices and sing a song that includes C'. Have students:

• Listen to the song, identifying the singers' voices as changed or unchanged. (verses: changed; refrains: unchanged)

• Name the six instruments mentioned in the refrain. (drums, cymbals, horns, bassoon, pipes, flute; point out that the word *pipes* means *bagpipes*.)

• Sing the refrain with pitch syllables. Name the pitch that goes below the tonal center (low *so*) and the highest pitch (*so*).

• Identify the distance between low *so* and *so* as being an octave.

• Name the same two pitches with letter names. (C, high C)

• Sing the song with words.

MOVEMENT: *"Macnamara's Band"*

Formation: two lines, partners facing

Verse: Individually, perform a repeated pat-clap-snap-clap pattern with the beat.

Refrain: (Verbal Cue—*right, own, left, own*) **Measure 1:** Partners clap right hands, clap own hands. **Measure 2:** Partners clap left hands, clap own hands. **Measures 3–4:** (Verbal Cue—*heel, toe, heel, clap*) With weight on L foot, tap R heel on floor, then cross R foot over L and tap R toe on floor. Tap R heel again, clap partner's hands. **Measures 5–8:** (Verbal Cue—*slide, 2, 3, 4; home, 2, 3, 4*) Partners join

hands, slide step four times in one direction, then four times back. **Measures 9–16:** repeat sequence.

PLAYING INSTRUMENTS: *Unpitched*

Verse: play the drums with the beat.
Refrain: perform this ostinato.

CELEBRATIONS

SPRING

SELECTION
TREE SONG, *page 344*

LESSONLINKS

Tree Rhyme *(15 min)*

OBJECTIVE Create and choose meters for a rhythmic speech pattern

Reinforcement
tone color, *page 265*
changing meter, *page 277*

MATERIALS
Resources Resource Master C • 6
(practice)

Tree Song *(20 min)*

OBJECTIVE Sing a song with an octave skip

Reinforcement
octave, *page 179*

MATERIALS
Recording Tree Song   CD8:9

Arbor Day is a holiday to honor trees.

TREE SONG

Words and Music
by Ken Medema

344

MEETING **INDIVIDUAL** NEEDS

BACKGROUND: *Arbor Day*

Julius Sterling Morton was a newspaperman in Nebraska during the 1800s. He believed in the importance of trees and suggested a special day to encourage people to plant trees. On the first Arbor Day celebrated, more than a million trees were planted. The exact date of Arbor Day depends on one's location. In Nebraska it is celebrated on Morton's birthday, April 22. In California, it is celebrated on March 7, the birthday of Luther Burbank, a plant breeder who developed many successful varieties of fruit trees, vegetables, and flowers.

PLAYING INSTRUMENTS: *"Tree Rhyme"*

Have students name classroom instruments made of wood and select four with different tone colors. Have them plan a different instrument to play Beat 1 of the first and third measures of Lines 1–3 of their tree rhyme. Have them play all four instruments together with the rhythm of Line 4. Finally, have them read the poem with this accompaniment.

344   Celebrations SPRING

This is the song that my tree friend sang to me.

Refrain

I've got roots grow-ing down to the
shade from the hot sum-mer

wa-ter, I've__ got leaves grow-ing up to the
sun-down. I__ am nest for the birds of the

sun-shine, and__ the fruit that I bear is a
heav-en. I'm__ be-

sign of the life__ in me.__ I am

com-ing what the Lord of Trees has meant me to

be:___ A strong__ young tree.

Tree Rhyme

Create and choose meters for a rhythmic speech pattern. Have students:

• Select 14 other trees to fill in the following skeleton. (Optional: Use **Resource Master C · 6**, which includes the skeleton and a list of possible trees.)

			and beech
			and peach

• Practice speaking the tree rhyme while performing a pat-clap pattern with the beat.

• Observe that they were performing the pattern with two beats per measure.

• Try speaking the pattern in different meters, such as in three, and try changing meters with different measures. (As a variation, students may rearrange the tree names to fit different meters.)

Tree Song CD8:9

Sing a song with an octave skip. Have students:

• Sing a D major scale, drawing the ascending pattern in the air with their hands and imagining they're climbing a tree while they sing.

• Repeat the scale, leaving out *ti* and hearing it internally, or singing it only in their heads.

• Repeat the scale again, leaving out both *la* and *ti,* then *so la ti,* and so on until they sing only low and high *do.* Each time they should sing the skipped pitches silently, only in their heads.

• Find the octave skip in the song (Measures 8–9) and discuss how its placement there might emphasize the meaning of the words *growing tall and strong.*

• Practice the refrain, noticing the key words and using them as memory devices (*roots, leaves, fruit, shade, nest*).

• Sing the entire song.

SCIENCE CONNECTION: *Trees*

In collaboration with a science or classroom teacher, have students study the functions of each part of the tree mentioned in the song—roots, leaves, fruit. Have them discuss what trees give, both practically (nest for birds, oxygen, shade) and aesthetically (beauty, a special place to sit and think).

SOCIAL STUDIES CONNECTION: *Community Trees*

In San Francisco, the Friends of the Urban Forest offers an extensive tree planting service to beautify city streets. When neighbors decide they want trees planted, this organization brings the trees and sells them cheaply, then helps plant them and teaches how to care for them. Over 28,000 trees have been planted in San Francisco neighborhoods as a result of their efforts. Have students find out if there are similar initiatives in their area.

MUSIC LIBRARY PLANNER

MORE MUSIC!

The *Music Library* is a collection of special sections for use throughout the year. Materials reinforce and provide alternate experiences with concepts and skills introduced in Units 1–6. All *Music Library* materials are cross-referenced to lessons within the units.

CONTENTS

MUSIC LITERACY IN *SHARE THE MUSIC*, GRADE 4

Music literacy is carefully developed on an ongoing, sequential basis throughout Units 1–6 in the following ways. *(For a full listing of skills covered and for specific references to lessons, see the Skills Overview that directly precedes each unit.)*

In UNIT 1 students develop music literacy in the following ways:

READING
- See graphic notation for duple meter, four beats to a measure, beat and rhythm
- Read rhythm pattern with known rhythms
- Sing with pitch syllables from notation
- Match graphic notation to phrases
- Study notation to find *la*
- Put notated phrases in correct order

WRITING
- Make score with graphic notation
- Write 4-measure patterns in duple meter
- Notate composed melodies

In UNIT 2 students develop music literacy in the following ways:

READING
- Follow visuals of melodic contours
- Find similar phrases and read sixteenth notes
- Read graphic notation of beat and rhythms with sixteenth notes
- See and listen for notated melodic theme
- See notated meter change
- Perform an ostinato with sixteenth notes from notation
- Identify upbeat
- Read, sing, and play D E G A B from notation
- Identify treble clef
- Find tonal center, *la*, *so*, in notation
- Sing letter names and pitch syllables from notation

WRITING
- Practice writing rhythms with sixteenth notes
- Practice drawing treble clef

In UNIT 3 students develop music literacy in the following ways:

READING
- Read rhythm notation
- See symbols for and sing A B sections
- See dynamics in notation
- Read pitches C D E F G on staff
- Read patterns in duple compound meter
- Sing song and perform ostinato from notation in duple compound meter
- Identify key signature, flat
- Clap rhythm from notation in duple compound meter
- Identify and follow dynamic markings in notation
- Review bar lines

WRITING
- Devise graphic notation for dynamics
- Write rhythm patterns in duple compound meter
- Create and notate unpitched ostinatos
- Devise graphic notation for sounds, dynamic levels

In UNIT 4 students develop music literacy in the following ways:

READING
- Read graphic notation of beat and rhythm
- Observe key signature of D major
- See symbols for A, B, C sections and coda
- See eighth-quarter-eighth syncopation
- See *Da Capo al Fine*
- Read and sing from notation of syncopation
- Label C, C¹ on staff
- Identify chord roots, chord names on notation
- Read graphic notation for chord changes
- See notation of melodic theme of improvisation

WRITING
- Write patterns with known rhythms including tied and syncopated rhythms
- Notate ostinato with C, C¹
- Notate rap graphically

In UNIT 5 students develop music literacy in the following ways:

READING
- Read graphic notation of meters and known rhythms
- See notation of duple and triple meter, dotted rhythms
- Identify *la ti do¹* in notation
- Compare two key signatures
- Identify eighth rest
- Read notation with ties
- Identify dotted rhythm in notation
- Match rhythm notation to familiar melodies
- Read and perform from notation in triple meter with dotted quarter-eighth note rhythms
- Identify key signatures and scales in F major, D minor
- Identify B♭ in notation
- Read C, F, G major scales

WRITING
- Practice writing meter signatures
- Write *la ti do¹* pattern
- Write dotted and tied rhythms
- List rhythms of selection

In UNIT 6 students develop music literacy in the following ways:

READING
- Follow notation with introduction, repeats, coda
- See notation with changing meter signatures and patterns that include sixteenth notes
- See *Da Capo al Fine*
- Identify accidentals in notation
- Read E major and E minor scales
- Identify songs in major, minor
- Identify whole note
- Compare same song written in different meters
- Read graphic notation of rhythm, melodic ornamentation
- Follow listening map of theme and variations with expressive qualities, orchestral families

WRITING
- Write new verses
- Write rhythms in augmentation
- Write down changes in meter, rhythm, dynamics, tempo, ornamentation, instrumentation

▶ In "More Songs to Read," the musical concepts presented in the units are reinforced in carefully structured activities that build security in reading and writing musical notation.

USE WITH	Unit 1, Lesson 1, pp. 12–15	Unit 1, Lesson 2, pp. 16–19	Unit 1, Lesson 4, pp. 24–27
FOCUS	Duration/Meter p. 346	Form, phrase length p. 347	Duration—quarter note, eighth note, half note p. 348
SELECTIONS	I Love the Mountains	Go 'Round the Mountain • Night Song	Night Song • Babylon's Fallin'
CONCEPTS AND SKILLS	• Pat with the beat • **Pat with the strong beat to identify meter** • **Conduct in ⁴⁄₄.** • Play a melodic accompaniment • *Play a harmonic accompaniment*	• Move to the beat • **Identify phrases** • Move to show melodic direction of phrases	• **Identfiy ²⁄₄ meter** • **Identfiy quarter and eighth notes** • **Read quarter and eighth notes** • Conduct in ²⁄₄ time

USE WITH	Unit 2, Lesson 4, pp. 72–75	Unit 2, Lesson 5, pp. 76–79	Unit 3, Lesson 1, pp. 108–111
FOCUS	Duration—sixteenth notes p. 352	Pitch—low *so* and *la* pp. 353–354 Rhythm p. 354	Pitch, melodic movement p. 355
SELECTIONS	Ida Red	Trail to Mexico • Lady, Come Down and See • Old Chisholm Trail	Old Tar River
CONCEPTS AND SKILLS	• **Find ♩♫ and ♫♩ rhythms** • Identify form as being A B • **Perform patterns with sixteenth-note rhythms** • *Play patterns with sixteenth-note rhythms*	• Identify a song by reading rhythms and pitches including low *so* and *la* • Read patterns with *so, la, do re mi so la* • **Identify and read sixteenth-note rhythm patterns**	• **Sing and identify repeated notes, steps, and skips** • Practice inner hearing • Find and sing low *so* and low *la* • Sing solos • *Play melodic rhythms on contrasting instruments*

USE WITH	Unit 4, Lesson 1, pp. 158–163	Unit 4, Lesson 2, pp. 164–167	Unit 4, Lesson 4, pp. 172–175
FOCUS	Duration, ♪♩♪ (*short long short*) p. 360	Pitch, octave p. 361	Rhythm p. 362
SELECTIONS	Old Dan Tucker	Heave-Ho Me Laddies • My Dame Hath a Lame, Tame Crane • To Stop the Train	Before Dinner
CONCEPTS AND SKILLS	• Echo-clap rhythms including the *short long short* pattern • **Signal aural recognition of the short long short pattern** • Read *so, la, do re mi so* with pitch syllables and hand signs • **Create and play 4-measure rhythms with at least one short long short pattern** • *Play a recorder descant*	• **Define and find notation of octave skips** • Move to show melodic direction • **Signal aural recognition of an octave skip** • **Find the short long short pattern** • Sing in canon	• **Identify the *short long short* pattern** • Identify call-and-response form • Read and play three rhythm patterns with a song • *Practice patterns including mi, so, la,*

USE WITH	Unit 5, Lesson 4, pp. 218–221	Unit 5, Lesson 5, pp. 222–225	Unit 6, Lesson 1, pp. 254–257
FOCUS	Pitch, *ti* p. 366	Rhythm p. 367	Expressive Qualities—tempo, dynamics p. 368
SELECTIONS	Lots o' Fish in Bonavist' Harbor • Alleluia, Amen • San lun tsa	John Kanaka • To Stop the Train	Ah, Poor Bird • Chickalileeo
CONCEPTS AND SKILLS	• Sing a major scale with pitch syllables • Identify *do* and *ti* in notation • Sing in unison and two-part canon	• Identify the *short long short* pattern • **Identify and read dotted quarter-eighth patterns** • Identify fermata • Read pitches including *fa* and high *do* • Sing in unison and in two- and three-part canon	• **Plan dynamics and tempos for expressive effects** • **Read minor songs with pitch syllables** • **Signal to show aural identification of major or minor**

SKILLS OVERVIEW

Unit 1, Lesson 5, pp. 28–31	Unit 2, Lesson 1, pp. 58–61	Unit 2, Lesson 2, pp. 62–65
Pitch—*do re mi so la* p. 349	Pitch—*do re mi so* p. 350	Duration—Four sounds to a beat p. 351
Night Song • Babylon's Fallin' • Page's Train • I Am a Cat	Down the Road (A section) • Lady, Come Down and See	Dinah
• Identify pitches used as being *do re mi* • **Read songs with pitch syllables *do re mi so la*** • Accompany with quarter-note, eighth-note, or half-note pulses • Experiment with *accelerando* and *ritardando* • *Sing two-part canons*	• Read *do re mi* patterns with pitch syllables and hand signs • Aurally identify a pitch below *do* • *Practice inner hearing*	• **Identify and pat four sounds to a beat** • **Identfiy beats with four sounds** • **Identify a phrase by its rhythm** • Find *do* and read pitches *do re mi so* in rhythm • Play accompaniment patterns with four sounds to a beat

Unit 3, Lesson 2, pp. 112–117	Unit 3, Lesson 4, pp. 124–127	Unit 3, Lesson 5, pp. 128–131
Rhythm/Meter p. 356	Pitch—*fa* p. 357	Duration pp. 358–359
Heave-Ho Me Laddies	My Horses Ain't Hungry	The Derby Ram • Lots o' Fish in Bonavist' Harbor
• Pat equal and unequal sounds to a beat • **Identfiy meter as being ²⁄₄ or ²⁄₂** • Recognize similar phrases	• Recognize a skip below low *so* and identify low *mi* • Read *mi, so, la, do re mi* with pitch syllables and hand signs • **Identify *fa*** • **Sing and play an ostinato containing *fa*** • *Compare two songs with different meters and styles*	• **Identfiy meter as being ⁶⁄₈** • **Speak, pat, and play rhythm patterns in ⁶⁄₈ meter** • Read a song including low *so* and *low* la • Move to a song in ⁶⁄₈ meter

Unit 4, Lesson 5, pp. 176–179	Unit 5, Lesson 1, pp. 206–209	Unit 5, Lesson 2, pp. 210–213
Pitch, octaves p. 363	Meter p. 364	Pitch, major and minor p. 365
Sarasponda • Hop Up and Jump Up	Oliver Cromwell • Who's Got a Fishpole? • My Horses Ain't Hungry	Boll Weevil
• **Find and identify octave skips** • **Sing octaves with pitch syllables** • Pat a rhythm ostinato with a song • **Play an octave accompaniment**	• **Conduct songs in ⁶⁄₈, ³⁄₄, ⁴⁄₄** • **Read rhythms in ⁶⁄₈, ³⁄₄, ⁴⁄₄** • **Create movements in ³⁄₄** • Read pitches including *fa* • Sing a call-and-response song	• Aurally identify major and minor scales • Determine whether a song is in major or minor • Plan different dynamics and tempo for each verse • *Play a recorder accompaniment*

Unit 6, Lesson 2, pp. 258–261	Unit 6, Lesson 4, pp. 266–269	Unit 6, Lesson 5, pp. 270–273
Texture, accompaniment p. 369	Pitch, minor p. 370	Rhythm, augmentation and diminution p. 371
Artsa Alinu	Artsa Alinu • Korobushka	O musique • Alouette
• Discuss properties of dance music • Determine phrase form • Find the *short long short* pattern • Find dotted quarter-eighth patterns • **Perform two ostinatos to change a song's texture**	• Clap the rhythm of songs with the *short long short* and dotted quarter-eighth patterns • **Read pitches of two minor songs** • *Create codas*	• **Determine if a song is in major or minor** • Read pitches including octave skips • **Sing a song in augmentation, patting with the beat** • *Learn about dotted eighth-sixteenth rhythm*

MUSIC LIBRARY
MORE SONGS TO READ

RELATED ARTS | MOVEMENT | **THEATER** | VISUAL ARTS |

LESSONLINKS

For use after Unit 1, Lesson 1, pp. 12–15

FOCUS Duration/Meter

OBJECTIVE Identify meter as $\frac{4}{4}$ and take turns conducting

MATERIALS
Recordings
I Love the Mountains   **CD8:10**
I Love the Mountains
  (performance mix)   **CD11:11**

Instruments resonator bells, Orff instruments, or other pitched instruments

---

1. Introduce "I Love the Mountains" CD8:10
Have students:

• Listen to the song without looking at it, patting with the beat and listening for the strong beat.

• Listen again, patting only the strong beat to decide the meter. ($\frac{4}{4}$)

• Look at page 346 to test their answer and to recall the meaning of the $\frac{4}{4}$ meter signature. (four beats in a measure)

• Count how many times the word *I* is heard on the strong beat. (five)

• Sing the song, patting with the strong beat.

2. Conduct in $\frac{4}{4}$. Have students:

• Compare the conducting patterns on page 346.

• Practice conducting in $\frac{4}{4}$ with both hands.

• Take turns conducting as the class sings the song.

3. Play a melodic accompaniment. Have students:

• Observe the key. (F)

• Find measures with similar melodic shapes and rhythms. (Measures 1–6)

• Watch as you notate the first pitch of each of these measures as a whole note on a staff on the board.

• Volunteer to play these pitches while the class sings the song. Take turns until all have had a chance to play.

More Songs to Read

Feel the Beat! Conduct the Meter!

I Love the Mountains
Traditional Round

I love the moun-tains, I love the roll-ing hills,
I love the flow-ers, I love the daf-fo-dils;
I love the fire-side when all the lights are low.
Boom-dee-ah-da, Boom-dee-ah-da, Boom-dee-ah-da, Boom-dee-ah-da.

346

MEETING **INDIVIDUAL** NEEDS

PLAYING INSTRUMENTS: *Harmonic Accompaniment*
Have students accompany "I Love the Mountains."

ENRICHMENT: *Expressive Gestures*
Have students plan gestures for key words in "I Love the Mountains." Sing the song in unison and canon with the gestures. One group can sing the last line as an ostinato as the rest sing in unison and in canon, with gestures.

Practice with Phrases

Three-tone
d r m

LISTEN to find the phrases in these songs. How many different pitches does each song use? 3

GO 'ROUND THE MOUNTAIN

Illinois Play Party Song

Leader
1. Go 'round the moun-tain;
2. Swing 'round your part-ner;

Group
To-di-did-dle-um, To-di-did-dle-um,

Leader
Go 'round the moun-tain;
Swing 'round your part-ner;

Group
To-di-did-dle-um, To-di-did-dle-um-dum.

3. Back 'round the mountain; . . .
4. Girls through the window; . . .
5. Boys through the window; . . .
6. Find you a new love; . . .

Three-tone
d r m

NIGHT SONG

German Folk Song

All through the night, the moon is sil-ver bright.

Crick-et sings his ti-ny song, sings it through the

whole night long. All through the night.

Music Library *More Songs to Read* **347**

LESSONLINKS
For use after Unit 1, Lesson 2, pp. 16–19

FOCUS Form, phrase length

OBJECTIVES
• Identify phrases
• Identify number of pitches in songs

MATERIALS
Recordings
Go 'Round the Mountain   CD8:12
Night Song   CD8:11

Resources Orff Orchestration O • 18
(Night Song)

1. Introduce "Go 'Round the Mountain"
CD8:12. Have students:

• Listen to the song.

• Echo you saying the words. (Start slowly and gradually increase tempo.)

• Listen again, singing the nonsense words.

• Sing the song and perform the movement. (See *Movement* below.)

• Describe the length and melodic direction of each phrase. (two measures; downward)

• Tell how many different pitches are in the song.

2. Introduce "Night Song" CD8:11. Have students:

• Listen to the song and tell how it suggests a night scene. (moon, crickets)

• Listen again to hear how many different pitches it has.

• Describe the length and melodic direction of each phrase. (two measures; Phrases 1, 2, 5—downward; Phrases 3, 4—upward, then downward)

• Sing the song, maintaining its mood while gesturing to show the melodic direction of each phrase.

• (Optional: To add an instrumental accompaniment, identify the chords in each measure and play them on autoharps, bells, or Orff instruments.)

MOVEMENT: *"Go 'Round the Mountain"*

Formation: single circle of partners, facing clockwise, boy ahead of girl

Verse 1: Circle moves clockwise, stepping to the beat. **Verse 2:** Partners face each other and do locked-elbow swings, 8 beats with L elbow, 8 beats with R. **Verse 3:** Circle moves counterclockwise, girl ahead of boy. **Verse 4:** Boys take one step into circle and raise joined hands to form "windows." Girls move clockwise, weaving in and out of the "windows." **Verse 5:** Same as Verse 4, but girls form windows, boys weave. **Verse 6:** Boys promenade in "skating" position with nearest girls as their new partners.

ORFF: *"Night Song"*

See **O • 18** in *Orchestrations for Orff Instruments*.

MORE SONGS TO READ

LESSONLINKS

For use after Unit 1, Lesson 4, pp. 24–27

FOCUS Duration—quarter note, eighth note, half note

OBJECTIVE Identify and perform quarter, eighth, and half notes

MATERIALS
Recordings
Night Song   CD8:11
Babylon's Fallin'   CD8:13

Resources
Resource Master R • 1 (practice)
Orff Orchestration O • 19 (Babylon's Fallin')
Recorder Master R • 7 (Babylon's Fallin')

1. Identify rhythms in "Night Song" CD8:11.
Have students:

• Sing the song, patting with the beat.

• Identify the meter as ²₄.

• Identify each note as a quarter or eighth note, and recall that eighth notes are half as long as quarter notes.

• Read the rhythm of the song, patting with the beat. Say *song* for quarter notes, *the* for the single eighth note, and *cricket* for pairs of eighth notes.

• Sing the song again.

2. Introduce "Babylon's Fallin'" CD8:13.
Have students:

• Discuss the background of Babylon. (See *Social Studies Connection*, below.)

• Look at the song and identify the meter as ²₄.

• Listen to the song, patting with the beat and following the notation.

• Listen again, conducting in ²₄ with both hands.

• Read the words in rhythm, then sing the song.

• Take turns conducting as the class sings.

• (Optional: Use **Resource Master R • 1** to write the song's rhythm and chant city names to find beats of sound and silence.)

Reading Rhythm

IDENTIFY the meter and read the rhythm in this song. These are the rhythms used:

♩ quarter note

♫ two eighth notes

♩ half note

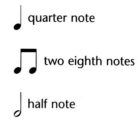

Virginia Folk Song

Bab - y - lon's fall - in', fall - in', fall - in',

Bab - y - lon's fall - in' to rise no more.

348

MEETING **INDIVIDUAL** NEEDS

SOCIAL STUDIES CONNECTION: *Babylon*

The ancient city of Babylon was located about 60 miles (97 kilometers) south of present-day Baghdad, Iraq. It was a major city of the region of Babylonia (southern Iraq), located in the fertile lands between the Tigris and Euphrates rivers. Have students locate this area on a map and research the lives of some of its renowned rulers—Hammurabi, Cyrus the Great, and Alexander the Great.

ORFF: *"Babylon's Fallin'"*

See **O • 19** in *Orchestrations for Orff Instruments*.

Reading *Do Re Mi So La*

SING two songs that use only *do re mi so la*.

la

so

mi

re

do

Pentatonic

d r m s l

Page's Train

1
D

North Carolina Folk Song

do

Pa - ge's   train   runs   so   fast,

2
D   A7   D

Can't   see   noth-ing   but   the   win - dow   glass.

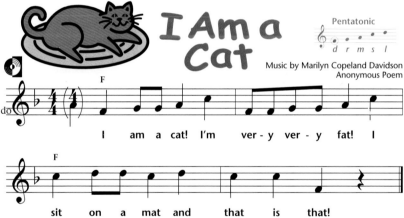

I Am a Cat

Pentatonic

d r m s l

Music by Marilyn Copeland Davidson
Anonymous Poem

F

do

I   am   a   cat!   I'm   ver - y   ver - y   fat!   I

F

sit   on   a   mat   and   that   is   that!

Music Library *More Songs to Read* **349**

ENRICHMENT: *Comparing Pitches with "Fed My Horse"*

Have students use **Resource Master R • 2** to reinforce *do re mi so la*.

VOCAL DEVELOPMENT: *Singing in Canon*

Two songs in this lesson can be sung as two-part canons, the second part entering as follows:
"Night Song"—second part enters one measure later.
"Page's Train"—second part enters two measures later.

ORFF: *"I Am a Cat"*

See **O • 20** in *Orchestrations for Orff Instruments.*

LESSONLINKS

For use after Unit 1, Lesson 5, pp. 28–31

FOCUS Pitch—*do re mi so la*

OBJECTIVE Identify *do re mi so la* in songs

MATERIALS
Recordings
Night Song   CD8:11
Babylon's Fallin'   CD8:13
Page's Train   CD8:14
I Am a Cat   CD8:15

Instruments unpitched instruments

Resources
Resource Master R • 2 (practice)
Orff Orchestration O • 20 (I Am a Cat)

---

1. Read pitches in "Night Song" CD8:11 **and "Babylon's Fallin'"** CD8:13. Have students:

• Sing *do re mi so la* with hand signs, mirroring and echoing you.

• Sing "Night Song" to decide which three of these pitches it uses. *(do re mi)*

• Sing the song with pitch syllables.

• Repeat the process with "Babylon's Fallin'."

2. Introduce "Page's Train" CD8:14. Have students:

• Label the starting pitch as *mi*, then locate every *mi re* and *do* in the song.

• Sing the song, singing aloud only those three pitches and thinking the other two pitches silently.

• Name all the pitches in the song. *(do re mi so la)*

• Sing the song slowly with pitch syllables.

• Clap the rhythm, then sing the song with words.

3. Add accompaniments. Have students:

• Form three groups, each group assigned to accompany "Page's Train" with a different pulse: eighth-note pulse, quarter-note pulse, half-note pulse.

• Use contrasting timbres to perform their parts, either with body percussion or unpitched percussion.

• Experiment with *accelerando* and *ritardando*.

4. Introduce "I Am a Cat" CD8:15. Have students:

• Read the words in rhythm.

• Label the starting pitch as *do*, then sing the song slowly with pitch syllables.

• Sing the song with words.

Music Library MORE SONGS TO READ **349**

MUSIC LIBRARY
MORE SONGS TO READ

LESSON LINKS

For use before Unit 2, Lesson 1, pp. 58–61

FOCUS Pitch—*do re mi so*

OBJECTIVE Sing *do re mi so* and aurally identify a pitch below *do*

MATERIALS
Recordings
Down the Road (A section)   CD2:16
Lady, Come Down and See   CD8:16

---

1. Review *do re mi* patterns with "Down the Road" (p. 76) CD2:16. Have students:

• Sing the two patterns at the top of page 350 with pitch syllables and hand signs.

• Listen to "Down the Road" to find these two melodic patterns. (Measure 1, Measure 2)

• Look at the six patterns in the middle of page 350 and find *do*. (second line)

• Sing each pattern, then sing the patterns as you point to them in random order. (Patterns 5 and 6 can be sung one after the other as an ostinato with the song.)

2. Introduce "Lady, Come Down and See" CD8:16. Have students:

• Notice where *do* is and sing it. (second line)

• Listen to the song to find a pitch below *do*. (first pitch)

• Clap the rhythm of the song.

• Read the melody, singing the first pitch (the pitch below *do*) on a neutral syllable such as *loo* and the remainder with pitch syllables and hand signs.

• Sing the song with words.

Practice *Do Re Mi So La*

SING these two patterns with pitch syllables. Then listen to "Down the Road" to find each pattern.

SING these patterns.

1.    2.

3.    4.

5.    6.

Lady, Come Down and See

Traditional Round

La - dy, come down and see, the cat sits in the plum tree.

FIND the pitch below *do*.

350

MEETING **INDIVIDUAL** NEEDS

EXTRA HELP: *Inner Hearing*

To help the students internalize the sound of the pitches (called "inner hearing"), have them think the pitches silently and show the hand signs as you clap the rhythm of "Lady, Come Down and See." At this time, have them show the first pitch, the "mystery" pitch below *do*, with both hands out to the side and shoulders raised in a "Who knows?" gesture.

ENRICHMENT: *Singing in Canon*

When the students are singing "Lady, Come Down and See" in unison with security, have them sing it as a two-part canon. Invite them to sing it in three or four parts as they are able.

Four Sounds to a Beat

FIND the beats with four sounds.

Four-tone

d r m s

American Minstrel Song

No one in the house but Di - nah, Di - nah,

No one in the house but me I know.

No one in the house but Di - nah, Di - nah,

Play - ing on the old ban - jo.

Music Library *More Songs to Read* **351**

ENRICHMENT: *Practicing Four Sounds to a Beat*

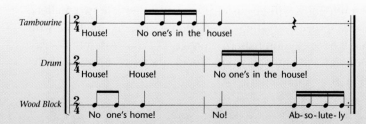

ORFF: *"Dinah"*

See **O • 21** in *Orchestrations for Orff Instruments.*

LESSONLINKS

For use after Unit 2, Lesson 2, pp. 62–65

FOCUS Duration—four sounds to a beat

OBJECTIVES
• Aurally identify four sounds to a beat and identify a phrase by its rhythm
• Read pitches *do re mi so*

MATERIALS
Recording Dinah   CD8:17

Instruments unpitched instruments

Resources Orff Orchestration O • 21 (Dinah)

1. Identify and pat four sounds to a beat.
Have students:

• Echo you on the following sequence: snap 4 quarter notes, clap 8 eighth notes, and pat 16 sixteenth notes with alternating hands.

• Step the beat with alternating feet as you perform the sequence again.

• Perform the sequence as you step with the beat.

• Signal the number of sounds per beat in each echoed example. (1, 2, 4)

2. Introduce "Dinah" CD8:17. Have students:

• Listen to the song to find beats with four sounds. (first beat of each phrase)

• Look at page 351 to see beats with four sounds.

• Listen as you perform the rhythm of various lines of the song (snapping, clapping, and patting as in the sequence above) and signal the number of the line.

• Read the words in rhythm.

• Observe where *do* is and read the pitches in rhythm.

• Sing the song.

3. Learn accompaniment patterns with four sounds to a beat. Have students:

• Echo you as you read the three patterns below. (See *Enrichment.*)

• Watch as you notate the patterns on the board.

• Identify which pattern you are speaking as you perform them in random order.

• Form three groups, one to perform each pattern with the song. When students are secure in speaking each pattern one at a time, have them speak all three at one time with the song.

• Switch and repeat so that all groups perform each pattern.

• Take turns playing the patterns on unpitched instruments.

Music Library MORE SONGS TO READ **351**

MUSIC LIBRARY
MORE SONGS TO READ

LESSON LINKS

For use after Unit 2, Lesson 4, pp. 72–75

FOCUS Duration—sixteenth notes

OBJECTIVE Perform sixteenth-note patterns and find them in a song

MATERIALS
Recording Ida Red   CD8:18

Resources Resource Master R • 3 (practice)

1. Perform sixteenth-note patterns. Have students:

• Echo-pat each pattern on page 352 while saying the vocal cues.

• Form three groups and perform the patterns, Group 1 twice through, alone, then Groups 2 and 3 twice through at the same time.

2. Introduce "Ida Red" CD8:18. Have students:

• Find the ♪♫ rhythm from Pattern 2 in the song. (Measure 1, Beat 2; Measure 3, Beat 1)

• Find the ♫♪ rhythm from Pattern 3 in the song. (Measure 3, Beat 2)

• Read the words of the song in rhythm.

• Name the form of the song. (A B, Refrain/Verse)

• Identify the pitches used, then read the pitches slowly with pitch syllables and hand signs.

• Listen to the song, then sing it.

• Form three groups and sing the song with the patterns, each group performing its pattern when appropriate.

• Create new verses, silly or sweet, using other colors.

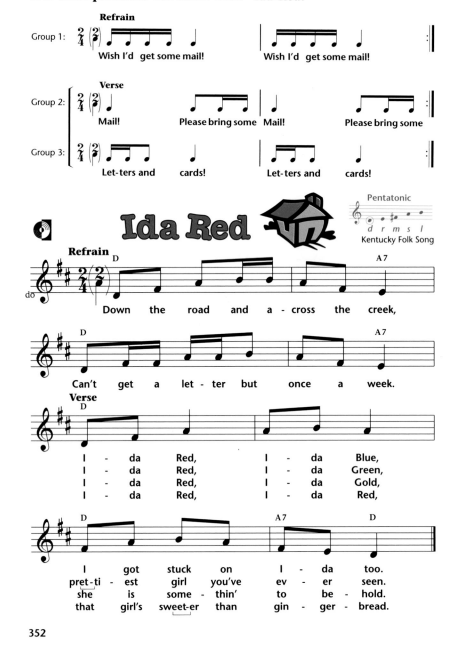

MEETING **INDIVIDUAL** NEEDS

PLAYING INSTRUMENTS: *"Ida Red"*

Playing rapid sixteenth notes will be easier if students alternate two mallets. Have students choose three contrasting unpitched instruments playable with two mallets. Transfer each rhythm pattern on page 352 to a different instrument. For example, play Pattern 1 on wood blocks, Pattern 2 on agogo bells or cowbells, and Pattern 3 on drums.

ENRICHMENT: *Composing with Sixteenth Notes*

Have students use **Resource Master R • 3** to create a coda for "Trail to Mexico" with sixteenth-note patterns.

Discover a Song

SING the pitches and rhythms of these phrases to discover the name of the song.

SING these patterns.

1.

2.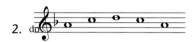

3.

4.

5.

6.

LESSONLINKS

For use after Unit 2, Lesson 5, pp. 76–79

FOCUS Pitch—low *so* and *la*

OBJECTIVE Identify a song by reading rhythms and pitches, including low *so* and low *la*

MATERIALS
Recordings
Trail to Mexico   CD2:14
Lady, Come Down and See   CD8:16

Resources Resource Master R • 4 (practice)

1. Identify "Trail to Mexico" (p. 74) CD2:14 **from its notation.** Have students:

• Silently think the pitches and rhythms at the top of page 353 to identify the song.

• Read and pat the rhythm aloud.

• Sing the pitches used in the song, going down and then up from *do*, then write each pitch on a staff on the board. (*do la, so,; do re mi so la*)

• Read the pitches with syllables and hand signs.

• Sing the song on page 74 with words.

2. Read "Lady, Come Down and See" (p. 350) CD8:16. Have students:

• Look at the song to see if it is in the same key as "Trail to Mexico" and find low *so*. (yes; first pitch)

• Sing the song with pitch syllables and hand signs, then with words.

3. Read patterns with low *so* and *la*. Have students:

• Find *do* in the patterns at the bottom of page 353, then sing these patterns with pitch syllables and hand signs.

• Listen as you sing the patterns randomly and signal the number of the pattern you sang.

ENRICHMENT: *Reading Rhythms*

Have students use **Resource Master R • 4** to put phrases of "Trail to Mexico" in the correct order.

MUSIC LIBRARY
MORE SONGS TO READ

RELATED ARTS | MOVEMENT | **THEATER** | VISUAL ARTS |

LESSONLINKS

For use after Unit 2, Lesson 5, pp. 76–79

FOCUS Pitch/Rhythm

OBJECTIVES
• Identify and read low *so* and low *la*
• Identify and read sixteenth-note patterns

MATERIALS
Recording Old Chisholm Trail   CD8:19

Resources Orff Orchestration O • 22 (Old Chisholm Trail)

---

1. Introduce "Old Chisholm Trail" CD8:19. Have students:

• Review the patterns on the bottom of page 353.

• Listen to the song.

• Figure out how the melodic patterns and the song are related. (The patterns are derived from the song and appear in order, without rhythm or repeated pitches. The patterns overlap.)

• Read the pitches of the song, recognizing that they have already read them on page 353.

2. Read sixteenth-note rhythms. Have students:

• Find beats with four sixteenth notes. (Verse: Measure 2, Beat 1; Measure 3, Beats 1–2; Refrain: Measure 1, Beat 2; Measure 3, Beat 2)

• Find the 🎵 rhythm. (Measure 1)

• Find the 🎵 rhythm. (Verse: Measure 4, Beats 1–2: continues into the Refrain; Refrain: Measure 2, Beats 1–2)

• Say the words of the song in rhythm.

• Sing the song with words.

3. Create skits. Have students:

• Listen as you tell them about the Chisholm Trail. (See *Background*.)

• Do more research, as desired, on the Chisholm Trail.

• Form small groups and write skits incorporating the song. Create and add their own verses to the song.

• Share the skits with the class.

---

354   Music Library MORE SONGS TO READ

Using What You Know

THE OLD CHISHOLM TRAIL

Pentatonic

s, l, d r m s l

Cowboy Song

Verse

1. Come a-long boys, and lis-ten to my tale.

I'll tell you of my trou-bles on the old Chis-holm trail.

Refrain

Come a ti yi yip-py, yip-py ay, yip-py ay,

Come a ti yi yip-py, yip-py ay.

2. I woke one mornin' on the old Chisholm trail,
A rope in my hand and a cow by the tail. *Refrain*

3. I started up the trail on October twenty-third,
Started up the trail with the old cow herd. *Refrain*

4. On a ten dollar horse and a forty dollar saddle,
I'm gonna punch those Texas cattle. *Refrain*

5. It's bacon and beans 'most ev'ry day,
I'd as soon be a-eatin' prairie hay. *Refrain*

6. It's cloudy in the west and it looks like rain,
And I left my old slicker in the wagon again. *Refrain*

7. I'm gonna see the boss, gonna get my money,
Goin' back home to see my honey. *Refrain*

354

MEETING **INDIVIDUAL** NEEDS

ORFF: *"The Old Chisholm Trail"*

See **O • 22** in *Orchestrations for Orff Instruments.*

BACKGROUND: *"The Old Chisholm Trail"*

From the 1860s to the 1880s, the Chisholm Trail went nearly 1,000 miles from San Antonio, Texas, to Abilene, Kansas, where cattle could be shipped by rail to the Northeast. Cattle were also brought north on the trail to better grazing in the Dakotas and Montana. Cattle drives took several months and cowboys on the trail sang to pass the long hours. This song is considered the classic example of those created during this era. There are hundreds of verses, since they were easy to improvise on the spot.

Steps, Skips, and Repeats

SING this song two pitches at a time. After every two pitches, tell if you just sang a step, a skip, or a repeated pitch.

Old Tar River

Pentatonic

s₁ l₁ d r m s

American Folk Song

1. Way___ down in North Car'-lin-a, } *Whistle*
2. My old dog he won't go with me,
3. Rac-coon, Pos-sum had a fray,
4. Old dog watch, smelled all a-round,___
5. Di-nah, I am going to leave you;

On the banks of Old Tar Riv-er, } *Whistle*
He'd rath-er hunt far's I can see.___
Fought all night un-til next day,___
Found Rac-coon just left the ground,___
When I'm gone don't let it grieve you,

Go from there to Al-a-bam-a, } *Whistle*
He smells some-thing up the hill,___
When day broke went Poss' to the hol-low,
Then he bark right up the tree,___
First to the win-dow, then to the door,___

For to see my old Aunt Han-nah. } *Whistle*
If I don't find it, he sure will.___
Rac-coon says, "I bet-ter fol-low."
Rac-coon says, "You can't catch me."___
Look-ing for to see my ban-jo.

Music Library *More Songs to Read* 355

LESSONLINKS

For use after Unit 3, Lesson 1, pp. 108–111

FOCUS Pitch, melodic movement

OBJECTIVES
• Read a song with low *so* and low *la*
• Identify repeated notes, steps, and skips

MATERIALS
Recording Old Tar River   CD8:20

1. Introduce "Old Tar River" CD8:20. Have students:

• Name ways one can perform a melody. (singing, playing, humming, and so on)

• Listen to the song to find out how the first verse is performed. (sung, played, and whistled)

• Listen again, whistling along as they are able.

• Sing and whistle the entire song.

• Find the ♩♫ rhythm. (Measure 3 of each line)

• Say and clap the rhythm of Verse 1.

• Practice inner hearing, singing parts with words and thinking whistled parts. Switch and repeat.

• Find low *so* and low *la*. (first note of Measures 1, 7, 15; third note of second measure in each line)

• Form two groups, one to sing the pitch syllables of the sung part and the other to sing those of the whistled part. Switch roles and repeat.

• Volunteer to take turns singing the sung phrases as solos.

2. Identify melodic movement in the song. Have students:

• Review what repeated notes, steps, and skips are.

• Form a circle and sing the pitches of the song in order, two at a time. After each interval, an individual labels it as repeated notes, step, or skip. For example, the song begins with *so₁ do* (skip), *do do* (repeat), *do mi* (skip), *mi re* (step). Continue until each student has had a turn.

PLAYING INSTRUMENTS: *Wood and Bell Sounds*

Have students perform the melodic rhythm of "Old Tar River" with instruments of contrasting tone colors. For example, use wood sounds (xylophones) for singing and resonator bells for whistling.

PLAYING INSTRUMENTS: *Recorder*

Have students play this part on soprano recorders with "Old Tar River."

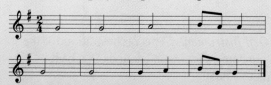

MUSIC LIBRARY

MORE SONGS TO READ

RELATED ARTS MOVEMENT | THEATER | VISUAL ARTS

LESSON LINKS

For use after Unit 3, Lesson 2, pp. 112–117

FOCUS Rhythm/Meter

OBJECTIVES
• Identify meter of a song in $\frac{2}{4}$
• Read low *so* and low *la*

MATERIALS
Recording Heave-Ho Me
Laddies · · · · · · · · · · CD8:21

Resources
Resource Master R • 5 (practice)
Orff Orchestration O • 8 (Come and Sing
Together)

---

1. Introduce "Heave-Ho Me Laddies"
CD8:21. Have students:

• Pat two equal sounds ♩♩ or two unequal sounds ♩. ♪ as you clap the beat, switching on your verbal cue.

• Listen to the song without looking at it. Pat with the beat to decide if the song is in $\frac{2}{4}$ or $\frac{2}{4}$· ($\frac{2}{4}$·; two unequal sounds to a beat is a prominent rhythm pattern.)

2. Read the pitches in the song. Have students:

• Notice where *do* is. (first space)

• Find where the melody skips from high to low *so*. (Line 3, Measures 1 and 3)

• Find two lines that are almost alike and recognize that the phrase form is a b c b' the first time and, on the repeat, a b c b. (Lines 2 and 4; form varies because the two endings differ.)

• Sing the song slowly with pitch syllables and hand signs.

• Sing the song at tempo with words.

• (Optional: Use **Resource Master R • 5** for more pitch reading.)

New Meter Ahoy!

LISTEN to this song to decide if you hear equal or unequal sounds to the beat.

356

MEETING **INDIVIDUAL** NEEDS

MOVEMENT: *"Heave-Ho Me Laddies"*

Have students create movement to illustrate the song and to follow its form. First, have them explore various work motions associated with sailors that could be performed with the song, such as pulling sail ropes, swabbing the deck, pulling in the anchor, or coiling ropes around an object to hold it tight. Then have them choose one movement for each different phrase, choose a formation for the group, and perform the movements while singing.

ORFF: *"Come and Sing Together"*

See **O • 8** in *Orchestrations for Orff Instruments.* This orchestration for the song on page 115 reinforces the concept of two equal sounds to a beat by incorporating one and two sounds to a beat.

Reading New Pitches

FIND a new pitch in this song.
Hint: It is below low so. *low mi*

My Horses Ain't Hungry

Pentatonic

Tennessee Folk Song

m, s, l, d r m

1. My hors - es ain't hun - gry, They won't eat your hay,
2. I know you're my Pol - ly, I'm not going to stay,
3. With all our be - long-ings, We'll ride till we come

So I'll get on my po - ny, I'm go - ing a - way.
So___ come with me dar - ling, We'll feed on our way.
To___ a lone - ly cab - in, We'll call it our home.

PLAY an ostinato with the song.

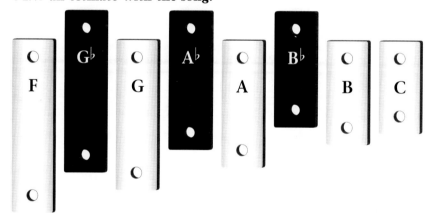

Music Library *More Songs to Read* **357**

LESSONLINKS

For use after Unit 3, Lesson 4, pp. 124–127

FOCUS Pitch—*fa*

OBJECTIVE Identify low *mi* and read and play an ostinato containing *fa*

MATERIALS
Recording My Horses Ain't
Hungry   CD8:22

Instruments resonator bells or Orff instruments

Resources
Resource Master R • 20 (hand signs)
Resource Master R • 6 (practice)
Resource Master R • 7 (practice)

1. Introduce "My Horses Ain't Hungry"
CD8:22. Have students:

• Say the words in rhythm.

• Notice where *do* is, find low *so*, and notice the pitch lower than low *so*. (first space; C; low A in Measures 2 and 6)

• Decide if the new pitch is a step or a skip below low *so* and name its pitch syllable. (skip; low *mi*)

• Sing the song slowly with pitch syllables and hand signs.

• Listen to and then sing the song.

2. Learn an ostinato containing *fa*. Have students:

• Watch as you write the following on the board.

• Recall the pitch between *mi* and *so* and its hand sign. (*fa*; refer to **Resource Master R • 20** for the hand sign. Use **Resource Masters R • 6** and **R • 7** for more practice with *fa*.)

• Sing the ostinato with pitch syllables, then practice playing it on the resonator bells on page 357.

• Take turns playing the ostinato on resonator bells or Orff instruments to accompany the song.

VOCAL DEVELOPMENT: *Vocal Ostinato*

Sing this vocal ostinato with "My Horses Ain't Hungry."

I'm rid - ing, rid - ing.

LANGUAGE ARTS CONNECTION: *Writing Stories*

Write about the person(s) singing "My Horses Ain't Hungry." Why are they leaving? From where? What adventures do they have?

CRITICAL THINKING: *Compare and Contrast*

Have students sing "Fed My Horse" (page 31) and compare it with "My Horses Ain't Hungry" in terms of meter and style.

RELATED ARTS MOVEMENT | THEATER | VISUAL ARTS

LESSON LINKS

For use after Unit 3, Lesson 5, pp. 128–131

FOCUS Duration

OBJECTIVES
• Speak and pat rhythm patterns in ⁶⁄₈ (²⁄♩.)
• Read a song containing low *la* and low *so*

MATERIALS
Recording The Derby Ram — CD8:23

Resources Resource Master R • 8 (practice)

1. Introduce "The Derby Ram" CD8:23.
Have students:

• Observe the meter signature and the predominant rhythm pattern. (⁶⁄₈; ♩ ♪)

• Listen to the song, following the notation.

• Read the words of the first verse in rhythm.

2. Sing with pitch syllables. Have students:

• Identify *do* and hum it. (first space)

• Sing the pitches used in the song, following your hand signs.

• Notice the words in the verse that go below *do*. (*As, Derby town all, that's ever fed*)

• Sing the song slowly with pitch syllables and hand signs.

• Sing the song with words.

3. Pat the rhythm. Have students:

• Form five groups.

• Assign each group one verse on which they are to pat the rhythm. (Suggest that they pat lightly, alternating hands, on the floor or on their desks.)

• Sing the song again, each group patting the rhythm of one verse.

• To reinforce the rhythm, count off by twos and start in scattered formation. 1s walk with the beat through shared space while 2s stand still and pat the rhythm of the melody. Switch roles on each verse.

Reading in ⁶⁄₈ (²⁄♩.) Meter

THE DERBY RAM

Pentatonic
s, l, d r m s l

English Folk Song
Ozark Version

Verse

1. As I went down to Der - by town, all
2. The wool up - on this ram's_____ back It
3. The horns up - on this ram's_____ head They
4. The ears up - on this ram's_____ head They
5. Oh ev' - ry tooth this ram_____ had would

on a sum - mer's day,_____ It's there I saw the
drug_____ to the ground,_____ I hauled it to the
reached_____ to the moon, the butch-er went up on
reached_____ to the sky, the ea - gle built his
hold a bush-el of corn, And ev' - ry foot he

fin - est ram, that's ev - er fed on hay._____
mar - ket, And it weighed ten thou - sand pounds._____
Feb - ru - ar-y, And nev-er got back till June._____
nest there, For I heard the young ones cry._____
stood_____ on, Would cov-er an a-cre of ground.

Refrain

And if you don't be - lieve me,_____ And think I tell a lie,_____

Just you go down to Der-by, And you'll see the same as I._____

358

MEETING **INDIVIDUAL** NEEDS

ENRICHMENT:

Using **Resource Master R • 8**, have students sing the phrases of "One More River," which are printed out of order, then match each line with a phrase from the song.

LANGUAGE ARTS CONNECTION: *Hyperbole*

Hyperbole is a figure of speech so exaggerated that it obviously cannot be taken literally. Have students sing the song one time through. As they sing it a second time, have them stop every time they encounter hyperbole. For example, in Verse 2 they should stop on *it weighed ten thousand pounds* and in Verse 3 on *they reached to the moon*. Have students create their own hyperboles for the song and share them with the class.

A ⁶⁄₈ Song from Newfoundland

Lots o' Fish in Bonavist' Harbor
Newfoundland Folk Song

D major

d r m f s l t d'

Verse

1. There's lots o' fish in Bon-a-vist' Har-bor,
2. Oh, Sal-ly went to church ev'-ry Sun-day,

Lots o' fish right in a-round here.
Not for to sing nor for____ to hear.

Boys and girls are fish-in' to-geth-er,
But to see the fel-ler from For-tune

For-ty-five from Car - bon-ear.
What was down here fish-in' last year.

Refrain

Oh, catch-a-hold this one, catch-a-hold that one,
Dance a-round this one, dance a-round that one,

Swing a-round this one, swing a-round she;

Did-dle dum dee dum, did-dle dum dee.

Music Library *More Songs to Read* 359

1. Introduce "Lots o' Fish in Bonavist' Harbor" CD8:24. Have students:

• Listen to the song, patting with the beat, to find sounds two beats long. (first note of Lines 1, 5)

• Read the words in rhythm, watching for those that suggest movement. (*swing around, dance around*)

• Listen as you tell that in Newfoundland, this song is often sung and danced at weddings and other joyful occasions. Traditionally, people do a "Newfie" jig.

• Sing the song.

2. Add a rhythm ostinato. Have students:

• Watch as you write the rhythm of the jig step for the verse on the board. (See *Movement,* below.)

• Pat the rhythm with fingers, alternating hands, saying "Right-Left-Right, Left-Right-Left."

• Play the rhythm with the verse on unpitched instruments, alternating hands or mallets as they did in patting the rhythm.

MOVEMENT: *"Lots o' Fish in Bonavist' Harbor"*

Formation: partners facing, scattered formation

Verse: "Newfie" Jig: R foot steps to R side; L foot closes next to R; R foot steps in place; repeat to left.

Refrain: Swing R elbow with partner; then swing L elbow; repeat.

Have students use the two-beat sounds at the beginning of the Verse and Refrain to switch positions from facing to elbow swings and back.

MUSIC LIBRARY
MORE SONGS TO READ

LESSON LINKS

For use after Unit 4, Lesson 1, pp. 158–163

FOCUS Duration, ♪ ♩ ♪ (*short long short*)

OBJECTIVES
- Identify and clap the *short long short* pattern
- Read the pitches of a song

MATERIALS
Recordings Old Dan Tucker   CD8:25
Old Dan Tucker
  (performance mix)   CD11:12

1. Introduce "Old Dan Tucker" CD8:25.
Have students:

• Echo you in clapping rhythm patterns with the *short long short* pattern. (See *Composing*, below.)

• Listen as you tell them that Daniel Emmett, a favorite minstrel songwriter of the 1800s, is credited with having written "Old Dan Tucker." The song was one of Abraham Lincoln's favorites, probably because of the humorous nature of the nonsense words. Emmett, an Ohio native, also wrote "Dixie."

• Listen to the song and raise a hand when they hear the *short long short* pattern. (Measures 1, 5, and 6 of the Refrain)

• Listen to the song again and clap the *short long short* pattern when it occurs.

• Discuss the nonsense words in the song.

• Sing the song, still clapping the *short long short* pattern.

2. Read the pitches of the song. Have students:

• Observe the position of *do* and list the pitches used in the song. (Line 2; *so, la, do re mi so*)

• Sing the song with pitch syllables and hand signs.

• Sing the song with words once again.

• Form groups and create four-measure rhythms that include at least one pattern from *Composing*, below.

• Transfer their rhythms to unpitched instruments and take turns playing with the refrain. (Have one student play the beat.)

Find the *Short Long Short* Pattern

LISTEN for the *short long short* pattern.

Old Dan Tucker

American Folk Song
Folk version of Dan Emmett's minstrel song

Verse

1. Old Dan Tuck- er's a fine old man.
2. Old Dan Tuck- er be - gan in ear- ly life, To

Washed his face in a fry - ing pan,
play the ban - jo and the fife. He'd

Combed his head with a wag - on wheel And
play the boys and gals to sleep, And

died with a tooth - ache in his heel.
then in - to his bunk he'd creep.

Refrain

Get out the way, Old Dan Tuck- er, You're too late to

get your sup- per. Sup- per's o- ver and din- ner's cook- in' And

Old Dan Tuck- er's just stand- in' look- in'.

360

MEETING **INDIVIDUAL** NEEDS

COMPOSING: *Using Syncopated Patterns*
Have students use these patterns in creating their own rhythms.

PLAYING INSTRUMENTS: *Recorder*
Have students add this descant to "Old Dan Tucker."

Octave Skips

My Dame Hath a Lame, Tame Crane

G major
s, l, t, d r m f s

Traditional English Round

My dame hath a lame, tame crane.

My dame hath a crane that is lame.

Pray, gen-tle Jane, let my dame's lame, tame

crane sing and come home a-gain.

To Stop the Train

F major
s, d r m f s

English Round

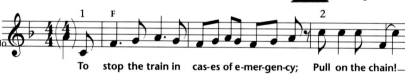
To stop the train in cas-es of e-mer-gen-cy; Pull on the chain!—

Pull on the chain!— Pen-al-ty for im-prop-er use, five pounds.

Music Library *More Songs to Read* **361**

ENRICHMENT: *Octaves*

Have students work with octaves on **Resource Master R • 9.**

MOVEMENT: *"To Stop the Train"*

MOVEMENT

Have students perform these motions with the lyrics: *stop*—hold arm out as if stopping traffic; *train*—pump arms back and forth rapidly at sides, elbows bent; *cases of emergency*—palms facing out, close and open fists rapidly; *pull on the chain*—one arm up as if grasping a high handle, on *chain*, move arm down, then up; *penalty for improper use*—shake finger; *five*—show five fingers; *pounds*—hand out, palm facing up. As a challenge, have students perform the song as a silent canon with motions.

LESSON LINKS

For use after Unit 4, Lesson 2, pp. 164–167

FOCUS Pitch, octave

OBJECTIVES
• Signal to identify octave skips
• Sing songs in canon

MATERIALS
Recordings
Heave-Ho Me Laddies   CD8:21
My Dame Hath a Lame,
   Tame Crane   CD8:26
To Stop the Train   CD8:27

Resources Resource Master R • 9
(practice)

1. Review "Heave-Ho Me Laddies" (p. 356)
CD8:21. Have students:

• Recall what an octave is. (a skip from one pitch to the next of the same name)

• Find the octave skips in the song. (Line 3, Measures 1 and 3)

• Sing the song, showing the melodic direction of Line 3.

2. Introduce "My Dame Hath a Lame, Tame Crane" CD8:26. Have students:

• Share any tongue-twisters they know.

• Listen to the song, signaling when they hear an octave skip. (Line 4, Measure 1, first two pitches)

• Echo you on the words.

• Sing the song, following the notation.

• When secure in singing the song in unison, sing it as a two-part canon.

• (Optional: Challenge students to sing this song as fast as they can without missing any words. Sing the song at regular tempo, in aug-mentation, and in diminution. When secure in singing it as a two-part canon, sing it as a four-part canon.)

3. Introduce "To Stop the Train" CD8:27. Have students:

• Listen to the song, signaling when they hear an octave skip. (last measure)

• Find the *short long short* pattern. (Phrase 2)

• Sing the song with pitch syllables, then words.

• When secure in singing the song in unison, sing it as a two-part canon, then a three-part canon.

Music Library MORE SONGS TO READ **361**

MUSIC LIBRARY
MORE SONGS TO READ

RELATED ARTS **MOVEMENT** | THEATER | VISUAL ARTS

LESSON LINKS

For use after Unit 4, Lesson 4, pp. 172–175

FOCUS Rhythm

OBJECTIVE Read rhythm of song containing four sixteenth notes and the *short long short* pattern

MATERIALS
Recording Before Dinner   CD8:28

Instruments agogo bells or two cowbells, shakers or maracas, drums

Resources Orff Orchestration O • 23 (Before Dinner)

1. Introduce "Before Dinner" CD8:28. Have students:

• Look at the song and decide how it is to be performed. (call-and-response form)

• Tell which part is always the same. (response)

• Identify the *short long short* pattern. (first measure of the response)

• Say and clap the rhythm of the words.

• Listen to the song.

• Form two groups and sing the song in call-and-response form. Switch parts and repeat.

2. Introduce unpitched instrument parts. Have students:

• Read the agogo part, clapping the lower notes and snapping the upper with alternating hands.

• Clap and snap the pattern with the song.

• Practice the other two parts without, then with, the song. (Clap the shaker part; pat the drum part.)

• Form three groups, each taking one part and doing the body percussion with the song.

• Take turns playing the parts on instruments with the song.

Using What You Know

FIND the measures with the *short long short* pattern. Then identify and read the pitches.

ADD these instrument parts to the song.

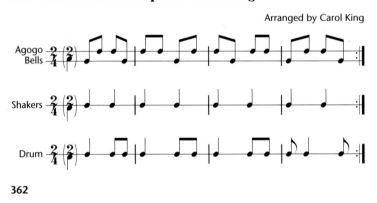

362

MEETING **INDIVIDUAL** NEEDS

NOTATION: *"Before Dinner"*

Have students identify *do* and recognize that the pitch set is *mi, so, la,*. Then, have students practice singing various combinations of pitches as you point to them on a staff. (Check accuracy with a pitched instrument, if necessary.) Finally, sing the song with pitch syllables in unison and then in call-and-response form.

ORFF: *"Before Dinner"*

See **O • 23** in *Orchestrations for Orff Instruments*. The first two parts on page 362 are included in the orchestration, and the third part is preparation for the other parts in the orchestration.

Hearing and Using Octaves

RAISE your hand when you hear these pitches.

FIND the octave skip in the song below. Sing the song with pitch syllables. Then, accompany it with an octave pattern.

Shaker Song

Hop up and jump up and whirl 'round, whirl 'round,

Gath-er love, here it is all 'round, all 'round,

Here is love flow-ing 'round, catch it as you whirl round,

Reach up and reach down, here it is all 'round.

Music Library More Songs to Read **363**

LESSONLINKS

For use after Unit 4, Lesson 5, pp. 176–179

FOCUS Pitch, octaves

OBJECTIVE Identify pitches, including octave skips, and play an octave accompaniment

MATERIALS
Recordings
Sarasponda   CD4:11
Hop Up and Jump Up   CD8:29

Instruments Orff or other pitched instruments

Resources Orff Orchestration O • 24 (Hop Up and Jump Up)

---

1. Review "Sarasponda" (p. 167) CD4:11.
Have students:

• Silently think the pitches at the top of page 363.

• Sing the song, signaling when the pitches occur.

• Decide how they knew when they heard the pitches. (They heard the octave.)

• Name the octave's pitch syllables. (*do, do'*)

2. Introduce "Hop Up and Jump Up" CD8:29 **and add an octave accompaniment.** Have students:

• Find the octave skip. (Line 3)

• Sing the song with pitch syllables.

• Listen to the song.

• Sing the song with words.

• Pat the following pattern with the song:

• Take turns playing the pattern on low and high C with the song.

• When secure in singing the song in unison, sing it as a two-part canon, the second part entering one measure after the first.

MOVEMENT

MOVEMENT: *"Hop Up and Jump Up"*

Formation: circle

Measure 1: 2 step hops (step R, hop R, step L, hop L). **Measure 2:** Turn in place. **Measure 3:** 2 step hops. **Measure 4:** Extend R, then L arm up and out. **Measure 5:** 2 step hops. **Measure 6:** Turn in place. **Measure 7:** Reach up, then down. **Measure 8:** Extend R, then L arm up and out.

ORFF: *"Hop Up and Jump Up"*

See **O • 24** in *Orchestrations for Orff Instruments*. This orchestration incorporates the octave accompaniment taught in the lesson. Also, the instrument parts are structured to help teach the movement sequence.

MUSIC LIBRARY
MORE SONGS TO READ

RELATED ARTS | MOVEMENT | THEATER | VISUAL ARTS

LESSONLINKS

For use after Unit 5, Lesson 1, pp. 206–209

FOCUS Meter

OBJECTIVES
• Conduct in ²⁄, ³⁄, and ⁴⁄ and create movement in ³⁄.
• Read songs with *fa*

MATERIALS
Recordings
Oliver Cromwell   CD8:30
Who's Got a Fishpole?   CD8:31
My Horses Ain't Hungry   CD8:22

Resources
Resource Master R • 10 (practice)
Orff Orchestration O • 25 (Oliver Cromwell)

---

1. Introduce "Oliver Cromwell" CD8:30
Have students:

• Read the words in rhythm.

• Read the song with pitch syllables, then words.

• Listen to the song, conducting in ²⁄.

• When secure in singing the song in unison, perform the song in canon with the second part entering one measure after the first. They can also sing it as a solo/group song, with the group singing the *hee haw* phrases.

2. Introduce "Who's Got a Fishpole?"
CD8:31. Have students:

• Read the words in rhythm.

• Read the song with pitch syllables, then words.

• Form two groups, one to sing the questions and the other to sing *We do*.

• Listen to the song, conducting in ⁴⁄.

• (Optional: Use **Resource Master R • 10** to improvise melodically in ⁴⁄.)

3. Review "My Horses Ain't Hungry"
(p. 357) CD8:22. Have students:

• Read the song.

• Form groups, each to create a 3-beat movement pattern. Share their patterns as all sing the song.

• Listen to the song, conducting in ³⁄.

Reviewing Meter

Oliver Cromwell
English Folk Song

1. Ol - i - ver Crom-well lay bur - ied and dead, Hee haw,
(2.) ap-ples were ripe___ and read - y to fall, Hee haw,
(3.) sad-dle and bri - dle, they lie on the shelf, Hee haw,

bur - ied and dead. There grew an old ap - ple tree
read - y to fall. There came an old wo - man to
lie on the shelf. If you want an - y more you can

o - ver his head, Hee haw, o - ver his head. 2. The
gath - er them all, Hee haw, gath - er them all. 3. The
sing it your-self, Hee haw, sing it your-self.

Who's Got a Fishpole?
American Song

1. Who's got a fish-pole? We do. Who's got a fish-pole? We do.
2. Who's got a line?___ We do. Who's got a line?___ We do.
3. Who's got a hook?___ We do. Who's got a hook?___ We do.

Who's got a fish-pole? We do. Fish - pole needs a line.
Who's got a line?___ We do. Line___ needs a hook.
Who's got a hook?___ We do. Hook___ needs a worm.

364

MEETING **INDIVIDUAL** NEEDS

ENRICHMENT: *Conducting in* ³⁄₄

ENRICHMENT: *Dramatizing "Oliver Cromwell"* THEATER
Have groups of six to eight create ways to dramatize the song.

ORFF: *"Oliver Cromwell"*
See **O • 25** in *Orchestrations for Orff Instruments*.

Major or Minor?

A major

Southern Folk Song
Arranged by Mary Goetze

m, s, l, t, d r m

Verse

1. The Boll Wee - vil am a lit - tle black bug from
2. The first time I saw Boll Wee - vil,_____ He was
3. The Boll Wee - vil to the farm - er said, "You'd
4. The mer - chant took_____ half the cot - ton._____ The

Mex - i - co they say. Come all the way to Tex - as just to
sit - tin' on the square. The next time I saw Boll Wee - vil, He had
bet-ter leave me a - lone. I done eat all your cot - ton, Now I'm
Boll Wee-vil took the rest. He on - ly left the farm - er Just a

Refrain

find a place to stay.
his whole fam' - ly there. } Just a look - in' for a home.
start - in' on your corn."
sin - gle rag - ged vest.

Just a look - in' for a home.

Just a look - in' for a home.

Just a look - in' for a home.

Music Library *More Songs to Read* **365**

SOCIAL STUDIES CONNECTION: *The Boll Weevil*

Have students research the boll weevil in Texas, Oklahoma, and the South to discover why there is a monument to this insect in Enterprise, Alabama. (It forced the farmers to raise peanuts, which were eventually more profitable.)

PLAYING INSTRUMENTS: *Recorder*

Have students play this part on soprano recorders.

Refrain

LESSON LINKS

For use after Unit 5, Lesson 2, pp. 210–213

FOCUS Pitch, major and minor

OBJECTIVE Aurally identify major and minor scales and identify a song as being in major

MATERIALS
Recording Boll Weevil   CD8:32

Instruments chromatic pitched instruments such as resonator bells, keyboards, or recorders

Resources
Resource Master R • 11 (practice)
Resource Master R • 12 (practice)

1. Introduce "Boll Weevil" CD8:32. Have students:

• Listen to the song, following the notation.

• Describe characteristics of the boll weevil and possible feelings of the farmer.

• Read the words in rhythm, patting the beat.

• Sing the song.

• Plan different dynamics and tempo to reflect each verse, then sing the song again as planned.

• (Optional: Use **Resource Masters R • 11** and **R • 12** to review pitches and meter.)

2. Discover whether the song is in major or minor. Have students:

• Listen as you play an A major scale (A B C♯ D E F♯ G♯ A); then an A natural minor scale (A B C D E F G A).

• Decide if "Boll Weevil" is major or minor. (major; You can reinforce this by playing or singing the melody of "Boll Weevil" in A minor: disregard the sharps in the key signature and perform it without using any black key notes.)

• Watch as you write the A major and A minor scales on the board, then take turns volunteering to play one or the other for the class to identify.

MUSIC LIBRARY
MORE SONGS TO READ

LESSON LINKS
For use after Unit 5, Lesson 4, pp. 218–221

FOCUS Pitch, *ti*

OBJECTIVE Identify a song containing *ti* and identify *ti* in songs

MATERIALS
Recordings
Lots o' Fish in Bonavist' Harbor   **CD8:24**
Alleluia, Amen   **CD8:33**
San lun tsa   **CD8:34**
Recorded Lesson:
  Pronunciation for "San lun tsa"   **CD8:35**

Resources Resource Master R • 13
(practice)

1. Identify "Lots o' Fish in Bonavist' Harbor" (p. 359) CD8:24. Have students:

• Watch you write a C major scale on the board.

• Sing a scale with pitch syllables as you point to each pitch.

• Sing pitches you indicate until they identify the song.

• Sing the song.

2. Introduce "Alleluia, Amen" CD8:33. Have students:

• Look at the song to find *do* and *ti*. (C; 17th note)

• Read the pitches with syllables and hand signs.

• Sing the song in unison and as a two-part canon.

• Name and write missing pitches including *ti* using **Resource Master R • 13.**

3. Introduce "San lun tsa" CD8:34. Have students:

• Look at the song to find *do* and *ti*. (D; 10th note)

• Read the pitches with syllables and hand signs.

Recorded Lesson CD8:35

• Listen to "Pronunciation for 'San lun tsa.'"

• Listen to the song.

• Say the words in rhythm.

• Sing the song in Mandarin or English.

• (Optional: Play this recorder part with the song.)

Tunes with *Ti*

FIND *do* in each song. Where is *ti*? *ti*

ALLELUIA, AMEN

Traditional Round

1. Al - le - lu - ia, al - le - lu - ia,

2. A - men, a - men.

San lun tsa
Three-Wheeled Taxi

Taiwanese Folk Song
Collected and Transcribed by Kathy B. Sorensen
English Version by MMH

Mandarin: 三 輪 車 跑 得 快 上 面 坐 個 老 太 太
Pronunciation: san luen chər pau di kwai san mien juɔ gər lau tai tai
English: **Shall I come?— Shall I go? East or West I do not know!**

要 五 毛 給 一 塊 你 說 奇 怪 不 奇 怪
yau wu mao gei yi kwai ni shuɔ chi gwai bu chi gwai
I am lost all a - lone, Three-wheeled tax - i,— take me home!

366

MEETING **INDIVIDUAL** NEEDS

EXTRA HELP: *"San lun tsa"*

Notate the pitches of the first two measures on the board (D E F♯ A B C♯ D'). Have students sing pitches as you point to them. Begin scale-wise, then vary the order, using parts of the song. Next have students sing only the first pitch in each measure, thinking the others. Then, again sing the first pitch, but also sing the last three. Finally, sing the entire song with pitch syllables.

PRONUNCIATION: *"San lun tsa"*

ɑ f<u>a</u>ther	e ch<u>a</u>otic	ɛ p<u>e</u>t	i b<u>ee</u>	o <u>o</u>bey
ɔ p<u>a</u>w	u m<u>oo</u>n	ə <u>a</u>go	ɾ flipped r	

Reading Rhythms

Pentatonic

d r m s l d'

American Sea Chantey

Verse D

do

1. I   heard,   I   heard   the   Old   Man   say,
2. We'll work   to - mor- rer, but no work   to - day,
3. We're bound a - way   for 'Fris - co   Bay,
4. A   Yan - kee ship wid a Yan - kee crew,
5. Oh, haul a - way,   oh, haul a - way!

D   A7   D

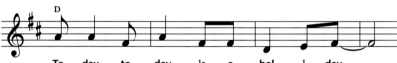

John   Ka - na - ka, na - ka, Tu - lai - ay!

D

To - day, to - day   is a hol - i - day,___
We'll work to - mor- rer, but no work to - day,___
We're bound a - way at the break of day,___
Oh, we're the buck-os fer to push 'er through.___
Oh, haul a - way,   an'___ make your pay.___

D   A7   D

John   Ka - na - ka, na - ka, Tu - lai - ay.

Refrain
D   G   D

Tu - lai - ay,   Oh!   tu - lai - ay,

D   A7   D

John   Ka - na - ka, na - ka, Tu - lai - ay.

Music Library *More Songs to Read* 367

MOVEMENT: *"John Kanaka"*

Formation: double circle, partners facing

Verse: Meas. 1–4: Partners do-si-do R shoulders. **Meas. 5–8:** *John*—stamp foot, *kanaka-naka*—pat knees, *Tulai*—clap own hands, *ay*—clap partner's hands. **Meas. 9–16:** Repeat 1–8. **Refrain: Meas. 17–20:** Outside circle takes 2 sliding steps L to face new partner. **Meas. 21–24:** Repeat 5–8.

ORFF: *"John Kanaka"*

See **O • 26** in *Orchestrations for Orff Instruments.*

LESSONLINKS
For use after Unit 5, Lesson 5, pp. 222–225

FOCUS Rhythm

OBJECTIVE Identify the *short long short* pattern and the dotted quarter-eighth pattern

MATERIALS
Recordings
John Kanaka   CD8:36
To Stop the Train   CD8:27
Resources
Resource Master R • 14 (practice)
Resource Master R • 15 (practice)
Orff Orchestration O • 26 (John Kanaka)

1. Introduce "John Kanaka" CD8:36. Have students:

• Listen as you tell them about the song. (In the 1700s, whalers convinced some desperately poor Polynesian Islanders to "rent" their children as ship workers. Often, the children were never returned home and worked more as slaves than employees. These children were often listed anonymously as "John Kanaka." The name is similar to our "John Doe.")

• Listen to the song, patting with the beat, to find the *short long short* and the dotted quarter-eighth rhythm patterns.

• Listen to Verse 1 again, raising a hand on the *short long short* pattern. (begins Measures 1, 9)

• Listen again, raising a hand on the dotted quarter-eighth pattern. (Measure 2; It is natural to hear the ♩ ♪ pattern as the dotted pattern.)

• Look at page 367 to see the patterns, then say the words of Verse 1 in rhythm.

• Find the *fermata* and identify the pitch. (*do'*)

• Read the song with pitch syllables, then words.

2. Review "To Stop the Train" (p. 361) CD8:27. Have students:

• Find the *short long short* and dotted quarter-eighth patterns in the song, then read the rhythm.

• Read the song with pitch syllables.

• Sing the song with words in unison, then sing it as a two- or three-part canon.

• (Optional: Use **Resource Masters R • 14** and **R • 15** for further work with the dotted quarter-eighth pattern.)

MUSIC LIBRARY
MORE SONGS TO READ

RELATED ARTS MOVEMENT | THEATER | VISUAL ARTS

LESSONLINKS

For use after Unit 6, Lesson 1, pp. 254–257

FOCUS Expressive Qualities—tempo, dynamics

OBJECTIVES
• Plan dynamics and tempo for expressive effect
• Aurally identify songs as being in minor
• Read the ♩♫ pattern

MATERIALS
Recordings
Ah, Poor Bird   **CD8:37**
Chickalileeo   **CD9:1**

Instruments resonator bells or Orff instruments

Resources Orff Orchestration O • 27 (Chickalileeo)

---

1. Introduce "Ah, Poor Bird" CD8:37. Have students:

• Read the song with pitch syllables.

• Read the words and discuss the feelings they convey. (sadness, hope)

• Discuss what they think the tempo and dynamics should be. Choose a tempo and tap the rhythm of the melody.

• Listen to the song to compare it with their ideas.

• Indicate by a show of hands whether the song is in major or minor. (minor)

• Decide on dynamics and tempo for the song and sing it in unison and in canon.

• Take turns accompanying the song with a cross-over bordun.

2. Introduce "Chickalileeo" CD9:1. Have students:

• Read the song with pitch syllables.

• Read the words and discuss the feelings they convey. (humor, longing)

• Discuss what they think the tempo and dynamics should be. Choose a tempo and tap the melodic rhythm.

• Listen to the song to compare it with their ideas.

• Indicate by a show of hands whether the song is in major or minor. (minor)

• Decide on dynamics and tempo, then sing the song.

Tools for Expression

AH, POOR BIRD

D minor
Old English Melody

1. Ah, poor bird, take your flight, Far a-bove the sor-rows of this sad night.
2. Ah, poor bird, as you fly, Can you see the dawn of to-mor-row's sky?

Pentatonic
s, l, d r m

From GROWING WITH MUSIC, Book 3 TE, by Wilson et al. © 1970 Prentice-Hall, Inc., Englewood Cliffs, NJ. Arrangement adapted.

Chickalileeo

Southern Folk Song

1.–4. La la la chick - a - li - lee - o,
La la la chick - a - li - lee - o.

(1.) I'm goin' to mar - ry who I please,
(2.) I'm goin' to mar - ry lit - tle John - ny Green
(3.) He's gone off to the war a - way,
(4.) Yon - der he comes I do be - lieve,

La la la chick - a - li - lee - o.

Bet you I will if you mar - ry me,
He's the prett - 'est boy I've ev - er seen,
He'll come back some pret - ty fair day,
I hope he will mar - ry me,

La la la chick - a - li - lee - o.

368

MEETING **INDIVIDUAL** NEEDS

MOVEMENT: *"Ah, Poor Bird"*

Formation: circle, all kneeling, sitting "back" on heels

Verse 1: Measure 1: Create a large circle in the air by first crossing R arm in front of L side of body, then lifting arm up over head and lowering it down R side of body. **Measure 2:** Repeat with L arm, crossing in front of R side. **Measure 3:** slowly raise body to kneeling. Arms cross in front and cir-cle up and out at same time. **Measure 4:** slowly lower body down to heels as arms drop. **Verse 2:** Repeat Verse 1 but come to standing in Measure 3; sway in Measure 4 while lowering arms.

ORFF: *"Chickalileeo"*

See **O • 27** in *Orchestrations for Orff Instruments.*

Adding Parts, Changing Texture

ADD an accompaniment to change the texture of this song.

Tambourine

Drum

D minor

s, l, t, d r m f s l

Artsa Alinu
Our Land

Israeli Dance Song
English Version by MMH

Dm

Hebrew: אַר - צָה עָ - לִי - נוּ, אַר - צָה עָ - לִי - נוּ,
Pronunciation: aɾ   tsa   a   li   nu   aɾ   tsa   a   li   nu
English: **Ar - tsa a - li - nu,   Ar - tsa   a - li - nu.**

Dm   Am   Dm

End
(Fine)

אַר - צָה עָ - לִי - נוּ.
aɾ   tsa   a   li   nu
Ar - tsa   a - li - nu.———

Dm   Am   Dm

כְּ - בָר חָ - רַשׁ - נוּ וְ - גַם זָ - רַע - נוּ,
kəvar   xa   ɾash   nu   vɛ   gam   za   ɾa   nu
To   our   land,   we   come   to   our   land.———

*Go back to the beginning
and sing to the end
(Da Capo al Fine)*

Gm   Am   Dm

אֲ - בָל עוֹד לֹא קָ - צַר - נוּ.
a   val   od   lo   ka   tsaɾ   nu
Here   we   have   plowed   and   plant - ed.

Music Library *More Songs to Read* **369**

ORFF: *"Artsa Alinu"*

See **O • 28** in *Orchestrations for Orff Instruments*. Students may use this to add pitched instrument textures to the song. (These pitched instrument parts are not compatible with the recorded instrumental part.)

PRONUNCIATION: *"Artsa Alinu"*

ɑ f<u>a</u>ther   ɛ p<u>e</u>t   i b<u>ee</u>   o <u>o</u>bey   u m<u>oo</u>n   ə <u>a</u>go   ɾ flipped r
x guttural h, *Hebrew* <u>H</u>anukkah

RELATED ARTS **MOVEMENT** | THEATER | VISUAL ARTS

LESSONLINKS

For use after Unit 6, Lesson 2, pp. 258–261

FOCUS Texture, accompaniment

OBJECTIVES
• Read *short long short* and dotted quarter-eighth patterns
• Add ostinatos to a song

MATERIALS
Recordings
Artsa Alinu   CD9:2
Recorded Lesson: Pronunciation
for "Artsa Alinu"   CD9:3
Artsa Alinu (performance mix)   CD11:13

Instruments tambourines, drums

Resources Orff Orchestration O • 28
(Artsa Alinu)

1. Introduce "Artsa Alinu" CD9:2. Have students:

• Listen to the song and discuss what makes it feel like dance music. (rhythmic drive, accents, clearly defined phrases)

• Determine the phrase form. (a a b b c c a a)

• Find the *short long short* pattern, then the dotted quarter-eighth pattern. (Measures 1, 3, 5, 11, 13; Measure 9)

• Clap the rhythm of the song.

Recorded Lesson CD9:3

• Listen to "Pronunciation for 'Artsa Alinu.'"

• Sing the song.

• Sing the song again, conducting in ².

2. Change the texture. Have students:

• Learn two ostinatos by echoing or mirroring you. (For example, clap the tambourine part and pat the drum part.)

• Add the ostinatos to the song one at a time.

• Describe how adding the ostinatos changes the song. (Texture is thicker.)

3. Perform a circle dance. Have students:

• Learn this movement, which is not traditional but reflects what is typically done.

Meas. 1–4: 2 grapevine steps (Verbal Cue: *side, back, side, cross*) *side*—R foot to R side; *back*—L foot steps behind R; *side*—R foot steps to R side; *cross*—L foot crosses in front of R. **Meas. 5–8:** 4 steps into center, 4 steps out. **Repeat** Meas. 1–8. **Meas. 9–12:** (Verbal Cue: *side, back, side, lift*) Repeat grapevine step, except replace *cross* with *lift*—lift L leg slightly. Repeat with opposite foot. **Repeat** Meas. 9–12. **Meas. 13–16:** 4 sways, weight equal on both feet, with the half-note beat (R, L, R, L). **Repeat** Meas. 13–16.

MUSIC LIBRARY
MORE SONGS TO READ

RELATED ARTS **MOVEMENT** THEATER VISUAL ARTS

LESSON**LINKS**

For use after Unit 6, Lesson 4, pp. 266–269

FOCUS Pitch, minor

OBJECTIVE Read pitches in minor songs

MATERIALS
Recordings
Artsa Alinu   **CD9:2**
Korobushka   **CD9:4**
Recorded Lesson:
    Pronunciation for "Korobushka"   **CD9:5**
Korobushka (performance mix)   **CD11:14**

Resources Resource Master R • 16
(practice)

1. Read pitches in "Artsa Alinu" (p. 369)
CD9:2. Have students:

• Find *do.*

• Clap the rhythm of the song.

• Name all pitches used and notate them on the board. Sing them in order, up and down from *do.*

• Practice singing pitches as you point to them.

• Slowly sing the song with pitch syllables.

• Sing the song at the regular tempo.

2. Introduce "Korobushka" CD9:4. Have students:

Recorded Lesson CD9:5

• Listen to "Pronunciation for 'Korobushka.'"

• Follow the steps above to learn the song.

370

MEETING **INDIVIDUAL** NEEDS

PRONUNCIATION: *"Korobushka"*

ɑ f<u>a</u>ther	e ch<u>a</u>otic	ɛ p<u>e</u>t	i b<u>ee</u>
ɪ <u>i</u>t	o <u>o</u>bey	ɔ p<u>a</u>w	u m<u>oo</u>n
ə <u>a</u>go	ɾ flipped r	ʒ plea<u>s</u>ure	

MOVEMENT: *"Korobushka"*
See *Movement* on the bottom of page 257.

ENRICHMENT: *Create a Coda*
Have students create a coda with **Resource Master R • 16.**

Exploring Augmentation

~ O musique ~

French Folk Song
English Version by MMH

E minor

m, s, l, t, d r m s

French: O mu-si-que no-tre a-mie, Sour-ce pure et frai-che.
Pronunciation: o mü zi kə nɔ trɑ mi sur sə pü ɾe fɾɛ shə

Alouette

French Canadian Folk Song

F major

s, t, d r m f s l

Refrain

French: A - lou-et - te, gen-tille a - lou-et - te,
Pronunciation: ɑ lw ɛ tə ʒɑ̃ ti ya lw ɛ tə

A - lou-et - te, je te plu - me-rai.
ɑ lw ɛ tə ʒə tə plü mə ɾe

Verse *Leader*

Group

1. Je te plu-me-rai la tête, Je te plu-me-rai la tête,
ʒə tə plü mə ɾe la tɛt ʒə tə plü mə ɾe la tɛt

2. Je te plu-me-rai le bec, Je te plu-me-rai le bec,
ʒə tə plü mə ɾe lə bɛk ʒə tə plü mə ɾe lə bɛk

Leader *Group*

No repeat first time

Go back to the beginning and sing to the end
(Da Capo al Fine)

1. Et la tête, et la tête. A - lou-ette, a - lou-ette. Oh!
e la tɛt e la tɛt ɑ lw ɛt ɑ lw ɛt o

2. Et le bec, et le bec.
e lə bɛk e lə bɛk
Et la tête, et la tête.
e la tɛt e la tɛt

3. Le nez lə ne
4. Le dos lə do
5. Les pattes le pat
6. Le cou lə ku

Music Library *More Songs to Read* **371**

NOTATION: *Dotted Rhythms*

Have students find the dotted eighth-sixteenth pattern in "Alouette" (Measure 2). Guide them to see that the dotted eighth is like three sixteenths tied, so this pattern is like the dotted quarter-eighth pattern in diminution. Read the rhythm in this song and in "Go 'Round the Mountain," page 347.

PRONUNCIATION: *"O musique" and "Alouette"*

ɑ f<u>a</u>ther	e ch<u>a</u>otic	ɛ p<u>e</u>t	i b<u>ee</u>	o <u>o</u>bey	ɔ p<u>aw</u>
u m<u>oo</u>n	ə <u>a</u>go	ɾ flipped r	ü lips form [u] and say [i]		
ʒ plea<u>s</u>ure	~ nasalized vowel				

LESSONLINKS

For use after Unit 6, Lesson 5, pp. 270–273

FOCUS Rhythm, augmentation and diminution

OBJECTIVES
• Sing a song in augmentation and diminution
• Read a song with dotted rhythms

MATERIALS
Recordings
O musique   CD9:6
Recorded Lesson:
    Pronunciation for "O musique"   CD9:7
Alouette   CD9:8
Recorded Lesson:
    Pronunciation for "Alouette"   CD9:9

Resources Resource Master R • 17

1. Introduce "O musique" CD9:6. Have students:

• Listen to the song to decide if it is in major or minor. (minor; ends on *mi*)

• Find *do* and read the song with pitch syllables.

• Listen as you read about the song's meaning. ("Music, our friend, a pure, fresh spring.")

Recorded Lesson CD9:7
• Listen to "Pronunciation for 'O musique.'"

• Sing the song in unison, patting with the beat.

• Discuss augmentation. (Values are doubled.)

• Sing the song in augmentation, patting (or stepping) two beats for each note. (Optional: (Augment rhythms on **Resource Master R • 17.**)

• Listen as you explain that diminution means all note values are halved.

• Form three groups and sing the song this way: Group 1—once in augmentation; Group 2—twice as written; Group 3—four times in diminution. Switch parts and repeat.

2. Introduce "Alouette" CD9:8. Have students:

• Listen as you read them the meaning of the words. (*alouette,* lark; *gentille,* lovely; *je te plumerai,* I will pluck your feathers; *tête,* head; *bec,* beak; *nez,* nose; *dos,* back; *pattes,* claws; *cou,* neck)

• Listen to the song, following the notation to find the cumulative measure. (last line, Measure 1)

• Find *do* and read the song with pitch syllables, finding the octave skips. (Line 4)

Recorded Lesson CD9:9
• Listen to "Pronunciation for 'Alouette.'"

• Sing the song with you as the leader.

MUSIC LIBRARY
CHORAL ANTHOLOGY

The Path to the Moon

1. Introduce the song CD9:10. Have students:

• List ways a person can travel from one place to another. (car, plane, walk, skip, and so on)

• Discuss ways to travel to the moon. (rocket, imaginary "light ship")

• Tell what they know about the moon. (238,700 miles from Earth, orbits around Earth, reflects sun's light)

• Read page 372.

• Listen to the song, then discuss the meaning of the words. (Are people traveling to the moon? Why is a ship on the sea being used? How does the text play with the image of traveling to the moon?)

• Describe what musical decisions they might make if they were to compose a song about traveling to the moon. (Focus on choice of sounds, tempo, and dynamic contrasts.)

• Listen again with attention to how the accompaniment contributes to expressing the idea of traveling over the sea.

• Listen again with attention to the vocal range, legato musical style, and use of many melodic sequences.

• Sit or stand in correct singing posture and sing the song. (Encourage supported and accurate singing of higher and lower pitches.)

Choral Anthology

The words of this song link the image of the moon with the image of the sea. The long smooth melody also suggests moonlight, while the gentle rhythms might suggest the sea.

What are some words from the song that describe the moon and the sky? The wind and the sea?

LIST two words to describe how you want to sing this song.

Music by Eric H. Thiman
Words by Madeline C. Thomas

372

MEETING **INDIVIDUAL** NEEDS

VOCAL DEVELOPMENT: *Breath and Range*

The wide range of this composition and the generally high tessitura offer an opportunity for students to expand their ability to use their voice in an expressive manner. Many students will be comfortable singing the lower pitches of this song but may experience some difficulty singing the higher ones. Effective posture and breath management are very important to expressive performance of this composition in general and for the higher passages specifically. To expand students' vocal range and to increase their ability to sing wide leaps accurately, have students sing the following

vocalise, gradually moving higher and lower in their vocal range:

Continue up by half steps to E or F.

I love— to sing! I love— to sing! I love— to sing! *etc.*

Emphasize singing with accurate pitch, sustained breath support (see *Vocal Development,* pages 13, 18) and good vowel placement (see *Vocal Development,* pages 131, 210).

Sil - ver the sails to car - ry me,
Tra - vel - ing on for man - y a day;

to car - ry, car - ry,

car - ry me o - ver the sea.

Sil - ver the sails to car - ry me,

to car - ry, car - ry,

car - ry me o - ver_____ the

sea._____

• Identify places where a melodic motive is repeated. (Measures 1–2 repeated in 19–20, 9–12 repeated in 21–26 with extension)

• Sit or stand in correct singing position and echo-sing as you or a volunteer model either motive.

• Evaluate and identify ways they could sing more expressively. (See *Vocal Development,* page 372.)

• Identify where melodic sequences are present. (Measures 9–11, 21–23)

• Echo-sing as you or a volunteer sings these measures.

• Evaluate and identify changes they could make which would lead to more expressive singing.

• Sit or stand in correct singing posture and, using the recording, sing only the measures with melodic motives and sequences.

• Identify and describe the part of the song they have not learned. (Measures 3–8; no motive or sequence)

3. Sing the song. Have students:

• Sing the song without the recording or other assistance, listening carefully to evaluate their performance.

• Sing the song again, emphasizing breath management, legato singing, and an even quality of sound throughout their vocal range. (Optional: Use "The Path to the Moon" Performance Mix **CD11:15**.)

Reinforcement
melodic motive, *page 87*
§ rhythms, *page 143*
octave, *page 167*

ENRICHMENT: *Composing or Arranging*

Have students expand the discussion of the composer/ arranger presented in Step 1, bullet 6 above. Focus on the concept that composers and arrangers make decisions about sound in order to express ideas. Sometimes ideas come from words. Have students select their favorite texts and, in small groups, explore reading each text with different expression. Have group members identify which reading is most effective and make suggestions about musical sounds that could be used to support or replace the text to express the same idea.

MUSIC LIBRARY
CHORAL ANTHOLOGY

The words to this song were written by the author of "Winnie-the-Pooh." As you look at the song, find places where you think the composer is describing the wind.

Wind on the Hill

1. Introduce the song CD9:11. Have students:

• Listen to the song several times.

• Read the words and discover the rhyme scheme. (*aaabbaaa*)

• Analyze the melody to identify its form. (A B A; review *D.S. al Fine* as meaning "Go back to the sign and sing to the end.")

• Listen again, tracing the melodic contour on the page with an index finger, and tell if the melody moves mostly by steps or wide leaps. (stepwise)

2. Learn the song. Have students:

• Sit or stand in correct singing posture. (See *Vocal Development,* page 8.)

• Sing the song with the recording.

• Evaluate their performance and identify passages, especially stepwise ones, performed incorrectly.

• Practice those passages identified as having been sung incorrectly, then sing the song again, emphasizing accuracy.

• Compare this performance with the previous one.

• Listen to the recording to hear when the singers breathe, then practice breath management for musical phrasing. (See *Vocal Development,* below.)

• Observe the dynamic markings.

• Sing the song again, emphasizing posture, accuracy, phrasing, and dynamic contrasts to enhance expressive singing. (Optional: Use "Wind on the Hill" Performance Mix CD11:16.)

Reinforcement ⁶⁄₈ meter—aural, *page 117*

Wind on the Hill

Music by Victoria Ebel-Sabo
Words by A. A. Milne

No one can tell me, no-bod-y knows____ Where the wind comes from,____ where the wind goes,____ goes,____ where the wind goes. It's fly-ing from some-where fast as it can.____ I could-n't keep up with it,____ not if I ran.____ No one can

374

MEETING **INDIVIDUAL** NEEDS

VOCAL DEVELOPMENT: *Breath Management*

Have students use this activity to improve their ability to manage their breath through long musical phrases. Have them practice inhaling air as if through a straw for four counts and then managing the release of air by making a hissing *s-s-s-s* sound for four counts. As they exhale, have them keep the intensity and dynamic level of the *s-s-s-s* sound the same. Repeat several times, inhaling for four counts and exhaling for 6, 8, 12, and finally 16 counts. Apply breath management techniques to enhance singing the phrases in the song.

BIOGRAPHY: *A. A. Milne*

A. A. Milne (1882–1956) was a British author famous for his poems and stories for children. He based his stories on his son Christopher Robin and the boy's stuffed animals, particularly the bear Winnie-the-Pooh. Milne's collections of children's poems, *When We Were Very Young* and *Now We Are Six,* are classics.

LOOK at the song and decide its form.

Does the rhythm of this song use mostly short or long sounds? Consider the rhythm when deciding what singing style to use.

G minor

Hasidic Round
Arranged by Henry Leck

Hai-da hai-da hai-di-di dai-da   hai- da   hai- da hai-da

hai- da   hai- da   hai - di- di dai- da   hai- da   hai- da hai- da

hai - da   hai - di- di dai- da   hai- da   hai- da hai- da

last time to Coda

hai - da   hai - di- di dai- da   hai- da   hai- da hai- da

Coda

hai- da   hai- da   hai - da____

Like the word *lah*, the syllables traditionally sung in "Haida" are without specific meaning.

Haida

1. Practice rhythm reading CD9:12. Have students:

• Listen to the song.

• Echo-clap the rhythms of selected measures from the song: Measures 1, 2, 5, and 9–10.

• Read the rhythms (notate them on the board), first speaking each pattern on a neutral or rhythm syllable, then clapping and speaking each one.

• Examine the notation to locate, identify, and perform each of the rhythm patterns.

• Form two groups and clap the song in call-and-response form. The two groups clap alternate measures, then alternate every two measures, then every four measures. Groups take turns starting first.

2. Practice singing a round. Have students:

• Practice the rhythm patterns for the whole song.

• Locate the repeat and determine when to go to the coda.

• Form two groups and perform the round.

3. Practice pitch reading in minor. Have students:

• Practice speaking each rhythm pattern with pitch letter names, saying *sharp* for F♯ and *flat* for B♭, and discover similar pitch patterns.

• Listen to the words of the song.

• Sit or stand in correct singing posture and, using the recording, sing the repeat of each two-measure pattern.

• Sing the entire song, focusing on accuracy.

• Form two groups and sing the song as a round. (Optional: Use "Haida" Performance Mix CD11:17.)

Reinforcement
sixteenth-note rhythms, *page 75*
canon, *page 139*

PLAYING INSTRUMENTS: *Percussion*

Help students enhance their study of the rhythm patterns by using different percussion sounds for different note values in "Haida." Have students select percussion instruments that can produce sounds of various durations. Then ask them to assign the instruments to the note values of sixteenth, eighth, quarter, and whole notes found in the song. Guide them in reading and playing the song's rhythm with the chosen percussion. Have them evaluate their performance for rhythmic accuracy and suitable instrument choices.

BACKGROUND: *"Haida"*

This arrangement is based on a Hasidic round. The Hasidim are a Jewish group known for mysticism and intense spirituality. Songs such as this one are typically sung to inspire Hasidic worshipers in religious services. Traditionally, such songs begin slowly and speed up, gradually becoming very excited and emotional.

Allundé, Alluia

1. Introduce the song CD9:13. Have students:

• Listen to and discuss a portion of the recording without looking at the notation. Discuss the language, possible continent of origin, and musical characteristics.

• Look at the notation and read the words.

• Identify the musical form. (Refrain, Verse 1, Refrain, Verse 2, *D.S.*, Refrain, Coda; Call attention to *D.S.*, Coda, and repeats, reviewing symbols as needed.)

• Listen to the song again, following the notation.

2. Learn the song. Have students:

• Listen, then echo-sing, as you or a student volunteer sings the refrain phrase by phrase.

• Identify and define this song as being in call-and-response form.

• Form two groups and sing the refrain in call-and-response form.

3. Improvise in call-and-response form. Have students:

• Listen and echo as you or a volunteer improvises a "call" phrase in the musical style of the refrain. Maintain the gentle rhythmic quality found in the refrain.

African Lullaby/Prayer
As sung and arranged by
Margaret Campbelle-Holman

376

MEETING **INDIVIDUAL** NEEDS

ENRICHMENT: *Improvising*

Improvisation is frequently found in African music. By using calls and responses as in "Allundé, Alluia," students can gain confidence in improvisation. Begin by singing or having a volunteer sing or "call" their street address. Then have the class "respond" appropriately. Encourage students to expand the range and musical qualities they use in their calls as they continue to experiment with this form of musical expression.

PRONUNCIATION: *"Allundé, Alluia"*

ɑ f<u>a</u>ther   e ch<u>a</u>otic   ɪ <u>i</u>t   u m<u>oo</u>n   ʊ p<u>u</u>t

TRANSLATION: *"Allundé, Alluia"*

The words to this song mean "O God of the sunrise, as I have given of myself to my baby, will You watch over and protect us through the night. If he or she wakes when the sun greets the earth, he or she will grow to be an adult and will take up the responsibilities in the world."

Verse

1. Jé pu wah yé   yé ku-sah,
ʒe pu wa ye   ye ku sa

2. Man-dé a-qua-qua a-qua-qua man-dé,
man de a kwa kwa a kwa kwa man de

Ai-yai-yai yé _____ al-lun-dé. _____
ai yai yai ye   a lun de

% for D.S.—pp

Ai-yai-yai yé.   ai-yai-yé al-lun-dé.
ai yai yai ye   ai yai ye a lun de

| 1. | *to Refrain* | 2. *D.S. to 3rd ending* | 3. | *to Refrain and Coda* |

Coda ⊕

Al-lun-dé, al-lu-ia. _____

Coda ⊕

lu-ia.   Al-lun-dé, al-

Al-lun-dé, al-lu-ia. _____

lu-ia. _____ Al-lun-dé, al-lu-ia. _____

4. Perform the refrain. Have students:

• Form two groups and sit or stand in correct singing posture.

• Perform the refrain with one group singing the calls and the other the responses. Switch parts so that each group gets to sing each part.

5. Perform the entire song. Have students:

• Form two groups and sing the entire song with the recording, listening closely to their pronunciation.

Recorded Lesson CD9:14

• Listen to "Pronunciation for 'Allundé, Alluia.'" Focus on the text for the verses.

• Echo as you sing the words of each verse.

• Practice the melody of each verse on a neutral syllable such as *ye*, then sing each verse with words. (This is a good opportunity to have individuals sing all or a portion of each verse.)

6. Perform the song. Have students:

• Form two groups or choose a leader and group for singing the refrain. Choose volunteers to sing the verses as soloists or in small groups.

• Sing the song, then evaluate their performance in terms of accurate pronunciation, style, and rhythm. (Optional: Use "Allundé, Alluia" Performance Mix **CD11:18**.)

Reinforcement
call-and-response, *page 19*
performing with percussion, *page 171*
Orff accompaniment, *page 265*

ORFF: *"Allundé, Alluia"*

See **O•29** in *Orchestrations for Orff Instruments*. The arrangement is the one heard on the recording. Using both pitched and unpitched percussion instruments to accompany "Allundé, Alluia" can greatly enhance its expressiveness.

ENRICHMENT: *Pitch Reading*

The refrain uses pitches of a pentatonic scale, *do re mi so la do'*. Have students read the pitches of the top part of refrain using pitch syllables and hand signs. After they are comfortable reading the top part in unison, have students form two groups and read the two parts in harmony with pitch syllables.

MUSIC LIBRARY
CHORAL ANTHOLOGY

And Where Is Home?

1. Introduce the song CD9:15. Have students:

• Listen to the song and list repeated words. (*lai, home, where is home*)

• Looking at the notation, observe the form of the song, reviewing multiple endings, verse and refrain, and *D.S. al Fine.*

• Identify similar melodic phrases from the notation. (Measures 1–2, 3–4 of unison section; Measures 1–2, 5–6 and 3–4, 7–8 of verse)

• Learn and sing the introductory unison section using the first ending.

2. Learn to sing the song. Have students:

• Speak the words in rhythm for *Voice II* in the refrain.

• Recognize the repeated rhythm patterns in *Voice II* and examine the melody to find repeated melodic patterns.

• Echo-sing the melody of *Voice II.*

• Sit or stand in correct singing posture and, with the recording, sing the introduction and *Voice II* with accurate rhythm and pitch.

• Practice the verses without accompaniment. (Encourage music reading: there are repeated phrases and they have heard the melody several times.)

• Sing the entire song with the recording, singing *Voice II* of the refrain.

• Describe and discuss *Voice I* of the refrain. How is it similar to *Voice II*? How is it different? (It shares some unison passages with *Voice II*; it uses longer note values and harmonizes with *Voice II* by being higher or lower.)

And Where Is Home?

D major

Words and Music by Margaret Campbelle-Holman

378

MEETING **INDIVIDUAL** NEEDS

ENRICHMENT: *Music Reading*

Help students develop music reading skills by analyzing steps, chordal skips, and repeated notes in this song. Have students speak the pitch names in rhythm, sing on pitch names, and sing scales in D major to establish tonality. Using a pitch ladder such as on **Resource Master R•19**, have students read and sing melodies from this song or melodies similar to the ones in this song.

PLAYING INSTRUMENTS: *Recorder*

Have students play *Voice I* and *Voice II* on recorders. (Teach them how to finger F♯ if appropriate.) The limited range, especially of *Voice I*, provides a good opportunity for students to read music on an instrument.

- Discuss the role of the composer in deciding to include two voice parts for the refrain. (It creates musical contrast and interest and develops musical independence on the part of the singers.)
- Read and sing *Voice I* of the refrain.
- Form two groups to sing the refrain in harmony, one on each voice part. Switch parts and repeat.
- Sing the entire song with the recording.

3. Experiment with tone color. Have students:

- Identify and describe various characteristics of their voices. (possible answers: thick, thin, big, small, clear, breathy)
- Form groups based on similar vocal characteristics. Experiment with the qualities of sound created when different groups sing *Voice I* of the refrain.
- Describe and discuss the words. (reflective, yearning)
- Select the group with voice characteristics most appropriate for singing *Voice I*.
- Using the group selected for *Voice I*, form two groups, sit or stand in correct singing posture, and sing the entire song again. (Optional: Use "And Where is Home?" Performance Mix **CD11:19**.)

Reinforcement
vocal tone color, *page 23*
♩. ♪ rhythm, *page 225*

ENRICHMENT: *Composing Descants*

Have students use the simple harmonic structure of the refrain to begin developing additional descants to add to the refrain. Encourage students to listen closely to the harmony of the refrain. Have them hum or sing on *oo* to create other melodies or descants that harmonize with the two parts of the verse. Finally, have them choose words from or based on the text to use with their new descant.

LANGUAGE ARTS CONNECTION: *"And Where is Home?"*

Have students identify books, poems, plays, and movies that deal with the content of the words in this song. Discuss how other creative artists have presented this concept in their artworks.

MUSIC LIBRARY
CHORAL ANTHOLOGY

Don't Let the Music Stop

1. Introduce the song CD9:16. Have students:

• Listen to the song, paying attention to the musical form. (Introduction, A section, interlude, B section, A and B sections combined, brief Coda)

• Compare and contrast characteristics of the melodies of the A and B sections. (A is more staccato, has more dotted and syncopated rhythms, and is more like a traditional melody than B. B has more long notes and fewer words; the words are repeated exactly.)

• Discuss the musical style as being "popular," that is, written in a style similar to a song from a Broadway show.

• Listen again, singing Melody A softly and then Melody B.

2. Practice the A section. Have students:

• Practice singing in a staccato style with well-focused vowels, using rhythm patterns from Melody A. (See *Vocal Development*, below.)

• Sing Melody A, using the words and emphasizing staccato singing.

• Evaluate their performance and make suggestions to improve their musical style, such as using crisper diction and contrasting the few long notes with the many short notes.

• Sit or stand in correct singing posture and, with the recording, sing Melody A when appropriate throughout the entire song.

LOOK at both parts of "Don't Let the Music Stop."

One part uses mostly long notes and the other uses mostly short notes. Use your voice to emphasize the difference between them. Learn to sing the parts separately and then combined.

Words and Music
by Eugene Butler

380

MEETING **INDIVIDUAL** NEEDS

VOCAL DEVELOPMENT: *Staccato Style*

Consonants and crisp articulation are keys for singing Melody A. Active use of the teeth, tongue, and lips are crucial for creating crisp-sounding consonants. Have students sing:

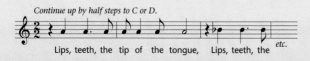

ENRICHMENT: *Partner Songs*

Invite students to expand their ability to sing in parts by singing other partner songs. See "Winter Fantasy," page 314, and "Orchestra Song," page 98.

Don't let the mu-sic stop,___ don't let it ev-er

I hear___ A-mer-i-ca sing - ing, I

cease, 'Cause the mu - sic that I sing makes the

hear her sing - ing, Var - ied

world go round,___ It brings love and joy___ and peace.

car - ols I hear.___

SING the first part of the song in a legato style and the second part in a staccato style. Is this easy or difficult? Identify why the composer wrote each part in a different style.

3. Practice the B section. Have students:

• Practice singing in a legato style with well-focused vowels using rhythm patterns from Melody B.

• Sing Melody B, using the words and emphasizing legato singing.

• Evaluate their performance and make suggestions to improve their musical style, such as better breath management and well-focused vowels.

• With the recording, sing Melody B when appropriate throughout the entire song.

4. Perform the song. Have students:

• Form two groups. Have each group sing first Melody A and then Melody B with attention to appropriate musical style.

• Decide which melody each group sings more accurately and assign each group Melody A or Melody B.

• Create harmony by having one group sing Melody A and one Melody B. Switch parts so that each group sings each part.

• Sing the entire song. (Optional: Use "Don't Let the Music Stop" Performance Mix CD10:1.)

Reinforcement
syncopation, *page 187*
♩. ♪ rhythm, *page 225*

MUSIC LIBRARY
LISTENING ANTHOLOGY

YOU'RE INVITED

LESSONLINKS

OBJECTIVE Discuss choral concerts and concert behavior, and listen to a concert sampler

Reinforcement
vocal tone color, *page 23*
changed voice, *page 171*
vocal styles, *page 281*

MATERIALS
Recordings
Le chant des oyseaux (excerpt)
by C. Janequin (listening)   CD9:17
Hallelujah Chorus (excerpt) from
Messiah by G. Handel
(listening)   CD9:18
Turtle Dove (excerpt) by R.
Vaughan Williams (listening)   CD9:19

YOU'RE INVITED
Choral
CONCERT

CHORAL CONCERT

Clément Janequin   Le chant des oyseaux
(about 1485-1560)   (excerpt)

George Frideric Handel   Hallelujah Chorus
(1685-1759)   (excerpt) from *Messiah*

Traditional/Arranged by
Ralph Vaughan Williams   Turtle Dove
(1872-1958)   (excerpt)

PROGRAM   NOTES

Le chant des oyseaux
Clément Janequin

Clément Janequin wrote many songs that imitate sounds of everyday life, including Paris street noises, bird songs, battles, and hunting expeditions. Can you tell what is imitated in this song?

382

MEETING **INDIVIDUAL** NEEDS

BACKGROUND: *Formal Concert Etiquette*

Discuss audience etiquette at a formal concert: keeping hands and feet still; not talking or whispering during the performance; watching the musicians perform; showing appreciation at the proper times by applauding, but not by shouting or whistling; listening with a purpose in mind.

LANGUAGE ARTS CONNECTION: *Words in Music*

Have students work in groups. Choose or write poems about any subject. (circus, argument, car ride) Discuss what the music might sound like. Have some students read the

poem while others use their voices or instruments to create sounds that imitate or evoke a mood. Encourage students who read the poems to use their voices in different ways. (whisper, change the pitch, change the tempo, sing)

ENRICHMENT: *A Choral Concert*

Have students give a choral concert for another class, parents and teachers, and friends. Help them select the music and a conductor for each piece, choose performers and ushers, and write a program that includes notes on anything they find interesting about the songs or composers.

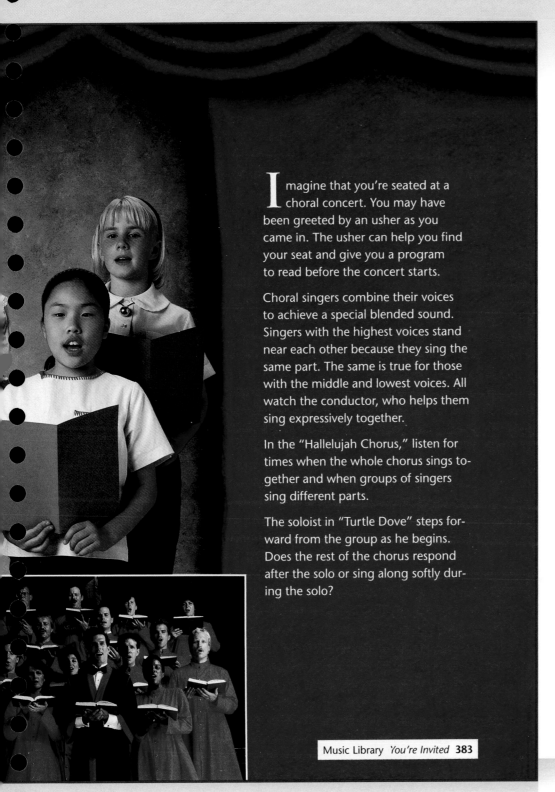

I magine that you're seated at a choral concert. You may have been greeted by an usher as you came in. The usher can help you find your seat and give you a program to read before the concert starts.

Choral singers combine their voices to achieve a special blended sound. Singers with the highest voices stand near each other because they sing the same part. The same is true for those with the middle and lowest voices. All watch the conductor, who helps them sing expressively together.

In the "Hallelujah Chorus," listen for times when the whole chorus sings together and when groups of singers sing different parts.

The soloist in "Turtle Dove" steps forward from the group as he begins. Does the rest of the chorus respond after the solo or sing along softly during the solo?

Music Library *You're Invited* **383**

TEACHING SUGGESTIONS

1. Discuss choral groups and concerts. Have students:

• Look at the photographs of two choral groups performing and name and describe choirs they have sung in or heard. (singers' ages, sizes of groups, dress, settings, accompaniment, music sung)

• Discuss audience behavior in different settings. (Participation, seating, formality; see *Background* on the bottom of page 382.)

2. Listen to a choral concert sampler. Have students:

• Read the first paragraph on page 383 and the program notes for "Le chant des oyseaux" (lə shã dɛz wa zo). (The Song of the Birds) Listen to the excerpt **CD9:17**.

• Read about and listen to excerpts of "Hallelujah Chorus" **CD9:18** and "Turtle Dove" **CD9:19**.

3. Discuss the concert. Have students:

• Discuss how reading about music before the concert prepared them for listening.

• Tell what sounds were imitated in "Le chant des oyseaux." (birds)

• Describe the part-singing in "Hallelujah Chorus" and the soloist in "Turtle Dove." (male and female voices heard entering at different times in "Hallelujah Chorus;" rest of chorus sings along softly during the solo in "Turtle Dove")

• Discuss the relationship between the subjects and sounds of the pieces. (imitation of birds in "Le chant des oyseaux;" loud, bright music of "Hallelujah Chorus;" smoothly flowing music of "Turtle Dove") (See *Language Arts Connection* on the bottom of page 382.)

• Explain why it is important for the singers to watch the conductor. (starting and stopping, dynamics, expressing the meaning of the words) (See *Enrichment* below.)

ENRICHMENT: *Follow the Conductor*

Have students play "Follow the Conductor." One student at a time is the "conductor." The conductor leads the class in singing the word *watch* on the pitch F and signals when to begin and end; holds out the vowel sound *ah* as long as he or she likes; signals a crescendo and then a decrescendo.

BIOGRAPHIES: *Three Composers*

Clément Janequin (**klɛ** mã ʒɑ nə **kɛ**) was a French composer of the Renaissance period. He was most popular in his time for his *chansons,* or songs, that imitated nature and

everyday life. In these pieces, the sounds of the words were as important as the meaning of the words. He was a storyteller and humorist through his songs.

Ralph Vaughan Williams (1872–1958) was an English composer who often arranged traditional folk songs like "Turtle Dove" for chorus or orchestra. His musical themes were rooted in the musical traditions of England, including folk songs, while his style continually explored modern ideas of tone color, instrumentation, and harmony.

For information about George Frideric Handel and "Hallelujah Chorus," see pages 385A–B.

MUSIC LIBRARY
LISTENING ANTHOLOGY

SELECTIONS

BAROQUE:
Hallelujah Chorus from *Messiah* by *George Frideric Handel (1685–1759)* pages 385A–385B

CLASSICAL:
Symphony No. 35 ("Haffner"), First Movement (excerpt) *by Wolfgang Amadeus Mozart (1756–1791)* pages 385C–385D

ROMANTIC:
Erlkönig *by Franz Schubert (1797–1828)* pages 385E–385F

EARLY TWENTIETH CENTURY:
The Shrovetide Fair (excerpt) from *Petrushka* by Igor Stravinsky (1882–1971) pages 385G–385H

MUSICAL THEATER:
The Dance at the Gym (Mambo) from *West Side Story* by Leonard Bernstein (1918–1990) pages 385I–385J

CONTEMPORARY:
Island Rhythms (excerpt) *by Joan Tower (b. 1938)* pages 385K–385L

Listening

Some of the music listed below is very old, and some is new. Listen to these pieces. Which type of music would you like to learn more about?

Hallelujah Chorus
from *Messiah*
GEORGE FRIDERIC HANDEL
1741

Symphony No. 35 ("Haffner")
First Movement (excerpt)
WOLFGANG AMADEUS MOZART
1782

Erlkönig
FRANZ SCHUBERT
1815

384

MEETING **INDIVIDUAL** NEEDS

LISTENING ANTHOLOGY

Pages 384 and 385 are followed in this Teacher's Edition by six *Listening Anthology* lessons on pages 385A through 385L. Each lesson is based on one of the listening selections shown on these two pages of the Pupil Edition.

For each listening selection, a Listening Map Transparency and Listening Map Resource Master are available. Students can watch as you point to the symbols on the transparency while the selection is played the first time. On subsequent listenings, students may follow their copies of the maps.

This *Listening Anthology* offers a sample of music performed at professional concerts and provides strategies that help students become actively involved listeners—and thus, develop appropriate concert etiquette.

You are encouraged to use these listening selections and listening maps often during the school year. One goal might be to choose a number of favorite selections and challenge students to learn to recognize the melody, the title, and the name of the composer by the end of the school year.

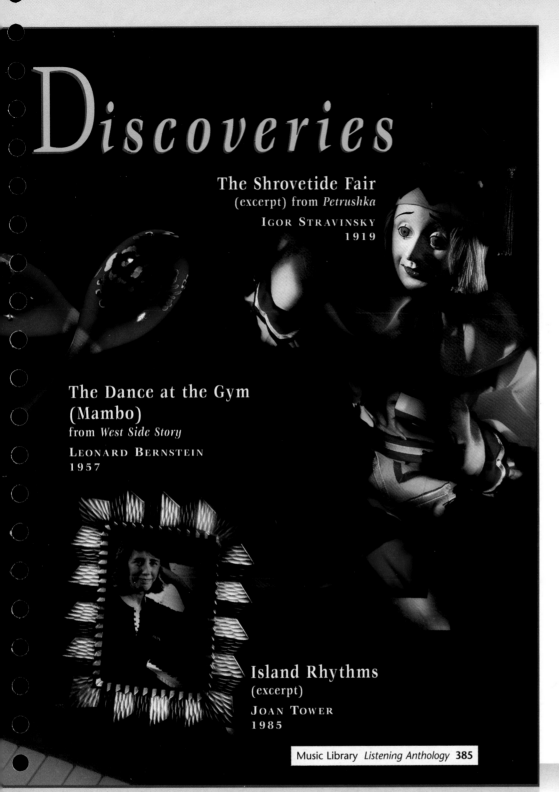

Discoveries

The Shrovetide Fair
(excerpt) from *Petrushka*
IGOR STRAVINSKY
1919

The Dance at the Gym
(Mambo)
from *West Side Story*
LEONARD BERNSTEIN
1957

Island Rhythms
(excerpt)
JOAN TOWER
1985

Music Library *Listening Anthology* **385**

ABOUT THE PUPIL PAGES
Each listening selection is represented by a picture on the pupil page.

HALLELUJAH CHORUS
interior of St. Paul's Cathedral, London

SYMPHONY NO. 35
porcelain dancers performing a minuet

ERLKÖNIG
piano keys

THE SHROVETIDE FAIR
harlequin marionette

THE DANCE AT THE GYM (MAMBO)
maracas

ISLAND RHYTHMS
photograph of Joan Tower

All maps are available as Listening Map Transparencies. Listening selections in this program are listed in the Classified Index.

MUSIC LIBRARY
LISTENING ANTHOLOGY

HALLELUJAH CHORUS from *MESSIAH*
by George Frideric Handel

LESSON LINKS

OBJECTIVES

OBJECTIVE 1 Distinguish between male (tenor and bass) and female (soprano and alto) voices

OBJECTIVE 2 Distinguish between full chorus and parts sung alone

Reinforcement
vocal tone color, *page 23*
changed voices, *page 171*

MATERIALS
Recording Hallelujah Chorus from *Messiah* by G. F. Handel (listening)   **CD9:20**

Resources
Listening Map Transparency T • 12
Resource Master LA • 1 (listening map)

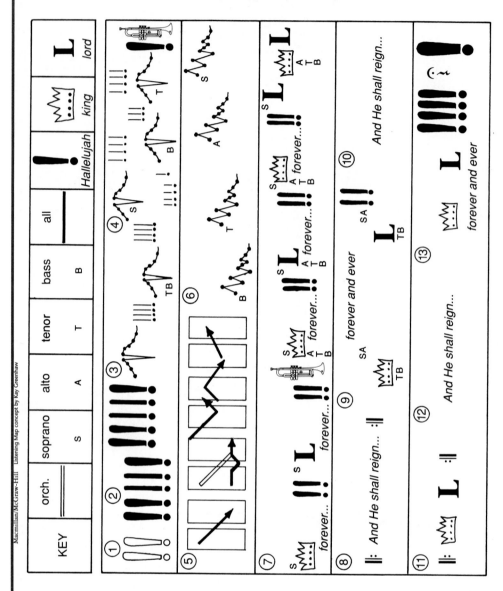

Hallelujah Chorus from *Messiah*
by George Frideric Handel

MEETING **INDIVIDUAL** NEEDS

EXTRA HELP: *Following the Map*

Explain each element of the key. Focus on the symbols that stand for words of the text (exclamation mark for *Hallelujah*, crown for *king of kings*, L for *Lord of Lords*). *All* represents the whole chorus and orchestra. Point out that the size of the exclamation mark indicates the duration of the voices singing the *Hallelujah* theme. Note the recurring melodic contour graph (sections 3, 4, and 6), and the melodic contour shown by the arrows in section 5. Follow the musical events by pointing to the exclamation marks for each *Hallelujah*. Have students find the repeat signs.

BACKGROUND: *"Hallelujah Chorus"*

The "Hallelujah Chorus" is from the end of Part II of Handel's *Messiah*. The libretto, which consists of selected scriptures, was by Charles Jennens. The work became so popular after its premiere performance in Dublin, the city issued special traffic regulations for the horse-drawn carriages of ticket holders. The ladies were even asked to come without the hoops in their skirts so there would be more room. It is said that when King George II first heard the "Hallelujah Chorus," he was so moved that he stood up. It is still customary to stand during the "Hallelujah Chorus."

TEACHING SUGGESTIONS

1. Learn about male and female voices.
Have students:

• Describe where and when they have heard people singing in a group, such as a choir. (concerts, religious services, and so on)

• List the different kinds of singing voices that they have heard in a group. (Explain to students that voices can be classified as male and female, lower and higher: higher female—soprano; lower female—alto; higher male—tenor; lower male—baritone/bass.)

2. Introduce "Hallelujah Chorus" CD9:20.
Distinguish between male and female voices and signal when each kind of voice sings alone. Have students:

• Preview the map, looking at the key and explaining that the letters S A T B represent the voices—soprano, alto, tenor, and bass.

(Use **Listening Map Transparency T · 12** or **Resource Master LA · 1**.)

• Explain what the other symbols on the map represent. (words from the text)

• Locate all the symbols from the key in the listening map.

• Listen to the music, watching you follow the map on the transparency.

OBJECTIVE 1 Informal Assessment
• Have the girls pretend to sing (lip-sync) along with the sopranos and altos and the boys along with the tenors and basses.

OBJECTIVE 2 Informal Assessment
• Listen again, having the boys stand when they hear tenors or basses singing without women (beginning of section 6), and the girls stand when they hear sopranos singing without men (beginning of section 7).

THEME

BIOGRAPHY: *George Frideric Handel*

George Frideric Handel (jɔrj **fri** de ɾɪç **han** dəl), 1685–1759, was born in Germany. His father, a barber and surgeon, did not want Handel to become a musician. Handel studied law in Germany to please his father and concentrated on music only after his father died. After studying music in Italy, Handel became a great composer in the Italian style of opera, not in his native Germany, but in London. Later in his career, he began composing oratorios in the English language. Unlike operas, with their many dance numbers, costumes, and stage sets, oratorios are performed in a concert setting. Oratorios involve very little acting, if any, and have less of a continuous dramatic plot than operas. Many of Handel's great oratorios are based on Biblical themes: *Israel in Egypt, Saul, The Resurrection, Jephtha*.

All Handel's oratorios contain great choral numbers, but the glorious "Hallelujah Chorus" from *Messiah* is one of the best known. Handel composed *Messiah* in 1741, completing it in less than a month. The first performance was at a benefit for people in debtor's prison.

MUSIC LIBRARY
LISTENING ANTHOLOGY

SYMPHONY NO. 35 ("HAFFNER"), FIRST MOVEMENT (excerpt)
by Wolfgang Amadeus Mozart

LESSON LINKS

OBJECTIVE Aurally distinguish between the dynamics piano (*p*) and forte (*f*)

Reinforcement
orchestral instruments, *page 71*
dynamics, *page 139*
octaves, *page 179*

MATERIALS

Recording Symphony No. 35 ("Haffner"), First Movement (excerpt) by W.A. Mozart (listening)   **CD9:21**

Resources
Listening Map Transparency T • 13
Resource Master LA • 2 (listening map)

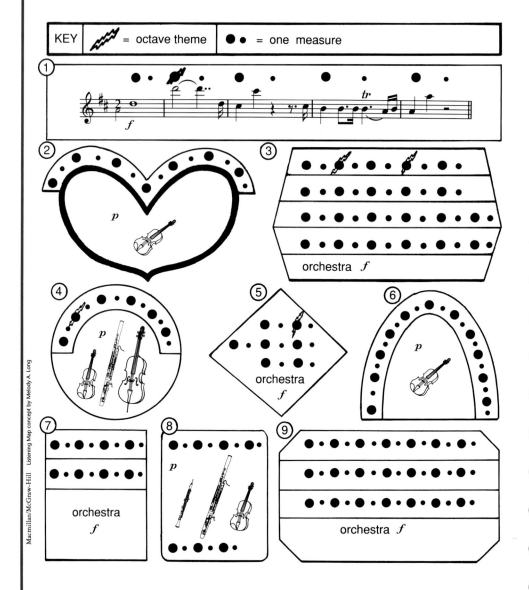

MEETING **INDIVIDUAL** NEEDS

EXTRA HELP: *Following the Map*

Identify the symbols in the key. Explain that the lightning bolt represents the ascending octave leap of the theme. Note that each pair of dots represents 1 measure in ²₂ Each dot represents 1 beat. Then, to read the map, begin at the top left. Point out the written theme and, if possible, play it by using the recording or a piano. Have students name the different instruments pictured on the listening map. (violin, bassoon, cello, oboe) Listen for the change in instrumentation or dynamics as a cue to move to the next section. (for example, in the first section—full orchestra, forte; in the

second section—violins only, piano) Have them locate the sections in which the full orchestra plays. (numbers 1, 3, 5, 7, and 9)

BACKGROUND: *Classical Style*

The Classical era in music spans the period from about 1750 to 1825. It is a period in which elements of form still in use today were developed by such great composers as Haydn and Mozart. Characteristics valued in the Classical style of composition include balance, grace, and an emphasis on melody and form.

TEACHING SUGGESTIONS

1. Review dynamics. Have students:

• Say this rhyme in their normal speaking voice the first time, in a soft voice the second time, and then in a loud voice:

Peter Piper picked a peck of pickled peppers. How many pickled peppers did Peter Piper pick?

• Use the terms for dynamics, *piano* and *forte,* to describe what they just did. (piano the second time and forte the third time they spoke the rhyme)

• Tell different ways a composer might vary the dynamics in a piece of music. (varying instrument sections, adding or subtracting instruments, playing solo or in groups, having all play piano or forte)

2. Introduce the "Haffner" Symphony
CD9:21. Signal to distinguish piano from forte. Have students:

• Preview the map, locating the theme and finding the piano and forte sections. (Use **Listening Map Transparency T • 13** or **Resource Master LA • 2**.)

• Listen to the music, watching you follow the map on the transparency.

OBJECTIVE Informal Assessment
• With eyes shut, raise a thumb during the piano sections and raise a whole hand during the forte sections. (As an alternative, students can hold hands with palms close together for piano, far apart for forte.)

THEME

BIOGRAPHY: *Wolfgang Amadeus Mozart*

Wolfgang Amadeus Mozart (**vɔlf** gang a ma **de** us **mo** tsart), 1756–1791, was born in Salzburg, Austria. When Mozart was three, his father recognized that his son had unusual musical ability. Young Mozart learned to play the harpsichord at age four and then the violin. By the time he was five, he was composing his own music. Mozart's talent was so extraordinary that he was asked to play his music throughout the capitals of Europe and became quite well known as a child prodigy. After settling in Vienna, Mozart continued to compose. His music includes many different genres. Although he only lived to be 35, Mozart produced more than 25 string quartets, 20 operas, 40 symphonies, and 17 piano sonatas. In 1782, Mozart composed the "Haffner" Symphony. He wrote it to celebrate the occasion on which his friend Sigmund Haffner of Salzburg was raised to the ranks of the nobility.

ENRICHMENT: *Identifying Instruments*

As students listen, have them imitate playing the instruments that they hear.

MUSIC LIBRARY
LISTENING ANTHOLOGY

RELATED ARTS | MOVEMENT | **THEATER** | VISUAL ARTS |

ERLKÖNIG
by Franz Schubert

LESSON**LINKS**

OBJECTIVES
OBJECTIVE 1 Identify a motive in piano accompaniment
OBJECTIVE 2 Identify a male voice, singing in different ways to tell a story

Reinforcement
motive, *page 87*
changed voice, *page 171*
dynamics, *page 257*

MATERIALS
Recording Erlkönig by F. Schubert (listening)   CD9:22

Resources
Listening Map Transparency T • 14
Resource Master LA • 3 (listening map)
Resource Master LA • 4 (script)

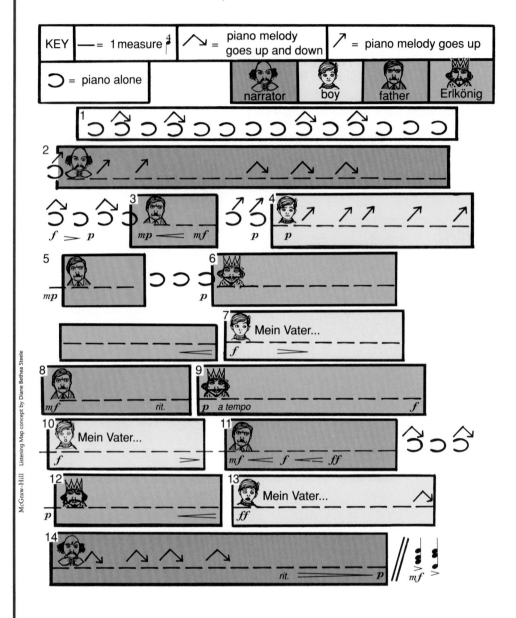

McGraw-Hill   Listening Map concept by Diane Bethea Steele

MEETING **INDIVIDUAL** NEEDS

EXTRA HELP: *Following the Map*

Cover all of the map except the row being sung. Move the cover down and show each row as it is heard. Have students listen for the pounding triplets in the piano accompaniment, which suggest both the galloping horse's hooves and the frantic worry of the father. Also listen for the increasing dynamic level of the words *mein Vater* as the terrified child cries to his father. On a subsequent listening, have students follow the dynamic markings on the map, pretending to whisper during sections marked *p*, *mp* and to shout during sections marked *mf*, *f*, *ff*.

BIOGRAPHY: *Franz Schubert*

Franz Schubert (fɾɑnts **shu** bəɾt), 1797–1828, was born in Vienna, Austria. His early musical training was at a school for singers in Vienna, but when his voice changed, he had to leave the school. Unlike other composers of his time, he never held a position as a musician in a court or wealthy household. Instead, he managed a meager existence as a private tutor, sold a few compositions to publishers, and obtained a few commissions. Even though he died at age 31, he composed piano, chamber, and orchestral works, and over 600 art songs.

TEACHING SUGGESTIONS

1. Introduce "Erlkönig" CD9:22. Describe how one voice can be used to sound like different characters. Have students:

• Listen as you play the opening piano part (about 20 seconds) and describe the mood that the music creates. (gloomy, eerie)

• Listen as you paraphrase the opening of the story. (The father is carrying his sick son while riding on horseback to get the boy home. Explain that they will hear the story sung as a mini-drama by a male singer who performs all four parts—those of the narrator, the father, the son, and the Elf King, or Erlkönig (ɛrl kö nɪç).

• Describe how they think one voice can be used to express the sounds of the different characters in the story. (The voice can change from low to medium to high; it can change from smooth and soft to forceful and louder, from detached to excited, using full voice or half voice.)

2. Identify the motive played by piano. Have students:

• Read the key of the map. Locate the arrows, which represent the melodic shape of the motive, and the horseshoe, which indicates when the piano is heard alone. (Use **Listening Map Transparency T • 14** or **Resource Master LA • 3.**)

• Discuss the dynamic markings on the map. (*p*—soft; *mp*—medium soft; *mf*—medium loud; *f*—forte; *ff*—very loud)

• Find on the map the phrase *Mein Vater* (mɑɪn **fɑ** təɾ), which is German for "my father." (Explain that this song is sung in German.)

• Listen to the music, watching you follow the map on the transparency.

OBJECTIVE 1 Informal Assessment
• Pretend to play the piano or pat the rhythm of the motive when they hear the piano alone.

3. Identify the different characters as portrayed by the singer. Have students:

• Listen again, then tell how the mood of the music changed to fit the story. (Optional: Make a transparency of **Resource Master LA • 4**, the English script for "Erlkönig," before listening to the recording, then uncover one line at a time as a student reads the script aloud, not revealing the last line until they listen to the recording.)

OBJECTIVE 2 Informal Assessment
• Divide into four groups, one for each character, and stand only when they hear their assigned character.

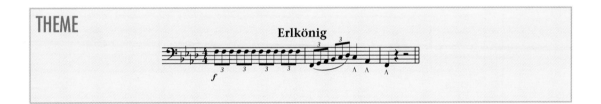

THEME

Erlkönig

BACKGROUND: *"Erlkönig"*

Johann Wolfgang von Goethe (**yo** han **vɔlf** gang fɔn **gö** tə) was a German poet who wrote the poem "Erlkönig." The poem inspired Schubert to compose the art song when he was only eighteen. According to Danish legend, the Erlkönig (or Elf King) only shows himself to someone who is dying. Sometimes he is considered to be merely a hobgoblin; in this case, parents tell their children that the Erlkönig will get them if they don't behave.

BACKGROUND: *Romantic Art Songs*

The Romantic period in music lasted from about 1825 to 1900. German Romantic literature was the inspiration for many Romantic compositions for voice, as in Schubert's "Erlkönig." An art song like "Erlkönig" is a vocal solo with a specifically composed accompaniment (not improvised or arranged), for piano or occasionally for orchestra.

ENRICHMENT: *Using Stick Puppets*

Have students make stick puppets with which to act out the story of "Erlkönig."

MUSIC LIBRARY
LISTENING ANTHOLOGY

RELATED ARTS | **MOVEMENT** | THEATER | VISUAL ARTS

THE SHROVETIDE FAIR (excerpt)
from *PETRUSHKA*
by Igor Stravinsky

LESSON LINKS

OBJECTIVES

OBJECTIVE 1 Recognize the sounds of the flute and the clarinet

OBJECTIVE 2 Identify the theme (at different tempos)

OBJECTIVE 3 Draw melodic contour

Reinforcement
orchestral instruments, *pages 71, 265*
sixteenth notes, *page 75*
tempo, *page 217*
clarinet, *page 273*

MATERIALS

Recording The Shrovetide Fair (excerpt) from *Petrushka* by I . Stravinsky (listening) CD9:23

Resources
Listening Map Transparency T • 15
Resource Master LA • 5 (listening map)
Musical Instruments Masters—flute, clarinet

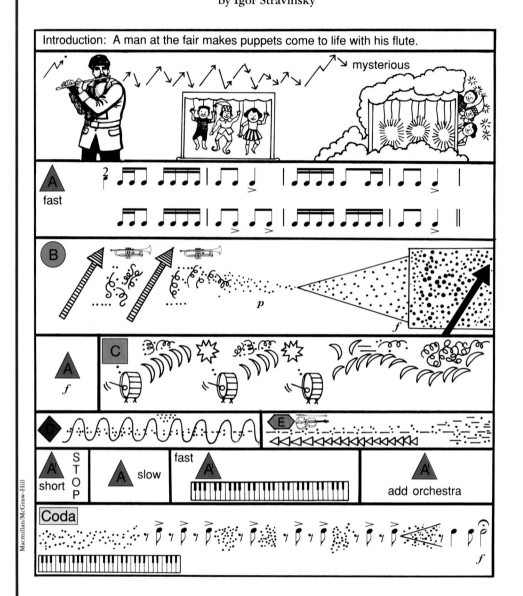

The Shrovetide Fair (excerpt) from *Petrushka*
by Igor Stravinsky

MEETING **INDIVIDUAL** NEEDS

EXTRA HELP: *Following the Map*

Point out the flute and the arrows showing the melodic contour of the flute solo. Below the contour lines is the puppet theater containing the puppets. The next puppet theater shows the magic spell taking effect. This mysterious music ends with three pairs of short piccolo notes shown by little sparkles. Each pair of notes brings one puppet to life. The characters then begin to dance the Russian theme shown by A. Point out the places where the theme (A and A') occurs. Focus on the different tempos indicated for the theme. The first two arrows in section B are ascending xylophone glis-

sandos. In section C, point out the bass drums and the bursts (cymbals). The melodic contour lines in section D represent the clarinet arpeggios. The wedges in section E represent the many short French horn crescendos accompanying the violin solo.

MOVEMENT: *Puppet Movements*

Have students improvise movements of a marionette just brought to life. After they practice their movements, they can perform them with the Russian dance theme.

TEACHING SUGGESTIONS

1. Practice echo-clapping rhythms from the excerpt. Have students:

• Echo-clap these rhythm patterns:

• Echo-clap all the rhythm patterns in sequence. (This sequence is the rhythm of the beginning of the Russian dance theme.)

2. Introduce "The Shrovetide Fair" CD9:23. **Recognize the sound of the flute and clarinet and identify the A theme.** Have students:

• Preview the map, starting with the flute solo. Tell what they know about the flute. (a woodwind instrument with a wide range and with high pitches) Similarly, ask what they know about the clarinet. (a single-reed instrument of the woodwind family) Have students identify all other instruments on the map. (trumpets in the B section, bass drums in the C section, violin in the E section, and piano keyboards in the second A' section and coda) (Use **Listening Map Transparency T · 15** or **Resource Master LA · 5.**)

• Find the A theme shown by the rhythmic notation the first time, and by the A and A' in triangles elsewhere.

• Listen to the music, watching you follow the map on the transparency.

OBJECTIVE 1 Informal Assessment
• Pantomime playing the flute during the opening flute solo and the clarinet during the D section, represented by the wavy line.

OBJECTIVE 2 Informal Assessment
• Raise their hands when they hear the A (Russian dance) theme. (It is heard six times. The fourth is slow; the others are fast.)

3. Draw melodic contour. Have students:

• Tell where they see lines on the map going up and down. (the flute solo and the D section) Explain that the lines show melodic contour.

OBJECTIVE 3 Informal Assessment
• On a subsequent listening, draw the melodic contour in the air with their hands (during the flute solo and the D section).

THEME

BIOGRAPHY: *Igor Stravinsky*

Igor Stravinsky (ĭ gôr strȧ **vĭn** skĭ), 1882–1971, was born in Russia. His father was a famous opera singer, so he was exposed to classical music throughout his childhood. He studied law until he was 19, when he began to study music seriously. Many of Stravinsky's most popular pieces were written for a Russian ballet company then performing in Paris. Stravinsky lived in Paris, Los Angeles, and New York. Unlike many other composers, Stravinsky worked in various genres and styles, incorporating some jazz elements into some of his works, and was successful and famous in his own lifetime.

BACKGROUND: *Petrushka*

Composed in 1911, *Petrushka* vividly depicts the atmosphere of pre-Lenten carnivals at St. Petersburg in Russia. A typical attraction at a carnival was a puppet theater. This ballet features three life-sized marionettes—Petrushka, the Moor, and the Ballerina. They are brought to life by a flute-playing magician. The Moor and Petrushka are both in love with the Ballerina. In the end the Moor kills Petrushka with a sword. This excerpt depicts the magician's flute music and the Russian dance the puppets perform.

MUSIC LIBRARY
LISTENING ANTHOLOGY
RELATED ARTS | MOVEMENT | THEATER | VISUAL ARTS

THE DANCE AT THE GYM (MAMBO)
from *WEST SIDE STORY*
by Leonard Bernstein

LESSONLINKS

OBJECTIVES
OBJECTIVE 1 Pat the steady beat while listening to syncopated rhythms
OBJECTIVE 2 Signal to show recognition of a motive in a listening selection

Reinforcement
motive, *page 87*
syncopation, *page 187*

MATERIALS
Recording The Dance at the Gym (Mambo) from *West Side Story* by L. Bernstein (listening)   CD9:24

Instruments unpitched rhythm instruments

Resources
Listening Map Transparency T • 16
Resource Master LA • 6 (listening map)

The Dance at the Gym (Mambo) from *West Side Story*
by Leonard Bernstein

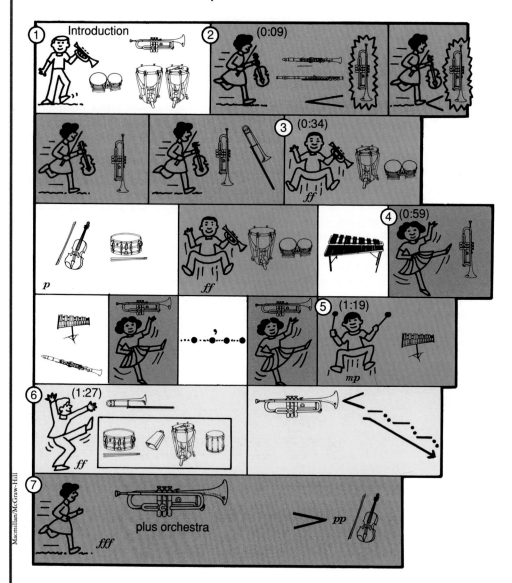

Macmillan/McGraw-Hill

MEETING **INDIVIDUAL** NEEDS

EXTRA HELP: *Following the Map*

Ask students to identify the instruments on the listening map. (trumpet, bongos, timpani, violin, clarinet, flute, trombone, snare drum, xylophone, and cowbell) Instruments shown are the main instruments heard or featured in any given box. The length of each box on the map is related to the duration of that section of music.

BIOGRAPHY: *Leonard Bernstein*

Leonard Bernstein (1918–1990), born in Lawrence, Massachusetts, was a composer, conductor, and pianist. He composed music for a variety of performing groups, including orchestra, choir and orchestra, and musical theater. He also had a highly acclaimed career as a conductor and conducted the New York Philharmonic for 15 years. Bernstein believed in educating children about classical music and for several years produced the *Young People's Concerts* for television.

TEACHING SUGGESTIONS

1. Introduce "Mambo" CD9:24. **Pat with the steady beat while listening to syncopated rhythms.** Have students:

• Tell about dances they like.

• Listen as you briefly tell the plot of *West Side Story.* (See *Background* below.)

• Listen to "Mambo" without looking at the listening map, patting with the beat.

• Tell if they heard syncopation.

• Name the instrument families they heard playing the syncopated rhythms. (mainly strings, brass, and percussion, but also woodwinds at times)

2. Play rhythm instruments with the beat. Have students:

• Preview the map, learning that there are three main motives represented by figures in three different dance poses. (The figures in sections 2 and 7 show one motive, sections 3 and 5 show the second motive, and section 4 shows the third motive. Similar motives are shown with the same color on the transparency.) Use **Listening Map Transparency T • 16** or **Resource Master LA • 6**. (See Extra Help, on the bottom of page 385I.)

• Divide into three groups, each group playing rhythm instruments with the beat, either when they hear their motive or when you point to their dance pose on the map. (Use the CD indexing for sections 2, 3, and 4. Play each motive a few times to help each group identify their motive.)

OBJECTIVE 1 Informal Assessment

• Listen again through the first five boxes (sections 1–2), patting with the beat.

OBJECTIVE 2 Informal Assessment

• Listen to the selection with eyes closed and raise a hand to signal hearing their motive.

THEME	Mambo

BACKGROUND: *West Side Story* THEATER

West Side Story, composed in 1957, was one of the first Broadway musicals (plays with music) to combine dance, drama, and music successfully. It is based on the tragic love story of Shakespeare's *Romeo and Juliet.* Set in the 1950s in New York City, the warring factions are two boys' gangs and their girlfriends. A boy and girl from opposing gangs fall in love, and because this love is forbidden, tragedy follows for both of them. The "Mambo" is heard at a dance organized by a teacher to help the two gangs get along better. The dance turns out to be a competition instead.

ENRICHMENT: *Creating a Dance* MOVEMENT

Have each of the three groups create dance steps for the motive in their section. Have the whole class create a movement for those sections that contain music other than these three motives. (Possible movement: stand in place, tapping a toe and snapping fingers.)

MUSIC LIBRARY
LISTENING ANTHOLOGY
RELATED ARTS MOVEMENT THEATER **VISUAL ARTS**

ISLAND RHYTHMS (excerpt)
by Joan Tower

LESSONLINKS

OBJECTIVES
OBJECTIVE 1 Recognize tone color of each instrument family
OBJECTIVE 2 Aurally identify when a musical element (tone color, dynamics, rhythm, pitch level) stays the same and when it changes

Reinforcement
orchestral instruments, *page 71*
tempo, *page 217*

MATERIALS
Recording Island Rhythms (excerpt)
by J. Tower (listening)   CD9:25

Resources
Listening Map Transparency T • 17
Resource Master LA • 7 (listening map)
Musical Instruments Masters—brass
family, string family, percussion family, woodwind family

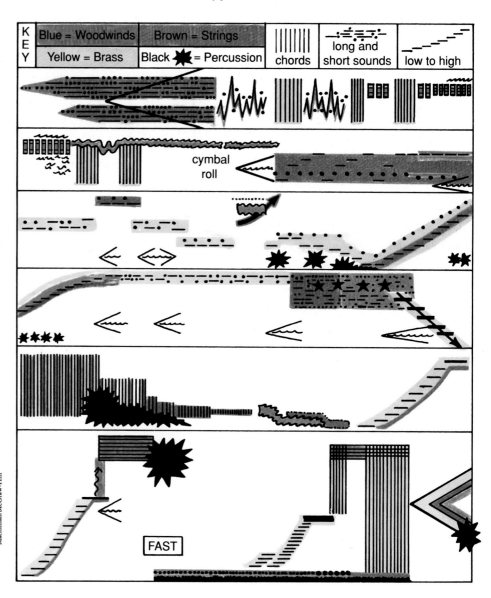

Island Rhythms (excerpt)
by Joan Tower

Macmillan/McGraw-Hill

MEETING **INDIVIDUAL** NEEDS

EXTRA HELP: *Following the Map*

Discuss the key with students, then have them identify the instrument families by their colors on the map. Also discuss the three symbols representing melodic patterns. Have students find examples on the map. Point out how each symbol may differ at different places in the map. Discuss what the differences are: the vertical bars are all one color in some places (all same family) and multi-colored in another area (many families playing together). Point out the eleven crescendo signs on the map. Explain that the vertical placement of the symbols indicates relative pitch.

BIOGRAPHY: *Joan Tower*

Joan Tower (b. 1938) was born in New Rochelle, New York, but she was raised in South America. South American music influenced her rhythmic style. She attended Bennington College and received a doctorate in composition from Columbia University. She was composer-in-residence with the St. Louis Symphony Orchestra from 1985 to 1988. Tower is currently a professor of music at Bard College. She has written for a wide variety of instrument combinations, including flute, clarinet, piano, violin, woodwind quintet, solo instruments and piano, orchestra, and percussion ensembles, small and large (up to 54 players).

TEACHING SUGGESTIONS

1. Introduce "Island Rhythms" CD9:25. Recognize the sound of each instrument family. Have students:

• Name the orchestral instrument families and list some members of each family. (Woodwinds, strings, brass, percussion; you may wish to use the Musical Instruments Master for each of these families.)

• Preview the map, finding the instrument families in the key.

• Listen to the music for the contrasting tone color of each family, watching as you follow the map on the transparency. (Use **Listening Map Transparency T • 17** or **Resource Master LA • 7**.)

OBJECTIVE 1 Informal Assessment

• Form four groups, one group for each instrument family, and pretend to play appropriate instruments upon hearing the assigned family.

2. Aurally identify when a musical element (tone color, dynamics, tempo, pitch) stays the same and when it changes. Have students:

• Listen as you play C, D, and E on the piano or another pitched instrument. Then listen as you sing C, D, and E.

• Identify what was the same (pitch level) and what was different (tone color) about the two versions.

• Listen as you clap steadily, slowly, and very loudly. Then listen as you clap quickly and very softly.

• Identify what was the same (tone color) and what was different (dynamics and tempo).

• Discuss how composers might use these elements to create effects that are the same and different. (Use instruments with contrasting tone colors or pitch ranges; use fast and slow tempos to change the mood, change the dynamics; vary rhythms by using steady beats or syncopation; contrast solos and large groups.)

3. Use the map to identify similarities and differences of given musical elements within the selection. Have students:

• Look at the map and study the three symbols, noticing the similarities and differences. (Similar symbols, such as all the vertical bars, all the long/short patterns, or all the ascending patterns, contain similar melodic material but may have different tone color, for example.)

• Listen to the music, focusing on same/different patterns shown by different symbols on the map, watching you follow the map on the transparency.

OBJECTIVE 2 Informal Assessment

• Create and perform body movements for each of the three symbols while they listen to the selection.

THEME

Instead of a simple melodic theme, "Island Rhythms" uses recurring blocks of sound textures and rhythmic patterns. These were combined to inspire exciting images of oceans and islands in the listener's mind.

BACKGROUND: *"Island Rhythms"*

This work was commissioned by the Florida Orchestra for the opening of Tampa's Harbour Island in 1985. Of the work, Tower says, "This was an attempt to depict an underwater swimmer gradually rising to the water's surface from a very deep place in the ocean."

ENRICHMENT: *Create a Listening Map* VISUAL ARTS

Have students create their own listening map of Joan Tower's "Island Rhythms." Students can create the maps individually or in small groups. You may wish to divide the class into six groups, one group for each row of the listening map on **Transparency T • 17** or **Resource Master LA • 7**. Each group can use the symbols in their row as a guide to the structure, then create an underwater or island scene to tell a story that goes with the musical events. For example, the large percussion symbol in row 5 could be an underwater volcano erupting. Students should feel free to use their imaginations (and what the composer said about the piece) to create underwater and island scenes.

MUSIC LIBRARY
MUSICAL

LESSON LINKS

OBJECTIVE To contribute to the production of a musical play by taking part as a member of the cast or crew

MATERIALS
Recordings

Happiness	CD9:26, 9:27, 9:34
No Matter What	CD9:28, 9:29, 9:32
Things That Grow	CD9:30
Barter Song	CD9:31
Bird in the Water	CD9:33

Performance Mixes for all songs	CD11:20–26

Other Performance Mixes	
Processional	CD11:27
Fanfare	CD11:28
Clown Waltz	CD11:29
Clown Jig	CD11:30

Resources
Resource Master S•1 (script)

An original musical by Linda Worsley based on a story by the Brothers Grimm

HAPPINESS

Words and Music by Linda Worsley

386

PRODUCTION SUGGESTIONS

SETS: Scene I takes place in a forest. Trees may be painted on a backdrop or created by using corrugated paper as the trunk and branches with leaves cut from green paper. Scatter branches and sticks on the floor of the stage for Ned and Tess to pick up. If you use a painted backdrop, you may want to make a large, papier-mâché rock to hide the golden goose until the traveler tells Ned where to find it. A wooden bench should be placed on one side of the stage.
Scene II takes place in the palace courtyard. You will need a castle wall with a window for the princess to look out. You may place the window at stage level or use portable stairs behind the wall to achieve a balcony effect. If using stairs, make the sure the princess is seated or otherwise positioned safely. The king's throne should be on one side of the stage, the courtyard gate on the other.

USING THE RECORDINGS: Use the performance mixes of the songs for full stereo arrangements of the accompaniments **CD11:20–26**. Additional instrumental tracks **CD11:27–30** are provided for the processions of characters stuck to the goose, for setting Scene II, and for the clown routines in Scene II.

Feel it and it will be here! When you are will-ing,
Feel it and it will be there! May-be a ship is
Reach out a hand and take it! *Tess:* May-be our house will
Feel it and it will be here! *Chorus: as in I, to end*

when you be-lieve it, you'll make it through,
wait-ing to take us far, far a-way!
burn to the ground! Or may-be we'll freeze,

And when you do, You will dis-cov-er
Tess: May-be I'll stay! *Ned:* Or there's a treas-ure
Ned: Or if you please, You'll be a he-ro

you can a-chieve it, Make up your mind,
just for the ask-ing! May-be I'll find...
may-be the king will Ask you to tea!

then you will find, Hap-pi-ness! And ad-ven-ture,
Tess: May-be you're blind! *Ned:* Hap-pi-ness, and ex-cite-ment,
Tess: That I've got-ta see!

Reach out, help each oth-er, Some-where,
I just looked a-round me, Sud-den-ly,

some-one needs you, Strang-er, or friend or broth-er.
in a mo-ment, hap-pi-ness came and found me.

Music Library *Musical* **387**

TEACHING SUGGESTIONS

1. Introduce *The Golden Goose* and begin plans for producing it on stage. Have students:

• Recall what they can about the story of the golden goose.

• Read the script, or follow along as you read, stopping before each song.

• Listen to each song as it appears in the story.

• Discuss the characters of the story and how their wishes and outlooks differ.

• Review elements of producing a musical. (cooperating; rehearsing lines, songs, and movement; making props, costumes, and sets; and so on)

2. Introduce "Happiness" CD9:26. Have students:

• Look at the song and notice that the repeat sign is for Version II (CD9:27) only.

• Listen to the song (Version I).

• Practice the dotted rhythm of *happiness* by clapping and speaking the word.

• Practice the quarter rests at the beginning of Measures 2, 6, 10, 14, 26, and 30. Clap the rhythm of these measures, spreading hands apart on Beat 1 to indicate the silence represented by the quarter rest.

• Practice both the soprano and alto parts at the end until they are comfortable with both lines, then combine the two parts. (If the group will be singing in unison, either line works as an ending to the song.)

PERFORMING FORCES: *The Golden Goose* may be performed by a group of any size. To include more students, you may add more guards and ladies-in-waiting who could share the parts. The chorus may be as large or small as needed to accommodate the number of students available for the performance.

STAGING: Ned and Tess enter after the chorus finishes Version I of "Happiness." They are gathering firewood. During Version II, the traveler enters. She or he applauds at the end of the song. Tess leaves after Ned offers to share his lunch with the traveler.

USING THE RECORDINGS: The three recordings of "Happiness" use the same melody with different words. Version I is the opening chorus, Version II is the first song in Scene I and features the characters Ned and Tess, and Version III (CD9:34) is the finale of the production. Have students sing along with the recording of Version II to understand the repeats and solos. As students follow the script and hear the songs for the first time, have them sing the song again where directed, using the words for Versions II and III. For a production that uses performance mixes, Versions I and III make use of the same track.

MUSIC LIBRARY
MUSICAL

continued from previous page

3. Introduce "No Matter What" CD9:28.
Have students:

• Notice the repeat signs and first and second endings.

• Observe the places where Ned and the Traveler echo the chorus and discuss that this occurs in the repeat only.

• Listen to the song.

• Read pages 388 and 389.

• Talk about the importance of keeping promises and share examples of promises they have made.

388 THE GOLDEN GOOSE

PRODUCTION SUGGESTIONS

MOVEMENT: Have students brainstorm gestures that represent a promise—crossing your heart, raising your right hand, shaking hands with another person, and so on. Use one or more of their ideas each time the word *promise* occurs in the song.

WORKING BACKSTAGE: Ask for volunteers to be part of the backstage crew. Each task—scenery set-up, props, and lighting—will require one or more students. You may also want to have a prompter to help students remember their lines when necessary.

PROPS:

Firewood

Sandwiches tied in squares of cloth (2)

Goose—this can be a decoy or stuffed animal covered with gold cloth, or it can be created from papier-mâché

Pail for the milkmaid

Basket filled with carrots (plastic or real)

Handkerchief

Tray of fake jewelry and other trinkets

Bag of "gold"

- Clap the rhythm of the phrase *no matter what* in the second ending. Emphasize the silence on Beat 1 by spreading the hands apart.

- Sing the song in unison without the echoes.

- Sing the song again, singing only the echoes.

- Volunteer to sing the echoes as a soloist or in a small group.

- Listen as you tell them that Versions II, III, and IV are shorter and end at the *Fine*, then read the lyrics for Version III.

- Discuss how Tess' attitude differs from Ned's and how singers could express the difference in this song.

- Sing Versions II, III, and IV as directed while following the script. (Version II is sung by Ned and the milkmaid, Version III by Ned and Tess, and Version IV by Ned and the princess. Versions II and IV use the same lyrics as Version I but stop at the *Fine*. In a production using the performance mixes, Versions II, III, and IV make use of the same track.)

MEETING **INDIVIDUAL** NEEDS

SPECIAL LEARNERS: *Participation*

Being part of the cast of a play can be a wonderful boost to the confidence of a student with language or physical challenges. You can help ensure their success by assigning them to roles that capitalize on their strengths. If a student is truly uncomfortable speaking in public, let her/him be part of the chorus or the backstage crew. A student who has difficulty with motor skills might make an excellent prompter. Be sure to acknowledge the contributions of the entire cast and crew by asking each group to take a bow at the end of the performance and by listing them in the printed program, if you have one.

READING CONNECTION: *Literature*

The Golden Goose was inspired by a fairy tale written by the Brothers Grimm. Have students find and read the original. They may also share tales that have similar themes—the goose that laid golden eggs or King Midas.

SOCIAL STUDIES CONNECTION: *Golden Geese*

Medieval cookery included techniques for coloring food, both to disguise poorly preserved foods and to surprise and delight diners. Roasting meat and fowl were "gilded" by basting them with a paste of saffron, egg yolks, and flour.

MUSIC LIBRARY

MUSICAL

continued from previous page

5. Introduce "Things That Grow" CD9:30.
Have students:

• Define *call and response* and share examples of songs which are in that style.

• Observe the repeat sign and the endings.

• Read pages 390 and 391.

• Listen to the song.

• Notice the place where the singers go back to the sign and how the tempo changes from there to the end.

Ned finds the golden goose, who says, "Take me to the king!" On the way they meet a milkmaid. She wants a feather, but when she touches the goose she becomes stuck. Tess runs up to pull the maid away and can't let go. Both of them must now go with Ned to the king.

In another part of the forest, a farmer is singing of the joys of farming and his new harvest of carrots.

First time Farmer; on repeat, Chorus, with Farmer on echo phrases.

D major

Words and Music by Linda Worsley

Things that grow, (Things that grow,) In the gar-den, (In the gar-den,) Things that grow, (Things that grow,) In the sun. (In the sun.) Plant the seeds, when it's breez-y, pull the weeds, nice and ea-sy, hope for

390 THE GOLDEN GOOSE

PRODUCTION SUGGESTIONS THEATER

ASSIGNING ROLES: Many of the characters in the musical may be played by either boys or girls. Ned may become Nell, Tess may become Troy, and the sad princess could be a prince. Change the pronouns in the script to fit the needs of your production.

COSTUMES:

Ned: a rope in place of a belt
Tess: a scarf tied around her hair, or an apron
Traveler: ragged clothes, perhaps with patches sewn on
Milkmaid: a white apron

Farmer: a straw hat
Peddler: a drawstring bag at his waist
Guard: a plastic sword in a sheath at his waist, or a helmet and shield
Lady-in-Waiting: a tall, cone-shaped hat with a scarf attached to the tip
King: a crown
Princess: a smaller crown or tiara
Geppo and Sir Silly: funny hats and red foam noses
Chorus: scarves or aprons for girls, rope belts for boys

rain and the job will be done! In the

fall, (In the fall,) dig the car-rots, (dig the

car-rots,) Crisp and sweet, (Crisp and sweet,) ev-'ry

3rd time slower

one! (ev-'ry one!) Bless the sun and the

rain and bless the earth be-low for the

things that grow!

a tempo

things that grow!

D.S. al fine second time

6. Sing the song. Have students:

• Sing the responses, echoing you after you sing each phrase of the chorus part.

• Divide into two groups, with one singing the chorus part and the other singing the farmer's part.

• Switch parts and sing the song again.

• Volunteer to sing the farmer's part as a solo.

• Practice the harmony parts in the last two measures, so that all students are familiar with each part.

MEETING **INDIVIDUAL** NEEDS

MOVEMENT: *"Things That Grow"*

During this song, the farmer should pantomime the actions suggested by the words of the song. The chorus may make the same movements on the repeat, with the farmer imitating them. At the end of the song, the peddler enters from the opposite side of the stage while the farmer is struggling to lift the basket of carrots onto the bench.

CLASSROOM CONNECTION: *Science*

Have students plant carrot seeds in small containers. Ask each student to keep track of her or his plant's progress in a daily journal which could include amounts of water and sunlight the plant receives, measurements of the plant's height at various stages of development, and sketches of the plant as it grows. After a few weeks, send the plants home with students and give them instructions on transferring the plants to larger containers or to a garden.

MUSIC LIBRARY
MUSICAL

continued from previous page

7. Introduce "Barter Song" CD9:31. Have students:

• Define barter and discuss whether bartering is still done.

• Define *coda* and notice where it comes in the song; point out the signs that lead to the coda.

• Read pages 392 and 393.

• Listen to the song.

A peddler approaches with a tray of goods. The farmer admires a silver ring on the tray and the peddler eyes the bright orange carrots.

BARTER SONG

Words and Music by
Linda Worsley

C major

r m f s l t d'

I'll trade you three car-rots. (ten car-rots,) four car-rots, (nine
trade you five car-rots,(eight car-rots,) six car-rots, (Well,)

2nd time to Coda

car-rots,) five car-rots for one shin-y ring! (the ring is of sil-ver!) Or
Both: How a-bout sev-en for one shin-y ring?

brass! (With a dia-mond!) Or glass! but it's real-ly a

beau-ti-ful thing! Bar-ter, bar-ter and trade!

That's how bar-gains are made! Each side,

D.S. al Coda

giv-ing a lit-tle, un-til we can see, that we can a-gree. I'll

392 THE GOLDEN GOOSE

PRODUCTION SUGGESTIONS THEATER

STAGING: Encourage students to suggest ways to act out "Barter Song." The farmer could hold out carrots while the peddler shines the ring on his sleeve, holds it up to the light, and otherwise shows it off. The words of the song indicate when the farmer and the peddler should actually make the trade, and they may complete the deal with a handshake at the end of the song. Some of the lines may be spoken rather than sung, as well. After "Barter Song," Ned enters carrying the goose, with the milkmaid and Tess attached to it in a line. When the chain of characters with the goose enters and then exits at the end of Scene I, use "Processional" (CD11:27) as accompaniment music.

SCENE CHANGE: A blackout should occur at the end of Scene I. During the blackout, the stage crew should clear the stage by removing the bench, the peddler's tray, the farmer's basket, and any trees or sticks that are on stage. The castle wall should be set up near the center of the stage with the portable steps behind it. Place the king's throne and the courtyard gate at opposite ends of the stage. The princess should be in place before the lights come back up. Play "Fanfare" (CD11:28) as the king, guard, and lady-in-waiting enter to begin Scene 2.

Coda ⊕

Peddler / Farmer / Both

(Sold!) Sold! Hon-est and true! Se-ven

(One ring,

car-rots for you! That's how bar-gains are made when you

shin-y and new!)

bar-ter,_____ Bar-ter and trade!_____

The farmer and the peddler see Ned and the others, try to help, and become stuck.

Meanwhile, at the palace, the king is losing hope that anything will cheer his daughter. She is sad because she wants to be an ordinary person instead of a princess.

BIRD IN THE WATER

Words and Music by
Linda Worsley

Slowly

F major

King / Princess

It's im-pos-si-ble! I just

In tempo

have to be-lieve that it's pos-si-ble!

Music Library *Musical* **393**

8. Sing the song. Have students:

• Observe the sixteenth rests and notes in Measures 3 and 4, then clap the rhythm of the first eight measures.

• Notice that in Measures 19 and 20 the farmer and the peddler sing different words simultaneously.

• Say the words to the song in rhythm, with half the class as the farmer and half as the peddler, then switch parts.

• Sing the song in unison, trading roles so that everyone has a chance to learn both parts.

• Practice the harmony part at the end of the song.

• Volunteer to be either the peddler or the farmer, and sing the song as a duet.

MEETING **INDIVIDUAL** NEEDS

COOPERATIVE LEARNING: *Sharing the Spotlight*

Create a variety of roles and tasks for the class, so that each student feels she or he is contributing something important to the production. In addition to the solos, speaking parts, and backstage crew, students can be dramatic coaches (to work with others on memorizing lines), stage managers (to cue entrances, exits, and help supervise scene changes), or director's assistants (to take notes on entrances from left or right as the director decides during rehearsals).

ENRICHMENT: *Attending a Performance*

Give students opportunities to be an audience as well as to perform. Students who are not performing in a given scene can watch the scene in rehearsal and in performance. Having alternate casts will allow students to watch an entire performance by their classmates. As an audience, students should be encouraged to listen attentively, to show approval at appropriate points in the performance, and to offer constructive comments after the performance by means of writing reviews or discussing suggestions.

MUSIC LIBRARY
MUSICAL

continued from previous page

9. Introduce "Bird in the Water" CD9:33.
Have students:

• Point out the repeat signs and the first and second endings.

• Notice that the notation of the last word of the song indicates that it is to be spoken or shouted rather than sung.

• Read pages 394 and 395.

• Listen to the song.

• Brainstorm other "impossible" animals or ideas.

394 THE GOLDEN GOOSE

PRODUCTION SUGGESTIONS

STAGING: Following "Bird in the Water," two clowns, Geppo and Sir Silly, enter one at a time to try and make the princess laugh. Have students create movement routines for the clowns. Some ideas include being so clumsy that they trip over their own feet and drop everything they pick up; trying (and failing) to perform magic tricks; doing silly dances such as the Swim, the Monkey, the Alligator, and the Funky Chicken; miming; or making funny faces. Be sure that the clowns do their acts so that both the princess and the audience can see them. Play "Clown Waltz" (CD11:29) and "Clown Jig" (CD11:30) as accompaniment to the two movement routines.

CHOOSING SOLOISTS: Finding students who can act or sing with confidence and expression can be challenging. The way a student behaves in a classroom does not always indicate her or his ability to perform in front of an audience. When you are preparing for a production, notice which students are reluctant to volunteer and personally invite them to audition for a speaking or singing part; they may just need a word of encouragement from you. Holding tryouts will help you identify those students who are best suited to the roles.

The princess bursts into laughter at the sight of Ned
and the others. The king rewards Ned with a farm.

10. Sing the song. Have students:

• Sing the song in unison, with everyone singing all the parts.

• Sing the song again with the class divided into four groups, one group to sing each part.

• Volunteer to sing the part of the king, the guard, the lady-in-waiting, or the princess.

MEETING **INDIVIDUAL** NEEDS

VOCAL DEVELOPMENT: *Preparing for a Musical*

Give your students many opportunities during the year to sing in front of the class. This is an excellent way to build self-confidence. It is also helpful in choosing students to portray the characters in the play. Select students who sing with a pleasant tone and match pitch well to be soloists or part of a small group. As you play the recordings and practice the songs, look for individuals who show an interest in a particular song.

ART CONNECTION: *The Golden Goose*

VISUAL ARTS

Ask students to illustrate one or more images from the song, then have them brainstorm their own ideas to illustrate. Display the artwork in the classroom or hallway on the day of the performance. Have students choose some or all of the drawings to create advertising posters and a cover for the printed program, if you have one.

RECORDER

PLAYING THE RECORDER CORRELATION

A summary of Recorder lessons referenced throughout this Teacher's Edition follows.

396

GLOSSARY

A

accelerando to get faster gradually, **215**

accent stress on a note or chord, **187**

accidental a flat (♭), sharp (♯), or natural sign (♮) that appears before a note and shows how the pitch should be changed, **267**

adagio slow, **215**

allegro fast, **215**

augment to change a rhythm by making it last twice as long, **270**

B

bar line (|) a line that divides notes into sets, showing the measures, **26**

bassoon a double-reed woodwind instrument that can play very low pitches, **216**

beat the pulse felt in music, **13**

C

call-and-response describes a song form in which each phrase sung by a solo leader is followed by a phrase sung by the group, **17**

canon song form with two or more voices performing the same melody but starting at different times, so that they overlap like a round, **21**

chord three or more pitches sounded together, **180**

chord root pitch on which a chord is built and that gives the chord its letter name, **182**

clarinet a woodwind instrument that uses a single reed, **273**

coda an ending section to a piece of music, **25**

crescendo (◁) to get louder gradually, **136**

cumulative describes a song form in which more words are added each time a verse is sung, **22**

D

decrescendo (▷) to get softer gradually, **136**

dotted quarter note (♩.) a note equal to one quarter note plus one eighth note, **128**

double reed two pieces of bamboo tied together, through which air is blown to produce the sound in some woodwind instruments, **216**

dynamics loudness and softness of music, **118**

E

eighth note (♪) two eighth notes (♫) equal one quarter note, **24**

eighth rest (♼) the symbol for a silence the length of an eighth note, **219**

397

GLOSSARY

F

flat (♭) a symbol in the key signature or in front of a note that means the pitch should be sung or played a half step lower, **133**

form the order of phrases or sections in music, **32**

forte (*f*) loud, **136**

H

half note (♩) a symbol for a sound the length of two quarter notes, **24**

harmony two or more pitches sung or played at the same time, **133**

heavier register a quality of speaking or singing that usually gives louder, fuller, and lower sound, **20**

I

improvise to make up music while playing it, **190**

interlude a short musical connection between sections or verses of a musical piece, **87**

J

jazz a style of music, often using improvisation and syncopation, that grew from the spirituals, work songs, and blues created by African Americans, **190**

K

key signature the sharps or flats at the beginning of each staff, **133**

L

ledger line a line added above or below the staff, **29**

lighter register a quality of speaking or singing that gives quieter, generally higher sound, **20**

M

major the sound of music that has do for its tonal center and uses the pitches of a major scale, **213**

major scale a specific set of eight pitches from *do* to *do¹*, **220**

measure the set of notes and rests between two bar lines, **26**

melody the tune; a series of pitches that moves upward, downward, or stays the same, **16**

meter signature a symbol that shows how many beats are in each measure and what kind of note equals one beat, **14**

mezzo forte (*mf*) medium loud, **136**

mezzo piano (*mp*) medium soft, **136**

minor the sound of music that has *la* for its tonal center and uses the pitches of a minor scale, **213**

minor scale a specific set of eight pitches from *la*, to *la*, **235**

moderato medium tempo, **215**

motive a short pattern used often in a piece of music, **85**

398

N

natural (♮) a symbol in front of a note that means the pitch should be played or sung as written, without a flat or sharp, **267**

O

oboe a double-reed woodwind instrument with a higher, sweeter sound than that of the bassoon, **216**

octave a skip of seven steps between two pitches; the distance between two pitches that have the same name, **166**

orchestra a large instrumental group, usually including four families of instruments: strings, woodwinds, brass, and percussion, **68**

ornamentation extra pitches or groups of pitches added to a melody to decorate it, **278**

ostinato a rhythmic or melodic pattern that repeats over and over, **40**

overture an instrumental piece that begins an opera or other large musical work; it often introduces the main musical ideas of the work, **85**

P

phrase a complete musical idea, **16**

piano (*p*) soft, **136**

pitch the highness or lowness of a sound, **16**

pitch syllable the name of a pitch, such as *do* or *mi*, **28**

presto very fast, **215**

Q

quarter note (♩) the symbol for one sound to a beat in ¼, **24**

quarter rest (𝄽) a symbol for a silence the length of a quarter note, **24**

R

reed a single piece of cane attached to the mouthpiece of some woodwind instruments, through which air is blown to produce sound, **273**

repeated notes one way a melody moves; to move by staying on the same pitch, **109**

ritardando to gradually slow down, **215**

S

sharp (♯) a symbol in the key signature or in front of a note that means the pitch should be played or sung a half step higher, **161**

sixteenth note (♬) four sixteenth notes equal one quarter note (♬♬), **72**

skip one way a melody moves; to move higher or lower by jumping over one or more pitches, **109**

spiritual a type of song created by African Americans, who combined African rhythms with melodies they created and heard in America, **168**

staff the five lines and four spaces on which musical notes are written, **29**

step one way a melody moves; to move by going to the next higher or lower pitch, **109**

Glossary **399**

GLOSSARY

syncopation happens when stressed sounds occur between the beats instead of on the beats of a rhythm pattern, **187**

T

tempo the speed of the beat, **215**

theme the main musical idea of a piece, **282**

theme and variations a musical form that has a main idea followed by changed versions of the idea, **282**

tie (‿) a curved line that connects two notes of the same pitch and means that the sound is held for the length of both notes, **173**

tonal center the home tone or pitch around which a melody is centered, **59**

tone color the sound that is special to each instrument and voice, **22**

treble clef (𝄞) the symbol at the beginning of the staff that wraps around the G line, **78**

U

upbeat a note or notes that come before the first complete measure of music, **75**

V

variation a changed version of a theme or melody, **282**

vibration a motion that creates sound, **166**

vocables sung syllables that have no specific meaning, **167**

W

whole note (○) a symbol for a sound the length of four quarter notes, **270**

400

SHARE THE MUSIC SEQUENCING:

Throughout *Share the Music* careful sequencing promotes successful music learning. Lesson-to-lesson and unit-to-unit, students enjoy enriching musical experiences that lead them through carefully planned sequence stages. The *Program Scope and Sequence* shows these stages for tested objectives and outlines presentation of other selected concepts. Specific activities are presented in the Unit Planners.

PREPARE

Experience the concept in all perceptual modalities (visual, aural, kinesthetic) without labeling it and without conscious attention being drawn to it.

Imitate and explore the concept, without labeling, gradually leading toward and ultimately reaching an understanding of it.

Describe the concept, characterizing it in students' own words, gestures, and/or pictures.

PROGRAM SCOPE AND SEQUENCE

MUSICAL ELEMENTS	CONCEPTS	UNIT 1 *WHERE IN THE WORLD?*	UNIT 2 *TRAVELING ON*	UNIT 3 *JUST IMAGINE*	UNIT 4 *CONNECTIONS*
EXPRESSIVE QUALITIES	**Dynamics**	• Experience contrasting dynamics (L6)	• Experience soft dynamic (L6)	• Experience (L2), explore, describe, identify, practice, reinforce, create (L3), read (L7) dynamics	• Reinforce (L2), create (L7) dynamics
	Tempo	• Experience tempo changes (L2, 4) • Experience slow tempo (L5)	• Explore tempo changes (L2, 7)	• Experience slow tempo (L1, 6)	• Explore slow tempo (L2), tempo changes (L7) • Experience presto (L5)
	Articulation	• Legato (L2), short, crisp singing style (L8)	• Legato (L6, 8), staccato (L7), marcato (L8)	• Legato (L3), staccato (L4, 7), accent (L4), tremolo, glissando (L7)	• Staccato (L1, 5), accent (L7), legato (L8)
TONE COLOR	**Vocal/ Instrumental Tone Color**	• Woodwinds—Chinese flute (L2), orchestral instruments (L6), unpitched instruments (L1, 4, 6, 7, 8) • Heavier and lighter vocal registers (L3) • Tone color (L3)	• Orchestral families (L3, 7), unpitched instruments (L6)	• String quartet (L2), Renaissance instruments (L4), concert band (L5) • Tone color (L7)	• Woodwinds—Andean quena (L1), orchestral music (L5) • Vocables (L2) • Changed and unchanged voices (L3) • Tone color (L3)

AN OVERVIEW

LABEL

Identify and label the concept by name. Introduce hand sign, gesture, or symbol as appropriate.

APPLY

Practice the concept, using known material, now with the label or name used.

Reinforce the concept with new material, with label used.

Read or interpret visual representation, consciously using the concept.

Create, consciously applying understanding of the concept.

Maintain the understanding with more new material.

Bold = Tested Strand   ★ = Assessment of Tested Objective

UNIT 5 *MUSIC WITH A MESSAGE*	UNIT 6 *A WORLD OF CHANGE*	CELEBRATIONS	ENCORE/MUSIC LIBRARY
• **Reinforce dynamics (L2, 3, 5, 6)**	• **Reinforce dynamics (L1, 4, 8, 9)★**	• **Reinforce dynamics (307, 329, 341)**	• **Reinforce dynamics (368, 385D, 385F)**
• Explore (L1, 2), identify, practice, interpret visual representation (L3), reinforce (L7) tempos	• **Reinforce tempo changes (L1, 4, 8, 9)★**	• Fermata (329)	• **Reinforce tempo changes (368, 385H, 385L)** • Fermata (367)
• Staccato, legato (L3, 6) • Accent (L3, 5)	• Legato (L1, 4, 5, 6) • Contrasting articulation (L8)	• Legato (301)	• Legato (347, 366)
• Woodwinds—oboe, bassoon (L3), orchestral music (L6), Renaissance winds (L7)	• Tone color (L3, 8) • Orff instruments (L3), woodwinds—clarinet (L5), orchestral music (L5, 8) • Vocal ornamentation (L7)	• Heavier and lighter vocal registers (299), changed voice (343)	• Unpitched tone colors (52–53, 102) • Woodwinds—Native American flutes (150), saxophone (198), oboe, bassoon, English horn (247) • Changed voice (383, 385B, 385F) • Orchestral instruments (385D, 385H, 385L), woodwinds—clarinet, flute (385H)

(continued on next page)

MUSICAL ELEMENTS	CONCEPTS	UNIT 1 *WHERE IN THE WORLD?*	UNIT 2 *TRAVELING ON*	UNIT 3 *JUST IMAGINE*	UNIT 4 *CONNECTIONS*
DURATION	Beat/Meter	• **Experience, explore, describe, label, practice (L1), reinforce (L5, 9), read (L4) ⁴⁄₄*** • **Experience, explore, describe, label, practice (L1), read, reinforce (L4, 8, 9), create with (L8) ²⁄₄*** • Beat (L1, 2, 3, 6, 8)	• **Maintain ⁴⁄₄ (L2, 6, 7)** • **Maintain ²⁄₄ (L1, 6)** • Beat (L1, 2, 3, 4, 5, 6, 7, 8) • Meter changes (L3) • Upbeat (L4)	• **Maintain ⁴⁄₄ (L1, 2)** • **Maintain ²⁄₄ (L2, 3)** • **Experience (L1), explore, describe (L2), label, practice, create (L5), read (L5, 7), reinforce (L6, 7, 8) ⁶⁄₈*** • Beat (L2, 3, 4, 6) • Meter changes (L2)	• Beat (L1, 2, 3, 4, 5, 6, 7, 8)
	Rhythm	• **Experience, imitate (L1, 2), describe, identify, practice (L4), read (L4, 8), reinforce, create with (L8, 9) ♪♪, ♩, 𝄾, 𝅗𝅥*** • Rhythm of words (L1, 2, 3, 4, 6, 7)	• **Experience (L1, 3), explore, describe (L2), label, practice, read (L4, 9), reinforce (L4, 6, 7, 9), create with (L7, 9) sixteenth notes ♬♬, ♬♪, ♪♬**	• **Maintain ♪♪, ♩, 𝄾, 𝅗𝅥 (L4)** • **Maintain sixteenths (L4)** • **Experience (L1), imitate, explore, describe (L2), identify, practice, read (L5, 9), reinforce (L6, 7, 8, 9), create with (L5, 9) ♪♬, ♩ ♪, 𝅗𝅥***	• **Maintain ♪♪, ♩ (L9)** • **Experience, explore, describe, label, practice (L1), read (L4, 9), reinforce (L3, 4, 6, 9), create with (L9) ♩ ♩ ♪*** • Syncopation (L7, 8)
PITCH	Melody	• **Experience (L2), imitate (L2, 5), describe, label, practice (L5), read, reinforce (L5, 7), create (L7) do re mi so la*** • **Experience, imitate repeated notes, steps, skips (L2, 5, 7)** • Pitch (L2) • Melody (L2, 6, 7) • *Do' (L2, 5)*	• **Maintain do (L1), do re mi so la (L5), do re mi (L7)** • **Experience, imitate repeated notes, steps, skips (L1, 2, 4, 5)** • **Experience, imitate (L1), explore, describe, identify, practice (L5), read (L6), reinforce (L5, 6, 8, 9), create (L9) D E G A B*** • Melody (L1, 3, 4, 6, 8) • Melodic contour (L1, 6, 7) • *So₁ and la₁ (L1, 5, 6, 7, 8, 9)*	• **Maintain do (L4, 6), re mi so (L4)** • **Explore, describe, identify, practice, read (L1), reinforce (L1, 4, 9) repeated notes, steps, skips*** • **Maintain D E G (L4)** • **Experience, explore (L1), describe, identify, practice, read (L4), reinforce (L9) fa*** • **Experience, explore (L1, 4), describe, identify, practice, read (L4), reinforce (L8, 9) C F*** • Melody (L5, 8), melodic contour (L1, 4), so₁ (L4, 6) and la₁ (L4), do' (L1, 4)	• **Maintain do re mi fa so la (L5)** • **Maintain repeated notes (L2), steps (L9), skips (L2, 9)** • **Maintain F G (L6), C (L2, 5, 8, 9)** • **Experience, imitate (L1, 2), describe, identify, practice (L2), reinforce (L3, 5, 8), read (L5) octave*** • **Experience (L1), explore (L2), identify, practice (L5), create, read (L5, 9), reinforce (L5, 8, 9) C'*** • Melodic ornamentation (L1) • Melodic contour (L2) • *Do' (L5, 8, 9)*
	Harmony	• Countermelody (L5) • I-V harmony (L6, 7)	• Chord roots (L3) • Melodic ostinato (L4, 5)	• Harmony changes (I-V) (L6, 8)	• Chords, chord roots, chord names, chord changes (I-IV-V) (L6, 8) • 2-part singing (L2)
	Tonality major/minor	• **Experience minor (L2)** • Major (L5) • Tonal center (L7)	• Tonal center (L1, 5, 6)	• **Experience minor (L2, 7)** • Tonal center (L6) • Key signature (L6)	• Key signature (L1) • Tonal center (L8)
DESIGN	Texture	• Canon (L3, 7)	• Unpitched ostinatos (L3, 4, 6, 7)	• Canon (L7)	• Unpitched ostinatos (L1, 3, 4, 5, 7, 8)
	Form/ Structure	• **Experience (L1), imitate, label, practice, read (L2), reinforce (L5, 6, 7, 9) phrase*** • Phrase form—same, similar, different (L6, 7, 8), call-and-response (L2), cumulative song (L3), coda (L4), interlude (L8), ostinato (L8), introduction (L9)	• **Maintain phrase (L2, 8)** • Sectional form (A B, A B A) • Cumulative song (L3) • Overture (L7) • Motive (L7) • Interlude (L7)	• Phrase form (L1) • Sectional form (L1, 5, 6, 7) • Motive (L2, 4) • Coda (L3)	• **Maintain phrases (L4)** • Call-and-response (L1) • Sectional form (L, 2, 5, 8) • Coda (L2)
CULTURAL CONTEXT	Style/ Background	• African American song (L2) • Appalachian folk song (L5) • Music from 20th-century orchestral suite (L6) • Celtic music (L8)	• Turkish folk music (L2, 4) • 19th-century program music (L3) • Opera overture (L7) • Chinese folk music (L8)	• Mexican folk song, dance (L1, 6) • Native American music (L3) • Renaissance music (L4) • Concert band music (L5)	• Caribbean folk songs (L1, 2) • Andean carnivalito (L1, 4) • Rap (L7)

Bold = Tested Strand   ★ = Assessment of Tested Objective

UNIT 5 *MUSIC WITH A MESSAGE*	UNIT 6 *A WORLD OF CHANGE*	CELEBRATIONS	ENCORE/MUSIC LIBRARY
• **Maintain ⁴/₄ (L1, 9)** • **Explore, describe, identify, practice (L1), read (L5, 7), reinforce (L1, 2, 3, 5, 9), create (L9) ⁴/₄ ★** • Beat (L1, 2, 3, 4, 5, 8) • Changing meter (L3)	• **Maintain ²/₄ (L2)** • **Maintain ⁴/₄ (L5, 6)** • **Maintain ⁶/₈ (L6)** • Beat (L1, 2, 3, 4, 5, 8) • Changing meter (L3, 6, 8)	• **Reinforce ²/₄ (305, 321)** • **Reinforce ⁶/₈ (313)** • **Reinforce ³/₄ (303, 319, 326)** • Beat (297, 305, 333, 343) • Changing meter (345)	• Beat (199) • **Reinforce ²/₄ (348, 369)** • **Reinforce ⁴/₄ (346, 364)** • **Reinforce ⁶/₈ (358, 359, 364, 366)** • **Reinforce ³/₄ (364)**
• **Maintain ♫, ♩ (L5)** • **Maintain ♪♪ ♪, ♩ (L8)** • **Experience, explore (L1, 2, 5), describe, identify, practice (L5), read (L5, 7, 9), reinforce (L7, 9), create with (L8, 9) dotted rhythms ♩♪, ♩♩♪ ★**	• **Maintain ♫ ♩ ♪, ♩ (L6)** • **Maintain sixteenth notes (L1, 3, 4, 5)** • **Explore, describe, identify, practice, read (L5), reinforce (L5, 8, 9) augmentation★** • Whole note (L5)	• **Reinforce sixteenth notes (311)** • **Reinforce ♫♫, ♩ ♪, ♩ (313)** • **Reinforce ♪♪♪ (339)** • **Reinforce dotted rhythms (301, 303)** • Rhythm (297) • Syncopation (337)	• **Reinforce ♫ ♩, ♩ (348, 349)** • **Reinforce sixteenth notes (351, 352, 354, 362, 365)** • **Reinforce ♩ ♪, ♩ (356, 358, 359)** • **Reinforce ♪♪ ♪ (360, 361, 362, 367, 369)** • **Reinforce dotted rhythms (367, 369, 371)** • **Reinforce augmentation (371)** • Syncopation (360, 361, 362, 367, 369, 385J)
• **Maintain *do re mi fa so la* (L4)** • Melodic contour (L2, 4) • *Do'* (L4) • *Ti* (L2, 4, 8) • Major scale (L4, 8) • Minor scale (L8)	• **Maintain *do re mi fa so la* (L4)** • *La ti do'* (L4) • Melodic ornamentation (L7, 8)	• **Reinforce steps (333)** • **Reinforce *fa*, C, F (337)** • **Reinforce octave (301, 343)** • *So,* and *la,* (315) • *Ti* (325)	• **Reinforce steps, skips (101)** • **Reinforce octave (100)** • Melodic counter (101) • **Reinforce *do re mi so la* (349, 352)** • **Reinforce D E G A B (330, 332)** • **Reinforce steps, skips (347, 355)** • **Reinforce *fa* (357, 364)** • **Reinforce C F (357)** • **Reinforce octave (361, 363, 371, 385D)** • *So, la,* (353, 354, 355, 356, 358, 360) • *Do'* (361, 363, 364, 366, 367, 371) • *Ti* (366)
• Melodic ostinato (L8)	• Harmony (L4) • 2-part singing (L2), 3-part singing (L1, 4)	• Partner songs (315) • Countermelody (317) • Chords (323, 329) • Harmony (339)	• Melodic ostinato (357, 363)
• **Explore, identify, practice (L2), reinforce (L2, 5, 6, 8), interpret visual representation (L6) minor** • Tonal center (L4), key signature (L4), major scale (L4, 8), minor scale (L8)	• **Reinforce minor (L4, 8, 9)★** • Major (L1, 4, 8) • Major scales (L4) • Minor scales (L4, 9)	• **Reinforce minor (329)** • Tonal center (301) • Major (329)	• **Reinforce minor (365, 368, 370, 371)** • Major (365)
• Canon (L7)	• **Identify, practice (L2), reinforce (L2, 3, 8, 9) accompaniment★** • Canon (L6, 8)	• **Reinforce accompaniment (307, 333)**	• **Reinforce accompaniment (102, 352, 357, 359, 362, 363, 369)** • Canon (349, 350, 361, 363, 364, 366, 367)
• Sectional form (L1, 3, 6, 7) • Rondo (L2, 7) • Call-and-response (L5, 8)	• Coda (L1, 2) • Cumulative song (L3) • Sectional form (L4) • Theme and variations (L5, 8) • Movement from suite (L5)	• **Reinforce phrase (301, 307)** • Theme and variations (303) • Ostinato (307, 309, 343) • Sectional form (309) • Motive (317) • Introduction, coda (325, 341) • Cumulative song (331)	• Sectional form (150) • Call-and-response (200) • **Reinforce phrase (347)** • Call-and-response (362, 364) • Motive (385F, 385J) • Phrase form (356, 369) • Sectional form (352)
• Native American music (L5) • 19th-century orchestral music (L6) • Spiritual (L6, 8)	• American folk songs (L2) • Shaker song (L4) • 20th-century orchestral music (L5)	• Mexican Christmas (318) • Asian New Year (332)	• Native American flute (151) • African American jazz (199) • Choral concert etiquette (382) • Renaissance (359), Baroque (383, 385B), Classical (385D), Romantic (385F), 20th Century (383, 385H, 385J, 385L)

MOVEMENT SCOPE AND SEQUENCE

A SEQUENCED APPROACH TO MOVEMENT

Share the Music presents movement in a systematic way, to encourage children to develop movement skills as they learn music concepts and skills. This **Movement Scope and Sequence**, a first for any music series, shows how movement skills are sequenced throughout the lessons.

MOVING: A PRIMARY MODE OF LEARNING

All children are born tactile and kinesthetic learners, discovering their world through touch and movement. Visual and auditory learning become important, but some children remain primarily "movement" or kinesthetic learners. On the playground, hand jive, jump rope, hopscotch, ball tossing, and other movement games are the activities of choice. This energy, interest, and enthusiasm is available to us in the classroom: to present musical concepts in a fresh way, to get children physically involved in skill development, to motivate, illustrate and educate.

PARALLELS BETWEEN MUSIC AND MOVEMENT

Movement can provide clarity and reinforce understanding in music. Experiencing beat in movement can help a child learn to play an ostinato. Drawing the melodic contour in the air can help a child sing a melody. Creating a dance in ABACA form can prepare children to hear rondo form.

ELEMENTS OF MOVEMENT		UNIT 1 FOCUS: DIRECTION, BODY FACING	UNIT 2 FOCUS: LOCOMOTOR AND NONLOCOMOTOR
SPACE	Level		• Change arm levels in a dance (L4)
	Direction	• Change direction while moving in and out, and around a circle (L2)	• Create movement that changes direction (L2)
	Pathway	• Draw curved air pathway (L2)	• Walk straight, curved, or zigzag pathways (L2, 4) • Mirror, using air pathways (L8)
	Range		
	Body Design	• Define body design and change on cue (L1, 2)	
	Body Facing	• Face four different walls to show phrase (L2) • Practice body facing change (L2, 3) • Define body facing (L3)	• Face in and out of circle (L3)
GROUP FORMATIONS		• Double lines (L2, 5, 7) • Circle (L2) • Spokes of wheel (L6) • Scattered pairs (L3, 8)	• Scattered pairs (L2) • Three concentric circles (L2) • Broken circle (L4, 8) • Double lines (L5, 8) • Groups of four (L6, 8)
LOCOMOTOR		• Jump while changing body facing (L3, 8) • Walk or run in a dance (L2, 5, 6, 7)	• Walk and jog (L2, 7) • Perform folk dance with a walking pattern (L2, 4, 8)
NONLOCOMOTOR		• Create four movements to represent note values (L4) • Learn a "Hambone" pattern (L5, 6)	• Move arms like a windshield wiper (L2, 4) • Play hand game with partner (L6, 8) • Experiment with movement for head and arms (L8) • Mirror with partner (L8)
TIME		• Perform pat-clap-clap pattern (L1) • Show phrase through body facing change (L2) • Show meter by jumping (L2, 8)	• Respond to $\quarternote$, $\eighthnote\eighthnote$, and $\sixteenthnotes$ in movement (L2) • Create eight-beat pattern in movement (L2) • Play a game with beanbags (L6)
FORCE/QUALITY			• Change quality of movement by responding to adverbs (L5, 8) • Perform marcato and legato movements (L8)
RELATIONSHIPS		• Try four body facing changes with partner (L3) • "Step it down" with partner (L2, 5, 7) • Perform a dance in group of three (L6) • Create a movement ostinato with partner (L8)	• Do a clapping pattern with a partner (L1, 6) • Create dances in small groups (L2) • Play a hand game in groups of four (L6, 8) • Mirror with partner (L8)
SINGING GAME AND DANCE SKILLS		• Move in circle clockwise, counterclockwise, in and out (L2) • Use "step it down" step (L2, 5, 7) • Swing elbows with partner (L2, 5, 7) • Move to head and foot of the set (L2, 5, 7) • Counterbalance in a small circle (L6)	• Perform side-close step (L2, 4, 8) • Change body facing in a circle (L3) • Practice side, cross, side, touch, (L3, 5, 8)

UNIT 3 FOCUS: **RANGE**	UNIT 4 FOCUS: **FORMATIONS**	UNIT 5 FOCUS: **PARALLEL AND CONTRARY MOVEMENT**	UNIT 6 FOCUS: **FOLK DANCE STEPS**
• Change level to show harmonic change (L6)	• Change level using a bow in a folk dance (L4)		
	• Change direction of a movement pattern (L1, 2, 4, 5)	• Change direction while performing a step-hop (L3) • Experience changing direction (L5, 6)	• Change direction while performing Schottische step (L1, 4); while circling (L2, 6)
	• Leader chooses pathway for group to follow (L4)	• Experience parallel and contrary movement (L4, 5)	• In concentric circles, move in contrary motion (L1) • Draw circular air pathway (L5)
• Respond to melody by changing size of steps (L1) • Define range (L1) and change range of movement (L2, 3, 7, 8) • Use large and small movements (L8)		• Create parallel and contrary movement (L5, 6, 8)	• Change size of steps and air pathway to reflect augmentation (L5)
• Create body design individually and in small groups to interpret a poem (L3)	• Change body design on cue (L6)		
	• Form a line with two different body facings (L5)	• Change body facing while performing a step-hop (L3)	
• Scattered (L1, 3, 5) • Double lines (L4, 5) • Pairs (L8)	• Circles and double lines (L1) • Groups of three or four (L2, 4, 5) • Lines of six (L4, 6) • Square of eight (L5)	• Scattered pairs (L1) • Concentric circles (L1, 4, 6) • Circles of four (L3) • Lines of four or five (L5) • Circle (L4, 6)	• Concentric circles (L1, 4) • Circle (L2, 6) • Broken circle (L8)
• Use twirls and other locomotor movement with a poem (L3) • Gallop, skip (L8) • Hop (L6) • Jog to show ♫, gallop to show ♩ ♪, and walk to show ♩ (L5)	• Walk in a rhythm pattern (L1, 7) • Learn a step-hop pattern (L4)	• Walk ♩ through shared space (L1) • Step-hop (L3) • Perform ♫ ♫ ♫ ♩ pattern with feet (L5) • Perform Galliard step (L7)	• Learn Schottische step (walk, walk, walk, hop) (L1, 4) • Create a dance that uses walking steps (L2) • Walk ♩ ♩ ♫ ♩ pattern (L5); ♫ ♫ ♩ ♩ pattern (L8)
• Move hands and fingers (L3) • Create nonlocomotor movements (L5) • Use nonlocomotor movement to create a "storm" (L7)	• Practice arm movement— paddling, sweeping, pointing, pushing, waving (L6)	• High five movement with partner (L1) • Hand-clap pattern in ⅜ (L2, 3)	• Perform hand gestures to identify instruments (L3) • Raise and lower arms in a dance (L6)
• Clap rhythmic motive while walking through shared space (L2) • Clap ♩ while galloping (L5) • Clap ♫ while walking ♩ (L5)	• Change between walking to beat and walking the rhythm of words (L1, 7) • Play stone-passing game (L4)	• Create a four-beat pattern (L1) • Perform a three-beat pattern (L2, 3) • Perform movement as a canon (L3) • Change tempo in a dance (L3)	• Change tempo in a dance (L1, 4) • Perform body percussion to demonstrate augmentation (L5) • Move in canon (L6)
• Add energy to a swing (L1) • Make sudden, sharp movements (L3) • Change quality of movement to express a poem (L3)		• Create movement to capture quality of water or waves (L8)	• Ornament a simple dance by adding a stylized element (L7)
• In small groups, use body design and range to interpret a poem (L3) • Create movement with a partner (L4, 6, 8)	• Dance in small groups (L4, 2) • Perform game in groups (L4) • Create B section movement in groups (L5)	• Create a movement pattern with partner (L1, 5, 6) • Perform hand-clap game with partner (L2, 3, 4) • Perform dance in small groups (L3, 5) • Create movement in three groups (L8)	• In small groups, create a dance (L2) • Perform a folk dance with a partner (L1, 4) • Perform movement ostinato with a partner (L5)
• Form and walk under arches, do-si-do (L5) Kick-leap step (L8) • Use right and left elbow swing (L8)	• Practice side, close, side, touch (L1) • Step ♩ ♩ ♫ ♩ with alternating feet (L1) • Form right- and left-hand stars (L2, 5) • Step-hop (L4) • Allemande left to corner, right to partner (L5) • Do-si-do partner and corner (L5) • Perform a "Rip and Snort" (L5)	• Travel through shared space finding new partner (L1) • Step-hop (L3) • Form right- and left-hand stars (L3) • Form large circle from several small circles (L3) • Perform Galliard step (L7)	• Dance the Schottische (L1, 4) • Perform side, close, side, touch (L1, 4) • Practice leap, step, step (L4) • Circle clockwise and counterclockwise (L6) • Practice side-lift (L8)

MOVEMENT GLOSSARY

alignment   The position of body parts in relation to each other. Of special importance to good singing is the position of the vertebrae, head, shoulders, and feet in relation to each other.

allemande left   In a square set, couples turn back to back, join left hands with their "corners," swing around once, and return to their partners. An *allemande right* is the same sequence done with right hands.

body facing   The spatial orientation of body surfaces, most often the front.

> Whether or not one is moving, **body facing** exists at all times. The term refers to where various body surfaces are in relation to an outside reference.
>
> 1 partner or opposing line
>   · *front to front*
>   · *front to back*
>   · *back to back*
>   · *side by side*—with same or opposite outside reference
>   · *same*—both facing the same outside reference
>   · *opposite*—each facing opposite outside references
> 2 direction or line of motion
>   · *forward*—front facing the line of motion
>   · *backward*—back facing the line of motion
>   · *sideways*—side facing the line of motion
> 3 the area in which the person is located
>   · *front*—where the leader stands
>   · *back*—opposite to front
> 4 the group formation
>   · *inward*—toward the center of a circle or square
>   · *outward*—away from the center of a circle or square
>   · *clockwise*—to the left in a circle
>   · *counterclockwise*—to the right in a circle

body part   An individual section of the body. Each body part has its own function and potential for movement.

body percussion   The sounds created by using body parts as percussion instruments. Examples: pat, clap, snap, rub, stamp.

body shape   The design created by placement of body parts.
  curved rounded lines predominant
  angular straight and bent lines predominant

broken circle   A line of dancers with a leader who leads the group in curved pathways (often circular). The curved pathway remains unclosed.

circle dance   A dance done in circle formation without partners.

circle formation   A number of individuals standing or sitting equidistant from a center point.

close   Bring one foot next to the other. Can be done with or without transferring weight (either a step or a touch).

concentric circle formation   Circles inside other circles, without partners.

conduct   Direct the performance of musicians.

conducting pattern   A series of hand motions with a strong downbeat and a separate motion for the other beats. Used to direct musicians to play in a particular meter.

contrary motion   Term used to describe movements that go in opposite directions. Example: one arm going up as the other goes down.

corner   In a square set, the person standing next to a dancer who is not that dancer's partner.

counterbalance   Create equilibrium between two connected individuals. Partners can hold onto one another and lean away from each other, or lean against some part of one another's bodies. The partners depend on one another to keep from falling.

dance   A series of body movements usually performed to music. A dance could be structured or improvisatory, and may include visually perceptible themes (steps, gestures, or spatial designs) that are repeated and developed throughout its duration.

dancing   Doing a dance or moving with control over the form and visual design of body movements.

direction   The spatial orientation of the line of motion.

> When there is a line of motion, **direction** occurs. If an individual is still, there is no direction, only body facing. A direction is always in relation to a point of reference. The most common directions are:
>
> 1 in relation to a partner or facing line
>   · *toward*—approaching a partner or line
>   · *away from*—separating from a partner or line
> 2 in relation to a circle formation
>   · *clockwise*—following the hands of a clock
>   · *counterclockwise*—reverse of clockwise
>   · *in*—toward the center of the circle
>   · *out*—away from the center of the circle
> 3 in relation to an imaginary vertical line
>   · *up*—higher
>   · *down*—lower
>
> *Forward, backward,* and *sideways* are body facings in relation to the line of motion and are not directions.

do-si-do   Partners begin by facing each other, then move toward each other, pass right shoulders, step to the right, walk backward, pass each other again by the left shoulders, and return to facing position. Often done with arms folded across chest.

double circle A partner formation of concentric circles. Partners stand side by side or front to front. Dancers in the inside circle are connected to partners in the outside circle by holding a hand or both hands and/or moving together.

draw Trace a movement in the air.

elbow swing Link elbows (right or left) with partner and turn.

facing partner Front-to-front body relationship.

floor pattern or pathway An imaginary line resulting from locomotion across the floor.

foot couple The partners at the foot of the set or the end farthest from the music source.

formation A group spatial arrangement or design.

> Every dance or singing game has a traditional spatial arrangement called a **formation** that determines how the participants will stand or sit at the beginning of the dance or game. Some of these include:
> - *broken circle*
> - *circle*
> - *double circle*
> - *concentric circles*
> - *line*
> - *longways set (contradance lines)*
> - *scattered*
> - *square*
> - *square of four*

broken circle

concentric circles

longways set

square

galliard A vigorous Renaissance dance in 𝄋 or 𝄋. Basic movement sequence consists of six steps: four leaps followed by a hop and another leap, performed in the rhythm ♩ ♩ ♩ ♩ ♪♩

gallop A 𝄋 locomotor combination of a step and a leap. The step gets a quarter-note value; the leap gets an eighth-note value (♩ ♪). The same foot always leads in a gallop.

grand right and left A movement sequence with a single circle of partners facing one another: 1) partners grasp right hands; 2) walk past partner; 3) take the next person's left hand and release partner's right hand; 4) walk past that person; 5) take the next right hand; and so on around the circle until partners meet again.

grapevine step A series of weaving foot movements (cross/side/back/side): 1) left foot crosses right; 2) right foot steps open to right; 3) left foot steps in back of right; 4) right foot steps open to right. Step can be done to the left by crossing the right foot in front of the left to begin. A *modified grapevine step* begins with an open step to the side followed by a cross step either in front or in back.

group shape or group design The spatial outline created by a gathering of people. Related to formation, but not all group shapes are traditional formations.

hambone An African American "clapping play" in which, traditionally, the thigh (hambone) is slapped on the offbeat while a verse is being recited.

hand signs Specific hand gestures used to communicate. Both Native American sign language and sign language for the deaf provide an extensive lexicon of specific hand signs. Hand signs are also used to signal solfege syllables.

head couple The partners at the head of the set or the end nearest the source of music.

high five Gesture used as a greeting or a congratulation in which two people clap their right hands, maintaining contact as they raise their hands upward.

home Location from which the mover leaves and to which he/she returns.

improvise Create (movement) spontaneously, without prior planning.

in place In self space. Without leaving home.

jog A slow run variation where the knees come up a bit and the movement has a bouncy quality.

kick leap A leap in place with the free leg kicking out in front.

lean Shift body weight beyond the base of support. Part of the body can rest on an outside support such as a wall or another person.

leap   A basic locomotor movement in which weight is transferred from one foot to the other, with a moment in which neither foot is on the floor. A leap differs from a run because it is done for either height or distance, not speed.

line dance   Dance in which participants move next to one another, either side by side or front to back, forming a straight line. There are no partners.

locomotion   Going from one place to another, or traveling.

> Movement that allows us to get somewhere is called **locomotion.** Most locomotion involves the feet. Basic locomotor movements that use alternate feet include:
> - *walk*
> - *run*
> - *leap*
>
> Basic locomotor movements that do not alternate feet include:
> - *hop*
> - *jump*
>
> Other common forms of locomotion combine two of the basic forms and are distinguished by their rhythm.
> - *gallop*—step/leap, uneven rhythm (♩ ♪)
> - *slide*—sideways gallop
> - *skip*—step/hop, uneven rhythm (♩ ♪)
> - *step-hop*—similar to skip, even rhythm (♫ or ♩ ♩)
>
> Forms of locomotion that do not involve the feet include *crawl, scoot,* and *roll.* These are not considered basic forms.

longways or contradance set   Parallel lines of dancers usually facing each other.

mirror   Strive to move in perfect unison. Can be done by facing partners or by a group, usually with a designated leader. Mirroring without a leader is possible with practice.

mixer   A dance or singing game in which a participant gets a new partner with each repetition.

movement exploration   Improvised motion to discover movement possibilities, usually relating to a concept. Example: explore ways of going from point A to point B.

movement ostinato   A repeating movement pattern.

movement quality   The characteristic of movement that results from the interplay of time and force. Examples: strong, light, sudden, percussive, sustained, shaky, swinging, vibratory.

movement variation   A movement that has been changed but still maintains its original character. Example: an arm gesture done with the opposite arm, or at a different level or tempo.

nonlocomotor   Movement that does not involve traveling from one place to another. Sometimes called *axial movement* because it occurs around an axis at a joint in the body. Examples: bend, twist, stretch, sway, swing, reach.

pantomime   Movement, especially gestures, used to simulate an activity without the objects that would usually be present. Example: playing a trumpet without the trumpet.

parallel motion   Term used to describe identical movements that are performed at the same time and at an equal distance.

Example: partners walking down opposite lines of a longways set.

pat   Tap thighs with both hands.

pathway   An imaginary line created by movement.

percussive   A quality of movement created by a quick, short, explosive movement that stops instantly.

pinkie hold   Side-by-side partners link little fingers at shoulder height with elbows bent.

posture   Body alignment.

promenade   To perform this movement, a couple walks side by side, usually with skaters' hold.

range of movement   The size of a movement, or how much area is required to execute a movement. Examples: large, small.

right-hand star   A folk-dance figure in which a group (often four dancers) joins right hands in the center of a circle and moves clockwise around that center. Hands can be at waist height or higher. The *left-hand star* is the same but with left hands joined and movement in a counterclockwise direction.

rip and snort   All couples in a square set hold hands as the head couple goes under an arch made by the foot couple, taking the other dancers along. The head couple drops their hand hold and separates after going under the arch but everyone else stays joined. One side of the line goes right and the other left until the foot couple turns under their own arch and everyone is back home.

Head Couple

Head Couple

run   A basic locomotor form in which the transfer of weight from one foot to the other is fast, including a moment when both feet are off the ground.

scattered formation   A group of individuals or couples spaced randomly around the movement area.

schottische   A dance style based on a sequence of three steps and one hop in an even rhythm. Can be done forward, backward, or to the side.

self space   The area that an individual occupies. Used by that person only.

set   A formation for dancing. Examples: longways or contradance set, square set.

shared space   The total area through which more than one person is moving.

side-close   A movement sequence: 1) Step to the side with one foot; 2) step with the other foot close to the first foot.

side couples The couples to the side of the head and foot couples in a square set.

side-touch A movement sequence: 1) step out to the side with one foot; 2) tap the other foot next to the first but without a weight transfer.

sign language Communication involving movement, most often of the hands, and no spoken words.

skaters' hold A traditional position for dance in which partners stand side by side with same body facing, holding right hand with right hand and left hand with left hand to the front. This can be achieved easily by partners facing one another, shaking right hands and holding, doing the same with the left hands, and then facing the same way without dropping hands.

skip A locomotor combination of a step and a hop. The step has the value of a quarter note and the hop has the value of an eighth note (♩ ♪). The leading foot alternates.

square dance An early American country dance form still popular today. Dancers are positioned in a square set of four couples, each facing one other couple.

square of four Four dancers, each forming one side of a square.

square set Four dancers or four couples, each forming one side of a square and facing a partner or another couple.

step A basic form of locomotion in which weight is transferred completely from one foot to the other. A series of steps is *walking*.

step-hop A ⅜ dance step similar to a skip, except that each movement gets a full beat (even rhythm ♩ ♩).

step in place Walk without going anywhere.

step-it-down An African American movement sequence: 1) put one foot out in front as if to step on something but do not transfer any weight; 2) bring that foot back and step on it; 3) repeat the same two-beat movement leading with the other foot. This produces a syncopated back-and-forth motion with accents on beats 2 and 4.

steps Locomotor combinations and/or sequences making up a dance.

step-touch A dance step in which weight is transferred to one foot on one beat and the other foot taps the floor on the next beat without transferring weight. Variations of this include step-lift and step-kick.

style A quality of movement or a particular way movement elements are combined that make a dance (or other creative form) recognizable as unique. Styles can be influenced by the origin of the dance (example: Appalachian clogging), by the kind of music (example: jazz dance), or by the dancer (example: the style of Kris Kross).

supporting foot The foot that bears weight or supports the body.

sway Shift weight from one foot to the other without taking feet from the ground. Typically used with a slow to moderate tempo.

swing A dance step in which partners join hands or elbows and turn around each other.

three-step turn A movement sequence: 1) step to side maintaining original body facing; 2) step in the same direction on the other foot as you reverse body facing; 3) take the third step in the same direction and reverse body facing again. This turn travels in a continuous line.

through space Moving out of self space into shared space.

tiptoe A walk variation done on the balls of the feet, often with a light quality of movement.

touch Tap the floor with a foot without transferring weight to that foot. Also, physical contact.

trace Go over a preexisting line. Example: Using a finger, trace the melodic contour of a phrase of music shown in a book.

travel Locomote or go from one place to another. Examples: walk, run.

twist Turn a body part against a fixed point or point of resistance.

two-step turn A complete turn in just two steps. If turning to the right: 1) the left foot crosses over the right foot and steps to the right while dancer reverses body facing; 2) the right foot now crosses in back of the left foot while dancer reverses body facing, bringing the body back to its original facing.

unison movement At least two people moving identically.

walk A series of steps or alternating transferences of weight from one foot to the other. There is never a moment when both feet are off the ground.

walk variations The ways in which the basic walking step can be altered.

Some **walk variations** have well-known names:
 · *giant step/baby step* alters the range of movement
 · *tiptoe* alters the part of the foot touching the floor
 · *sneak/strut* alters the quality of movement
 · *crab walk* alters the body parts involved
 · *scurry* alters the tempo

weight transference A change in the body part that supports the weight of the body. Examples: A step changes the supporting surface from one foot to the other foot; sitting down changes the supporting surface from the feet to the buttocks.

wring the dishrag Partners face each other holding both hands and swing hands to one side and up. As hands go overhead, partners turn underneath their joined arms, face back-to-back, then bring the arms down, and resume front-to-front facing. The joined hands describe a complete circle in the air.

MULTICULTURAL INFUSION

MULTICULTURAL PERSPECTIVES

Share the Music is committed to teaching and spreading the joy of music through the expressions of many cultures. The musical selections in the series and the approaches to teaching music reflect our pluralistic society and the diversity of cultures.

As a multiculturally infused music series, *Share the Music* celebrates diverse modes of cultural expression. Varied vocal styles, for example, are used as appropriate. Students learn about both lighter and heavier vocal registers and determine which is most culturally appropriate for selected materials.

Students experience many facets of culture, including dance, fine arts, holidays, instruments, and aspects of daily life.

Making Multicultural Music Accessible in the Classroom

Share the Music includes authentic materials along with support tools to make them easy to use.

• **Context Information** leads students to respect, appreciate, and understand diverse peoples and cultures. This background is presented throughout the pupil books and in *Meeting Individual Needs.*

• **Recorded Interviews** bring musicians from diverse backgrounds into the classroom to introduce new material in a familiar, friendly way.

Easing the Use of Non-English Languages

In keeping with our commitment to presenting authentic music, *Share the Music* incorporates songs in over 60 languages. Songs in their original languages encourage positive self-esteem by honoring the languages of many cultures. With these songs, teachers receive important tools for using various languages with ease.

• **Recorded Pronunciation lessons** accompany every non-English song. In these lessons, a native speaker teaches students how to pronounce song words.

• **Singable English translations,** where appropriate, provide an alternative to using the original language.

• **The International Phonetic Alphabet** provides pronunciation at the point of use, underlaid beneath song notation. For each song, a customized key on the teacher's page provides a quick reference for pronunciation. In Grades 1–2, the pronunciation is printed on the reduced pupil page in the Teacher's Edition only.

Using the International Phonetic Alphabet (IPA)

The International Phonetic Alphabet (IPA) was developed in 1888 to facilitate the accurate pronunciation of all languages. It is commonly used by linguists, singers, and speech pathologists. IPA provides one consistent set of symbols for sounds from diverse languages, including non-English sounds that other phonetic systems fail to take into account. Thus, it helps provide greater multicultural authenticity. In IPA, each symbol represents one sound, and diacritic marks are minimized.

The IPA used in *Share the Music* was simplified by a linguist, working with over 100 multicultural experts, to retain English consonants wherever possible and to incorporate 12 main vowel symbols used in IPA. Special sounds that have no English equivalent are represented with special symbols. The use of simplified IPA limits the number of symbols students encounter, encouraging ease of use and success.

As the first major textbook series to use IPA, *Share the Music* helps students easily attain a greater degree of multicultural authenticity in their pronunciation of diverse languages.

PRONUNCIATION KEY

Simplified International Phonetic Alphabet

VOWELS

a	f<u>a</u>ther	o	<u>o</u>bey	æ	c<u>a</u>t	ɔ	p<u>a</u>w
e	ch<u>a</u>otic	u	m<u>oo</u>n	ε	p<u>e</u>t	ʊ	p<u>u</u>t
i	b<u>ee</u>	ʌ	<u>u</u>p	ι	<u>i</u>t	ə	<u>a</u>go

SPECIAL SOUNDS

ß   say *b* without touching lips together; *Spanish* nue<u>v</u>e, ha<u>b</u>a

ç   <u>h</u>ue; *German* i<u>ch</u>

ð   <u>th</u>e; *Spanish* to<u>d</u>o

ṇ   sound <u>n</u> as individual syllable

ö   form [o] with lips and say [e]; *French* adi<u>eu</u>, *German* sch<u>ö</u>n

œ   form [ɔ] with lips and say [ε]; *French* c<u>oeu</u>r, *German* pl<u>ö</u>tzlich

ɾ   flipped r; bu<u>tt</u>er

ī   rolled r; *Spanish* pe<u>rr</u>o

ǀ   click tongue on the ridge behind teeth; *Zulu* ṇg<u>c</u>wele

ü   form [u] with lips and say [i]; *French* t<u>u</u>, *German* gr<u>ü</u>n

ṻ   form [ʊ] with lips and say [ι]

x   blow strong current of air with back of tongue up; *German* Ba<u>ch</u>, *Hebrew* <u>H</u>anukkah, *Spanish* ba<u>j</u>o

ʒ   plea<u>s</u>ure

ʼ   glottal stop, as in the exclamation "uh oh!" [ʼʌ ʼo]

~   nasalized vowel, such as French b<u>on</u> [bõ]

˺   end consonants *k*, *p*, and *t* without puff of air, such as s<u>k</u>y (no puff of air after *k*), as opposed to *kite* (puff of air after *k*)

OTHER CONSONANTS PRONOUNCED SIMILAR TO ENGLISH

ch	<u>ch</u>eese	ny	o<u>ni</u>on; *Spanish* ni<u>ñ</u>o
g	<u>g</u>o	sh	<u>sh</u>ine
ng	si<u>ng</u>	ts	boa<u>ts</u>

BIBLIOGRAPHY

African American Music (See also Multicultural Music)

Bebey, Francis. *African Music: A People's Art.* Chicago: Chicago Review Press, 1975.

Edet, Edna S. *The Griot Sings: Songs from the Black World.* Collected and adapted. New York: Medgar Evers College Press, 1978.

Glass, Paul. *Songs and Stories of Afro-Americans.* New York: Grosset & Dunlap, 1971.

Johnson, James Weldon, and J.R. Johnson, eds. *The Books of American Negro Spirituals.* 2 vols. in 1. Jersey City, N.J.: Da Capo Press, 1977.

Jones, Bessie, and Bess L. Hawes. *Step It Down: Games, Plays, Songs, and Stories from the Afro-American Heritage.* Athens, Ga.: Univ. of Georgia Press, 1987.

Nketia, Joseph H. *The Music of Africa.* New York: W.W. Norton & Co., 1974.

Southern, Eileen. *The Music of Black Americans.* 2d ed. New York: W.W. Norton & Co., 1983.

Cooperative Learning

Gibbs, Jeanne. *Tribes: A Process for Social Development and Cooperative Learning.* Santa Rosa, Calif.: Center Source Publications, 1987.

Johnson, David W., Robert T. Johnson, and Edythe Johnson Holubec. *Circles of Learning: Cooperation in the Classroom.* Alexandria, Va.: Association for Supervision & Curriculum Development, 1984.

Slavin, Robert E. *Cooperative Learning: Student Teams.* 2d ed. Washington, D.C.: National Education Association, 1987.

Dalcroze (See also Movement)

Abramson, Robert M. *Rhythm Games.* New York: Music & Movement Press, 1973.

Aronoff, Frances W. *Move with the Music: Songs and Activities for Young Children, A Teacher-Parent Preparation Workbook Including Keyboard.* New York: Turning Wheel Press, 1982.

Bachmann, Marie-Laure. *Dalcroze Today: An Education Through and into Music.* Oxford: Clarenon Press, Oxford University Press, 1991.

Jaques-Dalcroze, Émile. *Rhythm, Music, and Education.* rev. ed. Translated by Harold F. Rubenstein. London: The Dalcroze Society, 1980.

Early Childhood Music

Andress, Barbara. *Music Experiences in Early Childhood.* New York: Holt, Rinehart & Winston, 1980.

Aronoff, Frances W. *Music and Young Children: Expanded Edition.* New York: Turning Wheel Press, 1979.

Bayless, Kathleen M., and Marjorie E. Ramsey. *Music: A Way of Life for the Young Child.* 3d ed. Columbus, Ohio: Merrill Publishing Co., 1987.

Birkenshaw, Lois. *Music for Fun, Music for Learning: For Regular and Special Classrooms.* 3d ed. Toronto: Holt, Rinehart & Winston of Canada, 1982.

McDonald, Dorothy C., and Gene M. Simons. *Musical Growth and Development: Birth Through Six.* New York: Schirmer Books, 1989.

Nye, Vernice T. *Music for Young Children.* 3d ed. Dubuque, Iowa: William C. Brown Publisher, 1983.

Kodály

Choksy, Lois. *The Kodály Context.* Englewood Cliffs, N.J.: Prentice-Hall, 1981.

—. *The Kodály Method: Comprehensive Music Education from Infant to Adult.* 2d ed. Englewood Cliffs, N.J.: Prentice-Hall, 1988.

Daniel, Katinka S. *Kodály Approach, Method Book One.* 2d ed. Champaign, Ill.: Mark Foster Music Co., 1979.

—. *Kodály Approach, Method Book Two.* Champaign, Ill.: Mark Foster Music Co., 1986

—. *Kodály Approach, Method Book Three.* Champaign, Ill.: Mark Foster Music Co., 1987.

—. *Kodály Approach, Method Book Two—Song Collection.* Champaign, Ill.: Mark Foster Music Co., 1982.

Szonyi, Erzsébet. *Musical Reading and Writing.* Translated by Lili Halápy. Revised translation by Geoffrey Russell-Smith. 8 vols. London and New York: Boosey & Hawkes Music Publishers, 1973–1979.

Listening

Copland, Aaron. *What to Listen for in Music.* New York:

McGraw-Hill Book Co., 1988.

Hoffer, Charles R. *The Understanding of Music.* 5th ed. Belmont, Calif.: Wadsworth Publishing Co., 1985.

Miller, Samuel D. "Listening Maps for Musical Tours." *Music Educators Journal* 73 (October 1986): 28–31.

Movement (See also Dalcroze)

Boorman, Joyce L. *Creative Dance in the First Three Grades.* Toronto: Harcourt Brace Jovanovich, Canada, 1969.

—. *Creative Dance in Grades Four to Six.* Toronto: Harcourt Brace Jovanovich, Canada, 1971.

—. *Dance and Language Experiences with Children.* Toronto: Harcourt Brace Jovanovich, Canada, 1973.

Joyce, Mary. *First Steps in Teaching Creative Dance to Children.* 2d ed. Mountain View, Calif.: Mayfield Publishing Co., 1980.

Weikart, Phyllis. *Teaching Movement and Dance: Intermediate Folk Dance.* Ypsilanti, Mich.: High/Scope Press, 1984.

Multicultural Music (See also African American Music)

Anderson, William M. *Teaching Asian Musics in Elementary and Secondary Schools.* rev. ed. Danbury, Conn.: World Music Press, 1986.

Anderson, William M., and Patricia Shehan Campbell. *Multicultural Perspectives in Music Education.* Reston, Va.: Music Educators National Conference, 1989.

Fulton Fowke, Edith, and Richard Johnston. *Folk Songs of Canada.* Waterloo, Ontario, Canada: Waterloo Music Company, 1954.

George, Luvenia A. *Teaching the Music of Six Different Cultures.* rev. ed. Danbury, Conn.: World Music Press, 1988.

Heth, Charlotte, ed. *Native American Dance: Ceremonies and Social Traditions.* Washington, D.C.: National Museum of the American Indian, Smithsonian Institution with Starwood Publishing, Inc., 1992.

Horse Capture, George P. *Powwow.* Cody, Wyo.: Buffalo Bill Historical Center, 1989.

Rhodes, Robert. *Hopi Music and Dance.* Tsaile, Ariz.: Navajo Community College Press, 1977.

Speck, Frank G., Leonard Broom, and Will West Long. *Cherokee Dance and Drama.* Norman, Okla.: University of Oklahoma Press, 1983.

Titon, Jeff Todd, ed. *Worlds of Music: An Introduction to the Music of the World's Peoples.* 2nd ed. New York: Schirmer Books, 1992.

Orff

Frazee, Jane, and Kent Kreuter. *Discovering ORFF: A Curriculum for Music Teachers.* Valley Forge, Pa.: European American Music Distributors Corp., 1987.

Keetman, Gunild. *Elementaria, First Acquaintance with Orff-Schulwerk.* Valley Forge, Pa.: European American Music Distributors Corp., 1974.

Keller, Wilhelm. *Introduction to Music for Children.* Translated by Susan Kennedy. Valley Forge, Pa.: European American Music Distributors Corp., 1974.

Nash, Grace C., Geraldine W. Jones, Barbara A. Potter, and Patsy S. Smith. *Do It My Way: The Child's Way of Learning.* Sherman Oaks, Calif.: Alfred Publishing Co., 1977.

Orff, Carl, and Gunild Keetman. *Music for Children.* English version adapted from Orff-Schulwerk by Margaret Murray. 5 vols. London: Schott & Co., 1958–1966.

—. *Music for Children.* Canadian (North American) version adapted from Orff-Schulwerk by Doreen Hall and Arnold Walter. 5 vols. London: Schott & Co., 1956.

Regner, Hermann, ed. *Music for Children.* Vol. 2, *Orff-Schulwerk.* Valley Forge, Pa.: European American Music Distributors Corp., 1977.

Shamrock, Mary. "Orff Schulwerk: An Integrated Foundation." *Music Educators Journal* 72 (February 1986): 51–55.

Recorder

King, Carol. *Recorder Roots* (Books I–II). Memphis, Tenn.: Memphis Musicraft Publications, 1978 and 1984.

Signing

Gadling, Donna C., Pastor Daniel H. Pokorny, and Dr. Lottie L. Riekehof. *Lift Up Your Hands: Inspirational and Patriotic Songs in the Language of Signs.* Washington, D.C.: National Grange, 1975.

Kannapell, Barbara M., and Lillian B. Hamilton. *Songs in*

Signed English. Washington, D.C.: Gallaudet College Press, 1973.

Riekehof, Lottie L. *The Joy of Signing.* 2d ed. Springfield, Mo.: Gospel Publishing House, 1987.

Sternberg, Martin. *American Sign Language.* New York: Harper & Row Publishers, 1987.

Weaks, Donna Gadling. *Lift Up Your Hands.* Vol. 2, *Favorite Songs with Sign Language Interpretation.* Washington, D.C.: National Grange, 1980.

Special Learners

Atterbury, Betty W. *Mainstreaming Exceptional Learners in Music.* Englewood Cliffs, N.J.: Prentice-Hall, 1990.

Cassidy, J.W., and W.L. Sims. "What's In a Name?" *General Music Today* 3 (3–1990). 23–24, 32.

Darrow, Alice-Ann. "Music for the Deaf." *Music Educators Journal* 71 (February 1985): 33–35.

Graham, Richard M., and Alice S. Beer. *Teaching Music to the Exceptional Child: A Handbook for Mainstreaming.* Englewood Cliffs, N.J.: Prentice-Hall, 1980.

Hughes, J.E. "Sing everyone." *General Music Today,* 4 (2–1991), 8–9.

Jellison, J.A. "A Content Analysis of Music Research with Handicapped Children and Youth (1975–1986): Applications in Special Education." In C.K. Furman (ed.), *Effectiveness of Music Therapy Procedures: Documentation in Research and Clinical Practice* (pp. 223–279). Washington, D.C.: National Association for Music Therapy, 1988.

——. "Functional Value as Criterion for Selection and Prioritization of Nonmusic and Music Educational Objectives in Music Therapy." *Music Therapy Perspectives,* 1 (2–1983), 17–22.

——, B.H. Brooks, and A.M. Huck. Structure Small Groups and Music Reinforcement to Facilitate Positive Interactions and Acceptance of Severely Handicapped Students in Regular Music Classrooms." *Journal of Research in Music Education* 39 (1984), 322–333.

——. "Talking About Music: Interviews with Disabled and Nondisabled Children." *Journal of Research in Music Education,* 39 (1991), 322–333.

——. "Writing and Talking About Children with Disabilities. *General Music Today,* 4 (1–1990), 25–26.

Lam, Rita C., and Cecilia Wang. "Integrating Blind and Sighted Through Music." *Music Educators Journal* 68 (April 1982): 44-45.

Pennington, H.D. "Acceptance and Expectations of Disabled Students in Music Classes" *General Music Today* 5 (1–1991), 31.

Technology

JVC Video Anthology of World Music and Dance. Victor Company of Japan and Smithsonian/Folkways Recordings, 1991. Distributed by New England Networks, 61 Prospect Street, Montpelier, Vt. 05602

MetroGnomes' Music (MS-DOS, 640K, CGA, or better display, 3.5" or 5.25" drive, hard drive and sound card recommended). Fremont, Calif.: The Learning Co.

Note Play (MS-DOS/Windows, MIDI keyboard optional). Available through Educational Resource, Elgin, Ill.

Piano Works (MS-DOS, 640K, CGA, or better display, 3.5" or 5.25" floppy drive and hard drive, MIDI interface and keyboard). Bellevue, Wash.: Temporal Acuity Products.

Soloist (MS-DOS, 286K, Sound Blaster sound card, microphone). Ibis Software, available through Educational Resource, Elgin, Ill.

Vocal Development/Choral Music

Bartle, Jean Ashworth. *Lifeline for Children's Choir Directors.* Toronto: Gordon V. Thompson Music, 1988.

Cooksey, John M. *Working with the Adolescent Voice.* St. Louis: Concordia Publishing House, 1992.

Heffernan, Charles W. *Choral Music: Technique and Artistry.* Englewood Cliffs, N.J.: Prentice-Hall, 1982.

May, William V., and Craig Tolin. *Pronunciation Guide for Choral Literature.* Reston, Va.: Music Educators National Conference, 1987.

Rao, Doreen. *Choral Music Experience Education Through Artistry.* Vol. 1, *Artistry in Music Education;* Vol. 2, *The Artist in Every Child; Vol. 5, The Young Singing Voice.* New York: Boosey & Hawkes, 1987.

Swears, Linda. *Teaching the Elementary School Chorus.* Englewood Cliffs, N.J.: Prentice-Hall, 1984.

OPTIONS FOR SCHEDULING   Grades K–5 (See p. 416 for Grade 6.)

FOR MUSIC SPECIALISTS   Music Once a Week   9- or 12-month schools

UNIT 1	UNIT 2	UNIT 3	UNIT 4	UNIT 5	UNIT 6
CORE Lessons 1, 2, 4, 5	CORE Lessons 1, 2, 4, 5	CORE Lessons 1, 2, 4, 5	CORE Lessons 1, 2, 4, 5	CORE Lessons 1, 2, 4, 5	CORE Lessons 1, 2, 4, 5
Lesson 9 Review and Assessment (optional)	Lesson 9 Review and Assessment (optional)	Lesson 9 Review and Assessment (optional)	Lesson 9 Review and Assessment (optional)	Lesson 9 Review and Assessment (optional)	Lesson 9 Review and Assessment (optional)

IN ADDITION TO CORE LESSONS, CHOOSE FROM	
ACROSS THE CURRICULUM	Curriculum integration activities after CORE Lessons 1, 2, 4, 5
ENCORE	After each unit
CELEBRATIONS	Seasonal, holiday, patriotic songs to integrate into the units
MUSIC LIBRARY	More Songs to Read Choral Anthology (Grades 4, 5, and 6) Listening Anthology Musical
HAL LEONARD SHOWSTOPPERS	Highly motivational popular songs

OUR AUTHORS RECOMMEND:
SEQUENCED INSTRUCTION for ONCE-A-WEEK LESSONS

TIME FRAME (36 weeks / 36 lessons)

- CORE Lessons 1, 2, 4, 5 in all six units in consecutive teaching order
- Review and Assessment—Lesson 9 in each unit (optional)
- Selections from TIME FOR SINGING!, ACROSS THE CURRICULUM, MORE SONGS TO SING, ENCORE, CELEBRATIONS, MUSIC LIBRARY, and HAL LEONARD SHOWSTOPPERS

FOR MUSIC SPECIALISTS   Music Twice a Week   9- or 12-month schools

UNIT 1	UNIT 2	UNIT 3	UNIT 4	UNIT 5	UNIT 6
CORE Lessons 1, 2, 4, 5	CORE Lessons 1, 2, 4, 5	CORE Lessons 1, 2, 4, 5	CORE Lessons 1, 2, 4, 5	CORE Lessons 1, 2, 4, 5	CORE Lessons 1, 2, 4, 5
Non-CORE Lessons 3, 6, 7, 8	Non-CORE Lessons 3, 6, 7, 8	Non-CORE Lessons 3, 6, 7, 8	Non-CORE Lessons 3, 6, 7, 8	Non-CORE Lessons 3, 6, 7, 8	Non-CORE Lessons 3, 6, 7, 8
Lesson 9 Review and Assessment	Lesson 9 Review and Assessment	Lesson 9 Review and Assessment	Lesson 9 Review and Assessment	Lesson 9 Review and Assessment	Lesson 9 Review and Assessment

IN ADDITION, CHOOSE FROM	
ACROSS THE CURRICULUM	Curriculum integration activities after CORE Lessons 1, 2, 4, 5
ENCORE	After each unit
CELEBRATIONS	Seasonal, holiday, patriotic songs to integrate into the units
MUSIC LIBRARY	More Songs to Read Choral Anthology (Grades 4, 5, and 6) Listening Anthology Musical
HAL LEONARD SHOWSTOPPERS	Highly motivational popular songs

OUR AUTHORS RECOMMEND:
SEQUENCED INSTRUCTION for TWICE-A-WEEK LESSONS

TIME FRAME (36 weeks / 72 lessons)

- CORE and Non-CORE lessons in all six units in consecutive teaching order
- Selected activities from *Meeting Individual Needs* sections of lessons
- Review and Assessment—Lesson 9 in each unit
- Selections from TIME FOR SINGING!, ACROSS THE CURRICULUM, MORE SONGS TO SING, ENCORE, CELEBRATIONS, MUSIC LIBRARY, and HAL LEONARD SHOWSTOPPERS

TO ORGANIZE TEACHING BY SPECIFIC THEMES, SEE THE *Thematic* INDEX AT THE BACK OF THIS BOOK.

OPTIONS FOR SCHEDULING

FOR CLASSROOM TEACHERS Grades K–5   9- or 12-month schools

UNIT 1	UNIT 2	UNIT 3	UNIT 4	UNIT 5	UNIT 6
CORE Lessons 1, 2, 4, 5 ▶ Basic Program activities	CORE Lessons 1, 2, 4, 5 ▶ Basic Program activities	CORE Lessons 1, 2, 4, 5 ▶ Basic Program activities	CORE Lessons 1, 2, 4, 5 ▶ Basic Program activities	CORE Lessons 1, 2, 4, 5 ▶ Basic Program activities	CORE Lessons 1, 2, 4, 5 ▶ Basic Program activities

IN ADDITION TO CORE LESSONS, CHOOSE FROM	
ACROSS THE CURRICULUM	Curriculum integration activities after CORE Lessons 1, 2, 4, 5
ENCORE	After each unit
CELEBRATIONS	Seasonal, holiday, patriotic songs to integrate into the units
MUSIC LIBRARY	More Songs to Read Choral Anthology (Grades 4, 5, and 6) Listening Anthology Musical
HAL LEONARD SHOWSTOPPERS	Highly motivational popular songs

OUR AUTHORS RECOMMEND:

SEQUENCED INSTRUCTION for ONCE-A-WEEK LESSONS

TIME FRAME (36 weeks / 36 lessons)

- Basic Program activities shown with ▶ symbol from CORE Lessons 1, 2, 4, 5 in all six units in consecutive teaching order
- Selections from Non-CORE lessons, TIME FOR SINGING!, ACROSS THE CURRICULUM, MORE SONGS TO SING, ENCORE, CELEBRATIONS, MUSIC LIBRARY, and HAL LEONARD SHOWSTOPPERS

FOR CLASSROOM TEACHERS Grade 6   9- or 12-month schools

CORE UNIT 1 Music Makers	UNIT 2 Musical Adventures	UNIT 3 The Keyboard Connection	UNIT 4 Our Musical Heritage	UNIT 5 On Stage
CORE Lessons 1–8 ▶ Basic Program activities	CORE Lessons 1, 2, 4, 5 ▶ Basic Program activities	CORE Lessons 1, 2, 4, 5 ▶ Basic Program activities	CORE Lessons 1, 2, 4, 5 ▶ Basic Program activities	CORE Lessons 1, 2, 4, 5 ▶ Basic Program activities

IN ADDITION TO CORE LESSONS, CHOOSE FROM	
UNIT 6 FROM RAG TO RAP	Eras of American music history
ACROSS THE CURRICULUM	Curriculum integration activities after CORE lessons
ENCORE	After each unit
CELEBRATIONS	Seasonal, holiday, patriotic songs to integrate into the units
MUSIC LIBRARY	More Songs to Read Choral Anthology (Grades 4, 5, and 6) Listening Anthology Musical
HAL LEONARD SHOWSTOPPERS	Highly motivational popular songs

OUR AUTHORS RECOMMEND:

SEQUENCED INSTRUCTION for ONCE-A-WEEK LESSONS

TIME FRAME (36 weeks / 36 lessons)

- Basic Program activities shown with ▶ symbol from CORE lessons in Units 1–5 in consecutive teaching order
- Selections from Unit 6, Non-CORE lessons, TIME FOR SINGING!, ACROSS THE CURRICULUM, MORE SONGS TO SING, ENCORE, CELEBRATIONS, MUSIC LIBRARY, and HAL LEONARD SHOWSTOPPERS

▶**Basic Program** activities for classroom teachers can be taught with a minimum background in music.

TO ORGANIZE TEACHING BY SPECIFIC THEMES, SEE THE *Thematic* INDEX AT THE BACK OF THIS BOOK.

OPTIONS FOR SCHEDULING Grade 6 (See p. 414 for Grade K–5.)

FOR ELEMENTARY OR MIDDLE SCHOOL MUSIC SPECIALISTS
9- or 12-month schools

CORE UNIT 1 Music Makers	UNIT 2 Musical Adventures	UNIT 3 The Keyboard Connection	UNIT 4 Our Musical Heritage	UNIT 5 On Stage
CORE Lessons 1–8	CORE Lessons 1, 2, 4, 5	CORE Lessons 1, 2, 4, 5	CORE Lessons 1, 2, 4, 5	CORE Lessons 1, 2, 4, 5
ALSO INCLUDE FOR TWICE A WEEK OR DAILY				
	Non-CORE Lessons 3, 6, 7, 8	Non-CORE Lessons 3, 6, 7, 8	Non-CORE Lessons 3, 6, 7, 8	Non-CORE Lessons 3, 6, 7, 8
Lesson 9 Review and Assessment	Lesson 9 Review and Assessment	Lesson 9 Review and Assessment	Lesson 9 Review and Assessment	Lesson 9 Review and Assessment

IN ADDITION, CHOOSE FROM	
UNIT 6 FROM RAG TO RAP	Eras of American music history
ACROSS THE CURRICULUM	Curriculum integration activities after CORE lessons
ENCORE	After each unit
CELEBRATIONS	Seasonal, holiday, patriotic songs to integrate into the units
MUSIC LIBRARY	More Songs to Read Choral Anthology Listening Anthology Musical
HAL LEONARD SHOWSTOPPERS	Highly motivational popular songs

FOR SEQUENCED INSTRUCTION, OUR AUTHORS RECOMMEND:

FOR ELEMENTARY MUSIC SPECIALISTS

TIME FRAME (twice a week, 36 lessons per semester)

- Unit 1 lessons in consecutive teaching order
- CORE lessons in Units 2–5 in consecutive teaching order
- Review and Assessment, Lesson 9, in Units 1–5
- Selections from Unit 6, TIME FOR SINGING!, ACROSS THE CURRICULUM, MORE SONGS TO SING, ENCORE, CELEBRATIONS, MUSIC LIBRARY, and HAL LEONARD SHOWSTOPPERS
- Selected activities from *Meeting Individual Needs* sections of lessons

FOR MIDDLE SCHOOL MUSIC SPECIALISTS

TIME FRAME (daily, 45 lessons per 9-week course)

- Unit 1 lessons in consecutive teaching order
- CORE lessons in Units 2–5 in consecutive teaching order
- Selected Non-CORE lessons in Units 2–5
- Review and Assessment, Lesson 9, in Units 1–5
- Selections from Unit 6, TIME FOR SINGING!, ACROSS THE CURRICULUM, MORE SONGS TO SING, ENCORE, CELEBRATIONS, MUSIC LIBRARY, and HAL LEONARD SHOWSTOPPERS
- Selected activities from *Meeting Individual Needs* sections of lessons

FOR MIDDLE SCHOOL MUSIC SPECIALISTS

TIME FRAME (daily, 90 lessons per semester)

- Unit 1 lessons in consecutive teaching order
- CORE and Non-CORE lessons in Units 2–5 in consecutive teaching order
- Review and Assessment, Lesson 9, in Units 1–5
- Selections from Unit 6, TIME FOR SINGING!, ACROSS THE CURRICULUM, MORE SONGS TO SING, ENCORE, CELEBRATIONS, MUSIC LIBRARY, and HAL LEONARD SHOWSTOPPERS
- Selected activities from *Meeting Individual Needs* sections of lessons

For Grades 7 and 8: The Grade 6 book can be used flexibly in Grades 7 and 8.

TO ORGANIZE TEACHING BY SPECIFIC THEMES, SEE THE *Thematic* INDEX AT THE BACK OF THIS BOOK.

THEMATIC INDEX

Stories and Tales. *Every culture has stories that are passed on through generations.*

Traditions. *Traditions enrich special celebrations as well as our daily lives. See* Classified Index: Folk Music; Holiday, Seasonal, Patriotic Music; Multicultural Materials

Travel. *Trips to places old and new can bring adventure.*

CLASSIFIED INDEX

Accompaniments. *See* Instruments, Playing; Ostinatos; Texture

Artists. *See* Biographies; Fine Art Reproductions and Architecture

Assessment
creative
Unit 1, 47
Unit 2, 95
Unit 3, 147
Unit 4, 195
Unit 5, 241
Unit 6, 289
formal
Unit 1, 46
Unit 2, 94
Unit 3, 146
Unit 4, 194
Unit 5, 240
Unit 6, 288
music journal
Critical Thinking, 27, 38, 63, 69, 81, 127
discussion of imagined rap, 185
discussion of musical elements, 211, 256, 259, 271
journal, 266
response to fine art, 26
response to listening selection, 121
Think It Through, 25, 39, 65, 79, 122, 133, 137, 171, 187, 225, 276
Write, 47, 95, 147, 195, 241, 289
portfolio
assessment ideas, 46, 94, 146, 194, 240, 288
composition, 38, 82, 137, 154, 186, 271, 284
conducting, 214
create, 47, 95, 147, 194, 195, 241, 289
graphic notation, 14, 20, 29, 137, 186
improvising, 189, 190, 236
instrumental performance, 19, 31, 38, 58, 77, 87, 115, 127, 129, 164, 169, 174, 181, 188, 211, 225, 229, 231, 256, 259, 261, 265, 266, 279
meters, recognition and use, 206, 208
movement performance, 43, 122
musical notation, 26, 27, 38, 78, 154
pitch names, recognition and use, 78, 126, 221
pitch syllables, recognition and use, 30, 34, 36, 82, 124, 178, 218
rhythm patterns, recognition and use, 64, 74, 130, 131, 142, 154, 173, 174, 224, 270
vocal performance, 20, 74, 159, 186, 236, 260, 261, 271, 284
Write, 47, 95, 147, 195, 241, 289

Bilingual Songs. *See also* Non-English Language Selections
En la feria de San Juan (In the Market of San Juan), 66

Hei Tama Tu Tama, 212
Somos el barco (We Are the Boat), 4

Biographies. *See also* Careers
artists
Bankhead, Irene, 201
Frankenthaler, Helen, 123
Haring, Keith, 277
Pressley, Daniel, 229
Rivera, Diego, 141
Shahn, Benjamin, 26
authors
Greenfield, Eloise, 184
Heide, Florence Parry, 251
Tolkien, John Ronald Reuel, 55
choreographer
Robinson, Cleo Parker, 103
composers
Bernstein, Leonard, 385I
Britten, Benjamin, 197
Carreño, Maria Teresa, 116
Cheney, Martha, 118
Copland, Aaron, 178–179
Dvořák, Antonin, 226
Ellington, Duke, 10
Grainger, Percy Aldridge, 130–131
Handel, George Frideric, 385A
Ives, Charles, 302
Janequin, Clément, 383
Mozart, Wolfgang Amadeus, 385D
Mussorgsky, Modest, 70
Palmer, Hap, 118
Poulenc, Francis, 217
Praetorius, Michael, 127
Prokofiev, Sergei, 32–33
Richardson, Anthony Q., 255
Schubert, Franz, 385E
Stravinsky, Igor, 385H
Sullivan, Sir Arthur, 96
Susato, Tielman, 232
Tower, Joan, 385K
Vaughan Williams, Ralph, 383
dancers
Fields, Gary, 152
Robinson, Cleo Parker, 103
historical figures
Edison, Thomas, 292
King, Jr., Dr. Martin Luther, 336
Lincoln, Abraham, 340
lyricists
Chavez, Julius, 120
Gilbert, Sir William, 96
performers
Armstrong, Louis, 10
Basie, Count, 10
Carreño, Maria Teresa, 116
Chavez, Julius, 120
Denver, John, 208
Fields, Gary, 152
Fitzgerald, Ella, 10
Kelly, Gene, 101
McFerrin, Bobby, 20

McPartland, Marian, 190
Miller, Glenn, 10
Monk, Thelonious, 200
Parker, Charlie, 198
Siva, Ernest, 150
Zurita, Edgar, 151
poets
Hoberman, Mary Ann, 270
Livingston, Myra Cohn, 155
Milne, A.A., 374
Sandburg, Carl, 307
Schupman, Edwin, 153
Thompson, Earl, 105

Body Percussion. *See* Duration/Rhythm; Ostinatos

Bulletin Boards
Be a Good Friend, 154
Challenge of Change, 250
Musical Journey, 8

Canons. *See* Rounds/Canons

Careers. *See also* Biographies
artist
Haring, Keith, 277
author
Greenfield, Eloise, 184
Heide, Florence Parry, 251
Tolkien, John Ronald Reuel, 55
choreographer
Robinson, Cleo Parker, 103
composer
Bernstein, Leonard, 385I
Britten, Benjamin, 197
Copland, Aaron, 178–179
Richardson, Anthony Q., 255
Tower, Joan, 385K
dancer
Robinson, Cleo Parker, 103
educator
Richardson, Anthony Q., 255
other
arranger, 21
composer, movie and television, 258
music journalist, 63
recording engineer, 295
session musician, 27
performer
Denver, John, 208
McPartland, Marian, 190

Chants. *See* Alphabetical Index of Songs and Speech Pieces

Choral Music. *See* Part Songs

Chords
based on *do* and *so,*, 133–134
based on *do, fa* and *so,* 323, 329
changes, identifying, 180, 182–183, 338
definition of, 180
playing, 183, 188, 323, 329
root of, 182, 323

PITCH AND RHYTHM INDEX

The Pitch and Rhythm Index provides a listing of songs for teaching specific rhythms or pitches. Songs that use only the rhythms or pitches under the heading are labeled *entire*. Specific measure numbers are indicated in parentheses when the rhythms or pitches apply to part of a song. The letter *a* indicates that the anacrusis to the measure is included.

Pitch Index: The pitch index is organized by teaching sequence. Within each category, the pitch sets are arranged alphabetically.

Rhythm Index: The headings in the rhythm index are listed by duration, from shortest to longest. Rhythms in § meter are grouped together at the end of the index. Other known rhythms used in the specified measures are listed after the meter signature of each entry.

Pitch

MI SO

Macnamara's Band (a1–2, a9–10, a17–18, a25–26), 342
'Way Down Yonder in the Brickyard (1–2, 5–6), 17

LA

mi so la
Before Dinner (entire), 362
California Song, The (a1–2, a5–6, a13–14), 48
Dale, dale, dale! (9–10, 13–14, 17–18, 21–22), 322
Fed My Horse (1–2, 5–6), 31
Mince Pie or Pudding, A (3–4), 311
Page's Train (1–2), 349
Pay Me My Money Down (a1–2, 9–10), 111

DO

do mi
Oh, Won't You Sit Down? (9–10, 13–14), 2
Who's Got a Fishpole? (1, 3), 364

do mi so
Hop Up and Jump Up (2, 4–5, 8), 363

do mi so la
Ida Red (5–6), 352
Lots o' Fish in Bonavist' Harbor (1–3, 6–7, 10–12), 359
When I First Came to This Land (1–4, 9–12, 21–24), 148

do so
To Stop the Train (3–4), 361

RE

do re mi
Ah, Poor Bird (2, 4), 368

Babylon's Fallin' (entire), 348
Bonhomme! Bonhomme! (a9–10), 312
Boogie Woogie Ghost, The (11–12), 304
Dormi, dormi (Sleep, Sleep) (1–4, 13–16), 328
Down by the Riverside (3–4, 7–8, 11–12, a19–23), 338
Down the Road (1–2), 76
Dry Bones (a1–9, a26–35), 308
Fed My Horse (9–12), 31
Go 'Round the Mountain (entire), 347
Hei Tama Tu Tama (1–6), 212
Hi! Ho! The Rattlin' Bog (a9–10, a13–14), 23
I Don't Care If the Rain Comes Down (1–2, 5–8, 11–12, 15–16), 108
La pájara pinta (The Speckled Bird) (9–10), 110
Michie Banjo (3–4), 264
Night Song (entire), 347
Oh, Won't You Sit Down? (5–16), 2
Tina Singu (3–4, 7–8), 158

do re mi so
Boogie Woogie Ghost, The (10–13), 304
Court of King Carraticus, The (a1–4, a7–8), 263
Dinah (entire), 351
John Kanaka (1–16, 21–24), 367
Lady, Come Down and See (a3–4), 350
San lun tsa (Three-Wheeled Taxi) (1), 366
Trail to Mexico (a5–6), 59
'Way Down Yonder in the Brickyard (1–8, 11–12, 15–16, 19–20, 23–24), 17

do re mi so la
California Song, The (a1–8, a13–16), 48
Fed My Horse (entire), 31
I Am a Cat (entire), 349
Ida Red (entire), 352
Little David, Play on Your Harp (9–13), 168
Martin's Cry (1–10), 336
Mince Pie or Pudding, A (3–8), 311
One More River (a9–16), 112
Page's Train (entire), 349
Sourwood Mountain (3–4, 7–8, 11–12, 15–16), 196

SO₁

so₁ do re mi
Alouette (1–4), 371

so₁ do re mi so
Lady, Come Down and See (entire), 350
Macnamara's Band (a1–4, a9–12, a17–20, a25–28), 342

so₁ do re mi so la
Heave-Ho Me Laddies (a5–17), 356
One More River (entire), 112

LA₁

la₁ do re mi
Artsa Alinu (Our Land) (1–4), 369
Eagle, The (a5–7, a22–29), 118

Hoe Ana Te Vaka (Paddle the Canoe) (3–4, 19–20), 181
Mongolian Night Song (entire), 19
Old Tar River (9–12), 355
Sir Duke (1–2, 5–6, 16–17, 20–21), 10

so₁ la₁
Trail to Mexico (vocal ostinato) (entire), 59

so₁ la₁ do
Swapping Song (1–4), 82
We Three Kings (13–16, 21–24), 329

so₁ la₁ do mi
Who's Got a Fishpole? (1–3), 364

so₁ la₁ do re mi
Bonhomme! Bonhomme! (a10–11, a14–15), 312
Chickalileeo (entire), 368
Down by the Riverside (a1–12, a19–23), 338
Down the Road (entire), 76
Hi! Ho! The Rattlin' Bog (1–6, a9–10, a13–14), 23
Oh, Won't You Sit Down? (entire), 2
Old Dan Tucker (1–12, a15–16), 360
Old Chisholm Trail, The (a5), 354
Old Tar River (1–4, 9–16), 355
Push the Business On (a1–4, a9–12), 245
Swapping Song (entire), 82

so₁ la₁ do re mi so
Old Dan Tucker (entire), 360
Old Tar River (entire), 355
Over the Sea to Skye (entire), 149
Singin' in the Rain (a1–12, a17–21), 100

so₁ la₁ do re mi so la
Derby Ram, The (entire), 358
Heave-Ho Me Laddies (entire), 356
Little David, Play on Your Harp (entire), 168
Old Chisholm Trail, The (entire), 354
Sourwood Mountain (1–8, 11–12, 15–16), 196
Trail to Mexico (entire), 59

so₁ la₁ mi
Old Carrion Crow, The (3–4, a7–10, 17–18), 62

DO'

do mi so la do'
Hop Up and Jump Up (entire), 363
This Is My Country (1–8), 7

do re mi so do'
I Don't Care If the Rain Comes Down (1–2, 5–8, 9–16), 108
San lun tsa (Three-Wheeled Taxi) (1, 3–4), 366

do re mi so la do'
Dale, dale, dale! (a1–4), 322
John Kanaka (entire), 367
Lots o' Fish in Bonavist' Harbor (1–3, 6–12, 15–16), 359

PROGRAM CONSULTANTS

Contributing Writer
Janet McMillion
St. Louis, MO

Consultant Writers
Teri Burdette, Signing
Gaithersburg, MD

Brian Burnett, Movement
Toledo, OH

Robert Duke, Assessment
Austin, TX

Joan Gregoryk,
Vocal Development/Choral
Washington, D.C.

Judith Jellison,
Special Learners/Assessment
Austin, TX

Jacque Schrader, Movement
Annapolis, MD

Kathy B. Sorensen,
International Phonetic Alphabet
Salt Lake City, UT

Mollie Tower, Listening
Austin, TX

Consultants
Lisa DeLorenzo, Critical Thinking
Upper Montclair, NJ

Nancy Ferguson, Jazz/Improvisation
Somerville, TN

Judith Nayer, Poetry
New York, NY

Marta Sanchez, Dalcroze
Pittsburgh, PA

Mollie Tower, Reviewer
Austin, TX

Robyn Turner, Fine Arts
Austin, TX

Multicultural Consultants
Judith Cook Tucker
Danbury, CT

JaFran Jones
Bowling Green, OH

Oscar Muñoz
Olympia, WA

Marta Sanchez
Pittsburgh, PA

Edwin J. Schupman, Jr.,
of ORBIS Associates
Spokane, WA

Mary Shamrock
Northridge, CA

Kathy B. Sorensen
Salt Lake City, UT

Visual and Performing Arts Contributors
Barbara Becker, Visual Arts
Los Angeles, CA

Karen Goodkin, Visual Arts
San Francisco, CA

David Robinson, Theater
Stockton, CA

Arlene Shmaeff, Visual Arts
Oakland, CA

Sue Walton, Theater
San Francisco, CA

Ancillary Contributors
Angela Broeker, Resource Masters
New Wilmington, PA

Teri Burdette, Signing
Gaithersburg, MD

Cindy Hall, Recorder
Whitefish Bay, WI

Jo Ella Hug, Recorder
Missoula, MT

Eleanor T. Locke, Songs to Sing and Read
Oakland, CA

Jerry Snyder, Playing the Guitar
Monte Sereno, CA

Patti Windes-Bridges, Playing the Guitar
Cave Creek, AZ

Lesson Contributors
Our thanks to these music educators for their contributions of classroom-tested lessons, materials, and strategies.

Sylvia Arieta (El Paso, TX), Margie King Barab (New York, NY), Patti Beckham (Lake Oswego, OR), Nancy Boone (Murfreesboro, TN), Ruth Boshkoff (Bloomington, IN), Madeline S. Bridges (Nashville, TN), Jay Broeker (New Wilmington, PA), Susanne Burgess (Memphis, TN), Randy DeLelles (Las Vegas, NV), Virginia Ebinger (Los Alamos, NM), Carol Erion (Alexandria, VA), Rhona Ewbank (Pasadena, TX), Cindy Hall

(Whitefish Bay, WI), Ruth Pollock Hamm (Mayfield, OH), Carol Huffman (North Olmsted, OH), Sarah Kastendieck (Fort Collins, CO), Susan Kennedy (San Francisco, CA), Robert Kikuchi-Yngojo (San Francisco, CA), Laura Koulish (New York, NY), Jeff Kriske (Las Vegas, NV), Judy Mahoney-Green (Albuquerque, NM), David Means (Northfield, MN), Karen Medley (Memphis, TN), Ellen Mendelsohn (New Milford, NJ), Isabel Miranda (Oxnard, CA), Janet L. S. Moore (Tampa, FL), Grace Nash (Tallahassee, FL), Konnie Saliba (Cordova, TN), Vicky Salmon (Pasadena, CA), Marcelyn Smale (St. Cloud, MN), Anna Marie Spallina (New York, NY), Todd Thompson (Northfield, MN), Wendy Ulmer (Woolrich, ME), Joy Yelin (Yonkers, NY), Alexis A. Zolczer (Orchard Park, NY)

Across the Curriculum Contributors
Our thanks to these teachers for their classroom-tested Across the Curriculum activities.

Patti Beckham (Lake Oswego, OR), Brenda Cook (Bakersfield, CA), Mary Jo Gardere (Dallas, TX), Elaine Hewes (Blue Hill, ME), Carol Huffman (North Olmsted, OH), Jane Livingston (Veazie, ME), Alice Bremer Moersch (Northfield, MN), Marilyn Moore (Normal, IL), Diane De Nicola Orlofsky (Troy, AL), Mary Sturbaum (Bloomington, IN)

Listening Map Contributors
Our thanks to these Texas educators for contributing listening maps to *Share the Music*.

Marilyn Buckner, Debra Erck, Kay Greenhaw, Rebecca Grusendorff, Melody A. Long, Sally K. Robberson, Diane Bethea Steele, Barb Stevanson, Debbie Tannert

National Music Advisory Committee
Our thanks to these music specialists, classroom teachers, and administrators for their valuable contributions in the development of *Share the Music*.

Betty Adkins (Shreveport, LA), Susan Ahmad (Alpharetta, GA), Carol Albright (Holidaysburg, PA), Earl Alexander (Lake Charles, LA), George Alter (Kansas City, MO), Claude Anderson (East Chicago, IN), Kathy Anderson (Mt. View, CA), Thom Antang (Campbell, CA), Christine Aparicio-Chaulsett (Los Angeles, CA), Sylvia Arieta (El Paso, TX), Saundra Ashworth (San Antonio, TX), Missy Atterbury (Edmond, OK), Eleanor Avant (Columbia, SC), Patti Beckham (Lake Oswego, OR), Sue Bertsche (Chicago, IL), Maureen Best (Chatham, IL), Patsy Biendenfield (Houston, TX), Ron Blackgrave (Indianapolis, IN), Victor Bobetsky (Hartford, CT), Judy Boelts (Fairbanks, AK), Earlene Brasher (Decatur, GA), Pat Brown (Knoxville, TN), Teddye Brown (Arlington, TX), Bruce Brumley (Mt. Sterling, KY), Bryan Burton (West Chester, PA), Doris Butler (Florence,

KY), Bettie Carroll (Dayton, OH), Jo Ellen Clow (Broken Arrow, OK), Deborah Cook (Roselle, NJ), Nancy Cox (Altus, OK), Robert Crisp (Detroit, MI), Don Davis (Jacksonville, AR), William Downes (Louisville, KY), Neiltje Dunham (Nashua, NH), Mary Frances Early (Atlanta, GA), Donya Easterly (Clear Creek, TX), Marie Esquibel (Albuquerque, NM), Laura Floyd-Cole (Carson, CA), Renée Forrest (Madison, WI), Enrique Franco (Los Angeles, CA), Sister Pat Gilgum (St. Louis, MO), Michelle Goady (Dallas, TX), Cathy Graham (Antioch, TN), Brian Halverson (San Antonio, TX), Katherine Heide (Kenosha, WI), Debbie Hess (Bloomington, IN), Peggy Horner (Altoona, PA), Anne-Marie Hudley (Bronx, NY), Karen Huff (Granville, OH), Jo Ella Hug (Missoula, MT), Janice Hupp (Wichita, KS), Joan Jemison (Minneapolis, MN), Steven Johns (Nokomis, FL), Sandy Jude (Winchester, KY), Nancy Kielian-Boyd (East Grand Rapids, MI), Dorothy Kittaka (Ft. Wayne, IN), Tom Kosmala (Pittsburgh, PA), Margaret B. LaFleur (Minneapolis, MN), Guido Lavorata (Chandler, AZ), Joanne Lawrence (Ellicott City, MD), Brenda Lucas (Lexington, KY), Lana Manson (Chicago Heights, IL), Doug Martin (Atlanta, GA), Sheridan Matheison (Lexington, MA), Cindy McCaskill (Boulder, CO), Sherry McKelfresh (Ft. Collins, CO), Dorothy Millard (Skokie, IL), Clayton Miller (New Rochelle, NY), Ruth Millner (Dallas, TX), Violeta Morejon (Miami, FL), Jim Morris (Athens, GA), Denise Moulton (Richardson, TX), Sharon Munson (Delavan, WI), Kathleen Myers (Altoona, PA), Darolyne Nelson (Tempe, AZ), Hal Nelson (Tampa, FL), Larita Owens (Topeka, KS), Mary Ozanne (Plano, TX), Paula Pheasant (Tyrone, PA), Josephine Poelinitz (Chicago, IL), Pam Price (Grapevine, TX), Yolanda Rippetoe (San Antonio, TX), Marcia Rober (Arlington, TX), Joe Royster (Lake City, FL), Juyne Sauer (Houston, TX), Ruth Sauls (Austin, TX), Kathleen Shepler (Louisville, KY), Linda Singleton (Nashville, TN), Gloria Sousa (Monterey, CA), Gwen Spells (Marietta, GA), Sue Stanger (Los Angeles, CA), Gwendolyn

Staten (Indianapolis, IN), Doris Stewart (Muncie, IN), Judy Svengalis (Des Moines, IA), Rose Marie Terada (Boulder, CO), Doris Terry (Macon, GA), Jean Thomas (Chattanooga, TN), Bonnie Thurston (Santa Cruz, CA), Doug Turpin (St. Louis, MO), Robert Ullom (Columbus, OH), Dianne Vernon (Dallas, TX), Barbara Waite (Evansville, IN), Mamie Watson (San Antonio, TX), Timothy Waugh (Bluefield, WV), Craig Welle (Houston, TX), Jo Welty (Amarillo, TX), Joann Whorwell (Kokomo, IN), Euranie Williams (Dallas, TX), Tobizena Williams (Dallas, TX), Charles W. Winslow, Jr. (Richardson, TX), Melinda Winther (Spokane, WA), Mary Wright (Omaha, NE), Pam Ziegler (Austin, TX)

Multicultural Advisors

Dennis Waring, Ethnomusicologist, Wesleyan University, Middletown, CT

Shailaja Akkapeddi (Hindi), Edna Alba (Ladino), Gregory Amobi (Ibu), Thomas Appiah (Ga, Twi, Fanti), Deven Asay (Russian), Vera Auman (Russian, Ukrainian), David Azman (Hebrew), Lissa Bangeter (Portuguese), Britt Marie Barnes (Swedish), Dr. Mark Bell (French), Brad Ahawanrathe Bonaparte (Mohawk), Chhanda Chakroborti (Hindi), Ninthalangsonk Chanthasen (Laotian), Julius Chavez (Navajo), Lin-Rong Chen (Mandarin), Anna Cheng (Mandarin), Rushen Chi (Mandarin), T. L. Chi (Mandarin), Michelle Chingwa (Ottowa), Hoon Choi (Korean), James Comarell (Greek), Lynn DePaula (Portuguese), Ketan Dholakia (Gujarati), Richard O. Effiong (Nigerian), Nayereh Fallahi (Persian), Angela Fields (Hopi, Chemehuevi), Gary Fields (Lakota, Cree), Siri Veslemoy Fluge (Norwegian), Katalin Forrai (Hungarian), Renee Galagos (Swedish), Linda Goodman, Judith A. Gray, Savyasachi Gupta (Marati), Elizabeth Haile (Shinnecock), Mary Harouny (Persian), Charlotte Heth (Cherokee), Tim Hunt (Vietnamese), Marcela Janko (Czech), Raili

Jeffrey (Finnish), Rita Jensen (Danish), Teddy Kaiahura (Swahili), Gueen Kalaw (Tagalog), Merehau Kamai (Tahitian), Richard Keeling, Masanori Kimura (Japanese), Chikahide Komura (Japanese), Saul Korewa (Hebrew), Jagadishwar Kota (Tamil), Sokun Koy (Cambodian), Craig Kurumada (Balkan), Cindy Trong Le (Vietnamese), Dongchoon Lee (Korean), Young-Jing Lee (Korean), Nomi Lob (Hebrew), Sam Loeng (Mandarin, Malay), Georgia Magpie (Comanche), Mladen Marič (Croatian), Kuinise Matagi (Samoan), Hiromi Matsushita (Japanese), Jackie Maynard (Hawaiian), David McAllester, Ellen McCullough-Brabson, Mike Kanathohare McDonald (Mohawk), Khumbulani Mdlefshe (Zulu), Martin Mkize (Xhosa), David Montgomery (Turkish), Kazadi Big Musungayi (Swahili), Professor Akiya Nakamara (Japanese), Edwin Napia (Maori), Hang Nguyen (Vietnamese), Richard Nielsen (Danish), Wil Numkena (Hopi), Eva Ochoa (Spanish), Drora Oren (Hebrew), Jackie Osherow (Yiddish), Mavis Oswald (Russian), Dr. Dil Parkinson (Arabic), Kenny Tahawisoren Perkins (Mohawk), Alvin Petersen (Sotho), Phay Phan (Cambodian), Charlie Phim (Cambodian), Aroha Price (Maori), Marg Puiri (Samoan), John Rainer (Taos Pueblo, Creek), Lillian Rainer (Taos Pueblo, Creek, Apache), Winton Ria (Maori), Arnold Richardson (Haliwa-Saponi), Thea Roscher (German), Dr. Wayne Sabey (Japanese), Regine Saintil (Bamboula Creole), Luci Scherzer (German), Ken Sekaquaptewa (Hopi), Samouen Seng (Cambodian), Pei Shin (Mandarin), Dr. Larry Shumway (Japanese), Gwen Shunatona (Pawnee, Otoe, Potawatomi), Ernest Siva (Cahuilla, Serrano [Maringa']), Ben Snowball (Inuit), Dr. Michelle Stott (German), Keiko Tanefuji (Japanese), James Taylor (Portuguese), Shiu-wai Tong (Mandarin), Tom Toronto (Lao, Thai), Lynn Tran (Vietnamese), Gulavadee Vaz (Thai), Chen Ying Wang (Taiwanese), Masakazu Watabe (Japanese), Freddy Wheeler (Navajo), Keith Yackeyonny (Comanche), Liming Yang (Mandarin), Edgar Zurita (Andean)

Consultants and Contributors for *Share the Music* 2000

Allison Abucewicz
Middletown, Connecticut

Millie Burnett
Mirasol, California

Steven and Kathleen Hoover
Edwardsville, Illinois

Donna Harrell Lubcker
Marshall, Texas

Ellen Mendelsohn
New Milford, New Jersey

Marvette Pérez
Smithsonian Institution
Washington, D.C.

James Weaver
Smithsonian Institution
Washington, D.C.

ACKNOWLEDGMENTS

Grateful acknowledgment is given to the following authors, composers, and publishers. Every effort has been made to trace the ownership of all copyrighted material and to secure the necessary permissions to reprint these selections. In the case of some selections for which acknowledgment is not given, extensive research has failed to locate the copyright holders.

Fran Smartt Addicott for *Let Music Surround You.*

Allyn and Bacon, Inc. for *The Wabash Cannonball* by William Kindt.

American Folklore Society for *Stone Pounding,* edited by T. Grame. Reprinted by permission of the American Folklore Society.

Argus Magazine for *I Wonder How It Feels to Fly* by Earl Thompson. Courtesy of Argus Magazine, Seattle, WA.

Association for Childhood Education International for I *Wish (aka The Shiny Little House)* from SUNG UNDER THE SILVER UMBRELLA by Nancy M. Hayes. Reprinted by permission of the Association for Childhood Education International, 11141 Georgia Avenue, Suite 200, Wheaton, MD 20902. Copyright © 1935 by the Association.

Irving Berlin for *It's a Lovely Day Today.*

Boosey & Hawkes, Inc. for *The Derby Ram* by Peter Erdei from 150 AMERICAN FOLK SONGS. Copyright © 1974 by Boosey & Hawkes, Inc. Reprinted by permission. For *Dormi, Dormi,* arranged by Mary Goetze. Copyright © 1984 by Boosey & Hawkes, Inc. This arrangement is made with the permission of Boosey & Hawkes, Inc. Reprinted by permission. For *The Path to the Moon* by Eric H. Thiman and Madeline C. Thomas. For *A Tragic Story* from FRIDAY AFTERNOONS by Benjamin Britten. © 1936 by Boosey & Co., Ltd.; Copyright renewed. Reprinted by permission of Boosey & Hawkes, Inc. For *Troika* from LIEUTENANT KIJE by S. Prokofiev. © 1936 by Edition A. Guthiel. Copyright assigned to Boosey & Hawkes, Inc.; Copyright Renewed. Reprinted by permission.

Marie Brown Associates for *Nathaniel's Rap* by Eloise Greenfield. Reprinted by permission of MARIE BROWN ASSOCIATES; © 1988 by Eloise Greenfield.

Margaret Campbelle-Holman for *Allundé, Alluia.* Arranged by Margaret Campbelle-Holman. For *And Where Is Home?* by Margaret Campbelle-Holman.

Canadian Museum of Civilization for *Feller from Fortune (Lots of Fish in Bonavist' Harbour)* from SONGS ON THE NEWFOUNDLAND OUTPORTS by Kenneth Peacock. National Museum of Canada, Bulletin 197, Anthropological Series 65, vol. 1, Ottawa 1965.

Cherry Lane Music Publishing Company, Inc. for *Calypso* by John Denver. © 1975 Cherry Lane Music Publishing Company, Inc. This Arrangement © 1994 Cherry Lane Music Publishing Company, Inc. All Rights Reserved. Used By Permission. For *Garden Song* by David Mallet. © Copyright 1975 Cherry Lane Music Publishing Company, Inc. This Arrangement © Copyright 1994 Cherry Lane Music Publishing Company, Inc. For *Take Me Home, Country Roads.* Words and music by Bill Danoff, Taffy Nivert and John Denver.

Choristers Guild for *Come and Sing Together* from CANONS, SONGS AND BLESSINGS by Helen and John Kemp. Copyright © 1990 Choristers Guild. Used by permission.

Vernon Clark for *Martin's Cry* by Vernon Clark. © 1991 Vernon Clark.

CPP/Belwin, Inc. for *Donna Donna* by Sholom Secunda and Aaron Zeitlin. Copyright © 1940, 1950 (Renewed 1968) MILLS MUSIC INC., c/o EMI MUSIC PUBLISHING. World Print Rights Administered by CPP/BELWIN, INC. All Rights Reserved. For *Petrushka* by Igor Stravinsky. Copyright © E.M. KALMUS ORCHESTRA SCORES. Used by Permission of CPP/Belwin, Inc., Miami, FL. All Rights Reserved. For *Singin' in the Rain* by Nacio Herb Brown & Arthur Freed. Copyright © 1929 (Renewed 1957) METRO-GOLDWYN-MAYER, INC., Rights Assigned to ROBBINS MUSIC CORP. All Rights of ROBBINS MUSIC CORP. Assigned to EMI CATALOGUE PARTNERSHIP. All Rights Controlled and Administered by EMI ROBBINS CATALOG, INC. International Copyright Secured. Made in U.S.A. Used by Permission. For *Sir Duke* by Stevie Wonder. © 1976 by JOBETE MUSIC CO., INC., and BLACKBULL MUSIC, INC., Hollywood, CA. International Copyright Secured. Made in USA. All Rights Reserved.

Dover Publications Inc. for *The California Song* from SONGS THE WHALEMEN SANG by Gale Huntington. © 1970 Dover Publications, Inc.

Follett Publishing Co. for *Voices of the World* by Stefi Samuelson, 1963 Follett Publishing Co., used by permission of Prentice-Hall.

Fox Film Music Corporation for *Somewhere in My Memory* by John Williams and Leslie Bricusse.

Ganymede Music for THE GOLDEN GOOSE. © 1999 by Linda Worsley.

Hap-Pal Music for *The Eagle* by Hap Palmer and Martha Cheney. © 1976 Hap-Pal Music. Harcourt Brace Jovanovich, Inc. for *Hi! Ho! The Rattlin' Bog* from HI! HO! THE RATTLIN' BOG AND OTHER FOLK SONGS FOR GROUP SINGING, copyright © 1969 by John Langstaff, reprinted by permission of Harcourt Brace Jovanovich, Inc.

HarperCollins Publishers Ltd. for *Roads Go Ever Ever On* from THE HOBBIT by J.R.R. Tolkien. Published by George Allen & Unwin Ltd., an imprint of HarperCollins Publishers Ltd.

Florence Parry Heide for *Rocks* by Florence Parry Heide. Copyright Florence Parry Heide.

The Heritage Music Press for *Don't Let the Music Stop* by Eugene Butler.

Houghton Mifflin Co. for *Roads Go Ever Ever On* from THE HOBBIT by J.R.R. Tolkien. Copyright © 1966 by J.R.R. Tolkien. Reprinted by permission of Houghton Mifflin Co. All rights reserved.

Neil A. Kjos Music Co. for *La Pájara Pinta* from CANTEMOS EN ESPANOL BOOK 1, © 1948, ren. 1975 Max and Beatrice Krone. Reprinted with permission 1992.

Rita Klinger for *Aquaqua del a Omar,* Israeli children's singing game, collected in Jerusalem, Israel, by Rita Klinger, 1980.

The Last Music Co. for *This Pretty Planet* by John Forster & Tom Chapin. © 1988 Limousine Music Co. & The Last Music Co. (ASCAP).

Limousine Music Co. for *This Pretty Planet* by John Forster & Tom Chapin. © 1988 Limousine Music Co. & The Last Music Co. (ASCAP).

Gina Maccoby Literary Agency for *Clickbeetle* from BUGS by Mary Ann Hoberman. Reprinted by permission of Gina Maccoby Literary Agency. Copyright © 1976 by Mary Ann Hoberman.

Margaret K. McElderry Books for *Finding a Way* by Myra Cohn Livingston. Reprinted with permission of Margaret K. McElderry Books, an imprint of Macmillan Publishing Company, from THERE WAS A PLACE AND OTHER POEMS by Myra Cohn Livingston. Copyright © 1988 by Myra Cohn Livingston. Used also by permission of Marian Reiner for the author.

McGraw-Hill Ryerson Ltd. for *The Old Carrion Crow,* a Nova Scotian folk song from TRADITIONAL SONGS FROM NOVA SCOTIA by Helen Creighton. © McGraw-Hill Ryerson Ltd.

Dale Marxen for *Waltzing with Bears* by Dale E. Marxen. © 1986 Dale Marxen.

MMB Music, Inc. for *The Cat Came Back* from THE CAT CAME BACK by Mary Goetze. © 1984 MMB Music, Inc., Saint Louis. Used by Permission. All Rights Reserved. For *Fed My Horse* from THE CAT CAME BACK by Mary Goetze. © 1984 MMB Music, Inc., Saint Louis. Used by Permission. All Rights Reserved. For *Mongolian Night Song* from SONGS OF CHINA by Gloria Kiester and Martha Chrisman Riley. © 1988 MMB Music, Inc., Saint Louis. Used by Permission. All Rights Reserved.

Page Mortimer for the movement instructions for *Down the Road.*

Music Sales Corporation for *Mambo* from WEST SIDE STORY by Leonard Bernstein and Stephen Sondheim. Copyright © 1957 (Renewed) by Leonard Bernstein and Stephen Sondheim. Jalni Publications, Inc., U.S. & Canadian Publisher. G. Schirmer, Inc., worldwide print publishers and Publisher for the rest of the World. International Copyright Secured. All Rights Reserved. Reprinted by Permission. For *This Is My Country.* Words by Don Raye. Music by Al Jacobs. Copyright © 1940 (Renewed). Shawneed Press, Inc. and Warock Corp. International Copyright Secured. All Rights Reserved. Used By Permission. For *Winter Fantasy* by Jill Gallina. Copyright © 1982 Shawnee Press, Inc. International Copyright Secured. All Rights Reserved. Used by Permission.

José-Luis Orozco for *En la Feria de San Juan (aka La Feria de Atitlán/La Pulga de San José).* © 1985 José-Luis Orozco. Music and Lyrics ARCOIRIS RECORDS, P.O. Box 7428, Berkeley, CA 94707.

Oxford University Press for *Festival* by John Kitching from LET'S CELEBRATE–FESTIVAL POEMS, edited by John Foster.

Plymouth Music Co., Inc. for *Haida.* Arranged by Henry Leck.

Marian Reiner for *Finding a Way* by Myra Cohn Livingston. Reprinted with permission of Margaret K. McElderry Books, an imprint of Macmillan Publishing Company, from THERE WAS A PLACE AND OTHER POEMS by Myra Cohn Livingston. Copyright © 1988 by Myra Cohn Livingston. Used also by permission of Marian Reiner for the author. For *To Meet Mr. Lincoln* from THERE IS NO RHYME FOR SILVER by Eve Merriam. Copyright © 1962 by Eve Merriam. © Renewed 1990 by Eve Merriam. Reprinted by permission of Marian Reiner.

Anthony Quinn Richardson for *I Can Be* by Anthony Q. Richardson. © 1991 by Anthony Quinn Richardson.

Roots & Branches Music, BMI for *Somos el barco* (We Are the Boat) by Lorre Wyatt.

St. Nicholas Music, Inc. for *A Holly Jolly Christmas,* Music and Lyrics by Johnny Marks. Copyright 1962, 1964 St. Nicholas Music, Inc., New York, New York, renewed 1990, 1992. All Rights Reserved. Used by Permission.

Scholastic, Inc. for *Boogie Woogie Ghost* by Nadine M. Peglar. Reprinted from INSTRUCTOR magazine, October 1973. Copyright © 1973 by Scholastic, Inc. Reprinted by permission of Scholastic, Inc.

Shawnee Press for *Sing a Song of Peace* by Jill Gallina.

Silver, Burdett & Ginn Inc. for *Michie Banjo.* English words by Margaret Marks, from MAKING MUSIC YOUR OWN © 1971 Silver Burdett Company. Used by permission. All rights reserved.

Kathy B. Sorensen for *Hoe Ana Te Vaka; San lun tsa; and Suk san wan pi mai;* collected and transcribed by Kathy Sorensen. © 1991 Kathy B. Sorensen.

Stratford Music Corp. for *Comes Once in a Lifetime* from SUBWAYS ARE FOR SLEEPING by Jule Styne (music), Betty Comden and Adolph Green (words).

Stormking Music, Inc. for *Song of the World's Last Whale* by Pete Seeger. © Copyright 1970, 1994 by STORMKING MUSIC INC. All Rights Reserved. Used by Permission.

Tempo Music, Inc. for *Things Ain't What They Used to Be* by Mercer Ellington and Ted Persons. Copyright © 1943 by Tempo Music, Inc. Copyright renewed 1969 by Tempo Music, Inc. Used by Permission. International Copyright Secured. Made in USA. All Rights Reserved.

The Touchstone Center for Children, Inc. for *Fire* by Patricia Taylor from MIRACLES: POEMS BY CHILDREN OF THE ENGLISH-SPEAKING WORLD. Edited by Richard Lewis. © The Touchstone Center, 1991.

Turnpike Tom Music for *City of New Orleans* by Steve Goodman.

Jerry Vogel Music Co., Inc. for *Macnamara's Band.* Unpub. American Version Copyright 1935 by Latham, Carlson & Bonham, renewed. Pub. American Version Copyright 1940 Jerry Vogel Music Co., Inc., renewed.

Warock Corporation for *This Is My Country.* Words by Don Raye. Music by Al Jacobs. Copyright © 1940 (Renewed). Shawnee Press, Inc. and Warock Corp. International Copyright Secured. All Rights Reserved. Used by Permission.

Word Music, Inc. for *Tree Song* by Ken Medema.

World Association of Girl Guides and Girl Scouts for *I Let Her Go, Go* from CANCIONES DE NUESTRA CABAÑA, copyright 1980 World Association of Girl Guides and Girl Scouts, reprinted by permission.

COVER DESIGN: Robert Brook Allen, A Boy and His Dog

COVER PHOTOGRAPHY: All photographs are by the McGraw-Hill School Division except as noted below.

Clarinet photograph by Jim Powell Advertising Photography for MHSD.

ILLUSTRATION:
Unit Planner Logo Art: Zita Asbaghi
Celebrations Planner Art: Jenny Vainisi
Technology Logo: Menny Borovski
Movement Glossary Illustrations: Network Graphics

PHOTOGRAPHY:
All photographs are by the McGraw-Hill School Division (MHSD) except as noted below.

Across the Curriculum Backgrounds: Scott Harvey for MHSD

Titus Kana for MHSD: 15A, 15B, 19A, 19B, 75A, 269A. Anne Nielsen for MHSD: xv (b.l. inset), 27A, 27B, 31A, 61B, 65A, 65B, 79A, 79B, 111B, 117A, 127B, 131B, 163B, 167B, 175B, 179A, 179B, 209A, 213B, 221A, 221B, 225B, 257B, 261B, 269B, 273A. Mark A. Philbrick for MHSD: xiv(b.). Robert Matheu/Retna Ltd.: xv (t.r.). Jim Stratford for MHSD: xiv (t.,m.).

Acknowledgments for Hal Leonard Showstoppers are on page HL17.

PUPIL EDITION

ART & PHOTO CREDITS

COVER DESIGN: Robert Brook Allen, *A Boy and His Dog*

COVER PHOTOGRAPHY: All photographs are by the McGraw-Hill School Division except as noted below.

Clarinet photograph by Jim Powell Advertising Photography for MHSD.

ILLUSTRATION
Steven Adler, 70, 84-85, 126-127; Zita Asbaghi, 192-193; Susan Ash, 128-129; Steve Atkinson, 76-77; Jim Kagan Batelman, 122-123; Karen Bell, 254-255; Doron Ben-Ami, 88-89; Bob Bennett, 292-293; (calligrapher) Steven Bennett, 46, 80, 56, 72, 122, 127, 172-173, 304, 316, 338; Ami Blackshear, 208-209, 239, 231; Karen Blessen, 298-299; Maxine Boll, 164-165; Sue Ellen Brown, 330-331; Thomas Buchs, 204-205; Shirley Chapman, 232-233; Judith Cheng, 272-273; Eva Vagreti Cockrille, 54-55; Sally Wern Comport, 104-105; Mary Collier, 300-301, 330-331, 344-345; Eulala Conner, 39, 71; Neverne Covington, 284-285; David Csiscko, 286-289; Margaret Cusack, 138-139; Dee Deloy, 14-15; Darius Detwiler, 20-21; David Diaz, 8-9; Nancy Doniger, 316-317; Janice Lee Durrand, 258-259; Allan Eitzen, 230; Nancy Freeman, 178-179; Brian Fujimori, 184-185; Manuel Garcia, 42-43; Jack Graber, 204-205; Griesbach & Martucci, 60-61; Jeffrey Gunion, 180-181; John Steven Gurney, 62-63; Randy Hamblin, 112-113, 318-319; Pamela Harrelson, 130-131; Dianne Teske Harris, 26-27; Kevin Hawkes, 30-31, 306-307; Mitch Heinze, 106-107; Cary Henrie, 182-183; Terry Herman, 1, 5, 12; Oscar Hernandez, 24-25, 260-261; Catherine Huerta, 120-121; Richard Hull, 22-23; Susan Huls, 233; Michael Ingle, 56-57, 386-387, 389, 390, 391, 392-393, 394-395; Ramona Jablonski, 114-115; Jakesevic and Lamut, 176-177; Shannon Jeffries, 190-191, 270-271; W.B. Johnson, 28-29, 36-37; Mark Kaplan, 186; Greg King, 214-215; Shannon Kriegshauser, 144-145; Dave LaFleur, 308-309; Barbara Lambase, 172-173, 320-321; Kathy Lengill, 206-207; Todd Leonardo, 58-59; Barry Maguire, 336-337; Mary Jo Mazzella, 166-167; Alan Mazzatti, 64-65; Sudi McCollum, 118-119; Francesca Moore, 338-339; Marjorie Muns, 66-67; Sal Murdocca, 132-133; Tom Nachreiner, 49; Randy Nelson, 68-69, 162; Carol Newson, 202-203; Nancy Nimoy, 236-237; Joseph Novach, 156-157; William O'Donnell, 217; Erik Olsen, 274-275; Edward Parker, 210-211, 230-231, 310-311; Bob Pepper, 262-263; Donna Perrone, 382-383; Bonnie Rasmussen, 74-75; Mike Reed, 108-109; William Rieser, 124-125; Robert Roper, 342-343; Robert Sauber, 32-33; John Schilling, 86-87; Fred Schrier, 324-325; Max Seabaugh, 92-95; Dorothea Sierra, 140-141; Michael Sours, 186-187; Randy South, 234-235, 282-283; Ken Spengler, 38-39; Gerardo Suzan, 80-81; Susan Swan, 21-213, 218-219; Glen Tarnowski, 222-223; Joseph Taylor, 136-137, 227; Kat Thacker, 40-41; Mary Thelen, 238-239; Gary Torrisi, 168-169; Elizabeth Traynor, 110-111; John Turrano, 44-45, 47; Jenny Vainisi,100-103, 224-225, 302-303; Randy Verougstraete, 16-17· Carolyn Vibbert, 228-229; Pam Wall, 314-315; Mei Wang, 18-19; David Watts, 150-151, 152-153; David Wehrstein, 304-305; David Wenzel, 82-83; Kris Wiltse, 158-159; Gary Yealdhall, 264-265.

Tech Art by TCA Graphics, Inc.

PHOTOGRAPHY
All photographs are by the McGraw-Hill School Division (MHSD) except as noted below.

i: r. © Artville. iv: l. © Artville; m. © Artville. v: r. © Artville. vi: l. © Artville; violin, © Artville; drumsticks, © Artville; vii: flute, © Artville. **Unit 1** 10: Photofest. 11: l. Photofest; r. Daryl Pitt/Retna Ltd. 18: Superstock. 20: Jeff Sealik/Outline. 26: The Phillips Collection, Washington, D.C. 30: Martin Fox for MHSD. 33: UPI/Bettmann Newsphotos. 36-37: FPG. 41: Ken Karp for MHSD. 42: Gordon Photographic Ltd. 50: l. © 1998 Smithsonian Institution; r. Steve Velasquez/National Musuem of American History. 51: Teodoro Vidal Collection/National Museum of American History. 52: t. Rick Vargas/Smithsonian Institution. b. Martin Koenig/Center for Traditional Music and Dance. 53: Alex Viega/Center for Traditional Music and Dance. **Unit 2** 68-69. Jim Powell Studio for MHSD. 70 Archive Photos. 80-81: Ken Karp for MHSD. 85: Ron Scherl/Bettmann Newsphotos. 90: Jack Vartogian. 90-91: Dallas & John Heaton Westlight. 91: r. Shanghai Museum. 100-101: Ken Karp for MHSD. 101: r. Motion Picture and Television Photo Archive. 103: De Croce Studio. **Unit 3** 116: t. Culver Pictures. 116-117: b. Karen Meyers for MHSD; bkgnd. Ken Karp for MHSD. 120: Mark Phillbrick for MHSD. 123: David Heald © The Solomon R. Guggenheim Foundation, NY./ Canal, 1963, Helen Frankenthaler. Purchased with the aid of funds from the National Endowment for the Arts, Washington, D.C.; matching gift, Evelyn Sharp, 1976. 124: Ken Karp for MHSD. 125:

Anne Nielsen for MHSD. 126: The Granger Collection. 127: The New York Public Library. 129: Ken Karp for MHSD. 130: A. R. Linden/U.S. Marine Band. 131: UPI/ Bettmann Newsphotos. 134: David Lavender. 134-135: Wesley Bocxe/Photo Researchers, Inc.; bkgnd. Ken Karp for MHSD. 138: Michael Yamashita/Westlight. 139: Marka/International Stock. 141: *Baile en Tehuankpec* by Diego Rivera, Los Angeles Country Museum of Art. Gift of Mr. & Mrs. Milton W. Lipper, for the Milton W. Lipper Estate. 142-143: Ken Karp for MHSD. 144-145: Bill Waltzer for MHSD. 150: b. Anna Lee Walter/courtesy Chronicle Books; m. Jim Powell Studio for MHSD. 151: Mark A. Philbrick for MHSD. **Unit 4** 143-155: Bill Waltzer for MHSD. 160-161: Bill Waltzer for MHSD. 162: t. Brissand-Figaro/Gamma Liaison; m.l. Faria Castro Haraldo/ Gamma Liaison; m.r. Olivier Pighetti/Gamma Liaison; b. Krzystof Wojcik/Gamma Liaison. 163: l. Brissand-Figaro/Gamma Liaison, r. Peter Frey/Image Bank. 169: Iraq Museum. 170: l. Jack Vartoogian; b. Tim Bauer/Retna Ltd. 171: t.l. Mertan Simpson Gallery; b.l. Collection of Virgil Young; LP Music Group. 174:Bill Waltzer for MHSD. 175 Caroline Davies/Liaison International. 177: Maerten van Heenskerck, *Anna Codde*; Rijksmuseum, Amsterdam. 179: Gordon Parks/Life Magazine/ © Time Inc. 160-161: Bruce Caines for MHSD. 186: Paul Natkin/ Outline. 188: inset David G. Hauser; bkgnd. Bill Waltzer for MHSD. 189: Joe Viesti. 193: Bill Waltzer for MHSD. 194: FPG; m.r. Photoworld/FPG. 195: r. FPG; b.r. Ken Karp for MHSD. 198: Frank Driggs/Archive Photos. 199: The Bettmann Archive. 200: Ken Karp for MHSD. 201: San Francisco Craft & Folk Art Museum. **Unit 5** 213: Derek Smith for MHSD. 214-215: Bill Waltzer for MHSD. 216: b. Harry Heleotis. 220: Bill Waltzer for MHSD. 221-222: Bill Waltzer for MHSD. 223: Jim Stratford for MHSD. 226: Archive Photos. 228: *Down by the Riverside* by Daniel Pressley, 1966/DMA Photographers, Schomberg Center for Research in Black Culture, Art & Artifacts Division, NYPL, Astor, Lenox, & Tilden Foundation. 232: *Boy Playing Flute* by Judith Leyster, Statens Kontsmuseer, Stockholm, Sweden. 247: Marcia Keegan/Stock Market; Royal-Athena Galleries. **Unit 6** 250-251: b. Lois Ellen Frank/Westlight; Kevin Kolcyznksi for MHSD. 256: t.l. NASA/Peter Arnold. 257: t.l. NASA/Peter Arnold; t.r. NASA. 265: Jim Powell Studio for MHSD. 268: American Museum, Bath England/Superstock. 272: Mayna Treanor Avent, *Off Franklin*/Tennessee State Museum. 273: Ken Karp for MHSD. 274-275: Bill Waltzer for MHSD. 277: © 1993 The Estate of Keith Haring. 278: m. Owen Franken/Stock Boston; b. Ken Karp for MHSD; t. Murray Alcosser/ Image Bank. 278-279: M. David Frazier/Stock market. 279: t. Frank Siteman/Stock Boston; r., m. Lynton Gardiner; b. Ken Karp for MHSD. 280: l. George Ancona/International Stock; r. Robert Frerck/Odyssey Productions; 281: b. Roland & Sabrina Michaud/Woodfin Camp & Associates, Inc.; t. Owen Seumptewa for MHSD. 286-287, 289: Bill Waltzer for MHSD. 292: l. Granger Collection. 292-293: r. Americana Stock/Archive Photos. 294: H. Armstrong Roberts. 295: Bob Daemmrich/Stock Boston. **Celebrations** 296: Ken Regan/Camera 5. 300: t. S. Dooley/Liaison International. 312: t. Hot Shots; b. Luc A. Couturier/Départ. 322-323: Ken Karp for MHSD. 328-329: Nancy Palubniak. 332: l. David A. Harvey/Woodfin Camp & Associates, Inc; r. Richard Shiell/Earth Scenes. 339: Roberta Barnes/Gamma-Liaison. 340-341: Steve Gottlieb Photography. 303: inset The Bettmann Archive. **Music Library** 382-383: t. Karen Meytes for MHSD; b. Superstock. 384-385: t.l. Angelo Hornak Photograph Library, London; t.r. Dresden/Meissen Antique Import Corporation of America. 385: t.l. MMB Music; b.l. © 1985 Steve J. Sherman; r. The Ballet Shop, New York/A. Royzman. 396: t. The Bettmann Archive; m. Herb Snitzer Photography; b. Ken Karp for MHSD.

McGraw-Hill School Division thanks The Selmer Company, Inc., and its Ludwig/Musser Industries and Glaesel String Instrument Company subsidiaries for providing all instruments used in MHSD photographs in this music textbook series, with exceptions as follows: MHSD thanks Yamaha Corporation of America for French horn, euphonium, acoustic and electric guitars, soprano, alto, and bass recorders, piano, and vibraphone; MMB Music Inc., St. Louis, MO, for Studio 49 instruments; Rhythm Band Instruments, Fort Worth, TX, for resonator bells; Courtly Instruments, NY, for soprano and tenor recorder; Elderly Instruments, Lansing, MI, for autoharp, dulcimer, hammered dulcimer, mandolin, Celtic harp, whistles, and Andean flute.

THEMATIC CORRELATIONS TO READING SERIES

Macmillan/McGraw-Hill: *McGraw-Hill Reading* © 2001

The following materials from Share the Music may be used with each unit in Macmillan/McGraw-Hill's McGraw-Hill Reading.

Unit 1 • Experience *REFLECTIONS Stories let us share the experiences of others.*

Boogie Woogie Ghost, The, 304
California Song, The, 48
Calypso, 208
Cat Came Back, The, 258
City of New Orleans, 56
Derby Ram, The, 358
Down At the Twist and Shout, HL12
El Marunguey (listening), 53
Erlkönig (listening), 384
Folktale from Kenya, A (story), 102
Golden Goose, The (musical), 386
Mongolian Night Song, 19
Oh, Susanna, 107
Old Carrion Crow, The, 62
Old Chisholm Trail, 354
Old Dan Tucker, 360
Old Joe Clark, 260
One More River, 112
Pay Me My Money Down, 111
Swapping Song, 82
Trail to Mexico, 59
Wabash Cannonball, The, 6
Waltzing with Bears, 242
When I First Came to This Land, 148
When I Was a Lad, 96

Unit 2 • Connections *SOMETHING IN COMMON Sharing ideas can lead to meaningful cooperation.*

Dancing in the Streets, HL4

It's a Lovely Day Today, 156
Let Music Surround You, 3
Simple Gifts, 269
Somos el barco (We Are the Boat), 4
Song of the World's Last Whale, The, 205
Take Time in Life, 206
Tree Song, 344
Voices of the World (poem), 8

Unit 3 • Expression *OUR VOICES We can each use our talents to communicate ideas.*

America, 302
America, the Beautiful, 300
At the Hop, HL2
Canoe Song and Dance (listening), 222
Comes Once in a Lifetime, 252
Don't Let the Music Stop, xvi
Donna, Donna, 291
Down the Road, 76
For the Flute Players (poem), 153
Garden Song, 290
I Don't Care If the Rain Comes Down, 108
I Wish (speech piece), 21
Land of a Thousand Dances, HL16
Martin's Cry, 336
Meet Joseph Shabalala (interview), 170
Music Alone Shall Live, 231
Nathaniel's Rap (poem), 185
No Matter What, 388
Sing a Song of Peace, 301
Singin' in the Rain, 100

Sir Duke ,10
Take Me Home, Country Roads, 12
Eagle, The, 118
Path to the Moon, The, 372
Star-Spangled Banner, The, 298

Unit 4 • Inquiry *JUST CURIOUS We can find answers in surprising places.*

And Where Is Home? 378
Dry Bones, 308
For the Record (encore), 292
I Wonder (poem), 105
Rocks (poem), 251
Wind on the Hill, 374

Unit 5 • Problem Solving *MAKE A PLAN Often we have to think carefully about a problem in order to solve it.*

Tragic Story, A, 197
Tum-Balalaika, 210

Unit 6 • Making Decisions *SORTING IT OUT We can make decisions that can lead to new ideas and discoveries.*

Barter Song, 392
Hosanna, Me Build a House, 166
I Can Be, 254

THEMATIC CORRELATIONS TO READING SERIES

Harcourt Inc: *Collections* © 2000

The following materials from Share the Music may be used with each theme in Harcourt Inc: Collections.

THEME 1

Down by the Riverside, 338
Finding a Way (poem), 154
I Can Be, 254
Martin's Cry, 336
Nathaniel's Rap (poem), 184
Proverbs by Aesop, 203
Richardson, Anthony (recorded interview), 266
Shabalala, Joseph (recorded interview), 170
Sir Duke, 12
Take Time in Life, 206
Voices of the World (poem), 9

THEME 2

Come and Sing Together, 115, 138
Finding a Way (poem), 154
Lincoln Portrait (excerpts) by A. Copland
    (listening), 340
Martin's Cry, 336
Nathaniel's Rap (poem), 184

Pay Me My Money Down, 111
Sir Duke, 12
Take Time in Life, 206

THEME 3

Eagle, The, 118
Garden Song, 355
I Love the Mountains, 322
Rocks (poem), 251
Song of the World's Last Whale, The, 39
This Pretty Planet, 257
Untitled (painting), 277

THEME 4

California Song, The, 320
Civil Rights Memorial (architecture), 339
I Can Be, 254
Lincoln Portrait (excerpts) by A. Copland
    (listening), 340
Martin's Cry, 336
Sir Duke, 12

Voices of the World (poem), 9
When I First Came to This Land, 323

THEME 5

Eagle, The, 118
Song of the World's Last Whale, The, 39
This Pretty Planet, 257
Untitled (painting), 277

THEME 6

Calypso, 208
Civil Rights Memorial (architecture), 339
Lincoln Portrait (excerpts) by A. Copland
    (listening), 341
Little David, Play on Your Harp, 168
Martin's Cry, 336
Sir Duke, 12
To Meet Mr. Lincoln (poem), 341

THEMATIC CORRELATIONS TO READING SERIES

Houghton Mifflin: *Invitations to Literacy* © 1996

The following materials from Share the Music *may be used with each theme in* Houghton Mifflin's *Invitations to Literacy.*

THEMATIC CORRELATIONS TO READING SERIES

Scholastic: *Literacy Place* © 1996

The following materials from Share the Music may be used with each unit in Scholastic's Literacy Place.

UNIT 1

California Song, The, 320
Calypso, 208
Heave-Ho Me Laddies, 339
I Can Be, 254
I Missed the Bus by J. Dupri (listening), 186
McPartland, Marian (recorded interview), 190
Nathaniel's Rap (poem), 184
Over the Sea to Skye, 341
Robinson, Cleo Parker (recorded interview), 103
Shabalala, Joseph (recorded interview), 170
Trail to Mexico, 59
When I First Came to This Land, 323
When I Was a Lad, 326

UNIT 2

Folktale from Kenya, A, 102
Lakota Legend, A, 152
Mañana Iguana by B. McFerrin (listening), 20
Shaker furniture (folk art), 268

UNIT 3

California Song, The, 320
Calypso, 208
Canoe Song and Dance (listening), 222
Concert Champêtre (painting), 126
Heave-Ho Me Laddies, 339
Martin's Cry, 336
Song of the World's Last Whale, The, 39
Voices of the World (poem), 9

UNIT 4

Boogie Woogie Ghost, The, 304
Cat Came Back, The, 258
Hi! Ho! The Rattlin' Bog, 23
Loco-Motion, The, HL8
Macnamara's Band, 342
Michie Banjo, 264
My Dame Hath a Lame, Tame Crane, 357
Old Dan Tucker, 333
Old Joe Clark, 260
Swapping Song, 83
Tragic Story, A, 342

UNIT 5

Calypso, 208
Fire (poem), 122
Landscape in the Style of Dong Beiyuan (scroll painting), 91
Le chant des oyseaux (excerpt) by C. Janequin (listening), 382
Rocks (poem), 251

UNIT 6

Civil Rights Memorial (architecture), 339
Lincoln Portrait (excerpts) by A. Copland (listening), 340
Little David, Play on Your Harp, 168
Macnamara's Band, 342
Martin's Cry, 336
Robinson, Cleo Parker (recorded interview), 103
Shabalala, Joseph (recorded interview), 170
Sir Duke, 12
To Meet Mr. Lincoln (poem), 341

THEMATIC CORRELATIONS TO READING SERIES

Scott Foresman Reading: *Seeing is Believing (Level 4)* © **2000**
(Addison-Wesley Education Publishers, Inc.)
The following materials from Share the Music *may be used with each theme in* Scott Foresman Reading.

THEME 1

Before Dinner, 362
Comes Once in Lifetime, 252
Finding a Way (poem), 154
It's a Lovely Day Today, 156
Mince Pie or Pudding, A, 311
Nathaniel's Rap by E. Greenfield
 (poem/listening), 184
Sing a Song of Peace, 301
Somewhere In My Memory, 327
Take Time in Life, 206
Tum-Balalaika, 210

THEME 2

Sir Duke, 10
Vocal Ornamentation Montage (listening),
 280
Voices of the World (poem), 8
Where in the World? (listening), 9

THEME 3

Martin's Cry, 336
Sing a Song of Peace, 301
Song of the World's Last Whale, The, 205

THEME 4

I Can Be, 254
Martin's Cry, 336

THEME 5

California Song, The, 48
Civil Rights Memorial (architecture), 339
Lincoln Portrait (excerpts) by A. Copland
 (listening), 340
Martin's Cry, 336
Over the Sea to Skye, 149
Pay Me My Money Down, 111
Sir Duke, 10
Trail to Mexico, 59

THEME 6

I Wonder (poem), 105
I's the B'y, 132
Let the Music Surround You, 3
Mañana Iguana by B. McFerrin (listening), 20
Nathaniel's Rap by E. Greenfield
 (poem/listening), 184
Now's the Time by C. Parker (listening), 199
Sir Duke, 10
String (fine art), 201
Take Time in Life, 206
Things Ain't What They Used to Be by M.
 Ellington (listening), 191
Dancing in the Streets, HL4
We Got the Beat, HL6

 TEACHER'S NOTES

TEACHER'S NOTES

TEACHER'S NOTES

TEACHER'S NOTES

TEACHER'S NOTES

 TEACHER'S NOTES

TEACHER'S NOTES

 **SHOWSTOPPERS**

HAL•LEONARD®

Land of a Thousand Dances

Dance Hits Through the Decades

Arranged by Mark Brymer Script and Choreography by John Jacobson

LAND OF A THOUSAND DANCES

RELATED ARTS | MOVEMENT | THEATER | VISUAL ARTS

LESSONLINKS

OBJECTIVE To sing popular dance songs of the mid-twentieth century and to contribute to the preparation and performance of a musical presentation

MATERIALS
Recordings
At the Hop	CDHL:01
Dancing in the Street	CDHL:02
We Got the Beat	CDHL:03
The Loco-Motion	CDHL:04
Bristol Stomp	CDHL:05
Down at the Twist and Shout	CDHL:06
Twist and Shout	CDHL:07
Land of a Thousand Dances	CDHL:08

Performance Mixes for each selection	CDHL:09–CDHL:16

The compact disc of Hal Leonard songs is located in the front of the Teacher's Edition.

Movement
Movement directions for each song are written in the Piano Accompaniments book.

Land of a Thousand Dances is a collection of popular dance songs from the mid-twentieth century. It has an accompanying optional script. This allows for flexibility in presentation, making it suitable for classroom or concert.

Announcement: *(over school loudspeaker)* Attention! Attention! All students! I regret to announce the 4th grade field trip to the shopping mall for market research has been canceled... *(students moan)* Also, there will be no recess today due to bad weather someplace, somewhere...*(students moan loudest)* Sooooo....*(very excited)* we're cancelling everything and having a sock hop like you'll never forget! *(students cheer)*

At the Hop

Words and Music by Arthur Singer, John Madara and David White

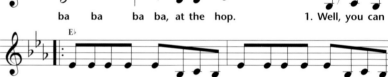

Ba ba ba ba, ba ba ba ba, ba ba ba ba, ba ba ba ba, at the hop.

1. Well, you can rock it, you can roll it, do the stomp and e-ven stroll it at the hop.
   swing it, you can groove it, you can real-ly start to move it at the hop.

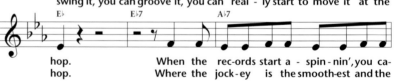

When the rec-ords start a-spin-nin', you ca-
Where the jock-ey is the smooth-est and the

HL2 LAND OF A THOUSAND DANCES

MEETING **INDIVIDUAL** NEEDS

SETS AND SCENERY

Land of a Thousand Dances is set in a school. The action takes place in the school's all-purpose room, gymnasium, or room suitable for a school dance. If you choose to have scenery, it should be reminiscent of a mid–twentieth century sock hop. For example, use large, paper cutouts resembling recordings of 45s of the era placed on the walls, balloons, and streamers.

USING THE RECORDINGS: *Instrumental Accompaniments*

Use the performance mixes of the songs for full-stereo arrangements of the accompaniments. If you use the recordings in performance, you may want to integrate it with the role of the DJ; for example, the DJ could pantomime placing the discs on the record player, etc.

lyp-so and you chick-en at the hop. Do the
mu-sic is the cool-est at the hop. All the

dance sen-sa - tions that are sweep-in' the na - tion at the
cats and chicks___ can___ get their___ kicks at the

hop. }
hop. } Let's go! Let's go to the hop!

Let's go to the hop! Let's go to the hop!

Let's go to the hop! Come on, let's go to the hop!

2. Well, you can Ba ba ba ba, Ba ba

ba ba, Ba ba ba ba, Ba ba ba ba, at the hop!

Hal Leonard Showstoppers **HL3**

TEACHING SUGGESTIONS

1. Introduce the basic story of *Land of a Thousand Dances*. Have students:

• Discuss what they know about the dances of the mid-twentieth century.

• Read through the script.

• Stop at each song and listen to it.

• Name the instruments they heard in the song.

• Find and explain how the song relates to dance.

• At the end, after reading the script and listening to each song, go back and name all the dances mentioned in the songs.

2. Introduce "At the Hop" CDHL:01. Have students:

• Find any repeat signs and first and second endings.

• Find any spoken phrases.

• Explain the word "Hop." (In the 1950s and early 1960s, it was a dance party for teenagers featuring the dance music of the time. Sometimes it was called a "sock hop" because the teenagers would take off their shoes and dance in their socks.)

• Listen to the song.

• Practice saying the words in rhythm.

• Practice singing the song. (You may want to practice the song in sections of intro, verse, and refrain.)

PERFORMING FORCES

Land of a Thousand Dances is very flexible. It may be performed with any number of students as long as the speaking parts are covered.

STAGING

This program is constructed to give multiple presentation options: chorus program, show choir, full staging, or any combination.

COSTUMES

It is not necessary to have costuming. However, one suggestion is to have the students dress in the style of bobby-soxers of the late 1950s and twisters of the early 1960s. You can create a separate appropriate costume for the DJ (oversized jacket, loud necktie or scarf, etc.).

continued from previous page

3. Introduce "Dancing in the Street"

CDHL:02. Have students:

• Find any repeat signs.

• Find all the natural signs and define the symbol. (A natural is a symbol in front of a note that means the pitch should be played or sung as written, without a sharp or flat.)

• Listen to the song.

• Practice saying the words in rhythm. (You may want to practice the words in phrases.)

• Practice singing the song. (You may want to practice the song in the same phrases you practiced the words.)

DJ: Hello Baby!! *(no response)*

DJ: I said....Hello Baaaaby!

All: *(shout)* Hello Baaaaby!

DJ: Now that's more like it! Welcome boys and girls, lads and lasses, moms and dads, teeny boppers and bobby soxers to the Land of a Thousand Dances! I'm DJ Howlin' Mac and in the Land of a Thousand Dances we're dancin' on the rooftops! We're dancin' on the ceiling and we're definitely....Dancin' in the Streets!

Dancing in the Street

Words and Music by Marvin Gaye,
Ivy Hunter and William Stevenson

Call - ing out___ a - round___ the world, "Are you

read - y for a brand new beat?" Sum - mer's here___ and the

time is right for danc - ing_____ in the streets.

They're danc - ing in Chi - ca - go,___

down in New Or - leans,___ up in New York Cit -

HL4 LAND OF A THOUSAND DANCES

MEETING **INDIVIDUAL** NEEDS

SOCIAL STUDIES CONNECTION: *Geography*

Have students locate on a map of the United States the cities mentioned in the song "Dancing in the Street," Chicago, New York City, and, New Orleans. Ask students which way they have to travel to find each city. (Chicago to New York City is east and New York City to New Orleans is south.) Ask the students to name the area of the country where each city is located. (Chicago is in the Middle West, New York City is in the East, and New Orleans is in the South.) Ask students to identify which of these three cities is closest to their school.

SOCIAL STUDIES CONNECTION: *Roots of American Popular Music*

Ask the students why they think Chicago, New York City, and New Orleans were mentioned in the song. Early blues and jazz were developed in New Orleans, Chicago, and New York City. When "Dancing in the Street" was written, these three cities were still the big centers for American popular music.

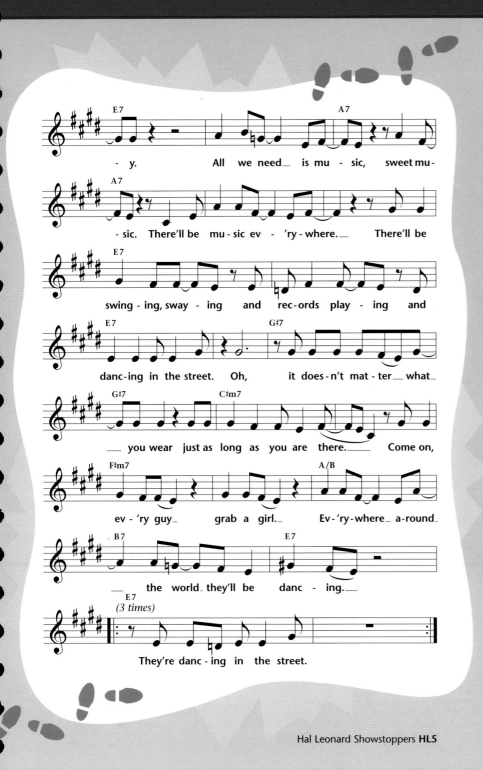

4. Sing the song. Have students:

• Echo back any phrases you identified as possible problem areas when you introduced the song.

• Echo the complete song in phrases, repeat if necessary.

• Sing the entire song without accompaniment.

• Sing the entire song without accompaniment at the intended performance tempo.

• Sing the song with the instrumental version: **CDHL:10.**

SPEAKING: *Diction*

Have students with speaking parts speak slowly and distinctly. Make sure they project so that they can be heard everywhere in the room. Of course, a student should never speak a part with his or her back to the audience.

MOVEMENT: *Classroom Management*

Notice the movement indications in the Piano Accompaniment book. These movements are to be done by the entire group, if possible. If the singers are on risers you will have to adapt some moves. Make sure the risers are compatible for the movements you choose. The risers should be strong, steady, large enough and safe enough to add movement to the songs. If you plan to perform all the movements, perform in an area on the floor. Remember when singing with movement, the song should be heard, not the movement. The movement should enhance the singing, not detract from it.

continued from previous page

5. Introduce "We Got the Beat" CDHL:03 .
Have students:

• Discuss the phrase "we got the beat."

• Find any repeat signs.

• Find any clapping indications. Practice the clapping rhythm.

• Find the parts for Group 1 and Group 2.

• Listen to the song.

• Divide the class into two groups, 1 and 2. Listen to the song again and have each group raise their hands when their group sings.

• Practice saying the words in rhythm together. (You may want to practice the words in phrases.) Always include the clapping section for practice.

• Practice saying the words in rhythm in Groups 1 and 2.

• Practice singing the song together. (You may want to practice the song in the same phrases you practiced the words.)

• Practice singing the song in Groups 1 and 2.

• Switch groups and repeat the practice steps.

Kid 1: *(like a rap to student dancing)* What's up?… What ya doin' there? Just the way you're movin' is giving me a scare!

Kid 2: *(like a rap)* When I hear the music I just got to move my feet! Can't sit still 'cause I've really got the beat!

Kid 3: *(Shouting like leading a cheer)* Who's got the beat?

All: *(shouting)* We've got the beat!

Kid 4: *(Shouting like leading a cheer)* Who's got the beat?

All: *(shouting)* We've got the beat! LET'S GO!!!!

We Got the Beat

Words and Music by
Charlotte Caffey

A(no3rd)

1. See the peo-ple walk-ing down the street;   fall in line just watch-
2. See the kids just get-ting out of school.   They can't wait to hang

A(no3rd)

- ing all their feet._ They don't know where_ they want to go, but they're
_ out and be cool._ Hang a-round 'til quar - ter af - ter 12. That's_

A(no3rd)   D(no3rd)

walk - ing in time.   They got the beat,_ they got the_
when they fall in line.   They got the beat,_ they got the_

G(no3rd)   F   C

beat, they got the_ beat,   yeah,   they got the beat.
beat, kids got the_ beat,   yeah,   kids got the beat.

HL6 LAND OF A THOUSAND DANCES

MEETING **INDIVIDUAL** NEEDS

ASSIGNING ROLES: *Considerations*

Either boys or girls may play all the roles in the program. The script represents ideas of what could be said. Like the entire program, it is flexible. You may modify it to suit your situation.

BACKGROUND: *The DJ*

The term DJ is short for disc jockey, a term coined in the 1950s. It typically referred to radio announcers who played rock 'n' roll recordings on their shows. Many of these DJs developed their own speaking style for hosting their shows and became famous.

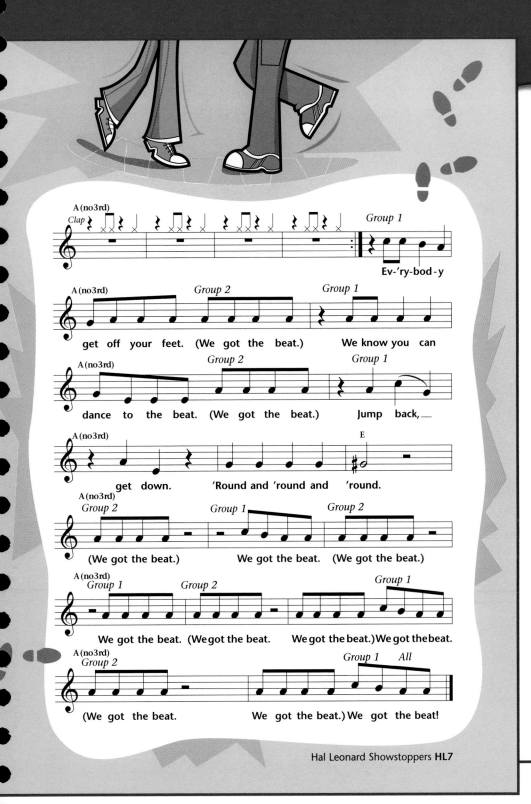

A(no3rd)
Clap
Group 1
Ev-'ry-bod-y

A(no3rd)   Group 2   Group 1
get off your feet. (We got the beat.) We know you can

A(no3rd)   Group 2   Group 1
dance to the beat. (We got the beat.) Jump back, ___

A(no3rd)   E
get down.   'Round and 'round and   'round.

A(no3rd)
Group 2   Group 1   Group 2
(We got the beat.)   We got the beat.   (We got the beat.)

A(no3rd)
Group 1   Group 2   Group 1
We got the beat. (We got the beat.   We got the beat.) We got the beat.

A(no3rd)
Group 2   Group 1   All
(We got the beat.   We got the beat.) We got the beat!

Hal Leonard Showstoppers **HL7**

6. Sing the song. Have students:

• Echo back any phrases you identified as possible problem areas when you introduced the song.

• Echo the complete song in phrases, repeat if necessary.

• Sing the entire song without accompaniment with both groups.

• Sing the entire song without accompaniment at the intended performance tempo.

• Sing the song with the instrumental version: **CDHL:11**.

BACKGROUND: *Dance Music*

Rock 'n' roll dance music typically has a very pronounced beat. This strong beat is usually heard in the drums and often the bass and rhythm guitars. The obviously pronounced beat facilitates dancing. Dancers liked to make sure they "had the beat" before they began dancing.

BACKGROUND: *Dances*

Rock 'n' roll dances were social dance forms with basic steps. The entire group would do the dance steps with only slight variations. As rock 'n' roll developed so did the dances. The dances became more personalized as a result of dancers doing their own individual variations on the basic steps. It has often been noted that as rock 'n' roll music developed over the years, dance partners put more and more space between each other.

continued from previous page

7. Introduce "The Loco-motion" CDHL:04.

Have students:

• Find all references to the coda. Define the term *coda.* (an ending section to a piece of music)

• Find the parts for Group 1 and Group 2.

• Listen to the song.

• Divide the class into two groups, 1 and 2. Listen to the song again and have each group raise their hands when their group sings.

• Practice saying the words in rhythm together. (You may want to practice the words in phrases.)

• Practice saying the words in rhythm in Groups 1 and 2.

• Practice singing the song together. (You may want to practice the song in the same phrases you practiced the words.)

• Practice singing the song in Groups 1 and 2.

• Switch groups and repeat the practice steps.

DJ: Line up everyone! It's time to do the Locomotion with me! *(All cheer)*

The Loco-Motion

Words and Music by
Gerry Goffin and Carole King

Group 1
1. Ev-'ry-bod-y's do-in' a brand new dance now.
2. Now that you can do it, let's make a chain now.

Group 2 / Group 1
Come on, ba-by, do the lo-co-mo-tion. I
Come on, ba-by, do the lo-co-mo-tion. A

know you'll get to like it if you give it a chance now.
chug-a-chug-a mo-tion like a rail-road train now.

Group 2 / Group 1
Come on, ba-by, do the lo-co-mo-tion. My
Come on, ba-by, do the lo-co-mo-tion.

HL8 LAND OF A THOUSAND DANCES

MEETING **INDIVIDUAL** NEEDS

COOPERATIVE LEARNING: *A Group Effort*

There are many different roles and tasks needed to create a successful program. Many of them are musical. However, there are many other important and creative roles to be filled and tasks to be done. There can be prompters and coaches to help with the speaking parts, stage managers to help with logistics, director's assistants, artists and designers, backstage crews, sound and lighting crews, and so on. Find roles and tasks for every student. Let the students know that a successful program is a group effort.

BACKGROUND: *Dance Songs*

Rock 'n' roll dance songs, such as "The Loco-motion," often had descriptive lyrics that depicted some of the steps done in the dance. An example of this is the phrase "A chug-a-chug-a motion like a railroad train." Many times, as in the case of "The Loco-motion," the title of the song was also the name of the dance.

Hal Leonard Showstoppers **HL9**

8. Sing the song. Have students:

• Echo back any phrases you identified as possible problem areas when you introduced the song.

• Echo the complete song in phrases, repeat if necessary.

• Sing the entire song without accompaniment.

• Sing the entire song without accompaniment at the intended performance tempo with both groups.

• Sing the song with the instrumental version: CDHL:12.

BACKGROUND: *Style*

Every type of music has a performance style associated with it. Just by knowing the type of music we can usually say something about how to perform the musical elements. The majority of rock 'n' roll dance songs are in two categories, loud and fast, and soft and slow. Ask the students what dynamic markings they might add to each song and why? Note there are no dynamic markings in any of the songs.

USING A MICROPHONE: *Considerations*

For many students this can be a new experience. If you choose to use microphones, it is important for the students to rehearse with them before the performance so they become accustomed to their amplified voice, not to lean in too closely to the microphone, and how to turn the microphone on and off. Test the microphones before a performance to see if they work and to avoid feedback.

continued from previous page

9. Introduce "Bristol Stomp" CDHL:05.

• Find all references to *D.S. al coda.* (*dal segno al coda,* repeat from the sign to the coda.)

• Listen to the song.

• Listen to the song again and ask the students to raise their hands when the *D.S. al coda* occurs.

• Practice saying the words in rhythm together. (You may want to practice the words in phrases.)

• Practice singing the song together. (You may want to practice the song in the same phrases you practiced the words.)

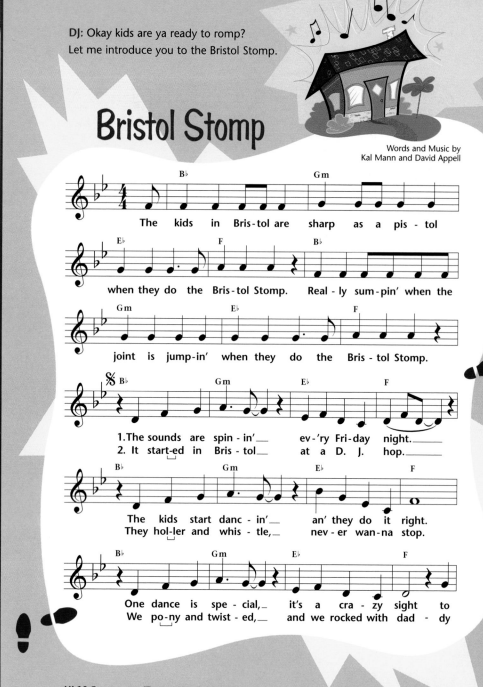

DJ: Okay kids are ya ready to romp?
Let me introduce you to the Bristol Stomp.

Bristol Stomp

Words and Music by
Kal Mann and David Appell

The kids in Bris-tol are sharp as a pis-tol

when they do the Bris-tol Stomp. Real-ly sum-pin' when the

joint is jump-in' when they do the Bris-tol Stomp.

1. The sounds are spin-in'___ ev-'ry Fri-day night.___
2. It start-ed in Bris-tol___ at a D. J. hop.___

The kids start danc-in'___ an' they do it right.
They hol-ler and whis-tle,___ nev-er wan-na stop.

One dance is spe-cial,___ it's a cra-zy sight to
We po-ny and twist-ed,___ and we rocked with dad - dy

HL10 LAND OF A THOUSAND DANCES

MEETING **INDIVIDUAL** NEEDS

VOCAL HELP: *Vocal Technique*

Students need to maintain good posture and vocal support as they sing. Although it is very basic, it may be helpful to review the difference between speaking, shouting, whispering, and singing voices. These songs require the singer to utilize chest, middle, and head voices. Stop the singers from carrying their chest voice into their head and from using their shouting voice. Because this music is popular dance music, the singers should sing with rhythmic vitality, and energy. For every style of vocal music, healthy vocal habits are important.

CHOOSING SOLOISTS: *Self-esteem*

Encourage all students to volunteer. Sometimes an encouraging word can make all the difference. Some students are not interested in being soloists. Those students should also realize how valuable their contribution is. Not matter what role a student has, self-confidence and a sense of pride in accomplishment are essential.

see_____ when they do the Bris-tol Stomp.
gee_____

Real-ly sum-pin' when the joint is jump-in' when they do the

2nd time to Coda 𝄌 E♭

Bris - tol Stomp. It's got that groov - y beat___

that makes you stomp y'r feet,___ so come on, get in

line,___ you're gon-na feel fine.___ And when you

dance with me,___ we'll fall in love, you'll see,___ the

D.S. al Coda

Bris - tol Stomp-'ll make you mine, all___ mine.

𝄌 **Coda**

Kids in Bris-tol are sharp as a pis - tol

when they do the Bris - tol Stomp.

Hal Leonard Showstoppers **HL11**

10. Sing the song. Have students:
- Echo back any phrases you identified as possible problem areas when you introduced the song.
- Echo the complete song in phrases, repeat if necessary.
- Sing the entire song without accompaniment.
- Sing the entire song without accompaniment at the intended performance tempo.
- Sing the song with the instrumental version: **CDHL:13**.

ABOUT THE ARRANGER: *Mark Brymer*

Mark Brymer is a composer, arranger, orchestrator, director, and producer. His areas of expertise include Broadway, Pop, and Show Choir. Brymer has published many best-selling educational choral works. He has been the Music Director of more than 30 musical revues for the Six Flags Theme Parks. This position includes complete show development. arranging, recording, and vocal coaching.

ABOUT THE CHOREOGRAPHER: *John Jacobson*

John Jacobson has choreographed, directed, and performed in numerous staged productions. He serves as guest clinician for hundreds of festivals, workshops, camps, and reading sessions. Jacobson works as consulting writer, choreographer, director, and performer for Walt Disney Productions. He authored *Gotta Sing, Gotta Dance* and *Puttin' on the Glitz,* wrote the production guides for many musical publications, and has a catalog of 42 Showcase Videos.

continued from previous page

11. Introduce "Down at the Twist and Shout" CDHL:06. Have students:

• Listen to the song.

• Explain ₂ (Two beats in the measure and the half note gets one beat).

• Listen to the song again and ask students to conduct a two pattern as they listen.

• Practice saying the words in rhythm together. (You may want to practice the words in phrases.)

• Practice singing the song together. (You may want to practice the song in the same phrases you practiced the words.)

Kid 5: Hey everybody let's go! I heard that the real fun is Down at the Twist and Shout!

Down at the Twist and Shout

Words and Music by
Mary Chapin Carpenter

Refrain

Sat-ur-day night_ and the moon is out._ I wan-na head on o - ver to the Twist and Shout, find a two-step part - ner and a ca - jun beat, when it lifts me up,_ I'm gon-na find my feet out in the mid-dle of a big dance floor. When I hear that fid - dle, wan - na beg for more. Wan - na dance to a band from a Loui-si-an'___ to-night._

HL12 LAND OF A THOUSAND DANCES

MEETING **INDIVIDUAL** NEEDS

BACKGROUND: *Down at the Twist and Shout*

Ask students in what state the "Twist and Shout" is located? (Louisiana) Name the three Louisiana cities mentioned in the song. (New Orleans, Lafayette, Baton Rouge) Identify other terms found in the song that are associated with Louisiana. (*Cajun* meaning Acadian—French Canadians who settled in Louisiana, and *Bayou*—a stream that flows slowly through marshy land found in the south central United States.)

BACKGROUND: *The Fiddle*

Ask the students to name the instrument mentioned in the song. (fiddle) Most rock 'n' roll bands in other parts of the country did not include fiddles. However, fiddle playing has a long history in Louisiana and is still played today.

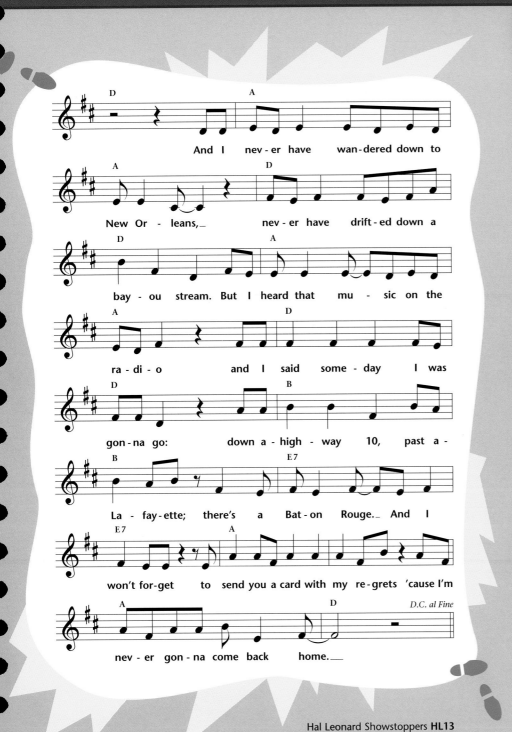

And I nev-er have wan-dered down to New Or-leans,__ nev-er have drift-ed down a bay-ou stream. But I heard that mu-sic on the ra-di-o and I said some-day I was gon-na go: down a-high-way 10, past a-La-fay-ette; there's a Bat-on Rouge.__ And I won't for-get to send you a card with my re-grets 'cause I'm nev-er gon-na come back home.__

D.C. al Fine

12. Sing the song. Have students:
• Echo back any phrases you identified as possible problem areas when you introduced the song.
• Echo the complete song in phrases, repeat if necessary.
• Sing the entire song without accompaniment.
• Sing the entire song without accompaniment at the intended performance tempo.
• Sing the song with the instrumental version: **CDHL:14.**

BIOGRAPHY: *Mary Chapin Carpenter*

The composer and author of "Down at the Twist and Shout" was born in 1958 in Princeton, New Jersey. Carpenter is a folk influenced, country singer/songwriter. She came into prominence in the late 1980s. In the early 90s, her song "Down at the Twist and Shout" became a number two single.

ENRICHMENT: *Different Styles of Dance Songs*

Give students the opportunity to listen to recordings of dance songs of many different styles. For help choosing selections refer to the Classified Index **Movement** under the subheading **patterned.** Play the recordings together with appropriate recordings you might bring from home. Have the students make a chart to compare and contrast the various styles. The chart could be arranged around the elements of rhythm, tempo, tone color in music.

continued from previous page

13. Introduce "Twist and Shout" CDHL:07.
Have students:

• Find all repeats and first and second endings.

• Find the parts for Group 1 and Group 2.

• Listen to the song.

• Divide the class into two groups, 1 and 2. Listen to the song again and have each group raise their hands when their group sings.

• Practice saying the words in rhythm together. (You may want to practice the words in phrases.)

• Practice saying the words in rhythm in Groups 1 and 2.

• Practice singing the song together. (You may want to practice the song in the same phrases you practiced the words.)

• Practice singing the song in Groups 1 and 2.

• Switch groups and repeat the practice steps.

DJ: Hold on boppers! No need to run!
Stay right here and have your fun!
I've got a number that will wear you out!
Come on everybody let's Twist and Shout!

Twist and Shout

Words and Music by
Bert Russell and Phil Medley

Well, shake it up ba - by, now.
(Shake it up ba -
- by.) Twist and shout.___ (Twist and shout.)___
Come on, come on, come on, ba-by now.___ (Come on ba-
- by,) Come on and work it on out.___ (work it on out.)___

HL14 LAND OF A THOUSAND DANCES

MEETING **INDIVIDUAL** NEEDS

BACKGROUND: *The Twist*

The twist became an immediate dance craze in 1960 after the singer Chubby Checker recorded the number one single "The Twist." Following the introduction of the twist hundreds of songs with the word "twist" were recorded.

MOVEMENT: *Teacher Tips*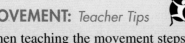

When teaching the movement steps, make sure students have enough room. Present each step slowly. It may be necessary to break down movements into several steps. Remember, if you are facing the students, they will do a

mirror image of your actions. In other words your right is their left. If this is a problem you may want to partially turn your back so that you are all going the same direction. Also it is a good idea to have the students point in the direction they will move before they move as a group.

MOVEMENT: *The Twist*

In order to do the twist, the dancers simply rise to the balls of their feet and twist their lower body in opposition to their upper body over and over again. Slow twist L or R simply means to perform the twist slowly, leaning toward stage left or right for any amount of counts.

Well, work it on out, _____ now. (Work it on out.)

You know you look so good. (Look so good.)

You know you got me go-in' now, (Got me go-

just like I knew you would. (Like I knew you would.)
- in')

Well, shake it up ba- Ah

Ah Twist and

shout! Twist and shout!
(Shake it up ba - by)

Hal Leonard Showstoppers **HL15**

14. Sing the song. Have students:

• Echo back any phrases you identified as possible problem areas when you introduced the song.

• Echo the complete song in phrases, repeat if necessary.

• Sing the entire song without accompaniment with both groups.

• Sing the entire song without accompaniment at the intended performance tempo.

• Sing the song with the instrumental version: **CDHL:15.**

BACKGROUND: *History of the Record*

The rise in popularity of the 45 rpm record and rock 'n' roll music go hand in hand. The record is referred to as a 45 because it spun on the turntable at 45 revolutions per minute. It was noted for the big center hole in the record. Unlike other record formats such as a 78 rpm (with a smaller spindle hole), a special spindle was required to play 45 rpm records. 45 rpm became popular with rock 'n' roll fans mainly because of the record's smaller size and affordable price. 45 rpm records contained only one song per side. The A side contained the "hit" song and the B side became known as the "flip side."

CLASSROOM CONNECTION: *Report on Technology*

Have students divided into three groups. Group 1 prepares an oral presentation for the class on the cylinder-playing phonograph invented by Thomas Alva Edison in 1877. Group 2 prepares an oral presentation on the disc playing gramophone beginning with the American, Emile Berliner's 1887 invention. Group 3 prepares an oral presentation for the class about the vinyl record playing record player, beginning with Columbia Company's perfected 12" long-playing vinyl disc in 1948. (As a starting point, students could read "For the Record," page 292–293.)

continued from previous page

15. Introduce "Land of a Thousand Dances" CDHL:08. Have students:

• Listen to the song.

• Find all spoken and clapped parts. Practice those parts.

• Find the *D.S. al Fine* and the sign. (Explain the term go back to the sign and sing to the *fine*, or end.)

• Count and name the dances referred to in the lyrics. (pony, mashed potato, alligator, Watusi, twist, and jerk; Explain the dance title, jerk, referred to the type of jerky or nonsmooth movements the dance called for.)

• Practice saying the words in rhythm together. (You may want to practice the words in phrases.)

• Practice singing the song together. (You may want to practice the song in the same phrases you practiced the words.)

Announcement: *(like the beginning)* Attention! Attention! The sock hop for today is just about over. Your reports on the influence of the Bristol Stomp on modern civilization are due Friday! *(students moan)*

DJ: Don't worry kids, I still have a little time. And lucky for you I have one more little rhyme! *(students cheer)*

DJ: When you're down, feeling out, and you don't like your chances, take a trip to the Land of a Thousand Dances! *(students cheer louder)*

Land of a Thousand Dances

Words and Music by Chris Kenner

You got-ta know how to po - ny___ like Bo - ny Mar - o - nie, Mashed Po - ta - to, do the Al - li - ga - tor. Put your hands on your hips, let your back-bone slip. Do the Wa - tu - si like my lit-tle Lu - cy.

HL16 LAND OF A THOUSAND DANCES

MEETING **INDIVIDUAL** NEEDS

PERFORMING THE SONG: *The Finale*

"Land of a Thousand Dances" as the last song of the musical presentation, could be considered the finale. It is a very high-energy piece designed to highlight the entire cast singing and dancing.

MOVEMENT: *Teacher Tips*

Often it is better not to teach the movement at the same time the students are learning a new song. One suggestion is to teach the song first, and after students are very secure on the song, teach the movement.

MOVEMENT: *Create a Dance*

Create a class dance. Use music in duple meter. Divide the class into groups of 4–6. Limit the dance to no less than two and no more than four. Limit the amount of space each group can use. Use an even number of steps. All the steps must be safe and easy to do. Discuss with the class that social dancing is done by everyone and should have appropriate moves that everyone can do.

16. Sing the song. Have students:

• Echo back any phrases you identified as possible problem areas when you introduced the song.

• Echo the complete song in phrases, repeat if necessary.

• Sing the entire song without accompaniment with both groups.

• Sing the entire song without accompaniment at the intended performance tempo.

• Sing the song with the instrumental version: CDHL:16.

Acknowledgments cont'd

Land Of A Thousand Dances
Words and Music by Chris Kenner
© 1963, 1970 (Renewed 1991) EMI LONGITUDE MUSIC
All Rights Reserved   International Copyright Secured
Used by Permission

The Loco-Motion
Words and Music by Gerry Goffin and Carole King
© 1962 (Renewed 1990) SCREEN GEMS-EMI MUSIC INC.
All Rights Reserved   International Copyright Secured
Used by Permission

Twist and Shout
Words and Music by Bert Russell and Phil Medley
Copyright © 1960, 1964 Sony/ATV Songs LLC, Unichappell Music Inc. and Sloopy II Music
Copyright Renewed
All Rights on behalf of Sony/ATV Songs LLC Administered by Sony/ATV Music Publishing, 8 Music Square West, Nashville, TN 37203
International Copyright Secured   All Rights Reserved

We Got the Beat
Words and Music by Charlotte Caffey
Copyright © 1981 by BMG Songs, Inc.
International Copyright Secured   All Rights Reserved
Illustrations by Mitch Mortimer

Hal Leonard Showstoppers **HL17**

ACKNOWLEDGMENTS

Grateful acknowledgment is given to the following authors, composers, and publishers.

At the Hop
Words and Music by Arthur Singer, John Madara and David White
Copyright © 1957 (Renewed) by Arc Music Corporation (BMI) and Six Continents Music Publishing, Inc. (BMI)
All Rights Controlled by Arc Music Corporation (BMI)
International Copyright Secured   All Rights Reserved
Used by Permission

Bristol Stomp
Words and Music by Kal Mann and Dave Appell
Copyright © 1961 Kalmann Music, Inc.
Copyright Renewed
All Rights Controlled and Administered by Spirit Two Music, Inc. (ASCAP)
International Copyright Secured   All Rights Reserved

Dancing in the Street
Words and Music by Marvin Gaye, Ivy Hunter and William Stevenson
© 1964 (Renewed 1992) FCG MUSIC, NMG MUSIC, MGIII MUSIC, JOBETE MUSIC CO., INC. and STONE AGATE MUSIC
All Rights Controlled and Administered by EMI APRIL MUSIC INC. and EMI BLACKWOOD MUSIC INC. on behalf of JOBETE MUSIC CO., INC and STONE AGATE MUSIC (A Division of JOBETE MUSIC CO., INC.)
All Rights Reserved   International Copyright Secured
Used by Permission

Down At The Twist And Shout
Words and Music by Mary Chapin Carpenter
© 1990 EMI APRIL MUSIC INC. and GETAREALJOB MUSIC
All Rights Controlled and Administered by EMI APRIL MUSIC INC.
All Rights Reserved   International Copyright Secured
Used by Permission

Correlation to National Standards for Music Education, Grades K-4

Share the Music is sequenced for mastery of the National Standards for Music Education. Key standards are correlated at the end of each lesson, Units 1-6. The chart below lists examples of activities in Grade 4 that address the Standards throughout the book. *Share the Music's* multi-focus lesson structure enables teachers and students to gain the greatest possible exposure to music skill development. The authentic assessment model used throughout *Share the Music* validates that students have met the Standards.

CONTENT STANDARD 1
Singing, alone and with others, a varied repertoire of music

STUDENT ACHIEVEMENT STANDARD	TEACHERS EDITION PAGES
a Sing independently, on pitch and in rhythm, with appropriate timbre, diction, and posture, and maintain a steady tempo	15, 19, 23, 27, 31, 35, 39, 43, 47, 61, 65, 71, 75, 79, 83, 87, 91, 95, 111, 117, 123, 127, 131, 135, 139, 143, 147, 163, 167, 171, 175, 179, 183, 187, 191, 195, 209, 213, 217, 221, 225, 229, 233, 237, 241, 257, 261, 265, 269, 273, 277, 281, 285, 289
b Sing expressively, with appropriate dynamics, phrasing, and interpretation	15, 19, 23, 27, 31, 35, 39, 43, 47, 61, 65, 71, 75, 79, 83, 87, 91, 95, 111, 117, 123, 127, 131, 135, 139, 143, 147, 163, 167, 171, 175, 179, 183, 187, 191, 195, 209, 213, 217, 221, 225, 229, 233, 237, 241, 257, 261, 265, 269, 273, 277, 281, 285, 289
c sing from memory a varied repertoire of songs representing genres and styles from diverse cultures	15, 19, 32, 31, 35, 61, 65, 75, 83, 95, 111, 127, 147, 221, 225, 241
d Sing ostinatos, partner songs, and rounds	23, 75, 79, 117, 135, 237, 261, 277, 281, 285
e Sing in groups, blending vocal timbres, matching dynamic levels, and responding to the conductor	15, 19, 23, 27, 31, 35, 39, 43, 47, 61, 65, 71, 75, 79, 83, 87, 91, 95, 111, 117, 123, 127, 131, 135, 139, 143, 147, 163, 167, 171, 175, 179, 183, 187, 191, 195, 209, 213, 217, 221, 225, 229, 233, 237, 241, 257, 261, 265, 269, 273, 277, 281, 285, 289

CONTENT STANDARD 2
Performing an instruments, alone and with others, a varied repertoire of music

STUDENT ACHIEVEMENT STANDARD	TEACHERS EDITION PAGES
a Perform on pitch, in rhythm, with appropriate dynamics and timbre, and maintain a steady tempo	35, 39, 43, 47, 75, 79, 83, 91, 95, 117, 127, 265, 131, 139, 167, 171, 175, 183, 225, 229, 233, 281 285
b Perform easy rhythmic, melodic, and choral patterns accurately and independently on rhythmic, melodic, and harmonic classroom instruments	15, 19, 35, 39, 43, 47, 61, 75, 79, 83, 91, 95, 117, 123, 127, 131, 139, 147, 163, 167, 171, 183, 191, 195, 221, 225, 229, 233, 237, 265, 273, 281, 285, 289
c Perform expressively a varied repertoire of music representing diverse genres and styles	19, 71, 167, 171, 175, 187, 191
d Echo short rhythms and melodic patterns	167, 191
e Perform in groups, blending instrumental timbres, matching dynamic levels, and responding to the cues of the conductor	15, 19, 35, 39, 43, 47, 75, 79, 95, 117, 123, 127, 131, 139, 143, 147, 167, 171, 183, 191, 195, 217, 221, 229, 225, 233, 237, 265, 285, 289
f Perform independent instrumental parts while other students sing or play contrasting parts	15, 19, 35, 39, 43, 75, 79, 83, 117, 127, 131, 139, 147, 167, 171, 179, 183, 191, 225, 229, 233, 237, 261, 265, 273, 285

CONTENT STANDARD 3
Improvising melodies, variations, and accompaniments

STUDENT ACHIEVEMENT STANDARD	TEACHERS EDITION PAGES
a Improvise "answers" in the same style to given rhythmic and melodic phrases	91, 229
b Improvise simple rhythmic and melodic ostinato accompaniments	83
c Improvise simple rhythmic variations and simple melodic embellishments on familiar melodies	39, 43, 91, 187, 191, 237
d Improvise short songs and instrumental pieces, using a variety of sound sources, including traditional sounds and non-traditional sounds available in the classroom, and sounds produced by electronic means	187, 191, 195, 209

CONTENT STANDARD 4
Composing and arranging music within specific guidelines

STUDENT ACHIEVEMENT STANDARD	TEACHERS EDITION PAGES
a Create and arrange music to accompany readings or dramatizations	117, 123, 289
b Create and arrange short songs and instrumental pieces within specific guidelines	47, 95, 131, 139, 195, 241, 289
c Use a variety of sound sources when composing	47, 117, 123, 131, 139, 195, 241, 289

CONTENT STANDARD 5
Reading and notating music

STUDENT ACHIEVEMENT STANDARD	TEACHERS EDITION PAGES
a Read whole, half, dotted half, quarter, and eighth notes and rests in 2/4, 3/4, and 4/4 meter signatures	15, 19, 27, 39, 43, 47, 71, 75, 79, 83, 87, 91, 95, 111, 117, 123, 127, 131, 135, 139, 143, 147, 163, 167, 171, 175, 179, 183, 187, 191, 195, 209, 213, 217, 221, 225, 229, 233, 237, 241, 257, 261, 265, 269, 273, 277, 281, 285, 289
b Use a system (that is, syllables, numbers, or letters) to read simple pitch notation in the treble clef in major keys	15, 19, 31, 39, 43, 47, 71, 75, 79, 83, 91, 95, 111, 117, 123, 127, 131, 135, 139, 143, 147, 163, 167, 171, 175, 179, 183, 187, 191, 195, 209, 213, 217, 221, 225, 229, 233, 237, 241, 257, 261, 265, 269, 273, 277, 281, 285, 289
c Identify symbols and traditional terms referring to dynamics, tempo, and articulation and interpret them correctly when performing	117, 123, 139, 217, 229, 257, 285, 289
d Use standard symbols to notate meter, rhythm pitch, and dynamics in simple patterns presented by the teacher	39, 131, 147, 225, 233, 241, 289

CONTENT STANDARD 6
Listening to, analyzing, and describing music

a Identify simple musical forms when presented aurally	35, 83, 91, 95, 167, 171, 175, 179, 183, 187, 191, 217, 229, 233, 265, 281
b Demonstrate perceptual skills by moving, by answering questions about, and by describing aural examples of music of various styles representing diverse cultures	15, 19, 23, 27, 31, 35, 39, 43, 47, 61, 65, 71, 75, 79, 83, 87, 91, 95, 111, 117, 123, 127, 131, 135, 143, 147, 163, 167, 171, 175, 179, 183, 187, 191, 195, 209, 213, 217, 221, 225, 229, 233, 237, 241, 257, 265, 269, 273, 277, 281, 285, 289
c Use appropriate terminology in explaining music, music notation, music instruments and voices, and music performances	15, 19, 23, 27, 35, 43, 47, 61, 65, 75, 79, 83, 87, 91, 95, 111, 117, 123, 127, 131, 135, 143, 147, 167, 171, 179, 187, 191, 209, 213, 217, 221, 229, 237, 241, 257, 261, 265, 269, 277, 285, 289
d Identify the sounds of a variety of instruments, including many orchestra and band instruments, and instruments from various cultures, as well as children's voices and male and female adult voices	15, 19, 23, 71, 135, 163, 171, 233, 265, 285
e Respond through purposeful movement to selected prominent music characteristics or specific music events while listening to music	15, 19, 23, 27, 31, 35, 39, 43, 61, 65, 71, 75, 79, 83, 87, 91, 95, 111, 117, 123, 127, 131, 135, 139, 143, 147, 163, 167, 171, 175, 179, 183, 187, 191, 195, 209, 213, 217, 221, 225, 229, 233, 237, 241, 257, 261, 265, 269, 273, 277, 281, 285, 289

CONTENT STANDARD 7
Evaluating music and music performances

a Devise criteria for evaluating performances and compositions	47
b Explain, using appropriate music terminology, their personal preferences for specific musical works and styles	47, 135

CONTENT STANDARD 8
Understanding relationships between music, the other arts, and disciplines outside the arts

a Identify similarities and differences in the meanings of common terms used in various arts	125, 153, 179, 187, 201, 203, 269, 273, 281
b Identify ways in which the principles and subject matter of other disciplines taught in the school are interrelated with those of music	35, 43, 47, 71, 79, 91, 95, 111, 117, 123, 127, 131, 135, 143, 183, 191, 213, 237, 241, 257, 265, 281, 285, 289

CONTENT STANDARD 9
Understanding music in relation to history and culture

a Identify by genre or style aural examples of music from various historical periods and cultures	53, 91, 127, 163, 191, 201, 213, 233, 281, 335
b Identify ways in which the principles and subject matter of other disciplines taught in the school are interrelated with those of music	126
c Identify various uses of music in their daily experiences and describe characteristics that make certain music suitable for each use	126, 147
d Identify and describe roles of musicians in various music settings and cultures	27
e Demonstrate audience behavior appropriate for the context and style of music performed	383, 385, 395

TEACHER'S NOTES

ALPHABETICAL INDEX

Alphabetical Index of Literature

Alphabetical Index of Listening Selections

See the Classified Index for recorded *Assessments, Recorded Interviews, Recorded Lessons,* and *Performance Mixes.*